RACISMS ||||||||||||||

RACISMS

‖‖‖

FROM THE CRUSADES TO THE TWENTIETH CENTURY

‖‖‖

FRANCISCO BETHENCOURT

PRINCETON UNIVERSITY PRESS

PRINCETON AND OXFORD

Copyright © 2013 by Princeton University Press
Published by Princeton University Press, 41 William Street, Princeton, New Jersey 08540
In the United Kingdom: Princeton University Press, 6 Oxford Street, Woodstock, Oxfordshire OX20 1TW

press.princeton.edu

Jacket illustration: Abraham Ortelius (Oertel) (1527–1598). Title page of the "Theatrum Orbis Terrarum."
Map from: Abraham Ortelius, Theatrum Orbis terrarum, Antwerp, 1570. Kartenabteilung. Courtesy of bpk,
Berlin / Staatsbibliothek zu Berlin, Stiftung Preussischer Kulturbesitz, Berlin, Germany / Art Resource, NY

Library of Congress Cataloging-in-Publication Data

Bethencourt, Francisco.
Racisms : from the Crusades to the Twentieth Century / Francisco Bethencourt.
    pages cm
  Includes bibliographical references and index.
  ISBN 978-0-691-15526-5 (hardcover)
  1. Racism—History. 2. Race relations—History. 3. Race. I. Title.
  HT1521.B474 2013
  305.8009—dc23
                                            2013019883

British Library Cataloging-in-Publication Data is available

This book has been composed in Minion Pro and Dante

Printed on acid-free paper. ∞

Printed in the United States of America

10 9 8 7 6 5 4 3 2 1

FOR ULINKA
||||||||||||||||||||||||||||||||

CONTENTS |||||||||||||||||||||||||||||||||||||||||||||||||||||||||||||||||||||||||||||||||||||||||||||||||||||||||

ILLUSTRATIONS ||||||||||||||||||||||||||||||||||||||||||||||||||||||||||||||||||||||||||||||||||||||||

MAPS

ACKNOWLEDGMENTS

I began to seriously research this book during the 2004–5 academic year with a fellowship from the Calouste Gulbenkian Foundation. In 2008–9, sabbatical leave granted by King's College London contributed to making this work possible: several chapters were written during that period. I am extremely grateful to both institutions.

I would like to thank colleagues and friends who agreed to read extensive parts of the book for their advice: Sir John Elliott, Ludmilla Jordanova, Miri Rubin, and Jonathan Steinberg. Anthony Molho and Elisabeth McGrath read first drafts of chapters or parts of chapters. The anonymous reviewers of the manuscript raised important questions and pointed out significant details. They are not responsible for any remaining errors, but they certainly helped me to avoid mistakes and contributed to clarify my reasoning. Al Bertrand, the publishing director for Europe at Princeton University Press, has been enthusiastic about the book from the moment he decided to contact me. His support and vision have played a crucial role in this project. I am grateful to Helen Hancock for providing a reliable, competent, and engaging revision of my manuscript, as I am not a native English speaker.

The final text benefited from the discussion of papers I presented to various universities, particularly the seminar on world history at Cambridge University, the seminar on empires at the Institute of Historical Research in London, the Beyond Slavery symposium at the University of Liverpool, the J. H. Parry Lecture at Harvard University, the seminar on early modern history at the University of Pennsylvania, the seminar on early modern history at the University of Oxford, the seminar on races in Latin America at the University of Warwick, the seminar on global history at the University of Notre Dame's London Centre, the medieval and renaissance seminar at University College London, the humanities research seminar at Wolfson College Cambridge, and the seminar on history at the University of Manchester. The Racism and Ethnic Relations in the Portuguese-Speaking World symposium I organized with Adrian Pearce also provided a forum to debate the main theoretical issues. The students in my European Expansion: Civil Rights and Ethnic Prejudices as well as World History: Power and Inequality courses offered important feedback. I would like to further acknowledge conversations with Luiz Felipe de Alencastro, Sir Christopher Bayly, Harald Braun, Peter Burke, Michel Cahen, Diogo Ramada Curto, Richard Drayton, Rebecca Earle, Felipe Fernández-Armesto, Antonio Feros, Serge Gruzinski, António Sérgio Guimarães, Maria Concepción García Sáiz, Herbert Klein, Jean-Michel Massing, Joe McDermott, Anthony McFarlane, Kenneth Maxwell, Andrea Nanetti, Linda Newson, Maria Lúcia Pallares-Burke, José Pedro Paiva, Pedro Ramos Pinto, Lyndal Roper, Laura de Mello e Souza, Jorge Vala, and Peter Wade—all of which helped to refine my research.

The preparation of this book was a long journey, coinciding with the creation of my family. Ulinka has been an extraordinary companion, wife, and mother of our children, João and Sophie. They all made me discover the symbiosis of passion, love, and harmony. I can only say that the life of our family has been a blessing to me; it allowed me to develop this work within an entirely relaxed and loving atmosphere. As a historian, Ulinka asked me the most challenging questions, which contributed to developing my argument and theoretical framework. For all this I dedicate the book to her. My father passed away in the last stage of this book's preparation. Throughout our lives, we were united by strong love and the kind of complicity that survives death. He exemplified sensibility, sharp observation, confidence, loyalty, perseverance, humor against adversity, and an enjoyment of life that I will always carry inside me.

RACISMS

Introduction

This book represents a departure from the largely consensual view that the theory of races preceded racism. It also challenges recent revisionist scholarship, which traces the invention of racism back to classical antiquity. It rejects the idea of racism as innate phenomenon shared by all humankind. I argue that particular configurations of racism can only be explained by research into historical conjunctures, which need to be compared and studied in the long term. Racism is relational and changes over time; it cannot be fully understood through the segmented study of short periods of time, specific regions, or well-known victims—for instance, black people or Jews.

The notion of racism I will use in this book—prejudice concerning ethnic descent coupled with discriminatory action—provides the basis for this long-term approach, enabling us to chart its different forms, continuities, discontinuities, and transformations. I focus my research on the Western world, from the Crusades to the present. Internal ethnic prejudice and discrimination are visible in Europe from the Middle Ages to the twentieth century, while the European expansion created a coherent set of ideas and practices concerning hierarchies of peoples from different continents. I do not maintain that the reality of racism is exclusive to this part of the world; Europe simply provides a relatively consistent setting that will be compared to other parts of the world where similar phenomena have manifested themselves.

The book is based largely on the analysis of primary printed and visual sources, which can provide us with new clues to the past, while it benefits from the critical reading of an important and extensive secondary literature on racism carried out in various fields.[1] The main hypothesis guiding my research is that throughout history, racism as prejudice concerning ethnic descent coupled with discriminatory action has been motivated by political projects.

QUESTIONS

How is it that the same person can be considered black in the United States, colored in the Caribbean or South Africa, and white in Brazil? This question triggered my research on the history of racism twelve years ago. Arbitrariness struck me as the main issue, yet I had been trained to take forms of classification seriously. Classifications can shape human behavior at all levels of society. In this case, it seemed obvious that racial classification had an immense power to rank social groups as well as set constraints and possibilities for the population in the countries involved. I consulted the key comparative studies on racism by Pierre van den Berghe, Carl Degler, and George M. Fredrickson.[2] These works clearly identified common and divergent racial perceptions in the United States and Brazil—an example of divergence being that one drop of African blood defined black people in the United States, while in Brazil middle-class status whitened a person. But I felt that both the historical background and changing forms of classification had not been sufficiently explored. The current contrast between France and the United States is telling: racial classification has officially been abolished by the French, because it is seen as reinforcing racist prejudices, even as in the United States racial classification is part of all bureaucratic inquiries, particularly for people entering the country. Moreover, the noun race has been taken over by African Americans, and reinstated as an expression of collective identity and a political tool against discrimination. The idea of racial classification as a social construct to justify hierarchies and monopolize resources has been turned on its head.

As my work progressed, I realized that the question that had inspired it was based strictly on skin color; it did not include, for instance, Native Americans, whose skin color was arguably similar to many European whites. Again I felt trapped by the tricks of classification. When and how was the idea of red skin invented? How could the contrast between white and black skin be sustained despite all the obvious gradations, both in Europe and Africa? I also realized that racial classification, formulated in the eighteenth and nineteenth centuries in Europe and the United States for scientific purposes, was intended to include all people of the world in a relational, systemic, and hierarchical arrangement. This attempt went well beyond simple variety in skin color. I had to relate precise colonial experiences to this global vision of the peoples of the world. This defined my next set of questions. How were systems of racial classification produced? How did these systems vary in time and place? How far did they shape human action? How were racial classifications influenced by conflict and social interests? How did racial hierarchies reflect prejudices and stimulate discriminatory action?

This list of questions still left gaps in my inquiry. Jews, for example, rarely have been defined by skin color; they were not even included in the main theories of races produced in the eighteenth and nineteenth centuries. Yet Jews were the main targets for racial extermination in Nazi Germany. Racism, in light of this devastating case of genocide, cannot be understood within the confines of intellectual history. Instead, political and social practices are crucial. This is why I decided to study racism as ethnic prejudice as well as practice of discrimination and segregation. Racial classification cannot be discarded since it has been used to either legitimize institutional intervention or justify informal action by social groups. Therefore I needed to understand practices, stereotyping, and classificatory ideas as interlinked. Classifications feed on perceptions of other peoples of the world, which must be reconstituted. Next, I enlarged my research to other cases of genocide concerning the Herero in Namibia and Armenians in the Ottoman Empire. I realized that different forms of racism emerged in time and place, in relation to specific conjunctures. I had to break away from a perspective of linear and cumulative racism, which in turn led to the last crucial question: Under what conditions were discrimination and segregation transformed into racial extermination?

INTERPRETATIONS

The idea that the theory of races precedes racism—a relatively consensual view among historians—supposes that the idea of ethnic descent was developed in eighteenth- and nineteenth-century Europe by the theory of races, which defined a natural division of humankind into subspecies placed in a hierarchy.[3] It also argues that the theory of races became a major tool to create and justify discrimination and segregation. This approach considers previous ethnic conflicts to have been caused by religious divides, opposed to a modern, natural divide. Finally, it highlights the historical use of the noun race in contrast with the creation in the twentieth century of the noun racism.

In my view, classification did not precede action. Prejudice concerning ethnic descent coupled with discriminatory action existed in various periods of history, although I acknowledge the critical impact of the scientific framework provided by the theory of races. Notions of blood and descent already played a central role in medieval forms of collective identification, while the modern ethnic and racial divide was largely inspired by traditional religious antagonism. The theory of races was permeated by conflicting points of view, which is why I will address its subject in the plural. To speak about race before racism means to follow a nominalist approach; Lucien Fèbvre pointed out many years ago that content may exist before the noun that expresses it.[4] I will discuss the significance of vocabulary and explain my own choices later.

The assumption that racism is a modern phenomenon has recently been challenged.[5] Benjamin Isaac contests the widely accepted vision established by Frank Snowden that Greeks and Romans had prejudices against barbarians and black people, but that these prejudices were cultural rather than natural.[6] Barbarians were unable to speak Greek, which meant that they were not aware of the habits, ideas, and rules of behavior established by the Greek. Black people were labeled "burnt faces," the original meaning of the noun Ethiopian in Greek, but prejudices against skin color, according to Snowden, were not translated into policies of social exclusion. The division between free people and slaves, or between Greeks and barbarians, was more important. Against this vision, Isaac gathers a richly detailed argument for the existence of racism in antiquity. In Isaac's view, prejudices were produced steadily and spread widely, and were detrimental to their victims. This approach makes the case for rooted prejudices concerning collective descent, yet it fails to demonstrate consistent and systematic discriminatory action—the second crucial element of racism. It has the benefit of showing the importance of prejudices, however, with some of them anticipating ideas that historicists had placed as originating in the eighteenth century. Moreover, such prejudices were unstable, as they were successively applied to different peoples, according to changing political conjunctures. Isaac explains how prejudices are shaped by and serve specific interests.

The setting of the history of racism in a historicist (or compartmentalized) framework was decisively challenged by Fredrickson's first general history of racism in the Western world from the Middle Ages to the twentieth century.[7] This study breaks with an approach that looks at the past in slices, as it establishes connections and avoids anachronism. Fredrickson consistently distinguishes informal racism, as practiced by social groups in everyday life, from institutional racism, backed by the state and transformed into formal policy, as in the southern United States, Germany, and South Africa. He rightly highlights the breakdown of this institutionalized racism between 1945 and 1994, despite the persistence of informal racism. Fredrickson also stresses the medieval and early modern racial gaze, which placed blood and descent at the heart of the main prejudices and discriminatory action, basing these on lineage and genealogical inquiry. But he accepts the mainstream idea that religion was crucial to shaping medieval and early modern prejudices along with discriminatory action, while the scientifically legitimated idea of a natural hierarchy of races influenced modern political action.

In contrast, I contend that the modern realities of racism, particularly against Armenians and Jews, show that the separation between religious and natural hierarchies is much more blurred than generally acknowledged. Furthermore, Fredrickson did not consistently challenge the divide between nature and culture. Claude Lévi-Strauss had formally placed this separation at the center of anthropological study even in his posthumous books on Japan.[8] In my opinion, the divide is not universal; Japan itself is a country in which the ideal of a symbiosis between nature and culture has always been upheld. It required the thorough and convincing exploration of Peter Wade on race and racism in Latin America to further challenge the traditional division between nature and culture.[9] But this approach is far from completely accepted.

The main problem with Fredrickson's book is that nearly all references to medieval and early modern history are derivative, thereby creating a schematic and artificial framework. The historical context of prejudices and discriminatory action is not set out convincingly. There is a considerable gap in the book's narrative between the persecution of Jews in the Middle Ages, followed by the persecution of New Christians of Jewish descent in Iberia, and then the theories of races in the eighteenth century. The work focuses exclusively on discriminatory action against Jews and black people; Armenians, for instance, are not mentioned. This is an important problem, since prejudices concerning ethnic descent coupled with discriminatory action in time developed hierarchies of types of human beings. In my perspective, racism is relational, placing specific groups in contextualized hierarchies according to precise purposes. Finally, Fredrickson fails to address the impact of nationalism on racial theory and racist practices, except to say that racism is generally developed within a national framework. Nationalism is a crucial issue in the long period from the 1840s to 1940s, and this has increasingly brought historians of racism and nationalism into a productive conversation. As we know, the most extreme case of blending nationalism and racism was presented by Nazi Germany, which made the exclusion of Jewish people into a state policy, but we also need to consider the earlier cases of the Ottoman Empire, which had defined policies to exclude minorities, or Russia, which registered regular pogroms and massive deportations of ethnic/religious populations in the nineteenth and twentieth centuries.

This discussion leads to the main interpretative framework applied to racism as historical phenomenon. Many historians, explicitly or implicitly, consider racism to be a phenomenon shared by all humankind that emerges here and there under special circumstances, and is underlined by a natural pride of belonging and rivalry with competitors. This immanent approach regards racism as part of the human condition. Arthur Keith (1866–1955), an anatomist who served as the rector of the University of Aberdeen and president of the Royal Anthropological Institute, considered race and nation as the same, thus equating immanent racism with essentialized national character—an issue I will discuss at the beginning of part III. Keith placed race feeling as "part of the evolutionary machine which safeguards the purity of race; human prejudices have usually a biological significance."[10] From this vantage point, any history would need to limit itself to a phenomenological approach, since its framework would be provided by natural instincts and competition engendered in the emergence or assertiveness of nations/races. I reject this immanent vision, which is based on neither scientific ground nor historical evidence. I believe we need to investigate the specific circumstances of the emergence of both social practices that exclude targeted groups and racial theories. These practices and theories are not universal, and they do not carry the same configuration through time and place, as the enlargement of my look at China, Japan, and India will show.[11]

Marxist interpretation relates racism to relations of production. It considers prejudice concerning ethnic descent and discriminatory action as an ideological and political mainstay of the accumulation of capital, keeping wages low and justifying the exploitation of types of human beings considered inferior.[12] This is an intelligent update for modern times of the Aristotelian notion of natural slavery, which justified and created a natural framework for the existence of bound labor. The advantage of this interpretation—its clarity—is exactly its problem: a limited scope and explanatory power. It is strictly linked to economic relations; it contributes to the understanding of colonial and postcolonial aspects of the international division of labor, which maximized profits even as it minimized the costs of both production and political disruption. But it does not provide a global level of explanation. Immanuel Wallerstein, for instance, dismisses Nazi policies to exterminate Jews as irrational, since they do not fit the model of a racialized division of the workforce. Yet it is obvious that there are levels of rationality beyond strictly economic ones.

Political and social approaches provide better interpretative models. In the United States, racism has been analyzed as a political project that created or reproduced structures of domination based on racial categories, which are accepted at face value for structuring institutions and identities right up to the present.[13] Max Weber approached the problem with subtlety a century ago: he linked racism and racial theories to the monopolization of social power and honor, while he played a part in the exposure of the arbitrariness of racial classification in his own time.[14] It is the struggle for the monopoly of social power that is at stake with racism and racial theory. Prejudices concerning ethnic descent coupled with discriminatory action therefore are linked to political projects, even if they do not always become integrated and institutionalized by the state. These interpretations inspire my hypothesis that racism is triggered by political projects and connected to specific economic conditions. Racism can be fed or deterred by influential powers, and is channeled by a complex web of collective memories and sudden possibilities—a web that can change the forms and targets of racism.

SEMANTICS

The concepts used to analyze racism are themselves the products of history, which is why we need to contextualize them. The nouns racist and racism were created as recently as the 1890s and 1900s in order to designate those promoting racial theory along with a hierarchy of races. The division of humankind into groups of descent that supposedly shared the same physical and mental features was narrowed down to fit specific political contexts. These groups were placed in a relation of superiority or inferiority. In the 1920s and 1930s, the words racist and racism took on the meaning of hostility against racial groups. These linguistic innovations reflected segregationist policies in the southern United States and the development of nationalist movements in Europe based on racial theories—namely, the Nazi rise to power in Germany. The antonyms antiracist and antiracism were coined in the 1930s and 1950s, respectively, to express political protest against racial prejudices, discrimination, and segregation.[15] The unprecedented scale on which racial prejudices had been transformed into political action, resulting in many millions of deaths, was registered after the defeat of Nazi Germany in the Second World War. The discovery of the full extent to which policies of racial extermination had been taken led to the adoption of an antiracism that is now the norm.

While the noun racism thus acquired a precise content, the meaning of the noun race is extremely unstable. The word race started to be used in the Middle Ages as a synonym for caste, and was applied to the raising of plants and breeding of animals. In the late Middle Ages it was used in the definition of noble lineage in Italy and France. During the long Iberian struggle between Muslims and Christians, followed by overseas expansion, race acquired an ethnic meaning—first applied to people of Jewish and Muslim descent, meaning an impurity in the blood, and then applied to Africans and Native Americans. Therefore, the semantic content of the word was developed through a hierarchical ethnic system of classification within the Iberian context. In the eighteenth century, the noun race was used in Europe to denote female gender and, in general, varieties of human beings. Within the theories of races the noun acquired an ambiguous role in labeling subspecies, virtually transformed into species by scientific racialism in the mid-nineteenth century. By the late nineteenth and early twentieth century, as nationalism triumphed in the Western world, the noun race was imposed as equivalent to nation.[16]

The extraordinary devastation of the Second World War, which was largely inspired by racial theories, brought the scientific basis of such theories and the very notion of race into question. The debate triggered by the UN Educational, Scientific, and Cultural Organization in the late 1940s was not concluded with the mapping and sequencing of the human genome in 2000.[17] Nowadays, scientists question the biological basis of race, since genetic variation within traditionally defined races is larger than between races, but they accept the existence of specific clusters of ethnic dispositions with medical relevance in terms of immunity and exposure to illnesses.[18] In the meantime, as I have already discussed, the noun race has been used by African Americans to express their collective identity and turn the word's original derogatory use on its head. The issue of a "desire" for race has been examined in this political and cultural context.[19] It requires a reevaluation of the notion of identity as a relational perception of belonging that affects individuals, groups, and communities over time as well as across locations, in a permanent process of construction and reconstruction.[20] Racism certainly played a role among targeted groups, creating complex cross-references of resistant identities.

The exclusive connection of racism to Europe has been challenged by various studies on China, Japan, and India.[21] Conflicts between the Tuareg and African ethnicities in the Sahel region of West Africa have recently been interpreted through the idea of race and racial hierarchy, considered to predate the colonial inheritance.[22] While the Muslim expansion brought with it ideas of descent shared with Latin Christian peoples, the extension of this approach to analyze the genocide against the Tutsi requires deeper research into local traditions. The risk, here and elsewhere, is in reifying the notion of race.

The instability of the noun race proves that classification reflects historical context rather than defining it. The problem is that the noun race has become too contaminated by the political practices of segregation and extermination to be used by researchers unreflectively. This explains why anthropologists and historians have started to search alternative terms to designate collective groups outside the ideological and anachronistic constraints of racial classification. The noun ethnic has provided an obvious choice, since it was coined in the thirteenth century after the Latin Christian *ethnicus* (pagan or gentile), itself originating from the Greek designation of people, *ethnos* (nation or race).[23] This term promised to combine the notions of a collective identity and "otherness" without being loaded with racial prejudices. The problem raised by anthropologists concerns the risk of essentializing groups that have had fluid borders, and have gone through processes of fragmentation and reorganization. The coining of the noun ethnicity tried to address this notion of fluidity. I will use both ethnic and ethnicity to designate groups that identified themselves by common descent, stressing fluidity and recomposition through the noun ethnicity. In some cases, where recent researchers consider it most appropriate, I will use the noun lineage, such as in West Africa, where kinship played a role in structuring professional groups and traditional polities.

The notion of racism that I will use in this work results from a reflection on historical semantics as well as conceptual developments in the social sciences. Racism attributes a single set of real or imaginary physical and/or mental features to precise ethnic groups, and believes these features to be transmitted from generation to generation. The ethnic groups are considered inferior or divergent from the norm represented by the reference group, thus justifying discrimination or segregation. Racism targets not only ethnic groups considered inferior but also groups considered competitive, such as Jews, Muslims, or Armenians. The crucial elements of descent, prejudice, and discriminatory action can be found in the past, not only in practices, but in perceptions too: the nouns inferior, prejudice, exclusion, and separation were used in the late Middle Age, while the terms inferiority, stigma, segregation, and discrimination were coined in the sixteenth and seventeenth centuries.[24] The issue remains that prejudice related to ethnic descent does not sufficiently identify racism; such prejudice must be coupled with discriminatory action.

Racism distinguishes itself from ethnocentrism in that it does not refer to a disdained or feared neighborhood or distant community in the abstract; it generally targets groups with which the reference community is engaged—groups considered bound to rules of blood or descent. Ethnocentrism can express contempt for another community, yet it accepts the inclusion of individuals from this community, while racism considers that blood affects all members of the targeted community. The notion of ethnocentrism can be extended to cover the rivalry between religious, confessional, or national allegiances, although in some cases the notion of descent is deeply ingrained in the way groups perceive each other.

Genocide is the most recent noun used in this work, meaning the deliberate and systematic extermination (or attempt to exterminate) an ethnic or national group. The UN Convention on the Prevention and Punishment of the Crime of Genocide, approved in 1948, defined the phenomenon as "acts committed with intent to destroy, in whole or part, a national, ethnical, national or religious group." The acts listed include killing members of the targeted group, causing serious bodily or mental harm, deliberately inflicting conditions of life that will bring about the physical destruction of the group, imposing measures intended to prevent births within the group, and forcibly transferring children from the group to another group.[25] We will see how this precise definition covers different cases addressed in part V of this book.

SCOPE

The European expansion provides the framework for my research in time and space. The scope for prejudices concerning ethnic descent coupled with discriminatory actions was radically enlarged by the exploration of other continents; overseas expansion and colonial settlement stimulated the classification of the varieties of human beings that was essential for the definition and justification of hierarchies. This vast movement of populations motivated a new geography, a new cartography, and a new perception of peoples around the world—all measured according to the European yardstick and needs.[26] Latin European expansion was renewed with the Crusades. This massive process of conquest and migration targeted the Holy Land, and was linked to the re-Christianization of Sicily and Iberia. The integration of conquered territories required the inclusion or segregation of, or discrimination against, local populations. The process brought with it old and new perceptions of different peoples, shaping classifications and hierarchies. The first part of my book addresses this process, placed in the wider historical context of classical antiquity, the barbarian invasions, and Muslim expansion, since many prejudices have old roots. The tension between the universalism of the church or empire and local conflicts of interest over subjugation of populations lies at the core of this part, in which I will include European peripheries, relating internal to external colonialism.

The European overseas expansion, marked by the voyages of Christopher Columbus (1451–1506) to America and Vasco da Gama (1469–1524) to India in the last decade of the fifteenth century, represented a long-term process that allowed for the exploration of new seas, lands, skies, and varieties of human beings. Cartography shifted its center from Jerusalem to Europe, thereby symbolizing the new assertion of the old continent in relation to Asia and Africa as well as the New World. The myth of continents, already built up in the Greek and Roman world, was followed by the personification of those continents, bestowing on them attributes that configured a hierarchy of peoples globally. This momentous assertion of Europe during the sixteenth century would have major consequences in the long run, since it supplied the template for data collection about geography, the economy, and natural history. The second part of this study analyzes the early modern European vision of people and humankind, showing the importance of the notion of the purity of blood in Iberia, following the medieval perceptions of Jews and Muslims. It also studies perceptions and stereotyping related to Africans, Asians, Americans, and Europeans, because they expressed political projects of expansion and influenced classifications used in the theories of races.

The third part of the book discusses colonial societies from the sixteenth through the nineteenth centuries, analyzing the concrete processes of conquest, transfers of population, and the construction of new societies defined by white supremacy. It studies the classification of people emerging from local and regional conditions, in which the debasement of inferior *castas* in the Iberian world could reach a level of dehumanization via animal metaphors transferred to northern European colonial cultures. I will link forms of classification and ethnic structure in order to show the interdependent dynamic between social practice and taxonomy. This part explores the role of political projects, central and local policies, institutionalized discrimination and segregation, and the convergence and divergence of practices between the major European colonial powers—Portugal, Spain, Britain, France, and Netherlands. The slave trade, slavery, and Native resistance lie at the core of this analysis; the uniqueness of the American case will be compared with the European presence in Asia. As slavery shaped American colonial societies so prominently, I will look at abolitionism, its possible impact on the late eighteenth-century notion of human rights, and its relationship to prejudices concerning descent.

The fourth part scrutinizes theories of races along with their impact on societies and policies from the eighteenth to the nineteenth century. This part is necessarily connected to the history of ideas and history of science; the main characteristics of the theories of races from Carl Linnaeus to Houston Stewart Chamberlain are discussed. I highlight the first stage of the classification of varieties of human beings underpinned by the work of Georges-Louis Leclerc de Buffon, Immanuel Kant, Petrus Camper, Johann Friedrich Blumenbach, Georges Cuvier, James Cowles Prichard, and Alexander von Humboldt. The focus will be on different perceptions and the significance of key debates in which the instability of conceptual trends as well as doubts related to the definition of boundaries between races became obvious. The study of scientific racialism in the mid-nineteenth century allows us to see forms of classification as interlinked with political struggle—in this case, the growing tension between the northern and southern United States, expressed by the opposed policies of free and slave soil, which would lead to the Civil War. By looking at Charles Darwin in particular, I will show how the notion of evolution rendered the clash between monogenists (defenders of one single Creation) and polygenists (defenders of multiple Creations) outdated, only to be immediately converted into a system of ideas about social evolution and a hierarchical vision of the different stages of humankind.

The fifth part concerns the development of racial policies in specific countries from the late nineteenth century onward. A survey of policies of exclusion and extermination implemented in Europe under the late Ottoman Empire and in Nazi Germany will allow me to reflect on the impact of nationalism along with its fusion with notions of race, which proved to be lethal in these contexts. I will also analyze the reappearance on a massive scale of forced labor and slavery in 1930s' Nazi Germany and the Soviet Union as well as the deportation of whole populations. The final chapter is one of comparisons. It addresses European forms of racism after the Second World War, segregation policies in the United States up to the campaign for civil rights, the acts of genocide against the Herero in Namibia in 1904 and the Tutsi in Rwanda in 1994, and the emergence and decline of apartheid in South Africa. I end by considering the long-term phenomenon of prejudice concerning ethnic descent coupled with discriminatory action in three Asian countries that were not extensively touched by the European expansion until the nineteenth century: China, Japan, and India.

This book reconstitutes prejudices around ethnic descent because they provide the context for the emergence of racist action. When examining specific authors, I do not imply that they were necessarily racist. In many cases they engaged in stereotyping, debated prejudices, or introduced complexity into the perceptions of varieties of human beings; in other instances, they were involved in the theories of races but not in discriminatory action. This explains why I have tried to strike a balance between the analysis of ethnic prejudices and discriminatory action; the former were clearly more fluid and present than the latter, but discrimination could not be implemented without a context of prejudice.

The problems associated with massive migration, the integration of minorities, and relations between civilizations are far from solved in this world. As Marc Bloch said, we need to study the past in order to understand the present and prepare the future.[27] My hope is that rigorous historical analysis can contribute to ending the history of racism, which this book is about.

PART I

The Crusades

The Crusades brought renewed and intensive contact between Western Europe and the Middle East from the late eleventh to the late thirteenth century. They involved the emigration of some two hundred thousand people from West to East, increased trade in the Mediterranean, and produced political exchange and military engagement between Muslims and the Christians powers, both European and Byzantine. With this significant displacement of people, accompanied by intermittent war, religious and ethnic identification became crucial for negotiating daily survival. Phenotype features, forms of dress, and/or hairstyles linked to religious beliefs became the obvious criteria for identification—the first step in the assessment of different peoples. In a dangerous and shifting world, visual stereotypes served to identify threats and help people feel secure. The projection of permanent psychological features onto different peoples and their descendants was part of the process of building alliances and defining enemies.

Thus the Crusades created the conditions for a renewal of ethnic preconceptions in the context of war. Some forms of identification and even primary stereotypes, however, already had a long history. The Crusades adapted ethnic assumptions developed within the different contexts of classical antiquity, barbarian invasions, and Muslim expansion. As such, this part of the book starts with an abridged and necessarily schematic view of the history of ethnic prejudices to avoid falling into the usual trap of seeing in the Crusades the unique, particular configuration of an ethnic-religious vision. I will look at interethnic perceptions in the context of the Christian (re)conquest of Sicily, Iberia, and the Middle East. Then the focus of my analysis will return to Europe to understand the impact on ethnic prejudices of spiritual and political powers—the Catholic Church and the Holy Roman Empire—whose universal ambition was challenged by the constitution of feudal states and persistent fragmentary polities. The assimilation of political and religious peripheries will be an important object of study in these chapters. Finally, I will address early typologies of humankind along with the different models of discrimination and segregation practiced during the Middle Ages.

CHAPTER 1

From Greek to Muslim Perceptions

CLASSICAL ETHNIC IDEAS

Greek and Roman men of letters believed that human physical and mental features were shaped by external elements. Environmental theory played a major role in the perception and classification of peoples. The shape of the body, physical strength or weakness, hardness or softness of character, swift or slow intelligence, and independence of mind or a submissive attitude were all generally linked to climate and geography. Different peoples were supposed to reflect the conditions of the land where they had been born. The geographic position of Greece and Rome—in the temperate zone, between the cold North and hot South, and for the Greeks, between East and West (a most important separation from "arrogant," "corrupt," and "servile" Asia)—allowed their peoples to attribute to themselves the virtues necessary for their imperial projects. This vision was nuanced by the idea of opposition between people from the mountains (regarded as rude and antisocial) and those from the plains (urban and sophisticated)—an approach that introduced the reality of conflicting forms of behavior even between neighbors. This theory was further complicated by Greek and Roman attitudes to different ways of living—for example, nomadic behavior—and different forms of government—in particular despotic rule in the East, which was seen to reinforce dependency and weakness.[1]

This environmental theory could be combined with the notion of hereditary characteristics acquired by human beings. The discussion of lineage and autochthony developed by the Athenians, who held that they had always occupied the same land and were of pure ancestry, was projected by the Greeks and Romans onto other peoples, shaping their attitudes.[2] The idea of descent became crucial in two ways: as a link between blood and soil, which reinforced the perception of an identity based on appearance, language, and custom in the creation of an essential definition of peoples (*gentes*); and as a guarantee of the reproduction among a people of characteristics shaped by their original environment. This meant that the descendants of Syrians, for instance, would carry with them the basic mental and physical features of their ancestors, even when born abroad. The Roman prejudice against most Eastern peoples, considered natural slaves, was directed not only toward these peoples in their own environment but also toward migrants living in other provinces or at the center of the empire, in Rome. In general, the supposed connections between environment and heredity, or physical and mental characteristics, meant the refusal of individual or generational variation. The possibilities for variation were, to a significant degree, collective and tended toward decline: the idea of descent, explicit in the Athenian boast of pure lineage, was linked to a prejudice against people of mixed origin. Mixed lineage was considered to create inferior human beings, weakening original positive qualities. By the same token, a change of environment could only lead to the deterioration of the human beings involved and their descendants.

The application of these criteria nonetheless was quite loose and contradictory. We can find praise for the brave German, Gaul, or Hispanic warrior; indeed, the Germans were seen as a threat, because they had never been vanquished, thus keeping their warrior qualities intact. Yet the Germans were also believed to hate peace and serious work, while the Gauls were depicted as drinkers, fickle, and unruly, though they were considered good orators. In the Middle East, the idea of natural slavery was applied to various peoples, but not to the Parthians, who had never been conquered by the Romans, nor to the Jews, whose successive rebellions made them a case apart. The old Egyptian civilization was respected, but its people were considered wicked and odd because of their zoomorphic cult. The cleverness attributed to the Phoenicians and Carthaginians went together with unreliability, while the Syrians were portrayed as effeminate, perverted, and superstitious. Accusations of human sacrifice and anthropophagi were used to condemn, among others, the druids, but prejudice against the Jews was based on the ideas of antisocial behavior and an exclusive religion. Condemnation of usury, the main antisocial activity attributed to Jews in the Middle Ages, is absent from Greek and Roman sources; it appears to have been first coined in the twelfth century.

The shifting nature of prejudice is demonstrated in the Greek and Roman heritage, since Greek judgments on Eastern peoples were turned against themselves: the Romans considered the Greeks learned and artful, but at the same time arrogant, effeminate, corrupt, inconstant, and lacking in seriousness. The comparison of human beings (and peoples) with animals was another feature of Roman preconceived opinions. A prejudice against black Africans based on color had already emerged, as these people were considered burned by the sun—the Greek etymology of Ethiopian—an undesirable result of adverse climatic conditions in the extreme South. The important issue here is that prejudice in the Greek and Roman world was already linked to the notion of lineage and descent.[3] There is no evidence of systematic discrimination against distinct ethnic people, though; on the contrary, Roman attribution of citizenship was relatively generous.

The problem is to understand how this set of unstable and shifting prejudices against other peoples, built partly as a response to the needs of the Greek and Roman civilizations in their processes of expansion, was affected by the process of Christianization as well as the decline and collapse of the Roman Empire in western Europe. The concept of universal conversion set up by the early Christian Church significantly disrupted the previous identification of peoples with territory and religion. In spite of their recognition as a sect of the Jewish people, the Christians' initial handicap was that they were not seen as part of an old tradition with historic roots. After three centuries of repression and resistance, however, this novelty paid off. The recognition of Christianity and its adoption as the religion of the empire by Constantine (321–25), followed by the ban on paganism by Theodosius (392), marked the identification of the Christian multiethnic message with the imperial ideology of universal rule as well as the transformation of the church from a persecuted community to a dominant religion endorsed by political power.

THE IMPACT OF BARBARIANS AND MUSLIMS

The invasion of western Europe by successive barbarian peoples transformed the set of ethnic categories: new realities imposed new designations of peoples, such as the Goths, Ostrogoths, Lombards, Visigoths, Suebi, Vandals, Franks, and Saxons. This period of intense migration led to the emergence of new ethnicities with their origins in the East, and also to the constant regrouping of peoples in multiethnic confederations under a common name.[4] The issue of the changing or multiple identities of these peoples has become an object of study in the past twenty years.[5] The transfer of the axis of the surviving Roman Empire to Asia Minor and the Middle East rendered the perpetuation of prejudices against the Syrians and Egyptians problematic.[6] The conversion (and reconversion from Arianism) of the barbarian kingdoms, generally accomplished between the fifth and eighth centuries, defined a new set of ideas on ethnicity related to smaller political units within a universal religion. Amid these movements, the prejudices previously described temporarily lost their relevance.

In time, as social and political conditions changed throughout medieval Europe, and as a significant number of Greek and Roman texts were recovered, some of the judgments on other peoples inscribed in these texts were reinterpreted and adapted to new historical realities. One example of a new prejudice, for which the original medieval perception has lasted until the present day, is provided by the enduring words *vandal* and *vandalism*, meaning "cruelty," "ignorance," and "irrational destruction," after the barbarian people who established a kingdom in North Africa around Carthage (the future Ifriqiya) between 439 and 533.[7] If the classical system of prejudices applied to particular peoples became partly meaningless, its core of environmental theory and hereditary characteristics proved to be, as we will see, particularly resilient. Under these new conditions of barbarian transition, the unique survival of the Jewish people—despite persecution, forced conversion, and segregation—added new criteria for defining ethnic groups based on religion.[8]

The political, religious, and ethnic environment that developed in the Mediterranean area after the barbarian invasions was radically changed by the Islamic expansion from the seventh to tenth centuries and beyond. Most of the Middle East and North Africa, the most significant Mediterranean islands, and almost all of Iberia were conquered in a short period of time, dramatically reducing the reach of the Byzantine Empire and terminating the Christian Visigoth kingdom of Hispania. Islam carried a new message of universalism, laying claim to the legacy of the Jewish and Christian religions, which it represented as

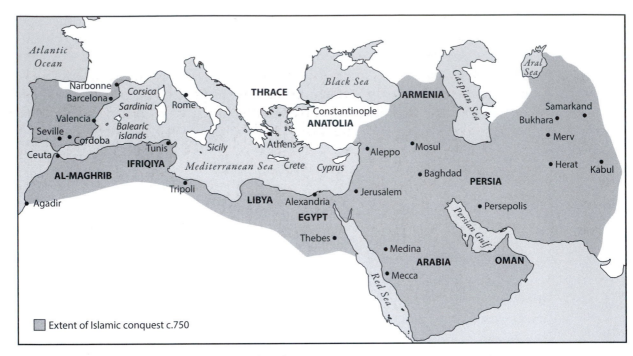

Map 1.1. Islamic expansion in the Middle East and Mediterranean, 632–750.
Sources: Angus Konstam, *The Historical Atlas of the Crusades* (London: Mercury Books, 2004), 10–11; Geoffrey Barraclough, ed., *The Times Atlas of World History* (London: Times Books, 1990), 120–21

the forerunners of the final and complete revelation sent by God to the prophet Muhammad. In around 700, the imposition of Arabic as the language of administration by the Umayyad Caliph 'Abd al-Malik reinforced the status of the sacred language of the Koran as the unifying element of Islamic countries (as had happened with Latin in western Europe and Greek in the Byzantine Empire), underlining the superiority of the Arabs as warriors and administrators who had assimilated the Syrians and Egyptians during their expansion. Pahlavi (Persian), though, kept its status as a major learned language, particularly after the transfer of the capital of the caliphate by al-Mansur from Damascus to Baghdad in 762. Its use later spread through India and Asia Minor—a sign of the important cultural role that the Iranians played in the Muslim world, most notably after the diffusion of Shiism in Iran (945 onward). The same phenomenon can be observed later with the Turks, whose language spread with the expansion of the Seljuks (between the eleventh and thirteenth centuries) and Ottomans (from the fourteenth century onward).[9] By contrast, the massive presence of Islamized Berbers in North Africa, Spain, and Sicily never carried with it any linguistic expression, even under the rule of Almoravid (1061–1163) and Almohad (1147–1269). Multilingual and multiethnic Islamic expansion, with its conversion of nomadic and seminomadic people like the Turks, integrated new ethnicities into large areas of Eurasia and North Africa. It built a new balance of forces between peoples and developed new perceptions of barbarians—a notion then applied to the Turkish Seljuks, Berbers, black Africans, and ultimately Crusaders.[10]

Islamic expansion brought with it the recovery of old Greek and Roman texts, which helped to shape a geographic and ethnic vision adapted to the necessities of a new civilization centered on the Middle East and extending from Iberia to central Asia. In spite of an easy process of conversion and egalitarian concept of the community of believers, new prejudices were visible in the classification of provinces (Arab and non-Arab) as well as districts and cities, and the definition of the main characteristics of their peoples. As early as the tenth century, the geographer al-Muqaddasī remarked on the refinement and delicacy of the people of Iraq, as opposed to the villainous qualities displayed by the inhabitants of Huzistān (nowadays southeastern Iraq), and the superior behavior of the people of Sam (Syria and Palestine, where he had been born), compared to the inhumanity and incivility of the inhabitants of Maghrib, not to mention the libertinism in Fārs, perfidy in Rayy, tyranny in Nisābīn, and stupidity in Hims.[11]

The vision of later Arab authors interested in geography (Al-Khwārismī, Abū Zayd al-Balkhī, al-Biruni, and al-Idrisi) emphasized a high level of correspondence between climates, stars, and peoples, embracing the classical division of the Earth into quadrants and updating the descriptions of the main civilizations: Persian, Syrian, Greek, Roman (to include the Franks), Libyan (African), Turkish and Khāzar, and Indian and Chinese. The skills of each people were also depicted in a schematic manner: the technical and artisanal abilities of the Chinese; the theoretical science of the Indians; the Greek philosophical inheritance of the Byzantines; the ethical and political vision of the Iranians; the capacity for war of the Turks; and the poetry and religion of the Arabs. Physical appearances, such as skin color (white, black, brown, or red), the shape of eyes (round or almondlike) or nose (long, large, or flat), the type of hair, and the scarcity or abundance of facial hair were already used to identify peoples, defining the major stereotypes later developed during the European expansion. Black Africans were already placed in opposition to the rest of humankind and labeled as savages, supposedly lighthearted and of inferior intelligence. Only the geographer Jāhiz of Basra (c. 776–869) offered an alternative to this vision, praising the superiority of black people over white, and including Chinese, Hindus, Abyssinians, and Sudanese in the former group. Particular prejudices against specific peoples also spread, often revealing the birthplaces of their main authors: the Turks were considered unfaithful, the Byzantines mean, the Khāzars impudent, black people unserious, Slavs cowards, and Indians unchaste. The only, but important, limit to this set of stereotypes was that they do not appear to have been based on the idea of inheritance or transmission of the same characteristics through generations.[12]

Islamic people were designated by the Jews and Romans as Saracens, from the late Latin *Saracenus*, which in turn came from the Greek *Sarakēnos*, and perhaps originally from the Arabic *šarkī* (eastern) or the Aramaic *surq[ly]īn*, meaning inhabitants of the desert.[13] Moor (*Moro* in Spanish and Italian, *Mouro* in Portuguese, *Maure* in French), from the Latin *Maurus*, designated the native of Mauritania in North Africa. In the Middle Ages, Moor meant not only a Muslim but also a person of an African physical type, with dark skin and black hair. In time, the term Moor took on a wide range of meanings: depending on the country, it might mean a mulatto, a horse or mare with a dark coat and a white blaze (or a dark head with a light-colored coat), wine mixed with water, a child who had not been baptized, a pagan, a hardworking person, a healer who used verses of the Koran in their practices, a round in a horse tournament, characters in a play, the enacting of fights between Christians and Muslims with music and dance, a Muslim from Sri Lanka, India, or the Philippines, or a type of monkey.[14] Centuries-old proverbs in Spain and Portugal are witness to the widespread use of the word Moro (and *Morisco*) to convey a huge variety of situations originally defined by ethnic prejudice and abuse, and they offer evidence of references to phenotype features from the earliest periods in these countries' history.

|||||||||||||||||||||||||||||||||||||||||||||||||||||||||||||||||||||||||||||||||||||||||||||||||||||||||||

CHAPTER 2

Christian Reconquest

The impact of Islam on Christian societies can be highlighted here in three areas: it inspired a major prophetic trend in western Europe; it spread the idea of holy war; and it provided a model of government based on the hierarchical coexistence of different religions. The swift Islamic conquest of Christian territories (mostly from 634 to 750), wiping out more than four hundred dioceses in the Middle East and North Africa, stimulated the output of an apocalyptic literature in western Europe.[1] The disappearance of Christian communities from the areas where most of the theological reflection of the early church took place, coupled with the Islamic dominion of Iberia and most of the Mediterranean area, had a long-lasting psychological effect, visible in the Western expansion of the late eleventh to the thirteenth centuries.

The idea of holy war as a personal and collective duty was alien to the Christian tradition.[2] Christ's teaching of peace and forbearance, set against the Islamic exhortation to holy war, was the main rhetorical argument propounded in the first Christian polemical texts produced in the Middle East, Byzantium, and Iberia that opposed the new religion.[3] The protection of Christians in the Middle East and access to the Holy Land were, seemingly, the only political issues at stake in Pope Urban II's preaching to the First Crusade in Clermont in 1095.[4] But the success of the First Crusade and consequent concentration of attention on Jerusalem fueled the Christians' obsession with the liberation of their holy places from the dominion of infidels for centuries to come. The idea of the Crusade was shaped by this specific ambition, feeding on the long struggle in Iberia between Christians and Muslims as well as the success of the Normans in recovering Sicily from the Muslims.[5] The disputed split of the Latin and Greek Christian churches in 1054 also played an essential role in the Latin expansion into the Middle East: it was only too present during the Crusades, contributing to both spiritual motivation and bitter reciprocal criticism.[6]

These complex internal and external contexts, within Christendom and in opposition to Islam, led to the juxtaposition of the traditional idea of pilgrimage as redemption of sins and the new idea of pious war for Christian access to the holy places. The crusading idea thus became crucial to Western expansion as a legitimate religious justification for the conquest of Iberia, the Mediterranean islands, and the Middle East that was to engage hundreds of thousands of Christian migrants.[7] The concept of a hierarchical coexistence of different religions, however, temporarily influenced the new Christian states of Iberia and Sicily as well as the Latin Kingdom of Jerusalem. The imposition of tributes on non-Christian populations along with the creation of serfdom or slave status in the conquered territories revealed the influence of previous Muslim practices.

The Crusades thus represented a major turning point for Christendom, not only because they gave ideological expression to an enormous process of expansion and conquest, but also because they unleashed new forms of religious persecution and new concepts of ethnic hierarchy. A significant reshuffling of peoples and ethnicities, individual and collective identities, accompanied the Crusades as a result of migrations, massacres, changes of status, reversals of hierarchies, the creation of new hierarchies, and massive conversions and reconversions. The expansion of Latin Christians in the Mediterranean area represented a first major shift in the self-perception of Europe: Jerusalem became commonly seen as the spiritual center of the world, despite the position of Rome as the headquarters of the church, and this had implications for geographic concepts and their cartographic expression.[8] The absorption of Islamic science into these fields, and also into mathematics, nautical navigation, and astronomy, resulted from new needs for orientation, information on peoples, and knowledge of territories.

SICILY

In 1145, King Roger II of Sicily donated two splendid sarcophagi carved out of porphyry marble to the cathedral of Cefalù. He indicated that one was intended for his remains, and the other for "the august memory of my name and the glory of the Church itself." When Roger II died nine years later, he was not buried in Cefalù, though: the project to transform the cathedral into a burial place for the kings of Sicily had failed. The diocese had been created by the antipope, Anacletus II (1130–38), who had controlled Rome and been recognized by Roger II. In 1139, Innocent II managed to reunify the church, and he excommunicated the Sicilian king. When Eugenius III agreed to reconciliation with Roger II in 1150, Cefalù became a political embarrassment. Only in 1166 was the diocese recognized by the pope and the bishop consecrated by the archbishop of Messina. Yet the bishop and cathedral chapter managed to put up a long fight to keep the sarcophagi as well as claim the fulfillment of Roger II's burial dispositions. It was only in 1215 that Roger II's grandson, Frederick II, king of Sicily and Holy Roman emperor, secured the removal of the sarcophagi from the cathedral of Cefalù and their transport to the cathedral of Palermo. Frederick II chose Roger II's sarcophagus for his tomb and the second memorial sarcophagus for his father (the emperor and king of Sicily, Henry VI, who died in 1197).[9]

The two sarcophagi represented an important innovation in the history of funerary art, but what concerns me here is the iconographic program for Roger II's first tomb. The decoration of the lid is rich in spiritual and imperial symbols.[10] But it is in the supports of the trough, the lowest part of the sarcophagus, that we find the most expressive symbols of dominion over peoples. The supports were carved as two pairs of lions facing in opposite directions, and holding a goat and human heads in their claws. The omnipresence of the lion was an obvious symbol of sovereignty: in the Greek and Roman traditions, the lion was a symbol of courage and strength, an emblem of the ruler, but also of victory, often used in triumphs.[11] This symbolism was widely reproduced in medieval Europe, and in Sicily the lion was a crucial element in the famous royal mantel of Roger II. The lion's double connotation of sovereignty and triumph is noteworthy. Yet the figures held by the lions are even more fascinating. The goat was a key symbolic element in Greek tragedy (*tragoidia*, literally meant goat song). The animal symbolized the obscure, ardent, prolific, and impulsive forces of nature. It was also used for sacrifices, implying identification with the metamorphoses of the gods. The Christian tradition reinterpreted the goat as symbol of impurity and diabolic nature.[12] It seems that two traditions converged here: the dominion over impulses or nature was coupled with tragic and sacrificial elements in the depiction of Roger II as protector of the Christians.

The three human heads most likely represented the peoples Roger II ruled over. Under the lion facing southwest (according to the actual position of the sarcophagus), there was a bearded head turned upside down. This head represented the Muslims defeated either in Sicily by the ruler's father or by Roger II's own project of expansion in North Africa, which started before the donation of the sarcophagus.[13] This interpretation is supported

Figure 2.1. A. Anonymous sculpture of a lion holding a bearded head upside down under its claws, probably representing defeated Muslims. Cathedral of Palermo, sarcophagus of Frederic II (previously carved for Roger II of Sicily in the 1140s), southwest support of the trough. B. Detail of figure 2.1A.
Photos: Francisco Bethencourt, with permission from Segreteria Ufficio Beni Culturali, Palermo

by the tradition of triumphs begun in Roman times, and perpetuated by the Byzantine, Western Christian, and Islamic powers: the standards of the conquered people would be reversed or turned upside down to signify their defeat.[14] Under the lion, facing southeast, there was a clean-shaven face that might represent the Latin Christians (mainly Normans) who had been involved in the conquest of Sicily and southern Italy, and who had settled in the region, to be strengthened by further migration. The human face depicted under the lion facing northwest is the most difficult to identify. It has lightly curled hair, but no beard, and may represent the Greek Christians, who were already undergoing a slow process of assimilation.

The second and actual sarcophagus of Roger II was not as splendid as the first one; it was probably built after his death. Both the spiritual icons and symbols of sovereignty were absent now, but the supports were once again figurative, being composed of four pairs of kneeling humans who carried the sarcophagus on their shoulders. The human figures, this time represented by a half-side view, were not as clearly carved as on the previous sarcophagus: one of them was wearing a turban and beard, in a clear reference to the Muslim community; another had lightly curled hair, probably a reference to the Greek community; there was a black African type with curled hair; and another man wore a cap and beard. The rest of the figures were clean shaven, and among them was a possible Asian face with almond eyes and straight hair, which would reinforce the universality of Roger II's imperial project.[15] As well as different ethnic types, these figures may represent different social types. They were distinguished from one another only by their faces and headdresses, though: they were similarly clad, in capes and short tunics, and had bare feet.[16]

The replacement of lions with human figures in the support of this second sarcophagus created a different political message: the vertical dominion of sovereignty, symbolized by the linking of political power with conquest and the dispensing of justice, was almost reversed in the new role given to the different types of people, who quite literally supported the king. Of course they were in an inferior position, but they were not under the claws of lions. The new iconographic program suggested a pact between the king and his vassals: the different peoples under the king's rule were expected to be loyal and submissive (on their knees), yet the king was expected to give them protection.

The insistence on a typology of peoples ruled by Roger II in the sarcophagi had another important function: it complemented his title of king of Sicily, Apulia, and Capua, referring exclusively to territories.[17] This title contrasted, for good reason, with those of other western European medieval rulers who were referred to as kings of a particular people: *rex romanorum*, *rex francorum*, and *rex anglorum*.[18] The Norman rulers of Sicily were not the leaders of a people more or less homogeneous from an ethnic point of view (even if homogeneity is always a political construct, contradicted by constant migration, as was particularly the case in rex romanorum). They ruled over multiethnic communities and were conscious of this fact, just like their contemporaries in Castile, Aragon, and Portugal, who assumed similar titles referring to their territories. In Sicily the ruler was also designated—from the beginning of Norman rule, when the title was that of count—"defender of God and protector of the Christian religion." This meant that the different ethnic communities ruled over by the Sicilian kings did not all have the same status—a fact underlined by the image of the defeated Muslim turned upside down on Roger II's first sarcophagus.

The consciousness of ethnic diversity represented in the sculptures under the two sarcophogi is confirmed by written sources. Differences between peoples were perceived as physical, religious, and cultural (language and clothing). In twelfth-century Sicily, Greeks, Arabs (Berbers), Normans, Lombards, and Jews were all extremely active, speaking their own languages (or the languages they had assimilated through time) and trying to preserve their identities. The Norman Conquest of Sicily meant that for a while, a Western Christian elite ruled over both an Islamic population, mostly concentrated in the western part of the Island, and a Greek population, concentrated in the eastern part. The position of Sicily as a hub of Mediterranean trade routes had brought, successively, the benefits of dominion by the Byzantines (until the ninth century, but with a longer-lasting military presence in the region), the Arabs (from the ninth to the eleventh century), and the Normans (whose conquest was relatively fast, from 1061 to 1091). On the mainland, where the Islamic presence before the Norman Conquest had been tenuous, the Greek and Roman culture had been perpetuated by the entrenchment of a Byzantine legacy that was only finally defeated by the Normans. Sicily was a composite commercial center, blending an Oriental-type trade in luxury goods with an Occidental-type trade in the products of agriculture. Commerce brought with it an influx of people who added to the ethnic mix—for example, Genoese, Pisan, and Venetian merchants. By 1184, the majority of the merchants in Palermo were still Muslims, while Messina had become a center for the Italian and Greek merchant communities.[19] Piracy and the slave trade would bring more Berbers, Greeks, Slavs, Tartars, and Albanians to the island, with some Russians, Bulgarians, and Turks—all of who would be replaced by black Africans during the fifteenth century.[20]

How did power relations between the main ethnic and religious groups evolve? The language of surviving royal documents gives us an idea of the increase or decline of the political influence of the three main communities in just one century: during the reigns of Roger I and Roger II, Greek, Arabic, and Latin were all equally used; under William I, only one in seven documents used Arabic; under William II it went down to one in ten; and by Tancred's short reign, all royal documents were in Latin.[21] By 1340, Arabic had almost totally died out among the Christian communities of Sicily, and from that time on, Jews and North African slaves were the only people who could read, write, or speak it.[22] The Jews comprised a small urban community whose numbers increased by migration from Iberia, after the invasion of the Almohads from the North of Africa during the second half of the twelfth century brought with it a new religious intolerance. Once enlarged, the community maintained an important presence in Sicily until the fifteenth century. The Greeks, on the other hand, were put under pressure to accept the Latin liturgy, and although they played a major role in the Norman administration and armed forces, especially in the fleet, which was often commanded by Greek admirals, their identity was eroded in the long run. In 1308, there still were more than a hundred Greek priests; their number was reduced to eleven in 1450.[23] The integration of the Greeks into Latin Christendom was slow and relatively smooth—with the exception, in 1168, of the riot of the Greek population of Messina against Chancellor Stephen of Perche.[24] But they lost their language and Orthodox religion. The initial Norman creation of Latin dioceses—in the five crucial cities of Troina, Agrigento, Catania, Mazara, and Siracusa between 1081 and 1088 alone—was a clear sign of a religious program to replace the Greek Orthodox Church.[25] The significant migration of Lombards and other peoples from Italy along with the Normans helped to impose a policy of Latinization.

The status of the Muslim population of Sicily after the Norman Conquest was more complex. The Norman rulers did not have clear religious objectives at the beginning. They were too busy with another military goal: conquering the territories of the Byzantine Empire in southern Italy. The turning point came in 1084, when Benavert, the Muslim ruler of Syracuse and Noto who resisted the Norman invasion of Sicily, decided to pillage the coasts of Calabria.[26] Benavert's fleet destroyed Nicotera and carried its inhabitants off into slavery; it plundered two churches near Reggio, from which it took images, vestments, and vessels; and it devastated the female convent of Rocco d'Asino, raping and abducting the nuns.[27] Pillage and enslavement were common practices on both sides, but the plunder of churches and abduction of nuns seemed to raise a strong sentiment among the Christians. From that moment, the Norman Conquest acquired a religious zeal never seen before, assuming the character of a holy war before the official launch of the First Crusade by the Pope Urban II in 1095 in Clermont. It is this religious zeal on the part of Roger I that probably explains why, in 1098, Urban II conferred on him the status of apostolic legate—a status claimed by his successors and recognized by successive popes. Although inevitably there was violence with the imposition of slavery on Muslims in certain circumstances and even, in the case of Butera, conquered in 1088, the exile of its population to Calabria, in many places a peaceful surrender was negotiated, allowing Muslims to maintain a significant presence in many towns.

The status of the Muslim community eroded quickly during the twelfth century, even though the Norman rulers of Sicily, and their Swabian successors up to Frederick II, were surrounded by Islamic artists, geographers, and philosophers, and during the reign of Roger II, the kingdom absorbed the best administrative innovations of Fatimid Egypt. Muslims were excluded from positions of power and lost control of their land, which was redistributed by the Norman rulers to those who had helped them in their conquest. They maintained a certain presence in the cities of western Sicily, as merchants and artisans (and in some cases, administrators), but in the countryside, most of them were reduced to serfdom or slavery. They were praised as warriors, mainly as infantry soldiers and horse archers: from Roger II to Manfred, including during Frederick II's expedition to Palestine, the Sicilian kings kept Muslim bodyguards and special troops; and Muslim troops fought with King Manfred in the decisive battle of 1266 against Charles I of Anjou.[28] The general decline of the Muslim population of Sicily was continuous, however, aggravated by the policies of conversion launched by Roger II in 1153, and renewed by papal bulls in 1199 and 1208, thereby stimulating emigration to North Africa.

The swift pace of the decline in their status explains the succession of revolts by the Muslims in Sicily: in 1189–90, during the weak government of Tancred; in 1197, after the death of Emperor Henry VI; in 1219–21, during the absence of Frederick II; and in 1243, again under Frederick II, in what was to be the final appearance of Muslims on the political scene in Sicily. The pattern was the following one: revolt, control of strongholds in the countryside (the mountains), a rallying of slaves and serfs, resistance for several years, and then final defeat with massacres and deportation. In 1221–24, Frederick II, after a violent repression, deported those Muslim communities accused of rebellion to North Apulia—mainly to Lucera. The same occurred in 1246, after three years of Muslim resistance. The Muslims then disappeared from Sicily, and the last colony in Lucera was destroyed by Charles II of Anjou in August 1300: the Muslims, who had revolted against the new ruler, were taken prisoner and transported to the ports of Barletta and Naples to be sold as slaves—an operation that probably involved ten thousand people.[29]

IBERIA

As we have seen, the relatively swift disappearance of Muslims from Sicily and southern Italy was complete by the beginning of the fourteenth century. In Iberia, however, the Muslim presence, which had begun in 711, lasted until 1492 as a political power, and Muslims continued to exist as a distinct religious community until 1502 in Granada and 1526 in Aragon. The different political histories of the two areas might be explained by the contrast between two hundred years of Muslim rule in Sicily and five hundred in most of Iberia (and almost eight hundred years in the Granada region). The swift Muslim conquest of Iberia, with the exception of the northern territories, in less than ten years can be contrasted with the sixty-plus years it took the Muslims to conquer Sicily—a process prolonged by strong Byzantine resistance. As a consequence, Islam became much more deeply rooted in Iberia, although the number of Christian communities was also significant, and the number of Jewish communities greater than in Sicily. Intercommunity relations in Iberia were thus based on the three religions of the book: Islam, Christianity, and Judaism.

Islamic rule in Iberia diluted the effect of the previous division of the peninsula under the barbarians into two communities: the Visigoths, and the Suebi, who were established in the northwest. The Basques had been the only exception to this division; they were never integrated into the Visigothic kingdom and maintained a fierce resistance to all forms of foreign domination for several centuries. It was close to their traditional territory in northeast Iberia that the intervention of the Franks had a particular impact in the second half of the eighth century. This intervention stimulated both Muslim dissidence and Christian resistance southwest of the Pyrenees, and in 801 the county of Barcelona was created by Christians to control territories on both sides of the chain of mountains up to Provence. Distance and the fragmentation of the Carolingian Empire made this county autonomous by the end of the tenth century—the same period that saw the emergence of the Catalan

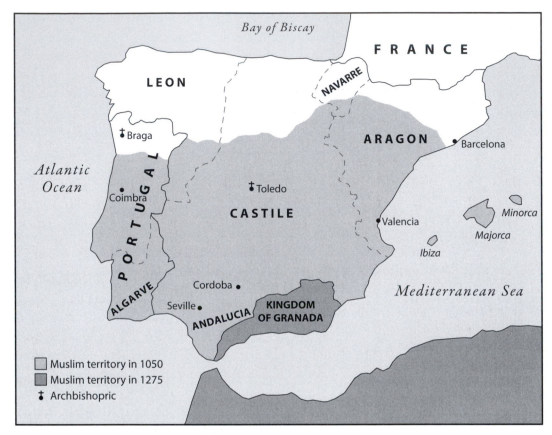

Map 2.1. Christian reconquest of Iberia (722–1492).
Source: Jonathan Riley-Smith, *The Atlas of the Crusades* (London: Times Books, 1991), 32, 73

language, although the *langue d'oc* continued to be systematically used to express a vibrant literature until the thirteenth century.[30]

The former Visigothic kingdom provided two essential tools for the reconquest of Iberia: Christianity, which had become rooted in the population after the conversion of King Recaredo from Arianism to Catholicism (c. 586) and the Third Council of Toledo (589); and the legacy of both Roman written law and elements of Hispanic and German customary law, which had been compiled into a unified code by the mid-seventh century—a significant achievement among the barbarian kingdoms. The Christian religion was the major vehicle of resistance against Muslim rule; the new Christian kingdoms adopted *lex gothica*, which maintained a long-lasting presence in Catalonia, as their legal and institutional framework. The Christian reconquest of Iberia created new forms of collective identity along the north-south axis of expansion from Asturias, a kingdom that had been created as a political refuge by the defeated Visigoths. The territories of Galicia and Portugal in the West, León and Castile in the center, and Navarra, Aragon, and Catalonia in the East of Iberia all became political entities between the eighth and twelfth centuries. With the exception of Portugal, though, which became an independent kingdom in the 1130s, these political entities were linked with one another throughout the process of reconquest and beyond. Galicia was integrated with León, which was associated with Castile in 1037 and finally united with it in 1230; Catalonia became associated with the kingdom of Aragon in 1150; and Navarra, a political entity from the ninth century and separated from Aragon in 1134, lost the territory south of the Pyrenees, which was conquered in 1512 by Ferdinand, then king of Castile and Aragon. Later, collective identities were built around the kingdoms of Castile and Portugal, but a Basque identity lived on without being embodied in an independent political entity, while Catalan autonomy subsisted under the crown of Aragon.[31]

The significant and constant migration to Iberia of Franks as well as other peoples from western and northern Europe throughout the period of Christian reconquest (legitimized by the pope as a Crusade in the twelfth and thirteenth centuries) had an impact on various aspects of the Iberian territories: the Christian political and ecclesiastical elite received an injection of new blood, since many Franks, Burgundians, or English became rulers and bishops in the area; the liturgy of the church changed, with the replacement of the Visigothic ritual by the Roman ritual; and the colonization of the reconquered territories was reinforced by the newcomers. These new immigrants were involved in the conquests of major cities, such as Toledo, Valencia, and Murcia, though in some cases cities fell to conquerors who were merely diverted from fleets of Crusaders on their way to the Holy Land, as happened in the conquest of Lisbon (1147), Silves (1189), and Alcácer do Sal (1217) on what would become the Portuguese coast. Nevertheless, the significant immigration of Christians from other parts of Europe did not leave many traces in terms of separate identities: although their arrival led to a few changes in place-names, the immigrants on the whole swiftly integrated into the Christian political entities. This phenomenon contrasted with Sicily, where as late as 1266, the chroniclers described the troops of Manfred as being composed of Germans, Lombards, *regnicoli* (inhabitants of the kingdom), and Muslims. Perhaps this can be explained by the Italian context: as the Muslim "threat" had fast disappeared, the different ethnicities may not have felt the need to integrate and instead maintained their separate identities. The constant presence of foreign powers and troops in Italy (Greeks, Germans, French, and Catalans) also helps to explain the difference, as do the long-lasting consequences of the barbarian kingdoms in the area—consequences that were expressed in the rooted identity of the Lombards.

Islamization and re-Christianization were complicated processes in Iberia. The Islamic conquest involved tens of thousands of warriors from North Africa, but at the beginning the conquerors were ruling over an overwhelmingly Christian society. Widespread conversion and the cultural Arabization of the Peninsula gained momentum in the tenth century—made easier by the migration to the north of Christian communities transformed into minorities. Re-Christianization followed reconquest: a frontier along the Douro River was consolidated at the beginning of the tenth century; the Tagus River was controlled by the end of the eleventh century, with the crucial conquest of Toledo in 1085 and the first conquest of Lisbon in 1093; and after a century (from 1147 onward) of setbacks in the struggle against Almohad rule, the isolation of the last Islamic power, in the region of Granada, was achieved by the mid-thirteenth century, with the conquests of Cordova, Murcia, Jaén, Seville, Cartagena, and Cadiz by Castile (1236–63), the conquest of the Balearic Islands and Valencia by Aragon-Catalonia (1229–45), and the conquest of Faro, the last significant Muslim stronghold, in the Algarve by Portugal (1249). As in Sicily, the status of Muslims after Christian conquest differed from community to community: it could mean sack, massacre, and enslavement; or under surrender and a pact (which was mostly the case), it could mean the maintenance of the Muslim community with an inferior social position, but with an agreement on taxes, property, and respect for its religion.[32]

Islamic resistance under conquest was apparently stronger than its Christian counterpart, since there were still a great number of Muslims in Valencia, Aragon, and Granada at the end of the fifteenth century. But in western and central Iberia, Muslim communities radically declined over two centuries due to irresistible religious pressure (all the large mosques were transformed into cathedrals, while minarets and muezzins were forbidden) and segregation laws. Muslims were excluded from municipal government, confined to specific neighborhoods, and banned from employment in the service of the king as well as from taking part in the Christian judicial system. Dress was strictly regulated. The surge of Christian conquests from the 1230s to the 1250s brought in its wake the expulsion of Muslims from city centers. In 1254 and 1276, Muslim revolts in Valencia were vigorously repressed. In 1264, a strong revolt among the Muslims of Murcia and Andalusia (this was still the first generation after the Christian conquest) was put down with enormous effort, triggering more expulsions from city centers, such as in Murcia. In 1287, the final conquest of Minorca was followed by the enslavement and deportation of the whole population. Massive expulsions of Muslims had already taken place after the conquest of the other islands in the 1220s and 1230s. In 1293, the cortes (parliament) of Valladolid outlawed the possession of land by Muslims; the latter were forced to sell their properties to Christians, obviously at a low price.[33]

Much more than in the case of the reconquest of Sicily, the conditions imposed by the Christian reconquest in Iberia shaped ethnic divisions along and across religious lines. Discrimination against the *mozárabes* or *moçárabes* (from the Arabic expression *must'arab*—literally, turned Arab), the Christian communities that had survived under Muslim rule in Iberia, became even more acute than discrimination against the Orthodox Church in Sicily and southern Italy. In many cities taken from the Muslims by the northern Christians, the mozárabe bishop was immediately replaced by a Latin bishop, in many cases a foreigner, who would impose the Roman ritual over the Visigothic one. This may seem a matter of small importance nowadays, but it was of major significance then. Different rituals expressed different identities—where a community had originally come from and how it had evolved. The triumph of their ritual represented the conquerors' new political dominion, and showed that while they had sometimes benefited from internal mozárabe help during the siege of a city, they nonetheless suspected their collaborators' intimacy with the enemy. In spite of being Christians, the mozárabes had to renegotiate their status with the new rulers, who redistributed military, political, and administrative jobs among their own followers.[34]

The difficulty of the mozárabes' position can be seen in one particularly key episode. In 1139, the ruler of Portugal, Afonso Henriques, conducted an audacious attack deep into Andalusia, more than a hundred miles from his headquarters in Coimbra. He defeated the Muslim troops in the mighty battle of Ourique, and carried off a huge booty that contained the spoils of war and the sacking of villages. Among the numerous prisoners destined for slavery were more than one thousand moçárabes (the chronicle explicitly only included males in the "estimate"). The liberation of these Christians was only obtained by the intervention of Teotónio, prior of the important convent of Santa Cruz de Coimbra.[35] This episode meant that the moçárabes' own protests and prayers had not been listened to. They were taken captive and thrown into chains, just as the Muslims were. There was another crucial episode during the conquest of Lisbon in 1147—a conquest that involved German, Flemish, English, and Norman Crusaders. After the surrender, a delegation of the different troops involved entered the city to collect the treasure that had been gathered by the defeated to offer in exchange for their freedom and consecrate the scene of their conquest with a procession. According to an anonymous Anglo-Norman Crusader, probably Presbyter Ralph, German and Flemish troops did not respect the agreement that had been reached, and entered the city in great numbers, sacking it, abusing the population, and committing violent acts that included the murder of the old bishop of the moçárabe community.[36] This episode demonstrates that the Crusaders did not respect the rights of the existing Christian community, which had clung to its own religion through the years of Muslim rule. The moçárabe bishop was eliminated and replaced by Gilbert, an English clergyperson who had traveled with the Crusaders.[37] After the violence, Muslims and Jews abandoned the city.[38]

The military presence in Iberia of the Almoravids (the puritanical Islamic power that invaded from northwestern Africa) after the Christian conquest of Toledo in 1085 brought with it religious intolerance (a ban on non-Islamic religious communities, restrictions on the public expression of religion, and rules governing dress) that provoked a new wave of Jewish and moçárabe migration to Christian territories. Warriors of another austere Islamic power from North Africa, the Almohads, were also drawn into conflicts in Iberia after the Islamic defeats of the mid-twelfth century, provoking an even more significant diaspora of Jewish communities, largely to Sicily and Italy. The Jews of Iberia had suffered extreme religious persecution in the last decades of the Visigothic kingdom; the Seventeenth Council of Toledo decided to disperse Jewish communities, reduce Jewish inhabitants to serfdom, and take children up to seven years old from their parents to be educated by Catholics.[39] Circumcision was considered such an infamous practice that the *lex visigothorum* punished the false accusation of "circumcised man" with 150 public lashes. In the same period, King Wamba decided to punish his restless soldiers accused of sacking and rape with circumcision.[40]

Having lived under this oppression, Jewish communities naturally greeted the Islamic invasion as liberation, but with the renewed persecution that arrived with the Almoravid and Almohad regimes, they turned to the Christian powers to obtain relief. In spite of local conflicts, between 1148 and 1348 Jewish communities in the Christian territories of Iberia enjoyed a degree of respect and lived relatively unmolested, participating actively in political life, as advisers, ambassadors, or royal ministers. They worked mainly as artisans, but also as merchants, doctors, tax collectors, contractors, and bankers. They played a role in the intellectual life of the main cities, such as Toledo, which they helped to turn into important centers for the translation of texts from Arabic and Greek into Latin.

This state of relative coexistence was disrupted in 1348, with the first large Christian assault on Jews taking place in the Jewish neighborhood of Barcelona, followed by similar actions in 1383 in Lisbon and in 1391 in Seville. The last of these assaults spread fast to the most significant cities of Castile and Aragon, and Palma de Majorca. The plunder and massacre of the Jews were the basic features of these Christian attacks, which defied the supposedly protective role of the royal authority. At the beginning, the kings managed to keep some control of the situation and punished those who promoted riots. Yet 1391 represented a major turning point due to the scale of the attacks and number of cities involved. From then on local outbreaks of violence persisted for the next eighty years.[41]

Widespread conversions resulted from the intimidation of Jewish communities through thousands of murders; the preaching of the Dominican saint Vincente Ferrer (1350–1419) took advantage of compulsory public debates on Christianity imposed on Jewish communities, such as the one organized at Tortosa in 1413–14. The violent integration of part of the Jewish population into Christendom was not a new phenomenon but it also had never been implemented on such a scale, and was contrary to all the precepts of peaceful and voluntary conversion established by canon law. The consequences of this series of acts were twofold: it divided the Jewish community, feeding the suspicion (or rather the prejudice based on the idea of innate qualities of descent) among the Christian community that Jewish converts would secretly return to their old faith; and it led to the division of the Christian community into Old and New (recently converted) Christians. The latter soon became stigmatized, facing the same prejudices that had targeted the ancestors.[42]

The wave of statutes of purity of blood, initiated in 1449 in Toledo by a riot of Old Christians against New Christians accused of collusion with the king for raising undue taxes, deprived the New Christians of access to public and administrative jobs, and defined a new line or "caste" divide within the Christian community across the different social orders—a specific feature of Iberian societies.[43] The expulsion of the Jews from Spain in 1492 and Portugal in 1496 (here forced to convert) sealed the fate of an extraordinary community that disappeared under the growing intolerance of a confident Christian political power unwilling to accept religious difference in the new "homogeneous" Iberia (for a more detailed analysis, see chapter 9).[44]

A comparison of the fate of the Jewish communities southwest and northeast of the Pyrenees is striking, because there was a gap of two hundred years between the two sequences of events that led to expulsion. During the 1010s, in the first wave of massacres, Jews were put to death in Rouen, Orléans, and Limoges as well as in Mainz and other cities of the

Rhine, but it was in 1096, after the launch of the First Crusade, that gangs of Crusaders decided to cleanse their land of the infidels who had denied the divine nature of Christ and delivered him to the Roman authorities to be crucified (a doubtful accusation drawn from the New Testament). Many cities in western and central Europe (France, Germany, and Bohemia) were devastated by pillage and murder, which left thousands of Jews dead and led to massive forced conversions. In certain cases, converted Jews were authorized by their rulers to return to their previous faith, because the legitimacy of the conversion procedure was questioned, although canon law condemned violent conversion even as it accepted its consequences. In 1146, the Second Crusade was better organized and did not replicate the opportunistic chaos of the First Crusade, although massacres still occurred in Cologne, Speyer, Mainz, Würzburg, Carentan, Ramerupt, and Sully. In 1188, the Third Crusade brought the pillage and massacre of Jewish communities to England (to London, York, Norwich, Stamford, and Lynn). The Crusade against the Albigensians in Provence (1209–29) also brought violence to local Jewish communities. Aborted Crusades in 1236, 1309, and 1320 left a trail of anti-Jewish assaults in various regions of Europe.[45] During this period, accusations that the water of wells had deliberately been poisoned, children kidnapped and ritually murdered, and the host desecrated were leveled against Jewish people.[46]

The expulsions of Jews decreed in England in 1290 and France (then a much smaller territory) in 1306 and 1394 set the seal on the first long, intense wave of anti-Semitism in Europe. During this period, two reasons explain the relative benignity of the Christians toward the Jews in Iberia: the Christians focused on the war against the Muslims, who represented a territorial power as well as a rival religion; and the Jewish communities were much stronger and better integrated into all levels of Christian society than in France, Germany, or England. The stabilization of Christian kingdoms and societies in Iberia after the mid-thirteenth century, following the destruction of internal Muslim resistance and reduction of the influence of Granada, started a shift toward a more intolerant religious policy, supported by new generations of poor people and inferior clergypersons who did not have access to the same benefits as the conquerors.

MIDDLE EAST

The status of the Jewish communities in the Middle East was also complex. They had suffered discrimination and segregation under the Byzantine Empire, and had been banned from Jerusalem. The Islamic conquest of the Holy City represented temporary relief from previous oppression, and meant that they could return there, despite the protests of the Orthodox patriarch, who had capitulated to the Muslims. Nevertheless, the Jews were subject to Islamic discrimination as were the Christians.[47] The terms of their status were defined by the famous "Pact" for the *dhimmīs* (non-Muslims living in Muslim lands) established under the caliphate of 'Umar ibn-al Khattab (634–44), the second successor of the Prophet Muhammad. The Pact decreed that non-Muslims were under the protection of Muslims. As

Map 2.2. The Crusaders' states at their greatest extension (c. 1144)
Source: Angus Konstam, *The Historical Atlas of the Crusades* (London: Mercury Books, 2004), 80–81

a result they were not allowed to use the Koran for mockery or misinterpretation, offend the prophet, deride the Islamic cult, touch or marry a Muslim woman, convert a Muslim or make an attempt against a Muslim's life or property, or help any enemy or give succour to enemy spies. Non-Muslims had to wear the *ghiyar*—a distinctive sign that was yellow for Jews and blue for Christians—were not allowed to build houses higher than those of Muslims, ring church bells, read their holy books aloud, drink wine in public, show their crosses, or ride horses, only donkeys and mules. Finally, they were obliged to bury their dead in silence.

The reproduction of the full list is useful, as we will see. The violation of any of the first six rules meant that the malefactor would henceforth be considered outside the protection afforded by the Pact; the violation of the second six rules could be dealt with by penalties.[48] By the late ninth century, dress restrictions were in force for dhimmīs. These forbade Christians and Jews to wear the *qabā'*, a garment of *khazz* silk, and the *aṣb* (turban), and imposed differentiation through the color of clothing and badges. The introduction of zoomorphic marks such as identifying badges explicitly intended to humiliate the wearer also occurred elsewhere in this period. In Ifriqiya, for instance, the Jews had to wear a patch with the image of an ape on it and the Christians a patch with the image of a pig, and in Egypt the Christians had to wear a tattoo of a lion on their hands.

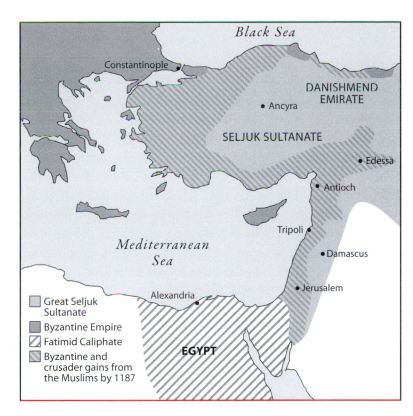

Map 2.3. Christian gains in the Middle East up to 1187. Source: Angus Konstam, *The Historical Atlas of the Crusades* (London: Mercury Books, 2004), 80–81

The long-lasting influence of this Islamic Pact on later Christian practices against Jews and Muslims can clearly be recognized.[49] The Jews of the Middle East also suffered from sporadic persecution during Muslim rule, the worst of which took place under the Fatimid caliph of Egypt, Hakim, who in 1012 ordered the destruction of all churches and synagogues as well as forbade the practice of religions other than Islam.[50] The temporary conquest of Palestine by the Seljuk Turks in the 1070s provoked a general devastation that did not spare the Jews. Following that, the first wave of Crusader conquests had a major impact on Jewish and Muslim communities: in every city that offered resistance, such as Jerusalem in 1099, Jews and Muslims were massacred and the survivors sold as slaves. Jewish communities survived only in those cities that capitulated, such as Ascalon and Tyre. They had to pay taxes, as all non-Christians, reproducing the Muslim practice concerning dhimmīs. After the second decade of the twelfth century, the ban on Jews settling in Jerusalem was relaxed and a small number were allowed to live in the city, but a proper community was only reestablished after Saladin conquered the city in 1187. Even then, most Jews lived outside the cities, mainly in the villages of Galilee. But the anti-Jewish legislation of the Third and Fourth Lateran councils was not applied in the Latin Kingdom of Jerusalem.[51]

The relatively benign treatment of the Jews by the Latin Christians in the Middle East after the first wave of conquests may be explained by the constant threat from the surrounding

Islamic world, the conquerors' lack of manpower, the scarcity of natural resources, and the relatively short duration of the colonial experience, from 1099 to 1291.[52] If we look at the other areas discussed in a similar, global context, this may explain the different policies along with different forms of integration or segregation to which conquered communities were subjected in each case. Sicily was an island eighty miles distant from North Africa, and it was close to southern Italy and the center of Latin Christendom. Iberia had a border with western Europe, but this was across the Pyrenees. Its border with North Africa, across the Strait of Gibraltar, was only eight miles long and was much more easily crossed. According to Ludolph of Sudheim, a pilgrim to the Holy Land (1336–41), the distance across the strait was so short that a Christian laundryperson and a Muslim one could quarrel and insult each other from their own sides.[53] The proximity of Iberia to Africa allowed important invasions in both directions, which may partly explain the long Muslim resistance in Iberia, while the distance of Sicily from Africa made the Norman Christian reconquest of that island easier, but Roger II's conquests in Ifriqiya difficult to maintain. The Holy Land, by contrast, was isolated from Latin Europe: it lay twelve hundred miles by sea from southern Italy, although it benefited from a connection with Christian Cyprus (latinized after the conquest of the island by Richard I of England in 1191) as well as the Venetian and Genoese colonial networks in the eastern Mediterranean.

The colonial experience of the Crusaders in the Holy Land was key: it was the first case of European expansion since the Romans in which Latin Christians had to deal with significant territorial conquest and administration in a hostile environment, faraway from their roots. The rule of an ethnic minority, the creation of local identities—visible, for example, in the chronicles of William of Tyre or Fulk of Chartres—the constant interaction with native population, including the Muslim majority, so well recorded by Usama Ibn Munqidh, and the maintenance of links with Europe defined a colonial model that would be replicated in the future.[54] The continuing influx of new migrants, regular renewal of links with European political and cultural elites visible in matrimonial alliances, attraction of new knights, and schooling of young people in Europe—these were the main features of a model that already dealt with the problems of alliance and integration, or segregation, between local communities and power elites.

The Latin Kingdom of Jerusalem had to manage a population that had been massively converted to Islam over the previous four centuries. In the repression of this population's religion, many mosques were transformed into churches. The fate of the Al-Aqsa Mosque, situated on the Temple Hill of Jerusalem close to the Dome of the Rock, gives an idea of the conquerors' systematic profanation and desecration of such sites: it was transformed first into a royal residence and then into the headquarters of the Templars. Sexual intercourse between Muslims and Christians was forbidden, and punished by castration; Muslims were not allowed to wear Frankish clothing; and they were forced to pay a poll tax.[55] The Latin kingdom also had to deal with a wide range of non-Latin Christian communities. There were the Greeks, who were present in all the territories of the kingdom, but mainly concentrated in the principality of Antioch, and who were backed by the Byzantine emperor.[56]

There were also the Armenians, who maintained an important presence in the county of Edessa and had their own political power in Asia Minor, where they managed to control an extensive territory after the victories over the Turks of the First Crusade.[57] And there were the Jacobites and Syriacs, who were present in the northern territories and beyond; the Georgians—although these Christians only had a symbolic presence in Jerusalem; the Nestorians, who were more important in Syria and Asia Minor than in Palestine, and famous for their missions to central Asia; the Maronites, who had their roots in the Lebanon; and finally, the Copts, whose most significant presence was in Egypt.[58]

The most important clash that the Latin Christians had with other Christians was with the Orthodox Greeks, who they refused to use in their administration or army, contrary to Latin practice in Sicily. This was probably because the Greek Christians of Palestine had, in the previous centuries, lost their political clout and been excluded from administrative functions, but under Latin rule they did not recover legal equality. The Greek religious hierarchy, which had managed to hold out through three centuries of Muslim rule, was almost completely obliterated from the Holy Land by the Crusaders' conquests, in spite of the proclaimed purpose of these: to rescue the Eastern Christians. Only the local Greek clergymen managed to survive, but in a reduced network, since a number of their churches and portion of their property were appropriated by the new Latin clergy in many cities and places of European settlement. It has to be said that Latin Christians did not force conversions and did not impose their rule on Orthodox communities.[59] The Greek monasteries, which were strongly established, were less affected by expropriation; in general they were respected, and some new ones were even created. Some communities, however, were removed from their establishments and lost their property during the creation of an impressive number of Latin regular as well as military religious communities.

After the conquest of Jerusalem, its Greek patriarch Simeon, who had fled to Cyprus before the arrival of the Crusaders (either by his own will or pushed by the Muslim rulers of the city), never returned; the Greek patriarchs of Jerusalem lived in exile in Constantinople. John, the Greek patriarch of Antioch, retired to Constantinople two years after the conquest of the city by the Crusaders. Throughout the existence of the Kingdom of Jerusalem, Latin Christians created an impressive number of dioceses: the archbishoprics of Caesarea, Nazareth, Tyre, Beisan, and Petra; and the bishoprics of Ramleh, Bethlehem, Gaza, Hebron, Sebaste, Tiberias, Banyas, Sidon, and Beirut. There were similar developments in the county of Tripoli, the principality of Antioch, and the county of Edessa, reaching a total of thirty-one dioceses.[60] In all these places, Greek patriarchs and bishops were evicted, and properties were seized, even though in some cases the power of local factions and necessity for alliances with the Byzantine emperor imposed the short-lived return of a Greek patriarch (as was the case in 1165 in Anthioc).[61] The only Greek bishop who managed to survive the Latin surge may have been the one in Gaza and Beit-Jibrin; the archbishop Melethos is recorded as being active there in 1164. The Orthodox Greeks only managed to recover part of their lost possessions in the Kingdom of Jerusalem when Saladin's conquest, in 1187, was followed by the departure of most part of the Latin clergy and the disappearance of almost all their monasteries.

The other Eastern Churches, such as the Armenian, Jacobite, and Syriac, suffered less than the Greeks.[62] They were each part of a different set of alliances, and did not represent significant political or religious competition. The Armenians were the most acceptable to the Latin Church, because they had recognized the authority of the pope, were traditionally in conflict with the Greek Orthodox Church, and had played a crucial political and military role against the Turks. It was not by chance that the Armenians immediately sought an alliance with the Franks who made up the First Crusade, offering a matrimonial alliance to the Crusader Baldwin (later the first king of Jerusalem) to secure the vulnerable territory of Edessa. The Jacobites were more tolerantly treated by the Franks than they had been under Byzantine rule, but they were still dispossessed of church property in the countryside. In general, the Eastern Christians were treated by the Crusaders as conquered natives. After the first decades, they were guaranteed legal protection—the same as that granted to the Jews and Muslims, in a Christian mimesis of the status of dhimmīs—for their life and property. Still, they never attained the status of "citizens," which was the prerogative of the Latin conqueror elite. Frankish suspicion of the Eastern churches was allayed by prudent behavior on the part of local religious leaders. For instance, the Jacobite bishop never resided in Antioch during the period of Latin rule, and the Copts only established a bishopric in Jerusalem after Saladin's conquest. The only way the Latin Christians managed to deal with difference was through assimilation or hierarchical association. Even the Lebanese Christian Maronites, although considered good soldiers and archers, were only fully integrated into the Crusaders' forces when they recognized the authority of the pope, as a result of persistent diplomatic action by the archbishop of Antioch.[63]

‖‖

CHAPTER 3

Universalism: Integration and Classification

Latin Christian political experiments in Sicily, Iberia, and the Middle East led to new prejudices and acts of discrimination: opposing religions such as Islam and Judaism were especially targeted, but Orthodox Greek and Eastern Christian churches were not spared either. The difference was that Eastern Christians were seen as competitors who needed to be curbed. The major issue was the recognition of the authority of the pope. There was no obstacle to the integration of Eastern Christians into the Latin ritual; in general they were not under suspicion of backsliding, because prejudices toward them did not include their descent. In practice, though, their treatment clashed with the claimed theory of Christian brotherhood. It is for this reason that I need to address the universalism of the Christian Church since this provided a theoretical framework, even if it was contradicted by policies on the ground. I will raise an equivalent issue concerning political relations between particular kingdoms and the universal aims of the empire. The Roman legacy had been perpetuated by the Byzantine Empire, while in Europe the Holy Roman Empire created by Charlemagne aspired to the same universal ambition. This logic had an impact on different levels of political action concerning ethnicities. Finally, I will return to Europe to see the process of assimilation on its peripheries in the Middle Ages, since some of the problems analyzed in the first two chapters were replicated by what has been defined as internal colonialism.

CHURCH AND EMPIRE

In 1461, Eneas Silvio Piccolomini, Pope Pius II (1458–64), wrote a letter to Mehmed II (Ottoman ruler, 1451–81), who had conquered Constantinople (1453) and what was left of the Byzantine Empire (Sinop and Trebizond, in that very year of 1461), inviting him to convert to Christianity in exchange for the title of emperor. The letter provides a fascinating manifesto on politics and international relations, in which the pope evaluated the balance of forces between Christians and Muslims. Pius II argued that the Turks could never conquer Europe, highlighted the number of Christians under their dominion, and pointed out the resistance they were encountering in Hungary, Bohemia, Dalmatia, Greece, and other regions where Christianity had become deeply rooted. He skillfully linked temporal power to salvation of the soul, with the latter being the privileged domain of the papacy. In his reasoning, war and the suffering of humankind spread evil plus prevented salvation; only conversion to Christianity could lead to religious homogeneity and universal peace. Piccolomini identified himself as the promoter of universal salvation for the Greeks, Latins, Hebrews, Saracens, and all the peoples of the world, including the enemies of Christianity. He promised Mehmed II both glory and salvation through conversion. He pointed out that a "small" gesture could transform Mehmed II into the most powerful person in the world: he should accept the water of baptism, adopt Christian rituals, and believe in the Gospel. The tradition of rulers who accepted conversion in order to secure or enlarge their imperium is made explicit in this letter: Emperor Constantine, who developed the model of unification of peoples under Christianity; Clovis I, king of the Franks; Stephen, king of the Hungarians; Richard, king of the Visigoths; Agilulf, king of the Lombards; and Ladislao, grand duke of Lithuania, who became king of Poland. Piccolomini underlined the role of his predecessors, popes Stephen, Adrian, and Leo, who encouraged Pepin III and Charlemagne to fight against the barbarians, and recognized the legitimacy of their power in the "liberated" regions. He hinted that were Mehmed II a Christian, he might have claimed succession to the throne of Bohemia and Hungary with papal support.[1]

At the heart of this letter is a model of temporal imperial power supported by the papacy's spiritual power (*maiestas pontificalis*)—a fine exercise in rhetoric by a pope who had made his political career as secretary to cardinals, popes, and Emperor Frederick III, thanks to his outstanding intellectual skills along with his oral and written eloquence. Piccolomini wrote geographic treatises on Asia and Europe, a history of Bohemia, and many didactic texts, biographies, and orations. These literary achievements culminated in the *Commentarii*, the only autobiography ever written by a pope.[2] Yet the letter displays Pius II's limited and distorted knowledge of Islam and its precepts: Piccolomini drew his main references from Juan de Torquemada and Nicholas of Cusa, who had recently compiled texts and produced new reflections on Islam, criticized as epicurean. Pius II also ignored (or decided to do so) the fact that in the tradition of the Byzantine rulers, Mehmed II presented himself as the legitimate emperor of a territory that included western Europe.

The letter to Mehmed II was most probably never sent. It was copied and corrected by the pope, who used it as propaganda to quell Turkophiles as well as assert his authority against the Holy Roman emperor and Italian powers. From the fall of Constantinople onward, both before and after he was invested as pope, Piccolomini engaged in a series of orations and actions in favor of a Crusade against the Turks. He died in Ancona while awaiting the Venetian ships that would enable him to command the Crusade himself—a defiant gesture in the face of the indifference or retreat of the Holy Roman emperor, king of France, and duke of Burgundy. The writing of the letter and preparations for invasion were not contradictory acts, since persuasion was always seen as a preliminary to violent action. Following the same line of reasoning, the impossible reenactment of the Constantinian model of conversion would have imposed on Mehmed II military engagement for the re-creation of an ecumenical Mediterranean based on the unity of the Christian Church. The medieval theocratic vision of Crusade was thus renewed to promote reform against Islam and prevent any political initiatives by the Christian powers that would challenge the authority of the church.

In his letter, Piccolomini addressed the issue of the Christian churches under Ottoman dominion—Armenians, Jacobites, Maronites, and Greeks. He accused these churches of having refused the decree of union of the Council of Florence (1439) and persevered in their "errors," specifically regarding their views of the Holy Ghost and concept of purgatory.[3] It is obvious that the universal scope of the Christian Church was to be imposed in an uncompromising way, through the strict implementation of the doctrine of the Church of Rome and assertion of the pope's authority. Nevertheless, the Councils of Constance (1414) and Florence (1439) played a major role in the universal projection of the Roman Church, since they placed the unification of all the Christian churches at the center of the church's concerns; the Eastern Churches, supposedly threatened by the Ottoman conquests and predicted fall of the last territories of the Byzantine Empire, were to be protected and, if possible, absorbed. These councils were thus transformed into forums for ecumenical discussion with invited Greek dignitaries, who received an attention not seen since the eleventh and twelfth centuries. This train of events seems like a strange and failed reenactment of the atmosphere and actions of the First Crusade, for which the catalyst was the Turkish invasion of Palestine. Universalism, however, did not prevent the pope from reproducing prejudices against the same peoples he declared to be responsible before God. In his letter to Mehmed II, Piccolomini praised the Turks as valiant warriors, supposedly descendants of the Scythians, but he denigrated "vice-addicted" Saracens, "crooked" Syrians, "effeminate" Egyptians, "weak" Arabians, and "naked Africans," all considered unprepared for war.[4]

If from the beginning the Christian Church had developed a universalist stance and considered itself as responsible for all the peoples of the world before God, the scholastic developments of the thirteenth century, particularly the work of Thomas Aquinas, integrated the Roman notion of natural law into legal theory.[5] The inclusion of the non-Christian *Homo naturalis* at the same level as the Christian *Homo renatus* liberated humankind from any Christological basis, stressing the common behavior and reasoning of humans as the essential basis for *humanitas*.[6] Yet universalism was accompanied by segregation. In Aquinas's work, Jews were assigned the status of perpetual slavery and blamed for usury, which was pointed to as their "only" source of income. Slaves of Jewish families who became Christian were to be immediately released from servitude. Aquinus, however, believed that no offense should be done to Jews and no tribute should be exacted in those places where there was no tradition of such a practice. He was adamant that unbelievers (Jews and heathens) "ought by no means to be coerced into the faith." He also held that Jewish rituals should be tolerated to show that "even our enemies bear witness to our faith," but declared that the rituals of other unbelievers should not be tolerated.[7]

These positions were in line with canon law—that is, with the collection compiled by Gratian in 1140 and the *decretales* compiled under Gregory IX in 1234. The rights of non-Christians were tackled in these—namely, the right to ownership of property. The first of these compilations opposed marriage between Christians and Jews. It also integrated the decision of the Fourth Council of Toledo from 633 that Jews should not be forced to convert. Yet once this had happened, even if it had been against their will, they had to remain Christians. The second compilation established comparability between the two religious communities of Jews and Muslims, imposing similar forms of segregation on them. The status of servitude, seen as mainly resulting from conquest, was clearly defined, justifying the legitimacy of expulsion later applied to the Jews.[8]

Sinibaldo Freschi, Pope Innocent IV (1243–54), a canon lawyer who contested the occupation of the Holy Land by the Muslims by force and justified the Crusades as defensive war, developed the notion of a just war. He also claimed the western lands of the Roman Empire as the rightful inheritance of the papacy, based on the donation allegedly made by Constantine, but that was exposed as a forgery by Dante Alighieri circa 1310 and then conclusively rejected by Lorenzo Valla in 1440.[9] Still, Innocent IV recognized the rights of non-Christians to property and self-government, considered to be rights for all people, and excluded war against unbelievers just because they were unbelievers, though there was an ambiguity in Innocent IV's vision, since he considered the pope to be responsible for the souls of all humans, Christians and non-Christians alike, which opened the door to intervention in infidel societies under certain conditions. This is why some canon lawyers later contested the rights of infidels and maintained that they should be subject to Christians. This debate was also influenced by the precepts of love toward all people and charity, which militated against the expulsion of non-Christians from their lands. Intervention in Muslims lands was thus only justified by the need to protect Christian communities.[10]

The ambiguity between the Roman Church's claims to universalism and its reproduction of ethnic prejudices, with their consequential discriminatory action, was also discernible in the imperial vision of the world. Byzantium reflected the shift of the axis of the Roman Empire to the Middle East and the maintenance of political positions in North Africa until the Muslim invasions. The theocratic nature of the Byzantine Empire, with the structural interdependence of church and state, blended religious and political universalism in a more systematic way than in the Western tradition of separated powers. Nevertheless, the inclusion of the different peoples of the world in the Byzantine overview did not mean an absence of the prejudices inherited from the classical legacy. This legacy ran parallel to the ideas about dark-skinned Eastern and trans-Mediterranean populations, but there was a higher ambiguity in this perception than in that of the Carolingian world in which the simple contrast of black with white had been developed. Anticolonialism mobilized by the Muslim invasions may have contributed to a relatively more egalitarian Byzantine perception of the peoples of the world: the representation of black-skinned people in Orthodox Greek illuminated manuscripts dealing with evangelization reinforced the universal message of the church. The political importance of this theme was reenacted annually: during the celebrations of the birthday of Christ at the Hippodrome of Constantinople, peoples from the known world were presented before the emperor.[11]

Figure 3.1. Illumination representing the Queen of Sheba with long flowing blond hair and black skin painted by a later hand, in Conrad Kyeser, Codex Bellifortis, fl. 122r (before 1405).
Photo: Universitätsbibliothek Göttingen

Ecumenical ideas had a significant influence in western Europe; they went together with the diffusion of the rituals and symbols of the Byzantine Empire, absorbed in different degrees by the royal courts and Holy Roman Empire. We saw how imperial projects in Sicily stressed different human types, including black Africans, as symbols of universal claims, creating the background for the political imagery circulated by Emperor Frederick II. In the meantime, the image of the queen of Sheba, who was portrayed as a symbol of the gentility wishing to convert to Christianity, started to become darker and eventually became black.[12] The enamel plaque by Nicolas of Verdun, *Salomon and the Queen of Sheba*, at the Chapter of Klosterneuburg (1181) is one of the first examples, but the extraordinary illustration in the manuscript illuminated by Conrad Kyeser before 1405, showing a black queen with blond hair, raises the question of the symbolic contrast of colors. In the long run, a visual ambiguity prevails, since the tempting, sensual black woman is juxtaposed with what had previously been a symbol of religious virtue. Also in the twelfth century, the three Magi started to be linked to the three parts of the world, although their names, unrecorded in the Gospel, would be interchangeable, as were the supposed regions of their origin: Melchior, offering gold, would be represented as a European old man with a long white beard; Caspar, offering incense, was represented as a young Asian with a tunic and later a turban; and Balthazar, offering myrrh, was represented with dark skin, becoming black in the thirteenth century.[13] The painting in Würzburg at St. Mary's Chapel (1514) is one of the finest examples of this tradition, well represented by the Polling alterpiece (1444).

The "Africanization" of one of the three Magi arrived along with the "Africanization" of Saint Maurice. A martyr of the Theban Legion who was put to death in the Roman Empire between 386 and 392 for refusing to abjure Christianity, the saint was soon the object of a cult, justifying the foundation of the abbey of Agaune in 515. The knight-saint became extremely important during the military instability of the Middle Ages as an alternative to the "English" Saint George or "Hispanic" Saint James: his name was given to sixty-two communes in the territory of what is now France, and became inseparably linked with the Frankish army; Otto I of Saxony chose him as the patron saint of the Holy Roman Empire; the German eastern expansion against the Slavs and Hungarians was placed under his patronage; he became patron saint of Magdeburg and Halle; a military order was created in his name in northern Italy; he was chosen as patron saint by the Swiss Federation; and Frederick II was anointed in Rome in front of the altar of St. Maurice at St. Peter's cathedral.

Originally a white saint, Maurice only started to become black in the thirteenth century. This innovation is embodied in the extraordinary statue of the black Saint Maurice at the cathedral of Magdeburg. Along with Cologne, Magdeburg was one of the most creative cities to develop imperial symbols and ideology. The Theban Legion was interpreted as Egyptian, and then reinterpreted as black, in a double process of Orientalization and Africanization. The saint was portrayed as black mainly in Germany as well as central and northern Europe, while in France, Flanders, and Italy he remained white. The support of the emperor was crucial for the purchase and offer of relics of the saint to the main centers of his cult. Many paintings, sculptures, illuminated texts, and later, engravings of the saint were ordered by the imperial, religious, and local elites.[14] The pictorial tradition can be observed, for instance, in the altar piece by Hans Baldung Grien of Saint Maurice and Saint George (1504), and the painting of Saint Erasmus and Saint Maurice by Matthias Grünewald (1520–24), both of which depict extraordinary portraits of black people. The impact of the Crusades and reputation of Saladin, praised as a conqueror in medieval literature, certainly played a role in the enthusiasm for things Egyptian in the thirteenth century, but the invention of the black African soldier and saint could only have been developed under the political auspices of the emperor.

Figure 3.2. Master of the Polling altarpiece, *Adoration of the Magi*, painting, oil on wood, 129 × 86 cm., 1444. Left panel of the triptych, lower part of the reverse. Alte Pinakothek, Munich, inv. nr. 1360.
© 2013. Photo: Scala, Florence; BPK Bildagentur für Kunst, Kultur und Geschichte, Berlin

Figure 3.3. Anonymous statue of the black Saint Maurice at the Cathedral of Magdeburg, limestone, c. 1240–50, 112 cm. high.
Photo: AKG-images, Berlin; Hilbich

The assembling of different peoples of the world to express imperial ambition shows a relatively continuous line from Byzantium to Sicily and the Holy Roman Empire. Dante, one of the authors in the Middle Ages who clearly supported the idea of a universal empire based on the separation of church and state along with the political autonomy of the emperor, revived Pliny's idea of the three parts of the world to talk explicitly about Asians, Africans, and Europeans.[15] Dante anticipated the divisions of humankind by two centuries; this vision would only be developed as a result of the European oceanic expansion. In the same context, the elevation of the black African to the status of saint and Magus, due to imperial symbolic investment, opened the way for the observation and portrayal of sub-Saharan Africans as real people in their common functions as slaves, servants, or soldiers in

Figure 3.4. Hieronymus Bosch, *The Garden of Earthly Delights*, triptych, central panel, c. 1503–4, triptych total size 220 × 195 cm. Museo del Prado, inv. nr. 2823.
Reprinted with permission from Art Archive, London; Museo del Prado; Gianni Dagli Orti

Europe. The stereotypical representation of black people on both sides of the condemned-saved divide in Hans Memling's *Last Judgment* showed equality in death and after.[16] But the climax of this new trend of a relatively neutral representation of black people may have been reached by Hieronymus Bosch, circa 1510, in the painting later titled *The Variety of the World* or *The Garden of Earthly Delights*, where black people were represented among dozens of other naked people without any visible stigma.[17] This new vision did not challenge major stereotypes fueled by the traditional symbolic meaning in Europe of the color black, used to express sin, evil, darkness, filthiness, unfaithfulness, mourning, penitence, misfortune, or ugliness. These prejudices around color were also spurred by the medieval reinterpretation of Noah's cursed son Ham, accused of disloyal behavior, whose lineage was located in Africa, and composed of black and unfaithful sinners, stained from generation to generation.[18] But when the emperor gave protective status to a black saint, his act at least created new possibilities for the representation of black people.

EUROPEAN PERIPHERIES

The ethnic prejudices that developed during the expansion of Latin Christian power were not limited to the regions of Iberia, Sicily, Ifriqiya, and the Middle East. It is true that the struggles in these regions against major powers shaped by other religions or other rituals, such as Islam and the Orthodox Church, created a specific framework in which the criteria for ethnic identification were mingled with religious prejudice. But the expansion of the Latin Christian powers through Europe created new peripheries to their zone of influence and led to new forms of interethnic perceptions in these peripheral territories, in a process defined as internal colonialism.[19] The difficulty of differentiating internal and external colonialism in medieval Europe was visible when dealing with the complex cases of Sicily and Iberia. Another difficulty concerns the particularity of regions shaped by the inclusive notion of Roman citizenship and early Christianization. I have briefly tackled the issue of the barbarian invasions and new ethnic realities that emerged in what had been the Roman Empire. Now I will look at the areas untouched by Romanization, which also saw the emergence of new ethnicities, and which were exposed to their first experience of Christianization during the Middle Ages. And whereas in the first chapters of this part I analyzed interethnic prejudices in the contexts of rivalry between different religions and different Christian churches, I will now examine some interethnic prejudices that developed within a less competitive religious framework.

The Christianization of the European fringes resulted from a complex set of events that need to be carefully examined. For example, the Vikings, who were active roughly between 800 and 1050, and were depicted by other peoples as ferocious, had played a central role in the territories of Scandinavia, the British Isles, and the northwestern coast of France; they had established regular trade with Constantinople, influenced the future Russia, and even reached Iran.[20] The Viking territories therefore cannot be considered a wild periphery; the Vikings were engaged in regular, peaceful trade with distance regions. The same argument is valid for other peripheral regions. By the same token, the relations between Christianized Germans and Slavs in eastern Europe at the beginning of the thirteenth century cannot be reduced to the depiction of the latter by the former as barbarians engaged in the practice of scalping their victims.[21] The purpose here is to briefly observe the forms that Christianization took in these areas, the new perceptions of peoples that were shaped by the process, and the gap between religious integration and political goals that could give rise to new forms of prejudice and discrimination.

The forced conversion of the Saxons to Christianity by Charlemagne's troops in northern Europe set an example that was followed five centuries later by the activities of the Teutonic military order against the Prussians and Lithuanians, who resisted conversion until the fourteenth century.[22] The Polish Christian nobility sent protests to Rome about the behavior of the Teutonic knights, denouncing their ruthless pursuit of territorial conquest and political ambitions. An alliance between the Poles and Lithuanians led to their victory against the Teutonic knights in Tannenberg in 1410. The levies exacted by the Teutonic knights, who laid claim to all the lands occupied by infidels and even violated agreements with converted peoples, as in Prussia with the Cumans, caused such protests that eventually the pope excommunicated them.[23] By contrast, the conversion of the Scandinavian peoples, achieved by the end of the tenth century, proceeded relatively smoothly, without invasion or military engagement. In the north and center of Scandinavia, however, there was resistance to Christianity by the Saami (Lapps, as they were called in a derogatory way), a hunter-gatherer people whose language belonged to the Finno-Ugrian group and who maintained a shamanistic religion until the eighteenth century.[24] This resistance defined a periphery within Scandinavia, not only in terms of religion, but also in relation to lifestyle. The seminomadic way of life of the Saami, shaped by the seasons as well as fishing and hunting expeditions, awakened in the Scandinavians the same ancient prejudices against otherness that had been developed by urban societies in classical antiquity. The conversion of Finno-Ugrian and Slav populations in central Europe also occurred during the tenth century without military intervention. The integration and conversation of the Cumans, who had reached Hungary from central Asia by the thirteenth century, occupying the central provinces and playing an important military role, took two centuries. The impact on the region of their costumes, hairstyle, and headdresses showed not only their resilience but also that a Christianized population could be tempted to return to barbarian habits.[25]

The conversion of the Bulgarians and Serbs (Slavs) as well as Romanians (non-Slavs) to the Orthodox Church did not prevent major military conflicts between the central areas and peripheries of the Byzantine Empire, just as the conversion of the Croats, Czechs, Moravians, and Poles (Slavs) along with the Hungarians (non-Slav Magyars) to Latin Christianity did not bring an end to the struggles between the major powers and the polities in central and eastern Europe—and the struggles between and within these peripheral countries. One example among many is the subordinate status of the Croats under Hungarian, Venetian, and Ottoman rule; another is the continuous struggle that the Magyars in Hungary, the Czechs in Bohemia, and Poles in Poland waged against the power of the Germans, Russians, and Ottomans. In Bohemia and Hungary, German immigrants brought with them their own laws and lived a separate communal life. After the fourteenth century, though, the balance of power shifted, and Germans in Bohemia were forbidden by the Bohemian rulers to marry into the local population, banned from citizenship of the towns, and excluded from certain offices.[26]

The zone of dispute between the Greek and Latin churches created a complicated political, military, and religious frontier across Europe, where discrimination was rife. The short-lived Latin Empire in Byzantium (1204–61) created several fiefdoms in Greece, such as the principality of Achaia (then Morea), in which the Greek serfs suffered judicial discrimination and were not allowed to bring accusations against their Frankish rulers. Then, at the beginning of the fourteenth century, the Catalans took control of the duchy of Athens, and created municipal oligarchies and dualist systems of law. For many years, the instability of the region allowed its systematic plunder and the enslavement of Christian Greeks, who the (Christian) Catalans sold in Italy and Iberia—a business that was only curbed by the king of Aragon after 1382.[27] This abuse contrasted with the Byzantine absence of formal legal stratification: the main division was between freepersons and slaves; there was no ethnic divide with Slavs, for instance, who were considered free.[28]

In other peripheral countries of western Europe, interethnic conflict among Christians was even more aggressive, as in the case of Ireland. The country was converted to Christianity in the fifth century, which meant it became Christian earlier than England. But sharing a faith did not spare the island from centuries of colonial wars, expropriation of land, political dependence, and collective humiliation at the hands of English colonizers, first triggered by the Anglo-Norman Conquest in 1169. Economic dispossession was a long process, which reached its height in the seventeenth century, yet ethnic prejudices came into being not long after the conquest. Legal discrimination embodied in a dualist legal system was introduced through the use of English common law by the settlers; the Irish could be accused but could not accuse. Contempt for Irish domestic architecture, allegedly without bricks or stone, the absence of gardens, and the lack of the sort of provisions that the settlers were used to can be found in medieval English texts, which spread the idea that the Irish had an inferior way of life. The Irish supposedly went unshaven and barefooted, with long hair, carried an enormous ax as their unique equipment for war, and engaged in bestiality and savage rituals of royal inauguration.[29] The English adopted policies of segregation and exclusion in the conquered territory early on: in 1366, the statutes of Kilkenny forbade marriage or cohabitation between the English and Irish, because mixed unions would tempt the English to lapse into degenerate Irish ways.[30] The vision of the Irish as a barbarian people was later used to compare them with the North American Indians, as in the writings of the American colonists Thomas Morton and Hugh Peter.[31]

‖‖

CHAPTER 4

Typologies of Humankind and Models of Discrimination

TYPOLOGIES

The main ethnicities in Norman Sicily, a region of Europe at the confluence of three civilizations exposed to war and migrations, were largely defined by their religion. Ethnic and religious identification generally came with political status, as the sculptures on the sarcophagi of Roger II suggest. But these representations did not reach the level of a typology of all humankind. They encompassed and classified only the peoples dominated by a particular sovereign power with imperial ambitions. The same phenomenon occurred during this period in other political entities on the frontiers of civilizations—for example, in the Christian kingdoms of Iberia, or the Latin Kingdom of Jerusalem, where a multireligious and multiethnic environment needed to be addressed and politically integrated. The classical world had no clearly defined typologies of humankind, but it witnessed a shift from the East-West divide conceived by the Greeks to a North-South divide conceived by the Romans. In the latter, the Nordic peoples were opposed to the peoples of the Mediterranean; there was a place for Asians as well as the black Africans brought through the small though constant flow of the slave trade into the Mediterranean.

The medieval period was a transitional one, leading to the typologies of humankind that resulted from the European oceanic expansion of the late fifteenth and sixteenth centuries. In the 1250s, the work of the sculptor Nicola Pisano in the cathedral of Siena may have expressed ideas that were current in this conjuncture: inside the dome of the cathedral, he sculpted four capitals in the form of heads, and each of these probably represented a different human type.[1] We are unable to identify clearly all the types. The stereotypical features attributed to the black African are the only distinctive ones: curled hair, thick lips, and a large nose. It would appear that the other three heads represent Nordic, Mediterranean, and Asian types. This hypothesis is inspired by pictures in Byzantine and western European illuminated books—in particular, the manuscripts describing the conquests of Alexander, the chronicles of the Crusades, and the *Chronologiæ Magnæ*—in which different types of head and different complexions were represented. In the 1310s, Dante was one of the first medieval authors to differentiate human types according to the notion of continents: Asians,

Africans, and Europeans.[2] This division, which corresponded to the implicit and sometimes explicit visual typology of the three Magi, took some time to become rooted.

Medieval authors interested in geography were familiar with the classical myth of the three continents, but they did not systematically put human beings into categories that coincided with the continents.[3] What they did was to develop certain criteria for identifying peoples (or ethnicities). As early as the seventh century, Isidore of Seville defined the major role of language in shaping behavior and building a sense of belonging: different peoples developed as a result of speaking their particular language, and not the other way around.[4] In the tenth century, Regino of Prüm indicated four criteria for ethnic identification: descent, customs, language, and law. The first of these criteria presents a clear proof that the classical idea of hereditary characteristics lived on in medieval western Europe.[5] The second evaluated something difficult to define—behavior, habits, and ways of doing things. Language was again indicated as the major vehicle for communication and culture. And finally, there were written law or oral rules—an institutionalized framework for action. Idrisi, the Muslim geographer who served Roger II, suggested a similar set of criteria, although these were more specific: physical appearance, natural disposition, religion, ornament, clothing, and language.[6] The development of these criteria is significant, since they stress the major role of religion—a feature that probably had not had the same importance in the barbarian kingdoms before these people's conversion to Christianity. The criteria also reveal a much more acute perception of detail in ethnic assessment—one where everything counts. Physical appearances, temperament, hair and beard styles, hair ornaments, fabrics, forms and pieces of clothing, and jewelry became the main descriptors. This extreme attention to detail was used to build up standardized prejudices against specific peoples. I will turn first to the impact of the criterion of physical appearance on historical practices and perceptions.

PHYSICAL APPEARANCES

In 1149, during a siege of the castle of Kerkyra (Corfu), which had been taken from the Byzantines by the Sicilian Normans, the troops of the allied Byzantine and Venetian assailants fell into a bitter quarrel that ended in battle. The defeated Venetians took refuge on their ships and ravaged the Greek coast, setting fire to and sinking the Byzantine fleet, which had been left at Euboia. According to Niketas Choniatēs, an imperial high officer turned chronicler, there was a further "monstrous" event:

> They stole the imperial ship, adorned the imperial cabins with curtains interwoven with gold thread and with rugs of purple, and placed on board an accursed manikin, a certain black-skinned Ethiopian. They acclaimed him as emperor of the Romans [Byzantines] and led him about in procession with a splendid crown on his head, ridiculing the sacred imperial ceremonies and mocking Emperor Manuel as not having yellow hair, the colour of summer, but

Figure 4.1. Anonymous portrait of Manuel I Komnenos, Byzantine emperor (1143–80), and his second wife, Maria of Antioch. Illuminated manuscript, Biblioteca Apostolica Vaticana, vat. gr. 1176.
Reprinted with permission from the Art Archive, London; Bibliothèque des Arts Décoratifs, Paris; Gianni Dagli Orti

instead being blackish in complexion, like the bride of the Song who says "I am black and beautiful, because the sun has looked askance at me."[7]

This mockery reveals the extent of anti-Byzantine prejudice among Latin Christians. The Byzantine emperor, Manuel Komnenos, who was personally present at the siege of Kerkyra, was ridiculed for his skin color (his dark complexion was underlined in a double portrait of him with his wife, Maria of Antioch, who was, by contrast, shown as white), small body, supposedly "effeminate" manner, and pompous ceremonial luxury. A black African, probably a slave, represented all this in order to underline the inferior condition of the emperor under his magnificent clothing and insignia. Choniatēs managed a riposte at the end of his description by using a biblical quotation from the Song of Songs.[8] The Byzantine chronicler was obviously aware of the patristic exegesis of the Song of Songs as an allegory for the church, such as in the work of the scholar Origen (185–232).[9] The reference allowed him to reverse the offense and place Komnenos as the defender of the church against the sacrilegious barbarians.

The Venetians' capacity for prejudice was consistent with that of other Latin peoples. William of Tyre, for instance, writing in the 1170s and 1180s, considered the Greeks idle and lacking in warrior virtues, responsible for the Muslim conquests, driven by their innate maliciousness and hatred of the Latin Christians, addicted to enigmatic questions and ambiguous answers, and given to delaying decisions.[10] The Byzantines did not mince their words either: they described the Latin Christians as "boastful, undaunted in spirit, lacking all humility, and trained to be ever bloodthirsty," and considered that they "nurtured an unsleeping hostility against the Romans [Byzantines], a perpetual raving hatred."[11]

The conflict between the Venetians and Byzantines had dramatic consequences: although Komnenos had to swallow the Venetians' offense in order to get them back to the siege and obtain Norman withdrawal from Corfu, he took revenge in 1171, when he ordered the arrest of all the Venetians in his empire and the confiscation of their property. This event left a trail of hate that lasted for several decades, with endless negotiations for financial compensation pushed by the Venetians; the compensation was accepted by the Byzantine rulers, but never entirely paid. Another traumatic event was the assault on the Latin quarter of Constantinople in 1182 by the Byzantine mob, which massacred the population it found there. In 1204, the Venetians easily managed to redirect the Fourth Crusade to the conquest of Constantinople, which was done with a scandalous sack of churches and sacred objects, followed by the nomination of a Latin patriarch.[12] Choniatēs also reported these events, describing the conquerors as savages and barbarians by nature. One of the most revealing episodes of this extraordinary event was the action of the Cistercian abbot Gunther Martin of the monastery of Pairis, in Alsace, which was reported by his biographer. Martin burst into the church of the Pantocrator, the burial place of Komnenos's mother, and forced the Greek priest to give him the relics after shouting, "Come on you old Infidel, show me where you keep your most precious relics. If you don't, look forward to death."[13]

Violence against the Orthodox Church broke out on other occasions. As early as 1098, after the conquest of Antioch, the leaders of the First Crusade had sent a letter to the pope complaining that their troops had managed to defeat the Turks and pagans, but not heretics such as the Greeks, Armenians, Syriacs, and Jacobites.[14] The frequent references to the Eastern churches as heretics or "infidels" by Latin rulers and clergypeople is striking; the Greek Orthodox Church had never been classified as such by the Church of Rome. The fact is that there was a rooted prejudice among Latin Christians against the Greeks, who were considered second-rate Christians, weak and unreliable, and easy victims of plunder, sack, and massacre. The conquest of Constantinople in 1204, which created a Latin Empire in the East, which was in turn terminated in 1261 by the Byzantine emperor, Michael Paleologus, defined relations between the Latin and Greek Christian churches for centuries to come: the Greek Church rightly considered that it could survive under Turkish but not Latin Christian rule. This is why various attempts to unify the churches were never concluded— for example, the Council of Ferrara-Florence in 1438–39, in which the dialogue between the two churches reached a climax. The Orthodox Church had been, with few exceptions, wiped out from all the territories conquered by the Franks in southern Italy, Sicily, Greece, and the Middle East; Norman, Venetian, and Catalan expansion in the western Byzantine territories meant the enslavement of the Christian Greeks (along with the Albanians and

Figure 4.2. Alfonso X "the Wise," king of Castile (1252–84), *Cantigas de Santa Maria* (1254–79), cantiga 46, scene 1, upper part, left side, second row. Illumination on vellum representing Muslims, Christians, an African, and a Jew next to the image of Saint Mary and Jesus. Biblioteca Monasterio del Escorial, Spain.
Reprinted with permission from AKG-images, Berlin; Album; Oronoz

Bulgarians), who were temporarily traded in western Europe, mainly in Italy and Iberia. Religious discrimination against the "schismatic Christians," as the Greeks were labeled in Rome, was used to justify political dominion and led to ethnic scorn, as revealed in these practices of enslavement.

Skin color was obviously important for the Venetians in the episode of revenge against the Byzantine troops, yet it is doubtful whether this criterion had the same significance in other regions of Europe, or under different circumstances. The illuminated manuscripts commissioned by the Castilian king Alfonso the Wise (1221–84)—the *Libro de Ajedrez* and *Cantigas de Santa Maria*—represented visible differences between Christians and Muslims based more on clothing than physical appearances.[15] Muslims were clearly identified by their turbans and large tunics, with the sleeves left open at the end, which disguised their body shape, as prescribed by Islamic tradition. Christian males did not have their head covered, and their tunics were more adjusted to fit the body, revealing the shape of the trunk and legs. Skin color was not irrelevant. The wide range of colors—white, light brown, dark brown, and black—depicted in various manuscripts indicates an acute perception of different complexions. Although the Muslims were depicted as brown and black more often than not, they were also portrayed as white. The reverse happened with the Christians.[16] This tendency is confirmed in the illuminated manuscript *Fueros del Reyno de Aragon*, compiled during the reign of Jaume I (1213–76): Muslims were represented as dark skinned. But color prejudice was not obvious. In the *Libro de Ajedrez,* one illumination depicted a game between a white and black man (not a Muslim): the black man, identified by the usual stereotypes—dark skin color, curled hair, thick lips, and large nose—had won the game and pointed his finger in a way that suggested he had given the other a lesson, while the white man was represented in a defensive position, acknowledging defeat with open hands. In the *Cantigas de Santa Maria*, a particular skin color was not required to identify Jewish people: they were represented as white, but with stereotypical beards and hooked noses.

The relative neutrality of the skin color in these representations is not consistent with the portrayal of skin in the *Lapidario*, another illuminated codex commissioned by Alfonso the Wise. The latter contains a disturbing image of an elephant with the head of a black man, and is perhaps one of the first representations of black people in which their features were mixed with those of African animals. It is true that the *Lapidario* is a complex book, clearly inspired by alchemy, which defined the range of colors in sequences of transformation and purification in which black, red, and white each acquired a special meaning. Still, in this case we cannot dismiss the link with other written sources that discussed black Africans. Ibn Khaldûn, writing a century later, expressed these prejudices against black people: "[They] are submissive to slavery, because [they] have little that is (essentially) human and possess attributes that are quite similar to those of dumb animals, [they] dwell in caves and thickets, eat herbs, live in savage isolation and do not congregate, and eat each other."[17] Ludolph of Sudheim, who wrote an account of his travels in the mid-fourteenth century, showed the same contempt for the "black Ethiopians," whose "men and women have monkey-like faces and breed tamed monkeys, as we breed dogs and chickens."[18]

Criteria of Identification

The *Catalan Atlas*, drawn in Majorca in 1375 by the Jewish cartographer Cresques Abraham, represents a striking combination of sea chart and *mappa mundi*, introducing the representation of human types in different parts of the world—an innovation later developed by the cartographers of Lisbon and Dieppe. This atlas represents the world as it was known to the Europeans in those days, from the Canary Islands to China. It shows the area of Catalan (and Aragonese) imperial ambitions in the Mediterranean, stretching from Barcelona and Valencia to the duchy of Athens, and including the Balearic Islands, Sardinia, and

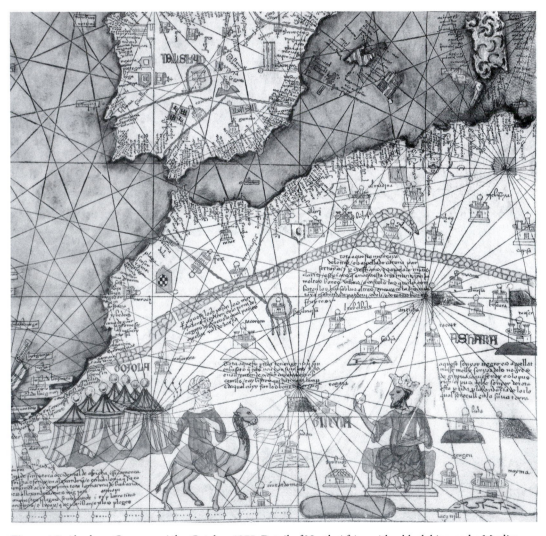

Figure 4.3. Abraham Cresques, *Atlas Catalan*, 1375. Detail of North Africa with a black king and a Muslim riding a camel.
© Courtesy of the Museu Marítim de Barcelona; Ramon Manent/Corbis

Sicily. It is obvious that in this politically defined environment, the description of territories and their cartographic representation went hand in hand with the description of peoples. There are no frontiers shown, but political entities are represented by castles and flags with the arms of the rulers. Several elements identify particular regions. In Morocco, there are royal tents along with a Muslim riding a camel with a turban, large tunic, and bare feet. Near Timbuktu, there is a black king with a scepter, golden crown, and golden globe. In North Africa, a black servant is leading a camel, the Muslim ruler of Ifriqiya is shown with a shield and large sword, there is an elephant, and the sultan of Cairo is represented with a pigeon on his hand. The Turkish sultan is placed in Asia Minor, and the queen of Sheba in Arabia. There is a sultan in Persia, two kings in India, and an elephant and the three Magi. There is a caravan with camels and men riding horses in central Asia, heading to Cathay (China). A white king is shown on the island of Java, and a brown king is depicted with an elephant on the island of "Taprobana" (later identified with Ceylon). In the Far East, the Antichrist is surrounded by kings and announced by the black trumpeters Gog and Magog. From Alexander the Great to savages and wild men, the range of humanity then recognize is shown.[19]

The biblical references are obvious, and come mainly from the Old Testament, but there also are precise references to contemporary events and practices. For example, we see the pilgrimage to Mecca made in 1340 by the king of Mali, Mansa Musa, famous for the luxury in which he traveled, the expedition of Jacome Ferrer to the Canary Islands the same year, and the communication network maintained across Egypt and Palestine through the use of carrier pigeons, well documented in the chronicles of the Crusades.[20] Most Muslim rulers are depicted as white, and it appears that clothing, headdresses, and animals for riding (camels, horses, and elephants) were particularly important to cartographers as symbolic markers of identity—although they did not ignore skin color. There is some indication, however, that northern Europeans might have seen things differently, confirming the Venetian view discussed above, since the Venetians occupied an intermediate position between the Mediterranean and central Europe. William of Rubruck, an agent sent by the French King Louis IX to the Mongol court in 1253, described the envoys of the people of Langa and Solanga who he saw at the court of Karakorum as "little brown men like Spaniards."[21] William of Rubruck was an excellent observer, on a level with Marco Polo. He tried to identify the different people he came across by noting such details as styles of house building, food habits, use of animals, clothes, codes of conduct, and court ceremonies.

The range of criteria for distinguishing between different peoples included far more than just skin color. Yet in transitional periods, the dividing lines between ethnicities based on religious allegiance were much more blurred than we suppose: by the end of the thirteenth century, in Lerida, the *Mudéjares* (meaning Muslims allowed to stay, from the Arab *mudaĝĝan*, or literally, tamed) dressed like Christians, while in Valencia, the Moriscos (converted Muslims or Moors, or Moros, as they were called in Iberia) dressed as Mudéjares, such as at their marriage feasts.[22] These cases clearly indicate conformism related to the different proportion of Muslims in each city's population: while in Lerida the Muslims were no longer the majority, in Valencia they still predominated. In Sicily, on the western side of the island, Christian women apparently continued to follow the dress code of Muslim women for a significant period of time after the Norman invasion.

ETHNIC CONTEMPT

It was common for people of the same religious allegiance to express ethnic contempt for one another. The Normans were labeled "the new Saracens" by the Byzantines.[23] The Calabrians were labeled cowards, and the Lombards perfidious by the Normans.[24] The Germans were feared in Italy as barbarians because they were supposed to exhibit irrational and violent behavior.[25] The Castilians were considered arrogant by their neighbours. An extremely long list of ethnic (and in some cases protonational) prejudices could be compiled for this period—a list largely shaped by political competition and conquest. Ibn Hawqal, a merchant from Baghdad, wrote a book about his travels in 977, at the time when Sicily was under Islamic rule although engaged in a continuous struggle against the Byzantine Empire. He considered the Sicilians as people of "limited capacity and weak brain power," eager to escape their duties of holy war.[26] This idea of second-rate Islamic Sicilians was reinforced after their defeat and subordination. Abd Allah Yaqūt, born in 1178, shared Ibn Hawqal's contempt, and he added the slur of untrustworthiness, due to the Sicilians' bad habit of constant dispute in their personal relations. He concluded that "for filthiness and dishonesty they even outdo the Jews," which underlines that prejudices are always relational.[27]

In the case of the Muslims of Iberia, defeat also generated contempt in the Arab world. Ibn Khaldûn, for instance, labeled them "weak-minded," a people who had lost their group feeling, instinct for cooperation, and ability to take power as a result of the annihilation of their Arab Dynasty. According to his words, which were doubtless inspired by the ideas of Cicero and Tacitus about the inevitable degeneration of conquered peoples, the Spanish Muslims had been enslaved by tyranny and become used to being humiliated. Ibn Khaldûn pushed his analysis further: "The [Muslim] Spaniards are found to assimilate themselves to the [Christian] Galician nations in their dress, their emblems and most of their customs and conditions. This goes so far that they even draw pictures on the walls and have them in buildings and houses. The intelligent observer will draw from this the conclusion that it is a sign of being dominated by others."[28] The politics of appearance could not have been better defined by an author who lived two years in Granada and visited the city of his ancestors, Seville: he was talking from experience. But the contempt for those who converted to Christianity was much worse, since they had abandoned their purity of faith.

Similar feelings are expressed in the records of Jewish communities in the Middle Ages, although local practices showed a great deal of flexibility between Hebrews and their relatives who had been converted to Christianity. Competition between the different religions of the book developed after the integration of the newly converted barbarian peoples. Yet even this integration had exceptions: the Arian king of the Ostrogoths, Theodoric the Great (454–526), viceroy in western Europe of the Byzantine Empire, excluded Romans from his army, forbade intermarriage between Romans and Goths, and kept two separate systems of law—a dualist state.[29] In the Middle Ages, suspicion against new Muslim and Jewish converts to Christianity was not uncommon. They were frequently considered to share the values, attitudes, and qualities of character of their ancestors—a prejudice against other peoples that was based on the idea of collective descent. In the anti-Muslim riots of 1275 in Valencia, the Moriscos (whose designation obviously underlined their ethnic roots) suffered as much as the Mudéjares. Converted Muslims were even called *tornadizos* (turncoats) by the Christians, despite such name-calling being forbidden by the *Partidas* (legislation compiled under Alfonso the Wise).[30] Converted Jews suffered similar abuse, being labeled *marranos* (probably meaning swine), new Christians and *cristãos lindos* (beautiful Christians, which was meant as mockery). Such name-calling was reciprocated by the Muslims: Ibn Jubayr, who was born in 1145 in Valencia, and traveled extensively in both Sicily and the Middle East, referred to King Baldwin IV of Jerusalem as the pig and his mother as the sow.[31] He labeled the Christians worshippers of the cross (which meant they were idolaters) and polytheists (due to the theological notion of the Trinity), both of which were common accusations made by Muslims against Christians.[32]

CONVERSION AND STIGMA

Suspicion against Muslim converts to Christianity could lead to persecution. Philip of Mahdia, who was born in North Africa, converted to Christianity in Sicily and became chamberlain to the king and admiral of the Sicilian fleet. In 1153, he conquered Bone in Ifriqiya, but was later accused of having been too benign toward the subjugated Muslims. By that time, King Roger II had changed his religious policy and favored a more militant church. He accepted the accusations of backsliding made against Philip and other former Muslim dignitaries of the royal court, and Philip was accused of systematic disrespect of Christian fasts while keeping the practice of Islamic prayers. He confessed his apostasy and asked for forgiveness, but the vengeful king confirmed the sentence against him. Philip was executed for committing a crime of *lèse-majesté divine*: he was dragged by a horse through the streets of Palermo, and burned at the stake with others who had been accused.[33]

This example of harsh treatment of a convert from Islam to Christianity was replicated in later periods of political turmoil, such as following the death of William I of Sicily, during the minority of his son, William II. This period saw the scandalous escape to North Africa of Gaito Pietro, a eunuch of the palace, royal chamberlain, and member of the council of regency, who probably saw little hope of surviving the ferocious intrigue around him.[34] At this point, a number of senior courtiers were accused of reverting to their previous Islamic faith. The most important target was Roberto of Calataboiano, who had worked with Pietro. Roberto was accused of apostasy, rape, homicide, adultery, robbery, and financing the restoration of the mosque in Castellamare. His relatives were tortured and died in prison, while Roberto had his properties confiscated.[35]

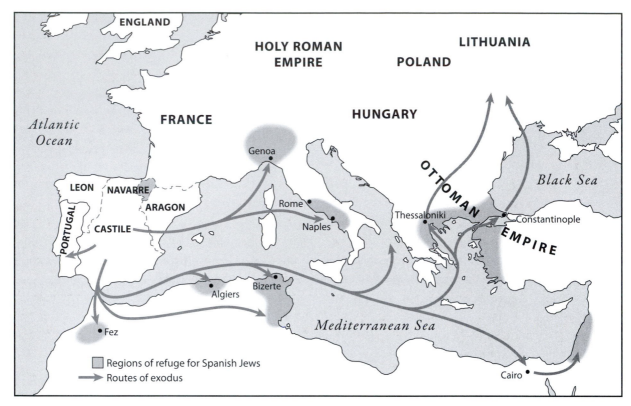

Map 4.1. Routes of the Jewish diaspora after the expulsion from Spain in 1492.
Source: Werner Hilgemann and Hermann Kinder, eds., *Atlas Historique*, trans. Raymond Albeck (Paris: Perrin, 1997), 150

Significant integration of converted Muslims occurred in Sicily, however, while individual cases were praised: al-Qāsim b. Hammūd, the last Islamic ruler of Agrigento and Castrogiovanni before the Norman Conquest, surrendered to Roger and became a Christian. He asked for land in the province of Melito, Calabria, and his request was granted. According to the chronicler Geoffrey Malaterra, "He lived a long time thereafter and proved himself time and time again guiltless of any deceit directed against our people."[36] Hammūd obviously survived constant scrutiny.

Anti-Muslim riots, led by the Lombards in 1161 and 1189, drove the victims out of the town centers of Sicily, mainly from the big cities like Palermo, in which they had long maintained a presence among the Christians and Jews.[37] After 1161, the central neighborhoods of Galca and Cassaro were reinforced as seats of power, with an exclusively Christian presence, while in the southern neighborhoods of Albergaria and Chalcia, Muslims, Jews, and Greeks coexisted for a while. Yet the Muslims who had survived the massacre of 1161 had to abandon those neighborhoods of Palermo and take refuge in the northern neighborhood of Seralcaldi during the riots of 1189.[38]

The segregation of Muslims after the Christian conquest in Iberia was much faster and more explicit. In the pact established by Alfonso I, king of Navarra and Aragon, with the Muslims of Tudela (a fortified town on the frontiers of Navarra, Castile, and Aragon conquered in 1119), the king confirmed the Islamic magistrates of the city in their functions and accepted the continuation of the community in their homes for one year. Nevertheless, the pact imposed the removal of the Muslims to a special neighborhood, to be built outside the walls, after that term. The Muslims were allowed to keep their property, on which they would be required to pay a 10 percent tax; they were allowed to depart for a Muslim country if they so wished; they would not be forced into military service or forcibly converted; the Jews were forbidden to sell Muslims as slaves; and finally, a dualist judicial system for Muslims and Christians was introduced.[39] Muslims and Jews in Christian Iberia ended up systematically segregated in separate neighborhoods, although in the case of the former, communities survived in the southern regions of Alentejo, Algarve, Granada, Valencia, and Aragon, while in the latter case, communities were spread across Iberia until their expulsion from Castile and Aragon in 1492, and from Portugal in 1496.

Segregation laws were drawn up to avoid the contamination of Christians and prevent new converts from reverting to their old faith. The Third (1179) and Fourth (1215) Lateran councils transformed the experience of discrimination and exclusion in Iberia, Sicily, and the Middle East into canon law, as did the *Decretales* compiled by Pope Gregory IX in 1234. This corpus of legislation, which included debate on the rights of non-Christians and justified the Crusades as defensive war, forbade the trade of arms and strategic materials into Islamic countries, service of Christians to Muslims or Jews (for example, as ships' captains or slaves), marriage of Christians with Jews or Muslims, and building of new synagogues. Jews and Muslims were required to wear distinctive badges and clothing; they could not appear in public during Holy Week; they were required to live in separate neighborhoods, and were excluded from the main judicial system.[40] Part of this legislation—namely, that portion dealing with Christian slaves and the performance of service for Jews—replicated an old tradition established by the Christianized Roman Empire as early as the fourth and fifth centuries.[41]

The stigma attached to Muslims and Jews was extended to stain their Christian protectors. Pope Innocent IV accused Emperor Frederick II of complicity with the Muslims; he also accused the emperor of allowing the "worship of Muhammad" (meaning Islamic prayers) in Jerusalem, although this was part of the agreement reached with the sultan of Egypt in order to recover political control of the city.[42] Manfred, the illegitimate son of Frederick II acclaimed king by the Sicilians, was derided as the sultan of Lucera after choosing the Muslim city of Apulia as one of his strongholds, storing the royal treasure there, and using local troops as his special guard. Peter III, king of Aragon, who defeated Charles of Anjou in 1282 and became king of Sicily as a consequence of the revolt against the French known as Sicilian Vespers, felt the full force of papal wrath when he was excommunicated and a Crusade was launched against him. The role of the Valencian Muslim troops in the defense of Gerona became legendary; they also provided part of the *almogávares* (from the Arabic *muğāwir*, militia), the special forces of the Aragonese army that defeated the French troops. The cardinal legate who accompanied the disastrous French "Crusade" bitterly accused the Aragonese king of joining with the Saracens against Christendom.[43]

✶ ✶ ✶

Although throughout the Middle Ages prejudices flourished between peoples of the same religious allegiance, there is no doubt that competition and constant war played an extremely important role in creating long-lasting hatred between people of different religions, mainly Christians and Muslims. The proliferation of prejudices among the peoples of western Europe is striking. This process was shaped by contempt for non-Christians, but also by projects of political dominion, as shown in the feelings of the Germans toward the Slavs, the English toward the Irish, the Scandinavians toward the Lapps, and even the peoples of northern Europe toward their southern counterparts. The virulence of prejudices between Latin and Greek Christians was even stronger, leading to the forcible replacement of people's religious structures after they were conquered, and even to their enslavement. Although these cases represent discrimination, they do not reveal prejudice concerning descent: Greeks and members of the Eastern churches converted to the Latin ritual were not stigmatized. An equivalent trend of prejudices and discrimination occurred inside the Muslim world, due to shifting centers of power and the definition of new peripheries in a period that saw the integration of a wide variety of nomadic or seminomadic peoples. Yet there was no stigmatization of people once converted, revealing an absence of prejudice concerning descent.

The old conflict between Christians and Jews (the latter's was the only religion to survive the Christianization of the Roman Empire) also became bitter in time. The respect for Jewish people as living witnesses of the religious roots of Christianity was transformed into hatred for their "stubbornness" in refusing to acknowledge the divine nature of Christ. The tension between integration by violent conversion (even though this was forbidden by canon law) and exclusion as well as segregation was visible in various parts of the Mediterranean. Permanent suspicion against converted Jews meant that they were the victims of prejudices built on the idea of ethnic descent: it was expected that they would continue to show the "qualities of character" of their ancestors, and would inevitably revert to their former faith. Permanent war on various fronts between Christians and Muslims also created a prejudice based on religious allegiance that deepened the idea of ethnic descent. Converted Muslims were the subject of suspicion, as were converted Jews.

Although pogroms, expulsions, and the enslavement of Jews and Muslims had been practiced during the Crusades and as a result of conquest, it was the last centuries of the Middle Ages, from the thirteenth to the fifteenth century, that saw the systematic segregation, violent conversion, and exclusion of communities of a different religious origin in Latin Christian areas. Prejudices against Jews and Muslims based on religious differences became linked to the idea of descent. These two religious communities also became connected in

Latin ecclesiastical legislation in a practical process of discrimination and segregation that lumped them together as "the enemy within."[44] Both communities were subjected to procedures of spatial, social, and professional segregation, sometimes even after they converted to Christianity. The notion of purity of blood became particularly rooted in Iberia, where it was used to discriminate against and segregate converted Jews and Muslims, showing how religion and ethnic descent had become entangled. This was the crucial case of racism in this period, since it contradicted the universalist ideal of the Christian Church, based on equality among believers from different ethnic origins. Finally, prejudice against black people is documented in the Mediterranean area from classical antiquity onward. Medieval Islamic and Christian writers renewed it, anticipating widespread scorn triggered by the increase of slave trade from Africa to Europe and then to America in the following centuries.

II

OCEANIC EXPLORATION

If the Crusades symbolically placed Jerusalem at the center of the world and reinforced ethnic prejudices based on religious allegiance, the oceanic exploration shifted the symbolic center of the world to Europe and built up the idea of white supremacy over the peoples of the other parts of the globe.[1] This process was a long one, characterized by a permanent tension between the identification of an increasing variety of peoples and the projection of stereotypical images onto African, American, and Asian peoples. In the seventh century, Isidore of Seville, in his encyclopedic summing up of the knowledge of the time, asserted that seventy-three peoples were descended from Noah, fifteen from Japheth, thirty-one from Shem, and twenty-seven from Ham.[2] Such mythical and biblically inspired genealogies of peoples were only challenged by the Renaissance experience of oceanic navigation. In 1512–15, Tomé Pires loosely mentioned more than ninety different peoples in the Indian Ocean in one of the first economic and political descriptions of the area.[3] In 1526–57, Gonzalo Fernandez de Oviedo identified more than sixty American "nations," although his ambiguous reference to native "provinces" (around three hundred) introduced an even greater diversity.[4] In 1594, André Álvares de Almada described with considerable accuracy thirty-seven different ethnicities in the region of the "rivers of Guinea" (roughly from present-day Senegal to Sierra Leone).[5] These authors were speaking from experience or information gathered locally: Pires was a pharmacist for the Portuguese royal family who worked in India as a royal factor and then in China as the king's ambassador; Fernandez de Oviedo was a courtier, writer, and official of the king who spent nearly forty years in the Americas; Álvares de Almada, a mulatto born on the island of Santiago in Cape Verde, pursued a military life in the region he described, having been promoted to captain and a member of the Order of Christ. In the 1590s, Giovanni Botero, who wrote one of the first reliable general geographic accounts of the world, dramatically multiplied the number of ethnic references then in use and declared there to be an infinity of peoples.[6] The diversity of humankind seemed to be at the core of the Renaissance, and the categorization of the different parts of the world, as we will see, emerged as a response to this apparent chaos. The reason for this paradox will be my first line of inquiry.

The definition of European whiteness is another important issue in this period, since permanent migrations and the mingling of peoples, mainly in the Mediterranean area, had given rise to a wide variety of phenotype features.[7] European internal ethnic stereotypes, mainly of the "white" North against the "mixed" South, were already visible in the Middle Ages, as the previous part of this book has shown. These internal prejudices increased as a result of oceanic expansion, but the harshest preconceived ideas were obviously reserved for the peoples of other continents. The Atlantic slave trade, which dramatically increased the numbers of slaves transported to southern Europe from the mid-fifteenth to the end of the sixteenth century, then redirected to the Americas from the sixteenth to nineteenth century, contributed to changing phenotype perceptions of Europeans inside and outside their continent. Definitions of ethnicities became even more based on skin color than before, although other traditional elements of identification, such as hairstyles and beards, clothing, shoes, ornament (jewels and tattoos), shapes and materials used in housing, food habits, and domesticated animals were still used. The evolution of the criteria employed for identifying peoples around the world will be my second line of inquiry.

We have seen how religious allegiance had been an essential criterion for ethnic identification in the Middle Ages. Even when people changed their religion, as a result of political conquest, social pressure, political shifts by elites, or personal choice, they could come under suspicion, accused of dissimulation of the old faith, or hidden reversion to it. After the fifteenth century in Iberia, Old Christians, whose language of discrimination and policies of exclusion created an atmosphere of ethnic prejudice that ignored a tradition of religious equality established by the water of baptism, particularly targeted New Christians of Jewish origin or Moriscos with their Islamic past. The issue here is to understand how this dividing line based on descent came to be constructed inside the Christian community—in what context it emerged, for what purpose, for how long, and with what consequences for the world outside Europe. The role of descent and caste divide will be my third line of inquiry.

I have used the sixteenth-century personification of the four parts of the world to structure these chapters. I will analyze European perceptions of Africans, Americans, and Asians, followed by perceptions within Europe, since stereotyping is crucial for understanding the dynamics of prejudices concerning ethnic descent. The mythical division of continents has been criticized.[8] But in this case I am simply following the line of the main sources, which will influence the division of humankind into three or four subspecies during the long period of the theories of races.

||||||||||||||||||||||||||||||||||||||||||||||||||||||||||||||||||||||||||||||||||||||||||||||||||||||||||||||||||||||||||||||

CHAPTER 5

Hierarchies of Continents and Peoples

PERSONIFICATION OF CONTINENTS

In 1570, Abraham Ortelius published the first significant printed atlas of the world, *The-atrum Orbis Terrarum*, one of the best sellers of its time in spite of its cost, with forty-one editions printed by 1612.[1] The illustrated frontispiece introduced a novelty in mapmaking: it personified the four parts of the world.[2] The allegorical figures are clearly placed in a hi-erarchy. Europe is at the top, sitting in front of the pediment, wearing an imperial crown. In her right hand she holds a scepter, and in her left hand, rather as one would use a rudder, she holds a cross that rests on top of a large globe. Behind her, vine leaves and grapes grow over an arched trellis, underlining her fertility and riches. This figure of Europe is the only one seated, fully clad, and with shoes. Her ruling position is further defined by the repre-sentation of two globes (celestial and earthly) at either end of the pediment, and it is under-lined by the symbols of liberality and labor (the plate and the ox head) on the entablature immediately below her.

Asia occupies the second position, well below but to the right of Europe, standing on the "marble" pedestal of the portal, in front of a column. She has an elegant headdress, is adorned all over with precious stones, and wears beautiful although rather transparent clothes that reveal her body. She is barefoot, and a censer rests on her left hand.

The third position, in front of the column to Europe's left, is assigned to Africa, her posi-tion symmetrical with that of Asia. Africa is represented as an almost-naked woman, with a ribbon on her head and a loose transparent piece of cloth that hardly covers her sex tied round her hips. The rays of the sun surround her head, underscoring the Greek etymology of the word Ethiopian as a burned face. She holds a branch of fragrant wood in her right hand—a reference to Egypt taken directly from Sebastian Münster's *Cosmographia*.[3] Only the nose is a stereotypical phenotype feature. Africa is represented in profile, in a reference to the Roman tradition of personifying Egypt in a woman's profile on coins and medals. On the colored versions of this title page, Africa is depicted in dark brown.

The fourth position is assigned to America, literally placed at the bottom of the portal, in front of the pedestal, lying down almost totally naked, with a stylized club in her right hand, while with her left hand she exhibits the severed head of a victim of cannibalism. America's

Figure 5.1. Abraham Ortelius, *Theatrum Orbis Terrarum* (Antwerp: Apud Ægid. Coppenium Diesth, 1570), title page representing the four continents. Staatsbibliothek, Berlin.
© 2013. Photo: Scala, Florence; Bpk Bildagentur für Kunst, Kultur und Geschichte, Berlin, 421

only "dress" is a feathered string wound round her head. She displays two other exotic ornaments: precious stones encrusted on her forehead, and a ring of small bells around one leg. Under her body lie a bow and two arrows, representing her as an Amazon warrior. Next to her is the naked bust of a woman attached to the top of a column that depicts a flame. This represents Tierra del Fuego, the mythical Australian fifth part of the world indicated in Ortelius's maps and inspired by the revolutionary world map published by Gerard Mercator in 1569.[4] The exotic scene is completed by the hammock hung on the wall behind the figures of America and Australia.

The iconographic program of this title page is extraordinary: it reveals how, in little more than a century of European oceanic exploration, the main stereotypes of other continents and peoples of the world had crystallized in a visually and powerfully compact way. The invention of these allegorical figures was extremely important. We will see how Ortelius was inspired by previous descriptions and representations, but what, in the long run, is striking is the impact that his frontispiece was to have on succeeding personifications of the continents, right up until the nineteenth century. The frontispiece functioned as a template that was used, with variants, in different forms of visual and performative culture—maps, drawings, engravings, royal entries, paintings, monuments, and public sculptures—without the assumption of the symbolism ever being challenged in any significant way. The reason was simple: the frontispiece underlined the superior position of Europe.

If we further analyze the iconographic program of the frontispiece, we can see how the portrayal of Europe concentrates ideas of wisdom, justice, ethics, and labor. The other allegorical figures are obviously quite lacking in these attributes. The vertical contrast between Europe and America, the latter literally placed as far as possible below the feet of the former, is the most telling of all. The scepter is a symbol of regal or imperial authority, implying the rightful exercise of justice. America uses a stylized club in place of a scepter to represent the total absence of moral authority or justice. The idea that she relies solely on the law of brutality, emphasized by the head of her victim, a wise, bearded old man, reinforces the contrast with Europe. The horizontal opposition of Asia and Africa to each other is also carefully staged: the first with fine clothes and an elegant headdress, insinuating luxury and idleness; and the second exhibiting roughness and savagery through her nakedness and careless head apparel. The opposition of the two figures is extended by the contrast of the branch of fragrant wood torn from a tree with the censer burning refined aromatics. There is a last, diagonal opposition between Europe/Asia and Africa/America defined by the setting of dressed against undressed and decorum against nakedness. Clothes, again, are a major element in identification and a carrier of prejudice.

But the opposition goes further, since Europe is presented as the example of work and decency, with sober clothes and shoes, contrasting with the sensual and idle Asia, with bare feet and transparent clothes. The symbolic meaning of the four elements is also in play in this iconography, in which every detail has been consciously chosen: fire is juxtaposed with the figure of Africa and connected to the figure of America, to represent the extreme nature of the climate and corresponding savagery of the inhabitants. Finally, it should be noted that while Europe is surrounded by the element earth (the vineyard), meaning stable roots along with a balanced and fruitful environment, Asia is surrounded by the element air, highlighted by the fuming incense, meaning levity, or better yet, a lack of seriousness.

There had been a long tradition of personification of the cities and provinces of the Roman Empire, leaving traces in some surviving (or reproduced) maps, such as the so-called Peutinger map on which allegorical figures of Rome, Constantinople, and Antioch are inscribed.[5] Medals and coins also presented personifications of the provinces of the Roman Empire, particularly North Africa, dominated by the image of Egypt as a female in profile, with an elephant as headgear, and a scorpion and censer, as reproduced by Antonio Agostini as late as 1592.[6] This type of image still shaped the allegorical figure of ancient Egypt on the corresponding map published in 1565 by Ortelius, who was well known as an antiquarian.[7] As we have seen, references to the Egyptian model were not entirely absent from the image of Africa in the *Theatrum Orbis Terrarum*, but the choice of the sub-Saharan black allegorical figure of Africa defined a shifting moment with long-lasting consequences. Although the mythical image of the rape of Europe by Zeus transformed into a bull was obviously well known, the allegorical positioning of the three parts of the world had not been

Figure 5.2. Hans Burgkmair, people from "Calicut" in *The Triumph of the Emperor Maximilian I*, wood-cut, c. 1517–18. British Museum.
© Trustees of the British Museum

personified in medieval art; there were only symbolic references connected to the three sons of Noah or the three Magi.

The surprising representation of the continents as female (and only sometimes male) figures had its beginning in the sixteenth-century ceremonies of royal triumphs, entries, weddings, and funerals—above all those connected to the emperor. In 1516, in Brussels, the funerary ceremonies of King Ferdinand of Aragon and Castile, organized by the Habsburg court artist Jan Gossaert, included a parade of masked Moors and Indians representing the peoples of conquered Granada and the Caribbean islands.[8] In 1517–18, the woodcuts by Hans Burgkmair of different peoples of the world for the triumph of Emperor Maximilian I renewed the medieval tradition, begun in western Europe by Roger II and developed by Frederick II, of depicting Africans and Asians as defeated peoples or vassals in order to enhance the imperial status.[9] In 1520, the entry of Charles V into Antwerp included a display depicting Africa and Asia kneeling before the ruler, who was represented embracing Europe. The image was flanked by anticipatory trophies of impaled North African Muslim and Ottoman heads. In 1526, in Seville, for the ceremonies held to mark the marriage of Charles V to Isabel of Portugal, a triumphal arch was constructed that represented a personified Glory crowning the emperor and empress, with Italians, Spaniards, Germans, Flemings, Moors, and Indians at their feet.[10] In 1539, in Florence, Charles V was received with a triumphal arch celebrating his position as emperor, with the personification of Spain, Mexico, Peru, Germany, Italy, and Africa as his vassals. Two years later, in Milan, Giulio Romano constructed a triumphal arch in which the emperor represented Europe, with an Indian (personifying the New World), Mauritanian (Africa), and Turk (Asia) at his feet. This is one of the first public representations of the four continents. In 1549 in Antwerp, during the entry of Charles V and his heir, Prince Philip, a pageant represented the three parts of the world subject to the prince, personified by female figures presenting a Turk as Asia and an Egyptian as Africa. The Indian signifying the New World was not presented, but there was an inscription referring to her. The unfolding pageant showed Philip chasing Turks, Moors, Arabians, Saracens, Africans, and Mamelukes off the stage, with the explicit purpose of liberating the provinces of Greece, North Africa, and Asia Minor. In 1558, in Alcalá de Henares, the funerary ceremonies of Charles V included the personification of the four parts of the world as the central point of an iconographic program in order to stress the imperial ideology embodied by the celebrated ruler.[11] In 1564, again in Antwerp, the *ommegangen* (a pageant in which boys and girls presented *tableaux vivants* depicting the city, the provinces of the Low Countries, and the trading nations) included for the first time a chariot bearing an allegorical representation of the four parts of the world (wheeled out again in 1566), significantly called *Theatre of the World.*[12]

This inventory of allegories of parts of the world predating Ortelius's title page is not complete, but it suggests that Antwerp was the main place for this iconographic innovation, although the Italian cities (and to a lesser degree, Spanish cities) also played a significant part. This is not surprising, because Antwerp enjoyed three extraordinary advantages in this period: it was the center of the European world system during most of the sixteenth century (roughly 1500–1585), benefiting from the Iberian oceanic explorations.[13] It was an important center of power during the reign of Charles V, playing the key role of mediator between southern and northern Europe.[14] And certain of its citizens accumulated an extraordinary expertise in crucial areas of knowledge, such as printing, engraving, emblem production (symbolic pictures with accompanying text), numismatics (the production and study of coins, medals, and paper money), geography, cartography, and mathematics.[15] All of these elements benefited from Antwerp's position in the densest urbanized region of Europe.[16] The intellectual resources of the city and their breadth are revealed by the extent of the circle of Ortelius's friends, associates, and correspondents, including: his patron, Cardinal Perrenot de Granvelle; the artists Pieter Brueghel the Elder, Philip Galle, Cornelis Metsijs, Dirck Coornhert, Lucas de Heere, Joris Hoefnagel, Hubert Goltzius, Frans Hogenberg, and Jan Sadeler; the printers Aegidius Coppen van Diest, Gerard de Jode, and Christoph Plantin; the poet Jan van der Noot; the legal consultant and politician Adolphe van Meetkerke; the Orientalist Guillaume Postel; the philosopher Justus Lipsius, the geographer and cartographer Gerard Mercator; the doctor, historian, and collector Johannes Sambucus, who resided at the court of Vienna; and the philologist Benito Arias Montano, who resided at the court of Madrid, to name only a few.[17]

Images of the peoples of the known world as subjects had been produced throughout the twelfth and thirteenth centuries in Sicily and Germany in order to enhance imperial projects (see chapters 2 and 3). The universal claims of these projects explain the involvement of peoples from other continents. This is why the images of black Africans or American peoples in this context were always ambiguous: savages but powerful, because they were considered as subjects or potential subjects that could be Christianized. As Ortelius lived in Antwerp, it was only natural that he absorbed the growing tendency to personify the four parts of the world. But it is undeniable that he played a major role in fixing the allegory of Africa, still hesitating between the Egyptian and the black African as well as the allegory of Asia, undecided between the Ottoman Turk and the Indian. The allegory of America made its way from the first representations in Burgkmair and Dürer to the public pageants of Milan and Antwerp, but the accumulation of written and visual references to the cannibalism of the natives, from the printed letters of Columbus and Amerigo Vespucci to Hans Staden's account of his sufferings as a prisoner of the Brazilian Tupinambas, is crucial to explain their figuration as the most barbarian peoples of the world.[18] In short, the publication of Ortelius's title page can be considered a visual act of major significance that shaped three centuries of visual strategies designed to legitimize European supremacy.

The immediate decades after Ortelius's frontispiece were crucial to diffusing the personification of the four parts of the world. Between 1572 and 1618, Georg Braun and Franz Hogenberg produced extraordinary title pages for the six volumes of *Civitates Orbis Terrarum*. These pages contained a vast program of architectural and urban celebrations of civic virtues and community values; the title page of volume 5 reproduced the main elements of the figures of the four continents, although in a way slightly less denigrating for the other three than that of Ortelius, perhaps due to the values of urbanity underlined at the bottom of the page by the representation of six seated wise men, including a Turk, engaged in pleasant conversation.[19] But there were alternatives to the allegorical personification of the four continents promoted by Ortelius.

The title page of the first comprehensive printed costume book, published by Hans Weigel in Nuremberg in 1577, featured a vigorous white, red-haired, naked European male with a huge roll of fabric under his right arm, a comb under his left arm, and a pair of scissors in his left hand.[20] This is in contrast with the other figures of an Ottoman soldier (Asia), Mameluke soldier (Africa), and Indian covered in feathers with a bow and arrows (America). These images stress the warrior attributes of the other peoples of the world, as opposed to the European inclination for continuous innovation in clothing, a topos in Renaissance literature that replicated the Roman concern about a decline in the qualities of its people. These images underline the reverse of the qualities I have been dealing with here, and they reinforced a strand in contemporary thinking about the peoples of the world, but they do not seriously challenge Ortelius's personification of the continents. It is only natural that as early as the sixteenth century, the subject of fashion would raise the ambiguous issue of change versus timeless qualities, and that innovative Europe would be contrasted with immobile Asia, Africa, and America—the latter an enduring topos that has been challenged by recent research.[21] The problem is that innovation, in the sixteenth century, was not regarded as a positive quality, while constancy was valued. By the same token, warrior qualities then defined masculinity.

Figure 5.3. Hans Weigel, *Habitus praecipuorum populorum . . . Trachtenbuch* (Nuremberg, 1577), hand-colored frontispiece by Joost Amman with allegory of the four continents. Reprinted with permission from the Art Archive, London; Biblioteca Nacional de España; Gianni Dagli Orti

The second comprehensive printed costume book, published by Abraham de Bruyn in 1581, replicated the main ideas of Ortelius's frontispiece and added significant elements that would have a long life.[22] The title page is conceived as a marble fountain with the emblem of a horseman trying to catch a flying woman with the words "c'est en vain" at its top. There could be no better symbol of the inconstant nature of fashion. On the superior right-hand side (to the spectator's left), Asia is dressed in rich clothes and a magnificent headdress, but she is barefoot. A parrot is perched on her left hand, and a camel is shown on top of the next column. At her feet, Africa leans on two seas, the Mediterranean and Atlantic; she is almost completely naked, with a loose tunic around her body. She wears sandals, and holds a fan of feathers in her left hand and in her right hand a pomegranate (a link to Carthage, as suggested by Valeriano). Africa is adorned with an elaborate collar, while her headdress is made out of corn. Her symbol is the elephant. On the superior left-hand side of the fountain is America, a robust woman, almost naked, with splendid feathers in her headdress and a tunic hanging from her shoulders, holding an arrow with her right hand and a bow with her left. She wears a beautiful collar around her neck and a ring of bells on her left arm. An opossum is depicted on the column next to America. Europe is placed on the inferior left-hand side, riding a bull, wearing sandals and a headdress of flowers, and holding a bull's horn in her left hand and a laurel in her right—a double gesture of domestication and glory. The symbol next to her is a horse. At the cente forefront of the image is a globe.

In this set of images, classical tradition was responsible for the mythical representation of Europe and the choice of fertile North Africa, depicted naked but without any sign of black physical stereotypes. This tradition would not completely disappear in subsequent imagery. The hierarchy of the continents was slightly less obvious in de Bruyn's frontispiece than in Ortelius's, yet there was another crucial element: the representation of animals connected with the parts of the world (the camel with Asia, the opossum with America, the elephant with Africa, and the horse with Europe). This human-animal connection corresponded to another old tradition, although one that had become fragmented, which used to stress the environment of human types and suggest that the animals sharing that environment had similar attributes. Now this connection became systematic, destined to have a long-lasting effect. The link between the personification of the continents and maps of the world was expanded, through dress, as an important element in the identification of peoples, cities, provinces, and countries. But it is helpful to observe more closely the impact of the visual act that Ortelius's title page of *Theatrum Orbis Terrarum* represented, since the allegories subsequently became quite autonomous, resulting in a specific visual genre.

The personification of the continents drawn by Marten de Vos and engraved by Adriaen Coollaert around 1589 developed the female allegories seen in Ortelius's work, placing them in a wider context. Europe is defined by the same attributes (imperial crown, scepter, full dress, and vineyard), and the background shows, on the one side, peaceful and prosperous agriculture and cattle breeding (cows, horses, and sheep), while on the other side a couple of bears with spears and muskets represent constant though orderly war. Asia sits on a camel, dressed as richly as Europe, but she does not wear a crown, and instead of a scepter she presents an incense burner. The symmetry of both images is replicated, on the one side, by the camels, giraffe, and elephants, and on the other side, war. Africa is again an almost-naked black woman, with the usual stereotypical physical features, holding a piece

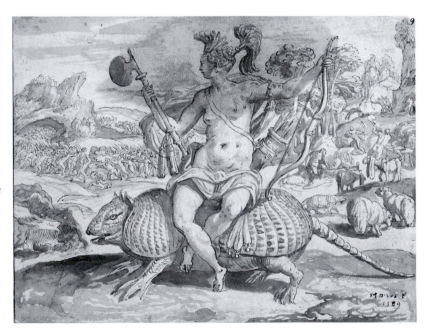

Figure 5.4. Marten de Vos, drawing of America from the series of personifications of the continents, 1589. Hessisches Landesmuseum, Darmstadt, inv. nr. AE440.
Photo: Hessisches Landesmuseum Darmstadt

of fragrant wood in one hand. She sits on a crocodile—a crucial element that generally represents voracity and destruction. The background scenes show a mixture of Egyptian references (obelisk and aqueducts), wild predators, and people living in caves. America is again depicted as an Amazon warrior, almost naked, with feathers on her head, holding an ax along with a bow and arrows. She sits on an armadillo—much more impressive and exotic than the opossum. Behind her, scenes of disorderly war against Europeans and cannibalism are portrayed.[23]

These images influenced the personification of continents in world maps for more than a century, particularly maps printed in the Low Countries. In 1652, the world map by Claes Janszoon Visscher still used de Vos's images almost unchanged, except for a simplified background. But even as this development was getting under way, other symbolic elements were being tried, and these would enlarge the scope of allegories. For example, the 1594 world map by Petrus Plancius was based on the same matrix. It included symbols of the liberal arts next to Europe, a seated Asia on a rhinoceros, and an America divided into Mexicana, Peruana, and Magallanica. This last element was a totally new and isolated image of a fully clad woman leading a war conducted on elephants, while the other images recycled previous representations of Aztecs, Incas, and cannibal Indians.[24] Plancius's inspiration for his association of Europe with the liberal arts remains unclear, but it is extremely important for the subject here: this new element expressed the idea of a superiority of European knowledge that would have a long life.

The allegories of the continents were further fixed by Cesare Ripa, whose *Iconologia*, first published in 1593, was widely used as a guide to symbolism by painters, sculptors, and engravers all over Europe in the following centuries, with the advantage of mixing explanatory texts and images for each entry, starting with the edition of 1603.[25] Ripa presented a synthesis of the non-European continents with the following basic attributes: Asia with flowers and fruits on her head, rich clothes and a headdress, a fuming censer in one hand along with a branch of fragrant wood, pepper, or cloves in the other, and a camel at her back; Africa with a simple, loosely draped garment, a collar of coral, an elephant's head as a hat, a cornucopia full of grain and scorpion in her hands, and at her back a lion and snakes (representing "Moorish" Africa, as the text underlines, although it indicates dark skin and curly black hair); and America with a loose tunic that hardly covers her sex, yellowish skin, holding a bow and arrow in her hands, with under her feet a head crossed by an arrow, a sign of cannibalism, and at her back an enormous lizard. This was no iconographic innovation, although the figure of Africa reveals some kind of mixture between fertile North Africa (based on the classical image of Egypt) and black Africa. But the figure of Europe is much more complex than the previous ones, concentrating more attributes, and correcting some of them, in a small vignette. First, on her right hand, she exhibits a temple: "true religion" is supposed to distinguish her from the other continents. Second, knowledge is highlighted at her feet, with the representation of an owl sitting on instruments of the liberal arts: set square, brushes, and a chisel. Third, she wears a sober dress, without jewels or ornament, showing the impact of the Protestant and Catholic reformations with their emphasis on subdued decorousness. The other elements are well known: the crown, this time multiplied to show the concentration of power in the world, including that of the emperor and pope; the ecclesiastical hats of bishop and cardinal; the cornucopias full of grain; and the horse with military trophies. The superiority of Europe here is underlined through the accumulated symbols of religion, wisdom, political power, and military strength.

The representation of the four parts of the world was quickly transferred to painting: in 1572–74 Giovanni di Vecchio executed a remarkable fresco for the world map room at the Palazzo Farnese, Caprarola (Turin) at the edges of which were allegories of the four continents (here, the black African is represented with a monkey at her feet); in 1584–86 Paolo Fiammingo used them in a series of four paintings commissioned by Hans Fugger for his castle in Kirchheim; in 1595, Paolo Farinetti painted a fresco on the same subject for Count Alvise della Torre at Mezzane del Soto (Verona); and around this date, Prospero Fontana (1512–97) painted a fresco with the same theme in Rome, for the Saletta Pompeiana at the Palazzo Firenze. These are just a few significant examples. In the following decades, the theme was further rooted in painting and passed to sculpture: Peter Paul Rubens painted a significant canvas on the subject around 1615; Frans Francken painted *Homage of the Earth and Sea to Apollo* (1629) and *Allegory of the Abdication of Charles V* (1636) and Gian Lorenzo Bernini sculpted the Four Rivers Fountain at the center of the Piazza Navona in Rome (1648–51).[26] The possibilities of painting allowed a more complex representation, but the subjects also imposed a certain discipline. For instance, in Franken's painting the focus was on richness, tribute, and gift. The splendid sculptural complex of the Piazza Navona expressed the possibilities of the personification of the "main rivers of the world" (again four) as another important vehicle for the allegory of the continents. It was organized around the Danube, Ganges, Nile, and Rio de la Plata, with each of them connected to animals (a horse, snake, lion, and crocodile, respectively), which were more important than the human figures defining, in a metonymic way, the attributes of each continent.

During the seventeenth century, a tradition of blending maps of the world (continents or regions) with images of the most significant cities and most "typical" peoples, generally represented around the edges by couples, became rooted in the work of the leading Dutch cartographers (Jodocus Hondius, Pieter van den Keere, Visscher, Willem Blaue, and Frederik de Wit, following Braun and Hogenberg). The costume books borrowed, yet also created, many images that were used in maps, atlases, and views of the cities of the world. In the long run, we see the invention of new genres of book, mixing in an almost perfect way the representation of cities and image of selected peoples. This is not the place to discuss the crystallization of stereotypical images of peoples through dress; it is sufficient to draw attention to the double register of phenotype features, headdress, and clothing as criteria for identification. The book published by Carel Allard around 1695, *Orbis habitabilis oppida et vestitus*, provides a good example of these innovations, since it systematically combined topographical plates with costume plates, representing a similar number (around twenty) of cities for each continent.[27] Its title page creates an interesting dialogue with the tradition established by Ortelius: the four continents are represented by couples, in the tradition of

Figure 5.5. Giambattista Tiepolo, fresco of the four continents, section on Asia, ceiling of the Stairway Hall in the Residenz at Würzburg, 1752–53. Detail of a slave in a manacle, next to an elephant, and a representation of Asia literally wrong-footed.
© Adam Woolfitt; Corbis

the costume book, with the usual symbols. The novelty is that the European female is represented as a "femme savante" who we can easily imagine in one of the Parisian salons already so critical for the republic of letters of the time. She does not exhibit any symbol of power, but she is the only figure who remains seated, and on who the movements or gaze of the other people converge, who bring her their gifts or tributes, like the black African couple, the enchained female carrying a turtle, and the male kneeling at Europe's feet offering her ivory. This is the costume variant of the superiority of Europe, in which the hierarchy of continents is underlined by posture, dress, or even chains.

Between the 1570s and 1790s, many works of art (drawings, prints, paintings, and sculptures) were executed using the personification of the continents. Sabine Poeschel has compiled 112 examples: 21 in the sixteenth century, 34 in the seventeenth, and 57 in the eighteenth—the vast majority of which were created in Italy (42) and Germany (39), followed by the Low Countries (15), France (12), and Spain (4).[28] It is impossible to analyze most of these works here, but I should highlight the symbolic meaning of Giambattista Tiepolo's masterpiece, the fresco painted in 1752–53 on the ceiling of the Stairway Hall in the Residenz at Würzburg, considered to be the largest and one of the greatest paintings in Europe.[29] The tributary position of Asia, Africa, and America in relation to Europe is clearly indicated by the choice of positions in relation to the stairs and the depiction of the figures: Europe is the only continent crowned, and the subsidiary figures gaze directly at the spectator. The established iconographic elements are used in the composition: a richly dressed Europe, yet with sober colors and ornament, is represented with the symbols of her origin (the myth of the rape by Zeus), tamed nature (the horse), true religion (the temple, miter, and cross, and the crosier of the prince-bishop), liberal arts (music, geography, architecture, painting, and sculpture, with portraits of Tiepolo and his collaborators, Neumann and Bossi), and capacity for war (a cannon and officer). Meanwhile, an almost-naked Africa sits on a camel, while an ape, ostrich, and pelican are depicted on the same freeze, which is completed by the figure of the Nile along with several scenes portraying Oriental and European merchants and local men smoking pipes. Asia, dressed in a turban, sits on an elephant, surrounded by a group of slaves, servant with a censer, tiger, and lion hunt, and there is a section indicating false religion represented by an obelisk and idol. Naked America sits on a crocodile with a headdress of feathers, placed in a large setting with musicians, fruits, and a servant holding a chocolate pot, and contrasted with an alligator hunt and scene of cannibalism rather oddly observed by the twisted European draftsperson. Alpers and Baxandall suggested that in the Asian scene, the slave with a manacle on his right wrist is clasping his own left wrist, which could mean that he is enslaving himself—an iconographic innovation that matches the traditional European idea of Oriental despotism and lack of freedom, and is also underlined by the pleading hands next to the manacled slave. What is striking is the opposition between Europe and the exotic continents, which are depicted with wild life, hunting, and cannibalism, but also crowded with trading elements (barrels, bales, balks of timber), parasols, turbans, conical hats, and strange headdresses, which across the freeze create an Orientalized atmosphere, even in Africa and America.

Exoticism is the crucial element in the contrast between Europe and the other continents in this history of the ideological foundations of European supremacy. The production of the exotic was an inherent element in the European expansion, which redefined cultural parameters and the criteria of civilization (as it would be called in the eighteenth century), downgrading other cultures and justifying political dominion wherever it was established.[30] In this construction of exoticism, Orientalism played a crucial role, as it had since classical antiquity, being renewed throughout the Middle Ages and Renaissance; it embodied a first contrast with western Europe and defined the main features of "strangeness" that would be elaborated in relation to the other continents.[31] Still, the European expansion brought new topics that were crystallized in the allegories of the four continents, and these were widely used until the first decades of the twentieth century.

I cannot follow all the steps of this process, which continuously renewed itself without major disruption. Jean-Baptiste Carpeaux (1827–75) sculpted its most famous representation in its final period; the prefect of Paris, Baron Haussmann, commissioned him to create a fountain for the Luxembourg Gardens (1867–74).[32] The public statue was based on gracious movement, with four female figures placed in a ring, circling round and holding

Figure 5.6. Jean-Baptiste Carpeaux, bronze sculpture on top of a fountain in the Luxembourg Gardens, Paris, 1867–74. Sculpted allegorical group of four continents supporting the globe. © Sergio Gaudenti; Kipa; Corbis

a celestial sphere aloft between them. It is one of the most "egalitarian" images of the four continents: all of them are naked (or almost naked). A certain hierarchy is expressed by subtle elements, though, such as hairstyle or different positions in respect to the spectator. Europe is represented in a frontal position, with long hair. Asia is seen almost from the back, with a long pigtail that underlines the exotic hairstyle of China (showing how this country had become prominent in Europeans' minds). America wears a feather headdress. Africa has a shackle on her right ankle with a broken chain attached, and has a long, rough piece of fabric as a headdress, within which lies a snake. Carpeaux obviously drew his inspiration from a tradition of representation, introducing new elements such as the broken chain to symbolize the abolition of slavery (in 1848, for the French colonies). The reference to cannibalism in America has disappeared, although Africa still exhibits some of the old symbols, and the broken chain is an ambiguous element, celebrating the abolition of slavery, but at the same time reminding viewers of the continent's inferior condition.

The good intentions of the sculptor were underscored by a separate bust that Carpeaux did of Africa, exhibited with the title "Why Be Born a Slave?" Nevertheless, the supremacy of Europe is reinstated in a new context: less hierarchical, supposedly more humanitarian, yet much more efficient from an imperialist point of view. The change of tone anticipated the new colonial era to be launched in the 1880s that would lead to European control, direct or indirect, of almost all of Africa and part of Asia.[33] By that time, Europe clearly needed not slaves but instead diligent subjects.

Hierarchies of Peoples

Visual culture expressed or even anticipated major intellectual developments. The personification of the continents had a long life from the sixteenth to the early twentieth century, framing the idea of European supremacy and a hierarchy of peoples of the world in an extremely simplified, stereotyped way. The advantage of these allegories was obvious from a European perspective: they synthesized the main prejudices against other peoples. But this was not the only possible representation of other peoples of the world. From the beginning of the European oceanic expansion there existed an alternative—or rather, complementary—hierarchy, based on a more complex classification of the world's peoples. This classification did not coincide with the continents, but was based on criteria that stressed the different stages of humankind, cutting across the four parts of the world. Yet it could be considered as complementary to the personification of continents, because it contributed to justifying the hierarchical principles of European supremacy in an elaborate way. It was based on an intelligent program of comparative ethnology, formulated for the first time in a systematic way by the Jesuit José de Acosta (1540–1600).[34]

Acosta was born into a New Christian family of merchants from Medina del Campo. He studied in the Jesuit college of his own city as well as the colleges of Salamanca, Plasencia, Lisbon, Coimbra, Valladolid, and Segovia. He completed his education in theology, law, canon law, and natural sciences at the University of Alcalá de Henares. Acosta lived in Rome, and taught at the colleges of Ocaña and Plasencia. In 1571, after several years of repeated requests, he was included in a mission to the Americas. He lived in Peru from 1572 to 1586, serving as rector of the college in Lima, *calificador* (consultant on theology) of the Inquisition, and Jesuit provincial. He visited the Jesuit colleges of the interior (Cuzco, Arequipa, La Paz, Potosi, and Chuquisaca) extensively, was introduced to the languages of the Quechua and Aymara, and was one of the founders of the first "reduction"—an Indian village created by the Jesuits at Juli on Lake Titicaca in 1578. On his voyage back to Europe, Acosta stayed in Mexico for one year, during which time he collected information on the natives of New Spain as well as the Chinese and Japanese. He met several missionaries who were returning from the Far East—in particular, P. Alonso Sánchez—and the Chinese who he came into contact with explained their system of writing to him. The scope of his research became comparative. Yet Acosta was not the only missionary interested in recovering the achievements of Amerindian knowledge after their deliberate destruction by the generation of the conquerors. The Franciscan Bernardino de Sahagun (1499–1590) was a major and extraordinary example of the persistent collection of ethnographic, linguistic, and historical knowledge about Nathuatl culture, based on a systematic inquiry among the older wise men of the native elite.[35] But Acosta was certainly well equipped to produce his series of books, which he explicitly compiled to prove Indian ingenuity.

Acosta was influenced by Bartolomé de Las Casas (1484–1566), who from the 1510s onward persistently denounced the illegitimacy of the Spanish Conquest, usurpation of the Indian dominions, and iniquity of the *encomiendas* (forced labor of Native Americans placed under the control of the conquerors), defending the rights of the Indians to property and self-government.[36] These claims had a surprising impact on the policies of Charles V, shaping a new raft of legislation aimed at protecting the interests of the Indians and controlling the tyranny of the colonists. The political consequences of Las Casas's vision may have been too radical to be pursued systematically by the king or elites, who benefited from the colonial system, but Las Casas's theological (and philosophical) reflections on the status of the Indians had a much deeper influence through the "school of Salamanca," created by the Dominicans Francisco de Vitoria (c. 1492–1546), Domingo de Soto (1494–1560), and Melchor Cano (1509–60), among others, who shaped the ideas of a second generation of Jesuits, including Luis de Molina (1535–1600) and Francisco Suárez (1548–1617). This school of thought asserted the human nature of the Amerindians, refuted the application to them of the Aristotelian notion of natural slavery, contested the fairness of war against them, advocated their freedom, and supported the idea of their capacity for self-improvement, due to their childlike nature.[37] They also defined the criteria for civil behavior, however, based on the existence of an urban environment, communication, trade, technological capacity, language, and written skills, and contrasted with human sacrifice, cannibalism, and savage nomadic habits (particularly concerning kinship and food). Different degrees of barbarism based on environment, custom, and a supposedly childlike nature became an issue open to debate. Las Casas and the school of Salamanca pointed out features shared by the Indians, the ancient inhabitants of Europe, and contemporary European peasants—a theme developed by missionaries in Italy, Spain, and Portugal.[38]

This was the context of Acosta's enterprise. Acosta's classification of non-Christian barbarians is the most important for the subject matter here, since it virtually comprehended the entirety of the known world. In the prologue to the book *De procuranda Indorum salute*, published in 1588, Acosta distinguished three types of barbarians. The first were rational peoples, with stable systems of government, public laws, fortified cities, prestigious magistrates, prosperous well-organized trade, and the use of letters. The Chinese, Japanese, and some of the peoples of India belonged to this first category. Acosta even talks about a common Euro-Asian culture, *instituta*, referring to principles, institutions, uses, and customs. These peoples are placed at the highest level in all respects, except in religious matters. The conversion of these peoples should be obtained exclusively through persuasion; violence or attempts at conquest would distance them from the Christian law.

The second category of barbarians were peoples without the regular use of letters, written laws, or philosophical or civil studies, although they did have a regime of government, magistrates, permanent settlements, political administration, military organization, forms of religious cult, and norms of behavior. In this category Acosta included Mexicans and Peruvians, whose systems of government, laws, and institutions were considered admirable. They compensated for their lack of letters with an ingenious system of signs (the *quipos*) to record their histories, rituals, and laws, also using them with the same skill as Europeans for mathematical operations. Minor kingdoms, principalities, or republics that created their own magistrates, such as the Araucanos, Tucapalenses, and other Chileans, were included in this category, since they lived in permanent settlements and had a notion of rights, even though they were believed to have much less intellectual reasoning and practical capacity. These peoples should be free, and be allowed to use their property and those parts of their laws that were not against nature or the Gospel. But they had to be converted with a mixture of violence and persuasion, and brought under the authority of Christian princes and magistrates, due to their monstrous customs (meaning human sacrifices).

The third category included savages, considered similar to beasts, who had human feelings but were without laws, kings, pacts, magistrates, or permanent regimes of government, and who moved continuously from place to place, like animals. They lived almost completely without clothing, were cruel to people who passed through their region, and fed on human flesh. Acosta asserted that innumerable "herds," as he put it, of this category existed in the New World: Caribes, Chunchos, Chiriguanas, Moxos, Iscaicingas (in Peru), Moscas (in New Granada), some of the peoples of Brazil, and the peoples of the Paraguay River, the extreme South, and most of Florida. He also included the inhabitants of the islands of the Oriental Indies, such as the Moluccas and the Solomon Islands. All these people, he asserted, needed education, so that, just as children, they could learn to be human. They had to be forced to live in settlements and receive the Gospel.[39] In the *Historia Natural y Moral de las Indias*, published in 1590, Acosta added some of the Otomites of Mexico to the second category, and the Pilcozones of Peru and Chichimecos of Mexico to the third category.[40] We can see the importance of the ideology of settlement and the prejudice against a nomadic style of life in these basic criteria of classification.

Acosta attributed the different degrees of barbarism to environment, relative isolation, and custom, reaffirming the principle that self-improvement and cultural evolution were promoted by communication.[41] He was the first to suggest that the Amerindian population might have migrated from Asia across a previously existing land link between the two parts of the world.[42] This assertion meant that the Amerindians were descendants of Adam and Eve—essential for later narratives of the monogenetic creation of humankind—and that they were the outcome of successive Asian migrations. Acosta also presented a phased model of different types of idolatry, based on the worship of natural phenomena, animals, and anthropomorphic images, as had already occurred in Europe, where savages had given way to Greeks and Romans, who were eventually prepared to receive the Christian message.[43] Finally, Acosta formulated a graded history of writing: first came pictograms based on images, signs, and mnemonics (Mexican and Peruvian); then, characters and ciphers based on an elaborate depiction of subjects, with supplementary signs, as the elements of an alphabet (Chinese and Japanese); and finally alphabets, based on phonology. This final form of writing was considered superior, since it was supposed to be the only one capable of reproducing all the words in any language (implicitly, the Greek and Latin forms of writing, but Acosta could also have included Hebrew or Arabic). He described the enormous efforts of the Chinese to memorize a minimum of 85,000 characters (scholars would need 125,000 to express themself, he wrongly stated), yet he belittled the possibilities of their writing: "there, to write is to paint"; "they write with brushes"; "their print is not well aligned"; and they were unable to "correctly" write foreign names like his own.[44]

What is striking about this astonishingly comprehensive system of classification of the peoples of the world is the juxtaposition of political, economic, and technological criteria of hierarchy with models graded according to religion and language. Las Casas had provided a first, tripartite typology of cultural betterment based on urban environment, civil behavior, and the use of law and written communication. He had equated savages with the barbarian invaders of the Roman Empire, but refused to include Amerindians in that category.[45] Acosta's classification was much more complex. It included all available knowledge in different fields and could virtually be applied to all the world's peoples. It clearly suggested a series of stages in cultural improvement to which, in one way or another, all the peoples of the world could be related. If we compare it to the personification of the continents, it implied a much more sophisticated level of definition of European superiority. The systematic valorization of the Mexica and Inca cultures, although always judged by European criteria of ingenuity, introduced a graduated perception that was naturally absent from the allegorical personification of the continents. By contrast, Acosta's discussion of the first reports on the excellence of Chinese and Japanese cultures that matched all the main European criteria highlighted the supposed limits of their writing systems. The outcome of this critique was to point up deficiencies in the best Asian cultures, making them vulnerable to supposedly superior European skills. Nonetheless, Acosta's main intention was to underline the human nature of all the peoples of the world along with their possibilities for self-improvement and different conditions for conversion. The precocious model of cultural improvement behind his approach was based on the idea of European superiority. This is why Acosta's criteria for classification would be so widely used until the nineteenth century.

These hierarchies framed European ethnic stereotypes in the period of oceanic expansion. In the following chapters we will see how European criteria—the political administration of significant territories, written law, recorded trials, military organization, urban planning, architectural skills, construction with "dignified" materials, industry and agricultural ability, cooked food and use of cereals, "proper" clothing and ornament, and "superior" forms of religion—shaped the European vision of other peoples, justifying different forms of discrimination and segregation. It is also important to acknowledge the subtleties of the interethnic dynamic on different continents, leading to either conflict or alliance with the Europeans. The tension between attempts to assimilate or put other peoples at a distance served different European purposes in time and place, reminding us that prejudices can be concealed or activated, according to precise conjunctures framed by trade, evangelization, or imperial projects.

‖‖

CHAPTER 6

Africans

FROM ASSIMILATION TO DETACHMENT

In 1488, the Wolof prince Bemoim was deposed. Bemoim ruled a territory near the mouth of the Senegal River, where the Portuguese came to trade slaves and gold. He had previously sent gifts and an ambassador to the Portuguese king, John II. After his deposition, he took refuge in a Portuguese caravel with a number of partisans and set sail for Lisbon to ask the Portuguese king for military assistance. John II welcomed him in a stately manner: he offered Bemoim clothing of the finest fabrics, ordered him to be served food on silver plate, and received him standing three steps from the throne, with his headwear slightly raised from his head, as he would have done for a European prince. Bemoim and his followers threw themselves to the ground to kiss the king's feet, and then took earth and put it over their heads in a sign of submission. The king asked them to stand up and listened to the prince's speech, which royal African interpreters translated on the spot. Rui de Pina, the chronicler who recorded these events, praised the words of the Wolof ruler, "which did not seem to be [proffered] by a black barbarian, but by a Greek prince educated in Athens." John II talked to the prince several times, promised the required military assistance, and offered feasts of bulls and canes in his honor as well as evening entertainments of masked theater and dance.

Bemoim was a Muslim, and it was decided that he should be converted to Christianity (in the words of the chronicler, "tratou-se de o converter"). Hence he was swiftly baptized a Christian, together with six of his followers, in the queen's chamber, with the king and queen, prince, duke of Bragança, papal nuncio, and the bishop of Tangier as godfathers. Bemoim received the name of Dom João (Dom was an Iberian form of address indicating noble origin), was knighted by the King and received a coat of arms. This was a golden cross on red field with the arms of Portugal. Bemoim declared his obedience and vassalage, and an account of his conversion was sent to Rome. Another twenty-four of his followers converted over the following days. Then Bemoim was dispatched to recover his dominion with twenty caravels commanded by Pero Vaz da Cunha—an enormous military effort involving at least one thousand soldiers. Besides the troops, the Portuguese took with them carved stone and wood to build a fort and churches. When they arrived at the mouth of the Senegal

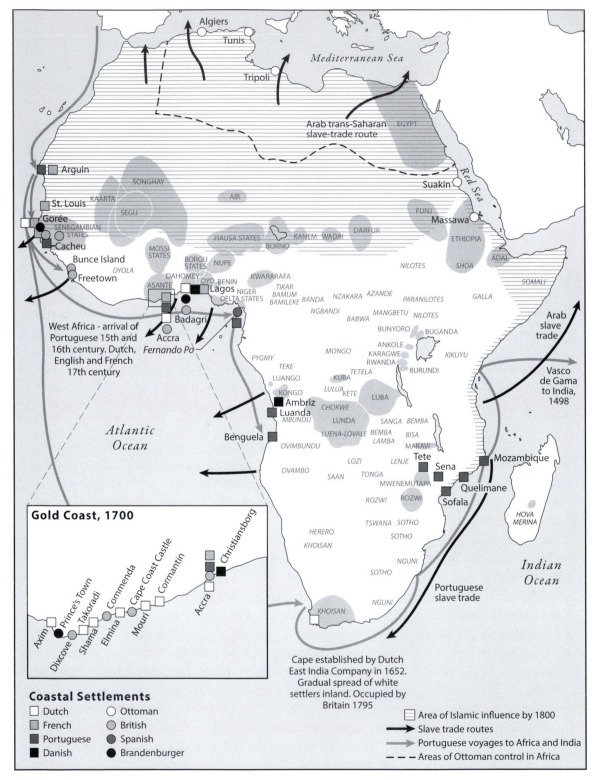

Map 6.1. Polities, enclaves, and movements of population in Africa, 1500–1800.
Source: Geoffrey Barraclough, ed., *The Times Atlas of World History* (London: Times Books, 1990), 166–67

River, the Portuguese captain and officers became suspicious of Bemoim, and they killed him before returning to Lisbon with their ships and soldiers. John II was disgusted by the captain's action, of which he strongly disapproved. In his view, the Wolof prince should have been brought back to be interrogated. But he did not dare punish the captain.[1]

This story is extremely revealing: the deposed ruler was received in state like a European prince; his noble and ruling status was recognized; he was integrated as a vassal of the Portuguese king and received a new identity as a Christian knight, while his conversion was undertaken by the Portuguese king in an act of propaganda to impress Rome. This early episode demonstrates the tension between the attribution to Bemoim of the European status of knight and ethnic prejudices against black Africans. Pina praised the "Greek" speech of Bemoim, but the captain of the expedition did not trust the Wolof ruler. The captain probably feared a trap in an unknown territory, or heard natural dissent against the project of building a fort and churches. The strength of ethnic prejudice at the royal court in Portugal might explain the king's inability to prosecute the captain. Yet it must be emphasized that John II was the most feared king in Portuguese history; he did not hesitate to kill his most powerful noble rivals, including a brother-in-law. This case reveals a further tension between the royal projects of recognition and subsequent assimilation for the native princes, and the practices of the Portuguese merchant-knights on the ground.[2] Merchant-knights were aware of the complexity of West African structures and frequent changes in local power relations, which justified a mixed policy of sack and trade. Finally, the granting of a European-type noble status to the black African ruler seems surprising in the context of a maritime slave trade organized from the 1440s on, strongly contributing to a derogatory image of black Africans as people who would sell their own children and relatives—one of the assumptions used to justify European pillage of the region.[3] But this recognition of nobility was part of a political project that required alliances in Africa in order to establish a steady presence in the field and prepare for future military operations. This is exactly what happened in Congo.

The first contacts of the Portuguese with the kingdom of Congo occurred during the same period, in the late 1480s and early 1490s. There was an exchange of gifts and ambassadors that led to a stable Portuguese presence in the region, helped by the existence of a structured and important regional power. The conversion of the local rulers was an explicit goal from the beginning: the Congolese king was asked to reject his idols and sorceries, "all this said in a soft way [recommended the Portuguese king] to avoid scandal due to the rudeness and idolatry in which he lived."[4] In 1491, the Portuguese expedition obtained authorization to build a church at the headquarters of Congolese power, the city of Mbanza-Congo, later called São Salvador. They converted the king, Nzinga a Nkuwu (baptized D. João), most of the royal family, and part of the nobility. This action was followed by a ritual destruction of "idols" performed by the Franciscans and consecrated by a victorious military expedition, assisted by the Portuguese, against rebellious vassals, the Bateke, near the Zaire River. Yet the last years of Nkuwu's reign were fraught with conflict: he reverted to his previous beliefs, probably because the imposition of monogamy created enormous social and political problems due to the tradition of building alliances between lineages through successive marriages—problems replicated among the nobility—and he clashed with his elder son, Mvemba a Nzinga, baptized Afonso, who had become firmly rooted in the Christian faith, and who Nkuwu exiled to the province of Nsundi. When the king died, his son Mpanzu a Kitima, who was not a Christian, received the support of the vast majority of the population and was probably chosen by the nobles of the kingdom who had elective powers. Afonso challenged this choice, entrenched himself in the capital, São Salvador, mobilized the Christian nobility, and engaged in a battle with the help of the Portuguese. Kitima was killed, and Afonso was enthroned, thereafter enjoying a long reign (1509–40) that favored the spread of the Christian faith in Congo.[5]

The Portuguese kings targeted the kingdom of Congo with a sustained flow of missionaries, soldiers, traders, schoolteachers, Christian books, liturgical vestments and hangings, European fabrics, arms, horses, agricultural tools, and even artisans (stonemasons and carpenters were especially appreciated). The Portuguese failure in the kingdom of Benin, to which a similar expedition was launched in the late 1480s and early 1490s, increased the investment in Congo. Here the Portuguese guaranteed a constant flow of people and received in exchange, mainly under special arrangements made in Afonso's reign, dozens of Congolese nobles, particularly members of the royal family, to be schooled in the Christian faith in Lisbon and learn the habits of the kingdom.[6] The Portuguese first projected the image of their own court onto that of the Congolese court, and then managed to reshape the latter according to their own set of administrative functions and jobs. The Congolese king received a coat of arms from Portugal and was allowed to give himself titles of nobility (duke, marquis, and count) in the European fashion. The Portuguese were given the second-best site in São Salvador to build their walled neighborhood, next to the main church and walled royal palace, surrounded by the houses of Congolese nobles in this capital city. These neighboring, privileged African and Portuguese elites had access to the main water sources.[7] Although the Portuguese king established the tradition of referring to the Congolese monarch as his "brother," the latter was placed under a kind of protectorate, which was an unusual situation in Africa, where in general the Europeans had to pay regular tributes for their presence in various regions until the nineteenth century. The Portuguese king advised the Congolese ruler to declare obedience to the pope and send an embassy to Rome, which he did, with Portuguese assistance. In an extraordinary conclusion to this whole episode, in 1518 the Portuguese king managed to convince the pope to nominate Afonso's son as Bishop Henrique.[8]

These early developments would suggest a long process of diffusion of the Christian religion in Central Africa, yet this was not exactly the case. In part III, I will discuss the devastating impact on Africa of the establishment of colonial societies in America that were based on the slave trade. I will also explore the Portuguese strategy in Central Africa that contributed to the deterioration of such encouraging beginnings (from the missionary point of view). But what I need to clarify here is that the special situation of evangelization in Congo did not have any significant or long-term impact on European perceptions of black people. Infante Henrique was the only black African to be elected bishop until the twentieth century. Black Africans or people of mixed race who achieved the status of clergypersons were few in number and were generally ordained as secular priests, without access to membership in the more prestigious religious orders. They had to cope with constant European abuse of their condition, being regularly accused of inferior knowledge, absence of morals, and involvement in the slave trade.[9] In the first century of interaction, European accounts avoided (with one Italian exception, apparently censored by the Portuguese chroniclers) any reference to cannibalism in Congo.[10] The evangelizing project assumed a good nature on the part of the people targeted. The erosion of the European and Christian presence in Congo changed this perspective. If we compare the first reports in the late fifteenth century with accounts published one and a half centuries later, the dramatic shift from closeness to distance, from a mirror image to an insurmountable strangeness, is striking.

Giovanni Antonio Cavazzi, a Capuchin friar who worked as a missionary in Angola and Congo in the 1650s and 1660s, wrote an influential account of the region that was first published in Italian in 1687. In a chapter dedicated to the "natural and moral defects of the inhabitants," Cavazzi announced that he was about to describe "strange things," of which it must be said that "barbarism makes them abominable" and "the total difference of customs to ours makes them incredible."[11] Here is the catalog of those defects: arrogance, shamelessness, laziness, ineptitude, refusal to work, lack of initiative, incapacity for inventing anything new, concupiscence, absence of the concept of legitimate children, use of procreation as a means to power, approval of robbery, malice, constant mendacity, the common practice of defamation, incapacity for study, lack of love for relatives, abandonment of newborn babies, and the regular practice of selling their parents, children, and siblings as slaves. This depiction was moderated by reference to the Christian habits of part of the population. The people of the cities were criticized more often than those living in the countryside, while men were considered much lazier than women, who worked the land. But Cavazzi's negative depiction was aggravated by extensive descriptions of human sacrifice and cannibalism attributed to the Jagas, a confederation of warriors from different ethnic origins who controlled part of what is now Angola and engaged in warfare with the different political entities on their borders, especially the kingdom of Congo.[12] The catalog of defects summed up Christian stereotypes concerning black Africans that would last until the twentieth century, and which was used to justify three and a half centuries of the Atlantic slave trade and the scramble for Africa of the 1880s.

Olfert Dapper's 1668 account of Africa proposed a comprehensive vision of the continent. It was widely read and in general projected a complex vision that tried to depart from previous stereotypes. It used all available Latin, Greek, Portuguese, Dutch, English, Italian, French, and Spanish texts on Africa to produce a new historical, ethnographic, and geographic synthesis. It duly acknowledged the diversity of peoples, physical appearance, costume, skin color, and habits, sometimes within a single area. North Africa and Madagascar were respectively identified with white and black peoples, while different shades of black, brown, and reddish skin color were related to different countries, such as Ethiopia. In certain cases, as in Egypt and Morocco, physical types were associated with a particular habitat: the light skin of fat, better-off people living in the cities or on the coast was contrasted to the dark skin of slim nomadic "Arabs" (Bedouins) or peasants (Berbers) in the countryside.[13] In North Africa, the colors of the turban defined religious allegiance, distinguishing Muslims from Christians and Jews. In Egypt, according to Dapper, Muslims wore a white turban, Christians blue or red, Jews yellow, and the descendants of the prophet green.[14]

This recognition of diversity led to a more nuanced scale of stereotypes, but did not change the latter dramatically. The people from Loango were labeled savages who used to eat each other, as sorcerers still did.[15] The people of Congo were "black as pitch," with curly hair and unimpressive height, but were well built, with black and blue eyes, and thinner lips than the people of Guinea, who Dapper considered the ugliest of all. The Congolese were portrayed as arrogant toward their neighbors, but civil and honest toward foreigners (meaning Europeans). They were supposed to have a tendency to get drunk easily on Spanish wine and eau-de-vie, and talk vividly, but not to be skilled with their hands. They were considered poor soldiers, without discipline, and given to theft and impunity. The Congolese ambassadors to Maurice of Nassau, the Dutch governor of Brazil, and the general states in the Netherlands were recognized as strong and agile, yet at the same time derided as rope dancers and gladiators who could jump and fence in extraordinary ways. They were also reported as representing the way that the king of Congo would sit on his throne for a long period of silence, during which he was adored by his subjects "according to ancient pagan superstitions."[16] According to Dapper, however, a Christian education and the recent presence of the Dutch had contributed to some improvement along with the introduction of law.

Dapper's perception of the peoples of the southern regions of Africa was also complex, defined by the traditional European views: the Hottentots were slim and ugly, although tall, with light to dark skin, like mulattoes and the Japanese. Their hair was curly and thick as wool, their eyes beautiful, black, and brilliant, and their teeth white as ivory, and they had good hands, "but unfortunately they have a flat nose and thick lips, especially the upper one," "the belly is hailing [swollen] and the bottom extremely big," "they let their nails grow, so they could be taken as the claws of an eagle," and "the married women have breasts so big that they can offer them to be sucked by their children behind their shoulders."[17] The Hottentots knew the laws of nations and nature, were praised for their lack of greed and sense of honor, and were seen as having benefited from contact with the Dutch. The people of Madagascar, favored with a long account due to recent explorations, were placed in a worse light, labeled as deceptive, simulators, flatterers, and liars.[18] The eastern coast of Africa was evaluated more positively, since the people of Sofala were considered more civil than the "Caffres" from the Cape of Good Hope.[19] The Christian Abyssinians, unsurprisingly, were depicted as peaceful, favoring justice and equity, clever, curious, and interested in learning. They were supposed to be better built than black Africans, live long lives and deliver children easily, have no flat nose or thick lips, and be similar to Europeans in all details except for their skin color, which was brown or olive. The conclusion of this praise was logically that "the best slaves are from Abyssinia." Yet they had some defects: they were dubbed

Figure 6.1. Olfert Dapper, *Description de l'Afrique* (Amsterdam: Wolfgang, Waesberge, Boom, and van Sommeren, 1686), engraving of a royal pageantry in Benin.
Reprinted with permission from AKG-images, Berlin; British Library

cowards; their country had more priests and monks than soldiers; and finally, they did not have any port, because the Mamelukes and Turks had captured the coast.[20]

The images in Dapper's book were much less nuanced than the text. The quantity of maps and views of cities was overwhelming, and the images illustrating the main rituals and daily life in different countries reinforced the sense of exoticism. The main themes were wild animals, ivory tusks, slaves (including tortured slaves), caravans to Mecca, pyramids, obelisks, sphinxes, kings dressed in leopard skins, kings being worshipped, kings receiving ambassadors, royal pageantry in Benin with dance, music, dwarfs and enchained leopards, royal funerals, bodies with tattoos or scarification, clothing and ornaments, feasts, dances, and human sacrifices. The contrast with contemporary European appearances was striking. The population of North Africa might have maintained the classical tunic, and the elite might be used to the finest fabrics, including silk, but in the second half of the seventeenth century, North African tradition was backward to the European eye: the long shirts doubled in winter, the dresses were narrow at the top and large at the bottom, and the narrow sleeves were closely woven at the wrist—all this was criticized.[21] The superiority of complex European modes of dress was implicit in this kind of statement, which consciously relegated Islamic fashion to the periphery, in favor of the pride (or vanity) of constant change that had finally spread from France and the Netherlands to more austere countries such as Germany and Spain.[22] In sub-Saharan Africa, with the exception of Abyssinia, parts of the body were represented more or less naked, although the spread of European fabrics was already a reality in many areas, where the materials were adapted to local traditions even as they also fostered new forms of identity.

AFRICAN LIVES IN EUROPE

European perceptions of the peoples of Africa need to be set against the realities of Africans living and working in Europe. In part I, I pointed out the significant number of African slaves brought to southern Europe, some of who ended up in other parts of Europe, but there were other slave routes, particularly through the Ottoman Empire and eastern Europe. The vast majority of slaves were servants and laborers, although there were also soldiers, musicians, skilled artisans, and courtiers. The most successful was perhaps Abram Petrovitch Gannibal (1696–1781), bought as a child slave in Constantinople, who became godson to the Russian czar, Peter the Great, a successful military commander, philosopher (corresponding with Voltaire [1694–1778]), diplomat, engineer and architect, and a confidant and adviser to the czar. His distinguished lineage included Russia's national poet, Alexander Pushkin.[23] The case I will highlight here concerns an earlier period, the first half of the sixteenth century, and a country directly involved in the slave trade, Portugal. It will show the ambiguities that Dapper would later report.

The ambivalent figure of João de Sá Panasco (this nickname meant rudeness revealed by clothes and/or manners), who served as a black slave to the infant D. Luís and jester to the Portuguese king, John III (1521–57), played a double role, mocked by the nobles of the royal court and mocking everybody else.[24] In the main collection of anecdotes recorded during that period, around sixty concerned black and mulatto people.[25] João de Sá is the protagonist in many of them, receiving constant racist abuse about his skin color, "disgusting" smell, and supposed incompatibility with a white *morisca* to who he had been married. But he was also able to reply and reverse the criticism. João de Sá derided his own position. When the king asked him who his best *privado* (favorite official) was, he replied, "The Castanhos among the *fidalgos*, the Carvalhos among the squires, and me among the blacks!" But when Baltasar de Morais, chamberlain of the duke of Bragança, maliciously regretted the death of "his" young black in Vila Viçosa, João de Sá responded that white people could not make a living without blacks. The inferior condition of João de Sá, stained by the initial status of slave, was constantly brought up and thrown in his face through jokes.

Still, he enjoyed the king's protection, and could do what was not allowed for anybody else: mock the courtiers with impunity. The series of his jokes that have come down to us show that João de Sá was the confidant of the king. John III was obviously an avid fan of gossip and liked an atmosphere of heavy mockery among his closest collaborators. He needed someone who did not depend on anybody else to keep him informed of what was really going on among the courtiers. João de Sá was the only one who could play the combined roles of gossiper, informer, and fool. Being a former slave and jester made him an unaccountable member of the royal court, pushing the margins of what it meant to be simultaneously an outsider and insider. He was much more dangerous for the nobles at court than they were for him. The fact that the king trusted him is reflected in the exceptional position that João de Sá achieved: not only was he married through royal favor, but he also acquired the privilege of wearing the attire of the military Order of Santiago, and he became famous

Figure 6.2. Anonymous, Chafariz d'el Rey in Alfama, Lisbon, Flemish painting, oil on wood, 93 × 163 cm., c. 1560–80. This painting includes a black horse rider wearing the habit of the order of Santiago. Collection Berardo, Lisbon. Photo: Collection Berardo, Lisbon

as the only black in Lisbon riding a horse in the prestigious gown of the order. João de Sá's capacity for humorous transgression paid off.

João de Sá is far from an isolated case of success or social mobility by black Africans at European royal courts. In the seventeenth and eighteenth centuries, we find a significant number of instances at northern and eastern European courts, and these were not connected to the traditional function of jester. But the modern stereotype of the happy and good-humored black had already been created, as is shown in one of the Portuguese anecdotes. According to this, when an unidentified papal nuncio returned from Portugal to Rome, he declared that he was coming from a country in which the slaves laughed while the free people cried. João de Sá achieved success through skillfully manipulating words and physical expressions in order to provoke laughter. His behavior fitted the stereotype of a jolly, careless black African, even in the face of daily experiences of clever and talented behavior.

A more rooted stereotype of Africans as savages needs to be addressed, however. The continent had been identified since the Greek and Roman times as the frontier between policed and barbarian societies, exposed to wilderness and uninhabitable hot regions. Supposedly extreme conditions of climate and soil favored the European vision of monsters and wild men used to reflect on the frontiers between culture and nature, human and animal, policed societies and wilderness. The case of a supposed "wild man" also comes from the European court society of the sixteenth century. It concerns a *Guanche*, a native of the Canary Islands, certainly not black, but nonetheless related to Africa in the European perception. Pedro Gonzalez, born around 1537 in Tenerife, in the Canary Islands, claimed to be of princely descent. This man had a particular genetic disorder, *hypertricosis universalis congenita*, which singled him out for life: he suffered from hair growing all over his face, ears, back, chest, arms, hands, fingers, thighs, and legs. Only his palms, the soles of his feet, and his lips were not covered in hair.[26] Gonzales's appearance matched the mythical image of the wild man (*homo silvestris* or *silvaticus*, the etymological origin of savage) created in classical antiquity to reflect on the difference between culture and nature, humans living in a community and humans living in the wilderness.[27] The image of the naked wild man, his body covered with long hair, his spirit prey to the most basic instincts and emotions, a figure close to the medieval stereotype of the giant, had been renewed, by coincidence, through the conquest of the Canary Islands in the fifteenth century. The revival of this topos was clearly expressed by the huge sculptures placed at the portal of the college of San Gregorio in Valladolid.

Gonzalez's appearance provoked enormous curiosity at the French royal court when he was offered to Henry II at the age of ten. He was examined especially by Julius Caesar Scaliger, who in 1557 published a treatise on his case. This was followed by an ambiguous reference to Gonzalez in Ambroise Paré's *Des monstres et prodiges* (1573). "Pierre sauvage," as he was then known, was educated. He learned Latin, proving that savages could become sophisticated. He performed so well that he reached a good position in the court as a sommelier (expert on wine). After the unfortunate death of Henry II, Gonzalez probably passed into the household of Catherine of Medici. Around 1573 he married a French woman, Catherine, and had at least five children, Henri, Madeleine, Françoise, Antoinette, and Paul, who all (with the possible exception of the last) inherited his genetic disorder.[28] In 1589, the death of Catherine of Medici forced him to search for another sponsor. Alessandro Farnese, the duke of Parma, took the Gonzalez family under his protection and sent them to Italy. There Gonzalez was registered as "Don Pietro Gonzales Selvaggio" at the court of Parma, which meant that from then on the Spanish aristocratic form of address, don, would be coupled with the word "savage" in Gonzales's life, as if he had found a way to compensate for his "naturally" inferior position. The sixth child, baptized Orazio (and also hairy), was born at the court of Parma in 1592. Gonzales tried to keep a discrete profile, but again was exhibited as a curious and valuable case, rescued from a half-animal condition. His daughter Antoinette (now Antonietta) passed into the court of the Marchioness of Soragna and was examined in Bologna by the naturalist Ulisse Aldrovandi, who wrote a long report later used by Bartolomeo Ambrosini in his *Monstrorum historia*, published in 1642. Aldrovandi left a portrait and manuscript reference to a girl "with a head hairy like that of a monkey and a glabrous [free of hair] body." The comparison is interesting for my argument: in Aldrovandi's chain of being, the peasant was the lowest grade of European human; the monkey was considered the animal closest to a human; the hairy girl was placed almost at the same level as the monkey. In 1592, Henri (now Arrigo), Gonzalez's first son, was sent to Rome at the request of Cardinal Odoardo Farnese, who made him an assistant in his chamber.

Figure 6.3. Agostino Carraci, *Arrigo peloso, Pietro Matto e Amon Nanno*, painting, oil on canvas, 97 × 130 cm., 1598–99. Museo di Capodimonti, Naples, inv. nr. Q369.
Photo: Fototeca della Soprintendenza Speciale per il PSAE e per il Polo Museale della città di Napoli

The social, intellectual, and scientific interest in the Gonzalez family is documented by successive portraits of the family produced from the 1580s onward: paintings by Dirck de Quade van Ravesteyn and Lavinia Fontana; and engravings by Joris Hoefnagel, Dominik Custos, and Stefano Della Bella. Curiously, the family became one of the most frequently depicted in late sixteenth-century Europe. But the extraordinary painting by Agostino Carracci, executed in 1598–99, titled in the inventory of 1644 *Arrigo peloso, Pietro matto, Amon nano et altre bestie* (Hairy Henry, mad Peter, dwarf Amon, and other beasts), clarified the function of the hairy "savage" at court: Arrigo was represented wearing a *tamarco* (a goat-skin overcoat worn in the Canary Islands), alongside a dwarf, a fool, two monkeys, two dogs, and one parrot.[29] Briefly, he was placed alongside the other human beings identified by (and derided for) their mental and physical "deformations"—all used as luxury accessories for the court and exhibited as strange phenomena of the natural world. But I should note that the Farnese fulfilled their obligations, and the clever Gonzalez family negotiated their position well: Arrigo, placed in Capodimonte at Lake Bolsena, Lazio, as an official in the cardinal's castle, became a powerful local notable involved in trade; in 1608 he managed to bring his family from Parma (his parents and three siblings, Madalena, Francesca, and Orazio); Arrigo married four times and had children; and the majority of his siblings also married and had descendants.

Visual Perceptions

These special cases of court society are defined by the ambivalence between prejudice and paternalism, inferior position and social achievement, social values and transgression. We have seen how visual culture helps us to go more deeply into the meaning of such cases. This is why I need to extend my inquiry into European perceptions of African peoples to works of art. The first series of woodcuts depicting African and Asian people was produced in 1508 by Hans Burgkmair to illustrate the travel account of Balthasar Springer, agent of the Welser family in Portugal, who sailed to India with the army of First Viceroy Francisco de Almeida.[30] In these woodcuts we find a family of Africans from Guinea depicted naked, with bracelets and rings on their arms and in their ears, the adult male throwing a wooden spear, and one of the children dancing—all placed in the middle of the woods, without any house nearby. The same setting was given to the Hottentots in Algoa Bay (southeastern Africa), represented half naked with leopard skins, headdresses of rough fur, and sandals, and the naked children held against the mothers' bodies by loose pieces of cloth. When Burgkmair decided to recycle these images and include them in his project for the triumph of Maximilian I (1517–18), the prejudices became clearer: non-European peoples were not only represented naked or almost naked but they were also surrounded by animals—goats, sheep, cows, bulls, parrots, and monkeys—in a deliberate confusion that made it difficult to distinguish between monkeys and the children negligently carried by the women. The overall aim was to situate Africans in nature.

Figure 6.4. (*Left*) Hans Burgkmair, *Africans in Guinea*, woodcut executed by Georg Glockendon, 1511. Staatsbibliothek, Berlin.
© 2013. Photo: Scala, Florence; BPK Bildagentur für Kunst, Kultur und Geschichte, Berlin
Figure 6.5. (*Right*) Albrecht Dürer, portrait of Katherina age twenty-one, silverpoint drawing on paper, 20 × 14 cm., 1521. Gabinetto dei Disegni e Stampe degli Uffizi, Florence, inv. nr. dis. 1060E.
Photo: Gabinetto dei Disegni e Stampe degli Uffizi, Florence; Bridgeman Art Library

This same message is implied in the *Miller Atlas*, created in 1519 by the Portuguese cartographers Lopo Homem, Pedro Reinel, and Jorge Reinel: on the map representing Africa, especially on West Africa, we see two ambiguous dark-brown figures, presumably monkeys, but reminding us of humans, in a suggestive ambiguity. The intention of the author, most likely the illuminator António de Holanda, might have been just to represent monkeys, but the idea of Africans placed in nature and mixed in among animals was already widespread in Europe.[31] The Flemish humanist Nicholas Cleynaerts, who lived in Portugal from 1533 to 1538, bought three black boys, taught them Latin, and used them as teaching assistants, yet he referred to them as "monkeys" in his correspondence, implying that they were able to imitate, but not create.[32] We will see later how this idea was contradicted by reality. It should be noted that even at this early stage, however, there were already successful attempts to portray black Africans with their own feelings and emotions. For example, Albrecht Dürer did two splendid drawings of a young man (1508) and a young woman identified as Katherina (1521).[33] Dürer's fascination for non-European artifacts and pieces of art is well known. It is not surprising that he treated these two subjects as he would have done to Europeans: he tried to get the proportions and the physical features right, at the same time providing an insight into their temperament. The young male African suggests serenity and resolution, while Katherina indicates melancholy.

The development of iconographic research into the seventeenth and eighteenth centuries reveals a majority of black people depicted at their normal tasks in the European context, as servants, soldiers, musicians, and laborers. There were a significant number of black saints represented according to their attributes. Yet there were also debasing

Figure 6.6. Antoine van Dyck, *Drunken Silenus*, oil on canvas, 107 × 91.5 cm., c. 1619–20. The painting includes a black man sticking his tongue out at a white woman. Gemäldegalerie Alter Meister, Staatliche Kunstsammlungen, Dresden, inv. nr. 1017.
© 2013. Photo: Scala, Florence; Bpk Bildagentur für Kunst, Kultur und Geschichte, Berlin; Elke Estel/Hans-Peter Klut.

stereotypes, probably fueled by feelings of superiority toward African slaves. I will refer here to a few instances of how black people were used to represent base feelings, uncontrollable emotions, and subordination to political dominion. Pietro Tacca sculpted four slaves (or blackamoors) for the base of Giovanni Bandini's marble statue of Ferdinand I in Leghorn (1607–26), solely for the purpose of symbolizing submission and political power.[34] In a painting of Silenus, circa 1620, Antoine Van Dyck (1599–1641) represented a black man sticking his tongue out at a white, female beauty and putting his hand on her shoulder, expressing unbridled lust.[35] Van Dyck also represented a black man during the martyrdom of Saint Sebastian in a scandalous attitude of mirth, expressing irreverence and lack of compassion; and he portrayed a black man with an ironic gaze of derision covering the naked torso of Christ with a coat after Pilatus offered him to the crowd with the words *Ecce Homo*.[36] In 1630, Jacob Jordaens (1593–1678) depicted a black man with a parrot laughing indifferently at the healing of a possessed person by Saint Martin; in 1660, Abraham van Diepenbeeck (1596–1675) showed the Ethiopian king, Ginmaghel, with goggle eyes, undermining the seriousness of African (and Christian, in this case) royalty; and Theodore Thulden (1606–69) represented a laughing black servant transporting the head of Saint John the Baptist on a tray. Black people therefore were used to express crudeness, idiocy, indifference, lust, malice, mockery, and cruelty. This iconographic trend emerged in the seventeenth-century Low Countries and spread through Europe during the eighteenth century, mainly in Germany and Italy.

I cannot confine the discussion to images with a predominantly negative meaning: the use of black people to embody negative emotions was always challenged by their representation in spirited or elevated human form. As evidenced in Diego Velázquez's work, artists could honor black and mixed-race people. Velázquez left a dignified portrait of his slave, the painter Juan de Pareja (c. 1650), whose gaze imposed respect as a human being (he would be manumitted).[37] A splendid anonymous portrait of a black woman in Bologna depicts her with a cage, showing compassion and ambivalent feelings about captivity and freedom. Antonio Verrio (c. 1639–1707) portrayed two black angels in *The Sea Triumph of Charles II* in Hampton Court, London. The seventeenth century also saw the emergence of black saints in iconography and literature.

By contrast, we can see the parallel development of the themes of abusive African princes, black people with open mouths expressing a lack of self-control, and images of black people in submissive positions. The illustrations of Voltaire's *La princesse de Babylone* by Charles Monnet (1732–1808), or Aphra Behn's *Oroonoko* by Clément Pierre Marillien (1740–1808), underlined rape and abuse.[38] There was also an insidious image of black Africans represented as mugs, lamps, chair legs, sofas, and supports for objects such as columns and vases, as if the slave condition had inspired such innovations in the decorative arts. One of the first examples of the use of a grotesque head of a black man as a mug, or perhaps as candlestick, is by Jan Brueghel I (1568–1625) in the context of a cabinet of curiosities.[39] The tradition of black people used as supports for tombs and tables (or caryatides in architecture) was re-created, for example, by André Brustolon (1662–1732) in his sculpting of a series of

Figure 6.7. (*Left*) Jacob Jordaens's workshop, *St. Martin Healing a Possessed Man*, painting, oil on canvas, 432 x 269 cm., 1630. The painting represents a black man holding a parrot and laughing in the back.
© Photo: Christie's Images; Bridgeman Art Library

Figure 6.8. (*Right*) Diego Velazquez, portrait of Juan de Pareja, oil on canvas, 81.3 x 69.9 cm., 1650. Metropolitan Museum of Art, New York, inv. nr. 1971.86.
© 2013. Image copyright the Metropolitan Museum of Art; Art Resource; Scala, Florence

enormous armchairs with the front arms and front legs decorated with black children and young people. He also specialized in full-size sculptures of black slaves in chains serving as vase carriers.[40]

Obviously, portraits of Africans in normal occupations were still being produced as well as compassionate visions of the African condition. In 1774, at the Venetian Scuola Grande dei Carmini, Giambattista Tiepolo painted an allegory of penitence, innocence, and chastity in which penitence was represented as a black woman holding a cross. The second half of the eighteenth century, generally considered the foundation period for theories of races, simultaneously witnessed the development of deep reflection on the human condition and universal values that led to the abolitionist movement. In 1798, Daniel Nikolaus Chodowiecki (1726–1801), who worked in Germany as a book illustrator—for instance, on J. F. Blumenbach's *Beiträge zur Naturgeschichte*, depicted an amazing love story between a

Figure 6.9. Andrea Brustolon (1662–1732), wood sculpture of a black captive carrying a vase support, 90 cm. high. Palazzo Ca'Rezzonico, Museo del Settecento, Venice. © 2013. Photo: Scala, Florence

white man and black woman that concluded with the white man throwing his book on the "system of human races" into the fire.[41]

COMEDIAS DE NEGROS

This permanent tension between ethnographic curiosity and an undermining gaze, a normal depiction in portraits and the use of black people to express cruelty or idiocy, is also found in literature. The compassionate gaze on black Africans (slaves or free peoples) found an unlikely place in the literature of the Iberian Golden Century, specifically in the genre known as comedias de negros.[42] With the character of Filipo, the protagonist of *El prodigio de Etiopia*, Lope de Vega (1562–1635) transformed the black African slave, thief, and gang leader into a warrior and king, capable of the most daring adventures, who finally came to be reconciled with God.[43] The play became such a success that the same protagonist was used as the subject of another play, this time by Juan Bautista Diamante (1625–87), *El negro más prodigioso*.[44] This new type of haughty African was reinforced by the character Antiobo in the play *El negro del mejor amo*, also written by Lope de Vega. Antiobo was a new black

Alexander, born a Muslim prince but converted to Christianity, thanks to the white slave who was his wet-nurse. He fought with the Sardinians against the Turks and died a saint, performing miracles after death and inducing the repentence of the white sinner, Doña Joana, who declared, "I am the black one here, you are already white."[45]

In the play *El valiente negro en Flandres*, Andrés de Claramonte (1580–1626) presented the stereotype of the brave and strong black soldier in Juan de Mérida, who reaches the heights of Spanish society when the king bestows the habit of the military Order of Santiago and the position of general on him in recognition of his military achievements, and thus he is enabled to marry a white aristocrat. The hero declares that "only region or climate differentiates them; if the whites exceed the unlucky blacks in perfection, it is because they have jurisdiction over them; in the same way the whites would be downtrodden and imperfect if they lived in submission to the blacks."[46] This play openly addressed and criticized prejudices against black people. The black soldier was portrayed as being close to the popular and marginal social types who opposed virtue to blood, merit to inherited privilege, and masculinity to mannerisms. Juan de Mérida (renamed Juan de Alba by the duke of Alba, who was his commander) even condemned Jews and Moors, boasting of his "clean blood"—a crucial topic among black Christians, who felt superior to converts from the other two religions of the book precisely because they did not have a previous religious stigma; they had simply been considered ignorant. Yet there were many cases of bad or ambiguous black characters in this Spanish genre. It is worth noting here a strange play, *Las misas de San Vicente Ferrer*, written by the New Christian Antonio Enríquez Gómez (1600–1663) under the pseudonym Fernando de Zárate. Enríquez Gómez depicted a sinister black slave, Muley, who was helped by the devil to seduce the sister of Saint Vicente Ferrer (1350–1419), the Dominican preacher who launched campaigns to convert Jews to Christianity.[47]

Traditional doubts about the religious beliefs of African peoples were reversed in another play by Lope de Vega, *El santo negro Rosambuco de la ciudad de Palermo*, in which he presented a new black hero chosen by God to prove the sincerity and strength of religious conversion.[48] It was based on the recent case of a Franciscan of slave origin, San Benito, who received regular visits in his convent in Palermo from nobles and even the viceroy, and who died in 1589 with the reputation of a saint. The play was written circa 1604, which means that the details of Saint Benedict's case had fast become widely known. The process of beatification started in 1594, but was only concluded by the Vatican in 1743. Lope de Vega portrayed the saint as a Muslim pirate defeated and enslaved by Christians, who converted and showed an extraordinary capacity for enduring abuse, and was able to intercede with God on behalf of sick people. This saint also influenced Luis Vélez de Guevara (1579–1644) in his writing of *El negro del Serafín,* while Friar Rodrigo Alvares Pacheco took the example of Saint Anthony of Noto in the play he wrote in 1641 under the same title.[49] These two saints were worshipped by confraternities of black people, not only in Europe, but also in America, which confirms the permanent relation between theater and reality.

Thus, black people could be heroes and saints in Spanish literature. In this highly gendered literary environment, in which all the good blacks were male, there was one final prejudice to be challenged: the supposed stupidity of Africans. It was challenged by the slave and professor of Latin Juan de Sesa, also known as Juan Latino, who reversed the symbolic meaning of black and white attributed to saints and devils in his poems, pointing out that white skin was despised in Ethiopia. Diego Jiménez de Enciso (c. 1585–1634) wrote a play titled *Juan Latino* (printed in 1652), in which he used the historical figure to deride the most common stereotypes concerning black people.[50] But if the comedia de negros challenged traditional stereotypes, we have to keep in mind that the good black was the one who assumed the values of white (or European) people—if possible, the ethos of white knights and clergymen, and that beside the main characters, there was often the caricature of a bad black or bad Moor. Good black characters were used as a literary device to show the reverse of fortunes, misdeeds of white people, possible change in roles, and redemption of black criminals through their faith, in contrast with the systematic relapses of white Christians. Even if the comedias de negros crossed ethnic barriers, their purpose was to reinforce the central system of values. Nevertheless, it is significant that Iberian society, largely defined by the notion of purity of blood, could allow the promotion of black individuals, expressed and endorsed in literature.

Northern European societies, although less involved in ethnic interaction in this period, were not detached from this literary movement. In some exceptional cases, they could go even further, turning color symbolism, along with social hierarchy, upside down. The African prince Oroonoko was depicted by Aphra Behn (1640–89) as an educated, gallant, and handsome man, with a skin of perfect ebony, like polished jet, "not brown rusty." Black women, like Venus Imoinda, Oroonoko's lover, were also praised as stunning beauties. But this novel was a special one: Behn imagined the enslavement of Oroonoko as a result of treachery by the English captain of the slave ship, portraying an intelligent, proud, and courageous man unjustly relegated to the bottom of Suriname's colonial society. Significantly renamed Caesar, the African prince manages to establish a reputation as a wise man. It is his engagement in the fight for freedom that brings about his final sacrifice. Oroonoko's denunciation of the slave condition is one of the most powerful in seventeenth-century European literature: "We are bought and sold like apes or monkeys, to be the sport of women, fools and cowards; and the support of rogues, renegades that have abandoned their own countries for raping, murders, theft and villainies."[51] The European stereotypical denigration of black Africans is here turned on its head to denounce the infamous slave trade, but not slavery itself. Although Behn's novel is set apart from the mainstream of northern European literature, the ambiguities of Oroonoko and the white values he embodied were not so distant from British literature and art relating to the empire.[52]

‖‖‖

CHAPTER 7

Americans

CANNIBALISM

It was Christopher Columbus (1451–1506) who coined the noun cannibal. In the diary of his first trip to the Antilles (1492–93), Columbus mentioned that the natives of the main islands (Cuba and Hispaniola) feared certain tribespeople who ate human flesh and were supposedly hunting them from the southern islands. These anthropophagi were identified as *caribes*, or *canibes* as they were designated in Hispaniola, in contrast to the peaceful

Figure 7.1. André Thevet, *La cosmographie universelle* (Paris, 1575), engraving representing cannibalism.
Reprinted with permission from the Art Archive, London; Biblioteca Nazionale Marciana, Venice; Gianni Dagli Orti

natives of the main islands, and were said to wear long lengths of hair attached to the back of a headdress of feathers plus be armed with bows and arrows.[1] In a letter to Luís de Santángel, dated February 15, 1493, Columbus stated that the anthropophagi came from an island called caribe.[2] Printed copies of the letter were made and the piece became a best seller, with two Spanish editions, nine Latin editions, three Italian editions, and one German edition, all in the space of four years (1493–97). The reference to eaters of human flesh did not go unnoticed.[3] In his account of his second trip (1493–96), Columbus mentioned the cannibals (in Spanish *canibales*), transforming the word into what was to become an accepted noun, which he repeated in all his accounts and correspondence with European kings.[4]

When Columbus arrived in the Antilles, the Caribs were settled farmers, fishers, hunters, and expert navigators who had spread from the northeastern coast of South America to the Caribbean islands and were driving away the Arawaks, who had previously settled there. Columbus may have reproduced the Arawak fear of the Carib as better equipped and more determined from a military point of view. Although Columbus praised the meekness of these people, who were supposed to be ideal recipients of the Gospel, he was also shocked by the "cowardice" of some Arawak communities. But the idea of anthropophagic practices served Columbus's own interests, clearly expressed in his account of the second trip. He suggested that the "cannibals" should be enslaved because they were infinite in number, and each of them would be worth three blacks from Guinea in strength and ingenuity (a "sample" group of Caribs was dispatched with the letter).[5] In 1494, Columbus sent a letter to the Catholic kings in which he suggested that an investment in caravels, personnel, cattle, and tools could be paid for by the resulting enslavement of the cannibals. The argument was that freed from "that inhumanity," the cannibals would be the best slaves; their expertise as rowers could be put to good use in the galleys that Columbus intended to build for travels on the Caribbean Sea.[6] In 1495, Columbus suggested enslavement of all Indians in a letter he wrote to the kings. Although he considered that the women of Hispaniola would not make good domestic slaves, he noted they would be valued as excellent workers on the land and in the manufacture of cotton fabrics.[7] The assertion that the natives were extremely lazy (*perezosos en grandísima manera*) was put forward for the first time in another letter of the same year, without Columbus noticing that it would contradict his project for enslavement.[8]

Columbus was familiar with the Portuguese model of trips to explore the west coast of Africa subsidized by the slave trade, the supply of which became the main purpose of those trips. He had lived in Lisbon and Madeira from 1476 to 1486, maintaining ties with the local elite through his marriage to Filipa Moniz, the daughter of a Portuguese captain of Porto Santo. Columbus claimed several times in his reports and even in the marginalia of his books that he had been in the Portuguese fort of Mina, in the Gulf of Guinea. Elmina, built in 1482, was a center for the gold and slave trades—a commerce that Columbus was trying to emulate in the Caribbean region.[9] In 1495, the same year that Columbus made his project explicit, he sent a cargo from Hispaniola of five hundred slaves, who were received and sold in Seville by his factors Giannotto Berardi and Amerigo Vespucci.[10] Queen Isabel temporarily suspended the auction, worried by its theological and political consequences—a compunction already expressed by the kings in their reply to a previous letter. In 1498–1500, Columbus insisted that the project should go ahead, adding brazilwood that he had seen on the coast of South America to the list of items to be traded. He drew attention to the fact that Castile, Portugal, Aragon, Italy, Sicily, the Canaries, and other islands "spent" a lot on slaves; those from this new source would be worth fifteen hundred maravedis each. The high death rate among enslaved Caribs, Columbus contended, was normal; the same had happened with the first black Africans and Canarians (guanches) sent to Iberia.[11] If the project of enslavement of the Caribs was never implemented, it was basically for three key reasons: the theological and political doubts of the kings (after all, these natives were their new vassals); the absence of the institution of slavery in the region, which meant that the natives refused the oppression, and in many cases preferred to die; and the existence of an established maritime slave trade with West Africa (later with Central Africa) that could be diverted from Iberia to the Antilles. Meanwhile, the Arawaks and Caribs were decimated by war, displacement, and the disease brought by the Europeans, which made Columbus's project pointless.

Columbus's description of the peoples he met in his explorations of the Antilles as well as the coasts of South and Central America was also important for European ideas about natives: he highlighted their nakedness, their absence of shame, the rudimentary cotton clothes and ritual feather headdresses, the body painting for war, the tattooing and piercing, and the necklaces and bracelets. He emphasized that the people were not black, despite the fact that they were living at the same latitude as people from Guinea. He described them as tall, with flat hair and almost white skin.[12] The persistent reference to skin color suggests that white was by then considered the standard in southern Europe. The Arawaks had tools made out of stone, houses made out of wood and palms, and hammocks as hanging beds. They cultivated the land and produced cotton fabrics. They were praised as ingenious and curious, despite their savage appearance. Besides the classical anthropophagi, Columbus also managed to locate Amazons in the Antilles (on the island of Matinino, the future Martinique), and referred to the existence of people with tails. He even understood a local Cuban joke against people who wore clothes, because they had some physical defect they needed to hide, like tails.[13]

Amerigo Vespucci's (1454–1512) letters reaffirmed the existence of cannibals and cannibalism in America. *Mundus Novus*, printed in 1503, turned into an immediate best seller, with editions in Venice, Paris, Augsburg, Nuremberg, Antwerp, Cologne, Strasburg, and Rostock. It was translated into Italian, German, Flemish, and French, and included in all the compilations of travel accounts published in the sixteenth century, most influentially in those organized by Francanzano da Montalboddo, Simon Grynaeus, and Giovanni Battista Ramusio. Vespucci's *Lettera delle isole nuovamente trovate* (1504), a longer and more elaborate text, was integrated in a Latin version by Martin Waldseemüller into the *Cosmographiæ Introductio*, published in 1507. It was Waldseemüller who gave the name America to the New World.[14]

Vespucci was a former associate of Columbus who traveled to America twice: in 1499–1500, with the Spaniards, and in 1501–2, with the Portuguese. On these travels, he explored a long section of the east coast of South America. Returning from his first trip, Vespucci brought Native American captives to be sold in Seville.[15] He declared that a particular community lived off human flesh (*vivono di carne umana*). When he described the peoples of the coast in general, he stated that the greater part of the meat they collectively ate was human (*la carne che mangiano, massime la commune, è carne umana*). He declared that he had lived twenty-seven days in a native village where he saw pieces of human bodies hanging from beams in houses, just as in Europe hams were hung for smoking. One man had told the visitors, probably through gestures, that he had eaten more than two hundred human beings (the number was enlarged to three hundred in *Mundus Novus*). The natives praised the human flesh for its superior quality, and marveled when the Europeans refused to join in the feast. At another point in the narrative of his travels, Vespucci claimed to have seen a confident young European being surrounded by local women who beat him to the ground and roasted him on the beach, to the despair of his companions, who were unable to help him, since hundreds of local warriors protected the scene.[16]

Vespucci's ideas about Native Americans had an even bigger impact on Europe than the ideas diffused through Columbus's texts. This was so for three reasons: Vespucci was able to organize a convincing and articulate argument; second, he reported on cannibalism with the authority of an eyewitness; and finally, some of the editions included astonishingly graphic images. It should be pointed out that the first editions of Vespucci's main texts, in Latin and Italian, did not include any significant images; they merely depicted ships landing and naked people on the shore. But the German translations of the texts, which were published immediately after, provided an extraordinary set of images portraying the murder of the young man and the roasting of human bodies. These images became powerful visual acts that were merged with the text, making it even more dramatic. They would be replicated and adapted in the sixteenth and seventeenth centuries, most prominently in Theodor de Bry's eleven volumes on *America*.

Vespucci's narrative and such visual acts contributed to a negative European conception of Native Americans. Although considered rational human beings, Native Americans were described as naked and idle, living by the laws of nature, without any order or faith, temples or religion (not even a mistaken worship of idols, Vespucci lamented), without notions of property, territory, boundaries, or rulers, without trade or money, and supposedly ignoring the immortality of the soul. They lived in communal houses, slept in hammocks, sat on the earth to eat, without a precise schedule for meals, ignored the institution of marriage and prohibition on incest, copulated freely in public like brute animals, urinated in front of their guests, counted the time by the cycle of the moon, ignored the rules of war, killed and devoured their enemies, could not communicate with other tribes due to the multiplicity of languages used, and abandoned the sick and old. Native Americans were accused of monstrous and bestial cruelty. Their wars did not even have the purpose of conquest or profit; instead, the revenge of ancestral wrongs and blind emotion were the sole motivations. The male faces were considered utterly ugly, because cheeks, jaws, noses, lips, and ears had been pierced in order to place stones or animal bones in them. Lustful women gave men herbal juices to inflate the penis, or (even better) placed venomous animals where they would bite the genital organ, with the risk to the males of "losing the testicles and becoming eunuchs." Briefly, concluded Vespucci, this was a "villainous liberty of living" (*scelerata libertà di vivere* in the Italian version of *Mundus Novus*). More positive attributes were the skin color, which was slightly dark and reddish like that of the lion, and would probably appear white were they dressed; ability to swim as well as produce ingenious bows and arrows (but without iron, since they did not know how to work metal); and supposed easiness with which the women gave birth, healthy bodies, and the habit of regularly washing in rivers.[17] This last naturally impressed Vespucci, used to the low European standards of hygiene. As we will see, most of Vespucci's assertions were baseless, particularly the Native Americans' supposed lack of religion.

Hans Staden's (c. 1525–c. 1579) account on his captivity by the Tupinamba, in Brazil, published in 1557 in Marburg, sealed the reputation for widespread cannibalism among the populations of the New World.[18] The book was reprinted in successive German editions, and more widely distributed through Flemish and Latin translations. The author had been engaged in a Spanish expedition to Rio de la Plata that was shipwrecked on the coast of Brazil. Rescued by the Portuguese, Staden became a bombardier at the small fort on the island of São Vicente, one of the main colonies, which was notable for its sugar mills. Captured by the Tupinamba, who were enemies of the Portuguese and allied with the French, he claimed to have lived among the "savages" for ten and a half months, under the continuous threat of being killed and eaten, until he was rescued by the French and sent back to Europe.

Staden provided extensive descriptions of daily life in the Indian community, correcting Vespucci in several respects: he added new information on family structure, sexual life, material culture, spiritual beliefs, and forms of identification through the names of animals, flowers, and fruits.[19] He also described how he negotiated his survival—first by stressing that he was not Portuguese, and then by playing with native "superstitions" to make them believe he was a sorcerer (contrary to Vespucci, he alleged that they had religious beliefs, spiritual guides, and idols). He benefited from an epidemic that killed part of the community and afterward maintained a precariously balanced relationship with his captors, who kept asking him to make his powerful God intervene in their favor. Staden told of several ceremonies in which prisoners, Indians, and Christians were ritually killed, stressing how the eating of human flesh was widespread and part of daily life (the Indians would take human meat on their expeditions). The Tupinamba constantly mocked their prisoners and indicated to them what lay ahead, simulating the eating of body parts, and feeding the prisoners in order to make them tasty.

The fact that Staden knew the Tupi language helped him enormously. The insertion of (duly translated) Tupi phrases in his account created an extraordinary effect of veracity. I quote two crucial ones. First, when he was brought before the Indians, they forced him to say in Tupi, "Here I arrive [or here I am] as your food!" (*a junesche been ermi vramme*, or in restored tupi, *ayú ichebe enê remiurama*). The second Tupi phrase concerned his discussion with the chief, who was eating human meat and invited Staden to join him. When Staden refused, saying that only an irrational animal would do this, the chief bit into the meat and replied, "I am a jaguar!" (given in Tupi as *jau ware sche*, or better, *yauara inchê*). The totemic relationship with the natural world was underlined in this anecdote, without excluding the possibility of derision, and in any case pointing out how easily the frontier between the human and animal conditions was crossed. Staden's illustrations increased the success of the book. He included more than fifty woodcuts that provided a visual expression of precise elements in the narrative. The material culture of the Indians was highlighted by these woodcuts. The ritual of cannibalism was detailed in its successive phases, closely following the text, and included the image of a club used for killing the victim.

GOOD SAVAGES

The experience of "France Antarctique," the colony that the French attempted to develop in the Guanabara Bay (now Rio de Janeiro) in the 1550s, during the same period when Staden was undergoing his ordeals in Brazil, resulted in two extraordinary texts—one published in 1557 by André Thevet (1516–90), and the other in 1578 by Jean de Léry (1536–1613)—which supplied material for philosophical and anthropological reflection for the following four and a half centuries.[20] Thevet and de Léry had different confessional points of view—the former was a Catholic, and the latter was a Protestant—but using similar images, they described and illustrated the same ritual of cannibalism, with de Léry claiming to have been an eyewitness and referring to specific cases. Both maintained that the Native Americans were moved not by hunger but rather by an extraordinary spirit of revenge against their ancestral enemies. The only difference between these accounts concerned the "moral conclusion." De Léry was the first to dispute the supposed European moral superiority. He pointed out that there had been many cases of Christians cruelly murdering their religious enemies. For example, during the St. Bartholomew's Day massacres in France, people had sold, roasted, and eaten parts of human bodies.

Michel de Montaigne (1533–92) integrated this comparison into his essay on cannibals, in which the common European contempt for the savagery of Native Americans was turned against its originators:

> What does sadden me is that, while judging correctly of their wrong doings, we should be so blind to our own. I think there is more barbarity in eating a man alive than in eating him dead; more barbarity in lacerating by rack and torture a body still fully able to feel things, in roasting him little by little and having him bruised and bitten by pigs and dogs (as we have not only read about but seen in recent memory, not among enemies in antiquity but among our fellow-citizens and neighbours—and, what is worse, in the name of duty and religion) than in roasting him and eating him after his death.[21]

He went further, declaring, "Every man calls barbarous anything he is not accustomed to; it is indeed the case that we have no other criterion of truth or right-reason than the example and form of the opinions and customs of our own country. There we always find the perfect religion, the perfect polity, the most developed and perfect way of doing things!" Montaigne lamented the corrupt taste of artificial sophistication and praised the natural habits of the savages:

> Those people have no trade of any kind, no acquaintance with writing, no knowledge of numbers, no terms for governor or political superior, no practice of subordination or of riches or poverty, no contracts, no inheritances, no divided estates, no occupation but leisure, no concern for kinship—except such as is common to them all—no clothing, no agriculture, no metals, no use of wine or corn. Among them you hear no words for treachery, lying, cheating, avarice, envy, backbiting or forgiveness. How remote from such perfections would Plato find that Republic he thought up.

He thus started a critical tradition of cultural relativism, but at the same time renewed the medieval idea of the golden age and good savage.[22]

The tension between the image of the good savage and that of the native prey of the devil was defined in the first accounts and representations of the Indians in Portuguese sources.

Figure 7.2. Vasco Fernandes, *Adoration of the Magi*, cathedral of Viseu, painting, oil on canvas, 130 × 79 cm., 1501–6. One of the magi is represented as a Native American. Museu Grão Vasco, Viseu, inv. nr. 2145.
© Direcção Geral do Património Cultural / Arquivo de Documentação Fotográfica, Lisbon

The letter written in 1500 to the king by Pero Vaz de Caminha concerning the first contacts between the Portuguese and Tupi on the coast of what is now Espírito Santo, in Brazil, could not have presented a more idyllic encounter: Native Americans were depicted as innocent, trustful, and generous, capable of communicating through music and dance.[23] Although "bestial beings of little knowledge," they were considered suitable subjects for evangelization. An *Adoration of the Three Magi*, painted in 1501–6 as part of the retable of the cathedral of Viseu, even represented one of the wise men as a Brazilian Indian, with feathers on his head, around his neck and at his waist, breaking with the late medieval tradition of the black African king.[24] This painting reinforced the image of the innocent Indian, who had somehow been separated from a civilized (or policed) environment and was in a fit state to receive the Gospel. Just a few years later, probably in 1510–20, another Portuguese painting representing hell depicted Lucifer as a Brazilian Indian with feathers on his head.[25] Here the demonized Indian was related to the supposed lawlessness of his country, where the Gospel had not been spread and the natives were prey to the devil. It is obvious that accounts of cannibalism had spread in the short, intervening period. The natives were now purportedly inclined by nature to persevere in a life without order—without faith, law, and king—as the accounts of the second half of the sixteenth century would reiterate.

It was, of course, the noun cannibalism that was invented by Europeans, not the practice. European classical narratives of anthropophagi and Native American narratives of people

Figure 7.3. Anonymous, *Hell*, painting, oil on wood, 119 × 217.5 cm., 1505–30. Lucifer is represented as a Native American. Museu Nacional de Arte Antiga, Lisbon, inv. nr. 432 pint.
© Direcção Geral do Património Cultural/ Arquivo de Documentação Fotográfica, Lisbon

as hunters and eaters of other people intersected. It is possible that the Arawaks were try-ing to lure the Europeans into their own unequal conflict with the Caribs, demonizing the aggressors and manipulating the Europeans against them. If that was the case, they soon discovered that the real intentions of the Europeans—to take their land—made all such manipulation pointless. But we also know that ritual cannibalism was a structural element of the Tupi-Guarani mythology in South America. The defeat of the tribe's enemies was part of the duties of a warrior—a part encouraged by Tupichauriya, a charismatic human-god figure. The ritual killing of captured enemies and ritual eating of their cooked bodies were considered important steps in the warrior's passage to the "Land without Evil," a paradise after death, a land of eternal happiness, where warriors would be rewarded and old people could recover their youth. In the European tradition, cannibalism was a crucial notion: it explored where the limits of human nature might be set, the most basic rules concerning what could and could not be consumed, what was considered dignified and what abject, what enhanced the human condition, and what degraded it. The taboo on human eating human was one shared by many cultures of the world. In many of these cultures, though, particularly in ancient Greece, the transgression of such basic rules was part of a framework that would permit extraordinary achievements. In the Tupi-Guarani mythology, the dif-ficult passage to the Land without Evil also required extraordinary deeds; the absorption of the strength and substance of their enemies was considered a necessary act to reach the prophesied land—an act that would ideally be repeated for better results.[26] This caught the imagination of the first Europeans, who could not find a better justification for their preten-sions to conquest and dispossession. If Native Americans were prone to the lowest instincts and unnatural behavior, they could not be allowed to govern themselves. For my argument, the construct of cannibalism formulated by the Europeans was the cornerstone of an ethnic contempt for Native Americans that lasted until the twentieth century. It became a striking symbol in the representations of America as a continent.

HUMAN SACRIFICE

While descriptions of cannibalism defined ideas about the first European encounters with Native Americans, mainly in the Antilles and eastern parts of South America, human sacri-fice became an important issue in the European conquest of Mexico. The phenomenon was reported in the first letter to Charles V by Hernán Cortés (1485–1547): he described the rit-ual of opening the victims' chests while they were still alive in order to take out their hearts and entrails, then burn them. Cortés calculated that three to four thousand people were sacrificed every year—some fifty people in each temple. He noted the annual imposition on each conquered people of a certain number of victims to be offered for sacrifice. During the war between the Spaniards and Nahuas, several imprisoned Spaniards were reportedly ritually sacrificed "to the idols," in the way that this took place in Zultepec and Tenochtitlán. The victims' heads were then ritually exhibited. Cortés claimed that he protested against

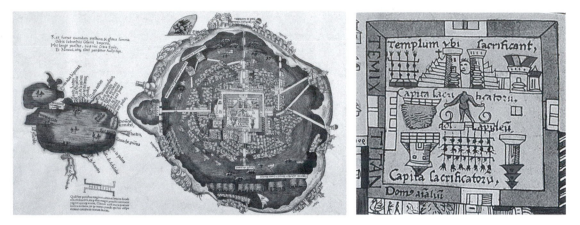

Figure 7.4. A. The city of Tenochtitlán, *Praeclara Fernandi de Nova Maris Oceani Hispania Narratio* (Nuremberg, 1524), woodcut. Staatliche Museen, Berlin, inv. nr. Mex-d dno 1. B. Detail of figure 7.4.A. A representation of the central temple and human sacrifice.
© 2013. Photos: Scala, Florence; Bpk Bildagentur für Kunst, Kultur und Geschichte, Berlin; Dietmar Katz

the practice and attempted to destroy the idols in Tenochtitlán while Montezuma still ruled there.[27] According to scholar Anthony Pagden, the ritual was relatively recent, apparently having started in 1483 when the Tzinacantepeca rebelled against the Mexica confederation. The ritual was more complicated than it appeared in the first reports: after the sacrifice, the body would be thrown down the temple steps, then stripped of its skin, cut up, and the parts offered for ritual consumption to the emperor and captor (if there was a captor).

The identification of the natives' idols as demons, justified by the widespread practice of human sacrifice, played a major role in the Christian suppression of local religions in Mexico.[28] We know that the Franciscans, and immediately after them the Dominicans, formed bands of young converted zealots who were key in campaigns to eradicate temples and idols; only six years after the conquest, five hundred temples had been destroyed, and twenty thousand "demon figures" were broken or burned.[29] This swift movement to suppress local religious monuments is defined by the historian Robert Ricard as a "spiritual conquest." Another historian, James Lockhart, criticizes this approach as giving too much emphasis to a top-down vision of planned and directed acculturation promoted by the Catholic monks.[30] Lockhart, in contrast, centers his analysis on the role of the *altepetl*, the preconquest local community, into which Christianity was integrated and used in a somewhat-different way than that intended by the Spanish clergy, leaving space for many forms of adaptation. A third historian, Serge Gruzinski, also acknowledges the importance of indigenous strategies for survival in the face of Christian rule, but stresses the enormous change imposed by the colonial religious and ideological enterprise.[31] We need to integrate these last two visions. The tradition of human sacrifice was obviously confronted with the Christological message of salvation: the sacrifice of the son of God had redeemed all humankind, making all other forms of sacrifice useless. This signaled a new departure and liberation from previous servitude. In one single phrase, the monks could establish a new religious standard and offer the superior perspective of their conception of salvation after death. By the same token, they would refuse the local religion as backward, devilish, and humanly unacceptable, trampling on the self-image of the conquered population.

Human sacrifice thus was a critical background on which the Christian vision of the world was imposed, in a region whose artisanal skills, agricultural activity, urban planning, and state organization had previously been recognized by Cortés and placed on the same level as those of classical antiquity.[32] This theme was repeated in relation to Mayan society, although the scale of human sacrifice in that society had been much smaller and Catholic zeal following the conquest less intense.[33] In the other American case of Tahuantinsuyo, known as the Inca Empire, we find a similar European contempt for local religion as idolatry—contempt reinforced by the (slightly different) practice of human sacrifice. The major rituals of inauguration and burial of the Incas as well as the festival of the Sun (Inti Raimi) would involve the sacrifice (*capacocha*) of young victims sent by the different parts of the empire to be buried alive either in Cuzco or their own locality after being purified at the political center. These victims were supposed to serve the deities and maintain the balance between the living and dead, the center and peripheries of the empire. Children were also sacrificed to the gods in various places, while human sacrifice was performed in crucial moments of the life cycle of native elites. The celebration of funerary rituals could include the sacrifice of widows, young women, and servants, who would be buried alive (or killed) with the notable person—a practice recorded even after the Spanish Conquest when it involved converted people.[34] The Spaniards were astonished when they executed the last Inca emperor, Atahualpa; all his wives committed suicide by hanging.[35]

Idolatry and human sacrifice fitted well with the Christian idea of false religion and devilish illusion. They became a major marker for the expression of ethnic prejudice and contempt toward people who were considered prey to the devil as well as suspected of relapsing into their previous beliefs. This ethnic prejudice framed the enterprise of evangelization in America, allowing strategies of adaptation and the survival of aspects of pre-Colombian religions under the facade of Christian rituals and saints, and even allowing private or familiar forms of worship by simply identifying them as superstitions, but irremediably breaking the overall traditional structure of beliefs as devilish, inferior, and inhuman.[36] The best example of spiritual colonization is Guaman Poma de Ayala (1534–c. 1617), who has been considered the champion of alternative political thought.[37] He spent the first chapters of his extraordinary work *Nueva corónica y buen gobierno* (New chronicle and good government) asserting his Christian allegiance, and praising the Christianity and princely genealogy of his father and half brother, Don Martin Ayala, who was of mixed race, being the first son of Guaman Poma de Ayala's mother and the Spanish captain Luís de Ávalos de Ayala, and who became a monk, devoting his life to sick people in the hospitals of Cuzco and Guamanga.[38] Guaman Poma de Ayala was Indian on both sides of his family, but his claims of princely descent through the Yarolvica Allauca Huánuco and Incas were never confirmed. He criticized the idolatry of the Incas as a recent, corrupt phenomenon in the region and praised

traditional local religion as being closer to Christianity. This was exactly the opposite position to that of Ayala's contemporary, the Inca Garcilaso de la Vega (1539–1616), a mestizo
of Inca and Spanish descent who acquired an erudite culture and spent most of his life in
Spain, reading and writing. Garcilaso credited the Incas with having prepared the country
for Christianity.[39]

What is interesting for my argument is how these two crucial authors who, together
with Pedro de Cieza de Léon (c.1520–54) and Juan de Betanzos (?-1576), provided the
best information on the region's historical past, religion, and culture, integrated European
ethnic prejudices into their thinking, or expressed quite new ones. Guaman Poma referred
to two Incas, Lloqui Yupanqui and Mayta Capac, as black, ugly, and weak; by contrast, another Inca, Uira Cocha, was described as a gentleman, white, bearded, and good-hearted.
But Guaman Poma went further: he analyzed professions along with social and ethnic
groups, vehemently criticizing Creoles, mulattoes, and mestizos. He considered them the
main source of evil: troublemakers, haughty, liars, gamblers, mean, uncharitable, deceivers,
thieves, and enemies of the Indians and Spaniards. Guaman Poma advocated a segregated
society in which the different ethnicities would not mix with each other. In his advice to
the king, Ayala recommended that mestizos should be used neither as royal officials nor
(under any circumstances) clergymen.[40] By contrast, Inca Garcilaso left few remarks concerning skin color. There is just one reference to the mother of Inca Viracocha, Mama Rantu
(mother egg), as having exceptionally white skin. In a more general way, Garcilaso insisted
that dance, clothing, and headdress defined social hierarchies and/or local identities in the
Andean environment.[41]

The peripheries of the Nahua and Tahuantinsuyo states were considered much more
barbarian, although the Araucanians (or Mapuche) were praised for their political organization and successful military resistance to Spanish expansion in what is now southern
Chile and Argentina.[42] The account of Ulrich Schmidel, who served with the Spanish armies
in the area that is now Argentina, Paraguay, and Bolivia from 1534 to 1554, did not report
any major cases of cannibalism or human sacrifice, except among the Carios around Asun-
ción (the first town created by the Spaniards in the region) and the Tupis when he crossed
the continent to the coast of what is now Brazil.[43] Curiously enough, major cases of cannibalism occurred among the Spaniards themselves, due to extreme hunger—a common
situation in shipwrecks and failed military enterprises. In the north of Mexico, the first
reports of the Chichimecas stressed the absence of royalty, the lack of houses or villages,
and a people living desolate lives in caves without agriculture, and so dependent on game,
roots, herbs, and other fruits of the land. The food was considered disgusting, especially
the eating of raw meat or meat that had been dried under the sun, and that included liz-
ards, snakes, and insects.[44] The contrast between raw and cooked food was seen as a major
criterion of civilization, and the inclusion of reptiles in the Chichimecas' diet was viewed
as particularly repulsive (a topos repeated in other contexts). Further north, the disastrous
Spanish expeditions to what is now Florida, Louisiana, Texas, and New Mexico, especially
those under the command of the *adelantados* Panfilo de Narvaéz (1527–37) and Hernando

de Soto (1539–42), revealed communities with few resources, living by hunting, fishing, and gathering, although some of them planted root vegetables or maize.[45] No widespread cannibalism was recorded, except for that among the starving Spaniards, who scandalized the indigenous people and risked being killed for the practice, while acts of bestiality and cruelty between enemy communities of natives were reported. From Narvaéz's expedition, only a small number of enslaved Christians (four out of four hundred) survived, managing to do so by pretending, like Alvar Nuñez Cabeza de Vaca, to perform demiurgic acts of healing. The Mississippi basin was perceived as relatively prosperous, while the descriptions of the Seminoles, Creeks, Sioux, and Dakota pointed to differences in family structure, the status of women, and ways of treating children that ranged from extreme love to savage abandonment or murder.

COMPARATIVE ETHNOGRAPHY

In 1590, Theodor de Bry published the *Briefe and True Report of the New Found Land of Virginia*, written by Thomas Harriot (1560–1621) and illustrated by John White. It was the first volume of de Bry's series on *America*, a lavish folio edition published in Latin, German, English, and French. The account benefited from the author's sharp eye. Harriot was a distinguished mathematician, astronomer, and cartographer, working for Walter Raleigh, while White drew extraordinary watercolor images from nature. Both had been in what is now North Carolina during the 1580s and spent time with the Algonquians, observing carefully their appearance, activities, costumes, manners, and rituals. The text and images supported each other, resulting in an extraordinary protoethnographic document. White benefited from becoming acquainted with the French artist, Jacques Le Moyne de Morgues, who had accompanied the expedition of Laudonnière to Florida in 1563–65 as recording artist and had escaped from the Spanish massacre to settle in England in the early 1580s.[46] White's watercolors, which survived in various versions, formed the best collection of drawings of North American Indians in this period.[47] They provided the basis for de Bry's illustrations, although they were slightly "domesticated" or Europeanized—a phenomenon visible in the depiction of faces and gestures, such as the way the Indians sat down to eat.

The title page of Harriot's account expressed important contemporary ideas and impressions. There is a Renaissance monumental portal surrounding the title, with an idol sitting on a goat's skull at the top of the pediment, worshipped by a "conjurer" or "juggler" and a "priest," the first half naked, with a fur covering his sex, a bird attached to his head, and the left hand pointing to his heart, and the second wearing a short cloak made of hares' skins, and his hands joined in prayer—a European gesture absent from White's watercolors.[48] At the base of the portal, an Indian chief stands with a skin around his lower torso, collars around his neck, and bracelets and tattoos. His head is shaved so as to leave a coxcomb of hair decorated with three feathers; there is a quiver with arrows at his back, held in place by a long animal tail; and he has a bow in his left hand and an arrow in his right. Standing

Figure 7.5. (*Left*) John White, Indian chief, watercolor, 26.3 x 15 cm., 1585–93. British Museum.
© Art Gallery Collection; Alamy
Figure 7.6. (*Right*) John White, Pictish warrior holding a human head, watercolor, 24.3 x 17 cm., 1585–93.
British Museum.
© Trustees of the British Museum

on the other side of the base of the portal, an Indian woman holds a gourd in her left hand, while the right one gracefully rests on the set of collars hanging from her neck; she also wears a skin around her waist, has tattoos on her body, and wears her hair long, with a fringe.

All these figures are depicted barefoot. The choice and adaptation of White's images for the title page reinforced the idea of idolatry and savagery, although the text contained nuances that caught the latest details, noting, "They have no such tools, nor any such crafts, sciences and arts as we; yet in those things they do, they show excellence of wit," and following this with an immediate assertion that the Indians found "our manner of knowledge and crafts to exceed theirs in perfection" while insisting that these people should "desire our friendship and love and having the greatest respect for pleasing and obeying us. Whereby may be hoped if means of good government be used, that they may in short time be brought to civility and the embracing of true religion."[49] This was a clear program of acculturation, soon to be confronted with reality. The text provided a much more detailed vision of the native way of life, taking in hunting, fishing, social types, sorcerers, shipbuilding, cooking, eating, feasts, rituals, villages, agriculture, idols, tombs of chiefs, and scarification—underlined by a second part that consisted of large engravings explained by long captions.

The main novelty of this account lay in the images of the last section, which portrayed Picts from Scotland to show that "the inhabitants of the Great Britain have been in times past as savage as those of Virginia." This approach was not totally new. Previous Spanish accounts had frequently made the comparison between the Nahuas or Quechuas and peoples described by Greek and Roman authors. But here the comparison was directly with the British people's ancestors, and for the first time, it was illustrated, lending the argument a weight it had never had before. The Picts were imagined as headhunters, who would cut the heads off their enemies in battle and carry them away. The men were depicted completely naked, their bodies painted all over with animals, and holding a spear, shield, and sword. The women were viewed as Amazonian warriors, holding the same type of arms, and exhibiting bodies painted all over with patterns, figures, and images of the sun and moon. The "neighbors" of the Picts were visualized with some kind of clothing, half naked, but without paintings on their body, indicating a further step toward civilization. Although Native Americans were represented as savages and idolaters, and denigrated through these general labels, the comparison with the Europeans' ancestors asserted the possibility of future improvement, showing no prejudice based on features permanently ascribed to specific peoples. This understanding was crucial in the early stages of a colonial project that needed to promote America and show its inhabitants in a favorable light in order to attract potential migrants. It undeniably had a long-term impact. In 1724, for instance, Jesuit Joseph François Lafitau would publish a treatise comparing the habits of the American savages with those of the Europeans of early times.[50] He maintained that early accounts of primitive Europeans could shed a new light on Native Americans, and that observation of the Indians could elucidate the unknown early stages of human life in Europe.

Native Americans were submitted to ethnic prejudices and discriminatory action from the beginning of the European overseas expansion, but it is also noteworthy that the image of the innocent Native American or noble savage was favorably compared to that of deceitful Europeans—an idea already present in the sixteenth century and diffused in Europe during the Enlightenment. In 1711, the *Spectator* reproduced a story included more than fifty years previously in Richard Ligon's *History of Barbados* about a British man shipwrecked on the coast of America who is helped by a sincere, loving Indian girl. The girl hides and feeds him until they can embark on a European ship, but is then sold as a slave by the man she has rescued.[51] This story should be related to Behn's approach in *Oroonoko*.

The literary idea of the innocence of savages was developed as the ignorance of vice in philosophical reflection. This idea, already formulated by Montaigne and Grotius, had been used by Richard Cumberland, Samuel von Pufendorf, and Montesquieu (1689–1755) against Thomas Hobbes and the idea of an unruly natural man dominated by passions. Yet it was Jean-Jacques Rousseau (1712–78) who developed the vision of the savage human at peace with nature and so could do without positive law, due to the absence of servitude and dominion.[52] The innocent or noble savage was generally placed in America. In *L'ingénu* (1767), Voltaire used a sincere Huron, identified later in the story as the offspring of colonists born in America and rescued by the Indians, to question the habits (particularly the religious practices) of the Europeans.[53] Robert Bage, who supported the rights of women and expressed a precociously libertarian critique of government and education, used his character Hermsprong (1796) to praise the "savage" way of life.[54] At the beginning of the nineteenth century, in successive novels and one long travel account, Chateaubriand (1768–1848), who declared himself a disciple of Rousseau, developed the idea of the European who refuses the permanent agitation of civilization to take refuge among Native Americans and live a calm life.[55] The notion of the savage in his writings is never pure: Atala was the daughter of a Spaniard and an Indian, raised as a Christian; and Chactas, patriarch of the Natchez, had been at Versailles in the time of Louis XIV. Imaginary America is a useful place to reflect on corrupt civilization, and that is why the civilized human who chooses to become a savage is one of the significant literary topics of this period.

||||||||||||||||||||||||||||||||||||||||||||||||||||||||||||||||||||||||||||||||||||||||||||||||||||||||||||||||||||||||||||||||||||||||||||||||

CHAPTER 8

Asians

INDIANS

In 1512–15 Duarte Barbosa, factor of the Portuguese king for the Malabar Coast, described for the first time in European terms the caste system, based on examples he had collected on the region.[1] Barbosa labeled the distinct social groups, each with their own laws, as gentiles, lineages, and castes. The semantic origin of the Portuguese and Castilian noun casta is "plant or animal species."[2] This concept was used as a metaphor for the steady inheritance of status and professions in India. The Italian translation of Barbosa's book was published by Ramusio in 1550 and was probably based on a manuscript with only a few references to casta. The translator preferred *lignaggio*, *di sangue*, or *sorti*, reflecting a free translation that did not, however, betray the content of the text.[3] Barbosa used the designation caste between one and four times in the six surviving manuscripts of the sixteenth century. But one instance of its use was decisive and common to all manuscripts: when he wrote about the set of eighteen social groups that he had managed to distinguish, he clearly indicated "eleven low laws," which "honourable people do not touch under penalty of death, with a great distance being kept between the ones and the others in order to avoid the mixing of one caste with another."[4] The noun caste soon replaced the other designations in descriptions of Indian social organization. It was systematically used by: the chronicler Damião de Góis (1566), who stressed the rigidity of professional boundaries imposed by the castes; the first provincial council of the archbishopric of Goa (1567), which denounced the immediate downgrading of any member of a high caste found eating or drinking with a member of an inferior caste as superstition; and Camões (c. 1524–80), who in the epic poem *Os Lusíadas* (1572, 7:37–39) related the interdiction on mixing castes in India to the supposed old Jewish refusal to touch the people of Samaria.[5]

These texts articulated crucial issues concerning the European view of India that would persist until the twentieth century. Góis was concerned with what we would nowadays call social mobility, allegedly suffocated by the caste system.[6] He had been influenced by João de Barros (1496–1570), one of the first chroniclers of Portuguese India, who developed his knowledge of Indian social organization in emulation of Barbosa, but who added a crucial element: the inheritance of professions, with particular professional lineages closed to marriage outside the group, so that, for instance, the son of the carpenter could not be a tailor but instead had to follow the way of life and job of his father, for religious reasons that Barros labeled superstitions. Barros also tackled the issue of the purity of the Nairs (warriors or Kshatriyas), nobles who could not touch or be touched by the lower castes. If this "disaster" occurred by mistake, he reported, the body of the Nair would be treated as a "glorified body" and the other's body as that of a "filthy animal." Barros compared this prejudice to that of the ancient Jews, but even if they touched a Samaritan, the former would not undertake as much purification as the Nairs.[7]

The clergymen in the Portuguese dioceses of the Estado da Índia were worried about the impact of the caste system on relations between Hindus and the Christian community, given that the converted were considered lower than the honorable castes because they had to mix with people of different origins. The resolutions of the above-mentioned synod of Goa in 1567 forbade Christians to feed Indians against their will; the intention of avoiding accusations of inflicting a deliberate stain on the higher castes in order to obtain their conversion was obvious.[8] Impurity that could not be washed out meant immediate exclusion. But the Indian principle of hierarchy, as opposed to the Christian and Muslim principle of equality among believers, would raise the issue inside the Christian communities of India, permeable as they were to the notion of purity. In turn, Camões was inspired by Barros when he poetically described the Hindu castes. He denigrated Hinduism as a "tissue of fables," reported that the people were almost naked, that they could not marry outside their caste, that the sons had to follow the occupation of their fathers until they died, and that the Nairs could not be touched and used a thousand rites to purify themselves, but that the Brahmans, their priests, would not kill any living creature and were not jealous of their wives. Camões made the comparison between the Nair and Jewish notions of purity even more strongly: "In the same way, the ancient Jews / Would not touch the Samaritan people."[9] This comparison between different historical periods supposed that rituals of purity and rules of segregation had resulted from a past practice that had been perpetuated in that part of the world. Yet the comparison transferred to the context of South Asia the same references to classical antiquity as had been used in the Spanish accounts of the Nahuas and Incas, coupled with Christian stereotypes concerning the Jewish people. The idea was repeated and enlarged a century later by the French merchant and traveler to Turkey, Iran, India, and Java, Jean Baptiste Tavernier (1605–89), who stated that a caste among the idolaters corresponded to a tribe among the Jews of ancient times.[10] This confirms my thesis that ethnic prejudices were never isolated; they belonged to a relational, hierarchical system concerning different ethnicities (and constructed races) in time and space.

The Portuguese notion of caste applied to the Indian social system was spread in the work of French, Dutch, and English authors throughout the seventeenth and eighteenth centuries. But the main ideas about the caste system were already present in Barbosa. The notion of purity and impurity was expressed through descriptions of the precise forms laid down for the treatment of food as well as cooking and for serving it to the higher castes; constant ablutions and rules for eating among the Brahmans (priests who did not eat meat or fish) and Nairs; taboos concerning the lower castes and respect for the Hindu interdictions on physical contact, with a simple touch carrying the penalty of death or social exclusion; and acceptance of these interdictions by the female members of the higher castes, who would denounce themselves should they make a mistake in the ritual, since the whole family would become polluted or "have the blood maculated," as Barbosa put it. The author also tackled the heavy consequences for the whole population, in terms of ritual, of the death of a ruler; servitude (labeled slavery) of the lower castes under the rulers or Nairs; family structures of the higher castes; forms of inheritance resulting from the supposed free relations of women among the Kshatriya; holding of virginity in abhorrence; common acceptance of the prostitution of women from the lower castes; and terrifying burning of widows with their deceased husbands in the higher castes. The different degrees of nudity, with more flesh exposed in the lower castes; widespread superstition along with constant use of sorcerers and diviners; and ferocious justice ordered by rulers without trial and constantly practiced by the higher castes to punish minor faults committed by the lower castes completed the European vision of Indians after Vasco da Gama that renewed classical stereotypes concerning the sensual and despotic East.

The allegedly superior status of the Brahmans in the caste system was accepted by the Portuguese missionaries, mainly the Jesuits, who had consistently espoused a top-down strategy of conversion. The problem was how to operate beyond the territories controlled by the Portuguese imperial state. Along the Pearl Fishery Coast in the extreme south of India from Cape Comorin to Mannar Island, the Franciscans have successfully converted the Paravar fisherfolk. When the Jesuits decided to establish a mission in the important interior city of Madurai, they were naturally rejected by the higher castes.

In the first two decades of the seventeenth century, the conversion strategies to be used in India were debated inside and outside the Society of Jesus. Roberto Nobili (1577–1656), an Italian noble and theologian, triggered the debate in the 1600s when he decided to adopt the lifestyle of a Brahman in Madurai. He lived in a separate house with local servants, dressed like a Brahman and ate the ritual food, performed the main ceremonies of purification, learned Sanskrit, and decided to teach the Gospel in a way that took account of the local culture.[11] He was immediately criticized by his older religious brother in Madurai, the Portuguese Gonçalo Fernandes Trancoso (1541–1619), who accused Nobili of going native and dissolving the Christian message in local superstition. Nobili mobilized his relatives in Rome and attracted the majority of the theologians called on to examine the case by the archbishop of Goa to his side. In the end, the Society of Jesus and pope recognized Nobili's method as valid. Nobili claimed that he was simply adapting to local cultural habits, the better to evangelize the population. But the distinction between culture and religion remained in dispute. Trancoso lost his battle for social and cultural reasons: Nobili was an erudite aristocrat with extraordinary persuasive skills, while Trancoso was a former soldier with poor training in theology and rudimentary knowledge of languages—he knew only Tamil, though he managed to read in translation and quote accurately the main Sanskrit texts of Hinduism. What Nobili tried to do in India was not completely new; he echoed previous experiments by Alessandro Valignano and Matteo Ricci, who took it on themselves to fill the role of the traditional figures of wise men (or men of letters) in Japan and China. Yet the caste system in India raised different issues. That is what Trancoso tried to point out in 1616, when he wrote an extremely dense treatise on Hinduism.[12] Not surprisingly, the treatise centered on Brahman ceremonies. Trancoso was obviously indicating that those ceremonies had a religious origin and purpose. What is important for the argument here, however, is that the ethnic prejudices against Hindus, expressed by the detailed descriptions of their "exotic" religious and social practices, did not prevent Nobili's experiment, which was even approved by the pope.

Barbosa acknowledged idolatry, but he did not develop this line of observation. Lodovico de Varthema (c. 1470–1517), an Italian traveler who in 1510 in Rome published his *Itinerario* from Egypt to Southeast Asia, described the sculpted figure of a "devil" worshipped by the Samudri of Calicut in a chapel decorated with paintings of other "devils" eating souls; the sculpture allegedly had four horns and four big teeth coming out of an enormous open mouth, with an awful nose, terrible eyes, curved hands like hooks, and feet similar to those of a cockerel.[13] The same line of crude depiction, obviously influenced by European Christian representations of the devil, was replicated one and a half centuries later by Tavernier. Although he acknowledged, like Varthema, that the Hindus believed in a single creator of heaven and Earth, who was the primary cause of all things and was omnipresent, Tavernier deplored the "foolish imagination" of those "idolaters" who attributed divine honors to cows, apes, and monsters, representing them with several arms and legs, beastly bodies, many heads, and long tails. Tavernier also criticized the Hindus for believing that gods had been born like men and possessed wives, thus imagining that they would enjoy the same pleasures as human beings. He introduced the idea of transmigrating souls, explaining that believers would be assigned another body to inhabit by God according to how they had led their previous lives—a process that could be repeated several times. The souls of the wicked and vicious could be assigned, as a penance, to contemptible beasts, such as donkeys, dogs, or cats. The Hindus held that there was some kind of divinity in cows, and souls would be happy in those bodies. Tavernier interpreted the repulsion they felt for the slaughter of animals as a precaution against the possible killing of some family member or friend doing penance in those bodies. By contrast, a virtuous life could propel a soul into a potent ruler's body, in which case the owner of the soul would enjoy the pleasures of this life.[14] It would take another century before there were the beginnings of a systematic study of Hinduism by Europeans. The philologists Anquetil-Duperron (1731–1805) and William Jones (1746–94) acknowledged the intellectual richness of Hindu religion and law, and translated some of the main texts, but at the same time laid the foundations for another stage in Orientalism.[15]

Visual culture will help us to better understand the prejudices entertained by Europeans toward different Asian cultures. The establishment of Portuguese colonies in the Indian Ocean and Far East provided Europeans with an ideal framework for a prolonged observation of the habits of peoples living on the shores of this vast though interconnected world.[16] The first anonymous Portuguese (in fact Luso-Asian) ethnographic and costume book was

Figure 8.1. Anonymous, Sacrifice of Indian People, Goan watercolor, 31 × 44 cm., c. 1550. Biblioteca Casanatense, Rome, ms. 1889, Disegni Indiani, 78–79 Photo: Ministero per i beni e le attività culturali Direzione Generale per i Beni Librari, gli Istituti Culturali ed il Diritto d'Autore; Biblioteca Casanatense, Rome

probably compiled in the 1540s, and showed a wide variety of peoples in areas stretching from the Cape of Good Hope to China. In doing so, it included scenes of war, leisure, religious rituals, human sacrifices, Indian deities, weddings, and economic activity. The captions were written in Portuguese, and the images showed a curious mixture of European and Asian illustrative techniques along with decorative elements. It is an extraordinary volume, with a vibrant and colorful set of seventy-five images depicting representative types of peoples in their customary dress, and pursuing their social practices through and for European eyes. The book was only published in the late twentieth century, using the single-known copy kept in Rome, but other copies had probably circulated in the Portuguese settlements in Asia, since they represented a first popular step that would lead to more sophisticated and formal images of Asian peoples. Three elements are crucial in this initial set of images: the variety of skin color, from dark brown to white (even the Hindu deities Vishnu, Hispar, or Siva as well as Brahma were represented in white, dark brown, and red); precision of the headdresses (turbans, bonnets, caps, hats, hoods, and veils), and hairstyles, confirming that they were key signs of identity; and variety of clothes (forms, patterns, and colors, which sometimes defined new identities, like that of the converted Christians of the Malabar Coast), and shoes or sandals, although most people were represented barefoot. For my argument, the critical images concerned human sacrifices in India, particularly the live burial of a widow with her husband (a practice of the lower castes, in contrast with the suttee or immolation of the widow on the funeral pyre of higher-caste husbands); sacrifice of a person's life under the wheels of a pagoda wagon pulled by thousands of people; and suicidal self-sacrifice in front of a temple, in which several techniques are shown.[17]

Jan Huygen van Linschoten most probably drew the images published in 1596 in his *Itinerario*, since he was a well-known draftsperson who had at one point received commissions to depict views of Portuguese ports.[18] But parts of the images must have been redrawn from previously made sketches, because Linschoten never left western India. Linschoten's position as secretary to the archbishop of Goa, the Dominican João Vicente da Fonseca, between 1583 and 1587, gave him a central viewpoint that may have allowed him to obtain information on an impressive variety of ethnicities from all the shores of Asia, but there were details in the drawings that he could not have grasped without direct observation. The twenty-six plates of the *Itinerario* represented different ethnicities and raise the same issues as the anonymous Luso-Asian costume book: the criteria used for choosing what to represent; and decision taken in some cases to represent complex people in a stereotyped manner.

Three engravings are especially important for my argument. The first depicts a Brahman couple. The man is almost naked, with a turban, a cloth around his lower torso, sandals, and the three distinctive skeins of thread hanging over the left shoulder and under the right arm. The wife is completely covered by a sari and cloak, while on one of her bare feet there is a bracelet around the ankle and rings on the toes. The landscape behind the couple represents an "idol" carved into a hill, which is being worshipped by naked villagers. The text underlines the superstitious nature of Indians, who are supposed to be skillful in mixing poisons and ready for any crime. The second image is the most powerful: it represents the ceremony of suttee, the immolation of the widow of a Brahman, who is throwing herself on to a burning pyre where she will be consumed with her husband's corpse, encouraged by the mourning of the crowd and rhythm of musical instruments. The text criticizes the "insane death" of women achieved by this "cruel and barbaric ordeal." Linschoten suggests that the ritual originally might have been inspired by fear of infidelity—a topic repeated to the point of obsession in the *Itinerario*, which dealt in the traditional European stereotypes of "sensual Asia." The third image represents an open pagoda, with an "idol," sacred cow, vivid

Figure 8.2. Jan Huygen van Linschoten, *Itinerario, Voyage ofte Shipvaert van Jan Huygen van Linschoten naar Oost ofte Portugaels Indien* (Amsterdam, 1596), 58–59. Engraving representing the suttee—the immolation of a Brahman's widow. © Robert Harding Picture Library Ltd.; Alamy

fire of incense, and group of worshippers—a scene separated by a palm tree from a strange mosque. The text abhors the "diabolical" and "terrifying" statues erected everywhere by the roadside and crossroads.

Linschoten's book was enormously successful, not only because it revealed the maritime itineraries used by the Portuguese in Asia, triggering regular Dutch and English voyages, but also because it provided maps and images of Asian peoples. It was translated into Latin, English, German, and French, and included in de Bry's series of volumes on Asia. The images of the suttee ceremony and Hindu temple were replicated throughout the seventeenth and eighteenth centuries, particularly in Bernard Picard's 1783 *Cérémonies et coutumes religieuses de tous les peoples du monde*.[19] The images clearly reinforced European prejudices against Indians as idolaters of exotic appearance who committed repulsive acts of human sacrifice based on self-immolation.

MUSLIMS

By the beginning of the sixteenth century, most of India already consisted of Islamic polities, but the development of the Mughal Empire created a powerful centralized political structure on the subcontinent that dominated it until 1720, before a long decline.[20] Hinduism stood up well under Islamic political dominion, but to European eyes the inexorable spread of Islam from the Middle East to Europe and South Asia was a major issue. Religious and political rivalry between Islamic powers, mainly between the Sunni Ottoman Turks and Shiite Iranians, defined an Islamic world that was not uniform or integrated. That is why in the sixteenth century the Portuguese, Spaniards, and Italians tried to establish good relations with the Iranian and Mughal emperors against the Ottomans, while the French king, François I, established a controversial alliance with the Ottomans against Emperor Charles V, following the example of the diplomatic compromise pursued by Venetians and Genoese as they tried to avoid their eradication from the eastern Mediterranean. The fall of Constantinople in 1453 had disrupted the medieval Christian world, although the Turks had already conquered nearly all of Asia Minor and most of the old Byzantine territories in Europe. The three-day plunder of Constantinople along with the widespread killing and rape of the population reinforced the reputation of "vile and brutish" Turks, even though this kind of behavior was common practice against cities that had refused to surrender.[21] The subsequent military expansion of the Turks in eastern Europe, North Africa, Egypt, Palestine, Arabia, and the Middle East, giving them control of the main Islamic holy cities (Mecca, Medina, and Jerusalem), helps to explain why Western interest in Islam was focused on the Ottoman Empire. Travelers Nicolas de Nicolay, Pierre Belon, André Thevet, and Guillaume Postel, who visited Turkey in the mid-sixteenth century with the French ambassadors, expressed their respect for the order imposed in the Ottoman Empire, discipline and restraint observed by the Janissaries (elite troops), frugal habits of the population, religious toleration (not praised, but noted), personal hygiene and decency of clothing,

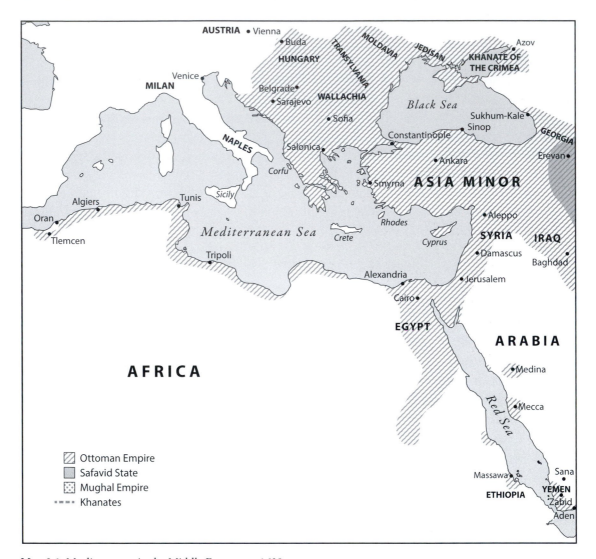

Map 8.1. Muslim power in the Middle East, up to 1639

equality among believers, and general hospitality and charity. They also addressed the main differences between the Christian and Islamic vision of the world.[22]

Idolatry was the major accusation made against Christians in the Islamic environment, proving how the old stigmatization of other peoples as "Pagans" or "Heathens" could be returned. For Islam, the visual representation of God was considered an offense against divinity, as was the representation of prophets (like Christ) and holy men (or saints). Orthodox Islam also prohibited the representation of rulers. The contrast between medieval Islamic and Christian tombs speaks for itself: the tombs of Islamic rulers have no carved or painted images. In public monuments, only the sacred words of the Koran could be used as decorative elements, along with geometric forms and representations of flora. This explains

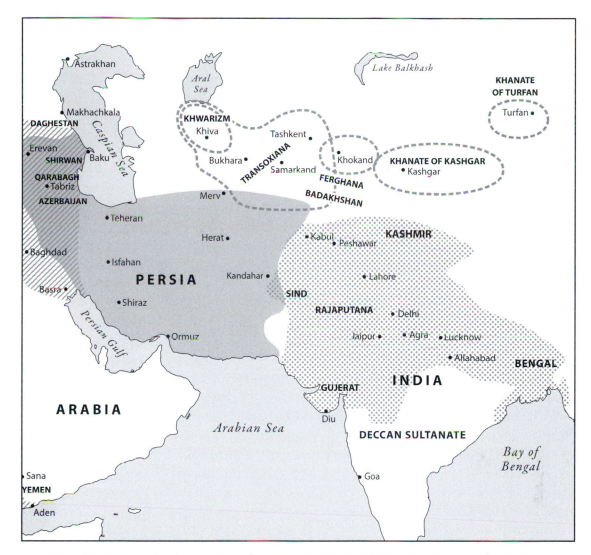

Source: Geoffrey Barraclough, ed., *The Times Atlas of World History* (London: Times Books, 1990), 170–71

why the illuminated books of the Mughal and Iranian emperors are so precious: the images in which the Islamic artists recorded the sovereigns and life at court are unique, although there were periods during which invitations were given to European artists, particularly Giovanni Bellini, who produced portraits of the Ottoman emperor Mehmed II (r. 1451–81), in paintings and on medals. The argument against idolatry propounded by the architects of the Islamic expansion was from its beginning so powerful that the Byzantine emperors launched successive campaigns of icon destruction in 730–87 and 815–43, following moves to suppress Christian art ordered by Caliph Yezid in 722–23. The debate on iconoclasm opened a divide inside Byzantine society as well as between the Christians of the East and those of the West.[23] The Reformation in the sixteenth century renewed this debate with similar contentions, but the Byzantine refusal of statues, contrary to the Western tradition, is interesting to note. This division gave rise to a colorful joke reported by Augier Ghislain de Busbecq, ambassador for Emperor Ferdinand to Constantinople from 1554 to 1562. When the ambassador and his companions saw Turkish workers destroying a Roman statue in order to use the stone and "showed ourselves displeased at their rude violence, they paid us with a jeer: 'What?' said the laborers, 'Will you bow down to worship this statue, as you Christians used to do to yours?'"[24]

Christian prejudices against Islam were built on ideas of despotism, sensual license, and superstition. The murderer of sons or brothers by old or new Ottoman emperors in order to suppress possible rivals—later called the "law of fratricide,"—is the first of the acts of tyranny noted by Christians.[25] Busbecq considered the sons of the emperor the most miserable creatures in the world, since they could not escape their fate. The ambassador gave a social and political reason for this practice: the Janissaries would use any living brother of an emperor to put forward their requests for new privileges, creating a feud that would force the emperors "to put their brothers to death and so begin their reign with blood."[26] The fundamental laws of the empire by the time of Mehmed the conqueror guaranteed the legitimacy of the procedure: the established course of action was for the successor to the sultanate to put his brothers to death in order to preserve the order of the world.[27] Busbecq, one of the sharpest observers of Ottoman institutions, was probably aware of this precept when he reported the successive murderers of children by Süleyman I (r. 1520–66) in detail. In Iran there was no such institution as the central palace of the Ottoman emperors, with a strictly segregated courtyard around which the wives, concubines, and children of the sovereign lived in seclusion—hundreds of people totally controlled by a guard of black eunuchs—but there was naturally a harem. The law of fratricide was not in place; rather, the emperor would blind his sons and brothers, since this handicap would exclude them from succession.[28] In both systems, the murder or blinding of potential rivals could be extended to nephews and uncles.

The systematic enslavement of young Christians and use of slaves to provide administrative as well as military service are other important elements in the accusation of despotism. The model for this practice was the military and political elite of the Mamelukes, a group of Christian slaves of Caucasian origin who were converted to Islam, and served as soldiers and administrators for the caliphs of Baghdad. Members of this group rose to rule Egypt from 1250 to 1517, and following the arrival of Ottoman power in Egypt in 1517, they maintained the status of a military caste until 1812. The advantage of this caste was that it did not have any roots in local elites, and theoretically would not get involved in acts of local or regional sedition. The Mamelukes were totally devoted to their military purpose, although they proved to be a source of political instability in the long run. The principle of recruiting slaves of Christian origin to serve as elite troops and administrators was pursued in a systematic way by the Ottoman Empire. When the recruitment of Christian slaves through conquest or war declined, the Ottomans introduced a regular levy of children among the Christian populations of all the empire. The early break with family ties, conversion to Islam, and education in religious, military, and administrative skills transformed these children into a privileged stratum exclusively devoted to the emperor. George Sandys (1577–1644) accused the

> barbarous policy whereby this tyranny is sustained . . . guided by the heads and strengthened by the hands of these slaves, who think it is a great honour to be so, as they do with us that serve in the courts of princes. The natural Turk (to be so called a reproach) being rarely employed in command or service; amongst whom there is no nobility of blood, no known parentage, kindred, nor hereditary possessions; but are as it were of the Sultan's creation, depending on him for their sustenance and preferment; who disposes, as well of their lives as their fortunes, by no other rule than that of his will.[29]

The supposed absence of hereditary landed nobility in the Ottoman Empire was an interesting issue. For Sandys, it indicated tyranny (despotism being a noun that was not in use until the end of the seventeenth century), because the sultan did not have to deal with regional powers with financial autonomy that could threaten their authority. The freedom of a landed aristocracy with rights of inheritance was implicitly seen as an important check that restrained the possible abuse of centralized power. The systematic promotion of slaves to the highest levels of the state, deliberately cut off from their original religious and family background, was seen as emblematic of a tyrannical power. Such slaves not only filled the military, administrative, and political central structures of the Ottoman Empire but they also were appointed to different levels of regional and local government for short periods of time. They received significant amounts of money for their service, yet could be removed at any moment.

Contrary to Sandys's impression, we know that most Ottoman troops were recruited by local powers, notables had an important role in the empire, and religious men were generally of Turkish or Arab origin, but the European ambassadors along with the scholars or travelers attached to them projected their own view of central institutions onto the empire. Belon (1517–64) had noticed the absence of landed nobility in European terms, although he reported it in a less critical light, since the issue for him was that only men with professional skills could earn their living in the Ottoman Empire. He noted that even the Janissaries could be required to perform mechanical tasks, and concluded that for any inhabitant, "it is useless in this country to fashion himself as gentleman." Belon nevertheless defined the tributary Christian communities, especially the vast Greek population, as "slaves" of the Turks, and considered the Egyptians, Syrians, and Arabs to be "slaves" too. The absence of nobility would explain, according to Belon, why no important country or urban villas were built; the main buildings were for religious purposes or the imperial bureaucracy. The fact that part of the wealth accumulated by the emperor's slaves would be returned to the ruler after their death (according to the rules of inheritance) helps to explain the lack of investment in private houses.[30] One century later, François Bernier developed a similar argument concerning Mughal India. He related the absence of private property in relation to uncultivated lands and considered this a main feature of diffused tyranny.[31]

Figure 8.3. George Sandys, *A Relation of a Journey* (London, 1615), title page representing the Ottoman emperor.
© British Library Board; Robana

The frontispiece of Sandys's travel book, published in 1615, expressed the Christian vision of Turkish despotism. Emperor Ahmed I (r. 1603–17), labeled "Achmet sive Tyrannus," is depicted next to the title on the right side of the portal, with a high turban, long tunic, and cropped beard. He is holding a globe in his left hand, a device for enchaining slaves in his right hand, and is trampling books underfoot. These may have been the books of law. Arbitrary rule and the enslavement of people were clearly indicated as the two distinctive features of the Ottomans. Although most of the European powers sent ambassadors to Iran to promote alliances against the Turks, the Safavid Dynasty was seen in a similar light. Tavernier, who boasted of having had friendly conversations with the shah, stated that "the government of Persia is purely despotic or tyrannical. For the king has the sole power of life and death over his subjects, independent of his council, and without any trials or law proceedings. He can put to what death he pleases the chief lords of the kingdom, no man daring to dispute the reason; nor is there any sovereign in the world more absolute than the king of Persia."[32]

Montesquieu (1689–1755) would further enshrine this tradition when he offered the opinion that Asia had naturalized despotism. He defined despotism in the context of the Ottomans, whose constitution was allegedly based on fear, restricted civil rights, and an imposed attachment of subjects through force and religion. The prince was considered the virtual owner of all Ottoman land, heir to his officers' wealth, and legal possessor of properties left without a male heir. Montesquieu attributed the greed of administrators to these succession laws, and saw the system as responsible for poor private buildings, lack of improvements in agriculture, and the abandonment of basic structures. The prince's siblings were simultaneously his slaves and rivals, since there was no clear rule of succession. "The royal family looks like the state; it is too weak and its head too strong; it seems extended but it is reduced to nothing." Montesquieu also pointed out the political effects of the secluded seraglio, in which the future heirs to the throne were excluded from any significant life experience and "where an old prince, every day more imbecile, is the first prisoner of the palace." But it was the supposed arbitrary justice that mostly occupied Montesquieu, who considered that in Turkey, there was no protection of the fortune, life, or honor of the emperor's subjects. He stated that "men are equal under a republican government; they are equal under a despotic government; in the former because they are everything and in the latter because they are nothing." He also condemned the vesting of exclusive executive, legislative, and judicial powers in Turkey in the sovereign, who was responsible for an "awful despotism." Montesquieu related the low levels of taxation in Turkey to the extreme servitude of people who could not tolerate more oppression.[33]

The second main set of stereotypes concerning the Islamic world targeted superstition. If Christians themselves were haunted by credulity concerning the properties and effects of certain practices or things (such as amulets and relics), they believed that Muslims gave free rein to their imagination and malice. Humanist Paolo Giovio implicitly derided the fast of Ramadan when he criticized the practice of eating at night and not during the day.[34] Postel wrote that Muslims indulged in astrology to choose the day of their wedding and the conception of children, sanctifying the practice with the name of Allah, in order to prevent the presence of the devil and corruption of the lineage. The precepts on regular ablution or purification of the body by washing were considered in the same vein. Christians also tried to turn the accusation of idolatry on its head. They considered the Muslim "horror of images" as a form of superstition, responsible for the concealment of the spectacular mosaics at the cathedral of Saint Sophie in Constantinople when it had been transformed into a mosque. The ritual obligation for Muslims to pray five times a day turned to Mecca was supposed to be reinforced by law and punished in case of failure. Dervishes, half naked and half dressed in furs and animal skins, who took part in shamanistic dances leading to ecstasy in which they wounded and mutilated themselves were singled out for criticism early on. Several authors depicted them with woodcuts as heterodox practitioners of Islam immersed in superstition.[35]

Busbecq compiled a curious set of accusations: papers were never left on the ground because the name of God could be written on them; Muslims believed that those papers (on which the name of God had been written) would protect them during the difficult passage to heaven through the red-hot iron gate. They would also collect fallen rose leaves from the ground, seeing them as the sweat of Muhammad. Christians who had sat on the Koran would be punished by death. The ritual preparation and rules concerning food were also considered as a superstition, and Busbecq regretted not having eaten some delicious-looking turtles because he was with Turks, and "they would have thought themselves so defiled that I know not how many washings would not have cleansed their imagined pollution." The graves were covered by stone but not filled with earth, so that the souls of the deceased could sit and discuss with the devil when called on to give account of their lives. Turks would seldom dress in black because it was seen as an unfortunate color. Madmen and fools were considered chosen for heaven. The absence of printing was related to the sacred character of the language of the Koran, while the absence of clocks and watches was related to the authority of the Muezzins. Pashas who fell from their horse could be removed from their office because the accident was viewed as a bad sign. The idea of fate or unavoidable destiny permeated the main decisions of the Turks. According to Busbecq, their refusal to act during a plague was due to the fatalistic idea that "every man's destiny is written by God on his forehead; so that it is a foolish thing in them to think to decline or avoid it."[36] Montesquieu returned to this critique of the concept of fate, which according to him transformed the magistrate into a calm and passive observer, yet he was more interested in the political issues concerning superstition. He observed that the Turks were not in control of their political life because "the pious consider victory or success to be divine judgement; thus nobody is sovereign by right but by fact." Montesquieu insisted that the Turks considered the result of the first battle in a civil war as a sign of the judgment of God, who decided everything in advance.[37]

Christians had for a long time accused Muslims of sexual license because they were able to marry more than one wife and legally enjoy concubines. Islam did not have sacraments; therefore marriage was not considered as such, although the Koran had established its rules. Postel imagined an enormous number of wives allowed for princes (seventy), rich people (twelve), and ordinary people (four to six) as well as all the slave concubines they could afford. In the seraglio at Constantinople, he thought, there were three hundred women for the sultan's pleasure. He pointed out the difference between a permanent marriage and one for pleasure, the latter being established as a contract for a temporary period of time. He acknowledged the reality of divorce; the *cadi* or judge had to be informed of the repudiation procedure on the grounds of sterility, suspicion of adultery, or incompatibility. Intercourse between a Christian and Turk was punishable by death, unless the Christian decided to become a Muslim. Curiously, Postel raised the issue of the oppression of women taken as war booty, sold as slaves in the market, and assigned an inferior status in daily life. He reproduced the saying that "twelve women are not worth a man."[38] Sandys went further and accused the prophet Muhammad of locating the happiness of life after death in bodily delights. Islam conceived of paradise as a place of eternal sensual felicity, in which virginity was recovered, and the elected restored to the age of fifteen (women) and thirty (men). The elected "shall spend the course of their happy time among amorous virgins, who shall alone regard their particular lovers."[39]

The main European prejudices against Islam in the Ottoman version were expressed in one single paragraph by Mary Montagu (1689–1762) in a letter to Alexander Pope written in 1717:

> But what can you expect from such a country as this, from which the Muses have fled, from which letters seem eternally banished, and in which you see, in private scenes, nothing pursued as happiness but the refinements of an indolent voluptuousness, and where those who act upon the public theatre live in uncertainty, suspicion, and terror! . . . Veins of wit, elegant conversation, easy commerce are unknown among the Turks; and yet they seem capable of all this, if the vile spirit of their government did not stifle genius, damp curiosity, and suppress a hundred passions that embellish and render life agreeable.[40]

This came from an informed author, the wife of a diplomat, who in many other letters expressed her admiration and sympathy for Ottoman culture and women. These stereotypes would last until the twentieth century, sometimes in modified ways. That is why I consider it useful to trace their origins and, whenever possible, purposes. The new knowledge accumulated by eighteenth-century European specialists on Asia—for instance, on sacred texts, the constitutional framework, and the functioning of Islamic institutions—allowed the establishment of a precarious basis for a more objective analysis of religious beliefs and political actions.[41] It contributed to overcoming some of the stereotypes I have described, but the main aspects of the Christian vision of Islam were not fundamentally challenged at that time.

Differentiation among Islamic societies—how Christians put Islamic societies into a hierarchy—is an important issue. The Portuguese and Spaniards were more confident in their relations with Mughals or Iranians, even after the conquest of Hormuz by Shah 'Abbas in 1622, than with the Turks, who were always regarded as the main enemy. The Portuguese and Turks fought crucial naval battles in the Indian Ocean at the beginning of the sixteenth century. The Spaniards and Venetians competed with the Turks in the Mediterranean, while the Germans, Hungarians, and other Christians competed with the Ottomans in the Balkans and eastern Europe. The French were the exception soon to be joined by the English, who sought political alliances and preferential trade agreements with the Ottomans. The Egyptians were seen in a more favorable light than the Turks, partly due to the prestige of having an older civilization than that of the Greeks and Romans. They had also played a key religious, political, and economic role during the Middle Ages. The final period of the Crusades had seen a redirection of military expeditions against Egyptian ports. The North Africans were fierce enemies of the Portuguese and Spaniards, who tried to expand along their coast and spent a great deal of money on successive campaigns, until the Portuguese suffered several setbacks and final defeat between 1541 and 1578. The permanent piracy by North Africans, which involved the enslavement of Christian captives and was carried out from the Mediterranean to the Atlantic and as far north as the British coast until the end of the eighteenth century, did not help to improve these peoples' image, although the Christians did much the same until the seventeenth century. Postel thus attacked the "Moors" (North Africans) as the "worst scoundrels, infidels and traitors among all the followers of Muhammad" (in fact *mahomediques*—a typical insult), who had supposedly done more to force Christians to convert than any other Muslims.[42]

CHINESE AND JAPANESE

European perceptions of China and Japan were quite different, because there was no background of religious strife. We have already seen how Acosta placed the Chinese and Japanese at the top of his hierarchy of peoples of the world. They were considered "policed" (ordered or urban, later labeled civilized) and to be almost perfect in all respects, except religion. Throughout the Middle Ages, Christian missionaries and merchants in India and central Asia reached China. Marco Polo had a major impact on European perceptions, due to his extraordinary travel account, recorded at the end of the thirteenth century.[43] But Portuguese contacts with China from the 1510s onward created a totally different framework,

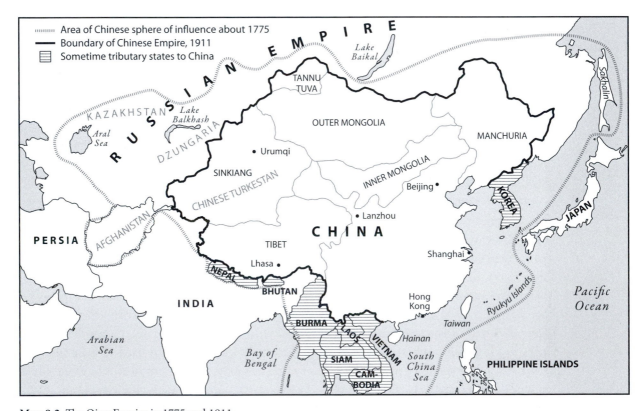

Map 8.2. The Qing Empire in 1775 and 1911.
Source: Marius B. Jansen, *Japan and China: From War to Peace, 1894–1972* (Chicago: Rand McNally and Co., 1975), 8

reinforced by the permanent establishment of Macau in the 1550s. This port became an important hub of maritime trade in the Far East, mainly between China and Japan (reached by the Portuguese in the 1540s), but also connected to Southeast Asia, the Philippines (from the 1570s on), and the Indian Ocean. It formed a base for regular missionary work in Japan and China by the Jesuits.

The first Portuguese accounts of China were compiled and developed by the Dominican Gaspar da Cruz (c. 1520–70) in a seminal work published in 1569. Da Cruz stressed that the Chinese exceeded all other Asians in the size of their population, greatness of their kingdom, excellence of their policies and government, and abundance of their possessions and riches. He admired the centralized administration of such a huge territory; social order to which the people adhered; righteous exercise of justice, supposedly without bribery or abuse of power; examination and selection for office of mandarins based on merit; checks made on all imperial functionaries, who were nominated for short periods of time to provinces distant from their homes, and regularly transferred without their families; urban planning, with great walls, houses with good stone foundations, and large streets that were geometrically laid out and paved; and river-based system of transport and communication, which was coupled with good roads and an extraordinary number of bridges. The skills of a hardworking population employed in intensive agriculture, industry, and trade were also praised by da Cruz as well as the hospitals and organized charity for old and handicapped people, which led to an absence of beggars on the street. The high number of characters in Chinese orthography was considered extraordinary, as was the fact that both peoples who spoke different dialects and the Japanese could read them. The case of an imperial verdict in favor of detained Portuguese merchants that went against previous decisions by local tribunals was considered unimaginable in a European country dealing with foreigners without any local attachment.[44]

Da Cruz inspired Bernardino de Escalante, Martin de Rada, and Juan Gonzalez de Mendoza.[45] Mendoza's book, published in 1585, became a best seller and major work of reference on China, and was translated into several languages. The invention of typography, paper, and gunpowder was duly credited to Chinese ingenuity, and the ancient foundations of Chinese civilization, older than that of the Greeks or Romans, started to be acknowledged. These authors agreed on the supposed main Chinese phenotype features: bodies of good disposition and well proportioned; broad faces, small eyes, and flat noses; and clean-shaven or scarcely bearded men. The Chinese from the interior were considered white, in contrast to the people from the south, particularly the province of Canton, who were considered brown, like the Moors. The Tartars were described by Mendoza as "very yellow and not so white"—an intriguing perception that might be linked to the much later idea of a "yellow" race. Some bizarre habits were pointed out: nails were left to grow long on the left hand, males wore their hair long, bound up on the crown of their heads, and small feet were fashionable among women, who "bind the feet so hard that they loose the form of them and remain half lame."[46] Idolatry and superstition were the main Chinese "defects." Mendoza declared his perplexity. How could people who showed prudence and wisdom in governing

Figure 8.4. Jan Huygen van Linschoten, *Itinerario, Voyage ofte Shipvaert van Jan Huygen van Linschoten naar Oost ofte Portugaels Indien* (Amsterdam, 1596), 32–33. Engraving representing Chinese Mandarins. Photo: Koninklijke Bibliotheek, The Hague H

their commonwealth, who were so subtle and ingenious in the arts, indulge in worshipping idols, accept astrological guidance, believe in fortune-tellers, cast lots, and engage in superstitious inquiries before they made any important decision?

The first Christians to visit Japan shared the same admiration for the people's ingenuity in arts and crafts, military capacity, and governmental and administrative skills. The arts of civility—manners, hospitality, entertainment, domestic cleanliness, self-presentation, rituals of daily life, and appearance and the use of the decorative arts—were depicted in an especially detailed way.[47] Jesuit Francisco Xavier's first letter on Japan noted the extraordinary sense of honor, relative poverty of the population including the nobility, regular use of arms, courteousness of daily life, monogamy, sense of hierarchy, restrained eating and drinking, exercise of justice, limited amount of criminality, and high degree of literacy. But Xavier also noted "idolatry"—information he obtained by engaging in debates with the Buddhist monks.[48] In a vivid account in his book *Peregrinação*, Fernão Mendes Pinto highlighted the Japanese curiosity and capacity for learning. In the early 1540s, in their first encounter with the Japanese, the Portuguese had left a harquebus as a gift for the governor of the island of Tanegashima. The governor had been extremely excited by the efficiency of the gun when he invited the Portuguese to go hunting, as there were then no firearms in Japan. When the

Portuguese returned after six months, they discovered that the gun had been replicated; when they left the island there were already six hundred; when Mendes Pinto went back to Japan in 1556, he was told that across all the islands, a total of more than three hundred thousand harquebuses was to be found.[49]

Behind this high praise lay missionary euphoria about the possibilities offered by the Far East and a wish to attract more evangelizers. The elation soon cooled, although the Japanese experience proved to be extremely successful, with hundreds of thousands of conversions by the beginning of the seventeenth century. Success was cut short, however, by the persecution of Christians launched by the central authorities in 1614 and sealed by the expulsion of the Portuguese in 1639.[50] In China, the Portuguese managed to maintain their position in Macau, although this was reduced to trade, and they accepted the small successes they had had with continental missions, even though recent work has challenged this view.[51] Ironically, the Chinese accused the Portuguese of cannibalism, because they bought young slaves smuggled into China by the coastal population.[52] The "barbarians of the south" were accused of the same awful unnatural crimes they attributed to the American Indians.

It is critical to understand the evolution of the perceptions of the Japanese and Chinese by the main missionaries. Valignano, the Jesuit visitor in Asia, played a crucial role in the expansion of the mission and opening of the company to native recruits. This was no minor breakthrough, since the refusal or acceptance of native recruits was a cornerstone of ethnic prejudices among religious orders, which generally excluded natives from continents other than Europe. Yet Valignano expressed his doubts about the sincerity of the Japanese people along with their supposed mixture of cruelty, dignity, depravity, and hypocrisy in several letters. He also declared that Japan was under martial law, with its population organized like an army of officers and soldiers.[53] For his part, Ricci lamented the effeminate nature of Chinese males, who could spend two hours doing their hair and dressing themselves meticulously; did not consider disputes, injuries, or insults as a matter of honor; placed the examination for military service significantly lower than that for civil service; and had vile and cowardly attitudes to war. Ricci also criticized the constant fear of foreign powers, which were much smaller than the Chinese, and the system of justice, which for him was defined by shameful and cruel punishments that could put a condemned person to death by a brutal whipping, and that provoked a constant fear among the population of being falsely charged.[54] But both Valignano and Ricci agreed that the Chinese and Japanese were of much better stock than Indians, who suffered corrupt government, a poor army, and inferior justice, and who were considered as little better than "brute beasts."[55] In an extraordinary phrase, Valignano defined the European assumptions concerning Indians and other Asian peoples: "A trait common to all these peoples (and I am not speaking now of the so-called white races of China or Japan) is a lack of distinction and character. As Aristotle would say, they are born to serve rather than to command."[56] It should be mentioned that for the most part, European accounts of Turks and Iranians considered these peoples as white or having "light dark" skin.[57] Valignano was probably not including these peoples in his declaration.

The prestige of China, which was already questioned by Ricci's nuanced vision, would be further eroded throughout the seventeenth and eighteenth centuries, although respect for the country's political and territorial power remained intact. The Dutch and Portuguese embassies to China in 1667 and 1670, reported by Arnoldus Montanus and Francisco Pimentel, signaled the transition to a "realistic" vision, as scholar Jonathan Spence has argued. The downgrading of the urban and architectural achievements of the Chinese was one of the results of these expeditions. Pimentel even declared that Peking was like a poor village in Portugal: muddy, without pavements (these had been removed by the Tartars), and consisting of badly built, low houses.[58] Montanus's account, magnificently illustrated and edited by Olfert Dapper, with the inclusion of extensive information collected from earlier sources, is also quite critical, especially of the Chinese culture of bribery, superstition and idolatry, and torture and brutal justice. The evaluation of Chinese knowledge is one of the outcomes of this enormous volume, which fixed the European vision of the Middle Empire for centuries to come:

> Of the Chinese knowledge we cannot speak but darkly, because there are no such authors found among them as Plato, Aristotle and other philosophers which keep an order or method in their writings; besides, they make no mention of liberal arts or other arts (except those that aim at the welfare of the state) and, as Martinus witnessed, the Chinese in many experimental things fall far short of the European.[59]

Montanus, however, acknowledged the superiority of Chinese physicians, who considered the European practice of bleeding veins to be a great mistake. He declared that the Chinese excelled in chemistry as well as arts and crafts. Montanus pointed out the Chinese invention of the printing process and gunpowder. He also praised their husbandry, land cultivation, and canal building. But Montanus considered that the Chinese were inferior in the arts of painting (they did not use shadows, and had no knowledge of mixing colors with oil) and sculpture (there was no rule to measure the parts of the body). The basis for a nuanced (and stereotyped) vision of China was set in this period.

||||||||||||||||||||||||||||||||||||||||||||||||||||||||||||||||||||||||||||||||||||||||||||||||||||||||||||||||||||||||||||

CHAPTER 9

Europeans

SOUTHERN EUROPEANS

When Mendoza described the skin color of the Chinese, he compared them to Europeans and North Africans: those from the province of Canton (the south) were brown, like the Moors, but those from the areas further inland were like the Germans, Italians, and Spaniards— white and pink, yet tending to be swarthy.[1] The author might have been hinting here at the slightly darker complexions of the Spaniards, or the variation in tones of white and pink found among the European population. The ambiguity was dispelled by a Dutch traveler we have already encountered: Linschoten. He observed that those who lived on the coast, near Macau and Canton, had dark skin, like the "white" Moors of Africa and Barbary, and to some extent, the Spaniards, while those from the interior of the country were like the Dutch and Germans (meaning white).[2] This comparison drew on internal European ethnic stereo- types, based partly on skin color. John Evelyn (1620–1706), for instance, on May 30, 1662, commented in his diary on Queen Catherine of Braganza and her ladies-in-waiting: "The Queen arrived with a train of Portuguese ladies in their monstrous farthingales, or guard- infantes, their complexions olivader and sufficiently unagreeable."[3] Curiously enough, Ginés Pérez de Hita, who wrote *Historia de los bandos de los Zagríes y Abencerrajes*, the history of the civil war that preceded the fall of Granada, described the skin color of the aristocratic Moors as swarthy, greenish black (*moreno* or *verdinegro*).[4] But the features of Queen Cath- erine's ladies-in-waiting with their extreme fashion provoked other comments. Writing a few days before Evelyn (on May 25, 1662), Samuel Pepys noted the English disappointment at the young Portuguese women. He mentioned having seen some of them at the Triumph Tavern, and although he did not say anything about their complexion, he added something important: "They are not handsome and their farthingales a strange dress. . . . I find noth- ing in them that is pleasing. And I see they have learnt to kiss and look freely up and down already, and I do believe will soon forget the recluse practice of their own country."[5] Pepys introduced here an essential idea about Portuguese women: their supposed seclusion. The parallel with the confinement of Muslim women observed by many travelers in different places is obvious.

Probably the Muslim influence in Iberia was being implicitly touched on in the reference to the dark complexion of the population and supposed seclusion of women. But after the Christian (re)conquest of the area, the Jewish influence was the second element of the ethnic prejudice held by northern Europeans against the peoples of Hispania. Portuguese merchants of Jewish origin were labeled *gente de nação* in Iberia, meaning "people of the nation," which is worth noting, since the word nation was at that time and in that area used to denote the Jewish community. In an ironic twist, in northern Europe the Portuguese as a whole had been labeled Jews since the sixteenth century, likely because most of the Iberian merchants trading in that area were of Jewish descent. The internal stigma against converted Christians of Jewish origin was turned upside down and transformed into an external stigma against the Portuguese. But prejudice against, and the segregation of, Iberian Muslims and Jews who had converted to Christianity must be seriously addressed here.

Moriscos

The Muslims had been dispossessed of their property and most of their rights during the Christian (re)conquest of Iberia. Their treatment after the fall of Granada in 1492 was not markedly different from previous defeats, despite the moderate terms of surrender imposed by the Christians: the religion, habits, and laws of the Muslims would be respected, and most of their property would not be touched. The reality proved to be different: Christian nobles who had participated in the conquest received the traditional *repartimientos*—concessions in the form of territories (*señorios*) in which they would collect rents and taxes; minor conquerors were allotted rents from villages, parishes, convents, and churches resulting from the expropriation and (re)consecration of mosques. The civil status of the Muslims was not radically different from the status of Native Americans after their conquest: they became inferior vassals. The growing religious and political pressure made the wealthiest families sell their property and migrate to North Africa. Those who stayed suffered a decline due to the following sequence of events. In 1498, the city of Granada was formally divided into two: one section for the Christians, and the other for the Muslims, in line with medieval rules of spatial segregation. In 1499, the archbishop of Toledo, Francisco Jiménez de Cisneros, launched a campaign of violent mass conversion. In 1500 and 1501, this campaign triggered Muslim riots in Alpujarra, Granada, Ronda, and Almería, and these were the pretext for the formal suspension of the surrender terms agreed to by the Catholic kings. In 1501 and 1502, general decrees imposed religious conversion in Granada and all the territories of Castile. Following their violent conversion, Muslims were labeled Moriscos, a classification meant to stress their previous condition of Moros (or Moors) and point to their traditional Islamic beliefs. It was a way of denying the integration of the newly converted into the Catholic community, and defining a category of people whose supposed blood inheritance gave them the same attributes as their ancestors.

The following decades saw the unfolding of a project for a homogeneous Christian society, although the Morisco elites managed to maintain a certain power of negotiation that enabled them to obtain the suspension of the laws devised to create this society or a delay in their implementation. In 1508, a time limit of six years was decreed for the abolition of "Muslim customs," but there were successive prorogations of this. In 1516, a first attempt to forbid the use of the Arabic language failed. In 1521–23, Germanías, the revolt in Valencia, opposed the landed nobility (supported by their Muslim vassals) to the old Christian urban population. The result was a violent mass conversion of Muslims. In 1526, the Arabic language along with traditional costumes and baths were forbidden in Granada, but implementation was again postponed following a payment of eighty thousand ducados. In the same year, two other decisions were much more effective: Charles V decided to abolish the Islamic cult in the territories of the crown of Aragon (consisting on the mainland of the kingdoms of Aragon and Valencia as well as the principality of Catalonia); and the Inquisition decided to transfer the district tribunal of Jaén to Granada. Two years later the prohibition of the Arabic language in Valencia failed. It took another generation, and the change of political culture at the center introduced by the reign of Philip II, to see another escalation of prohibitions, in the 1560s. These prohibitions were followed by determined implementation, which led to revolt: in 1560 Moriscos were forbidden to have Moors and black slaves; the law of 1553 forbidding Moriscos to have guns was finally implemented, and in 1563 in Aragon as well as in 1565 in Granada, Morisco houses were searched for forbidden guns; in 1564, the cortes of Valencia ordered the burning of books written in Arabic; in 1565, a vast inquiry into titles to property in the region of Granada was launched, which ended up with many Moriscos being fined or having their property confiscated to the benefit of the king or public domain; and in 1566, the synod of Granada launched a rigorous religious inquiry into the beliefs of the Moriscos. In 1567, the decisions of 1526 prohibiting the speaking, reading, and writing of Arabic were implemented: all books written in Arabic were controlled, and many contracts in Arabic nullified. Traditional Muslim clothing, Muslim feasts and holidays, and Muslim names were prohibited. The Muslim public baths were destroyed.[6]

This accumulation of political and cultural repression triggered a revolt in 1568 in the Alpujarras (the mountain region of Granada), which spread through both the interior of the province and the coastal area. The immediate murder of dozens of priests and the public reestablishment of Islam indicated that religion was the major tool of resistance. The resistance of the Morisco population was extraordinary, and the local Christian forces were unable to solve the problem. Philip II was forced to recruit an army and ask his half brother, Don Juan de Austria, to command it. It took almost two years to quell the revolt, with massive atrocities committed on both sides. Around thirty thousand people were killed during the war, more than 10 percent of the population of the region. Around two thousand defeated Moriscos were sold as slaves, but the largest part of the Morisco population (between eighty and a hundred thousand) was deported to Castile and divided into small communities to prevent further rebellions. Coinciding with a particularly harsh winter and typhus epidemic, the process of mass deportation resulted in high mortality: probably 40 percent of the deported died on the journey. War, repression, expropriation, deportation, death, and dispossession did not bring about the subordination and integration of the Moriscos.

The events resulted in Islam becoming even more deeply rooted and reinforced Muslim convictions about the evils of Christianity. On the Old Christian side, the revolt left a long-lasting fear of possible riots in Valencia and Aragon coupled with the conviction that the Moriscos could not be assimilated. The common practice of *taqiyya*, the Muslim principle that under repressive conditions, one is allowed to simulate the acceptance of another faith, fueled resistance, but spread the idea of permanent dissimulation by Moriscos among Christians. Obviously we should not overestimate the all pervasiveness of this community divide: there was a significant minority of Moriscos who integrated into the larger Christian society, abandoning their previous religion; and there was a tiny minority of Old Christians—for example, the first archbishop of Granada, Hernando de Talavera—who interacted with the Moriscos and were against violent conversion, preferring moderate efforts at evangelization. Neither can we project a homogeneous vision of the Morisco communities onto the whole of Spain, since there were huge differences between the autonomous communities in Castile and Valencia and the more integrated communities in Catalonia, with Aragon presenting an intermediate case. But the majority of members of each community became rooted in their convictions. The Muslims were persuaded of the superiority of their religion, based on a single god and simple principles of worship. They rejected the idea of the Trinity, the mediation of saints, the use of images (considered as idolatry), Mary's virginity, the divine nature of Christ (considered as the prophet who preceded Muhammad), and the possible incarnation of God. For their part, Christians criticized the supposedly low origins of the Arabs, with their descent from Ismael, the illegitimate son of Abraham and his slave Agar; the "false" prophet Muhammad, who legitimized polygamy; and the "sensual" nature of Islam, which imagined a life after death based on the delights of the flesh.[7]

The decades that followed the war of the Alpujarras saw a dramatic increase in inquisitorial repression, which had been launched against the Moriscos as early as the 1520s, but that became more intense after the 1560s with the new, more centralized political culture, stressing religious homogeneity.[8] The war of the Alpujarras had provided a pretext for the breaking down of seigniorial support for the Moriscos and action against community elites that previously had been relatively protected. These Morisco elites were the core of religious and cultural resistance, as many trials revealed. Inquisitorial intervention was aided by a growing fragmentation of the Morisco clans and generational divisions among them. Inquisitorial repression, in turn, contributed to this fragmentation, even though Morisco communities revealed a stronger cohesion than converted Jewish communities.

The Inquisition, though, never reached the same levels of violence in its repression of Moriscos as it did in its treatment of converted Jews—neither in the total numbers nor the severity of punishments (the toll of excommunication and execution was much higher for converted Jews). It is true that repressive measures against converted Jews reached their peak between the 1480s and 1520s, while those against Moriscos were implemented between the 1560s and 1600s. Yet a comparison of what happened to these two major ethnic community victims of the Inquisition shows a less violent approach to Moriscos, formally defined by precise instructions from the general inquisitors Manrique and Valdés. There were two reasons for this: a large majority of Moriscos were highly efficient agricultural workers or specialist artisans in the ceramic, textile, and silk industries, and were not always in direct competition with Old Christians; and the Moriscos had the support of the Muslim kingdoms of North Africa and the Ottoman Empire—a fact that played a crucial role in their relations with the Old Christian community. International politics, in this case Mediterranean politics, made a huge difference to the treatment of Moriscos, whereas the converted Jews of Spain were totally unprotected. International politics also played a major part in the outcome of the measures against Moriscos: many migrated to North Africa (between 1492 and 1568, two hundred thousand went from the region of Granada alone); and a significant number kept in constant communication with their communities in North Africa, helped the corsairs in their raids on the Spanish coast, and asked for military support in case of revolt.

In 1609–10 Philip III decided to expel the Moriscos from Spain, first from Valencia, then from the kingdom of Castile and kingdom of Aragon, and then from the principality of Catalonia. The two reasons indicated in the royal decrees were the persistent apostasy of the converted Muslims and permanent threat to the security of the kingdom represented

Figure 9.1. Pere Oromig and Francisco Peralta, *Boarding of the Moriscos in the Port of Vinaroz*, painting, oil on canvas, 110 × 173 cm., 1612–13. Bancaja Collection, Valencia.
Reprinted with permission from Bancaja Collection, Valencia, Spain; photo: Juan Garcia Rosell

by their supposed plotting with Muslim princes, particularly the Turks, against the Catholic king. The expulsion involved 300,000 people, roughly 125,000 from Valencia, 100,000 from Castile, and 75,000 from Aragon and Catalonia.[9] These figures do not include those who perished during the journey to the coast, although evidence survives of organized robbery, murder, and enslavement by gangs of Old Christians. The misery of the Moriscos did not finish at the ports: they had to wait for transportation, pay heavily for the trip, and sometimes were forced to disembark in inconvenient places, faraway from the main ports. In several cases local Muslim authorities did not welcome them. In any event, the decision to expel this significant minority involved a formidable diplomatic and military operation—first, Philip III, or rather his State Council, established treaties of peace (or truces) with France, England, and the Netherlands, and then the State Council defined a military framework for the expulsion in order to avoid riots. Hundreds of ships were requisitioned for the operation. This required significant financial investment. The king also decided to use the lands that the Moriscos had vacated to compensate the local nobility, who had lost a considerable amount of money in rents.

We have to keep in mind that this was the second exclusion of a large minority; the first had taken place in 1492, when the Catholic kings decided to expel the Jews from their kingdoms. But there is an important difference between these two expulsions: the Moriscos had been violently baptized and were considered Christians. Their expulsion was an enormous confession of failure, after centuries of pressure and (minor) efforts at evangelization. Ironically, the decision could have been perceived as a victory for persistent Muslim resistance: its adherents were finally sent to North Africa to live their faith. From the Old Christian point of view, this punished stubbornness, since the Moriscos were no longer allowed to live in the "paradise" that was Iberia.

Fernand Braudel still sets the terms of the debate about the expulsion: Spain got rid of an industrious minority because it could not be assimilated.[10] In his view, the decision was guided not by racial hatred but rather by religious and civilizational hatred. Samuel Huntington took up this perspective in his questionable vision of the clash of civilizations.[11] Braudel's contribution represented an essentialist approach to Christians and Muslims, ignoring social and religious nuances as well as the different possible political outcomes, as if the expulsion had been the inevitable result of collective rejection. Recent research demonstrates successful cases of full Morisco integration—the most striking one at Villarubia de los Ojos, near Ciudad Real, Castile-La Mancha.[12] I have already indicated the different regional features of the Morisco communities, their successive fragmentation, and local breakdown of resistance. But I could also point to opposition to the expulsion from the landed nobility and tribunals of the Inquisition, both eager to keep their best clients, laborers, and victims, who represented rents or the profits of financial extortion. As scholar Rafael Carrasco ably demonstrated, more than 60 percent of the income of the tribunal of Valencia between 1566 and 1609 came from the Moriscos.[13] Moreover, opposition to the expulsion may have touched other areas of Christian society, as indicated by Miguel de Cervantes in the second part of his famous novel *Don Quixote*, in which he introduced the character Ana Félix, a beautiful young woman expelled from Spain with the other Moriscos, who kept her Christian faith in Algeria and was allowed to go back to Iberia to recover the treasure of her family. Captured with her galley near Barcelona, Ana was rescued by the intervention of the viceroy and met her father, who had recovered the treasure and found a place in Germany for the family to live in peace.[14]

My own view conflicts with Braudel's. The designation of the Moriscos as an alien community situated within Christianity in Iberia was not simply a religious issue. These people were not formally Muslims, and they were not expelled because they were Muslims. They were Christians suspected of apostasy and feared as rebellious because part of them refused to assimilate in cultural, religious, and political respects. The suspicion had been there right from the beginning, embodied in the noun Morisco, which underlined their Moorish origins. It was the first crucial case (alongside that of the converted Jews) in the Christian community of a persistent internal divide based on the notion of descent. The Moriscos were supposed to have inherited the traditional features attributed by Christians to the Moors (meaning Iberian Muslims whose origins lay in a specific mixture of Arabs, Berbers, and converted Visigoths). The same ethnic prejudices shifted from Muslims to Moriscos, as if conversion had no effect. It was a clear case of the stigmatization of a converted population, targeted by a caste divide that transformed them into second-rate Christians, underlining their subordinate position as conquered, subject, discriminated, and segregated. The expulsion exposed a sequence of contradictory acts; it probably coincided with the best period of relative integration of a significant minority among Moriscos, showing how the issue was as political as religious, managed without a plan or long-term coherence.

How can we understand the genesis of the dividing line or internal frontier inside the Christian community? Christianity had traditionally integrated new members from different ethnicities, many of them converted collectively, in an egalitarian framework, following the teachings of Saint Paul. Carrasco highlights the issue of identity. He posits that the Moriscos did not refuse the Christian culture and forms of life but instead the opposite: the Old Christians were immersed in a complex process of assimilation during and after the conquest, and were experiencing the dissolution of their identity. This is why they asserted themselves through the concept of purity of blood, identifying an ethnic exclusivity for themselves that necessarily provoked the Moriscos' reaction.[15] To displace the issue from the Moriscos to the Old Christians reverses the traditional approach of the process that led to the Moriscos' expulsion. But the notion of identity is again taken in a rather essentialist way, as if the Christian loss of identity were a fact, or as if the reassertion of that identity could only have taken that form.

Historical disruptions may lead to the breakdown of old identities and the emergence of new ones, while some features of group identity may prove quite resilient in specific contexts. In the case of the Christian conquest of Iberia and integration of the defeated Muslim population into the new order, it is highly questionable whether the process led to a crisis of identity among the conquerors. It was rather the need to assert the rulers' power and territorial control that accounted for the first forms of segregation and deportation, while the strategy of religious integration, followed by exclusion, revealed the tension between assimilation and domination in the quest to perpetuate the subordinate status of the conquered population. The creation of a caste divide resulted from the struggle to access land in rural areas and property in urban areas, yet also from competition between social and ethnics groups—Muslims and then Moriscos were responsible for extremely profitable industries in various areas, especially tapestry, ceramic, gilded leather, and silk production. In any case, we need to distinguish between the first centuries of Christian conquest, with massive Muslim conversions (mainly in the eleventh century) followed by relative integration, and the disruption that followed the period 1492–1502 in Granada.

The change to a political ideology that favored a centralized government within a religiously homogeneous population played a significant role in the new, more violent forms of conversion and internal ethnic segregation that accompanied them. In this instance, the definition of the enemy as (internal) stranger as well as the limits of trust (and mistrust) between ethnicities in the process of conquest and settlement must be related to the issue of re-creating identities under exceptional historical conditions.[16] The hatred toward Moriscos fueled by (probably) the majority of Old Christians in the lower strata of urban society and lower-ranking clergymen contrasted with the support given them by landlords and part of the social elite. To some extent, the counterreformist faction in the church and the royal court used the struggle against Moriscos to impose its political project and vision of Spain. This historical process proves how identity can be shaped through a series of conflicts. The courses of action open to the victors in the wake of these conflicts formed a long trail, narrowing the set of choices at each stage. On the Moriscos' side, their political segregation and repression at the hands of the winning Old Christian faction fueled their resistance (a phenomenon rightly stressed by Carrasco). This resistance was also encouraged by the international phenomenon of strong Muslim political powers in the south and eastern Mediterranean.

NEW CHRISTIANS

The parallel history of the Jewish communities in Iberia may shed more light on the dividing line between Old and New Christians in relation to the tradition of equality of believers defined by the New Testament letters of Saint Paul concerning gentiles. The expulsion of the Jews from Spain in 1492 and (alongside Muslims) Portugal in 1497 was explicitly related to the supposed contamination of converted Jews. The background to these crucial events started in 1391 in Spain with a wave of anti-Jewish riots that spread from Andalucia to Valencia, Aragon, Catalonia, and Majorca, leaving an unprecedented trail of mass murders and violent conversions. Violent conversions had taken place before, but not on this scale. Between 1411 and 1416, the preaching of Dominican saint Vicente Ferrer, specifically directed toward Jewish communities, replaced terror by persuasion, although these communities were compelled to attend Christian preaching. The result of this confluence of violence, pressure, and persuasion over several decades was the creation of a significant community of converted Jews in Castile and Aragon. But the conversions did not settle the conflict; they simply moved it within the Christian community. The fact was that the converted Jews were soon excelling at new jobs now open to them as Christians—jobs that went far beyond their traditional areas of tax and rent collection, banking, trade, arts, crafts, and limited agricultural investment. They soon reached the highest positions as royal officials, bishops, abbots, judges, and officials of municipal councils. If the regular medieval riots were fueled by urban competition, moneylending, and/or tax and rent collection, the violent conversions exacerbated that same competition at all levels of public life previously reserved for Christians. Soon a new caste division was defined, separating the converted Jews, who were labeled New Christians or *marranos* (from the Arabic *muharram*, meaning declared "anathema," but also meaning "pig" in Castilian), when they were not simply defined as *judios* (Jews), as if the conversion had never taken place.

The political context of the fifteenth century in Castile, with constant factional conflict at the royal court and civil war in the country, dramatically affected the urban areas where Jewish and converted communities lived and worked. The next wave of ethnically inspired riots in Castile was launched primarily against New Christians. It started in Toledo in 1449, in a period of political instability, when King John II sent his constable Don Alvaro de Luna to collect a major new tax. The local elite of Old Christians, who refused the tax, accused the New Christians with high positions as merchants, bankers, and farmers of plotting against the city, attacked their houses, and murdered many of them. Pedro Sarmiento, governor of the castle of Toledo, published the first statute of purity of blood, excluding New Christians of Jewish origin from public positions in the municipality or as notaries, and fifteen lost their jobs. The king supported the New Christians and applied to Rome, where Pope Nicholas V published the bull *Humani generis inimicus* against divisions of blood within the Christian community. The setback did not last long, and new riots against New Christians occurred in 1465 in Seville, 1467 in Toledo and Ciudad Real, and 1473 in Cordoba, raising again the issue of purity of blood and exclusion of New Christians from public jobs. This period coincided with civil war, in which the king and local nobility protected the New Christians against urban Old Christians—their direct competitors.

The reign of Isabel the Catholic (1474–1506) and Ferdinand of Aragon ended the civil wars, completed the conquest of Granada, and centralized power. Stable political life did not protect the New Christians any better. The establishment of the Inquisition in Castile and Aragon in 1478 gave a new impulse to statutes of purity of blood. In 1485, the Inquisition proceeded against New Christian members of the Order of St. Jerome, denounced as still professing their old Jewish faith and practicing their rituals in the convents. The appearance of these people as penitents in the auto-da-fe of Toledo that same year created a significant scandal, since the order played a central role in the royal court. The following year, the chapter of the order approved a statute of purity of blood, but the decision was the subject of protests to both the king and pope by a strong minority of people. Yet Pope Alexander VI, who was of Spanish origin and approved the statute in 1495, broke this resistance.

The legitimacy of the exclusion of New Christians from a religious order was established for the first time at the highest level, and the consequences spread to both ecclesiastical and civil institutions.

The expulsion of the Jewish communities from Castile and Aragon was part of this repressive atmosphere; the proximity of the Jews was considered a major cause of the New Christians' relapse into their old beliefs. The decree issued on March 31, 1492 defined a period of four months within which all communities were supposed to abandon these two kingdoms or convert to Christianity. It is impossible to establish the precise number of those who converted or went into exile; after all the persecutions and forced conversions of the fourteenth and fifteenth centuries, the Jewish community was probably below 150,000 people (2–3 percent of the total population). Recent research has revealed the impact of persecution on geographic dispersal and economic decline. Jews favored small towns and even villages, invested in agriculture and animal breeding, kept to small trades and niches in the crafts, and lost their positions as bankers and financiers.[17] This decline, however, has been disputed at the regional level, mainly in Valencia, where signs of redress in the fifteenth century have been identified.[18] By the time of the expulsion, it is possible that the community of New Christians had reached 250,000 people.[19]

The decree of expulsion further split the Jewish community: some converted immediately; many perished on the way into exile, since the expulsion coincided with one of the deadly epidemics so common in the last decades of the fifteenth century; and an awareness of mortality must have encouraged further conversions, outweighing the converts' fear of the Inquisition's treatment of New Christians. A significant percentage of those exiled went to Portugal, where no significant riots or forced conversions had taken place, with the exception of the massacre of 1449 in Lisbon—an event not followed by forced conversions due to the decisive intervention of the authorities. The Portuguese king John II agreed to receive 600 rich Jews against payment of a tax, and many others followed under similar conditions. Maria José Ferro Tavares estimates the total number of Jews exiled from Spain to Portugal in 1492 at 30,000. A similar number of Jews was already in Portugal when their coreligionists from Spain arrived—meaning that the total Jewish population in Portugal would have risen to 60,000.[20] The number of refugees must have been higher than 30,000: first, because many escaped during the 1480s from Andalusia under the threat of the Inquisition; and second, because the available documents do not give a complete picture. The Jewish population of Portugal may have reached 80,000 people—that is, 8 percent of the total population—and they would have been quite visible, since the Portuguese urban network was not as densely populated as those of Castile or Aragon.

In December 1496, a decree of expulsion against the Jews and Muslims published by King Manuel of Portugal put an end to the existence of religious minorities in that country. They were given until October 1497 to leave under threat of confiscation of property and the death penalty. The Jews had for many years maintained a segregated (although under relatively peaceful conditions) community in Portugal, mainly in the north and center of the country, whereas most of the Muslims had either escaped or been forcibly integrated, subsisting only in tiny communities in the south. This pattern matches the situation in Castile, Navarra, and Aragon. If we look at maps of the distribution of Jewish and Muslim communities in Iberia up to the 1490s, there is a striking concentration of Jews in the north and Muslims in the south. In the Portuguese case, the conversion of Jews did not precede but instead was imposed by their proposed expulsion. The tactics used by the Portuguese king to obtain conversions were the most vicious of all: first he promised the Jews transport from three ports, and then he decided to take all their children up to the age of fourteen years and have them brought up in Christian homes.

In the meantime, he forced the Jews to gather in Lisbon, but did not provide the promised transportation from the port. Members of the community who had resisted previous abuse were enslaved, and only managed to recover their freedom and children through conversion. In exchange for this, the king promised twenty years without any religious inquiry into people's beliefs. The result was not an expulsion as defined by the decree; it was a forced conversion imposed through threats, abuse, and manipulation. The situation was so scandalous that more than seventy years later the chronicles of the reign of Manuel written by the two distinguished Portuguese humanists Damião de Góis and Jerónimo Osório, the latter, bishop of Algarve, condemned the conversions as illegitimate according to Christian law.[21] Portugal's Muslim communities disappeared from the map, proving that in their case the decree had been implemented.[22] Violence generated violence; in Lisbon in 1506, popular riots manipulated by the Dominicans against the New Christians ended in major massacres of the converted.[23] In 1498, the expulsion of the Jews from Navarra (still an independent kingdom) demonstrated the interconnection of decisions concerning religious minorities in Iberia.

The line of divide between New and Old Christians was reinforced by the statutes of purity of blood coupled with the activity of the Inquisition. From the 1480s to 1520s, New Christians accused of returning to their old faith were by far the main target of the tribunals of the Inquisition in Castile and Aragon. This first wave of terror meant an enormous disruption of the urban and social fabric of those countries—a situation that has not been adequately evaluated by the historiography. The New Christians were exposed to increasing stigma, officially sanctioned, even though many had married Old Christians, including landowners and even titled aristocrats. This social mix had a long-lasting impact: by the end of the sixteenth century, the so-called *libros verdes* in Spain denounced the "stained" bloodline of aristocratic families that had married New Christians. The percentage of New Christians persecuted by the Inquisition dramatically decreased after the 1530s, although the migration of Portuguese New Christians after the Iberian union of crowns in 1580 again caught the attention of the inquisitors. In the 1730s and 1740s a significant percentage of New Christians was still persecuted by the Holy Office, and then the phenomenon disappeared from the records. Despite the long-term decline of repression against New Christians, they still received the harshest sentences and most sermons of the autos-da-fe concentrated on the problems of Judaism, even where no sentences related to Judaism were involved. In the Portuguese case, the Inquisition played an even more important role in the long run when it came to the stigmatization of New Christians. Created only in 1536, almost sixty years after the Spanish tribunals, the Portuguese Inquisition did not launch a terror wave, husbanding this reserve of clients as a major resource over two centuries, during which the New Christians represented between 60 and 80 percent of all victims of the tribunals. In the Portuguese case, the percentage of New Christians among those prosecuted by the Inquisition declined significantly only after the 1740s.[24]

Purity of Blood

The notion of pollution or impurity of blood was further entrenched by the Catholic kings in 1501, when they decided that those convicted by the Inquisition along with their children and grandchildren should be excluded from access to major universities and prestigious offices, such as royal counselor, judge in the royal courts, secretary, governor, treasurer, or prosecutor. The same policy was followed in Portugal, where conviction excluded descendants from several professions and public positions. The policy to proclaim the infamy of the convicted and their relatives was systematically implemented by the Inquisition in both Spain and Portugal, which regularly checked on the effective display and maintenance of the *sambenitos* of the condemned in their parish churches. New Christians (and Moriscos) were repeatedly forbidden to travel overseas, but the Inquisition tribunals were only too pleased to launch investigations against those who managed to obtain licenses to settle in Lima, Mexico, or Goa. The disruption of New Christian networks in Lima, Cartagena, and Mexico City in the 1630s and 1640s played a major part in the reorganization of the Atlantic trade networks, while the contemporary persecution of New Christians in Portuguese India further weakened the Estado da Índia, already under threat by the Dutch expansion. Despite all this accumulation of repression and stigma, the New Christians of Jewish origin were never expelled from Portugal or Spain. The Inquisition tribunals rejected several projects around the time of the expulsion of the Moriscos, but the main issue was that New Christian communities were much more entangled in the urban fabric and difficult to distinguish from Old Christian ones, while there was no political justification for the idea that they might encourage an external threat.

Analysis of the statutes of purity of blood, however, is crucial to an understanding of the importance of prejudice concerning descent in the Iberian case. The notion of purity of blood had already defined medieval Christian behavior concerning Jews: they were considered a source of pollution. Jews could not touch food at the market, had to receive special authorization to use water from wells, and were excluded from baking in communal ovens.[25] Many riots in Europe were triggered by rumors concerning the contamination of water by Jews.[26] In early modern Europe, even Jews confined to ghettos did not escape stigma. Christians would not shake the hand of Jews in Venice when they signed a contract with them, but this was only one sign of a general fear of touch and body repulsion.[27] In Spain, the notion of purity of blood emerged in the thirteenth and fourteenth centuries, the crucial turning point in the Christian reconquest. Military confraternities created in Alcaraz, Ubeda, Baeza, and Jaén imposed a need on their members to preserve the purity of blood. But it was the growing community of New Christians in the fifteenth century, sequence of urban riots, and papal and royal final acceptance of the statutes of purity of blood that rooted this new line of divide inside the Christian community.

The Dominican convents followed the example of the Order of St. Jerome, although their statutes were recognized in a patchy way, with several setbacks, in which popes revoked previous licenses, over a long period from the 1490s to 1570s. In 1525, the Observant Franciscans obtained a papal brief forbidding the admission of new Christians, but the Benedictines only established the rule of purity of blood in 1565. The Jesuits held out for longer against this trend, which divided communities and exposed religious orders to fierce debate along with accusations at the local level, where the market for aristocratic and bourgeois investment in new churches and colleges was crucial. They only defined the rule of purity of blood at the fifth general congregation of 1593. Meanwhile, statutes of purity of blood had been adopted by chapters of cathedrals, such as Badajoz in 1511, Seville in 1515, Granada in 1526 (supported by Charles V), Cordoba in 1530, and Toledo in 1548 (approved by the pope in 1555 and Philip II in 1556). The movement spread to the cathedrals of Osma, León, Siguenza, Oviedo, and Santiago, but failed in Zamora, Jaén, Salamanca, Burgos, and Tuy, either because of local opposition or papal refusal. In Aragon, exclusion based on stained blood did not become so rooted; the cathedral of Valencia was probably the only one to adopt a statute of purity of blood. The exclusion of New Christians became even more important in military orders, major colleges and major universities, municipalities, guilds, and confraternities. It was clearly pushed by the representatives of the cities in cortes throughout the late fifteenth and sixteenth centuries. What is interesting is that in a country without a visible New Christian population, after the 1740s, the statutes of purity of blood became mainly an emblem of ancien régime, more ideological than efficient. In 1764, the gilders of Barcelona decided to refuse access to descendants of Jews, Muslims, or heretics, while in 1775 the guild of the druggists of Mataró imposed a requirement for proofs of purity of blood. The rules of inquiry into purity of blood for the military orders were still confirmed by Charles IV and Ferdinand VII in the early decades of the nineteenth century.[28]

The Portuguese case was quite different, slower, and even less homogeneous. In 1558, the first-known papal brief concerning purity of blood in Portugal forbade the access of New Christians to the order of the Franciscans. The pope extended this prohibition in 1572 to access to the military order of Christ. In 1574, the municipality of Vila Flor, Trás-os-Montes, established the first statute of purity of blood. But it was only during the union of Iberian crowns, from 1580 to 1640, that these statutes began to spread, slowly reaching royal jobs, universities, *misericórdias* (confraternities sponsored by the king), municipal councils, cathedral chapters, guilds, confraternities, and religious orders. If in Spain the statutes of purity of blood did not reach all institutions, in Portugal their spread was even more limited, although the urban elites also clamored in the cortes for the exclusion of New Christians and supported the Inquisition in the period of its suspension by the pope, between 1674 and

1681. In any case, the purity-impurity axis never reached the same prominence in Portugal as it did in Spain. Marginal exemption of New Christians from institutionalized exclusion were arguably more practiced in Portugal than in Spain, particularly in several cases of New Christians whose blood had been explicitly "cleansed" and even ennobled by the king, who also intervened as governor of the military order of Christ to waive the rules of blood purity (estimated at a rate of 2 percent of exemptions). When the marques of Pombal decided to abolish the distinction between Old and New Christians in 1773, only the University of Coimbra protested, but it too had to comply. After the fall of Pombal the distinction was never reinstated.[29] In the case of Spain, the statutes of purity of blood were only formally abolished by a string of laws from 1835 to 1870.

In Spain, the New Christians were much more entangled with the urban elites, aristocratic families, and ecclesiastical structures. The issue here concerned the status of different layers of Old Christians, some of who were not prepared to compete with the converted Jews for work. The social elites of Iberia were a poorly defined grouping, owing their status more to a loose interpretation of "noble lifestyle" or, in the strongest instances, an ambiguous idea of *hidalguia/fidalguia* (literally, descendants of someone implicitly important) than to a clear title or status bestowed by the king. Their poorly defined status was related to the tradition of upheavals and social reorganization following conquest. These factors might explain the importance of the statutes of purity of blood in defining internal frontiers, and their use to enhance ancestry (or blood) in the absence of other clear criteria of nobility beyond the limited number of titles given by the king.[30] Purity of blood also contributed to raising the lower strata of Old Christians to and confirming them in a status of superior descent. By the same token, this trend turned the issue of the New Christians into one of descent, relegating these people to the bottom of society, even though in some cases their financial resources would have put them well above this level.

As has been shown in the work of Dominguez Ortiz, Jaime Contreras, Rafael Carrasco, and David Nirenberg, the debate around purity of blood in Spain evolved from a cultural (or genealogical) to a natural (or biological) interpretation.[31] I think this opposition of culture to nature has to be challenged. Blood was the key argument, involving generation, birth, and lineage; it shows how the notions of nature and culture were entangled. Moreover, mental and physical attributes of different varieties of people were situated in nature. Purity of blood in Iberia was not a simple genealogical issue. It carried with it both a positive promotion of pure descent and negative vision of ethnic mixing, with the latter clearly refused. The segregation of converted Jews and Muslims was established in the face of the tradition of a universal Christian Church envisaged by Saint Paul. What distinguished Christianity from other religions before Islam was exactly this universality: ethnic origins did not matter; the converted people would be considered equal and saved by their faith. The direct transfer of the smear against Jews to New Christians, considered cowards, liars, mean, vain, envious, revengeful, and sanguine, reveals that stigma had not shifted to the slightest extent by the water of baptism. Under the conditions of Christian reconquest of Iberia, purity of blood was simultaneously a natural and cultural notion, used for a clear political project: first, to elevate the population of poor Old Christians; second, to deny converted Jews and Muslims access to public and ecclesiastical offices; and third, to exclude them from economic, social, and political resources.

The precarious and permanently threatened existence of New Christians, first in Spain and then in Portugal, led to a constant flow of people to North Africa, the Ottoman Empire, France, Italy, and the Netherlands, both during the long periods of strict prohibition on migration and the few short periods in which authorization to depart was obtained through significant payments. The New Christian elite of merchants and bankers established an international network with links stretching from Amsterdam to Leghorn, Lisbon to Goa, the Cape Verde Islands to Cartagena de Indias and Bahia, Luanda to Rio and Buenos Aires.[32] They were involved in the trade of spices, precious stones, gold, silver, and slaves. They operated all around the Atlantic Ocean. The peak period for these activities was from 1550 to 1650. Again, the Inquisition played a huge role in dismantling this network: the prosecutions brought against the main bankers and traders in Lima and Mexico, in the 1630s and 1640s, disrupted previous connections. The Inquisition was used to settle scores and regulate competition between ethnic groups, under the pretext of religious heterodoxy. Research has shown how the beliefs of the New Christians in this network varied, well beyond stereotyped assumptions about the strict Catholicism or Judaism espoused by members of this stigmatized group.[33] The connection with the Dutch Empire reinforced the allegiance to Judaism, first in Brazil, and then on the Caribbean islands.[34] The constant inquisitorial repression in the Iberian world had two effects, separated in time: in the first two centuries, it enhanced resistance and structured a largely hybrid consciousness from a religious point of view; in the long run, it provoked a constant flow of refugees to other European countries or other continents, integrating the remaining descendants of the group into the two Iberian societies as Christians.

JEWS

I have looked closely at converted Iberian Muslims and Jews, because they represent clear cases of racism. The presence of Muslims in western Europe (leaving aside the European territories of the Ottoman Empire) would not reoccur until the twentieth century with decolonization, although there were thousands of Muslim slaves in French, Italian, and Spanish Mediterranean galleys as well as in the Habsburg Empire as a consequence of wars with the Ottoman Empire.[35] But the presence of Jews increased in the early modern period. They discretely returned to England in the sixteenth century and were tacitly authorized to settle in London during Oliver Cromwell's regime, despite popular anti-Jewish agitation in 1656. Jews enjoyed the favor of political and economic elites, although British writers did not abandon anti-Jewish stereotypes—David Hume (1711–76), to quote just one example, labeled Jews as "fraudsters."[36] A second attempt, in 1753, to create a legal framework of naturalization and property rights for Jews failed, once again in response to popular pressure.

Literary images reproduced stereotypes and repulsion over centuries.[37] Jewish communities in Britain at least, though, did not suffer assaults, and could enjoy a stable and peaceful way of life. But we have to keep in mind that in this and all the other European cases, a good portion of Jewish people lived under poor conditions, surviving due to the charity of a handful of rich members of their communities.

Jews returned to France in significant numbers from the 1550s onward. They entered the country as Portuguese Christian converts, and settled in Bordeaux and Saint-Esprit (Bayonne). In spite of the reinstatement of the medieval French edict of expulsion in 1500 and 1615, these communities enjoyed tacit protection from the political elite until they were finally recognized as Jews in 1723 after large payments. The integration of further sizable communities of Jews followed the French occupation of Metz, Alsace, and Lorraine, not to mention the diplomatic arrangements concerning the Jews of Avignon and other cities in papal Provence. In the empire, the situation of Jews was even more ambiguous: they were expelled from Martinique in 1683, but tacitly accepted throughout the eighteenth century, although without being granted the status of citizens, which complicated matters of inheritance. French writers, particularly Montesquieu, proved to be more open to a break with traditional anti-Jewish stereotypes, despite the abuse constantly heaped on Jews by Voltaire.[38] Jews in the northern province of Saint-Domingue were only granted citizenship in 1783. The civil and political integration of the Jews was promoted during the French Revolution by Abbé Grégoire, who decisively supported the extension of French citizenship to Jews in 1791. Napoléon implemented this policy abroad, but limited it domestically. In the Low Countries, Jews established stable, dynamic, and recognized communities in the last decades of the sixteenth century, and these prospered for centuries without significant abuse from the Christian society in which they were embedded. This relatively peaceful situation was extended to the Dutch colonies in the Atlantic, where Jewish communities were accepted, especially in Brazil, New Amsterdam, Berbice, Demerara, Essequibo, Pomeroon, and Guyana. In the British colonies of North America, particularly Newport and New York City, the Jewish communities from the 1650s onward likewise enjoyed a relatively tolerant environment.[39]

In Sicily and Sardinia, Jews were expelled as a consequence of the Spanish decision of 1492. In Naples, the reception of the decree of expulsion took much longer to implement, in 1510 and 1541. After this date Jews were effectively excluded from southern Italy. Fragmented powers in central and northern Italy made the situation of Jewish communities variable according to time and place, although segregation in ghettos followed the Venetian example set in 1516. The Spanish dominion of Milan was reflected in edicts of expulsion in 1565 and 1590, and their influence in Genoa had already stimulated a similar decision. In Mantova, Ferrara, and Urbino, Jewish communities enjoyed a comparatively better situation, while in Tuscany restrictions on Jews in Florence and Sienna contrasted with the privileges granted to the Jewish community in Leghorn by the end of the sixteenth century, fueled by the political project of developing the port. In the Papal States, the convergence of Spanish influence and popes previously involved with the Roman Inquisition (Paul IV and

Pius V) created a period of persecution of New Christians in Ancona in the mid-sixteenth century (twenty-five New Christians were excommunicated and executed in 1556), while in Rome a ghetto was created in 1556. Orders to expel all Jews from the Papal States, with the exception of Rome, Ancona, and Avignon, followed in 1569 and 1593. The creation of the House of the Catechumens in 1543 proved to be instrumental in the long run in implementing the papal policy of Jewish conversion, with regular preaching that Jews were compelled to attend. Forced conversions and even the kidnapping of Jewish children were practiced with papal approval along with, in some cases, direct protection until the nineteenth century. Benedict XIV still recognized the ritual murder of children by Jews as a legitimate accusation. The pope pleaded in 1755 for the beatification of the victims. As late as 1900, the congregation of the Holy Office stated that ritual murder was historically proven.[40] There were no major assaults and massacres in the places where Jewish communities were allowed to live, but in general communities lived under constant pressure.

In Germany, where Jewish communities had managed to survive medieval persecutions, the Protestant Reformation did not favor their situation. Martin Luther (1483–1546), who hopeful of their conversion had written in favor of the Jews in his early career, became extremely critical in his later writings: he labeled them parasites and usurers, and endorsed the burning of synagogues, prohibition of Jewish cults, confiscation of Jews' holy books, and expulsion of communities. During the sixteenth century, Jewish communities were effectively expelled from Saxony, Brandenburg, and Silesia. In 1616, popular riots expelled Jewish communities from Frankfurt and Worms, but the authorities managed to impose the reintegration of those communities, and no major upheaval occurred again throughout the early modern period. In the main German courts, a new kind of Jewish banker emerged—managing to resist discriminatory practices and segregation. Discrimination did not disappear, however. In 1648, the Jewish community was expelled from Hamburg, though it was allowed to return some years later. Expansion of Jewish settlements occurred in the second half of the seventeenth century, even though impoverished communities were visible in the eighteenth century.[41] In the Habsburg Empire, conditions also became difficult. In 1670, the Jewish community was expelled from Vienna, though it was invited to return fifteen years later. In 1726, the Habsburg government decided to restrict Jews' right to marry to the eldest son, thereby provoking emigration to Poland and Hungary. The Jews were expelled from Bohemia in 1744 under the pretext that they were spying for Prussia. Yet the Habsburg Empire became more tolerant in the last decades of the eighteenth century: Joseph II published edicts of tolerance for Protestants (1781) and Jews (1783).

The persecution of Jews in eastern Europe started much later than in England and France: they were expelled from Warsaw and Kraków in the 1480s, and there was an attempt to expel them from Lithuania at the same time. Jewish communities had become rooted in Poland during the fifteenth century, though, and they increased their numbers in the following centuries, probably accounting for 10 percent of the population by the mid-eighteenth century. They were not confined to ghettos and in fact owned land, were active in various arts and crafts as well as commercial and industrial professions, and enjoyed the basic rights of citizenship; they could even carry arms. In 1648, the insurrection of the Ukrainian peasants was coupled with systematic pogroms that wiped out Jewish communities east of the Dnepr. Many Jews were sold as slaves to the Turks. The disruption of the Polish state went hand in hand with the disruption of Jewish communities, and this started a long period of economic decline, expressed in the influence wielded by Sabbataï Zevi's messianism and the important schismatic movement of Hassidism. The partition of Poland sparked further massacres of Jewish communities, and renewed medieval accusations of ritual murder of Christian children and host desecration. In Russia, Jewish communities were banned from early on, following the "Judaizing" heresy in Orthodox Novgorod in the last decades of the fifteenth century. The heretics denied the divinity of Christ, rejected the idea of the Trinity, and destroyed icons. This became an "affair d'état" and was repressed by Ivan III; the leaders of the sect were burned in 1504. Russian rulers consistently refused to tolerate the presence of Jews, although they had to accept the reality of extensive communities in the newly acquired eastern European territories from the 1770s onward.[42]

I have concentrated here on policies concerning Jewish communities, since these make for an easier identification of assumptions, stereotypes, and discriminatory actions. The complexity of relations between Christians and Jews has been widely acknowledged.[43] In art, the use of inscriptions in Hebrew and contemporary Jews as models for biblical scenes was part of a long tradition renewed in the seventeenth century, particularly by Rembrandt. On this subject, contrasting interpretations of philo- or Anti-Jewish positions have been replaced by a critical vision of the context of artistic experiments, especially the reflection on classical texts.[44] The enormous variety of references to Jews in European literature also reinforces a nuanced vision. This is particularly important for the second half of the eighteenth century and first decades of the nineteenth century in France and Germany, when Jews were used for exploring the limits of secular universalism, civil rights, and citizenship. In the German case they were even included in a major Orientalist trend, though this has escaped previous theoretical essays, notably by Edward Said. The project of extension of rights advanced in 1781 by Christian Wilhelm Dohm, *On the Civic Improvement of the Jews*, has been aptly identified under the idea of testing the frontiers of civil rights. Research has shown the persistence of Christian anti-Jewish stereotypes, but the inclusion of Jewish communities in secular universalism also triggered an internal debate. Major Jewish philosophers and theologians, such as Moses Mendelssohn (1729–86) or Abraham Geiger (1810–74), challenged the exclusivist and universalist notions of modernity endorsed by the Enlightenment, and then by liberalism, calling attention to Jewish identity and cultural pluralism.[45]

Gypsies

The absence of written sources and identifiable links to the origins of Christianity makes stereotypes concerning Gypsies, or rather Romany or Roma, much more marginal. The

Au bout du comte ils reuuent pour defsin
Qu'ils sont venus dAegipte a'ce festin

Figure 9.2. Jacques Callot, *Encampment of Gypsies*, engraving, 1621.
Reprinted with permission from AKG-images, Berlin; IAM

Gypsies entered Europe through the Balkans in the Middle Ages, arriving in Germany in the fifteenth century and England at the beginning of the sixteenth century. They were believed to have come from Egypt, hence their name, but eighteenth-century linguistic analysis placed their origins in India. The first available descriptions highlighted their nomadic lifestyle, labeling them vagabonds—Enea Silvio Piccolomini (Pope Pius II) considered them "land pirates." They were perceived as dark or black, although in time it was recognized that their skin color had much to do with the amount of time they spent outdoors. In some accounts they were described as good artisans, serving as shoemakers, cobblers, smiths, and spinners. They were also involved in horse dealing. In the Ottoman Empire they earned their living mainly as metalworkers, but also as musicians, barbers, messengers, and executioners. They were soon targeted in Europe, though, as fortune-tellers, sorcerers, thieves, and spies. The main stereotypical Gypsy characters in literature (particularly in the works of Gil Vicente and Cervantes) were palm readers or fortune-tellers, and Gypsies were also depicted in this way by Titian, Benvenuto Garofalo, Correggio, and Pieter Brueghel the Elder.

The first decades of a relatively warm welcome for Gypsies were based on the supposition that they were on a seven-year pilgrimage to expiate their sins. Therefore they received alms and safe conducts. In later years, a climate of rejection and expulsion developed. As well as being subject to numerous local bans, Gypsies were expelled from the Holy Roman Empire in 1498, 1500, 1544, and 1551, different Swiss cantons between 1471 and 1530, Spain in 1499 (a ban renewed several times by Charles V and extended to Flanders), Portugal in 1526, 1538, and 1557, Navarre in 1538, France in 1539, different Italian states, including the

Papal States, between 1493 and 1553, Denmark in 1536 (a ban renewed in 1554 and 1561), Poland in 1537, Sweden in the 1540s, Scotland and Bohemia in 1541 and 1549, and Moravia in 1558. In England there was also a succession of acts promulgated against Gypsies from the 1530s to 1550s, and fifteen separate acts of deportation can be identified. Gypsies became seen as vagrants, and were included in the act of 1562 concerning vagabonds. The repression continued in various countries throughout the seventeenth and eighteenth centuries, specifically in France and Germany. The passing of successive laws reveals how difficult it was to implement these.

In Spain, the issue from the outset was to impose a settled behavior on these people: the laws of 1633, 1717, and 1739 insisted on this, finally forcing Gypsies into work in the naval arsenals. The Portuguese systematically deported Gypsies to the African colonies and Brazil, but ended up legislating against them in Brazil in 1760. The continuous presence of Gypsies in Portugal, despite successive bans, is revealed by the widespread use of the word *gajo*, indicating another person or "guy," derived from the Romany *gadzó* (foreigner). Gypsies were prepared to adapt freely to local religion: they were Christians in Europe, and Muslims in the Ottoman Empire. Despite their closed community, which was based on the idea of purity and fear of contamination or pollution, they were rarely touched by the Roman or Iberian Inquisitions, which considered their fortune-telling a simple exploitation of public credulity. In Hungary, Gypsies were treated better there than in any other country, and were recognized as metalworkers and manufacturers of weapons. But generally in Europe, Gypsies were seen as vagrants and assigned the status of vermin, supposedly carrying the plague or syphilis, and engaged in the kidnapping of children and even cannibalism.[46]

✶✶✶

Oceanic exploration radically changed the European perception of the world. Elites started to represent themselves as being at the center of the world in terms of their cartography and geography. This shift from regarding Jerusalem as the symbolic center of the world in the late medieval period led to a restructured hierarchy of the peoples of the world, based on European criteria: written legal codes, civil administration, a recognized body of knowledge, an established religion, walled cities, metal weapons, a diet based on processed cereals, the use of technology for the creation of arts and crafts, transport systems, and a market-oriented economy. A nomadic lifestyle was equated with vagrancy and animal behavior, while settled populations were classified according to European criteria. The personification of continents expressed a ranking, with each allegorical representation concentrating all the prejudices concerning peoples native to that specific part of the world. America was defined by cannibalism and nakedness, Africa by slavery and uncivilized behavior, Asia by idleness and sensuality, and Europe by labor and sophistication. The hierarchy of continents was thus represented as a succession of stages, from the most barbaric to the most civilized or controlled.

The classification of the peoples of the world could cut across the different continents, based on a series of oppositions: settled versus nomadic, agriculture-based versus hunter-gatherer, organized religion versus sacrificial cults, written versus oral communication, cooked versus raw food, and dressed versus naked. The tension between the explosion of varieties of peoples encountered as a result of oceanic exploration and the arbitrary definition of their different types was visible as early as the sixteenth century. My inquiry into the European perception of peoples from different continents has shown detailed prejudice against and a progressive distancing of the peoples of Africa. The peoples of Asia were seen in a more elevated position at the beginning, with Chinese and Japanese considered at the same level as Europeans, but this view eroded in time. Oriental despotism became the cornerstone of European perceptions, meaning arbitrary rule, enslaved populations, backward sciences, and technology. The construction of prejudices concerning ethnic descent at the scale of the globe justified discriminatory action during the early modern expansion, and prepared the new wave of European colonialism in the late nineteenth and early twentieth centuries.

This period redefined internal ethnic frontiers in Europe. Jews were expelled in 1492 from Spain after one century of intermittent violence, in which a good part converted into Christianity, while large numbers of them were forced to convert in 1497 in Portugal. A new divide based on caste perceptions discriminated against and segregated converted Jews and Muslims in the Iberian world, creating a stigma based on stereotypes of mental features. *Conversos* and Moriscos were excluded from public office, religious orders, military orders, cathedral chapters, confraternities, and guilds. There were individual exceptions, but perceptions of different sections of society were shaped by lineage and blood, as if the supposed attributes of Jews and Muslims were perpetuated from generation to generation, even after they had converted. This was an early case of racism, meaning prejudices concerning ethnic descent coupled with discriminatory actions. The Old Christian population was not exempt from conflictive points of view on this matter, since landed aristocracy and some members of ecclesiastical hierarchy supported Moriscos and New Christians at the beginning of this process. The purpose of the lower, middle, and upper segments of the Old Christian urban population, which engaged in bottom-up actions leading to the diffusion of the statutes of purity of blood, was to consolidate different social interests in order to monopolize economic, social, and political resources. They stigmatized and targeted converted minorities, disrupting communities and imposing the entire reorganization of the social fabric. For the first time in history the ideal of a universal Christian Church, meaning equality of believers from different ethnic origins, was denied consistently in the long term. The Morisco population was finally expelled in 1609, although part had been assimilated, while the New Christians either escaped or integrated in the long run.

Peoples traditionally defined by religion and ethnicity proved to be quite resilient. Jewish communities managed to return to England and France, from where they had been expelled in the Middle Ages; they stabilized their situation in Germany and Italy, and flourished in the Low Countries. Yet they were only fully emancipated by the French Revolution. The best conditions for Jewish communities existed in Poland, where Jews enjoyed rights unknown elsewhere. But the Ukrainian peasant revolt of 1648 led to massacres of Jews and their long-term decline in that area, while the partition of Poland had a major impact on the destiny of the country's Jewish communities. In France and Germany, the Jews were used to experiment with the limits of secular universalism and civil rights in the last decades of the eighteenth and first decades of the nineteenth century, showing the tension between traditional stereotypes along with the individualistic stance of the Enlightenment and Liberalism.

Gypsies were consistently persecuted all over Europe throughout this period because of their nomadic lifestyle. They were dehumanized as vermin, and portrayed as living off the proceeds of theft and fortune-telling. This is another significant case of early ethnic discrimination, clearly not based on religious conflict, since the Gypsies were Christians, but rather on their way of life and descent. Prejudices based on the manner in which people lived had been expressed in medieval Europe against the Lapps, and they were perpetuated in discriminatory action against peoples on the social and political peripheries, such as the Irish, although in this last case without the same focus on descent. Meanwhile, skin color became more and more important due to the massive transatlantic trade in African slaves. While medieval Europe had already developed prejudices based on dark skin—for example, against the Byzantine emperors—Oceanic exploration and competition between maritime powers made dark skin a key element in the set of prejudices developed by northern Europeans toward the peoples of southern Europe—linked to the classification of peoples from other continents.

||||||||||||||||||||||||||||||||||||||||||||||||||||||||||||||||||||||||||||||||||||||||||||||||||||||||||||||||||||||||||||||||||||||||||

PART III

Colonial Societies

"The same set of manners will follow a nation, and adhere to them over the whole globe, as well as the same laws and language. The Spanish, English, French and Dutch colonies are all distinguishable even between the tropics," stated David Hume (1711–76) in his essay "Of National Characters."[1] Hume opposed the deterministic vision of climate shaping the physical and moral features of peoples advocated by influential writers such as Montesquieu—a vision that would dominate reflections on human diversity until the nineteenth century. He pointed out the different skin colors and shapes of the human body that existed under similar climates, and different moral characteristics to be observed in neighboring countries. Hume also acknowledged significant historical changes among particular peoples, such as the transfer of science and knowledge from southern to northern Europe. He argued for the imitative nature of the human mind, highlighting the way manners spread. He recognize the influence of difficult working conditions and specific cultures of different professional groups, like priests or soldiers, who were supposed to share similar features in distinct religious or political environments. Nevertheless, Hume was convinced that each nation had a peculiar set of manners, influenced by the nature of its government, the revolutions in its public affairs, and its general conditions of plenty or penury. Hume attributed an essential nature (set of manners) to each European power, so rooted that it shaped colonial societies. This idea had already implicitly been used in Europe in descriptions of Portuguese, Spanish, English, and Dutch colonies during the sixteenth and seventeenth centuries. Hume made it explicit and formalized it in a synthetic way that was to frame much historical reasoning up until the present day. Yet this projection of essentialized national values onto the world prevents serious research on colonial societies, local conditions, different interethnic relations, the variety of prejudices, and specific forms of discriminatory action.

Adam Smith (1723–90) suggested a slightly different approach when he reflected on the causes of the prosperity of the new colonies: "The colonists carry out with them a knowledge of the agriculture and of other useful arts, superior to what can grow up of its own accord in the course of many centuries among savage and barbarous nations. They carry out with them too the habit of subordination, some notion of the regular government which sup-ports it, and of a regular administration of justice; and they naturally establish something of the same kind in the new settlement."[2] Smith assumed that the colonists were always the changing and driving force, carrying with them superior knowledge, responsible for fast agricultural growth, superior government, and the administration of justice, meaning a respect for property and the protection of investment necessary for the creation of a stable environment. He rejected political imperial projects, dismissing them as a waste of money and distortion of markets as well as a nuisance for his uncompromising liberal vision of a free expanding world economy. But Smith's analysis, though less nationally oriented, justi-fied the centrality placed by Hume on European colonists, paving the way for a historical reasoning that went beyond Hume's original intentions: historical change and discontinuity were to be identified with the history of Europeans, even in other parts of the world.[3]

The mainstream of historical work in the twentieth and even early twenty-first century supposed (and often still supposes) that the Portuguese, Spaniards, and English carried with them their "national" features, and reproduced them in different colonial contexts.[4] The Portuguese and Spaniards thus were believed to be more open to native populations than the English, because they had had the experience of mixing with the migrants who came with the Arabs from North Africa and the Middle East, renewed by successive waves of Islamic military effort. Another component of the historical mix was the constant flow of African slaves traded into Iberia since the Middle Ages. The natives of Iberia, then, were believed to be more adaptable to tropical environments, due to the assimilation of Arab and North African historical experiences.[5] This approach ignores the conflictive interethnic process of assertion of Portuguese and Castilian identities, in which Jews, Muslims, and converted people were discriminated against and segregated. Moreover, other peoples of Europe were also shaped and reshaped through a constant flow of migrants of different origins, having their identities modified as a result of displacement, mixing, and division. There is no such thing as stable or autochthonous populations settled in specific regions from times immemorial: from a political perspective, it is possible to talk about collective identities, but it is difficult to project notions of nation and "national character" onto the past eighteenth-century. The point here is that identity is an ever-evolving process; Euro-pean collective identities were not crystallized before the European expansion, and the dif-ferent peoples involved in that process continued to redefine their self-perceptions.

Catholicism in Portugal and Spain is usually taken to explain a supposedly greater fre-quency of sexual intercourse and intermarriage with local populations. The alleged promis-cuity of Catholicism is opposed to British and Dutch Protestantism as cultures of sexual restraint and stricter rules concerning the choice of partners. Puritanism is supposed to be responsible for the exclusion of native people, since its higher standards of evangelization were incompatible with the mass baptism without previous indoctrination practiced by Catholic priests.[6] These assumptions suffer from anachronism: the religious divide within Christianity occurred one century after the beginning of the Iberian expansion, and the dif-fusion of Calvinism did not have a linear history. The precise configuration of ethnic mixes in the different continents partly contradicts these assumptions. The French case blurs the purported divide between Catholic and Protestant behavior, while Dutch and British practices vary in Africa, Asia, and America. I will look at the different trends of European migration to other continents, ratio of men to women, and different types of settlement—major indicators that have not been studied in a comprehensive way and that explain the distinct forms of sexual behavior much better. I will also analyze the impact of religion on interethnic exchanges, particularly the influence of confraternities on manumission and the marginal moderation of abuse.

The essentialist approach to European colonialism is wrong because it leaves native people out of the picture. It is true that the Europeans brought with them their languages, and in many cases managed to impose them, yet they also had to negotiate other languages and learn from them. European laws and institutions were exported in order to build the colonial framework, but in many cases they had to be adapted, while local laws, institutions, and administrative practices preserved their existence for longer than is generally acknowledged. Therefore colonial law has been defined as multicentered and multilayered, with the integration of previous local rules, norms, and habits.[7] European technology was important in the New World, but not in Asia, with the exception of artillery, until the nineteenth century. A Eurocentric approach ignores the agency of native people, local capacity for political, economic, and social negotiation, and permanent mediation that in many places defined the new configurations of colonial societies that did not match either previous European experiences or local traditions. Local realities significantly shaped European experiences on other continents, imposing different colonial practices, settlements, and ethnic configurations. The Portuguese settlements in Asia were distinct from those in Africa and even more distinct from those in America. By the same token, the British experience in Asia bore little resemblance to what happened in America, not to mention the divergent experiences of the Dutch in South Africa and North America.

This critical vision is extremely significant if we wish to clear a field obstructed by national and racial prejudices. Colonial societies created different environments, with specific interethnic features, which were not simply transferred from one place to the other; they were built and rebuilt according to their own dynamic, confronted by a vast set of previous experiences, both in Europe and overseas. The purpose of this part of the book is to study new ethnic prejudices raised by the establishment of European colonial societies. I will start with an analysis of the ethnic taxonomy created in those environments, which immediately reveals the level of interethnic violence along with the specific social and political configurations created. Next, I will discuss the magnitude of the slave trade across the centuries and its impact on different societies, mainly the American but also the Asian and southern European slave trade.

The integration of native populations and new structures resulting from the process of European settlement as well as the reorganization of the local economy and society will also be analyzed, in order to understand the shifts and logic of ethnic preconceived opinions. Instead of a pure transfer of European visions, colonial experiences led to the emergence of new stereotypes, and the rejection, reinterpretation, and displacement of transmitted ethnic prejudices. In this context, the creation of Creole societies in Central Africa and on the Caribbean islands presents an interesting laboratory for studying new forms of interethnic articulation and self-perception. Civil rights are also important to consider: To what extent did people have access to property, jobs, and houses? How did they suffer from spatial segregation? Could they marry people from other ethnicities? To what degree were they involved in or excluded from political action? Finally, this part will show how colonial projects impacted on interethnic and racial prejudices.

‖‖‖

CHAPTER 10

Ethnic Classification

CASTA PAINTING

The Mexican school of painting developed a series of social representations of castas or mixed-race people throughout the eighteenth century.[1] The purpose of this genre was to present a narrative, hierarchical vision of the process of racial mixing between the diametrically opposed types of Spaniards and "savage" Indians (living outside colonial society), spotlighting the triple mixture of Spaniards and Indians, Spaniards and black people, and Indians and black people. More than one hundred series have now gone through the process of scholarly referencing. The vast majority were produced in Mexico City, but some series were painted in the Mexican town of Puebla and Peruvian capital Lima. They were painted either on a single surface, like a kaleidoscope of different scenes joined together, or separate canvases or copperplates. Each scene in these series was given a number to highlight a hierarchy of purity of blood: generally from one to sixteen, yet the total could vary. Although the first extant paintings, by Manuel Arellano (1711), concentrated on individuals, sometimes with a child, all the other series depicted mixed couples with their offspring, one child, in an unexpected triumph of the nuclear family in the tropics. This visual act was efficient in a classificatory way: the race or caste of the male and female as well as the resulting different caste of the offspring could easily be identified by a caption, generally inscribed on the scene.

The first complete series known to us, painted circa 1715 and attributed to Juan Rodríguez Juárez, defined a model that was more or less replicated, but also rendered more complex, by successive experiments in this genre.[2] I will concentrate on the captions of each painting in this series; number one has the inscription "Spaniard and Indian produce Mestizo," and number fourteen, the last one, "Barbarian Indians." The series begins with the highest arrangement in the hierarchy, a Spaniard married to an Indian, and ends with the lowest, savage Indians living outside colonial society. The first set of three paintings presenting Spaniards mixing with Indians is completed by "Spaniard and Mestizo produce Castizo" and "Castizo and Spaniard produce Spaniard"—meaning a return to the original "pure" race at the end of the cycle. The mixing of Spaniards with Africans is the subject of the second set: "Spaniard and Black produce Mulatto," "Spaniard and Mulatto produce

Figure 10.1. (*Left*) Juan Rodriguez Juárez, *Spaniard and Indian Produce a Mestizo*, painting, oil on canvas, 80.7 × 105.4 cm., c. 1715.
Breamore House, Hampshire, UK; Bridgeman Art Library
Figure 10.2. (*Right*) Juan Rodriguez Juárez, *Spaniard and Morisca Produce an Albino*, painting, oil on canvas, 80.7 × 105.4 cm., c. 1715.
Breamore House, Hampshire, UK; Bridgeman Art Library

Morisco," and "from Spaniard and Morisco, Albino." In this case we do not have a return to pure Spaniard but instead an artificial and ambiguous (as we will see) whiteness. There remains an incomplete third set: "Mulatto and Mestiza produce Mulatto Return-Backwards," (*torna atrás*, meaning the result is darker than the mestiza), "Black and Indian produce Wolf," "Mexican Indians," and "Otomi Indians on the Way to the Fair." This series already stresses different clothes, hairstyles, headdresses, and in some cases, professional activity in order to identify the castes. The color of the skin is obviously considered an important means of portrayal. Among the lower castes, we already see agricultural products intended to be sold in the market. At this experimental stage, the idea of whitening is interesting to note as a model linked to the persistent presence of a Spaniard in successive generations resulting from Spaniards mixing with Indians or blacks. Yet this possibility is rejected by the presence in succeeding pictures of blacks and Indians without Spaniards.

The following series stabilized the format of the first set (Spaniards/Indians), rejected the possible whitening of the second (Spaniards/blacks), and developed the third (people of mixed-race descent), excluding the "Barbarian Indians." They focused on urban Mexican society, which saw the concentration of the castes phenomenon.[3] The series became more and more about mixed-race people and their hierarchy, in which Spaniards and Indians were placed at the top. Domestic and professional environments were better defined, while the inclusion of landscapes and agricultural products increased. Classification became more complex, although some designations were not stable, raising questions about the extent to which they really existed in daily life, even though the vast majority of them are attested to by other sources. The series of mixes between Spaniards and blacks was corrected in a

Figure 10.3. (*Left*) Juan Rodriguez Juárez, *Wolf and Indian Produce a Wolf Return-Backwards*, painting, oil on canvas, 80.7 × 105.4 cm., c. 1715.
Breamore House, Hampshire, UK; Bridgeman Art Library
Figure 10.4. (*Right*) Juan Rodriguez Juárez, *Barbarian Indians*, painting, oil on canvas, 80.7 × 105.4 cm., c. 1715.
Breamore House, Hampshire, UK; Bridgeman Art Library

concluding scene: "from Spaniard and Albino, Black Return-Backwards."[4] The temporary nature of the designation albino was highlighted and the tricks of nature unveiled. The possible return to purity of blood was then blocked in Spaniard/black descent, to be linked exclusively to Spaniard/Indian. Throughout the eighteenth century, new designations of mixed-race offspring were added: "from Wolf and Black, Chino," "from Chino and Indian, Cambujo" (also *genízaro*), "from Indian and Cambujo, Tente en el Aire (Suspended in the Air)," "from Cambujo and Mulatto, Albarrazado" (also *gíbaro*), "from Albarrazado and Indian, Barcino" (or *chamizo*), "from Barcino and Indian, Canpa Mulato" (also *zambaigo*), and "from Indian and Mestiza, Coyote."

The vocabulary used in this social taxonomy reveals a colonial society worried about the definition of internal frontiers in the context of mixed marriages. The elite was obviously not secure about its own definition, since belonging was mainly a matter of reputation and lifestyle, not of noble titles or established local aristocratic genealogy. Upward mobility could easily play with the flexibility of the system. The complicated taxonomy presented here had its origins in the sixteenth century, and its main features were developed in the seventeenth century; in the 1640s, the registers of baptism in the parish churches of Mexico City were already divided into Spaniards, mestizos, and mulattoes. The vocabulary inscribed on casta paintings is striking in three aspects: first, the animal metaphors constantly present in the representation of mixed marriages and their offspring; second, the transfer of established designations to other people; and third, the underlying genealogical tree, composed as a scale of tonalities of skin color.

Animal metaphors were used to debase interethnic offspring. The word mulatto comes from mule, the offspring of a horse and donkey—an offspring that cannot reproduce. The use of mule as a metaphor for the offspring of mixed couples of blacks and whites was meant not only to undermine the mix of races but also to underline the "degeneration" of human beings and stress the imagined uselessness of the mix. European theologians and nobles in Africa, America, and Asia in the sixteenth and seventeenth centuries sustained the idea that mixed marriages led to sterility within one, two, or three generations.[5] Coyote, the child of an Indian and mestiza, was a word taken from the Nahuatl vocabulary, used to designate a predatory canine mammal or prairie wolf of the deserts of North America. The deprecating attitude was obvious; the child was considered a wild beast. Lobo (wolf) was another case of the explicit use of an animal metaphor immediately suggesting contempt, based on the traditional attributes of the animal—wild, ferocious, and voracious. Cambujo was another word inspired by Nahuatl, designating a bird with black feathers and black flesh. Albarrazado signified animals with white spots, and Barcino was traditionally applied to cats, dogs, cows, or bulls with black and white hair.[6]

The application to castas of vocabulary traditionally used to indicate human physical handicap is part of the same tendency toward denigrating mixed-race people. Gíbaro was most probably inspired by *giba*, meaning "hunchback," used in colloquial Spanish as "nuisance" or "annoying person." Zambaigo was inspired by *zambo*, and the two adjectives could be used indiscriminately. Zambo originally designated the physical "defect" of being knock-kneed. These examples reveal the juxtaposition of animal and physical handicap metaphors in interethnic classification. The history of insults shows that these two sources of abusive language are still being drawn on in daily life today, even where there is no racial connotation. Prejudice concerning descent used this historical phenomenon to create a recognized system whereby different ethnicities and people of mixed race would be undermined.

Mestizo, from the Latin *miscere*, to mix, is an apparently neutral term, but with time the word became pejorative. The word *castizo* reflects the importance placed on genealogy in those days; it designates the third generation of mixed marriages between peoples of Spanish and Indian origins. The word directly expressed the idea of casta that structured Mexican society and Hispanic societies in America in general. We have here a metaphor from fauna (animal breeding) and flora (vineyards, the quality of grapes, and the practice of grafting) used in Iberian languages since the fifteenth century, and first applied in the following century to human societies in various contexts—for example, in India—and also Europe itself. It was common to see the inquisitors and commissioners in the Iberian trials from the sixteenth to eighteenth century ask what caste the witness or accused was. The transfer of names from recognized peoples, ethnicities, or social groups is shown in the way that Morisco designated a child of a Spaniard and mulatto: they were considered to be of light dark color, like the Iberian converted Muslims of North Africa origin. This use proves that in Iberia, the word Moor did not indicate the same degree of darkness that it did in northern Europe. *Chino* is another case of the transfer of a word just for the sake of taxonomy; the supply of possible words was not infinite. As we have seen before, the southern Chinese were credited with a kind of olive color. Some historians have identified chinos with the people of the Philippines, but the Chinese were well identified and differentiated from non-Chinese, particularly in the Philippines. They were brought to Mexico from the last decades of the sixteenth century onward.[7] Genízaro (or better *jenízaro*, and in English *janizary*) is another case of noun transfer, from the Italian *gianizzero*, which in turn came from the Turkish *yeniçeri*, "new troop," originally composed of the children of Christians, taken as tribute from their families and converted to Islam, who formed the sultan's guard and elite corps of the standing army. The "betrayal of origins" is the obvious meaning of this noun, which in the Mexican context expressed the prejudice against mixed-race people.

Prejudices concerning color also explain the designation of Albino, coming from the Latin *albus* through Castilian and Portuguese. The word traditionally meant an animal, plant, or person deficient in pigment, and thus white or pale. The child had a white color, but was not really white. The "risks" of mixed marriages were stressed by the designation of "Black Return-Backwards," a child of a Spaniard and an albino who had a darker skin than their parents, who was a throwback to an ancestor, understood as a joke, a revolt of nature, and nature's punishment of the fake white. Chamizo meant a half-burned or scorched tree, but also kindling for the oven. In this case we have a metaphor from flora to express the darkness of skin, matching the Greek etymology of Ethiopian as a burned face. In the hierarchy displayed by the casta paintings we can see tonalities of color as an organizing principle, from the whiter to darker—two symbolic poles of good (virtue) and bad (evil).

Genealogy was another organizing principle, since a decline from generation to generation could be depicted through the "wrong" succession of mixes, while the minute possibility of "whitening" could only be achieved by the "right" choice in each of a succession of marriages with Spaniards. The constant mixing defined a curious pattern of continuously changing labels, expressing the idea of repeated new departures toward the configuration of another casta, thus creating an ongoing state of ethnic instability, as if order could never be reached, in contrast with Europe, where the ethnic and social status of people could be more or less easily identified. This permanent state of ethnic instability, I have to add, could not have been better illustrated than by the category *tente en el aire* (suspended in the air), which meant more or less at the same level of the parents, but without knowing what direction the product of mixed race would take.[8]

The notion of purity of blood was also inscribed in the colonial context, although in a particular way, since the Indians were theoretically placed above converted Jews and converted Muslims—both groups that alongside Gypsies, were prohibited from migrating to America.[9] This hierarchy of blood expressed the supremacy of political reasoning: to enhance their status as vassals of the king, the Indians were recognized as the first inhabitants of the land, or those who had occupied it before the Spaniards. Genealogy, generally linked to purity of blood in the Iberian context, was also drawn on to represent proximity to, or distance from, the "superior" Spanish and white status imposed by colonial realities. Although generally formulated through the standard set of complicated labels, genealogy was used to express the principles of descent in an arithmetic way: the Peruvian series of casta paintings was labeled straightforwardly "Spaniard and Mestiza produces Quarterón (one-fourth) of Mestizo," "Cuarteron de Mestizo and Spaniard produces Quinterona (one-fifth) of Mestizo," and "Spaniard and Quinterona (one-fifth) of Mestizo produces Spaniard or Requinterona (new-fifth) of Mestizo."[10] The same logic was applied to the other sets (Spaniard with black, and mixed-race people), showing how distant the case of Lima was from the Mexican model, since it had to include the strict genealogical classification consecrated by the inquisitorial inquiries into purity of blood, estimating quarters and fifths of Indian (or black) blood. The Peruvian case (exemplified in only one series, I have to say) also calls attention to the possibility of whitening the blood, even through different kinds of mix, contrary to the Mexican refusal of widespread upward mobility.

The series of paintings were organized according to a triple hierarchy of blood, color, and occupation, combined with way of life. This last aspect is quite interesting, because in the anonymous series kept at the Museo de America in Madrid, the first painting represents a kind of European landscape composed of noble houses with towers and domesticated nature in which the family is presented in a dignified manner—a "noble" Spaniard, an Indian, and their mestizo child, all well dressed. The details in this painting show the prejudices against mixed marriage: the Spaniard has a noble attitude, stressed by the delicacy of his gestures, refined gait, and fine European clothes with their austere colors (black and white), set off by red buttons and a red hat brim; the Indian, dressed in colorful colonial clothes (red, white, orange, and blue), hesitates in her step, probably because she is not used to European shoes, and tries to straighten her head scarf with the right hand in a clumsy gesture; the child is dressed up as a Spanish noble, a small copy of his father, but he cries; as a matter of fact, he is one of the few crying children in the series. The only violent scene is in painting number four ("from Spaniard and Black, Mulatto"), in which the black wife of the Spaniard tries to kill him in the kitchen by hammering a huge nail into his head. The social level of this Spaniard is already "inferior" to that of the noble: he may be a shopkeeper. In another series, precisely the same scene is depicted in a restaurant.[11] In the other paintings, the dress and the decor of the family scenes emphasize the homogeneity of professions along with types of mixed marriages within each level of the caste society: a shopkeeper with a mulatto, a merchant with a Morisco, and a high official with an albino.

The men in these first seven paintings are Spaniards; all the others down through the social and ethnic scales are of mixed blood: porter, tailor, vendor, shoemaker, confectioner, artisan, and weaver of baskets and tapestries. The Spaniards are generally depicted in refined environments, inside good houses with rugs, elegant furniture, and paintings hanging on the walls, or in their landscaped gardens or parks. The shopkeepers are portrayed with their goods—rugs, glasses, animals, vegetables, and fruits. The fruits of the land are copiously represented in the scenes of mixed-race people, whose professional occupations have been added to so that they include peasants, vendors at the marketplace, tobacco rollers, rowers, laundrypersons, water carriers, bakers, textile workers, ceramic and metalworkers or vendors, stable workers, owners of food stalls at the market, musicians, and comedians. The representations of Spaniards include painters, sailors, and army officers. The lower castas are depicted barefoot and with ragged clothes—in this case, more the men than the women. In some of the later series, black men are shown with good clothes, identical to those of the

Spaniards, underlining the blurring of frontiers between the races, since some of them have married Spanish women—a possibility not considered in the earlier series.[12]

It is obvious that the casta paintings represent an extreme case of overclassification of mixed-race people. The paintings were created and developed in a specific urban context, Mexico City, which was home to perhaps the most complex concentration of mixed-race people in all America, with its extensive mix of Indians, blacks, and Europeans. It is true that significant percentages of mixed-race people could be found in other Hispanic urban environments, but not in the same elaborate arrangement, with different sections even having their own institutions (guilds, markets, and confraternities) as in Mexico City. The question has always been, "How accurately do these paintings represent reality?" which is never the right question in art history. It is obvious that as a genre, the paintings developed the subject of racial mix in their own terms, by accumulating and exaggerating stereotypes. Yet most of the categories used, although they had no formal status, can be found in other documents. As usual, the genre developed its own criteria, but it was inspired by social reality. The question of the paintings' reality has been redirected to parallel issues: Who was interested in this type of multiethnic or multiracial representation? Who commissioned these works?

García Sáiz has put forward good arguments for the theory that senior Spanish administrators—viceroys, archbishops, bishops, jurists, and officers responsible for areas such as customs or the post—commissioned the paintings. All the patrons who have been identified, even though only forming 10 percent of the total, came from this tiny group of the Spanish elite nominated by the king. They generally returned to Spain with an interest in pointing out the complex ethnic reality they had been dealing with. The paintings were intended to address the metropolitan public of the royal court and social elites (aristocracy and senior officials) involved in the administration of Hispanic America. The opposite perspective (put forward by Miguel Ángel Fernández, Ilona Katzew, and Jorge Klor de Alva) has stressed the endogenous process of the creation of this genre, developed by local painters with local themes, who promoted a vision of a complex casta society degenerating and threatening chaos, but at the same time projecting a colonial identity and proud vision of the products of the land.[13] These two visions should not be seen as incompatible, since the artists could not have been given a strict set of instructions by patrons nor could have invented this system of representation from scratch.

An interesting element to note is that as far as I can see, not a single painting bears the word Creole, or Spanish descendant, which is what the vast majority of the colonial elite came to be called. It is true that increasing conflict opposed Creoles, as Spanish descendants born in America, to Spaniards born in Europe throughout the eighteenth century, particularly as a result of the promotion of the latter by the Bourbon reforms. Those who commissioned the paintings might have left their imprint here; it is debatable whether the Creoles would have liked this label, since they always emphasized their Spanish descent. The word Spaniard was more in tune with the logic of colonial social hierarchy. Briefly, casta painting cannot be considered a simple representation of an actual system of classification embedded in daily life but rather a reminder of, or a pointer toward, the internal frontiers that the Creole and Spanish elite wished to highlight, supported by groups of mixed-race people who wanted to distinguish themselves from as well as claim higher status than other groups. It offered a global form of hierarchical representation of colonial society shaped by the elite's vision.

The most recent debate on this topic raises an even more relevant question for my argument: What was the role of casta painting in natural history? Two decisive elements drew attention to this issue. First, in 1770, a series of casta paintings commissioned by the viceroy of Peru, D. Manuel Amat y Junyent (1761–77), was sent for inclusion in a planned Royal Cabinet of Natural History, a display only formally created in 1776. And in 1799, the painting the *Natural, Civil, and Geographic History of Peru*, now at the Museo de Ciencias Naturales in Madrid, assembled two maps, four images of sets of fish, sixty-four images of land animals, ninety-two birds (and plants), and thirty-two types of human beings—in this case, individuals identified by different physical features and clothing. These two representations of the classification of castas or human beings were literally placed within a natural history context. In 2004, the organizers of an exhibition of casta painting at the Museo Nacional de Antropologia in Madrid decided to reevaluate the links between casta painting and natural history since the start of the art form, thus looking at it from a different perspective—one also suggested by Katzew.[14] The result was quite striking, not for the Peruvian series, which included few decorative elements, but instead for the Mexican series, rich since its beginnings in the "fruits of the land"—in some instances with those products identified and listed

Figure 10.5. Louis Thiebaut, *Cuadro de historia natural, civil e geografica del Reyno de Perú*, painting, oil on canvas, 325 × 115 cm., 1799. Museo Nacional de Ciencias Naturales, Madrid.
Photo: Museo Nacional de Ciencias Naturales, Madrid

Figure 10.6. Luís de Mena, *Castas and Fruits of the Land in Mexico under the Patronage of the Virgin of Guadalupe*, painting, oil on canvas, 119 × 103 cm., c. 1750.
Reprinted with permission from AKG-images, Berlin; Erich Lessing

in writing on a scene, as if the classification of castas were part of the general classification of the "products of the land."[15] This original approach justified the title of the exhibition, Fruits and Castas.

If this hypothesis is correct, the observation of human beings as part of nature developed a precocious momentum in Hispanic America in the first decades of the eighteenth century, well ahead of the European Enlightenment's obsession with the systematic classification of all minerals, flora, and fauna, including human beings, triggered by Linnaeus (1707–78) in 1735 (see part IV).[16] Hispanic America functioned as a laboratory for the classification of human beings and their development through interracial pairing that was later expanded to a world scale. In this process, names were invented for mixed races, and ethnic groups were labeled in a hierarchical manner according to the convenient judgments of the social elite. The tension between scientific development and classificatory stereotypes was already visible in this period.

Nevertheless, there are two crucial issues that cannot be neglected when we compare castas with racial construction: the definition of castas is local, not universal; and it does not suppose an immutable transmission from generation to generation of features. The definition of castas does not pretend to establish a hierarchy of types of human beings beyond the frontiers of Mexico (and Peru). It concerns the specific interethnic mixing that emerged in these colonial societies, basically in Mexico, where this mixing reached greater complexity due to local conditions. In this respect, the definition of castas does not have any pretention to the universalism we will find informing the theories of races. The second issue is also telling: the definition of castas does not stipulate a rigid system; individuals could be declassified or could negotiate their way up the hierarchy, showing that castas were not locked into an inescapable notion of descent.[17] In sum, the casta system is an interesting case that draws attention to the early classification of inter-ethnic human types related to nature, but does not clearly prefigure or anticipate theories of race.

CLASSIFICATION IN AMERICA

The real extent of these interethnic constructions in colonial societies still has to be established, since the Spanish case in America, or rather Mexico, is a singular one. I need to address Portuguese, British, Dutch, and French racial constructs in different continents. Their proponents carried with them different experiences from Europe; they were confronted with specific contexts; and they reshaped their visions along the way. The noun Creole supplies a key to these different worlds. The word was coined in the sixteenth century in the Portuguese and Spanish empires. It belongs to the set of animal metaphors within racial taxonomy. In a Portuguese dictionary published in the first quarter of the eighteenth century, *crioulo* (Creole) is used to refer to a slave born in their owner's house, like a chicken born in a household, not bought outside.[18] The origin of the word is obvious, residing in the Latin *creare*—creare in Italian, *crear* in Spanish, *criar* in Portuguese, *créer* in French, and *to create* in English—which means, among other things, "to breed." The likening of the slave to a chicken is striking. But the development of the noun through the centuries has further interesting surprises. In Spanish America, for instance, *criollo* had at the beginning the same meaning as in Portuguese America, though it slowly started to be applied to Spaniards born in America to white parents. The original idea of breeding is maintained, but has traveled up the social hierarchy, from the slave to the Spaniard, designating white people born in colonial society.

Although the noun Creole was introduced into the English language in the seventeenth century, it was not really applied to white people or even to black slaves in British America, except in the context of the plantations of the Caribbean islands, where a significant amount of vocabulary was imported from the Spanish and French colonies. It was also used to designate the descendants of French settlers in North America, especially in Louisiana, where after the British took over the colony, they had to deal with a different language spoken by the white, slave, and native populations. This and other experiences explain the application of the noun Creole to the reinvention of European languages in a colonial context.

The linguistic notion of hybridism was related to social hybridism, since Creole was applied to native-born people of African or European ancestry, or native-born people of mixed European and black ancestry who spoke a Creole language.[19] In French, *créole* was a noun, likewise introduced in the seventeenth century. It designated a white person born on the Caribbean islands, as in the Spanish American context. But in the French colonies of the Indian Ocean, particularly in Mauritius, it designated "colored" people. The noun was used for the new languages created by slaves or native people as a result of contact with European languages, as in Senegal, where forms of Creole of Portuguese origin were identified, especially in Casamance.[20] The Creole languages were considered patois, or corrupted languages, though—a view that only changed in the second half of the twentieth century. The noun Creole evolved over time. In modern Brazil, *crioulo* designates, in practical terms, the popular masses with dark skin.[21] Mulattoes of the middle and upper classes are considered white, and understand themselves as white, although recent affirmative action in favor of black people has been changing this pattern.[22] This double racial and social classification of skin color and status can be traced back to the colonial period. In modern North America, by contrast, mulatto does not really exist from a taxonomic point of view: by the late eighteenth century, a person was classified as black in daily life, again with the exception of the Caribbean Islands, whereas mulattoes were labeled "colored."

I need to return to the Portuguese case, since it is the closest to the Spanish one in terms of complex forms of racial taxonomy. The key nouns *mestiço* and *mulato* are found, respectively, from the fourteenth and sixteenth centuries on, and were used in the empire to designate the offspring of white and Indian or white and black. The noun *pardo*, which can be found from the fourteenth century onward, was widely used in daily life. It was even added to personal names to designate a mulatto or person of dark skin, between white and black. Respected etymologies indicate Greek and Roman origins for the noun, but a Portuguese dictionary of the late eighteenth century related it to the bird *pardal* (sparrow), known for its dark feathers, yet also for its vivacity and smallness.[23] Moreno, used in Spain since the twelfth century and Portugal since the sixteenth century, had its origin in Moro or Mouro (Moor), meaning light dark skin, between white and pardo, though in some cases it could be used to designate a dark color, between pardo and black. It also indicated dark hair, between brown and black, or simply black, the equivalent of the French and English brunette. The word is commonly used nowadays in Brazil and Portugal.

The colonial environment stimulated a major development in ethnic or racial taxonomy: in Brazil the offspring of a white and an Indian parent was also labeled *mameluco* (Mameluke), a clear reference to the Egyptian military elite constituted by Caucasian Christian slaves converted to Islam. The reference to a betrayal of origins was obvious, since many mamelucos were active hunters of Indian slaves for the Portuguese. *Caboclo* originally meant Indian, but soon came to mean, in the Amazon basin and northeast of Brazil, either the descendant of a white and an Indian or an Indian who could speak the homogenized Língua Geral, or general language, a Jesuit standardization of the Tupi language. *Carijó* was an original designation for the Indian Guaranis who inhabited the regions of southern Brazil. In the Tupi language it designated, simultaneously, the descendant of a white man and a spotted bird with black and white feathers. In the eighteenth century in Minas Gerais, the noun was applied to the offspring of an Indian and a black. In the same region, the offspring of a white and an Indian was designated a *Curiboco*, meaning a *mestiço* with copper skin and straight black hair.[24]

The Portuguese (Brazilian born or residents) made wide use of native vocabulary, particularly in their internal conflicts. In 1708–9 in Minas Gerais, during the civil war between the people of São Paulo, who claimed exclusive rights to the gold in the area, and the foreigners from other parts of Brazil and Portugal, the foreigners were designated *emboabas*, a noun inspired by the Tupi word for band of aggressors. In 1710, during the civil war that broke out in the region of Pernambuco between the landlords of Olinda and merchants of Recife, the former were designated *mazombos*, a noun directly taken from the African Kimbundu language, meaning a taciturn, rustic, brute, or backward person, while the latter were labeled *mascates*, a reference to the Persian Gulf port designed to undermine the status of the merchants by suggesting they were peddlers. *Cafuso*, another designation for the offspring of a black and an Indian found in nineteenth-century Brazil, was probably inspired by the Kimbundu *kufunzaka*, meaning to discolor, which reveals the African view of the process of racial mixing.[25]

The constant use of Native American and African languages for racial taxonomy is one of the main characteristics of the Portuguese system, more developed than the Spanish one from this point of view, but even less stable in its meanings. According to some recent studies, racial nomenclature in Brazil could designate more than 150 categories by the end of the colonial period, but the problem is to locate these in precise spatial and historical contexts, understanding their evolution or disappearance. There was nothing similar to the Mexican casta painting in the Portuguese colonies, yet it is difficult to say whether this was due to dissimilar interethnic environments or the generally acknowledged Portuguese deficit in visual culture when it came to secular or civil themes. It took the Dutch occupation of most of northeast Brazil, from 1630 to 1654, to see the first lavish depictions of Indians, blacks, and mixed-race people by distinguished northern European painters such as Frans Post, Albert Eckhout, and Zacharias Wagener, invited by Count Johan Maurits van Nassau-Siegen, governor-general of Dutch Brazil from January 1637 to May 1644. The typology we see in their series of paintings, however, is simple compared to the Mexican one.

Eckhout was the artist who created a more complete series of human types, based on couples, but with each partner depicted separately: Indian savages (Tapuya), integrated Indians (Tupi), black Africans, and mixed-race people of European and Indian origin (Mamelukes). The hierarchy was established by the background scenes of nature, the gestures, and the subjects' appearance. The Tapuyas were portrayed in the forest, almost naked and certainly without any European clothes. The male is represented among wild animals, such as the boa snake or bird spider, wearing traditional Indian weapons—the club, darts, and throwing board. The penis is visible, decorated with a string of plant material, contrasting with the headdress of parrot feathers and adornment of rhea feathers at the back. He has two white bones inserted into the cheeks, and a blue-green stone or piece of resin inserted under the lower lip. The female holds a severed hand and carries a basket of plant fibers containing a severed foot—clear signs of cannibalism. She has a rope belt with green leaves covering her sex and wears, as does the male, sandals of plant fibers. Between her feet a domesticated dog is represented, brought by the Portuguese, and thus perhaps a sign of transition. The naked relatives of the tribe are seen in the background, significantly between her legs, while the natural scene around her abounds in native trees, plants, and fruits.

Figure 10.7. (*Left*) Albert Eckhout, Tapuya woman holding a severed hand and carrying a basket containing a severed foot, painting, oil on canvas, 272 × 165 cm., c. 1641. Ethnographic Collection, National Museum of Denmark, Copenhagen, inv. nr. N38A2
© National Museum of Denmark
Figure 10.8. (*Right*) Albert Eckhout, Brazilian Tupi woman holding a child with a basket on her head, painting, oil on canvas, 274 × 163 cm., 1641. Ethnographic Collection, National Museum of Denmark, Copenhagen, inv. N38A4
© National Museum of Denmark

By contrast, the female Tupi wears a skirt of European cloth, which immediately distinguishes her. The rest of the body is naked, but a striped headband holding back her hair is as distinctive feature. She holds a child with her right arm and a basket with the left one, carrying native gourds, boxes, and a hammock. The child is wearing a similar striped headband. The background illustrates a European farm with orderly rows of trees, cows, and laborers working the fields. Next to her are an imported banana tree and native animals. The male wears breeches of European cloth, carries a European knife, and holds a native bow and arrows, signaling his intermediate position. In the background, we see a European sailboat and Tupis washing European clothes. Again, products of the natural world familiar to the Tupis are depicted next to integrated Indian.

The black couple portrayed by Eckhout is more intriguing. The female is represented with an African straw basket of fruits, among them a papaya from Brazil. She also wears what was probably a Javanese hat with peacock feathers. The skirt and elegant belt of dyed-red cotton around her waist are already a mixture of European and African clothes and forms. A pipe is stuck into the belt, suggesting a female African habit that was shown in the imagery of Dutch cartography of the seventeenth century, and was still being depicted in the photos and postcards of the late nineteenth century, particularly in Cape Verde. The female's ornaments are remarkable: a collar of coral, double pearl collar, pearl earrings, and bracelets. The son, curiously of a lighter skin color than his mother, displays a head of maize in one hand and a red-faced lovebird native to Central and West Africa in the other. They are surrounded by native trees and fruits. In the background there is an image of a port and farway ships at the sea, referring to the passage from Africa. The male is represented with an African Akan (from what is now Ghana) ceremonial sword in a sheath of stingray skin, a belt of African cloth, assegai (in Portuguese, *azagaia*), and a slender, iron-tipped spear of hardwood of the kind used by southern African tribes. He is surrounded by the tusk of an African elephant, dates, a palm tree, and shells from the South Atlantic, underlining his origins but also introducing an exotic note, since the shells were used both as money and for divination.

The mixed-race couple of Mamelukes, the last creation by Eckhout in this series of colonial couples, is illustrated with some splendor. The male is barefoot, with slightly curly

Figure 10.9. Albert Eckhout, Brazilian mestizo with rifle and sword (Mameluke), painting, oil on canvas, 274 × 170 cm., 1641. Ethnographic Collection, National Museum of Denmark, Copenhagen, inv. N38A5 © National Museum of Denmark

hair, which means that he has some African blood besides white and Indian. He could not be better dressed, with a shirt and skirt of white European cloth as well as a sleeveless leather coat. On his left side, a sophisticated rapier is held in a baldric of jaguar skin, while on the right side one can see the handle of a dagger. His left hand holds a musket. It is an arrangement that would have been entirely suitable for the militia commander, plantation supervisor, or slave hunter who had reached an important position in colonial society. Significantly, his surroundings include the sugarcane introduced by the Portuguese along with native trees and fruits. In the background, there is an impressive beach and European ships on the sea. The female is also barefoot, but wears an elegant, long Asian dress of white cotton, an attractive European collar with jewels, bracelets, and a headband with flowers. She has the same type of hair as the male, which suggests a similar mixed origin. She holds a basket of bamboo with flowers in it, and is surrounded by trees, fruits, and animals (native or imported by the Portuguese). The scene is set in an agricultural environment, with farms in the background.[26]

Art historian Peter Mason has already pointed out that these images are composites; they result from a "marvellous montage" or staging in the context of exotic visual formations.[27] Northern painters such as Eckhout embroidered racial or ethnic "reality," enhancing the richness and fantasy of the portrait with pieces from their own collection, or from the cabinets of curiosities of their patrons. This is the key to understanding the puzzling heterogeneous origins of many elements in the paintings; they cannot be read as "ethnic documents," since they were composed by the artist. This is clearly the case with the African couple, but also with the Mameluke pair, especially with the sophisticated guns that the male is portrayed with. But there is something else that is important for my argument: fifty years before the creation of the casta painting in Mexico, these painters in Dutch Brazil already portrayed racial types in a natural environment, in the middle of plants, trees, and animals, as one more significant product of the land.

CLASSIFICATION IN AFRICA AND ASIA

Iberian America, this amazing laboratory of the colonial interethnic mix, racial taxonomy, and images of human types, needs to be set in a wider context. Prejudices embedded in forms of classification were transferred from one continent to another. Native Americans, for instance, were constantly referred as *negros da terra* (blacks from the land), meaning that they shared with Africans their savagery and backwardness. In Portuguese Asia, this transfer occurred in an entirely official way: the lists of people on the payroll of the king included an estimated list of the inhabitants of each fort, divided into two major groups of "white" and "black" married people, meaning converted Asians who had some element of Portuguese descent (basically mestiços) and converted Asians without European blood. The same prejudice based on skin color was thus transferred from Africa to America and from America to Asia; native people, even when converted and integrated into colonial society, never ceased to be considered blacks (or barbarians). The subtlety of this classification is that mestiços of European descent were considered as whites in Asia, due to the particular configuration of the Portuguese empire in the region, which was very much dependent on local human resources.[28]

In East Africa, the ethnic diversity of what is now Mozambique resulted from frequent African migrations, but also from the presence of Muslims and Indians (in many cases Indian Muslims, particularly from Gujarat), who were already in the region before the Portuguese arrival. These Muslim and Indian ethnicities, who were concentrated in commerce, were abusively called *monhé* (from Macua *m'monhe*), Muslim, and *caneco*, offspring of an Indian and a European, meaning among other things a devil—a noun that is found in the nineteenth century yet probably had older origins. In Angola, since the eighteenth century, the specific situation in Luanda had been expressed in a simple casta system based on skin color: white, mulatto, and black, complicated by two more categories, *Cabrito* (offspring of a white and a mulatto with light dark skin) and *Cafuso* (offspring of a mulatto and a black).[29] Cabrito is another example of an animal metaphor, since it means young goat. We saw above the later adaptation of Cafuso in Brazil, where it was used to indicate the offspring of an Indian and a black.

In Dutch trading posts in the Gulf of Guinea, the taxonomy was not very different from the one used in Angola; we have to keep in mind that the Dutch, who occupied Elmina in 1637 and Luanda for a short period (1641–48), adapted to the previous Portuguese practices in the field. Negro was translated as *swert*, Moor, or *donker* (dark), while moreno or *baço* was translated as *bruin* and *olijff coleur*, and mulattoes as *mulacken*. Moor in Dutch probably shifted its semantic content from black African to Muslim, even being applied in the East Indies by the end of the seventeenth century, but it later returned to its original meaning.[30]

In the British colonial world, the basic ethnic and racial taxonomies were also imported early on from the Spanish and Portuguese vocabulary—namely, black, negro, Moor, black Moor, mestizo, mulatto, or sambo (offspring of an Indian and a black, from the Spanish and Portuguese *zambo*). But there was autonomous development of verbal abuse. For instance, the proverb "God made the white man, the devil made the mulatto" was widely disseminated in the eighteenth century, confirming the low esteem in which mixed-race people were held in the Anglo-Saxon world.[31] There are also striking sayings and proverbs concerning black people, or playing on the contrast between black and white, such as "black as the devil," which is to be found from the fourteenth century onward, or "every white has its black, and every sweet its sour," which has been quoted since the eighteenth century.[32] This analysis leads to the symbolism of colors, which had a relatively autonomous dynamic: black was always linked to cultural and religious contexts, traditionally death, and in the case of Christianity, the representations of sinful and devilish creatures.[33] In conclusion, European colonialism in Africa and Asia did not produce such a wide variety of interethnic and racial taxonomy as in America, because of its more limited impact. Yet it reflected local interethnic competition, projected local designations, and adapted the vocabulary received from other sources.

CRITERIA AND PURPOSES OF CLASSIFICATION

The last issue to tackle is the relation between skin color (real or imaginary), phenotype features, and mental and behavioral attributes in the idea of descent. This is crucial if we are to understand the ambiguities of the process of ethnic definition and racialization. Historian Jack B. Forbes has pointed out the absence of the concept of race in the premodern world and consequent absence of the concept of racial mix. In his view, racial differences were not as important as national or religious differences, as expressed by the terminology used for Saracens, Jews, Christians, mozárabes, Mudéjares, and so on. I contest this vision, which is based on the assumption that race is strictly physical. As we saw in the introduction, the noun race has been in circulation since the Middle Ages, and has meant first lineage and then subdivisions of humankind. It was applied in Iberia to Muslims, Jews, and black people to mean stained descent. It was not strictly based on phenotype features; Muslims and Jews could be identified as Christians if they wore the same dress. In the case of conversos and Moriscos, as people who were discriminated against and segregated after forced conversion, the intermingling of race, religion, and politics is even more visible. In those times, a former religion was a major marker for defining attributes and behaviors that were supposed to be transmitted from generation to generation, showing a departure from the Christian tradition of equality between believers. It meant that the memory of previous religious allegiance was used by political and social interests to create a line of divide within the Christian community. This division was based on the idea of descent. Genealogy was crucial, but genealogy is the construction of lineage, which means that culture itself is trapped in representations of nature (in this case, through sexual reproduction), basically engaged in the arrangement and rearrangement of ancestry. This makes it a good case study for the interconnection between nature and culture.[34]

With the European expansion, phenotype features became a major aspect of the definition of different types of humankind. Along with phenotype features came a stereotyped description of attitudes and behaviors that would be absorbed by the theories of races (see part IV). The other peoples of the world were placed in a hierarchy according to the main European criteria of policed or civilized behavior. These criteria were expressed through the idiom of skin color, due to the opposition of white to black, reinforced by the colonial experience. The wide variety of color designation—for instance, in the Iberian world—did not imply an absence of the notion of race but rather exactly the opposite: it reflected an intermingling of physical and mental features. The difficulty of matching skin tones with precise professions and occupations was part of the intense interethnic engineering produced by the colonial period in Iberian America.

The solution found in the late eighteenth and nineteenth centuries in the United States of reducing interethnic variety to two races, whites and blacks, was political, confirming the relationship between classification and social conflict. The downgrading of all mixed-race people, classified as black or Indian, reinforced the notion of pure white blood. This process of racialization was simple, visible, and efficient from the point of view of the interests of white people in southern slave societies. In Iberian America, a complicated classification did not mean that the process of racialization was nonexistent; it only meant that the inter-ethnic structure was much more complex, due to the integration of Native Americans as vassals and the relatively centralized political model, which forced the conversion of slaves and transformed all Christians into vassals.

||||||||||||||||||||||||||||||||||||||||||||||||||||||||||||||||||||||||||||||||||||||||||||||||||||||||||||

CHAPTER 11

Ethnic Structure

A colonial society generally means a new community created in overseas territory by European migrants. The Greek model was the result of overpopulation in a particular area, which would trigger the search for an ideal site that could provide a community with water, land, and a harbor. It supposed an agricultural community supported by an urban environment, but there were older examples of trading colonies in Egypt or on the Black Sea.[1] The latter model was reproduced by the Romans. The political and military conditions of an empire that stretched from the Atlantic to the Middle East stimulated new forms and functions of towns, in some cases founded on the site of military camps established in strategic positions. The barbarian invasions renewed the concept of colonization, as a result of the transfer of populations and reorganization of ethnic identities in rural and urban environments. In the Middle Ages, the Genoese and Venetian expansion in the Mediterranean was based on trading colonies, although the conquest and control of land showed traces of the ancient model. Portuguese and Spanish expansion allegedly followed different paths at the beginning, with trading colonies established by the former and colonies of occupation by the latter, but this was only because they were dealing with different realities overseas, and their colonial practices converged in America. They shared the same strategy of establishing forts and maritime control of the coast in North Africa, followed by Portuguese trading colonies or enclaves in West and Central Africa, Spanish settlements in America favored by the urban network of the Nahuas and Incas, and Portuguese control of key ports in Asia and agricultural colonies in Brazil. The Dutch and British created trading colonies in Asia, but they established agricultural communities in South Africa and America. It is obvious that local conditions played a major role in shaping different types of colonies, particularly the military type developed by the Portuguese in Asia to impose and protect privileged maritime trade.

Until the mid-eighteenth century, European expansion only created real colonial societies in America, with the exception of the Atlantic islands—the Canaries, Madeira, the Azores, and Cape Verde—the Cuanza River, the Zambezi valley, the Cape in South Africa, and part of the Philippines in Asia, to which one could add, to a certain extent, parts of Sri Lanka, Java, and a stretch of the northwest coast of India. Colonial rule, as it was imposed in India after the British conquest in the second half of the eighteenth century, did not necessarily mean the creation of a colonial society. This would have required not only political dominion but also a significant transfer of population and some sort of European social control of the new communities.

What I want to address here is the differentiated European migration into distinct continents from the sixteenth to the eighteenth century, the geographic distribution of African slaves massively transported to the New World, the impact of epidemics, war, and transfers of population in causing the dramatic demographic decline of Native Americans, and the contrast between new colonial societies in America and the resilient local societies and civilizations in Africa and Asia. The purpose is to understand the different ethnic and social conditions in which new ethnic prejudices as well as discriminatory action were developed. In some cases, Europeans built up new colonial societies from scratch; in others they created a new social and ethnic organization absorbing local structures. Sometimes the latter developed into hybrid societies that managed to create a certain degree of cultural variety.[2] Europeans involved local elites and, in certain circumstances, in Asia organized a system of indirect rule, while in Africa they accepted a relatively subordinate position until the nineteenth century. It is this diversity that will be studied in this chapter, since different models of discrimination and segregation were shaped by distinct forms of social and ethnic interaction.

EUROPEAN EMIGRATION

Spanish emigration to the New World probably involved 300,000 people up to the end of the sixteenth century, 400,000 in the seventeenth century, and 500,000 in the eighteenth century—that is, 1.2 million people in the early modern period.[3] The destination of these people from 1493 to 1600 is known in about 50,000 cases (mostly concerning people from Andalusia and Castile): 34.3 percent went to Mexico and Yucatán, 23.9 percent to Peru, 10.6 percent to the Caribbean islands, 9.8 percent to New Granada (Colombia, Venezuela, and Equador), 6.8 percent to Tierra Firme (Panama), 5.1 percent to Rio de la Plata, 4 percent to Central America, 3.6 percent to Chile, and 1.9 percent to Florida.[4] Two major changes occurred in the eighteenth century: the number of Catalans and Basques among the Spanish migrants dramatically increased, and their flow was redirected to Rio de la Plata, Chile, Venezuela, and Cuba, instead of Mexico and Peru.[5] The ratio of men to women, which had been extremely unequal in the first decades of emigration (18–15 to 1), moved toward greater equality during the second half of the sixteenth century (4 to 1). It is probable that the ratio became slightly more equal with the stabilization of European settlement and development of urban networks (the main feature of Spanish expansion). The short two-month trip from Spain to America and the low mortality rate gradually encouraged family migration. The Philippines were colonized from Mexico, involving a reemigration of the Spanish and Creole population. In Africa, emigration to the Spanish forts on the

Mediterranean coast was relatively insignificant, while the colonies in Equatorial Guinea and Western Sahara were established much later, and without a significant flow of migrants. Other cases of European migration to tropical regions resulted in a poor survival rate. Yet the capacity for reproduction of the white population in Spanish America was surprisingly high: 3 million white people have been estimated for 1760.

The Portuguese migrated in even greater numbers—probably 50,000 from 1415 to 1500, 280,000 from 1501 to 1580, 360,000 from 1581 to 1640, 150,000 from 1641 to 1700, 600,000 from 1701 to 1760, and 120,000 from 1761 to 1800, for a total over 1.5 million from a population five to six times smaller than the Spanish one.[6] The destinations were more diverse and changed more over time than in the Spanish world: in the fifteenth century, Madeira and the Azores attracted the vast majority of migrants, followed by the forts of North Africa; in the sixteenth century, the majority went to India, even though the mortality on board during the six-month trip was probably worse than in the Middle Passage. The success of sugar cultivation in Brazil and the second significant crisis in maritime trade from India directed the flow of migrants to South America from the last quarter of the sixteenth century onward. In the seventeenth century Brazil was the favorite destination, encouraged by the much lower mortality rate for a trip of two to three months. The discovery of gold and precious stones in Brazil explains the boom in emigration throughout the eighteenth century. Over time, the ratio of men to women was even more unbalanced than the Spanish one, and for the first two centuries the white population was concentrated more in rural than in urban areas, in contrast to Spanish America. Also, the relationship between migration and the development of a settled local population was much weaker than in Spanish America: in 1760, the white population in Brazil numbered around 390,000. This white population represented less than 30 percent of the total colonial population; white migration with a much higher men-to-women ratio than the Spanish one had created a large mulatto population.

The Portuguese were the only Europeans who maintained a long-standing presence in Africa, mainly in the regions of the Cuanza River (Angola), Zambezi valley (Mozambique), Cape Verde islands, and rivers of Guinea and São Tomé, but due to disease there was never a significant flow of migrants. In more than one way, Africa was the reverse of America: resilient political systems were in place, while the mortality rate of the Europeans in certain areas could reach more than 40 percent (even 90 percent) in one year. Only the spread of the use of quinine in the second half of the nineteenth century, revolution in artillery, and development of repeating guns opened the way to large projects of conquest in Africa.[7] The total Portuguese population in sub-Saharan Africa after three centuries of colonization (1760) reached a mere 2,500.[8] Portuguese migration to Asia was extremely significant in the sixteenth century, reaching 2,000 people annually, but the flow dramatically declined throughout the seventeen century and never recovered during the eighteenth, because of Anglo-Dutch competition. The peak period for the Portuguese presence in Asia was probably the first two decades of the seventeenth century, but the average figure for the best decades must have been around 10,000 people, due to high mortality and a regular flow of returning emigrants. By 1760, the Portuguese numbered around 3,000, most of them in the military forces.[9] The wastage of European emigrants in tropical areas is well documented here.[10]

British migration to America started a century after the Spanish and Portuguese migrations. In the seventeenth century, it involved mainly English emigrants, but Scots and Irish also went. These proportions changed dramatically in the eighteenth century, with a predominance of Irish, Scots, and Germans moving to British America. The European migration to America during the seventeenth century has been estimated at 355,000, with nearly half to the mainland and half to the Caribbean islands. In the eighteenth century, 686,000 people migrated, the vast majority (84 percent) to the mainland. Over 1 million European migrated to British America during these two centuries. Most of these people were young, male, indentured servants, redemptioners, and convicts. The male-to-female ratio was unbalanced: among the British indentured servants it rose from 3 to 1 in the second half of the seventeenth century to 9 to 1 in the first half of the eighteenth century. Indentured servants were mainly directed to Chesapeake, following the boom in tobacco cultivation, while the colonizers of New England were typically British families with a much more balanced gender ratio that arrived in smaller numbers.[11] The European population in British America grew enormously throughout the eighteenth century from over 400,000 in 1700 to 1.5 million in 1750 and 2.7 million in 1770 (83 percent lived on the mainland).[12]

The migration to Asia under temporary contracts with the chartered East India Company (EIC), created in 1600, had totally different objectives, and the main emigrants were sailors, soldiers, officers, clerks, and trade agents expecting to return to Britain. Far fewer people sought work in India than in America; one-third returned, while the majority died in India. The number of migrants under contract must have been much smaller than in the case of the Dutch empire in Asia, because the EIC did not have a comparable number of trading posts, and before 1757 it did not engaged in territorial conquest. After this date the situation changed dramatically. The disproportion between the number of migrants and the settled population was striking: in 1780 there were only 3,000–4,000 British and associated Eurasians in the port cities. The number of ships and permanent employees on the ground (mainly the number of soldiers) increased significantly with the conquest of India, triggered by the occupation of Calcutta in 1757. The number of Europeans in the EIC armies grew from 5,000 in 1760 to 20,000 in 1800.[13]

The Dutch expansion was based on chartered trading companies. The employees had contracts that could be renewed, and some of them prolonged their service in Asia for decades, but the expectation was that they would return to Europe. The Verenigde Oostindische Compagnie (VOC), created in 1602, had 40 ships and 500 employees in Asia in 1608, with an average of 12 ships sent annually from Europe. In 1688 it reached a peak of about 7,500 soldiers, 2,400 sailors, and craftspersons, and 700 clerks and trading agents in the Asian territories under direct VOC control, not to mention hundreds of trading post employees outside VOC-controlled areas. In 1720, the number of ships sailing to Asia reached 24 per year, involving about 6,000 employees, while Asian interregional commerce involved 80 ships and 4,000 employees.[14] In total this amounts to 16,000 permanent VOC employees in Asia, if we exclude those working on the ships going backward and forward from Europe. Yet a significant number of soldiers and sailors were not European—a tendency that increased throughout the eighteenth century. During the whole period before 1800, around 1 million Europeans left for Asia under the VOC, although many would have been existing employees renewing their contracts. One-third returned, mostly sailors, since soldiers suffered a much higher mortality rate. The VOC did not encourage settlement and tried to avoid the presence of free burghers after the end of their contracts. The only exception was the Cape Province in South Africa, in which there were 16,000 colonists by the end of the eighteenth century. In Batavia, the center of the Dutch colonial enterprise, there were only 2,031 inhabitants of European origin in 1811, of which only 552 were born in Europe. Dutch migration to Asia was largely circular, but as we will see, there was more mixing with local populations than we might expect.

A similar commercial structure can be found in the Atlantic operations of the West-Indische Compagnie (WIC), created in 1621, although the Dutch tried to encourage migration to northeast Brazil, occupied between 1630 and 1654, in order to quell the resistance of a Portuguese population that had developed roots there. The results were meager, and the Portuguese ultimately defeated the Dutch, but the number of WIC employees reached 10,000 in 1639, and the free burghers numbered 3,000 in 1645. The same efforts occurred in Surinam, Guyana, and New Netherland in North America as well as on the Caribbean islands (mainly Curaçao) with varying results: New Netherland was clearly the most successful case of migration, with 9,000 white people in 1664, before the British conquered the area, but Curaçao, with 2,781 colonists at the beginning of the nineteenth century, was the most profitable colony, the hub of the Dutch trade in the region. The total Dutch migration to the Atlantic colonies up to 1800 has been calculated at 25,000.[15] But the quantity of people involved in the Dutch operations in the area was much higher. Recent research on employees under Dutch flags sent to western Africa by private companies and then by the WIC between 1599 and 1673 showed a solid estimate of 33,000.[16] During one period, 1623–36, the WIC recruited a high of 67,000 people for all its operations.[17] These data are consistent with the commercial needs for the transport of commodities and military effort required to protect the transport and undertake corsair activities; besides major actions, such as the capture of the Spanish silver fleet in 1628, valued at 11.5 million guilders, the WIC captured 547 Portuguese cargo ships between 1623 and 1638, and 249 more ships in the year 1647–48.[18] If we project these data, we arrive at least at 300,000 people recruited by Dutch operations in the Atlantic only in the seventeenth century, counting periods of crisis and decline. The vast majority, however, did not settle.

The French did not provide a significant flow of overseas migrants before the nineteenth century. That is why their several attempts to create colonies in Brazil (France Antarctique and France Equinoxiale) and Florida failed. In India, military efforts to halt the expansion of the British in the second half of the eighteenth century were not successful, partly for the same reasons, although the resources employed (ships and soldiers) reached an unprecedented level. The same thing happened in America during the Seven Years' War (1756–63) and the period in which the French assisted the Americans in their War of Independence, but the military effort was never matched by significant migration. It is difficult to assess the real impact of these troops on the ground. It is likely to have been relatively important in India, since the French intervened in local feuds, and less so in America, although the ring of French forts in the interior of the continent, particularly in the Great Lakes region, may have had some influence. The French did manage to root themselves in the seventeenth and eighteenth centuries in the area they called New France (Acadia, Quebec, and the Great Lakes) as well as in Louisiana, the Antilles, Guyana, and the Mascarene Islands of the Indian Ocean (Mauritius and Reunion). Estimates of French migration to the Americas between 1500 and 1800 vary, but they may have approached 100,000 if we include soldiers.[19] A comparison of the European population of New France and that of the thirteen British colonies of mainland America is revealing: there was a ratio of 1:23 or 18,500 to 430,000 inhabitants in 1715, and a ratio of 1:30 or 48,000 to 1,420,000 in 1744.[20]

These data clearly reveal the major destination of European migrants between 1500 and 1800: the New World attracted more than 3.5 million people. Given their greater access to capital and human resources, the Dutch and British increased the scant European presence in Asia during the Portuguese expansion, yet these people were essentially soldiers and sailors, with the trading agents and administrators being a small percentage of the total. The northern Europeans in Asia were not settlers, and few engaged in private trade, unlike the Portuguese and Spaniards, before 1800. The striking disproportion between the apparent resources and results—the European conquest of India and Southeast Asia—has already been pointed out; the systematic use of local resources is the key to this enigma, and I will return to this issue, since it had an impact on ethnic relations.[21] The Asian paradox only highlights the role of the New World in the absorption of European surplus population and, in the long run, creation of a market that fueled European growth.[22] But what matters for my argument is that the massive European migration to the Americas eradicated most of the native population, through war, enslavement, forced labor, forced military service, forced transfer of people, and epidemics of lethal European diseases, such as smallpox, against which the Indians did not have immunity.

NATIVE AMERICANS AND AFRICAN SLAVES

Estimates of the Native American population before the European arrival are fiercely disputed, but the most widely accepted numbers lie between 50 and 60 million people. The native population of the Caribbean islands, Mexico, and Peru suffered an immediate decline, but all America was directly or indirectly affected, depending on the degree of isolation of communities. By the mid-seventeenth century, the number of Native Americans is likely to have fallen to 5 or 6 million, or about 10 percent of the original total.[23] In 1492, the majority of the Native American population would have lived in Mexico (32 percent of the total) and the Andes (about 30 percent), judging by the intensive forms of agricultural production and urban networks that supported, for example, the capital of the Nahua confederation, Tenochtitlán, which probably had 200,000 inhabitants and was bigger than any European city of the time. The European impact was strongest on the Caribbean islands, where 3 million Native Americans disappeared in two generations. Nomadic or seminomadic peoples were clearly more vulnerable to epidemics in South and North America, yet even in the areas of intensive agriculture the European impact was devastating: in central Mexico the population decreased from 16.9 to 1.1 million, and in central Andes it went from 12.1 to 1.5 million in less than a century, with the people living in the lowlands being much more affected than those in the highlands.

The result of the dramatic decline of Native Americans was either to facilitate relatively homogeneous European settlements, as in mainland North America, or encourage the import of African slaves to areas where the plantation system had been introduced, mainly in Iberian America and the southern British colonies as well as on the Caribbean islands. Many Native Americans, though, were integrated into Iberian colonial society through mixed unions. The demographic recovery of Indian communities in Spanish America started between the 1590s and 1620s, mainly in Ecuador, Peru, and Mexico, but it is not possible to talk about a general movement, due to the different conditions at the regional and local levels. In any case, these areas, which had previously seen concentrations of the native population, particularly Mexico and Peru, proved to be more resilient, and demographic recovery (though never capable of restoring previous population levels) meant the maintenance of a significant population of Native Americans descended exclusively from pre-Colombian ancestors.

The slave trade also had an enormous impact on the New World. From the 1440s onward a first wave developed, from the west coast of Africa to Iberia, operated by Portuguese navigators. This commerce, which replaced the previous one in slaves from the Black Sea and east Europe, helped to prolong slavery in southern Europe (mainly the south of Portugal, Andalusia, and Valencia, but also southern Italy) in contrast to northern Europe. Recent research has pointed out that the total number of African slaves sold in Iberia might have been 250,000 to 300,000 people between 1440 and 1600.[24] The flow declined after this date, but did not stop until the second half of the eighteenth century. The successful transfer of sugar plantations from southern Spain and the Algarve to Madeira, the Canary Islands, and São Tomé, followed by Brazil and the Caribbean islands, created a new market for the African slave traders in the Americas.[25] The prohibition on enslavement of Native Americans enforced by the Spanish and then the Portuguese Crown throughout the sixteenth century responded to the previous absence of the institution in the New World along with the devastation naturally provoked by several decades of brutal colonial experience. The institution of slavery in Africa and traditional trade from equatorial Africa to North Africa and the Middle East, partly redirected by the Portuguese navigators to Iberia, offered an alternative source of forced labor. Expertise in the maritime trade of African slaves had already been established through a network of ports, agents, ships, and crews that could be redirected to the New World. The transatlantic slave trade quickly became more important than the trade to Iberia, reaching 152,373 people in 1576–1600 and 352,843 in 1601–25. The figures increased dramatically throughout the eighteenth century, from over 1 million slaves per quarter to more than 2 million in 1776–1800. Even during the period of the abolition of the slave trade, from 1807 in Great Britain to 1850 in Brazil, the numbers remained extremely high, with deliveries of more than 3.5 million slaves.[26]

The transatlantic slave trade involved a total of over 12.5 million Africans, mainly taken on board in west-central Africa (45 percent) and the Gulf of Guinea (42 percent), but also in Senegambia and Sierra Leone (9 percent) and southeast Africa (4 percent). The Portuguese were responsible for the transport of over 5.8 million slaves (47 percent of the total), followed by the British with over 3.2 million (26 percent), the French with over 1.3 million (11 percent), and the Spaniards, who transported around 1 million (8 percent). The Dutch, North Americans, and Danish had smaller stakes in this infamous trade.[27] The wastage of slaves imported to the Americas started as a result of the bad conditions on the voyage: only 10,702,656 arrived alive, for a loss of 15 percent. Over 5 million, nearly half the total, were disembarked in Brazil, while British America received over 2.7 million (26 percent), the French colonies over 1.1 million (11 percent), and Spanish America less than 900,000 (8 percent), followed by the Dutch and Danish colonies. But this division by colonial powers is misleading, since the second main destination of the slave trade after Brazil was the Caribbean islands, which absorbed more than 4 million slaves.[28] These data also require some qualification: a small proportion of the slaves sent to Brazil ended up in Spanish America as contraband.[29] Some of the ships that sailed under the Spanish flag, mainly in the period of the union of the Iberian crowns (1580–1640), were owned or operated by the Portuguese.

The slave trade to Brazil was always extremely high volume: the high mortality rate under the rough conditions of sugar plantation work did not allow natural reproduction; slaves had to be imported in huge numbers to maintain the strength of the labor force.[30] The conditions of labor in the British, Dutch, and French Caribbean islands were similar, but the boom in sugar began later, inspired by the success of the plantations started by the British in Barbados and Jamaica from the 1660s onward. The British Caribbean was still the hub of the British Empire when the American Revolution broke out. Nevertheless, the import of slaves had increased on the mainland, stimulated by the spread of rice cultivation in South Carolina and Georgia, though also by the eventual replacement of indentured labor by slaves on the Chesapeake tobacco plantations. The result was that on the eve of the American Revolution, there were more slaves on the mainland than on the British Caribbean islands—a trend accounted for by the much higher reproduction of slaves on the mainland, not by the trade.[31] The French imported slaves to Louisiana, but the main destination was the Caribbean islands, mainly Saint Domingue (the future Haiti), the major world producer of sugar in the eighteenth century. In this case, the combination of an extraordinarily unbalanced ratio of owners to slaves (even in the context of the Caribbean) and high pressure on the slaves provoked, first, the highest rate of maroons (runaway slaves) in America, and next, the revolt of 1791, which totally destroyed the colonial system. The Spaniards brought Africans to the depopulated regions: first to the Caribbean islands, and then to what are now Venezuela, Ecuador, Peru, and Mexico. But the increase in the slave trade occurred only with the later boom in sugar plantations on the Spanish Caribbean islands, from the beginning of the nineteenth century onward, thereby accounting for the extremely high figures from 1801 to 1866.

COLONIAL SOCIETIES IN AMERICA

All these movements of migration, depopulation, and forced transport of slaves to the New World created colonial societies—in some cases from scratch, and in other cases integrating old structures into a totally new framework dominated by Europeans. America presents a unique example that was replicated only partially in a few specific regions of other continents, mainly in South Africa, and up to a certain point in the Philippines, but without the same capacity for sowing the seeds of new multiethnic configurations that would endure for centuries to come. These configurations evolved enormously over time, as the brutal ethnic discrimination and segregation of the colonial period was developed even further in the second half of the nineteenth and first half of the twentieth centuries, mostly in the southern United States. But the processes of independence, civil war, and much later, racial democratization challenged the old values established by the slave system. What were the ethnic structures of different regions and their impact on social perceptions?

Despite the high mortality of African slaves in Brazil, the enormous numbers involved had a natural impact on the structure of the colonial society. In 1590, a total of over 100,000 people were divided into 30,000 Portuguese, 28,000 Indians, and 42,000 Africans, with the captaincies of Pernambuco and Bahia, in which sugar cultivation was already important, containing a concentration of Africans, but also a significant presence of Indians, many of them enslaved in the first decades of colonization.[32] At the beginning of the eighteenth century, the composition of the colonial society may have stabilized at around 25 percent white, 30 percent mixed race, and 45 percent black in a total population of 300,000 people. The estimates for this period do not include a separate category for Native Americans, some of who had been integrated into the category of mixed-race people or absorbed for several generations into the category of white people. A significant number of Native Americans were still living in autonomous communities, not only on the colonial peripheries, but also inside the colonial area of influence—for instance, in the village missions (*aldeamentos*) controlled mainly by the Jesuits until the secularization imposed by the government of Pombal in 1757.[33] In the second half of the sixteenth century alone, Jesuits created twelve villages around Salvador (then the capital of the state of Brazil), in which about 40,000 Indians lived.[34] By the early nineteenth century, when the total population had increased to 3,000,000, the proportion of white people has been estimated at around 28 percent, free mulattoes and blacks at 28 percent, slaves (mainly black) at 38 percent, and Indians at 6 percent.[35] The Amazon basin and southern captaincy of Rio Grande do Sul, on the peripheries of Brazil, naturally contained the highest concentration of Indians, while the free mulattoes

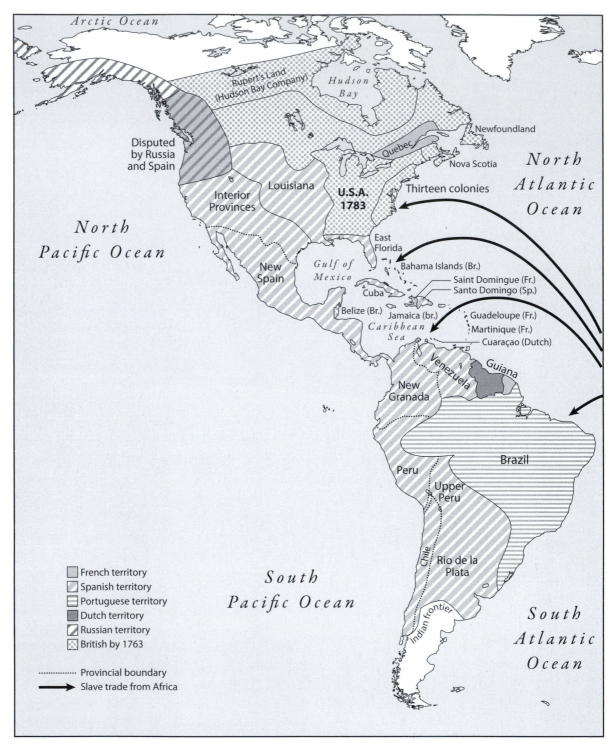

Map 11.1. Colonial America in 1763 (after the Seven Years' War)
Source: Geoffrey Barraclough, ed., *The Times Atlas of World History* (London: Times Books, 1990), 164–65

and blacks reached a percentage above the average in Pernambuco, Goiás, Minas Gerais, and Bahia. Black slaves reached a higher percentage in Bahia, Goiás, Maranhão—an effect of the recent boom in cotton and rice cultivation—Rio de Janeiro, and Minas Gerais. White people were overrepresented in Rio Grande do Sul, due to its minimal number of slaves, and Rio de Janeiro, which had become the capital of the state in 1763.[36]

These data reveal a high percentage of mixed-race people, mainly of white and black origin, but also some descendants of Indian origin. The 1808 census singled out "freedmen," which points to the social visibility of this group. The percentage of free people of slave origin was much higher than in the British and French American colonies, only paralleled by Spanish America. This high percentage is an important indicator of the regular practice of manumission (emancipation), especially through the wills of slave owners.[37] The extensive spread of confraternities also played a role in this practice, for these groups supported the purchase of freedom and put pressure on the slave owners.[38] The recognition of the category "mulatto" in the different censuses and estimates of population is also revealing: it indicates that mixed-race people had a social and political status in Portuguese America.

The Italian Jesuit Giovanni Antonio Andreoni (1649–1716) lived in Bahia during the last thirty-three years of his life and occupied some of the most senior positions in the religious order. He left an extraordinary treatise on the Brazilian economy and finance, *Cultura e opulência do Brasil por suas drogas e minas*, printed in 1711. In the first part of his treatise, on the sugar economy, Andreoni reflects on the organization of the plantation—namely, the significance of choosing the right supervisor and the duties of the team responsible for different activities. One of the central chapters concerns the different behaviors of the slaves. Andreoni classifies the capacities of the African peoples from different regions and places the mulattoes at the top for any office, but finds them haughty and vicious, capable of any abuse. He complains that mulattoes charm their masters because they have the same blood; they are considered spoiled. He accuses the sugar plantation owners of being governed by

Figure 11.1. Jean Baptiste Debret, *Voyage pictoresque et historique au Brésil* (Paris: Firmin Didot et Frère, 1834–39), vol. 2, plate 6 (lithograph). White house interior with young slaves as pets. Reprinted with permission from AKG-images, Berlin

mulattoes—a situation justifying the proverb "Brazil is hell for the blacks, purgatory for the whites, and paradise for the mulattoes." Andreoni acknowledges the fragile position of the mulattoes, since mistrust or jealousy may transform love into hate, followed by cruelty and despotism, but he insists that "one cannot give them a hand, because they would take the arm; from slaves they turn themselves into lords." He considers the manumission of restless female mulattoes to be foolishness, since they buy their emancipation with their bodies and once freed will ruin the men they ensnare.[39] Here we have a catalog of all the prejudices against mixed-race people, praised as collaborators of the white elite, but mistrusted for their ambiguous position as social mediators. The role of social buffer in a highly conflicted society, based on the extraordinary oppression of slaves, meant being subject to constant surveillance.

The extraordinary series of daily life portraits by Jean-Baptiste Debret (1768–1848) in his *Voyage pittoresque et historique au Brésil* makes a visual approach to this ethnic diversity possible, since he represented scenes of everyday public and domestic life in Rio.[40] During 1816–31, Debret was an official painter at the royal court in Brazil and a founder of the local Academy of Beaux Arts, where he staged both theater and royal ceremonies, having invented the ritual and dress of the new independent Brazilian imperial court. But he gained his reputation through the representation of Indians in their natural environment, a series of portraits of individuals from different African ethnicities (male and female), visions of female domesticity in the white man's house, crowded with relatives and slaves, the small black children treated as pets by the whites, vivid scenes of shops and street vendors, the transport of white people by slaves, and white families grouped formally with their slaves. The mulattoes are represented as supervisors and the intimate collaborators of their masters, but what dominates the series are the crude scenes of slave punishment, selling of slaves, and hard work imposed on black people. Despite the artist's extraordinary ability to observe social reality, it is misleading to consider his depictions as mere visual documentation of Brazilian colonial society: the Orientalist influence in many of his images is noteworthy.[41]

Figure 11.2. Jean-Baptiste Debret, *Voyage picturesque et historique au Brésil* (Paris: Firmin Didot et Frère, 1834–39), vol. 2, plate 5 (lithograph). Government employee with his family and slaves. Reprinted with permission from AKG-images, Berlin

Figure 11.3. Jean-Baptiste Debret, *Voyage picturesque et historique au Brésil* (Paris: Firmin Didot et Frère, 1834–39), vol. 2, plate 23 (lithograph). Slave trader's shop in Rio. Reprinted with permission from AKG-images, Berlin

Debret praised the Portuguese "humanitarian" treatment of slaves—a highly questionable topos of the 1820s and 1830s also reproduced by Georg Wilhelm Friedrich Hegel.[42] Yet it is precisely the brutality and misery of those racial and oppressive scenes, also portrayed by other artists in Brazil, particularly by Debret's contemporary, Johann Moritz Rugendas, that contrast with the representation of other Latin American peoples produced during the same period, showing the distinct flow and impact of the slave trade.[43] It is sufficient to consult the series of costumed scenes presented by Léonce Angrand in Lima, Raymond Quinsac Monvoisin in Argentina, and especially Claudio Linati, Johann-Friedrich von Waldeck, and Johann Rugendas (who traveled all over Iberian America) in Mexico to see the differences in human types.[44] They reveal the decline in slavery that had been taking place in those regions since the seventeenth century, and importance of Indians and castas in local society, visible in people's dress and behavior, while the misery of a society based on slavery had already become a distant memory. It should be mentioned that Debret, who received a small pension from the Brazilian government, did not hold back from criticizing the slave system and oppression of black people in everyday life, publishing sharp comments on the subject next to some of his images. He even reproduced the verbal abuse that was part of slave mistreatment, like "shut your mouth, black."

In 1789, the population of Spanish America is estimated to have been 14 million, of which 56 percent were Indians, 23 percent white, 8 percent mulattoes, 7 percent mestizos, and 6 percent black. Of this, 4.7 million, or 34 percent of the total, lived in an urban environment. In this case, the percentage of white people was almost on a level with the percentage of Indians, 36–37 percent, followed by mestizos (14 percent), mulattoes (9 percent), and blacks (4 percent).[45] Racial structure varied enormously from region to region. In Mexico, in 1810, in a population of around 6 million, 60 percent were Indians, 22 percent mestizos, and 18 percent whites (with a residual number of black people). High percentages of Indians were also found in Ecuador (65 percent of the total population), Peru (58 percent), Guatemala

Figure 11.4. Johann Moritz Rugendas (1801–58), *Market Scene in Mexico*, painting, oil on canvas, 56 × 70 cm., c. 1831–34. Hamburger Kunsthalle, Hamburg, inv. nr. 3494.
© 2013. Photo: Scala, Florence; BPK Bildagentur für Kunst, Kultur und Geschichte, Berlin; Elke Walford and Dirk Dunkelberg.

(58 percent), Bolivia (48 percent), and Honduras (41 percent). Low percentages of Indians were found in Colombia (20 percent), Venezuela (18 percent), and Chile (10 percent), which were closer to the Brazilian percentage. Mestizos and castas had an important presence in Honduras (53 percent), Colombia (48 percent), Venezuela (45 percent), Guatemala (38 percent), and Bolivia (31 percent). Apart from the Caribbean, black people maintained a significant presence only in Venezuela (16 percent), Colombia (8 percent), and Peru (7 percent). In all other cases on the mainland, the black population has been calculated at less than 2 percent.[46] On the Spanish Caribbean islands, sugar cultivation on a serious scale started only in the last decades of the eighteenth century. The sugar boom in the following century was concentrated in Cuba, which is reflected in the progression of numbers and percentages of slaves: 23–24 percent of the total population from the 1770s to 1790s; and 41–43 percent from the 1820s to 1840s. In the latter decades the number of slaves became, for the first time, higher than the number of white people, but the disruption of the slave trade and European emigration reversed the trend straightaway. The data on free nonwhites (the large majority mulattoes) are also revealing: 21–20 percent from the 1770s to 1790s, and 15 percent from the 1820s to 1840s. The data on other Spanish Caribbean islands show a much less significant number of slaves and higher number of free nonwhite people; in Puerto Rico, free nonwhite people represented 48 percent of the total population in 1775.[47]

We can see how Spanish America defined a multiethnic model based on an Indian and mixed-race population dominated by a white elite, in which, in the long run, the African element only maintained and increased an important presence on the Caribbean islands. On the mainland, the Indian population had a superior status to that of the mestizo, mulatto, and black strata from a political as well as religious point of view: they were allowed access to education; they were not to be questioned as to their faith; and they could gain entrance, under certain conditions, to the local ecclesiastical structure. For the Indian elite, the conquest opened up vast circles of world knowledge. Hybridism was the result

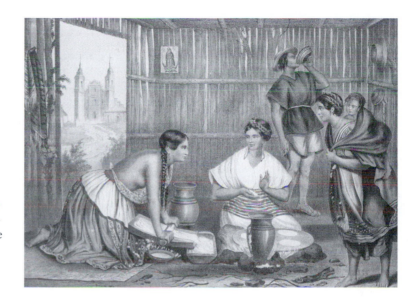

Figure 11.5. Jean-Fréderic Waldeck, *Mexican Women Preparing Tortillas*, lithograph, c. 1834.
Reprinted with permission from the Art Archive, London; Biblioteca Nacional de México; Gianni Dagli Orti

of prolonged interaction with the colonists. It was not limited to the physical creation of castas but instead had a cultural expression in literature, music, gastronomy, painting, and architecture.[48] This creative richness of new interethnic groups generally escapes analysis. At the same time, we should not forget that they still had to overcome the traditional ethnic prejudices of a colonial society based on the idea of white supremacy. There were particular differences from region to region, however, and possibilities that were eventually expressed in political action. Benito Juárez, a Zapotec Indian with a degree in law, served as president of the republic of Mexico for five terms between 1858 and 1872, resisting French occupation, securing the republic, and overseeing the modernization of the country. This would have been unthinkable in Brazil, dominated by the white elite and with only a small percentage of Indians in the population, even though here too national imagery built on the Indian foundations of the country in expressing its opposition to the former colonizing power. The significant presence of a mestizo or mulatto population—a specific feature of Spanish and Portuguese America—can be contrasted with the situation in the northern European colonies.

British America presented a clear division of ethnic structure between the four conventionally defined main areas, due to the impact of the plantation system in the south, which involved large numbers of slaves. In the northern colonies (New England, which included Nova Scotia, New Hampshire, Massachusetts, Rhode Island, and Connecticut), which relied for their livelihood on timber, furs, fishing, shipbuilding, and transport, the percentage of black people was extremely limited, representing between 2 and 3 percent of the total population during the whole of the colonial period. The middle colonies (New York, New Jersey, Pennsylvania, and Delaware) had a significant number of African people, due to a domestic urban market and well-developed rural activity, but this never reached the levels of the plantation system. In fact, it declined from 12 percent in 1640 to 6 percent in 1770.

The economy of the southern colonies (Maryland, Virginia, North Carolina, South Carolina, and Georgia) was based on the plantation system, although in the Chesapeake area tobacco cultivation was first developed by indentured labor. Rice and cotton production in the lower southern region was much more dependent on slave labor from the beginning. Throughout the eighteenth century, the increased cost of the indentured labor and relatively lower cost of slaves meant that slaves replaced the former type of labor. The percentage of black people in the population grew steadily from 5 percent in 1660 to 25 percent in 1710, and then 40 percent in 1760—and in 1790, they still accounted for 36 percent of the population. The Caribbean islands (Barbados, Antigua, Montserrat, Nevis, Saint Kitts, Virgin, and Jamaica) had an economy based on sugar cultivation, with a huge labor force of slaves from the beginning: black people represented 50 percent of the population in 1660, 83 percent in 1710, and 88 percent in 1760. The Atlantic islands (Bermuda and the Bahamas) followed the model of the South Atlantic colonies, with the percentage of black people rising sharply from 5 percent of the population in 1660 to 40 percent in 1710 and 47 percent in 1760.[49] The expansion of the United States to the west, which started under British colonial rule, led to the extension of cotton cultivation, based on slave labor, to the new southern colonies and states.

There is a problem as to how such data were originally produced, and how far they can be analyzed. The idea that Native Americans were totally segregated does not hold up, even if there are some illuminating stories of British refusal to mix with particular communities of Indians during the voyages of exploration. When Walter Raleigh narrated his voyage to Guiana, he boasted under an oath to God that none of his men had ever touched a native woman, but he did not restrain himself in his comments on Indian female beauty.[50] The fact is that local legislation in the colonies was much more favorable to the integration of Indians than to that of Africans. Sexual interaction across ethnic boundaries was probably influenced by the quantity of white women and degree of community control. It must have been much more widespread in Chesapeake than in New England. Throughout the seventeenth century in Chesapeake, there was a trend for manumission, probably of mixed-race people, and the freed slaves acquired land, reaching a status similar to that of white people. The reaction came at the turn of the century: the assembly of whites in Virginia forbade masters to free their slaves and firmly opposed miscegenation.[51] This is a clear example of how local legislation crushed the possible development of a relatively open interethnic system, reshaping normal behavior and forcing the various ethnicities into just two races, whites and blacks, with mixed-race people counted as black. In 1755, though, in Maryland, 8 percent of the slave population was recorded as mulattoes, and in Virginia the percentage was certainly higher, but mainland planters went on thinking in terms of two races.[52]

On the British Caribbean islands, mulattoes were classified as "colored," reflecting a tripartite racial concept, even if the numbers of mulattoes were probably not as high as in the Chesapeake area. The presence of an overwhelming majority of black people led to the acceptance of a certain social status for mixed-race people, who were present in rural areas as well as the lower- and middle-range urban professions. In 1810, so-called colored people made up 12 percent of the slave population on the main islands. Free nonwhites (the vast majority mulattoes) only started to be included in the population estimates in the last decades of the eighteenth century. It was a narrow category, because there was a significant portion of mixed-race people among the slaves. In Barbados, free nonwhites increased from 1 percent of the total population in 1786 to 7 percent in 1834.[53] In Jamaica, they maintained a steady percentage of 2–3 percent from 1758 to 1800, but by 1834 had reached 12 percent. In the British Empire, the slave trade was abolished in 1807 and slavery in 1833.[54] Manumission was extremely limited compared to its use in the Portuguese and Spanish American colonies, raising the issue of local policies and habits. The same pattern may be observed in the Dutch and Danish colonies. Mixed-race people—the vast majority of who were slaves—managed to control access to the most intimate positions of domestic service. The role of the Hemings family at Thomas Jefferson's Monticello is well known. But there were also other mixed-race groups, particularly traders from the African coast—the offspring of mixed white and black families.[55]

The ethnic structure of the French colonies in America was defined by the meager European migration to them, in contrast to the enormous size of the land claims in these areas, which surrounded the thirteen British colonies and ran through to Canada, the Great Lakes, Illinois, and Louisiana—the last of which included a huge area that followed the outline of the Mississippi valley. The contrast between colonial projects and the realities on the ground led to a permanent alliance with the Native Americans that was based on the continual offer of gifts, but stopped short of a policy of tributes. This dependence explains the much closer relationship between Europeans and their Indian allies, which led to some degree of sexual relations across ethnic boundaries, a certain number of unions, and young Frenchmen who joined Native American communities in much bigger numbers than their British counterparts, enjoying the attractions of the wild life.[56] The offspring of these unions, however, would be absorbed into the native environment, due to the more flexible nature of the customs, in which sexual hospitality to foreigners was a social institution favoring exchange and peaceful integration.

Enslavement of enemy Indians, often perpetrated by native allies of the Europeans, was another element of Canadian colonial society: 2,087 native slaves and 1,517 African slaves were recorded during the period of French dominion—limited numbers indeed.[57] In Illinois, the number of African slaves was more significant: they increased from 25 percent of the colonial population in 1726 to 32 percent in 1752.[58] The French defeat in the Seven Years' War resulted in the integration of Canada into the British Empire. Local communities of mixed-race people stayed where they were, but some French settlers moved to the high Mississippi and Missouri, where they mixed with the Sioux, Cheyenne, and Arapaho, while others went further south to the lands of the Kiowa and Comanche, creating new groups of mixed-race people allied to the Native Americans.[59] In Louisiana, the number of African slaves increased from 4,000 in 1740 to 6,000 in 1763, with most of them working in the plantations of indigo and rice around New Orleans. Due to the low numbers of white people, the ratio between white people and the black slaves in this area was four to one in the 1730s and two to one in the 1760s.[60] The French Caribbean islands followed the ethnic structure of the region, with a tripartite categorization of the multiethnic population. The sugar boom started much later than in the British and Dutch colonies, although during the eighteenth century Saint Domingue became the biggest world producer. The available estimates indicate the presence of free nonwhites—a category in which the large majority would be considered colored—but was also a minority of mixed-race people among the slaves. In 1789, two years before the slave revolt, Saint Domingue had 434,429 slaves (89 percent of all population) and 24,848 free nonwhite people (5 percent). Although the population as a whole was much smaller in Guadeloupe and Martinique, the percentage of slaves around that time was 84 and 87 percent, respectively while the percentage of free nonwhite people represented only 3 and 5 percent.[61]

COLONIAL SOCIETIES IN AFRICA AND ASIA

I turn next to European colonial societies in Africa and Asia in order to compare these data on a larger scale. The Portuguese mostly lived in ports or enclaves, dealing in slaves or gold, as in El Mina on the Gold Coast of the Gulf of Guinea. In each trading post there was a limited number of white people, who would have mixed unions and children with native women, but whose offspring would be reabsorbed into local native society, since there was no real colonial settlement of a minimum size. In West Africa, in the region of the Guinea rivers, there were many hundreds of Portuguese called *lançados* or *tangomaos* who settled into local communities. New Christians had a significant part in this migration. The tangomaos inserted themselves in local chieftaincies, and played an important role as mediators between African powers and the Portuguese or other European powers, smuggling and trading slaves.[62] They became natives with more than one identity, and their communities cannot be considered as colonial societies.

On the Cape Verde Islands, uninhabited before the Portuguese navigations, a colonial society was created in the last decades of the fifteenth century. The islands functioned for nearly two centuries as a platform for the slave trade from West Africa. In 1582, around 16,000 people lived on the islands, and the vast majority of them were slaves (87 percent of the total population). White and mixed-race people lived side by side in a curious grouping of 1,600 "neighbors," while there were already 400 free black married people and probably fewer than 200 white people. In 1731, the slaves accounted for only 15 percent of the population; the majority of inhabitants were free mixed-race and black people.[63] São Tomé e Príncipe, an archipelago in the Gulf of Guinea, was another case of a colonial society based on sugar cultivation, although the frequent slave revolts it experienced disrupted its economy several times. In the mid-sixteenth century it was estimated that there were 700 neighbors—which meant free people—but we do not know how many were white, while the 60 sugar plantations probably held a concentration of 10,000 slaves. In the eighteenth century, small farms of free black and mixed-race people spread through the islands on the peripheries of the big plantations.[64] As in Cape Verde, there were free black people from the beginning. They probably were Africans from the coast who conducted trade with their former communities and found a niche in Portuguese colonial society.[65]

On the mainland, the Portuguese maintained a strong presence in the kingdom of Congo, where they acted as clergymen, traders, and soldiers. The ease with which Christianity was accepted by the Congolese royal family, elites, and urban population was a unique case in sixteenth-century Africa that must be considered from the point of view of local mythology and the needs of political power.[66] There was a new, if temporary, identity based on a particular form of Christianity, integrating former religious practices and beliefs. What is critical for us here is that Portuguese military action on the southern peripheries of Congo as well as Portuguese structural dependence on the slave trade eroded relations with the African kingdom in the long run. A divergence of political projects explained growing European prejudices against native clergymen and native rulers. The relationship was disrupted in 1665 by the battle of Mbwila, in which the Congolese king was defeated by the Portuguese. This event was followed by a long political decline of the kingdom of Congo; there were no traces of Christianity by the beginning of the nineteenth century.[67]

In Angola, for two centuries Portuguese settlements were concentrated in Luanda, the Cuanza River area, and Benguela, rarely reaching more than 500 white people.[68] Portuguese influence in the hinterland grew throughout the eighteenth century, but in 1798 the city of Luanda counted only 562 Europeans, as against 1,259 mixed-race people and 5,383 Africans, the majority of who were slaves.[69] In the same period, the number of mixed-race people in the interior of what is now Angola may have reached 4,500 people, though fewer than 1 percent of the total population. These proportions would match much more precise statistical data from 1950: only 0.7 percent of the population of Angola was then mixed race. A similar historical situation existed in Mozambique, with a more dispersed Portuguese settlement, first inserted into the chieftaincies of the Monomotapa confederation, then reduced to the Zambezi valley, but with several trading posts on the coast and along the main rivers. Again, the extremely low proportion of mixed-race people lasted until the twentieth century; they represented only 0.4 percent of the population in 1950.[70] This is an important issue: mixed-race people were generally absorbed back into the global society in the African context—a structural difference from Brazil, where there was a specific place for interethnic groups.[71] It is true that in some crucial places like Luanda, mixed-race people maintained an important role for centuries, but this was not the rule across the vast African territories.[72]

The situation in the Portuguese Estado da Índia was different again. Due to their limited access in Europe to capital and personnel, the Portuguese depended heavily on local resources. From the beginning, the Portuguese based their presence on local alliances, local traders, bankers, and informants. The strategy of mixed-race marriages was implemented at local level in contradiction to the segregationist policy advocated by the Crown.[73] Policies of conversion became important to establish native groups that were relatively detached from traditional local political allegiances, and could form a bridge for Portuguese political interests and in certain cases be mobilized for military purposes. The next chapter discusses the policies of eradication of other religions and impact of the Inquisition, but it is essential at this point to note that a strong native Christian community existed in Goa from the 1560s to 1740s as well as small Christian enclaves, such as Macau. These contrasted with other colonies managed by a tiny Christian minority elite, particularly the Northern Province, a strip of territory on the northwest Indian coast, or Ceylon (Sri Lanka), which was mostly controlled by the Portuguese from the 1590s to 1620s. The inventories of Portuguese settlements in Asia, especially the detailed ones compiled by António Bocarro and Pedro Barreto Resende in 1635, reveal a division between white and black *casados* (married Catholic males): out of a total of 43,992 people, 4,937 were classified as white and 39,055 as black.[74] This classification needs some clarification: married people excluded soldiers (a good part of the Portuguese population in the forts supporting those settlements), and the category of married Catholic male implied that the number of relatives, servants, and slaves under the same roof should be multiplied by at least ten under Asian conditions, which would give us a total number of Catholics under Portuguese rule of around 450,000. But what is striking is that the white casados were mostly mixed-race people of European descent and that native converted people were labeled in an official report as black. The Portuguese depended on native people, mixed with them, and gave their offspring status, though they did not become less abusive in their vocabulary.

The pattern of the Spanish colonial presence in the Philippines was based on wide evangelization of the local population and control of the process of colonization by religious orders.[75] It is true that the population had been untouched by the religions of the book, with the exception of the Islamized southern islands; the territory was not rich in precious metals; and settlements were widely dispersed, which prevented the immediate impact of European diseases. These three factors contributed to comparatively lower levels of fighting, population transfers, and epidemics, although the decline in the population of the Visayas and Luzon has recently been recalculated by Linda A. Newson as being as high as two-thirds of the total—from what were probably 1.5 million inhabitants before the Spanish arrival to 500,000 in 1655.[76] The decline in the native population was significantly lower than in America, but the recovery started later. In 1571, the Spaniards transformed Manila into their headquarters and maintained their rule over the islands (with the exception of the south) until 1898, with a short yet decisive British disruption in 1762–64. The spread of Catholicism defined a colonial society based on a tiny Spanish elite (in 1588, 700 people, of who 300 were soldiers and 150 monks), a large community of Chinese migrants, and a significant percentage of mixed-race people (white and Chinese as well as white and Tagalog).

The Dutch and English in Asia and Africa mixed extensively with native peoples, contrary to common assumptions about segregation having been in place from the beginning. In 1650, Johan Maetsuyker, the Dutch governor of Ceylon, who was still fighting the last strongholds of Portuguese resistance, reported that there were 68 free burghers married to local women, mostly of Portuguese descent. Another 200 free burghers married Indo-Portuguese women after the conquest of Colombo and Jaffna in 1656–58.[77] In Batavia and the trading posts of the Dutch Far East, the existence of extended mixed families could be observed throughout the seventeenth and eighteenth centuries, and many of the offspring married senior VOC officials, including governors-general.[78] Cornelia van Nijenroode, the daughter of a geisha and a Dutch merchant in Japan, presents the most extraordinary case of a wealthy woman who fought for her rights against her greedy second husband, a Dutch lawyer, in seventeenth-century Batavia.[79] In the last decades of the eighteenth century, well-known officers of the East India Company, like Major James Achilles Kirkpatrick, the British resident at the court of Hyderabad, or General William Palmer, resident at Poona, had Indian wives and families, and shared in most of the native rituals, clothes, food, and habits. It is estimated that by that time, one-third of the British in India had native wives or concubines, fathering mixed-race children.[80] Thus, the Portuguese were not the only Europeans in Asia to create mixed-race communities or establish an intimate relationship with local societies. The difference between the European powers in Asia lay in the political status attributed (or not) to those communities.

As early as 1612, Pieter Both, the first governor-general of the Dutch East Indies, advocated mixed marriages with native women and converted Christians (Catholics) from various parts of Asia, particularly Ambon. The Heren XVII (the governing body of the VOC) authorized the governor-general and his council to allow so-called time-expired men, such as merchants, clerks, soldiers, and sailors, to settle in Asia. These free burghers could trade in goods on which there was no monopoly—for instance, rice, sago, or livestock—and were expected to supplement the company's local garrisons in time of war. They first established themselves in the Moluccas, then in Batavia, Malacca, and Sri Lanka, following the course of the Dutch expansion. They were supposed to remain subject to the company's rules and jurisdiction, could be authorized to marry baptized Asian women, and their children were to be educated as Christians. But free burghers married to Asian women were not allowed to return to Europe. In 1644, slaves, mixed-race people, and mixed-race wives were forbidden to travel to Europe—a ban that was renewed in 1650 and in 1713. Even free burghers married to European women could only travel back to Europe with personal possessions. In 1672, the authorities in Batavia forbade the employment of Asian office clerks unless they had special permission—a ban that was renewed in 1715 and extended in 1718 to the descendants of Europeans. It was only in 1727 that the reverse process started: the promotion of Eurasians in VOC administered territories.[81]

Although these rules, which lasted up until the first quarter of the eighteenth century, indicate a segregation process, their primary purpose was to control the group of time-expired men who wanted to go on living in Asia. These ex-employees were considered potential competitors to company officials in terms of trade, smuggling, and piracy. This kind of legislation kept free burghers at the margins of the system, and indeed they never became an important social group. The VOC never depended on them in Java, Sri Lanka, or India, because Chinese, Gujarati, Bengali, and other merchant groups were much more efficient in local, regional, and interregional trade networks. Free burghers mainly invested in innkeeping, which offers some idea of the limited scale of their commercial activities. The only exception to this situation was the Cape Town colony, which operated as a supply point for the VOC navy on its way to Asia. In this case, the free burghers mixed extensively with the local population, used slaves from East Africa—particularly Madagascar—and created a solid basis for agriculture and livestock production. In western Africa, where the WIC, at the peak of its presence in the 1640s, had 1,170 employees on a permanent basis, with a high mortality rate of 68 percent per year, more and more mulattoes were used in time, first as soldiers and artisans, then as assistant trading agents, despite the constant pressure and concrete measures against sexual intercourse with the native population.[82] Some of them became important independent merchants or acquired an influential position in the Dutch establishments, even becoming members of the WIC council, as in the case of Jan Nieser and Jacob Ruhle at the beginning of the nineteenth century.[83] But this was a limited group in a specific context, used against a background for the exclusion of African people from any significant jobs or positions in the WIC; Africans were only used as slaves for loading and unloading ships, or at best as craftspeople. In the Asian cases where there is evidence of extensive mixed marriages after conquest, the group of free burghers did not develop as initially envisaged. Even in Sri Lanka, where mixed marriage was strongly encouraged, the Eurasian community did not remain stable and coherent for a significant period of time, although there are continuities of people of European descent.

The English case is more complicated because the empire in Asia was established quite late; until 1757, there was only a set of trading posts and forts without effective control of significant territory. Robert Clive's policy of conquest completely changed that situation, stimulating emigration from the British Isles and further contacts with local communities. The emergence of mixed families came quite late in comparison to the Portuguese and Dutch cases. It was considered a private matter, tolerated and managed on an individual basis for a short period of time. Mixed families never became "communities," because the English had the capital (mostly native capital, incidentally), personnel, and military technology to extend their political dominion in India without depending on a buffer of mixed-race people. The initial trend toward mixed families was confronted by the enshrining in law of ethnic prejudices by the end of the eighteenth century. In 1793, the decision to exclude mixed-race people from government service defined a policy of discrimination (and segregation) that set the course of social relations between colonists and native people for the nineteenth century.[84] The creation of mixed families was significantly reduced by the turn of the century, offering a good case study of the impact of legislation in bringing about change in values and human behavior.

One final issue cannot be considered in any depth here: the identification of different ethnicities and religions among Africans or Native Americans. The fact that the criteria for classification were almost monopolized by degrees of skin color did not mean that observers—governors, administrators, captains of ships, travelers, and writers—were not aware of the immense ethnic variety in Africa or America. Not only could many observers point to dozens of original ethnicities when referring to the African slave community in a specific place but they were also attentive to the different forms of religion practiced before the Middle Passage from Africa to America. Islam was the obvious religious issue for the slaves brought from West Africa. This religious allegiance, which had generally involved literacy and contact with the Koran, would naturally make conversion to Christianity—wherever it was practiced systematically—much more difficult. In certain cases Islam led to a sharper resistance amongst slaves.[85] Ethnic identification was also linked to another issue: the search for certain skills, particularly in mining or specialized arts and crafts, attributed to specific African lineages and ethnicities. The problem is that knowledge of such skills was not transformed into a taxonomic system; it was only used for practical purposes, and even then not in any consistent way. The main systems of categorization were based on skin color, because they were easy to use and not hindered by exceptions. This is why the history of race overshadowed the history of lineage and ethnicity; the latter was much more complex, based on constant migration, recomposition, and a fluidity of alliances.

‖‖

CHAPTER 12

Projects and Policies

It is important to analyze the projects and policies of the main colonial powers to understand how legislation (central or local, formal or informal) disrupted or reinforced interethnic practices on the ground, shaping colonial societies. Two main questions need to be answered: How did the European powers involved in world exploration conceive of their role, and how did they deal with structured political powers in other continents? How did local colonial powers experience everyday interaction with native populations? These questions suppose that ethnic constructions were not merely a spontaneous result of concrete interaction between European and native populations on the ground; in many cases, they resulted from the dynamic of social and political interests reflected in ideas and concrete policies defined by the central structures or local status groups.

IBERIAN MODELS

The competition between the Portuguese and Castilian kings in the exploration of the northwest and west coast of Africa set the template for the Iberian mode of world exploration: Iberian adventurers simultaneously explored the coasts, conquered or occupied major ports and forts, made temporary peace treaties with local powers, peopled uninhabited islands of strategic importance (Madeira and the Azores), and conquered, enslaved, assimilated, and virtually eradicated the native population of the Canary Islands. Due to a relatively peaceful period at home, which contrasted with the successive civil wars in Castile, Portugal was more successfully engaged in maritime exploration during this foundational period: from 1455 onward, a series of papal bulls legitimized the exclusive rights of Portugal to navigate and trade south of the Canary Islands as well as its jurisdiction over Muslim and pagan territories already conquered or to be conquered. But this intervention did not solve the Iberian disputes over rights of trade, navigation, and conquest, most bitterly fought over the Canary Islands, which were the target of several important military expeditions by both sides.

The marriage of Isabel of Castile to Ferdinand of Aragon in 1469, defeat of the Portuguese king (and his wife, Juana, pretender to the Castilian throne) at the battle of Toro in

1476, and succession of Isabel and Ferdinand to the thrones of both Castile and Aragon, in 1474 and 1479, respectively, established a new balance of power in Iberia. In 1479, the treaty of Alcáçovas recognized Portuguese rights to navigation, trade, and conquest south of the Canary Islands, while the Portuguese recognized the rights of the Spaniards to the conquest of the islands themselves. The rights to the conquest of the kingdom of Fez and possession of other Atlantic islands (Madeira and the Azores) were also recognized as Portugal's. This fragile balance was disrupted by the voyage of Columbus in 1492; the following year, the Catholic kings obtained recognition of their exclusive right to navigation to the west from Pope Alexander VI, who drew an imaginary north-south line 100 leagues west of the Azores or Cape Verde Islands demarcating the territory reserved for Spanish exploration. Latitude was replaced by longitude as the imaginary frontier, but the Portuguese king was not pleased. In 1494, he obtained a much more favorable deal with the Catholic kings in the treaty of Tordesillas, according to which the demarcation line was moved to 370 leagues west of the Cape Verde Islands, thus opening up the possibility of the discovery and conquest of Brazil. In exchange, the Portuguese king recognized the rights of the Catholic kings to conquer North Africa east of the Strait of Gibraltar. All other previous agreements were maintained.[1]

Maritime exploration thus was a private activity sponsored from the beginning by the royal family and supervised by the king. This activity required significant investment and represented an enormous risk, due to the possibility of shipwrecks and military defeats. Private investors played a major role in opening up the coast, managing to monopolize for a while the major part of the ensuing trade, but the kings reserved the right to oversee any conquest and distribute lands as part of their new seigniorial rights—as on the Canary Islands, where the rights of conquest were ceded to the Castilian kings by the Norman clan of the Béthencourt responsible for the first European settlement. The long resistance of the Guanches, the native inhabitants of the Canary Islands, postponed a total conquest of the islands, and the conquerors' resources were diverted to enterprises of enslavement to compensate for their defeat and losses. These enterprises were generally managed by local captains and governors. The political, economic, and personal rights of the Guanches were the first to be publicly discussed, but as would happen on the Caribbean islands, war and disease annihilated the native population.

The concession of royal rights to *adelantados*, frontiersmen who would risk armed investment for future recognition of their conquests, was a practice transferred from Iberia to territories overseas. Columbus is a case in point, although his rights as admiral and lord-governor were swiftly curbed by the Catholic kings with the appointment of regular magistrates in the Antilles. The succeeding generation was subject to the same political principles: Hernán Cortés rejected the lordship of Diego Velázquez, governor of Cuba, and managed to obtain direct recognition from the king for his conquest of Mexico; he even secured the title of marques, yet he lost the function of governor. The conqueror of Peru, Francisco Pizarro, followed the same path, but was murdered in factional fighting by other Spaniards. In the end, the king's determination to avoid further cases of uncontrolled distant rule prevailed.

The same pattern occurred in the Portuguese expansion: the first phase of land concessions to captains-donataries on the Atlantic islands, Brazil, and Angola, eventually ended in the subordination of these concessions to direct royal administration, or their integration into it. In India, from the beginning, the king controlled the enterprise, making the main appointments, although on the ground, the local governor and colonial elites defined the main policies.

I do not want to lay too much stress on an early, centralized imperial process in the Iberian case, because there was room for a significant number of relatively autonomous initiatives, like those that led to the conquest of the two most important native political structures in America. But it is undeniable that the expansion was shaped by the royal power, which supervised or legitimized the main ventures, often sponsored initiatives, even signed contracts for maritime exploration, and when conquest was accomplished, ended up directly controlling the political and administrative framework of the operation. Close supervision or intervention by the Iberian crowns did not inhibit local colonial powers; on the contrary, they gave them legitimacy. We will see how those powers could become quite autonomous with distance, developing their own policies for a while, and even imposing major strategic decisions that would eventually have significant consequences. The system allowed a tremendous amount of initiative, even if the standard period of governorship was limited to three years, yet sometimes renewed—though this happened more in the Spanish than in the Portuguese case, due to the time lapse in communication caused by distance.

As a result of this close supervision, royal power was accountable for what happened in the colonies, particularly in relation to native people. Enslaved Guanches, for example, immediately questioned the Catholic kings on the legitimacy of the procedure. In the case of the treacherous enslavement of the subjects of the Spanish-allied lord of Guimar, in Tenerife, the victims claimed to be free, peaceful people, who had signed treaties with the Spanish governor of Gran Canaria. This is one of the few documented cases in which the kings had to intervene and free people were justified in their protest.[2] This does not mean that the crowns were able or willing to systematically control colonial abuse. It is well known that an important number of Portuguese and Spanish expeditions sought to enslave Guanches right up to the end of the fifteenth century. Nevertheless, the new conquerors would be forced to come to terms with the issue of the rights of native peoples who had become subjects and been forced to convert to Christianity. In the Iberian cases, the imperial state has always been an ethnic or racial state, legitimizing ethnic constructions and hierarchies. The issue here is the extent to which close supervision by the royal power meant a real reduction in the most extreme abuse.[3]

The conquests of Mexico and Peru are good cases to consider. For example, the distribution of the native population among the conquerors who, as *encomenderos*, used these people's labor for their own purposes, gave rise to many protests over the obvious abuse this entailed. The first task of royal administrators was to define rules, curb the rights of the encomenderos, and protect the decimated Indians from further illegitimate impositions. The existence of a distant royal power was used as a justification for local protest, since imperial rule over native populations involved a political obligation to define and implement rights—the basis for the legitimacy of the whole system. This explains why the Crown decided to create the *república de indios*, recognizing the political rights at the local level of native communities in New Spain. The result was a local political power with an alcalde and other elected administrators invested by the king with all the attributes of a typical Spanish municipality, including communal land, a water supply, and urban infrastructure. The villages or towns—*pueblos de indios*—were built according to the same geometric grid imposed in all Spanish American cities, structured around the main square, with a church, municipal headquarters, and column for public punishment. Urban planning projected the new political order. The Crown forbade other races and castas (whites, blacks, and mixed-race people) to reside in these Indian communities (through the laws of 1551, 1563, 1578, and 1680). This segregation, which naturally failed in the long run, was intended to maintain a minimum basis for Indian political representation, the local exercise of traditional common law, and a local social and economic framework that could preserve the natives from a further decline in population.[4]

The ambiguity of these purposes is inscribed in the vast operation organized by the Spanish power in America to transfer and concentrate the native population. The creation of hundreds of new towns, many of which had to be reestablished due to poor environmental conditions, aggravated the health problems of natives already enfeebled by being subjected to epidemics.[5] It reinforced imperial control over native populations, creating a precedent for similar operations in modern times, although in the case of Spanish America the transfer was not to places thousand of miles away. In Spanish America, the idea was to maintain the relationship between a population and its original region, in order to create a colonial urban framework that would impose a totally new political hierarchy with different rules and types of behavior. It is obvious that the república de indios was a subordinated, hierarchical form of integration of native communities that excluded them from the top administrative layer of the various viceroyalties. The Crown, however, recognized the property rights of those communities and tried to protect the people from the heavy work that would further disrupt their social fabric. It was prohibited to employ Native Americans in sugar plantations and sugar mills. The Crown also opened up access to the universities, colleges, and schools to the assimilated native elites. Black Africans and mixed-race people of illegitimate descent were excluded from those educational structures. When the Inquisition was established in the New World, in 1569–70, Philip II excluded newly converted Indians from inquiries into their religious beliefs and practices. This was an exception that contrasted with the persistent inquisitorial persecution of New Christians of Jewish origin or Moriscos back in Spain—later replicated in the New World in relation to Judaism. It also contrasted with the practice of the Inquisition in the Portuguese Empire, which persecuted newly converted natives in Brazil and India.

In these acts of positive discrimination, the Spanish kings recognized the status of Native Americans as the first holders of the land, although this was balanced by the demand for tribute imposed on all conquered populations. Legislation often may not have been implemented, as people or local elites avoided laws that were contrary to their interests. But legislation also created a framework that shaped new forms of behavior and negotiation in daily life. In the long run, all these measures meant that castas would claim Indian descent when they were prosecuted by the Inquisition, while Indians would dress as castas, move to Spanish cities, and learn to speak Castilian in order to avoid tribute. In certain cases, as in Peru and Guatemala, the zambaigos (offspring of blacks and Indians) and *cholos* (offspring of mestizos and Indians) were obliged to pay tribute in the same way as the Indians.[6]

The role of towns supposedly reserved for Spaniards was also crucial from the administrative, political, and cultural points of view, since they were places where major decisions were taken, from which the rural world was colonized, and where cultural exchange took place. The hierarchy of the city was defined by the central square: the most imposing houses of the important families of encomenderos, administrators, or royal officers were located there or in the nearby streets. The most important crafts might have designated streets in the main cities. The poorest Spaniards would be relegated to the peripheries of the towns. The Indians would have their own neighborhoods outside the town. In many cases, religious orders, mainly the mendicants (Dominicans and Franciscans), established their own convents in the middle of these neighborhoods in order to give religious guidance and comfort to local communities, but also to maintain a certain control over these people's activities. The support of local Indians against other Native Americans in the wars fought by the colonizers was rewarded, in some instances, with privileged access to designated building lots around the main square. The hierarchy of the city did not change dramatically over time, but mixed-race people occupied more and more significant amounts of space on the peripheries of the towns, while Indians penetrated the fabric of the urban center.

The enslavement of Native Americans was forbidden by the Spanish Crown in response to protests against the enormous scale of abuse during and after the conquest by the religious orders, mainly the Dominicans. That is why the Spanish authorities encouraged the slave trade from Africa as a way to ease the pressure to enslave Native Americans under the pretext of a just war—the one possible door left open by the legislation. The transatlantic slave trade began to function on an unprecedented scale, exceeding the traditional caravan trade to Muslim countries. But what needs to be highlighted is the crucial role played by the Crown's decision to transform converted Native Americans into subjects (or vassals), who could not be enslaved, while black Africans could be transported to perform the heaviest duties. We know that the percentage of Africans in the American population varied enormously with time and place, and ended at a low level in New Spain in the long term. Yet the image of black Africans as the lowest stratum, virtually without any rights—though this assertion has to be qualified—was certainly reinforced by this policy. At the same time, the Spanish Crown encouraged Catholic marriages between Spaniards and Native American elites, and did not forbid marriage between mixed races or castas, although illegitimate children were to be excluded from higher education and public office, while those marrying black women were excluded from the civil service in 1687.[7]

The Catholic Church played an undeniable role in moderating colonial abuse, not only through the sacrament of marriage, but also through the promotion of confraternities among all strata of the population, including black slaves. The Dominican confraternities of the rosary, created for black people, whether slaves or freedpersons, intervened in major cases of brutality against slaves and helped them to pay for their manumission (emancipation). Spanish legislation favored manumission: there was no legal obstacle, and the variety of options was considerable—in the owner's will, through external work and payment by the slave, or in return for a contribution from a charitable institution.[8] The condition of slaves was not the exclusive affair of the owner; the slave could legally denounce brutal treatment, require a change of master, and request the intervention of the king. These legal possibilities were distant from daily practices, yet the structure of confraternities enabled a certain level of information and action.

The Portuguese case presented similar features, although the rights of Native Americans were never properly addressed: the king donated vast stretches of Brazil, declared as "my coast and land," from the coast to the interior, in order to attract European colonists, as if the land were totally empty of native rule.[9] The fact that the colonists were dealing with seminomadic populations helped them to maintain an enormous level of native enslavement under cover of pursuing a just war. Dominican champions of natives' rights, such as Las Casas, were not active on the Portuguese side, but the Jesuits later performed this role, causing several of them to be summarily shipped back to Portugal by the angry colonists of São Paulo and São Luís do Maranhão, the major centers for hunting native slaves. Jesuits promoted Indians rights, obtained the support of the Crown, and in the long run managed to curb the practice of native enslavement by the colonists. The Jesuits were not entirely innocent, though; they wanted to control access to Native Americans, and managed an indigenous labor force within their own missions, where they also had sugar mills and African slaves. They compromised with the colonists in some areas, such as Maranhão, sending "their" Indians from the missions to temporarily undertake private and public labor.[10]

If the Portuguese king wanted to establish his political dominion over poorly protected native subjects, whose rights to property were not recognized until the eighteenth century, the Jesuits had their own vision of the world based on an autonomous theocratic society, organized around missions, through which they finally managed to define their own territory in the region of what is now Paraguay, then a political fringe between the Spanish and Portuguese empires in South America. The clash came in the mid-eighteenth century, when the Portuguese government of Pombal (1750–77) engaged in secular policies against traditional religious interests: the missions were secularized, and the Jesuits were eventually expelled from Portugal and the empire. The impact of this action has only recently begun to be properly evaluated. Although the functioning of many communities was disrupted once they were without Jesuit supervision, other missions were successfully transformed into civil towns and villages, directly managed by Native Americans. New legislation favored Indians' rights to property and trade, abolishing formal discrimination. This period also saw, for the first time, the recognition of civil rights for New Christians of Jewish origin, whose segregation—including their exclusion from universities, military orders, confraternities, and public offices—was forbidden. The Chinese in Macau started to have access to public offices; Timorese women were authorized to migrate into Macau; baptized Asian Indians were given preferential access to public positions; and the slave trade into Portugal and slavery in Portugal, though not in the colonies, were abolished under certain circumstances.[11]

In Asia, Governor Afonso de Albuquerque (1509–15) designed the Portuguese policy of mixed marriages between Europeans and local elites. In 1510, when he conquered Goa, Albuquerque immediately encouraged mixed marriages between the Portuguese conquerors and local women with significant financial endowments. A faction of Portuguese nobles opposed this policy. They were scandalized by what they saw as an impure procedure, and denounced it to the king. D. Manuel asked Albuquerque to stop promoting mixed marriages, but all he could obtain from the latter was the suspension of royal endowments. Albuquerque argued that without mixed marriages, the Portuguese would never become rooted in Asia. He maintained that the Portuguese did not have enough labor power, and that the existence of the Portuguese Empire in Asia depended on these mixed marriages and the creation of a strong group of Portuguese descendants. This was the first clear political decision taken in favor of creating mixed-race people, although Albuquerque had to assert that he would only favor Muslims and Brahman women of light color; Iberian prejudice against people of dark skin color probably matched local prejudices (see chapter 19). This policy became deeply rooted, and the king ceased to bother the governor about it. The issue was never raised again, in tacit acknowledgment of the force of Albuquerque's contention.

In Asia, the constant process of negotiating treaties with local powers in order to obtain access to land, declarations of vassalage to the Portuguese king, and even wills that would give rights of succession to the latter, as happened in Ternate and Sri Lanka (the kingdom of Kotte), initially prevented major colonial abuse, although ethnic contempt and discrimination were commonly practiced. The attack on native rights generally concentrated on religion, considered by the Portuguese as the cement of their empire. In the 1550s and 1560s in Goa, the Portuguese viceroys conducted a vast campaign of destroying Hindu temples, breaking the alliance that the Portuguese had established before the conquest with local Brahmans against Muslims. The king established this policy as a way to impose Christianity. The Portuguese did not have the strength to implement such a policy in the other colonies in Asia, but the religious rights of native communities were never considered in a positive light. Despite the Portuguese structural dependence on native bankers and traders, religious reason always prevailed over political reason until the mid-eighteenth century. The tolerance for native religions was only actively implemented after the conquest of the territories around Goa in 1747–63.[12]

Portuguese policies in Africa were carefully formulated from the beginning due to the complexity of local political systems and high mortality rate of Europeans. The conversion of the Congolese royal family and nobility to Christianity benefited from a careful diplomacy that assigned similar status to both kings plus managed to project a Portuguese court society onto the African reality. Even when the Congolese king, Álvaro I, was defeated by the Imbangalas (called Jagas by the Portuguese) in 1569 and retreated to an island on the Zaire River, depending on Portuguese strength and military assistance to recover his kingdom, vassalage and tribute were not imposed. In 1595, the Congolese king, supported by the

Portuguese, obtained the creation of an episcopate from the pope based in São Salvador, the capital of the kingdom of Congo. The new religion had an undeniable impact on the local population, which was baptized in significant numbers. This relatively peaceful policy was eroded by the extraordinary boom in the slave trade throughout the seventeenth century and disrupted by the Dutch occupation of Luanda (1641–48). It contrasted with the policy of conquest developed further south against the kingdom of Ngola from 1571 onward.

The Portuguese settled in Luanda along with the valleys of the Bengo and Cuanza rivers, establishing alliances with local rulers, and systematically converted the people to Christianity, transforming them into vassals whenever possible. They sent missions to the Ngolas and Imbangalas, sometimes combined with similar Congolese initiatives. Christian influence in west-central Africa spread in a significant way, in many cases supported by local rulers. All this interaction resulted in ethnic changes, particularly the creation of an important and widespread group of Luso-Africans with mixed-race descendants who controlled a good part of the trade, military and administrative posts in the various kingdoms, and the secular priesthood. The Luso-Africans became significant mediators of the emerging Atlantic Creole culture, which mixed Christian and African religious as well as cultural elements.[13] The results of all these movements were uneven: the Portuguese and Christian influence on local African populations increased dramatically in the sixteenth and early seventeenth centuries, while the reputation of Africans among Europeans declined due to the slave trade and constant wars. The Europeans' projection of their own society onto Africa during the first hundred years of contact was replaced by a more distant attitude and stronger prejudices.

The new Portuguese governors of Angola after 1648, who were heroes of the Brazilian war against the Dutch, brought with them mixed-race troops immune to local diseases and carried on a consistent war against the kingdom of Congo, thus breaking off a long alliance. By the end of the eighteenth century, Christianity had almost disappeared from the region. White supremacy was, paradoxically, reinforced during the process of increasing the racial mix: the Portuguese kings maintained a fiction of municipal councils controlled by Portuguese, or "purely" Portuguese descendants. Yet policies concerning the armed forces were more relaxed; in 1684, a decree forbade ethnic discrimination among members of the garrison of Luanda.[14] In the archipelagos of Cape Verde and São Tomé, where a colonial society had been established, even the above-mentioned fiction could not be maintained due to the extremely limited number of white people. The king explicitly allowed mixed-race people to be elected to the municipal councils—a major breach of previous rules.

DUTCH AND BRITISH MODELS

The British and Dutch expansion to the east was based on companies created in 1600 and 1602 by shareholders who obtained a monopoly on trade from the state—hence they were called chartered companies. This financial and commercial structure defined a framework that differed from that of the previous Iberian expansion, in which the state supervised the whole operation in one way or the other. It is true that state trade monopolies, as in the Portuguese case, granted exclusive rights in contracts and concessions concerning certain products and voyages. But as in the Spanish case, the king controlled the *carrera de Índias*, where the stakes were especially high, since the major commodity being traded was silver. The Iberian crowns were always struggling with an operational deficit, due to the enormous investment in shipbuilding, armed forces, the construction of forts, and the bureaucracy—what one might call the protection costs of trade and administrative costs of dominion—but the overseas operations were profitable for most of the private agents who took part in them.

In principle, the Dutch and British companies were strictly motivated by the logic of profit, because they had to pay dividends to their shareholders, while the Iberian enterprise was partly motivated by the extension of imperial dominion and religious conversion as well as the redistribution of profits among loyal noble vassals and obliging merchant subjects, particularly bankers, benefiting from royal contracts and willing to help the king in financial and military crises. The Anglo-Saxon model in its early stages favored trading posts and peaceful trade over the construction of forts and territorial dominion. Despite this radically different organizational culture, the Dutch and British companies reproduced the previous practices of piracy and plunder, occupied strongholds that would give them access to markets, turned against each other, initiated wars against the Portuguese, Spanish, and French, tried to impose monopolies on trade, and finally established territorial dominion in order to control markets and exclude competitors. Throughout the eighteenth century, the Dutch were so engaged in territorial control that they lost the flexibility that enabled them to avoid the huge administrative costs of investments that were no longer profitable. The same happened to the British after the conquest of India in the second half of the eighteenth century, where the collection of land taxes became more important than maritime trade from a financial point of view.

The relative blurring of frontiers between the two organizational models could not be better expressed than by the expansionist policy of Rijkloff van Goens (1660–75) in Sri Lanka: it was based on legal claims of succession to previous Portuguese rights of conquest, and even to the rights of sovereignty bequeathed in 1580 to the Portuguese Crown by the Catholic king João Dharmapala of Kotte in his will. The Dutch replicated Portuguese policies—not only in Sri Lanka, but also in Ambon, Luanda, Malacca, and Cochin—concerning forced conversion (or reconversion), promotion of those who had been converted, support for European descendants (mixed-race people), and extensive use of native people for military purposes. Between 1650 and 1658, 268 free burghers married Christian Eurasian women in Sri Lanka.[15] In 1665 alone, in the district of Vanni, in the Tamil northern region of Sri Lanka, the Dutch reconverted 4,533 Christian adults converted by the Portuguese. The case of D. João de Castro, chief of the Mudalyares—administrators of the provinces—in Sri Lanka, is revealing: Castro was the descendant of a family converted by Portuguese missionaries who maintained their Portuguese name; he was a confidant of Governor Goens and played a role in the main embassies, functioning as counselor for relations with the kingdom of Kandy along with the nomination of natives to political and administrative jobs.[16]

How did differences in the organizational culture of both models of expansion—Dutch and British—have an impact on prejudices and discriminatory action? The comparatively small role played by aristocratic values in the Dutch operation in Asia, reflected in the social origin of its governors and captains, may have favored more ethnic mixing. Indeed, the administrative and military elite itself engaged in a certain degree of mixing, but this practice did not trickle down through the social ranks in the seventeenth century, with the exception of Sri Lanka, due to restrictive rules. Employees circulated through the colonies and returned to Europe in significant numbers. The Dutch and British had sufficient people and capital to avoid the Portuguese level of dependence on native human resources for their daily operations. They also negotiated with local traders and bankers—a practice that peaked during the British conquest of India, which was exclusively made possible by local money. Yet in general, they could afford a certain level of ethnic separation.

The Dutch saw the advantage of allowing time-expired employees to stay on the ground, become free burghers, and create an interface with local society. The VOC even encouraged marriage with Eurasian women, but they established clear boundaries to avoid the emergence of smuggling and trading competitors (see the previous chapter). Ethnic prejudices were obvious in several bans imposed throughout the seventeenth and early eighteenth centuries: slaves, mixed-race people, mixed-race wives, and free burghers married to Asian women were forbidden to travel to Europe (due to the laws of 1644, 1650, and 1713). The Batavian authorities also prohibited the employment of Asian and European descendants as office clerks (through the laws of 1672, 1715, and 1718), although the rules started to relax after 1727, coinciding with the decline of the Dutch power in Asia. In the eighteenth and nineteenth centuries, mixed-race people multiplied and found a more favorable social status in Dutch Asia and South Africa. Eurasians started to be classified as Dutch, and by 1850 their number may have reached more than half of that of the white population. In South Africa, where the white population mixed extensively with the Hottentots, the first signs of segregation did not come until 1787, when an exclusively white militia was constituted.[17]

The opposite process occurred with the British in Asia: the segregation of European descendants began with the decision to exclude mixed-race people from political, administrative, and military office in 1793. This policy was maintained for two generations, and can only be explained by the ideological and political debate over the East India Company in England, where it was accused of corruption at all levels, supposedly influenced by Indian practices fostered by mixed-race people. As pointed out by Christopher Bayly, this decision coincided with a series of regulations designed to separate the Indian and European worlds.[18] Racial exclusiveness became part of the ideology of the British structure of government in India and other colonies, such as Sri Lanka, shaped by the political debate on moral independence, civic virtue, and the separation of powers, but also influenced by the development of the new scientific definition of racial hierarchies (see part IV).[19] British sources widely attest to the absorption of Portuguese and Spanish abusive language, like the designation of Indians and Sinhalese as black people.

The British colonization of America was initially based on royal grants of land made to companies or groups under the patronage of a respected sponsor. The autonomy of these initiatives and difficulty of the first decades of migration combined with the dynamic of religious and political turmoil in England during most of the seventeenth century. Significant Puritan and even Catholic migration resulted in the creation of relatively autonomous communities that established some form of self-government, later organized in regional assemblies of representatives, loosely connected to the homeland. There was no general government in the Iberian style, although the ties with the Crown became tighter during the eighteenth century. Native Americans were never considered or treated as vassals by these communities, despite military alliances: the peace treaties recognizing native rights in specific territories were systematically violated by European expansion. Imperial dominion and the rights of Indians as subjects was never an issue in the way that it was in Spanish America. The rural settlements predominantly chosen by British America until the nineteenth century, in striking contrast to Spanish urban colonial society, defined a way of life that was very different from that of the seminomadic Native Americans. The segregation that followed was related to the colonial project of European settlers, but also with their religious background: Calvinism was not open to compromise, and conversion was about deep reflection on the holy scriptures and Christian way of life.[20] Regional colonial assemblies played a major role in relation to segregation. In Virginia at the beginning of the eighteenth century, for example, the assembly forbade masters to free their slaves and opposed miscegenation. In 1806, the same state decided to expel freed black men from the territory in an extreme demonstration of white fears of miscegenation.[21]

THE FRENCH CASE

The French case in America stands between the British and Iberian, since New France operated a clear policy of royal patronage for marriages with converted natives supported by significant dowries. These policies changed, however, pushing French colonial society toward the British model. The code noir (black code), established in 1685, was meant to regulate the treatment and position of slaves and black people in general, but it reinforced religious and ethnic prejudices: the Jews were expelled; all slaves had to be declared by their owners and converted to Catholicism; the public practice of other religions was forbidden; only Catholics could be masters of slaves; free men with illegitimate children by slaves would pay a severe penalty, loosing their slaves and children (the accused could escape the penalty by marrying the slave if he were single); marriage between slaves required the master's consent; the offspring of slaves would belong to the woman's master; the offspring of a married free man and female slave would be considered a slave; the slave was not entitled to any kind of property, not even personal objects, except with the consent of the master; the slave was declared as unfit for public service and judicial inquiries, but could be accused and prosecuted; a slave who attacked the family of his master would receive the death penalty;

runaway slaves would receive severe physical punishment up to death; free men protecting runaway slaves would be punished; masters were forbidden from torturing or mutilating slaves; masters would be prosecuted for murdering slaves; and slaves were considered mobile property to be exchanged, passed from master to master, and inherited, and they were a taxable asset.[22]

These regulations were more or less in line with Roman law. Manumission, which had privileged domestic and mixed-race slaves, was restricted via the control of external profitable activities undertaken by slaves, such as selling goods at market or offering their services outside their masters' properties. The black code accepted manumission, and attributed the same rights, privileges, and immunities to freedpersons as people born free enjoyed. It even accepted manumission by masters as young as twenty (the age of majority at that time was twenty-five). But the royal ordinances of 1721 and 1743 forbade all masters of modest numbers of slaves from liberating their slaves, and imposed judicial control and taxation on the procedure. In 1724, the black code for Louisiana forbade slaves to buy their manumission, which was a common practice in Iberian America. It labeled masters who accepted such payment as mercenaries. Yet the French legislators not only decided to restrict manumission; they also targeted interracial marriage, which had been permitted under the first black code. In 1681, a government official of Saint Domingue denounced such marriages as debauchery, even though they were accepted practice in Iberian-controlled areas. The marriage of whites to blacks was forbidden in 1711 in Guadeloupe and 1724 in Louisiana, becoming general law in the French colonies in 1734. Louis XIV revoked the titles of all nobles who had married "colored" women. Sumptuary laws, particularly in Louisiana in 1720, forbade black people from dressing in the same way as whites.

Mixed-race people, who had been assimilated into the category of whites in the seventeenth century, were classified as black in the eighteenth century—a practice imposed by royal decree in 1713. In 1733, mixed-race people (mulattoes) were excluded from service in tribunals and militias. In 1764, they were excluded from practicing medicine and surgery. This series of segregationist laws against mixed-race people was produced right in the middle of a period during which this interethnic stratum grew rapidly, and during which freedpersons and mulattoes started to get closer to the white professions, even acquiring plantations. Segregation policies were extended to France in the first half of the eighteenth century: black people could not have slaves; slaves could not marry; and a mixed-race battalion created in 1740 was swiftly dissolved. This was the result of white people's insecurity and horror of mixing, even where the number of blacks was insignificant: by the mid-eighteenth century there may have been five thousand black people in France in a population of twenty million, against twenty thousand in England in a population of eight million.[23] The legislation on manumission and interracial marriage shaped colonial French society throughout the eighteenth century, and dissociated the French model from the Iberian one.

||||||||||||||||||||||||||||||||||||||||||||||||||||||||||||||||||||||||||||||||||||||||||||||||||||||||||||||||||||

CHAPTER 13

Discrimination and Segregation

In colonial societies, discrimination means a prejudicial distinction that lessens the likelihood of, or entirely prevents, access to certain positions, professions, or occupations for defined categories of the population. Segregation, in contrast, means the physical separation or isolation of specific ethnic or racial groups from the main body of the population or from key social structures. This chapter charts the outcome of forced or voluntary migration, changes undergone by native populations, and the impact of political projects and colonial policies by looking at integration or segregation of various communities.

SPATIAL SEGREGATION

Spatial segregation is visible in Iberian American urban planning, which was based on a gridiron or chessboard, with a square at the center around which were concentrated the main political, administrative, religious, and economic institutions of the town or city: the church (or cathedral), town hall, column for judicial punishment (*picota* or *pelourinho*), and market.[1] In several cases, as in Cuzco, the Spanish gridiron was superimposed on a previously existing structure, and what had been an enormous ceremonial center was reduced to the scale of a normal plaza mayor. In the case of Mexico City, the Zócalo was built on the previous site of the main Nahua temple, opening up an enormous space in front of the cathedral and the palace of the governors. The scale of Spanish colonial structures—churches, convents, and palaces—was generally bigger than in Iberia; the colonizers had to come to terms with the enormous size of the Nahua or Inca temples and palaces. The Spanish population lived in the urban center, while mixed-race people were banished to the peripheries. Outside the town or city walls, Native Americans could create their own neighborhoods, generally organized by ethnicities, and structured around the convents of religious orders, which exercised a control over these areas.

By the end of the seventeenth century, the Indian neighborhoods outside the walls of Mexico City were home to forty to fifty thousand people. The Mixtecs and Zapotecs were under the tutelage of Dominicans, and the Meztitláns under that of the Augustinians. In the

Andes, the tradition of separation by original ethnicity was even more carefully maintained. La Paz had three Indian neighborhoods outside the walls, Cuzco eight, and Potosi fourteen. In each case, the numbers matched those of the provinces that paid *mita* (from the Quechua *mit'a*), a tribute consisting of one week's public work. As we can see, the number of neighborhoods and complexity of the population involved were related to the size and functions concentrated in the city. Each Indian neighborhood had its own square and church as well as its own autonomous political administration. In special instances, in recognition of Native support during the process of conquest, the ruling family was offered building plots on the Plaza Mayor. The *cacique* Aymoró had access to the main square of Sucre, the capital of the department of Chuquisaca (in the region of La Plata), and his Indian Yamparas were exempted from the mita and placed under the tutelage of the Franciscans.[2]

The size of the *manzanas*, or blocks of buildings, in Spanish American cities was immense. But even in this special context, some institutions, like the convents of the religious orders, operated out of locations that represented an enormous portion of urban property. The convent of San Francisco in Lima, for instance, occupied no less than eight blocks—a concentration that included several churches, buildings used by members of the Third Order, houses for meditation, prayer, and other spiritual exercises, and orchards and vegetable gardens. By the end of the eighteenth century, Mexico City could boast 150,000 inhabitants with 100 churches, 50 convents, and 17 hospitals, not to mention its university, colleges, seminar, theaters, circus, and bullfight rings. Despite all these amenities, which were concentrated around the viceroy's headquarters, spatial segregation in Mexico City was gradually eroded throughout the seventeenth and eighteenth centuries; the blocks tended to be reduced in size, and urban property went through a process of fragmentation.[3] The penetration of mixed-race people and even Native Americans into the city center was the outcome of not only urban reform but also elite decline through several generations: courtyards, enclosures, and abandoned lots were occupied by the new groups in return for rents and services. For Native Americans, their arrival at the center, followed by the acquisition of language skills and European clothes, represented the opportunity to invent a casta identity and avoid tribute. The ideal of segregation was thus eroded in the last period of colonial dominion. The urban reforms launched by the archbishop of Mexico, Francisco Antonio de Lorenzana y Butrán, conceived in the 1760s and implemented in 1771, ignored the traditional division between Spaniards and Indians altogether.

It is difficult to neatly distinguish between *urbs* (the built city) and *civitas* (the political and social community).[4] A focus on civitas, however, allows us immediately to identify the notion of *vecino* (neighbor) as a citizen well rooted in the Spanish Empire, linked to an urban community formally recognized by the king.[5] Only vecinos were entitled to benefit from the *encomienda* or *repartimiento*, the allocation of native labor for private work, not to mention the distribution of land that had been part of the former Nahua state territories, former elite properties, or communal land abandoned by decimated, disrupted, or relocated villages.[6] Vecinos controlled the main administrative functions of the towns and played a major role at the local political level, negotiating their interests with the *audiencias* (regional tribunals) and the viceroyalty. These citizens can be defined as a Creole elite of Spanish descent that perpetuated its local political grip, even when for financial reasons the Crown systematically auctioned off the main town jobs.

This notion of citizenship was replicated in the república de indios and Indian neighborhoods, which had their own *alcaldes* and *regidores* of justice.[7] The former Nahua elite who aligned themselves with Cortés, particularly the descendants of Montezuma, and the elite of Tlaxcala, who played a crucial role in the conquest, were recognized as native nobility and allowed to establish a direct connection with the Spanish king as privileged vassals. The Indian towns or neighborhoods were privileged through "positive segregation," meaning that white or mixed-race people, even including the encomenderos, were forbidden to live in these areas, and there was a defined area around these urbes in which houses, farms, and other urban structures could not be built. The Indians were protected from enslavement, although we know that the practice did continue, despite royal legislation, mainly in the peripheries. They were also excluded from service to black or mixed-race people. The Spanish king recognized their property and other basic rights, and treated them as vassals, since they had been forcibly converted to Christianity. Nevertheless, the political and administrative scope of the república de indios was quite narrow: it basically concerned the interests of small communities. Members were treated as second-rate citizens, even if their children enjoyed privileged access to schools, seminars, and universities. The crucial point is that there were no obstacles to marrying Spaniards and becoming part of the colonial elite in one way or another. But by this point Natives were not Natives anymore.

The series of riots that took Mexico City by storm—in 1537, 1549, 1624, and 1692—indicated the difficulties of integrating a segmented population defined by castas who often lived at the limits of survival. The size of the city both facilitated communication and offered space for political action, generally connected to the marketplace. Black and mixed-race people were usually accused of the riots, revealing white fear of uncontrolled slaves and discomfort at the upward social mobility of those Natives who were present at the city center disguised as mixed-race people. The main social issue was the high percentage of illegitimacy among mixed-race people, which excluded them from access to the educational and religious systems. Most of these people had been born outside wedlock, undermining the sacrament of matrimony and established Catholic order. The paradox here is the presence of Natives among mixed-race people. From a political point of view, Natives were privileged over mixed-race people and black Africans. But in their towns and neighborhoods they had to pay tribute, while residence as mixed-race people in the colonial center meant they avoided tribute and improved their chance of entering domestic service.

The reports concerning the major riot of 1692 point to the breakdown of segregation along with widespread penetration by mixed-race and Native people of the city center. Priests were the main informants about these events. Father Barnabé Nuñez de Paez, from the parish of San Pablo, lamented that Indian women wore Spanish skirts instead of the traditional *huipil* (between a blouse and a tunic), while men wore socks, shoes, *valonas* (huge collars reaching down over the back, shoulders, and chest), and overcoats, letting their hair

Figure 13.1. Cristóbal de Villal-pando, *View of the Zócalo of Mexico City*, painting, oil on canvas, 180 × 200 cm., c. 1695. This painting includes the ruined facade of the vice royal palace after the riot of 1692 (superior center-right section with the market). Reprinted with permission from the Art Archive, London; Lord Methuen

grow into *melenas* (long chunks of hair coming down over the face to cover the eyes, and reaching to the shoulders at the back and sides) in order to be identified as mixed-race people. Clothing and physical appearances, particularly hairstyle, were considered the main criteria of identification. The priest especially regretted the wearing of overcoats, which in his opinion caused the Natives to act with great haughtiness, while the use of *mantas* (or ponchos) made them more humble and obedient, as they looked less like mestizos. These comments, which offer a catalog of colonial prejudices, continued to lament that Natives had learned Spanish and made themselves ladinos, "the beginning of all boldness (or insolence, *atrevimientos*), because while they speak their own language they are much more humble." The white perspective was also expressed by Father Agustin de Betancur, priest of the parish of San Juan: "Blacks, mulattoes and mestizos . . . are restless men of bad habits, thieves, gamblers, addicted to vice, lost people," who mistreat Indians in their villages and "teach them bad habits and laziness."[8] Language, clothing, and hairstyle could indeed transform a person, meaning that phenotype features were not crucial, and confirmed the idea that individuals in Spanish colonial society could play with different identities, or simply change identity, not necessarily breaking with the loose casta system, but rather negotiating their position according to the informal rules.

The status of the Indians in Portuguese America was not so well defined due to the lack of any complex native political or urban system before the conquest, although the king addressed these people as vassals when they had been converted. The prohibition on enslavement, reiterated several times in royal decrees, was constantly violated under the pretext of a just war. The slave-hunting expeditions of the Paulistas (people from São Paulo) continued until the end of the seventeenth century, and the practice of enslaving Indians was still in place throughout the eighteenth century in the poorer captaincies of Maranhão and Grão Pará in the Amazon basin. As a result, Indians were either expelled to the peripheries of the colonies or were assimilated into the colonial system without leaving any trace. The converted Indians were visible only because they were concentrated in large numbers by Jesuits and other members of religious orders (Franciscans, Carmelites, and Mercederians) in the missionary villages. Even there their status was not clear, suspended between religious tutelage and pressure from colonists to use their forced labor.

It was only in 1755, during the government of Pombal, that secular imperial policies were clearly formulated concerning the Indians' status. The hold of the missionaries was broken; villages were secularized and placed under civil administration. In those villages that were transformed into towns, Indians were allowed to apply for municipal jobs, including the judicial system. The symbols of political power were introduced (a town hall, punishment column, and jail), along with the accepted form of urban planning (central square and gridiron layout). Disruptions occurred, but for the first time parts of this important urban network became connected.[9] In 1757, the directory of Indians introduced a policy of integration based on civil rights, which defined the emancipation of all Indians, granting them the same rights as white people, including the rights to property and trade. The directory encouraged a policy of miscegenation, since it did not make any provision for spatial segregation, and explicitly favored relations between Indians and white people. The other side of this policy of integration—or its logical consequence—was that Indians had to abandon their language in favor of Portuguese and pay taxes. Under these new conditions, the Crown expected to obtain the integration of the Indian labor force into colonial society.

In Asia, spatial segregation was visible in the new towns built by the Portuguese inside (or protected by) their fortifications, which were reserved for Christians, and contrasted with native towns nearby.[10] A clear example of this is Cochin; the Portuguese controlled the harbor there, built a significant fort, and organize the city inside its walls. The native city was close by, upriver, and was home to not only Hindus and Muslims but also Jews and other non-Christians ruled by the raja, who in turn was protected by the Portuguese. For a long time, Cochin served as the main port for the *carreira da Índia* (the spice fleet controlled by the king), even after Goa became the capital of the Estado da Índia, since it was close to the main areas of pepper production. The same division between the Christian and native city can be observed in Diu or Daman; this division was replicated in nearly all the places occupied by the Portuguese where a native town with a significant population had previously existed. The case of Goa was quite exceptional, since the Portuguese managed to use their political power in the 1550s to transform the preexisting city into a Christian one, destroying all non-Christian temples. In Malacca, the Portuguese reserved the royal palace and central neighborhoods for themselves, taking advantage of the disruption of the local elite. But as in most Asian ports, a tradition of neighborhood divisions according to the different ethnicities of the traders already existed.

Religious allegiance was the main criterion for integration. Converted natives and mixed-race people enjoyed a special status in Portuguese Asia, being accepted in the Christian

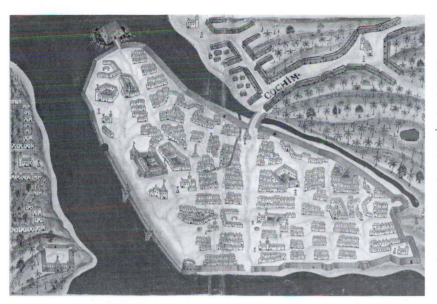

Figure 13.2. Pedro Barreto de Resende, *View of Cochin*, watercolor, 1635, in António Bocarro, *Livro das Plantas de todas as fortalezas cidades e povoações do Estado da Índia Oriental*, Biblioteca Pública de Évora, Portugal, manuscripts, CXV/2-1. The native city was further to the interior, separated from the Portuguese city.
Reprinted with permission from Biblioteca Pública de Évora, Portugal

neighborhoods or towns ruled by the Portuguese. In Sri Lanka, where the Portuguese controlled most of the island from 1597 to 1630, the city of Colombo functioned as the administrative capital, attracting slaves and converted natives; the city maintained its mixed ethnic features after the Dutch conquest. Despite the integration of converted natives and mixed-race people, ethnic prejudice remained part of normal daily life, still visible in the modern designation *black burghers* (people of Portuguese, African, and native descent). In Manila, the same practices of spatial segregation inside and outside the city walls, created in 1590, were visible from the beginning, with the tiny Spanish presence reinforced by a vast program of native conversions by the religious orders.[11] The main fear concerned the sizable Chinese community, which reached 10,000 people in 1586, far outnumbering the 800 Spaniards present at the time, and increased to 20,000 inhabitants in 1621, despite a massacre suffered in 1603, followed by others in 1639 and 1662 at the hands of the Spaniards and Tagalogs. The Chinese, who controlled trade with China and some of the urban professions, were given a special quarter of the city, Parian, but this did not prevent intermarriage with the native population.[12] Religious allegiance was the main feature of the Iberian expansion in Asia. There was a division between Christians and non-Christians, inside and outside the walls of cities, although the blurring of boundaries progressed with the spread of Catholicism.[13]

Spatial segregation in British and Dutch America became much more rooted than in Iberian America, since the colonial projects of these two powers and the characteristics of their settlements were totally different. The rural nature of the long British period of settlement contrasted with the strong urbanization that existed from early on in the Spanish areas of expansion. In the latter case, 330 towns were created before 1630, while there was nothing comparable in British America a century later. The size of the Spanish cities in comparison is also revealing: by the end of the seventeenth century, Mexico City had around 100,000 inhabitants, Boston 6,000, New York 4,500, and Philadelphia 2,200. By the mid-eighteenth century, the situation had not changed dramatically: Boston had 16,000 inhabitants, New York 11,000, and Philadelphia 13,000, well below seven Spanish American cities (Mexico, Lima, Havana, Quito, Cuzco, Santiago de Chile, and Caracas) and four Portuguese American cities (Salvador, Rio, São Paulo, and Ouro Preto).[14] Weak urbanization meant fewer opportunities for interethnic contact, due to the limited spread of markets and services. The relative ethnic homogeneity of the British and Dutch urban areas was likewise a consequence of their size. The predominance of rural areas and the plantation system in the southern colonies maintained a relatively secluded population that kept an indentured labor force and then African slaves under its control. This control was reinforced by local and regional legislation creating obstacles to manumission, and consequently the free circulation of people.

The case of Madras, nowadays Chennai, on the Coromandel coast of southeast India is well known. Founded in 1639–40 by the East India Company outside the fishing village of Madraspatnam, it evolved according to the previous Portuguese colonial model that had been experimented with in Africa and Asia. The fortified trading post protected the Europeans, while the natives built their own neighborhood outside the walls. In 1706, following several attacks by Nawab Daud Khan, Madras was walled. White Town and Black Town, as the British authorities explicitly labeled them, experienced a difficult coexistence, since they needed each other, but did not coincide in their goals. The native town was divided by religion (into Hindu and Muslim sections) and along caste lines. The porous frontier between the two towns was exposed by the short-lived French conquest in 1746: the French resettled Black Town four hundred yards away from the gates of White Town, creating an intermediate zone that was maintained by the East India Company when it reoccupied the city two years later. The extra space established by the ruthless French operation allowed the British to develop a complex Vauban-style fortification. In the aftermath of the reconquest, the British also decided to settle their differences with the Portuguese and Armenians, who had sided with the French, and these people were expelled from the white city.[15]

Madras presents a striking case of a color divide revealing ethnic prejudices coupled with segregationist actions. This related to the previous Portuguese classification of people and urban practices in Asia, rather than to the British experience in the Atlantic. New York provides an example for the relatively homogeneous British and Dutch cities in North America. It was founded by the Dutch as New Amsterdam in 1624–26, and taken over by the British in 1664. In 1658, a wall was built to protect the city from both the Indians and the British colonists of New England. Laws forbade the Indians from lingering in the area to the south of the wall during the night, in line with similar prescriptions passed in other North American towns. An exception were the "praying towns" of Massachusetts, where fourteen communities of converted Indians were set up in the mid-seventeenth century by the Reverend John Eliot—an interesting experiment that still needs to be compared with the missionary villages of Iberian America.[16] British towns in America were inhabited by a vast majority of Europeans, although black slaves were employed in varying numbers in domestic service.[17] Control of this "restless" racial group was a major issue for the local authorities, who were confronted in certain cases, like that of New York City, by spontaneous settlement outside

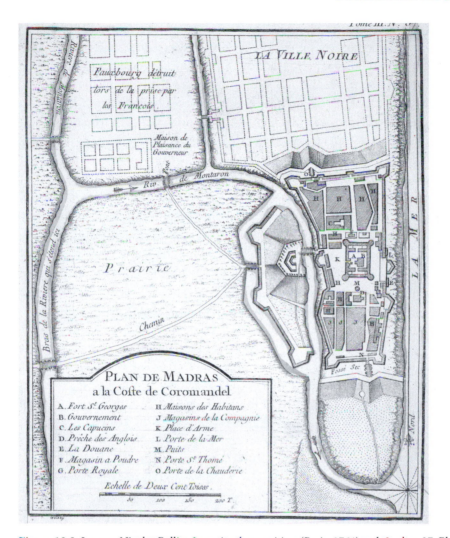

Figure 13.3. Jacques Nicolas Bellin, *Le petit atlas maritime* (Paris, 1764), vol. 3, plate 37. Plan of Madras after repossession by the British. The British city was inside the wall, separated from the indigenous or "black" city. © British Library Board; Robana

the walls. This explains the decision during the 1710s to force black slaves to live inside the walls. Slave owners were reminded of their responsibility to lodge the slaves in their household. Social control over slaves remained a private matter; the creation of urban, informally segregated areas was left to a much later period.[18]

CIVIL RIGHTS

Civil rights are the second crucial issue, closely related to spatial segregation. In the Iberian world, converted natives were vassals of the king, creating a claim on monarchical justice and protection. The fact that African slaves were converted also created a link between them and the Iberian monarchs. This is an obvious paradox, since slaves were considered the property of their owner and excluded from civil rights, even though their human condition was acknowledged, and the authorities had a duty to interfere in cases of unjustified brutality or murder by the owner. But this general obligation could be taken further, as shown by the puzzling series of Portuguese royal documents in which the king granted mercy in response to requests from slaves and freedpersons in Brazil.[19] The slaves' religious allegiance certainly played a major role in this implicit recognition of basic civil rights. The fact that slaves could not testify in judicial inquiries matched the exclusion of conversos and Moriscos from the right to make religious accusations against old Christians. Both these ethnic groups had diminished rights in the religious judicial sphere: they could be accused, but could not accuse. These groups were also excluded from access to religious orders, ecclesiastical positions, and public service (see chapter 9). New Christians were excluded from colleges, universities, and certain professions too; the descendants of conversos punished by the Inquisition suffered the same lack of rights as their ancestors. Conversos and Moriscos were forbidden to travel to America and India—a form of discrimination that underlined their inferior status from a religious and ethnic point of view. New Christians managed to circumvent the prohibition following special authorizations by the king. They also took advantage of the union of the Iberian crowns (1580–1640) and renewed communication between the two empires to increase their influence in the merchant networks that spanned the Atlantic. But in the 1630s and 1640s they were caught by the Inquisition, which targeted New Christians as the main single group of victims in that area and Iberian Asia.[20]

The integration or exclusion of natives and mixed-race people is the touchstone of interethnic policies. I have already analyzed the advantages and limitations of the república de indios. The república was adapted to other territories of the Iberian empires, particularly the Philippines, as a kind of local indirect rule. Its subjects were often placed under the tutelage of a religious order. Their status as vassals of the king provided Indians with privileged access to schools, colleges, and universities, which was denied to all black people as well as mixed-race people born out of wedlock. While converted natives managed to gain access to the secular priesthood in Asia and Africa, they were systematically undermined and largely excluded from the more prestigious religious orders. This general view has to be qualified, however. The exclusion of Asian Indians from religious orders was only implemented in the late sixteenth century, after which it was practiced throughout the seventeenth and most of the eighteenth centuries. The access of Native Americans to positions as secular and regular clergymen occurred in the first decades after the Spanish Conquest. It was then forbidden by the first two provincial synods of Mexico and the second provincial synod of Lima, and the prohibition was taken up by nearly all religious orders in the second half of the sixteenth century. Japanese and Chinese converts benefited from much better integration into religious orders, reaching various levels, although they never gained top positions. There was no native secular clergymen in Mozambique until the twentieth century, in contrast to the significant number of ordained natives in Congo and N'gola. Africans were ordained in west-central Africa, but not in America. The fact that Native Americans' access to positions as secular clergymen was blocked contrasted with significant native access in Portuguese India.[21]

As we can see, Acosta's hierarchy of the peoples of the world was projected through the degree of exclusion from, or access to, positions in the clergy, although the refusal of full-blooded Native Americans did not follow the model. The importance of rivalry and competition emerges clearly in some episodes: in the 1630s and 1640s, Portuguese regular clergymen in Asia blocked the appointment of native missionaries and even opposed the installation of the native bishop, D. Mateus de Castro (bishop of Chrisopolis *in partibus infidelium*), ordained in Rome and promoted by the Propaganda Fide.[22] The bishop, a Goan Brahman who traveled to Rome several times seeking support for his fight with the Portuguese clergy, was insulted by his main adversary, D. Afonso Mendes, the Jesuit patriarch of Ethiopia, as "a negro with his bottom uncovered" (*negro de rabo ao léu*), suggesting that Castro was not only "stained" by his skin color but could not even dress properly.[23] These vicious, unchristian insults against a fellow bishop who had been ordained by the pope reveal the extent of ethnic prejudice. The explicit idea, quite common among regular European clergymen, was that natives had neither the moral standing nor intellectual capacity to be ordained priests. Contempt and base insults were widespread, being denounced not only by Castro in his reports to Rome but also by some members of the colonial elite, who realized the importance of native clergymen.

Ethnic prejudices were well known in Rome and could stimulate some blunt interpretations. In various reports and accounts from the 1620s, 1630s, and 1640s, Francesco Ingoli, secretary of the Propaganda Fide, denounced the opposition to native access as a machination of Portuguese clergymen who did not want to share their rents.[24] Religious orders also argued that the admission of natives to the clergy would alienate the European colonial elite, who were responsible for most of the donations to the church. Ingoli may have exaggerated the importance of material interests to missionaries who benefited from Iberian royal patronage, but there was a basic element of competition. In the Philippines, where Spanish dominion benefited so much from the prevention of the worst military excesses by missionaries, the access of natives to the priesthood was largely blocked by religious orders that kept the monopoly of most local parishes until the nineteenth century. In 1870, only 181 out of 792 parishes were administered by native clergymen. The accumulation of wealth by the religious orders was such that the authorities launched several inquiries during the eighteenth century, in which they met obdurate refusals by the European clergy to accept judicial decisions. Discrimination experienced by native clergypersons was one of the grievances that lay behind the rise of the nationalist movement in the late nineteenth century, and thus secularization became the movement's clarion call.[25]

Mixed-race people were also largely excluded from both the secular and regular clergy positions, but they were apparently considered by the Spaniards to operate at a higher intellectual level than Native Americans. This prejudice allowed a certain number of mixed-race people to be ordained, since they knew the native languages. The opposition of most European clergymen to the access granted to these mixed-race clergy by certain bishops was expressed in a succession of petitions to the king and reflected in the prohibitions issued by the first provincial synods. In the 1560s and 1570s, Philip II sent several letters reprimanding the bishops for ordaining mestizos, which meant that the petitions had had an impact. In 1578 Philip II went one step further: he produced a decree (*cédula real*), addressed to all archbishops and bishops, which excluded mestizos from holy orders. The royal decree was followed by action on the part of the royal audiencias: the bishop of Quito was notified not only to refrain from ordaining new mestizos but also to remove those who had been given benefices such as *curatos* and *prebiendas*. The members of the audiencia went even further, stating that if the bishop did not remove the mestizos, they would do it themselves. They also ordered the encomenderos not to make payments to mestizo priests and the Indians not to give them food. This is the most extreme case of discrimination against mixed-race priests, totally humiliated by the royal power in the eyes of the population. But this action raised a crucial issue: the competence of the king to interfere in the strictly religious sphere.

The royal decree clashed with the pronouncements of the Council of Trent, which mentioned no ethnic or racial restrictions in the requirement for receiving holy orders. It also clashed with a bull issued two years earlier by Pope Gregory XIII, in which the bishops of the Indies were granted the right to ordain those speaking native languages as clergymen even if they were illegitimate. Those supporting the royal decree felt that it was justified by the church's royal patronage; this was mentioned by the audiencia as *cédula real del patronato*. The conflict over the decree reveals just how tremendously important access to positions in the clergy was in colonial society. The link between spiritual, social, and political issues was clearly established in this case.

The reaction of a notable group of mixed-race priests in Peru was surprisingly effective: in 1583 they wrote a letter to the pope, in faultless and elegant Latin, in which they contested the prejudices underlying the royal cédula. They showed their ability and education. They contradicted the main accusations and denounced the calumnies produced by the Spanish clergymen, describing them as ambitious and egotistic priests who had more interest in personal advancement than in the salvation of souls, and who left the area as soon as they became rich. This extraordinary document anticipated similar accusations leveled against Portuguese missionaries by the secretary of Propaganda Fide, Francesco Ingoli, by more than forty years. The letter was sent by the pope to the nuncio in Spain. Naturally, the pope took advantage of this protest to question whether the boundaries of intervention in religious matters had been breached by royal action. In 1582, mixed-race priests had already mobilized notable Spanish clergymen in support of their movement: they launched *probanzas* (proofs based on testimonies) to demonstrate their ability as priests during the third provincial synod of Lima. In Cuzco, the confraternity of the *Santa Misericordia* launched a parallel probanza. Philip II, who was probably aware of this movement, did not immediately bow to the papal request, but in 1588 he issued a new decree which authorized the admission of mixed-race people (meaning the descendants or offspring of Spaniards and

Indians) to holy orders as long as they were of legitimate birth and responded to all requirements established by the Council of Trent.

The access of mestizos to major ecclesiastical positions, mainly those involving crucial rents, was much more difficult. The case of Don Gonzalo Garcia del Zorro, the first mestizo appointed a canon at the cathedral of Santa Fe in New Spain, took more than ten years of petitions to the king and pope. Zorro faced all kinds of abuse, including periods of detention, and had to travel to Europe several times in order to finally overcome the ruthless opposition of the cathedral chapter, against clear orders from the king and pope. But the royal resolution of 1588 did not terminate this debate. In 1636 a new decree excluded mulattoes, mestizos, and illegitimate people from ordination—a decision reinforced in 1676. It was only in 1697 that the ordination of descendants of Indian rulers and mestizos was authorized again. Local resistance from the European clergy was still in place by 1769, when a royal decree established that a third or quarter of admissions to seminaries should be reserved for Indians and mestizos, although there are no clear records of the implementation of this decree.[26]

CHAPTER 14

▏▎▏▎▎▏

Abolitionism

OLAUDAH EQUIANO'S TESTIMONY

"I lost at once a kind interpreter, an agreeable companion, and a faithful friend; who, at the age of fifteen, discovered a mind superior to prejudice; and who was not ashamed to notice, to associate with, and to be friend and instructor of one who was ignorant, a stranger, of a different complexion, and a slave'![1] This is how Equiano (1745–97), the famous abolitionist black freedman, expressed his feelings of loss for the first friend he had made while a ten-year-old slave on a trading ship. The stigma that marked black people was acutely observed by Equiano, who received constant humiliation and abuse. In this case, his friend, a young white man, a native of America whose family owned slaves, had obviously broken the normal rule of ignoring or mocking the young black slave. This encounter bridged social, ethnic, and cultural distances built on prejudice. What Equiano tells us is that slaves were placed at the bottom of colonial society, objects of permanent command and contempt: they were supposed to be inferior, and this feeling was imposed on them; they were supposed to perform services and satisfy the master's requirements; they were not supposed to receive any instruction unless there was a motive for it; and they were not suppose to be befriended by whites.

The extraordinary autobiography written and published by Equiano served the abolitionist cause. Although fellow black freedmen—Briton Hammon, James Albert Ukawsaw Gronniosaw, Phillis Wheatley, Ignatius Sancho, John Marrant, and Ottobah Cugoano—had published books or poems related to this issue since the 1760s, both in America and England, it was Equiano who voiced most clearly a nostalgia for the original African society he had known while exposing the dreadful conditions of the Middle Passage, cruelty of the slave owners, and deep-rooted unfairness of colonial society. This was the direct testimony of a former black slave who had learned to read and write, worked at many different jobs, managed to purchase his own freedom, fought against constant abuse in the West Indies, even after manumission, become a subject of the British king, and finally was recognized as a campaigner for the rights of black people, publicly promoting and presenting several petitions to Parliament and king. His was the voice that white abolitionists needed to advance

Figure 14.1. Olaudah Equiano, *Interesting Narrative* (London, 1789), engraving with the portrait of the author. © British Library Board; Robana

the cause: a self-educated African who could prove the intelligence of his race and expose the iniquities of the slave trade through his own experiences.

The Interesting Narrative reveals Equiano's religious piety, conversion to Methodism, and moral standards. Equiano embraces what were considered the best values of British society: honesty, fairness, moderation, endurance, and perseverance. Several times in his book he calls attention to the important role played by the Quakers and British Protestants in the abolitionist movement.[2] He belonged to a prominent circle of abolitionists, led by his friend Thomas Clarkson, who campaigned for the suppression of the slave trade with a member of Parliament, William Wilberforce. Equiano also makes shrewd comments about the subordinate position of the Greeks under the Turks, comparing it to the relationship between blacks and whites in the West Indies.[3] In an open letter to the *Public Advertiser*, published in 1788, he stated that "the glorious system of the Gospel destroys all narrow partiality, and makes us citizens of the world, by obliging us to profess universal benevolence."[4] Equiano could not have expressed a more radical and cosmopolitan detachment from the constraints of racial classification.

The vast list of subscribers to Equiano's book, more than thirteen hundred people over nine editions, included members of the royal family, nobility, members of Parliament, officers, bishops, clergymen, scholars, and merchants. The list speaks tellingly of the spread of abolitionism among the British elites. Although abolitionists were no more than a growing minority in these years, Equiano and his friends were well supported. The list reflects the sophisticated British market for books and information, fueled by the widespread publication of political tracts and newspapers. It also represents a nonconformist civil society based on associations, less constrained by censorship than other European countries, used

Figure 14.2. Jasperware medallion of a humble kneeling slave with the inscription "Am I not a man and a brother?" by Wedgwood for the British Society for Effecting the Abolition of the Slave Trade, 1787. British Museum. © Trustees of the British Museum

to vigorous public argument about political and religious issues, in which former slaves could achieve public expression.

Petitions concerning the abolition of the slave trade began to be presented to Parliament in 1783, exactly at the end of the American War of Independence, which opened a new space for moral reflection.[5] In 1788, the year after the establishment of the Society for Effecting the Abolition of the Slave Trade, there were more than 100 petitions. In 1792, at least 519 petitions were presented, involving more than 400,000 people, many of them women, from every single English county along with Wales and Scotland.[6] The abolition of the slave trade was finally approved in 1807, but it was imposed by successive campaigns supported by growing numbers of petitions. These campaigns influenced the abolition of the slave trade by Denmark and the United States in the same year. The final abolition of slavery in the British West Indies between 1833 and 1838 involved millions of petitioners in England (one petition was signed by 700,000 women), who imposed clear choices on candidates during the parliamentary elections.[7]

The abolitionist movement also projected a remarkable iconography, such as the diagram of the slave ship *Brookes*, with its representations of the cramped conditions of slaves as well as the medallions, medals, and plates with dignified portrayals of slaves and freedpersons that were meant to contrast with the slave owner material culture of African heads as clay pipe bowls, tobacco jars, beer mugs, and drinking cups.[8] If we look at spiritual forms of art, it is striking how the equality of human beings became a vital topic. In his *House of Death*, for example, William Blake depicted bodies with different phenotype features, all of them equally measured by God.[9] This popular abolitionist movement is astonishing when compared to extreme discretion in the Netherlands, the "heavy" silence in Portugal and

Figure 14.3. William Blake, *The House of Death*, print finished in pen, chalk, and watercolor, 479 × 603 mm., c. 1795. Fitzwilliam Museum, Cambridge, UK.
© Fitzwilliam Museum, Cambridge, UK

Spain—silence prolonged throughout the nineteenth century—or the limited debate on this subject that grew up in France, even during the revolution.[10]

THE CATHOLIC DEBATE

There was no historical precedent for a systematic debate about the African slave trade and African slavery conducive to abolitionism in the Catholic world. The classical idea of freedom based on natural law conflicted with Aristotle's notion of natural slavery. Aquinas is a good case of the ambiguity involved here, since he accepted the belief that some human beings should be subordinate to others, and that there were differences in human beings' merit and social needs, even though he did not adopt the Aristotelian view on this subject. We have seen how Las Casas, the school of Salamanca, and later the Jesuits systematically fought against the enslavement of Native Americans, and sought to promote their basic freedom. But a debate on the same level was not extended to the African slave trade and black slavery, with the exception of Las Casas, who left manuscripts condemning the African slave trade but never took a public position on the issue.[11]

In the sixteenth century, the vast majority of theologians and political writers accepted the use of African slaves in the European colonies as necessary. They also asserted the legitimacy of slavery as a result of war, debt, and the selling of oneself or one's relatives when the means of subsistence were entirely lacking. Dominicans and Jesuits raised doubts about the legality of enslaving free people, whether perpetrated by Africans or Europeans. Domingo de Soto, Tomás de Mercado, Diego Covarrubias, and Luis de Molina condemned the purchase of slaves who had been taken captive by violence, but did not question slavery as institution.[12] Francisco Suarez also expressed concerns about the legitimacy of the status of many slaves, following Aquinas when he opposed the law of nations, based on practical needs and expediency, to natural law, defined by eternal principles. Bartolomé Frías de Albornoz went further, questioning the classic reasons given to legitimate enslavement. In a treatise about naval construction, Fernando Oliveira condemned the slave trade and the use of African slaves, yet his was a lone voice. Friar Alonso de Montúfar, archbishop of Mexico, wrote to Philip II critiquing the double standard relating to Native Americans and African slaves, but the matter was not pursued. The Jesuits Gonçalo Leite and Miguel Garcia were expelled from Brazil because they opposed the use of African slaves, but there is no trace of their argumentation. In the seventeenth century, when Alonso de Sandoval (1576–1652) reproduced the doubts of his colleagues concerning the legitimacy of enslavement in Africa, he quoted Molina, although did not question slavery as an institution.[13]

We have to wait until 1682 to find two powerful treatises against the slave trade and use of African slaves in colonial societies—written by the Capuchin friars Francisco José de Jaca and Epifanio de Moirans.[14] These two priests systematically went through the main arguments in favor of slavery, demonstrating the illegitimacy of the slave trade and advocating for the liberation of converted slaves. Jaca maintained that masters, under penalty of excommunication if they disobeyed, should manumit their slaves with indemnities. Moirans used the Bible to demolish the idea of the natural slavery of African people based on the legend of Ham, since Noah's curse concerned Canaan and his descendants in the Middle East, not in Africa. The case of these two Capuchins, based in Venezuela, became public because they expressed their opinions in their sermons and refused the sacrament of penitence to unrepentant slave masters. They were sent away to Cuba, where they again continued to publicly declare their opinions. This time they were detained, excommunicated, and deported to Spain, but they overturned the excommunications and managed to regain their freedom. They were forbidden to return to America, although they appealed to the congregation of Propaganda Fide in Rome, asking for a clear decision on the legitimacy of the slave trade and African slavery.

This petition coincided with another one presented by Lourenço da Silva de Mendonça, procurator of the confraternities of black people in Brazil, Lisbon, and Madrid, who raised similar concerns and asked for the perpetual outlawing of slavery for Christians.[15] The Propaganda Fide declared itself incompetent on doctrinal matters, and in 1686, another petition by Mendonça triggered a consultation with the congregation of the Holy Office. The Roman Inquisition decided that illegitimate enslavement was unacceptable, but refused to order the liberation of converted slaves. When the Propaganda Fide sent the result of the consultation to the bishops of the Iberian empires, it was confronted with the reality of royal patronage: the congregation had no jurisdiction over those bishops. Curiously, the Catholic debate on slavery was reduced to the traditional issue of the "Christian treatment" of slaves throughout the eighteenth century, with the exception of the Capuchin friar José de Bolonha, who was expelled from Bahia in 1794 for publicly declaring the slave trade unlawful due to the illegitimate conditions of enslavement. It was only in 1839 that Pope Gregory XVI condemned black slavery. Yet the Catholic Church did not take any initiative on the subject until the final abolition in Brazil in 1888.[16]

Turning to political thought—and here we need to look at both sides of the Christian divide—Jean Bodin was the only author in the sixteenth century who clearly rejected slavery, equated in *The Republic* with cruelty, corruption, and a threat to the state. Bodin directly challenged Aristotle and the scholastic tradition, dealing with the main arguments in favor of slavery one by one; he advocated the emancipation of all slaves, who should receive an education so that they could earn their livelihood and become fully integrated into society.[17] Bodin's position was not influential, which only confirms the nonlinear development of the history of ideas. Hugo Grotius declared that people cannot be slaves by the law of nature, but he accepted slavery under the law of nations as a result of human activity, even as he recognized the moderating influence of religion among Christians and Muslims, who refrained from enslaving their brethren captured in war.[18] Hobbes considered slavery to be part of the traditional system of authority. He also asserted the principle of equality among people, while accepting the historical reality of slavery under despotic rule.[19] Pufendorf saw slavery as a matter of fact that was included in the idea of social discipline.[20] John Locke rejected slavery as a matter of principle in the first phrase of the *Two Treatises of Government*, defining it later in the text as a state of continued war, yet he accepted the institution in a colonial environment, which he placed outside the social contract.[21] Montesquieu, like Bodin, demolished the traditional assertions in favor of slavery, declared that all humans were born free, rejected slavery in ordered societies, and associated it with political despotism. Yet Montesquieu ambiguously justified its existence in colonial societies as part of his climate theory.[22]

Colonial slavery was thus accepted among the most widely read political thinkers of the early modern period, although Bodin, Locke, and Montesquieu had in principle rejected slavery. The *Encyclopédie* developed Montesquieu's reasoning against slavery, defined as a right based on and perpetuated through violence, including civil and political bondage. For the first time slavery was placed in opposition to not only natural law but also the law of nations. As a consequence, all sales of human beings were considered null and void. The *Encyclopédie* broke with all previous ambiguity concerning the reality of slavery.[23] Rousseau equated slavery with dehumanization. He considered the idea that liberty could be denied as absurd, illegitimate, and invalid. Rousseau defined slavery as abusive violence against nature. According to his analysis, slavery was part of arbitrary and corrupt rule; he coined the notion of rights for all humankind.[24] Abbé Raynal and his collaborators, especially Denis Diderot, grounded their critical vision of the European expansion on the defense of antislavery. The conditions of the slave trade and slavery in America were analyzed and criticized, and the liberation of slaves by the Quakers in Pennsylvania was reported in detail as an important precedent.[25] Marquis de Condorcet anonymously published one of the most forceful attacks on slavery. He defined the institution as a crime, proposed its abolition, and refused indemnities because they would reward illicit trade and illegitimate property.[26]

A NEW SYSTEM OF VALUES

Slavery was often used as a convenient metaphor to designate despotic rule and contrast it with European (or British) liberties. Adam Ferguson, in his essay on civil society, was one of the main authors who introduced slavery as a political metaphor, mostly based on classical references. When he analyzed "rude" or barbarian societies, he referred to American native societies, as described by Pierre François-Xavier de Charlevoix and Lafitau, but he did not reflect on contemporary colonial slavery.[27] In a certain way, Ferguson represented the culmination of a long tradition of legal and political thought, established in the fourteenth century by Bartolo da Sassoferrato, according to which Europe had long ago abandoned the enslavement of prisoners of war, and he was followed by English and French authors who praised the suppression of slavery in their territories.[28] This tradition would lead to several famous judicial decisions during the eighteenth century, mainly in the United Kingdom, against the maintenance of the status of slaves brought to the metropolis, which had an impact on the colonies, fueling the abolitionist movement there.

The major ideological blow to the institution of slavery during the Enlightenment came perhaps from the new liberal economic thought. Hume demolished the traditional idea that there had been a larger population in antiquity than in modern times due to the supposed fertility of the slaves, thereby decisively contributing to the idea of the economic archaism of slavery.[29] Benjamin Franklin (1706–90) followed the same line of reasoning and, for the first time, submitted slavery to an economic analysis, from which he arrived at the conclusion that slaves were more expensive than free labor. In 1790, the year of his death, Franklin intervened in the debate about abolition with a parody of a Muslim minister from Algiers, who supposedly replied to a Christian sect's request to ban slavery by stating that the indemnities to slave owners would be enormous, only slaves could work in hot weather, and in any case, Christians were slaves in their own land, and surely they would prefer to be slaves in Algiers, exposed to the true faith and treated with humanity.[30] Comte de Mirabeau and the Physiocrats denounced the destruction of populations along with the depletion of the soil caused by colonial agriculture. For them, slavery had corrupted colonial labor and colonial commerce, leading to unreasonable cost and waste, monopoly and privilege. According to their reasoning, free trade was paramount. François Quesnay had compared the circulation of goods to the circulation of the blood.[31]

This background proved to be important. Adam Smith clearly stated that the work of slaves, apparently cheap since it cost only the latter's maintenance, was unproductive and comparatively more expensive than free labor. The reasoning was that the slave had no interest but to eat as much as possible and work as little as possible; only violence would squeeze work out of them. Smith elaborated on this principle when he referred to the vast investment in slaves in colonial America, stating that the Quakers in Pennsylvania had been able to set their African slaves free because the numbers were not significant. He pointed out that the extraordinary profit on sugar and (to a lesser extent) tobacco meant that the expense of cultivation through slave labor was affordable, implicitly suggesting that these profits would be even higher with free labor.[32] Thomas Clarkson, founder of the abolitionist movement in England, argued that slavery was contrary to economic interests, but the main propaganda of the movement stressed the moral issue based on human dignity. The economic issue was renewed much later, from a Marxist perspective, by Eric Williams, who stated that slavery had become unprofitable.[33] Although the profitability of slavery has been reassessed, and its decline contested—particularly in view of the huge profits produced by the slave-based economies of Cuba, Brazil, and the southern states of the United States in the first half of the nineteenth century—it is undeniable that there was a new economically minded discourse atmosphere that found expression in Smith's reasoning.[34]

The abolitionist movement could not have been triggered without a significant change in the European system of values, as David Brion Davis has highlighted. Economic change, with the emerging ideals of free labor and free trade, and political change, with the new vision of a society of citizens free and equal before the law, had already created a stimulating environment. Yet there was also a fundamental ethical change, which meant that slavery was considered unacceptable—a manifestation of corruption, sin, and the violation of the human dignity. The central place of human integrity in this critical vision of slavery was preceded by the development of the notion of religious tolerance. Protestant thought had at least the same impact on abolitionism as the reasoning of influential *philosophes* and economists, although the questioning of slavery came from minority currents in Protestantism, and only became effective toward the mid-eighteenth century. The founders of Protestantism did not innovate in this field, but the issue of the legitimacy of trading slaves had been discussed since the first decades of the seventeenth century. William Perkins and Samuel Willard dismissed Aristotle's idea of natural slavery, as had the Catholic school of Salamanca in the previous century.

The Protestant synod at Rouen in 1637 rejected "overscrupulous" ideas about the illegality of the slave trade, which suggests that the issue had been widely discussed. Catholics like Jean-Baptiste du Tertre accused Protestants of refusing to baptize slaves because they might claim emancipation. Richard Baxter and Morgan Godwin refused to accept this criticism, aligning Protestant doctrine with Catholic doctrine on this issue, which was reflected in British colonial legislation. Eliot had created villages for converted Indians in New England in the 1630s, but it was considered inappropriate to force African slaves to convert. It took several campaigns, triggered by Godwin in the 1680s, to spread the practice of converting slaves in the Protestant colonies, where the colonists finally accepted that such methods could contribute to preventing resistance and insurrection. Successive programs of conversion insisted on treating slaves well—a topic developed by the Philanthropists, the Anglican Society for Promoting Christian Knowledge, the Society for the Propagation of the Gospel in Foreign Parts, and the German Pietists who migrated to America. The creation of schools for black people was part of this movement, in which Moravians and Quakers played a major role. The resistance of established colonists remained strong. In 1740, for instance, South Carolina passed a law making it illegal to teach black people to write.

The significant delay in Protestant debates and action is surprising in comparison to Catholic practices with regard to conversion, evangelization, and even the education of slaves. To use the law to maintain the illiteracy of slaves, because access to knowledge might lead them to rebel, was a thought that would not have occurred in Iberian America—where censorship was considered more efficient, as confession and consultation could solve any crisis of conscience among scrupulous colonists. This Catholic institutional framework, with permanent checks and balances, meaning inertia and compromise with the current social order, contrasted with the public debate among Protestants. That is why the development of the Protestant fear of sin in tropical environments proved to be more powerful in the long run, capable of breaking with the main premises of the colonial order—that is, the plantation system, urban labor system, and domestic service, all of which were based on slavery.

In 1736 the Quaker Benjamin Lay labeled the slave trade and slavery "a hellish practice," "the capital sin," and "the very worst part of the old whores' merchandise."[35] He equated religious purity with antislavery and launched what was to be the first serious campaign against slavery. The Quakers were particularly equipped to take on the debate about slavery, having questioned the practice among themselves since the 1680s. They were moved by ideas of inner light, equality of the human condition, absence of ecclesiastical authority, pacifism, nonresistance, personal responsibility, and social regeneration through the reform of habits and behavior, which included the refusal to pay tithes, take oaths before magistrates, and bow or doff their hats to superiors. They shared with the Jewish and Christian traditions of asceticism and millenarianism their refusal of the inevitable consequences of original sin, the idea that corruption was caused by bondage, the notion of liberation from servitude, the search for the perfection of the soul, and the vision of a world based on equality and love. Their principles were inimical to the acceptance of precedent or compromise with ancient customs. But it took another generation of dissenters and the Seven Years' War to precipitate real action, following the Quakers' refusal to fight or pay taxes. Quakers resigned from public office in Pennsylvania; in 1757 the London Yearly Meeting launched an inquiry into members involved in the slave trade; during the following year, the Philadelphia Meeting excluded members who bought and sold slaves; in 1760, the New England Quakers made the import of slaves a disciplinary issue; and in 1780, Pennsylvania abolished slavery, followed by New York (1799) and New Jersey (1804).

Protestants from other confessions contributed to the debate. In 1700, Samuel Sewall, a judge in Massachusets, published a pamphlet against slavery after a long trial that ended in the freeing of a slave. In Boston, he reproduced the *Athenian Oracle*, an English periodical edited by John Dunton that in 1705 had included a long article attacking the slave trade and questioning all the arguments justifying slavery. In the meantime, the new ethic of benevolence, introduced by the Dutch Arminians, English Latitudinarians, and German Pietists, had promoted a vision of redemption as a historical process in which humans could improve moral standards and reach eternal reason. The impact of the Restoration explains an interest in "primitive societies" as models of natural innocence and virtue. Primitivism in literature followed its own line of argument in the works of authors such as Thomas Tryon, Aphra Behn, Baron de Lahontan, John Dennis, James Thomson, and Daniel Defoe. But this trend had been started by the theologians' search for an inherent moral sense, natural virtue, and empathy with the misfortunes of others, in contradiction to Hobbes's idea of egotistic humans dominated by their own interests and emotions.

It was this tradition, built up by scholars and clergymen like Benjamin Whichcote, Isaac Barrow, Henry More, and John Tillotson, which contributed to the placing of virtue at the heart of theological debates, blending sentimentalism with rationalism. The suffering of black slaves, a major theme of the flood of antislavery literature that swelled throughout the eighteenth century, was highlighted by this theological debate and combined with developments in moral philosophy, particularly through the output of Francis Hutcheson and James Foster. In 1762, when the Quaker Anthony Benezet published *A Short Account of That Part of Africa Inhabited by the Negroes* in Philadelphia, the intellectual atmosphere in Britain and the British northern American colonies were ripe for the launch of a serious abolitionist campaign. In 1769, Granville Sharp, a lawyer involved in major legal battles to free black slaves in England, published the strongest rejection of slavery, *A Representation of the Injustice and Dangerous Tendency of Tolerating Slavery in England*, which set the stage for the years to come.[36]

SLAVE REVOLTS

Abolitionism, however, was not just motivated by major changes in European and American ethical, political, and economic thought. Black slaves contributed to their own liberation. They had their own aspirations, which expressed themselves in constant resistance, pleas for manumission, protests against bad treatment, individual or collective escapes, the organization of maroon communities, and riots and revolts, some of them large in scale. The increased import of slaves in the second half of the eighteenth and first half of the nineteenth centuries only served to increase these efforts, as in Cuba between 1789 and 1815. Yet it was only after the outbreak of a war of independence in Cuba in 1869 that a Spanish law supplying partial emancipation was passed in 1870, as slaves needed to be recruited as fighters in return for the promise of manumission. The peace agreement of 1878 freed all slaves, and was followed by a general law of emancipation in 1880.[37] On mainland Spanish America, resistance to abolition was less vigorous due to the much lower numbers of African slaves. The wars of independence in the 1810s and 1820s represented a major disruption of the slave system, since the widespread military recruitment of slaves on both sides meant that the latter possessed a new bargaining power, which resulted in the gradual and total abolition of the slave trade and slavery in those years.[38]

The most important urban slave riots and occupations of land in Brazil took place between 1798 and 1835 in Bahia, although a far greater number of slaves had been involved in escapes and the setting up of maroon communities in the area over its three centuries of slavery.[39] The resistance to abolition was fueled by the prosperity of the plantation system, now facing less competition from the French and British Caribbean islands, whose economies greatly declined after 1791 and 1807. The abolition of the slave trade was only implemented in 1850, following military action by the British Navy, which systematically searched slave ships and blockaded Brazilian ports.[40] Slavery itself was only abolished in 1888—the last abolition in the Americas. The outcomes of the American Civil War and Cuban War of Independence were not sufficient to deter Brazilian rulers and slave owners, but did have an impact on the belated spread of the abolitionist movement there in the 1870s and 1880s, thereby launching a successful campaign for "free soil" in Ceará. As a result of this policy, the slavery system had clearly been disrupted by the 1880s, with the spread of collective flight, which was responsible for a 40 percent decrease in the total number of slaves.[41]

In Portugal, whose merchant class dominated the Brazilian slave trade, the abolition of human traffic was only officially decreed in 1836, also as a result of British naval action, although it took a blockade of the Brazilian ports to implement it, and even then only partially. The abolition of slavery in the African colonies was only decided through a tortuous string of laws passed between 1853 and 1875. Early abolition of the slave trade into Portugal in 1761 and abolition of slavery in the metropolis in 1773 (under the principle of "the free womb": the granting of freedom to children born to slaves) failed to set a precedent for the colonies.[42] There was no public abolitionist movement in Portugal given that the slave trade interests were so entrenched. In Spain a movement did not arose until the mid-nineteenth century, and it was limited to the liberal middle class and anticlerical elites. The same absence of an abolitionist movement occurred in the Low Countries, where slavery was only abolished in 1860–63, despite increasing slave unrest in Suriname.[43]

The slave revolt in the French colony of Saint Domingue (Haiti) in 1791 surpassed any previous riot in America in its level of violence, scale of slave engagement, and political outcome. The destruction of two thousand plantations by fire and murder of one thousand masters at the beginning of the revolt set the stage for the many thousands of killings on both sides in the years to come. These actions were transformed into a revolution supported by a victorious army; the autonomous and, in the end (1804), independent state managed to resist several French attempts to reconquer Haiti.[44] The level of brutality on both sides temporarily deterred liberal ideas on slavery among the white colonial elites in America, but the argument against slavery as violence that fuels further violence made progress. The revolt stimulated the first French abolition of slavery, in 1794. Although this was not effectively implemented in most colonies, and was reversed by Napoléon in 1802, it involved slaves, former slaves, and nonwhite peoples in the ideals of emancipation and citizenship,

Figure 14.4. Anonymous, slave revolt in Saint Domingue, print, c. 1791.
© RMN, Grand Palais; Agence Bulloz; Bibliothèque nationale de France

creating a new reality in the Atlantic world.[45] The French abolitionist movement was never as vigorous as the British or North American movements, and lost all its impetus in the first decades of the nineteenth century. The abolition of the slave trade, agreed to by France in 1815 at the congress of Vienna, was not implemented until 1831, while slavery in the French colonies was only finally abolished in 1848.[46]

In the British colonial world, the 1816 Barbados revolt, which destroyed plantations but killed virtually no masters, slowed down the antislavery movement in England, while the fierce repression of the Demerara revolt in 1823, with hundreds of executions along with the detention and death in prison of a white missionary who supported the slaves, struck a sensitive cord among the British, arousing indignation and further abolitionist action. Jamaica's "Baptist War" in 1831–32 repeated the pattern of the Demerara revolt on a larger scale, with the restraint shown by the slaves contrasted with brutal repression and executions, further fueling abolitionism in the United Kingdom and leading to the emancipation of slaves in 1833. The extension of abolitionism to India was, by contrast, a top-down operation sparked by British public opinion, but was initially opposed by the colonial authorities, fearing the reaction of local elites. In 1843, the British decided to suppress the legal framework sustaining slavery, making it a criminal offense to sell captives. In the United States, although slave revolts were few in the decades that preceded secession (1860) and Civil War (1861–65), the Union's declaration of freedom for Southern slaves dramatically increased the flight of slaves from the Confederation. This led the Union to recruit two hundred thousand former slaves as soldiers, who contributed to the northern victory. The final abolition

Figure 14.5. Anne-Louis Girodet-Trioson, portrait of the Deputy Jean-Baptiste Belley, free black from Saint-Domingue at the National Convention, painting, oil on canvas, 158 × 113 cm., 1797. Musée National de Versailles.
© 2013. White Images; Scala, Florence

of slavery in the United States (1865) put an end to the internal slave trade and heralded the end of slavery in the Americas. In this case, a massive mobilization of northern abolitionists after the 1830s, supported by a significant number of European migrants who shared the ideal of free soil, contrasted with a no less determined and massive mobilization of pro-slavery opinion in the southern states.[47]

The antislavery and abolitionist process faced enormous resistance from established interests that included planters, investors, slave traders, shipowners, sailors, and merchants. Plantations based on slave labor were a powerful economic system that represented millions of pounds of capital invested in land, crops, and slaves, not to mention the enormous commercial profits and fiscal benefits that the trade in cotton, sugar, tobacco, and coffee represented to the states in which the plantations were located. Even the popular abolitionist movement in the United Kingdom had to overcome rooted political interests linked to the plantation system that made their influence felt in successive rejections by the House of Lords of legislation that had already been passed by the House of Commons. The Declaration of Independence of the United States in 1776 and French Declaration of Human Rights in 1789 might have established once and for all a new system of values based on the equal dignity of human beings, but those declarations were obviously addressed to the white population.[48] Nevertheless, they did provide slaves and abolitionists with new assertions within a surge of ideas that proved unstoppable, impelling opinion toward the extension of these rights to all races.

THE IMPACT ON HUMAN RIGHTS

What matters for my argument is an understanding of the abolitionist movement's impact on ethnic and racial hatred. Did it diminish prejudices and discriminatory action? Did it really spread the notion of human rights applied to all races? Abolition of slavery certainly meant the destruction of an economic system based on slave labor, but that destruction was not implemented from one day to the next. Abolitions were gradual in most cases, with periods of apprenticeship under the former slave owner. In many cases slavery was replaced by forced labor, not only in the Americas, but also in Africa. In this sense the situation was prolonged in some European colonies well into the twentieth century. Former slaves were involved in all these transitional and prolonged processes to free labor. Dehumanization was replaced by segregation: black people would still be at the bottom of the economic system for many years to come, which perpetuated the material conditions for contempt. The replacement of slavery with indentured labor on the European colonial islands of the Indian and Atlantic oceans throughout the second half of the nineteenth century, with the organized migration of many Indians and Chinese, also meant that prejudices against Asian peoples were renewed, coinciding with new and large imperial projects in the East.

In England the vast abolitionist movement managed to overcome many previous prejudices, but proslavery opinion continually voiced ideas about the racial inferiority of black people. Among first-generation abolitionists, this prejudice was implicitly accepted: they favored gradual abolition in order to create conditions in which the slaves would learn to use their freedom well. This is one of the reasons for the movement's focus on the abolition of the slave trade rather than the abolition of the slave system, although there were also reasons of political expediency for this emphasis. In France, in a manifesto of 1789, the *Société des Amis des Noirs*—created in 1788 by Jean-Pierre Brissot, who involved Condorcet, Mirabeau, marquis de La Fayette, duc de La Rochefoucauld, and Olympe de Gouges—explicitly ruled out the abolition of slavery: black people were not ripe for freedom; they were to be prepared.[49] The first generation of abolitionists was motivated by the idea of the shared dignity of humans, including all races, even though some races had to be elevated to the supposedly superior position of the white man. The idea of the grateful slave was implicit in many literary and political texts.[50] This philanthropic attitude distinguished abolitionists from the supporters of slavery: the latter held that black slaves were locked into their servitude, for not only were they inferior, but they also could never elevate themselves to the level of white people. In a certain way, this debate at the end of the eighteenth century, prolonged into the nineteenth and twentieth centuries, renewed the argument between Las Casas and Juan Ginés de Sepúlveda concerning the American Indians in which the idea of childlike behavior was set against the notion of natural slavery. But the inferior condition of black slaves in particular and black African people in general, whether mutable or immutable, was a conception shared by nearly all white people.

This idea can be illustrated by looking at the works of the main Enlightenment authors. Montesquieu wrote a strange section in *De l'esprit des lois*, starting, "If I had to justify the right to enslave black people." He mocks the prejudices against people of black color through exaggeration: we cannot imagine that God would place a soul inside a black body; blacks have such squashed noses that we cannot even pity them; and black people prefer glass to gold necklaces, serving as proof of their lack of common sense. Montesquieu wrote these ironic statements in the section about the Egyptians exterminating red-haired people in order to underline the arbitrariness of prejudices concerning color, yet the exercise remains ambiguous.[51] Rousseau praised the innocence of native Africans and Americans, reevaluating the writings of Montaigne along with the primitivist literature of the late seventeenth and early eighteenth centuries. He criticized European civilization through the promotion of the noble savage—noble but savage nonetheless.[52] Voltaire shared this disillusioned vision of European civilization as corrupt and constantly involved in inexplicable wars caused by greedy rulers, but his constant use of the noble savage topos was clouded here and there by irrepressible mockery.[53] Abbé Raynal, who launched one of the most consistent attacks on slavery, depicts Africa as a desolate continent, with poor houses, furniture, and clothing, and an extremely limited agriculture carried out by slaves in the middle of vast uncultivated fields, while the population lives in ignorance and idleness, immersed in local superstitions, without any idea of the art of politics.[54] Condorcet, who also criticized slavery, considered that freed slaves would have to be subject to severe discipline, since they had lost part of their capacity for reasoning, and had been corrupted and made idiots as a result of constant oppression and debasement by their masters. It is true that Condorcet always talks about the effects of slavery; he does not reproduce the idea of ignorant and barbarian black Africans; and he even dedicated his book to black slaves, addressing them in the opening letter as friends and brothers. But the future freedmen were not conceived of as citizens or landlords. The necessity for a long period of integration was implied.[55] Even Alexis de Tocqueville, who always positioned himself as an abolitionist, criticizing slavery as a corruption of the dignity of human beings, tried to accommodate the interests of the white colonists in the French parliamentary debates of the 1830s and 1840s: not only was he in favor of financial compensation, but he also proposed to exclude freedmen from access to property for a certain period of time in order to avoid a dramatic increase in wages. Tocqueville knew what he was doing, since he had declared in *Democracy in America* how important rights of property and succession were. It is obvious that he favored a long transitional period for freedmen to become full citizens.[56]

These arguments against slavery were mainly formulated from the point of view of natural law, or after the 1770s and 1780s, from the notion of human rights coined by Rousseau and spread by the American Declaration of Independence as well as the French one. But antislavery positions were also taken by those seeking to end the competition between free labor and slavery, or between free soil and slave soil, as it came to be phrased in the United

States during the prolonged disputes over the status of the new states created by migration to the west. Although the question of slavery was left to be decided at the level of each state, in order to avoid further tensions that might break down the federal project of the United States, it became the main underlying political issue that led to the Civil War. The rush of European migrants to the Northern states reinforced the movement for free soil, but the generous abolitionist movement also had to contend with the suggestion that they were opposing slavery in order to maintain a strictly white or "unstained" population. In the independent Iberian American countries such as Brazil, the policy of attracting European migrants, who arrived in increasing numbers after the abolition of slavery, was explicitly defined as a project to "whiten" the population. This idea was dominant in Brazil until the 1930s, when Gilberto Freyre launched a new vision of a happy and successful population of mixed-race people.[57]

The extension of human rights to all races as a political ideal and practice was solved neither in the period of revolutions nor the long nineteenth century. Abbé Grégoire's *Essai sur le régénération physique et morale des Juifs*, published in 1788, was one of the first Catholic public statements in favor of the formal integration of Jews into the French state, thereby preparing the ground for their full recognition as citizens after the revolution. Grégoire was also involved in granting citizenship to black and mixed-race freedmen in 1790 and 1791. His *De la noblesse de la peau*, published in 1826, was one of the few books that directly addressed the issue of prejudice against black Africans without in any way compromising with the dominant idea of inferior races, concluding that true nobility is virtue, the privilege of humans of all colors. It included references to the caste system in India as well as the division between Old Christians and New Christians in Iberia. It stated that the idea of "nobility of the skin" had succeeded the idea of "nobility of the blood" as a result of colonial greed to justify slavery—or as Grégoire observed, "This prejudice seemed to white people a wonderful invention to prop up their domination."[58] But Grégoire, a Catholic and Republican, who proved too radical for Napoléon's taste and was forced into retirement after the restoration of the Bourbon monarchy, did not represent the mainstream of public opinion.

The progressive inclusion of other races in human rights was a long process. Native Americans, for instance, were only recognized as American citizens well into the twentieth century. The antislavery and abolitionist movement stimulated, as a reaction, the development of arguments to justify slavery, mainly in the southern United States, where the ideological debate was carried to great lengths. The first contentions about the depiction of slavery in the Bible were difficult to sustain, due to major reinterpretations of scripture and the process of secularization affecting Western society. The assertions concerning slaves as property were much more effective and persistent. Slaves were considered part of an economic system that could not be dismissed from one day to the next. There were too many interests at stake, from the investments of individuals to trade routes distributing the products of slavery, not to mention the fiscal benefits for the state. The major point of discussion was the possible indemnities to the slave owners given the precedent created by the British in 1833. Southerners made use of massive estimates of the compensation that would have to be paid for abolition in the United States to deter any serious initiative. Even in France, where investment in slaves were less than one-tenth of the capital invested by the United States, the government only managed to pass a law abolishing slavery under the special conditions of 1848, when its success was due to the efforts of Victor Schœlcher, an exceptional undersecretary of state for the navy, who was exiled by the Second Empire and dedicated his life to fighting slavery.

The main arguments of the proslavery camp, in the United States and elsewhere, were based on the supposed racial inferiority of black Africans and their descendants, incapacity of black slaves to become citizens, and irreconcilable gap in intelligence, manners, and feelings between white and black people. This was the line developed by the southerner John Caldwell Calhoun (1782–1850) in the senate of the United States long before the Civil War.[59] The debate on slavery fueled scientific theorizing about race, showing how pressing political interests could interfere in new fields of knowledge, particularly the classification of species. Racial prejudice and discriminatory actions enormously benefited from this scientific support, which succeeded in prolonging the debate and the practices involved. The conclusions of this chapter are thus mix: on the one hand, abolitionism created new ideological and political conditions for the spread of the concept of human rights, preparing the field for the inclusion, in the long term, of nonwhite races under the notion of citizenship; on the other hand, attempts to justify slavery stimulated a scientific definition of racial hierarchies that contributed to perpetuating forms of segregation and discrimination.

✶✶✶

Colonial societies were only created from scratch in the New World. Elsewhere the European expansion had a variable economic and political impact, save for a few exceptions, without effectively restructuring social configurations in the long term. In the Americas, European migration involved 3.5 million people up to 1800, while more than 12.5 million African slaves were imported up to the 1860s, and Native Americans were reduced to 5 or 6 million people in the first century of European intervention. The presence of women was significantly higher among the British than among the Spanish and Portuguese migrants, and this fact helps to explain higher levels of European mixing with natives and Africans on the Iberian side. Different political models also help to explain divergence among colonial societies: while in British North America colonial communities were quite autonomous, with loose relations with the central government until the beginning of the eighteenth century, the presence of royal institutions in Iberian America from the beginning stimulated forced conversions of Native Americans and African slaves. The former were transformed into vassals, and the latter into members of the Catholic Church.

Settled native populations in Mexico and the Andes decisively contributed to the interethnic model of Spanish America. The creation of the República de Indios meant positive segregation, but in general Iberian colonial societies were shaped through hierarchical interethnic integration and discrimination based on white supremacy along with a graduated scale of mixed-race people. In North America the Indians were classified as aliens until the late nineteenth century, while African slaves were not subject to systematic Christian conversion until the last decades of the eighteenth century. From the start, seminomadic natives were segregated. Mixing with African slaves followed the same model in the long run: mixed-race people ended up segregated and classified as black, while emancipation was forbidden in certain colonies, like Virginia, where freedpersons were expelled after independence. Formal laws against mixed marriage sealed the British model of segregation. The French case, which began closer to the Iberian one due to policies of mixed marriages with natives in New France, reverted to the British model of segregation throughout the eighteenth century. In the Caribbean, these models showed some interaction, but the continental experience had shaped the main policies.

The importance of the American colonial experience is obvious for three reasons: the systemic relation with Europe, from an economic, social, demographic, and political point of view; the amount of slave and indentured labor, which contributed to defining whiteness and blackness as opposite poles; and the policies concerning native people and mixed-race people, which shaped new forms of interethnic classification. Slavery became identified with blackness, and the color black became synonymous with native people under the framework of the European expansion, applied to Native Americans and Asians, with the exception of the Chinese and Japanese. Segregation in British, Dutch, and (later) French America contrasted with relative integration coupled with discrimination in Iberian America. The long-term process of excluding those of mixed race in British America led to a binary classification of white and black people, while Natives Americans were simply considered aliens.

Casta painting reflected an obsessive interethnic classification structured by opposite poles—white/black; integrated Indian/savage living in the wilderness—but one that revealed an enormous flexibility in the system, defined by gradations, possible reversals of the process of descent, and status change. It is a Mexican artistic genre that cannot be taken at face value, since it developed its own system of classification, but it can be related to taxonomies found all over Iberian America, which confirm the flexibility of interethnic hierarchies. Purity of blood, well represented by genealogical fictions, certainly contributed to the assertion of white supremacy, while interethnic classification contributed to the Enlightenment obsession with taxonomy and observation of human beings as part of nature. Still, the claim of precocious racial construction does not withstand analysis, since casta hierarchies have a local rather than a universal scope, and do not promote the idea of immutable features transmitted from generation to generation that would eventually inform the theories of races.

Local conditions and colonial projects shaped different societies, but both dual and multiple systems of interethnic classification placed black people at the bottom of the social hierarchy. The status of freed and mixed-race people varied in different colonial societies, not only in America, but also in Asia and Africa. The Portuguese financial and demographic dependence on natives and mixed-race people in Asia gave these people a status denied in Dutch and British colonies and on trading posts, with their greater European labor pool. While prejudices were not impacted, discriminatory action was less visible in the

Portuguese case. The Portuguese case is also useful for contrasting African and American colonial experiences: while mixed-race people in Africa, with the exception of Luanda, were generally integrated into local society, in Brazil they created a distinct segment of colonial society that enjoyed significant social status.

These colonial experiences had various effects on European perceptions, but in one way or another they confirmed the vision of blackness as an inferior human type, while the integration of Native Americans in Mexico and Peru did not wipe out the vision of an American type defined by cannibalism and savagery. Discrimination and segregation in different parts of the world where the Europeans managed to build colonial societies or enclaves caused ethnic prejudices coupled with precise forms of debasement or blatant exclusion to take root. In the last quarter of the eighteenth century, slavery was finally challenged by an impressive British abolition movement, which coincided with the spread of the notion of human rights. Yet this campaign for the dignity of African slaves did not diffuse the perception of equal rights. In the long run, abolitionism helped to spread human rights among emancipated people, but vicious debates stimulated by economic and political interests based on slavery contributed to the perpetuation of prejudices as well as new forms of segregation.

||||||||||||||||||||||||||||||||||||||||||||||||||||||||||||||||||||||||||||||||||||||||||||||||||||||||||||||||||||||||||||||||||||||||||||||||

PART IV

THE THEORIES OF RACE

Figure 15.1. H. Kinsbury, portrait of Linnaeus "in a Lapp costume," engraving, 1805, after Martin Hoffman's portrait (1737).
Reprinted with permission from the Art Archive, London

In 1737, Carl Linnaeus (1707–78) commissioned a portrait of himself in which he was depicted wearing a Saami (Lapp) costume, with a long fur coat plus accessories that included a round leather beret, extraordinary leather boots, and a native belt from which hung a runic calendar, a knife, birch-bark boxes, pouches of reindeer fur, and a shaman's drum. Another essential item, placed in his right hand, was the white flower from a small Arctic plant he had named *Linnea borealis*, which would become his trademark.[1] In one single but complex image, Linnaeus established his credentials as botanist, traveler, and researcher. The picture explicitly referred to Linnaeus's travel to Lapland five years previously, which had been subsidized by the Royal Society of Sweden, and represented a turning point in his scientific interests and career. The portrait was produced halfway through Linnaeus's long stay in the Netherlands (1735–38), during which he obtained a doctoral degree in medicine, worked with the main botanists of the time, established his European scientific network, and published some of his main books, particularly the first edition of the *Systema Naturæ*.[2] His work, with its classification of plants expanded to cover the classification of animals, including human beings, has been described by Michel Foucault as the cornerstone of the classical age (the seventeenth and eighteenth centuries) episteme.[3] The portrait hints at the major processes of this order of knowledge—observation and collection, analysis and classification—but is clearly dominated by the ethnographic gaze: the observer is disguised as the observed, or to put it in other words, the civilized is dressed as the savage. In fact, the Saami were still considered savages at this time, one century after a rough process of colonization that saw the opening up of mines with forced labor, the transfer of populations, and a Christianization involving the radical suppression of shamanist practices. Lapland was, indeed, the Swedish West Indies.

This visual statement reverses the usual representation of savages: their clothing acquires a new dignity when worn by a white man of science. The portrait has been interpreted as a highly successful marketing operation addressed to Linnaeus's colleagues.[4] But the obvious risk for him was not to be taken seriously. Since the famous festival of the Tupinambá staged in Rouen for the pleasure of the French royal court in 1550, in which Native Americans were paraded together with Normans, all almost naked except for feathers, there had been an irrepressible pleasure in engaging in native ways in the face of prudish Christian horror.[5] In Linnaeus's portrait he was covered from head to toe, although at the time his classificatory system, based on the sex of plants, was considered useful but indecent. While marketing may have played a role, the portrait was not just strategic: during those years, Linnaeus described Saami costumes, habits, and ceremonies in a sympathetic way.[6] Even though he might express his disgust at the local standards of hygiene, or unkindly refer to the "frog skin" of a "dark" woman who helped him, he praised Saami clothing and shoes as much more natural and adequate than Swedish dress, with its rigidity and obstruction of agility as well as muscle development. He was impressed by the speed of Saami walking and running. On special occasions he would wear Saami costume in Uppsala, and he took it with him on his trips. This was not just for showing off: he used it as a statement about natural apparel, adapted to the climate and body. The portrait thus draws attention to the multidimensional personality of Linnaeus along with the different types of discourse he used as a botanist, ethnographer, economist, doctor, and theologian.[7] His experience with the Saami provided Linnaeus with a first, crucial reflection on the relationship between nature and culture that marked him for life, and contributed to defining his ethos as a natural historian.

The development of natural history in the eighteenth and nineteenth centuries triggered the long-term establishment of chemistry, comparative anatomy, physiology, biology, and geology as disciplines that defined new frameworks of thought that changed the vision of humans. Perceptions of time changed dramatically: biblical creationism and Christian chronologies of the world, already questioned in the seventeenth century, were put under pressure to accommodate increasingly complex accounts of peoples and kingdoms as well as the archaeological discovery of civilizations more ancient than the Hebrew. Geology played a crucial role, bursting the limits of time. The vision of fossils as ancestors of contemporary animals or lost forms of animals took time to be accepted, while the study of strata of sediments placed humans in a wide chronological framework.[8] The impact of Sir Isaac Newton's concept of the universe took decades to be absorbed and developed into new ideas about the cooling down of Earth that could not have been contained in biblical assumptions of time, challenging the literal understanding of the six days of the Creation. The enormous stretch of time already hinted at by Buffon (1707–88) in 1749—although he never dared to publish his calculations of the age of Earth, which reached 10 million years (we now know it is 4.5 billion years)—was linked to the issue of space.[9] The location of paradise had entertained many European authors and readers from the Middle Ages to the Enlightenment, although the discovery of the New World, the exploration of Asia and Africa, and finally the discovery of Oceania—developments that had led to the identification of an enormous variety of communities of human beings—had challenged the idea of the descent of humans from a single couple, Adam and Eve.[10] Several authors advocated the existence of human beings before Adam, particularly Isaac de La Peyrère (1596–1676), who tried to find justification for his thesis in the Bible.[11] This vision had been preceded in the sixteenth century by the theories of Paracelsus and Giordano Bruno, who developed ancient ideas of spontaneous generation transmitted by Avicenna, Diodoro Siculo, and Pietro Pomponazzi.[12] The issue of multiple creations, both biblical and nonbiblical inspiration, became related to the inquiry into the variety of human beings in the world.

The debate between those who claimed a plural creation of humans (polygenists) and those who clung to a unique descent (monogenists) flared up across the eighteenth and nineteenth centuries, only to be relatively damped down, but not terminated, by the evolutionary perspective introduced by Charles Darwin (1809–82).[13] In this debate polygenism radically challenged the Judeo-Christian narrative of the Creation, opening the door to the natural division of humankind, which carried with it a natural hierarchy of human types. Monogenism could accommodate a long formation of human beings, thereby questioning the literal reading of Genesis without contesting the uniqueness of humankind, which was considered to have reached different stages of differentiation and complexity. Religious issues were crucial here: widespread reference to biblical creationism meant that monogenists were always dominant.[14] In the eighteenth century, the idea of degeneration, used to justify variation within the same species, originated by perfect, divine Creation, began to be challenged by the idea of improvement and perfectibility.

In the same period, the classical idea of the chain of being was also being contested.[15] According to this notion, inanimate minerals along with living plants and animals, from the elementary level to the more complex forms, were all believed to be linked through a progressive and imperceptible gradation, implying hierarchies, subtle forms of transition, continuities, and plenitude. In this vision, humans were not separated from nature. Aristotle, for instance, classified humans among animals, stressed the common structure of the quadrupeds, and suggested an analogy of faculties between all animals. In one of his references to the varieties of human beings, generally based on the distinction between Greeks and barbarians, he even corrected Herodotus's error of attributing a different color of sperm to black people.[16] The idea of the chain of being accommodated the Judeo-Christian notion of humans created in God's image, although natural historians such as Buffon separated humans from the other animals for physiological reasons—intelligence, language, manual skills, and the expression of emotions. The notions of physiological operations, interactions between functions, and the relationship between organs contributed to disrupting the artificial system of nature conceived by the chain of being, favoring the study of connections. Methodologically controlled description, analysis, and classification of nature within the limited comparative scope preferred by Cuvier, who separated the animal world into four different branches, became influential, but was immediately challenged by Jean-Baptiste Lamarck's (1744–1829) concept of acquired characteristics and the transformation of organisms due to changing environment, while the systematic comparative methods developed by Geoffroy Saint Hilaire (1772–1844) led to the idea of a unique plan encompassing all animals. Human beings were involved in this increasingly comparative research into nature, in turn spurring interest in their origin and the causes of variety.

Ethnology was created through dialogue with the main developments in natural history. In many cases, ethnologists were also natural historians, as we have seen with Linnaeus; a creative interaction of knowledge was developed by such figures as Kant (1724–1804), Johann Gottfried von Herder (1744–1803), and James Cowles Prichard (1786–1848). Reflection on humankind was part of this increasingly open discussion of nature. Systems of classification were naturally based on stereotypes concerning different types of human beings; they carried with them a presumption of rigorous tabulation of nature that affected the hierarchical way in which varieties of human beings were to be described. Scientific study multiplied methods and assumptions to explain differences between humans. It was no longer sufficient to describe phenotype features as well as supposed degrees of intelligence, habits, and behavior. Skulls were collected and measured; skeletons were compared; and a hierarchy of differences between human beings was established according to a scale of proximity to or distance from apes. This general framework of measure—or better, mismeasure, as it was labeled by Stephen Jay Gould—lent new credibility to forms of classification expressed through the notion of race.[17] In this context, the noun race acquired a scientific status that contributed to essentializing differences: phenotype features were believed to defy the influence of external circumstances, while intellectual and moral capacities were inextricably linked with physical appearance.[18]

The purpose of part IV of this volume is to understand the development of competing theories of races through the analysis of the most influential authors; the way humans were positioned in relation to other animals; and the way variety in human beings was defined, crystallized, and organized into a hierarchy. This process covered most of the eighteenth and all of the nineteenth centuries, leaving an indelible imprint on the twentieth century—only disrupted by World War II and the Holocaust. We need to place this process in its changing intellectual framework. The depiction of God as a transforming force in the eighteenth century meant that acceptance of the existing social order started to be questioned, while history was seen as a creative process. These ideas clashed with static perceptions of the old, perfect order, thus stimulating the development of natural history and new disciplines of science. But in no way can we speak of a linear progression of ideas, as the analysis of new and old assumptions, racial constructions, and renewed prejudices concerning descent will demonstrate.

||||||||||||||||||||||||||||||||||||||||||||||||||||||||||||||||||||||||||||||||||||||||||||||||||||||||||

CHAPTER 15

Classifications of Humans

FOUNDATIONS

In 1735, in his *Systema Naturæ*, Linnaeus placed human beings at the top of the animal kingdom, heading the classification of quadrupeds, immediately above *simia* (monkey). The publication was composed of six dense folio sheets covered with tables preceded by a brief introduction on nature. The content was presented in three parts: rocks and minerals, the vegetable kingdom, and the animal kingdom. The latter was divided into quadrupeds, birds, amphibians, fishes, insects, and worms. Man was classified in four categories: European, defined as white; American, defined as red; Asiatic, defined as dark; and African, defined as black.[1] The crudeness and brevity of this classification is striking, and probably was the reason for its success. There were no descriptions, justifications, or explanations. The fact was that humans were integrated into nature and related to other animals in an implicit hierarchy. And it was this hierarchy of nature that mattered.

The *Systema naturæ* became more sophisticated in later editions, and descriptions were included, eventually filling several volumes. Man was then defined not just as homo but rather as Homo sapiens, heading mammals and primates. Two other categories, surprisingly, were added at the beginning and end of the classification of human beings: the wild man, classified as four-footed, mute, and hairy; and the monstrous man, "varying by climate and air." Among the latter, Linnaeus distinguished small, active, and timid mountaineers, large and indolent Patagonians, less fertile Hottentots, beardless Americans, conical-headed Chinese, and flat-headed Canadians. The four initial categories continued, but were developed with the inclusion of physical and psychological attributes: the American was defined as copper colored, choleric, and erect, with black, straight, thick hair, wide nostrils, a harsh face, and a scanty beard; as content and free; and as painting themselves with fine red lines, as regulated by custom. The European was fair, sanguine, and brawny, with flowing yellow or brown hair, and blue eyes; they were light, acute, and inventive; and they covered themselves with garments with fastenings, as regulated by custom and law. The Asiatic was sooty, melancholic, and rigid, with black hair and dark eyes; they were severe, haughty, and covetous; they clothed themselves in loose garments; and they were governed by opinion. The African was black, phlegmatic, and relaxed; they had frizzy black hair, silky skin, a flat nose, and tumid lips; they were indolent, negligent, and crafty; they anointed themselves with grease; and they were governed by caprice.[2]

The difference between this and the previous classification of man by Linnaeus is extremely interesting. In the first instance, the hierarchy was established by skin color, from white to black—which placed the American and Asiatic types in the middle. In the second, the hierarchy was redefined by the introduction of the two new types, wild and monstrous, with the first being an implicit intermediate stage between human and monkey, and the second an expression of degeneration, both completing the sequence in this context of ambiguous detachment from the idea of the chain of being. Neither of these types was new—they both had a long literary tradition from antiquity to the Enlightenment, although the monsters included stereotypes accumulated through the European expansion, which influenced the perception of Hottentots. The physical and psychological description of the four human races synthesized prejudices developed over the past three centuries, even though the origins of the African and Asian types may be found in classical antiquity—playful and careless on the one side, greedy and authoritarian on the other, and embodying the traditional perceptions of inconsistent Africa and Oriental despotism. Political stereotypes thus completed the picture: the American was regulated by custom, the European was controlledd by law, the Asian was guided by opinion, and the African was governed by caprice. Linnaeus further stressed the supposed superiority of the European: muscular, inventive, and acute. The geographic model for these types was not new either. It was merely built on the allegorical personification of the continents (or the four parts of the world) created in Europe throughout the sixteenth century (see part II). But the scientific context of exhaustive classification of nature was certainly new, creating a different framework for old stereotypes.

Gould argues that these four human races represented a geographic model that would later be transformed into the hierarchical order, discussed below, of five races defined by Blumenbach (1752–1840). As we have seen, the geographic and hierarchical model had already been constructed in the Renaissance, and had received a new meaning in Linnaeus's classifications, the first organized by skin color, and the second by supposed physical, psychological, and political attributes. The immediate development of theories of races did not match Gould's schematic narrative either: Buffon, who in 1749 published the first three volumes of a new, extensive natural history, which had an enormous impact on Europe, criticized Linnaeus's obsession with classification. Buffon was interested in describing the variety of human beings across the continents; his purpose was to understand the impact of climate, food, habits, and migrations on man.[3] He identified several types he indifferently named races, nations, or varieties, which did not conform to the geographic model of the continents. Buffon probably found inspiration for this vision from the French physician and traveler François Bernier (1625–88).[4] Northern peoples living next to the Arctic on both the old and new continents, including the Lapps (or Saami) and Eskimos (or Inuit), were labeled as savages and believed to have similar features (small, large, with dark skin, and with different degrees of deformity). Tartars were distinguished from northern Europeans by their different food and habits, which stimulated a different physical and psychological configuration, although they lived on similar latitudes. Tartars were marked as vagabonds and thieves, living in tents, small but robust, with a scanty beard, without religion, and in some cases still involved in the slave trade. The Mongols, who had conquered China, were considered the most civilized and best-proportioned people among the Tartars.

In the 1777 edition, Buffon further distinguished the Danes, Norwegians, Swedes, and Russians from the Polish, Germans, and other peoples of Europe, since the second group had undergone infinite diversification due to miscegenation—an opinion curiously opposed to nineteenth-century racial constructions. Buffon also attributed the distinction he made between Tartars and Chinese to differences in habitat, since the phenotype features were not so dissimilar—although the Chinese were believed to be better built and to have a skin color that varied from north to south. The custom of binding women's feed—enforcing lameness for an ideal of beauty—is also mentioned. In the 1777 edition, Buffon pointed to miscegenation between Tartars and Russians. He also stressed similarities between Chinese and Japanese, based on common habits and civilization, although the latter were believed to have a stronger complexion and darker skin, due to their more southerly position. Indians were considered physically similar to Europeans despite their different skin color, and were defined by bizarre customs, such as food rituals, loose clothing, and promiscuous behavior (only Mughal women were seen as chaste). South Asian and Southeast Asian migrations were taken into account in Buffon's vision of the populations of the area, while particularly robust people, like the Javanese, were singled out as noteworthy.

The exploration of Oceania, especially the vast continental mass of Australia (then New Holland), occurred in the eighteenth century, and Buffon immediately integrated descriptions of its different communities into his work, specifically the Australian aborigines. Black people were identified in various parts of Oceania (only labeled as such in the nineteenth century), Southeast Asia, and South Asia. Buffon equated them with the black peoples of Africa as showing the effects of hot temperatures on different continents, while the Australian aborigines were likened to the South African Hottentots. Buffon highlighted variations of skin tone in Turkey, Persia, and Arabia as well as different degrees of civilization, considered higher in the first two cases, since he related Arabs to Tartars. In the 1777 edition, however, he included a long section on the Arabs to improve his initial schematic view. The existence of savages on different parts of the old continents (Europe and Asia) was explained by extreme conditions of climate (the Arctic), peripheral position in mountainous regions (for example, in Formosa or on the northern Japanese islands), or relative isolation in the case of islands. Diverse phenotype features in Africa were attributed to climate and food, since the monsoon winds tempered the climate of the east coast. This is why Buffon identified North Africans as white and distinguished blacks (from Sudan along with West and Central Africa) from Kaffirs (East Africans, Bushmen, and Hottentots)—a subject developed in the 1777 edition (he failed to note the Abyssinian Christian faith).

Different degrees of civilization were first related to physical appearance, although set in the context of a variety of customs, manners, and technical abilities. The designation savages was reserved for black people living in the interior. The diversity of human types in America was considered less marked than in Africa; Buffon attributed the absence of black people in America to the benign climate compared to the excessive heat in certain regions of Africa. He stressed the unique source of the New World's native population as Asian (Tartar) migration to the New World across the Bering Strait. Buffon's first impression of a diminished American nature, with inferior animals, plants, and human beings (always categorized as savages, with the exception of Aztecs and Incas) compared to other continents, had an impact on Cornelius de Pauw and Raynal, who proclaimed the degenerative effect of the New World—according to the former, even on European migrants.[5] Yet Buffon, who never went as far as these authors, corrected his first view in the 1777 edition, in which he explicitly criticized de Pauw's unfounded judgments concerning the brutality, stupidity, and inferior human complexion and intelligence of the American Indians. He revised his vision of Native Americans, refusing to apply the notion of degeneration to the New World, although he maintained his vision that there existed fewer species and smaller quadrupeds (he compared the puma with the lion, lama with the camel, and tapir with the elephant). Buffon implicitly accepted the protests of Benjamin Franklin, US ambassador in Paris in 1776–82. Franklin, who had an extraordinary sense of humor, once asked Raynal and the other guests he had invited for dinner to stand up. He pointed out that all the American guests were much taller than the French, thus mocking the idea of the degenerative effect of the New World.[6]

It is obvious that Buffon had his own criteria of classification, even if they were much more flexible than those of Linnaeus. He was keen to establish comparisons that would show continuities of human types from one continent to another. Contrasts between extreme human types were identified within the same continent, as in Africa or Asia. He was one of the few natural historians who highlighted the impact of migration, distancing himself from the essentialized vision of autochthonous societies supposedly living in the same territories for centuries, if not millennia. Buffon was also interested in cultural change. He pointed to Mexico and the Philippines as the regions with the greatest variety of human types in the world; he did not criticize miscegenation, refusing the common prejudice against mixed-race people. Instead, he studied the curious cases of albinos in various settings, as he was trying to understand the accidents that might produce "monsters" or "giants," renewing the sixteenth-century researches of Ambroise Paré and Ulisse Aldrovandi. Prejudices against certain types of human beings are clearly recognizable in Buffon's writings, particularly concerning the smelly, disingenuous but cheerful black people, the ugly, stupid, and superstitious Lapps, the ceremonious, idle, and dependent Chinese, the strong, civil yet vain Japanese, the fierce, resilient, and rough Tartars, and the promiscuous, superstitious, and bizarre Indians. Buffon broke with the common vision of Jews as dark-skinned people; he clearly stated that they adapted to different climates, and only Portuguese Jews maintained a dark skin color, while the German Jews had become white. He pointed out other changes, especially in habits, quoting the example of the Russians, who had once been slaves—rough, brutal people without courage and lacking manners—but who had become civilized, interested in the arts and sciences, trade, and ingenious novelties.

Buffon maintained that white was the primordial color of nature, suggesting that the Europeans were the most balanced and perfect of all the human beings because they lived in the temperate region between the latitudes of forty and fifty degrees. He integrated, without quoting, the traveler Jean Chardin's view of Caucasian women as the most beautiful in the world, drawing on their reputation as white slave concubines and wives to the rulers of Persia and Turkey.[7] He reproduced the usual stereotypes against various peoples of the world, especially blacks, Native Americans, and Eskimos, while introducing new ones concerning the peoples of Oceania. Buffon also replicated traditional assumptions against nomadic and seminomadic people, considered vagabonds and thieves. Nevertheless, he recognized the devastating impact of the European conquest on the Native American population, and was inspired by Montaigne's and Rousseau's respective visions of the virtuous, innocent savages. Buffon, moreover, underscored the enormous differences between humans and apes as well as a monogenist vision of a unique stock of human beings spread all over the globe. He insisted on reproduction between different types of humans as the key definition of the species, separating it from all other animals. Buffon explicitly questioned the brutal treatment of slaves by European masters. Finally, he defended the concept that all human beings were perfectible.

Buffon had an overwhelming impact on both researchers and public opinion in Europe and America. He was a central figure at the French royal court and scientific establishment, constantly visited by statesmen, politicians, and diplomats. But there were visions that competed with his and were disseminated to a wider public. Voltaire, who rightly defined prejudice as an opinion without judgment, subscribed to de Pauw's view of American nature and human beings. The idea of the noble savage developed by Voltaire's adversary Rousseau was used to criticize European religion and customs, but never taken seriously, left suspended by an ironic, condescending vision of an anthropophagic yet innocent savage. As a polygenist, Voltaire helped to naturalize the variety in human beings, attributing different human types to different creations. Although he wrote on tolerance, rejecting religious persecution and the Inquisition, extensively mocked in *Candide*, he reproduced traditional anti-Jewish stereotypes in the *Dictionnaire philosophique*, where Jews were seen as slaves and victims of their superstitions whose mind-set had been reproduced by Christianity.[8] Voltaire's perception of Jews, to which he held despite constant exchange with several members of the community, especially Isaac Pinto, is a reminder of the extent of public prejudice that bubbled under the surface throughout the eighteenth century.

Kant is another key author who was widely read in Europe. He taught philosophy, physical geography, and anthropology at the University of Königsberg, and his writings contributed to the reflection on theories of races. Kant accepted Buffon's rule of reproduction in the definition of natural species, although he introduced a principle of regeneration or degeneration concerning an original "single phylum" (basic original community). Races were defined by the principle of irreversible differentiation or degeneration of subspecies, revealed through the persistent reproduction of features from generation to generation or in variations resulting from mixing. By contrast, strains always preserved the original phylum in all transplantations and mixing with others, supporting the idea of regeneration. Finally, varieties were determined by possible though not persistent regeneration. This notion of race is exemplified by the mixture of black and white, which necessarily results in the begetting of half-breed children (mulattoes), while blonds and brunets are considered not different races but rather different strains of whites, because they can beget either blond or brunet children. Kant believed that the quality of soil and nutrition introduced hereditary differences, which could become varieties or disappear in several generations following environmental change.[9] He distinguished four races—white, black, Hunnish (Mongolian or Kalmuckian), and Hindu (or Hindustani)—but underlined the idea that whites and blacks were the two basic races. Whites included Moors from North Africa, Arabs, Turkish-Tartaric peoples, Persians, and Asian peoples not included in other races. Blacks included the natives of sub-Saharan Africa and New Guinea. Huns, also called Kalmuckians, Mongols, or Eleuts, included the pure Koschuts, whose blood was mixed with that of the Tartars in the Torguts and even more so in the Dzungarians. The Hindustani race was considered pure, one of the oldest human races, originating in Tibet, and distinct from the people of the opposite side of the Indian peninsula. We have to keep in mind this early distinction between the pure race of northern India and darker races of the south (though they were not explicitly labeled as such by Kant) when I turn to Aryanism in the next chapter. Kant considered that all other hereditary ethnic characters derived from these four races. The Hindustani blood, for instance, in being mixed with Scythian and Hunnish blood, might have generated the mixed races of the southern Indians, Tung-Chin, and Chinese.

Kant suggested that "germs" and a predisposition to being affected by environmental conditions were responsible for differences in body shape and skin color. Humid cold was related to northern European blonds, dry cold to American copper-red skin, humid heat to Senegambian blacks, and dry heat to Indian olive-yellow skin. The small Laplanders, "a subsidiary phylum of the Hungarian people" derived from the Hunnish race, had been shaped by the cold Arctic conditions. The Kalmuckian bulging elevation under the eyes, beardless chin, flattened nose, thin lips, semiclosed eyes, and flat face had resulted from an adaptation to cold air. The Americans were considered to be a Hunnish race not yet fully adapted to the differences in environment between the north and south of the New World since they carried their features from Northeast Asia and northern America to South America.

The critical issue for the environmental explanation was that similar regions did not contain the same races. Kant's idea was that once a race had taken root and suffocated other "germs," it would resist transformation. His second essay on human races developed these arguments, but Kant added a critique of polygenism, arguing that if the races had been created to fit different environments, there was no justification for their unfailing transmission of their own differential characteristics in their mixing. The capacity of human beings to adapt to all climates and soils could only be explained by a single first phylum containing within it all the predispositions eventually developed in different parts of the world. Kant insisted on the unfailing hereditary differences of races. He reproduced old stereotypes, such as the "strong odour of the Negroes, which cannot be helped through any cleanness," and tried a scientific explanation for black skin as saturated by "phlogistized air" from thick forests and swamp-covered regions in west Africa.[10]

Herder, whose work had a long-term impact on European philosophical and political thought, did not take up the debate on human races, but he produced a vast work related to the subject, partly based on the philosophy of language. He was a monogenist and religious person, yet refused to accept the divine origin of language. Herder regarded language's genesis and development as a human phenomenon, set in the context of nature, in an animal-human world, and being part of the progressive process of human formation—"human beings were animals until they found words."[11] He labeled the Laps, Finns, and Estonians as the residual savages of Europe, because they supposedly used half-articulated and unwritable sounds, just as the Hurons and Peruvians did. Herder also essentialized people's ways of thinking when he considered that barbarian peoples always turned abstractions into mishmash: "What became of Aristotle in the hands of the Arabs? What did papacy become in China? The former a Muslim, the latter a living Confucianism."[12] But he believed in common predispositions shared by all human beings and a shared human capacity for perfectibility—"a single progressive whole" with "a distinctive characteristic plan"—stressing the enormous changes to the earth (its form, surface, and conditions) as well as changes in race, manner of life, manner of thought, form of government, national taste, sensations, and needs.[13]

It was Herder who first formulated in a clear way the principle of cultural relativism when he claimed it was necessary to "leave one's own time and one's own people in order to judge remote times and peoples," and refused to measure the virtue of the ancient Egyptians with the criteria of another time and land.[14] He developed Montaigne's critique of ethnocentrism: the noun barbarian is analyzed as a watchword of contempt for foreigners who do not speak our language, do not share our ways of thinking and doing, are not our equals in wisdom or bravery, with all this revealing not only ignorance and pride but also insecurity through a rejection of everything that contradicts our manner of thought.[15] Herder mocked the pretensions to progress and universalism of the French philosophers, exposing the devastation, waste, and enslavement imposed on three-quarters of the world, while Europe itself had banned slavery because it was less expensive to use free labor. The complexity of Herder's thought is revealed by his criticism of the obliteration of national characters in favor of cosmopolitanism, lament over social mixing along with the upward drive of the lower classes "to the place of withered, proud and useless high ones in order soon to be worse than these," feeling of repulsion toward the egalitarian trend in which "we are all becoming brothers," and praise for tradition, limited knowledge, and arts and crafts against the increasingly pervasive ideas of rationalization, efficiency, and industrialization.[16] Herder sowed the seeds for considering different cultures on their own terms, helping to challenge the hierarchies of peoples of the world, although his vision had little impact in his own time.

MEASUREMENT AND DIVERGENCES

In the meantime, mainstream research on the variety of human beings was being pushed further thorough the measurement of racial difference. Petrus Camper (1722–89) took the first step to creating an allegedly scientific measure of different human types.[17] He criticized polygenism and supported the idea of a common origin of humankind. Camper agreed with Buffon's aesthetic hierarchy of human types. He contributed to debunking the myth of the role of continents in the creation of races: the Laplanders were of a tawnier complexion than the Javanese; many Persians were not darker than the Spaniards; the Kaffirs were remarkably different from the Angolans and Nubians; the American tribes derived their origin from the northern countries of Asia (he mentioned Cook's map of the Asia-America passage); the Moluccans seemed to have blended the characteristics of Africans and Asians—a description that opened the way for Blumenbach's Malay type. He also accepted the existence of national and regional physiognomic types, although in many cases—for example, Holland—migration had blurred the distinctions. The same line of reasoning stated that peripheries saw the continuation of particular features long after they had disappeared from the big population centers. Curiously, Camper played down the importance of skin color. In his view, color was not "material"; it merely resulted from the refraction of light. But no other author picked up on this assertion. Camper underlined the importance of manners, costume, and education in shaping the body as well as the significance of food, climate and disease, war, colonization, trade, navigation, and shipwrecks in differentiating or blending humankind. This is a rough résumé of a complex reasoning, but nothing in Camper's view fundamentally contradicted Buffon's flexible system of classification; the latter was simply enlarged and placed in a framework that enhanced its separation from the idea of the chain of being and metaphysics.[18]

Camper was both a professor of anatomy and sculptor in Amsterdam, and was interested in the representation of the human body in a much more rigorous way than his naturalist colleagues. This is the point at which innovation occurred. Camper created a "machine"—a quadrangular table composed of a network of horizontal and vertical lines—in which he

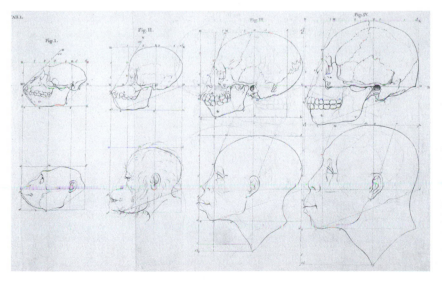

Figure 15.2. Petrus Camper, *The Works of the Late Professor Paetrus Camper on the Connection between the Science of Anatomy and the Arts of Drawing, Printing, Statuary,* trans. T. Cogan (London: C. Dilly, 1794), plate 1, I 32. The plate depicts the angle face, and a comparison of human and ape skulls. © British Library Board; Robana

projected the skulls of human types so that the different configurations could be easily spotted. The advantage of this invention was that the configuration of eyes, noses, and faces in general was for the first time clearly related to the platform of bones on which muscles and tissues were placed. The quadrangular table was supposed to objectively measure skulls and then compare them according to the different angles produced at crucial points—the entrance to the hearing channel, the cheekbone, the first vertebra of the neck, the front teeth, and the occipital bone. Camper invented the notion of a facial angle as measurable space between the line from the nasal bone to the front of the head and the line from the nasal bone to the ear.

The problem was that Camper compared the skulls of two apes with those of an African, Mongol, and European. This exercise was inspired by the idea of sequences and gradual differences, but assumed fundamental physical differences between these races and species. The types thus identified were not based on a serious sample but instead on a random collection of skulls of different ages, sexes, and nutritional backgrounds. Although Camper wanted to emphasize the differences between the African and ape, what resulted from this powerful image was the intermediary position of the African and Mongol skulls. Their facial angle measured seventy degrees between the fifty-eight degrees of the orangutan and

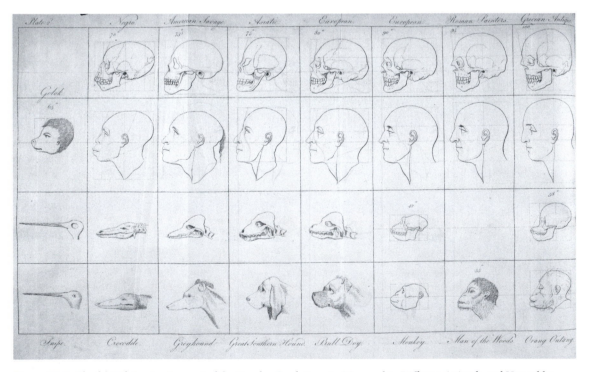

Figure 15.3. Charles White, *An Account of the Regular Gradations in Man and in Different Animals and Vegetables* (London: D. Dilly, 1799), plate 2. The plate shows a comparison of skulls and faces of humans, monkeys, and other animals.
© British Library Board; Robana

the eighty degrees of the European skull. But Camper also compared his measurements of skulls with measurements taken from Greek and Roman statues. He discovered that the Greeks had reached a maximum facial angle of a hundred degrees, while the Romans had stabilized their representation of human beauty at ninety-five degrees. He also compared the position of the upper and lower jaws, the position of the cheekbones, and the relative distances from the ear to the nose and the occipital bone. Camper discussed the models of beauty set out by classical writers. Yet the most prejudiced naturalists later recycled his images to prove the distance between the European skull (modeled on Greek statues) and the African one. Camper's innovative work was immediately replicated and used by naturalists who interpreted it as the first successful attempt to scientifically measure racial physical differences. Charles White (1728–1813), an English physician and polygenist, played a major role in diffusing Camper's model among British and American naturalists.[19]

Johann Friedrich Blumenbach (1752–1840) was a physician, anatomist, and anthropologist who taught medicine in Göttingen, and whose publications had a major impact on theories of races. He became one of the key writers on natural history after Buffon and before Cuvier. Blumenbach criticized Linnaeus for his ambiguous statements about the

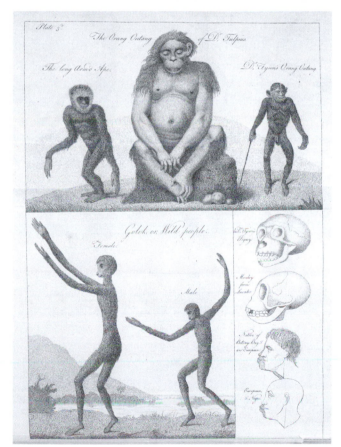

Figure 15.4. Charles White, *An Account of the Regular Gradations in Man and in Different Animals and Vegetables* (London: D. Dilly, 1799), plate 3. The plate illustrates a comparison of humans and monkeys, stressing the intermediate position of black people.
© British Library Board: Robana

separation between human and ape, defended the unity of the human species against poly-genists, and advocated the capacity of any human being—particularly the African—to im-prove their skills. Blumenbach questioned the arbitrary classifications of human variety and suggested a more complex scheme than Linnaeus's, underscoring similarities among types across different parts of the world, in line with Buffon's work. He also stressed the difficulty of marking the boundaries between varieties and accused polygenists of arbitrarily defin-ing differences. In the first edition of his treatise *De generis humani varietate natura* (On the natural variety of humankind), published in 1776, Blumenbach followed Buffon's clas-sification of four human types, but cutting further across continents. According to him, the first type included the Europeans, Asians west of the Ganges and north of the Amur River, and Americans closest to Europe; the second type included Asians beyond the Ganges and south of the Amur, and the inhabitants of the Pacific Islands and Australia; the third type consisted of Africans; and the fourth type covered the rest of America.

Blumenbach corrected this classification in the second edition of his book in 1781. He included the North African in the European/West Asian type, and was explicit about which Americans belonged to this type: the Greenlanders and Eskimos. He subdivided the East Asian type into two races—one in China, Korea, and Indochina, and the other embracing Siberians, Manchurians, Tartars, Kalmucks (or Mongols), and Japanese. The third type now included only the sub-Saharan African, while the fourth type comprised the rest of Amer-ica. In this edition, though, Blumenbach created a fifth human type located in the southern world, which included the Sunda, Molucca, and Philippine islands along with the Pacific archipelago. This type was divided into two tribes: on the one hand, the New Zealander, Friendly islander, and Marquesas islander, all humans of elegant appearance and wild dis-position; and on the other hand, the inhabitants of New Caledonia and New Hebrides, black, with curled hair, and in disposition more distrustful and ferocious. Blumenbach also reproduced previous stereotypes: the Asian had a brownish skin color, straight face, narrow eyelids, and scanty hair; the African was black and muscular, with prominent upper jaws, swelling lips, turned-up nose, and curly hair; and the American had copper-colored skin, a thin body, and scanty hair. Finally, Blumenbach included linguistic and psychological fea-tures: the Chinese were defined by their monosyllabic language, depravity, and perfidious-ness of spirit and manners.

It was in the third edition of his book (1795) that Blumenbach coined the notion of a Caucasian type, inspired by Buffon, explicitly based on aesthetic judgment. This type was placed at the top of a hierarchy that included the Mongolian, Ethiopian, American, and Malay. The Finns, Lapps (Saami), and Eskimos (Inuit) were relocated under the Mongols, while the denomination Malay replaced the previous southern types (Southeast Asians and Pacific Islanders). The Caucasian was considered the original—"primeval"—type, and fixed at the center point of a continuum along which the others were placed. The Mon-golian was at one end of this spectrum, preceded by the American, and the Ethiopian was at the other end, preceded by the Malay. The degeneration of races, a major topic of debate in those days, was used to justify the superior white aesthetic and cultural model, contrasted with the inferior types that had resulted from adaptation to other climates and topographies.[20]

Blumenbach campaigned for the abolition of the slave trade, quoted Thomas Clarkson, challenged the notion of savages, met Olaudah Equiano, possessed a library of books by black writers, listed examples of excellent black authors and clergymen, and praised the perfectibility of Africans. He drew extensively on Buffon and contributed to weakening the prejudices about mixed-race people. This very influential author reproduced both old and new ethnic stereotypes about the mental and physical attributes of human types, but he established new methods of observation, discussed racial boundaries, mixed race fertility, and the degeneration and improvement of man placed in nature.

The disruption of the scientific establishment provoked by the French Revolution was followed, in 1793 and 1794, by the reorganisation and expansion of research, namely through the establishment of the Institut de France, the transformation of the Jardin des Plantes into the Musée d'Histoire Naturelle, and the creation of new chairs in Comparative Anatomy and Zoology. Georges Cuvier (1769–1832) thrived in this new environment: he was quickly nominated to the Musée d'Histoire Naturelle and to the Collège de France, holding a central position at the Académie des Sciences. Cuvier was probably the most influential scientist of his time. He became linked to Napoléon's regime, but managed to survive the Restoration with his prestige and institutional positions intact. He created a vision of nature that was both specialized and compartmentalized. He identified four different types of animals related to specific environment. He distinguished man from quadrupeds by his vertical posture, two hands—defined by their thumbs—voice and language. He acknowledged that man was only one species, and that this species' boundaries were determined by its capacity for reproduction. However, he considered that there were hereditary configurations of man that constituted different races, the most distinct of all being the white (or Caucasian), the yellow (or Mongolian) and the black (or Ethiopian). The first race comprehended most of the civilized and beautiful peoples, and was composed of the Aramaic, Indian, Celtic, and Tartar branches of humankind. The second was supposed to exhibit the same physical features—prominent cheekbones, flat face, narrow and oblique eyes, scanty beard (male gender was always the reference in these classifications) and olive skin color—and to be capable of creating large empires, but to have allowed its civilizations to stagnate. It was composed of Kalmucks, Chinese, Manchus, Japanese, Koreans and Malays. The third race, which inhabited Africa south of the Atlas Mountains, was defined by black skin, curled hair, a compressed skull and flat nose. Cuvier considered the black race, with its prominent muzzle and thick lips, to be close to apes; the bushman, equated with the Hottentot, was explicitly classified in an intermediate position between the white man and apes. The black 'peuplades' (tribes) had remained in a barbarian stage, which suggested permanent handicap. Eskimos and the Lapps were classified between Mongols and Tartars (or Scythes), while Native Americans were placed between Europeans and Mongols, though closer to the latter, without a defined race.[21] This demonstrates the volatile criteria of these classifications, which successively shifted peoples from one race to another, created or aggregated new categories, and placed some peoples between categories. Cuvier played a crucial role in the racialization of humankind and reinforcement of old prejudices, particularly those concerning the permanent barbarian state of the black Africans and stagnation of Asian civilizations.

Cuvier's precise discourse, which served his scientific paradigm of specialized knowledge detached from philosophy, can be contrasted with the reflections of his older colleague at the Musée d'Histoire Naturelle, Lamarck, on the development of life, from the simplest to the most complex organisms, proceeding by a gradual succession of more and more complicated forms, with increasingly specialized organs due to the exercise of certain functions. In Lamarck's vision, environmental changes create new needs, leading to the adaptation, reduction, or development of organs in the animal world. In a world defined by the transformation of life-forms, Lamarck pointed out the significance of the nervous system and its growing complexity as an important element of differentiation among animals. He considered the study of the human brain along with its parts and functions as the main challenge for scientific research.[22] Saint Hilaire, also a researcher at the Musée d'Histoire Naturelle, followed a different path, undertaking extensive comparisons of animal forms, and thus leading him to support the idea of a unique organizational plan based on his observation of connections and related functions as well as his refusal of a priori considerations. He pointed out, for instance, the correspondence between the organs of fishes and those of superior animals. The conflict with Cuvier, who rejected this approach as speculative reasoning, led Saint Hilaire to reevaluate Lamarck's transformist ideas. The debate between Saint Hilaire and Cuvier at the Académie des Sciences in 1830 had repercussions all over Europe, and was immediately acknowledged by Johann Wolfgang von Goethe as the crucial event of that year—more important even than the French Revolution of July.[23] Lamarck and Saint Hilaire were not especially interested in the variety of humankind, but contributed to the integration of human beings, in general, in nature. Lamarck even maintained that humans were just a temporary end point on the animal scale, destined to be superseded by more advanced forms—a statement used to accuse him of atheism.[24]

The religious framework for the conception of nature was eroded during the second half of the eighteenth century and the first decades of the nineteenth century. Natural history became more and more autonomous, with the development of specific fields of knowledge providing new data that stimulated reflection on the transformation of organisms and a unique plan for the organization of nature. Nevertheless, Cuvier's vision favored a steady typology of perfectly created animals, refusing any evidence of transformism; for him, fossils were the remains of extinguished animals, not the ancestors of living animals. This scientific stance was challenged from the 1820s onward. The 1830s and 1840s brought new developments in the order of knowledge. Etienne Serres (1786–1868), an embryologist who taught comparative anatomy at the Musée d'Histoire Naturelle in Paris, maintained that the embryos of the higher classes of animals successively recapitulated the forms of those of the inferior classes.[25] In the meantime, Romanticism brought with it spiritual needs and a renewal of a religious inquiry that had always been important in Germany, where Pietism (the tradition of Lutheran emphasis on individual piety and strong Christian life renewed in the late seventeenth century) played a major role. This is why biblical creationism was always present, in one way or another, in the major debates throughout the nineteenth century.

A complex political, cultural, and scientific background between the 1820s and 1840s defined the important period for the classification of humans. Julien Joseph Virey (1775–1846), a medical doctor who published *Natural History of the Human Species* in 1801, expanded into a three-volume edition in 1824, may serve as a guide.[26] Virey was not a scholar who had a significant influence on the main academies and schools, but he published extensively, addressing a literate public interested in the sciences, particularly through his articles in encyclopedias and dictionaries. He reengaged with the tradition of the naturalist philosopher, expressed by his participation in the monumental reediting of Buffon's works. Virey did not share all of Lamarck's or Saint Hilaire's ideas, yet he was attentive to the progress of scientific ideas in the German countries and Britain, leading him to develop both a physiological and anthropological project.

Virey held to an ambiguous vision of the origins of humankind, somewhere between monogenism and polygenism, based on the progressive creation of species from monkeys to apes (orangutans), followed by the Hottentot along with blacks and whites. "Monkeys," he wrote,

> seem to be the root of humankind, preceding original man: human beings were created and organised progressively, either the most perfect deriving from the less noble and less accomplished during the ancient ages of our planet, or each species being formed independently of the others, with its own degree of natural perfection. Nevertheless, we see a gradation from the white to the black, the hottentot, the orang-utan and the other monkeys; we cannot deny this progression, either in its descent or its ascent.[27]

Virey's limited polygenism was based on the opposition of white to black: black was considered not just a distinct race but also a different species, since his/her intellectual, behavioral, and physical features did not change with continent, climate, or circumstances.[28] Virey depicted him as stupid (an adjective he repeated several times), an imitator, just like the monkey, incapable of industry, sensual ("he feels more than he thinks"), voluptuous, carefree, lazy, ugly, filthy, and stinking—a condition aggravated by the regular application of tallow or use of raw putrefying hides as clothing.[29] The contradiction between supposed laziness and suitability for slavery is reinforced through the comparison between sugar and honey production, with blacks being equated to bees.

Virey discussed the practice of taking human measurements. He refused the volume of the skull as a criterion of intelligence since it depended on individual physical features. He noted the alleged resemblance, however, between the heads of the Botocudos, a tribe of Brazilian Indians, and those of orangutans. Virey agreed with Blumenbach's doubts concerning the pertinence of Camper's facial angle theory, since many cases fell outside the supposed norms. Yet he built up his own definition of two human species using these norms, including the white, yellow, copper, and brown races (Arabs, Indians, Celts, Caucasians, Chinese,

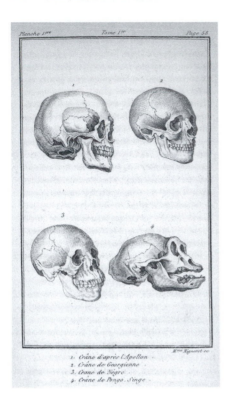

Figure 15.5. Julien Joseph Virey, *Histoire naturelle du genre humain*, 2nd ed., 3 vols. (Paris: Crochard, 1824), book 1, plate 1, 58. Lithograph with the skulls of Apollo, a Georgian, a black, and a monkey.
© British Library Board; Robana

Mongols, Americans, Malays, and Polynesians) in the first species, with a facial angle of around eighty-five degrees, and the black races (Negroes, Kaffirs, Hottentots, and the people of Papua) in the second species, with a facial angle of between seventy-five and eighty degrees.[30]

Virey also accepted Cuvier's notion that the black human pelvis was close to that of the orangutan, while he maintained that the occipital orifice of black people was set further back than that of whites, which meant that Africans were not upright, bending down in a way that was halfway toward the transverse position of monkeys.[31] This idea was exposed as totally baseless by Willem Vrolik and Karl Otto Weber, Dutch and German pathologists and anatomists, whose arguments were used by Victor Schœlcher (1804–93) in 1847, many years after Virey's original publication, and a year before the final abolition of slavery in France, showing how scientific debate was related to policy. Schœlcher, a famous journalist and abolitionist, wrote the French law that abolished slavery under the special conditions of the 1848 revolution. A change of political atmosphere could also have an impact on science. By 1831, Virey received his first criticism at the hands of Saint Hilaire, who accused him of betraying the "true-speech" of a scientist, while the naturalist Bory de Saint Vincent (1778–1846) criticized him for claiming a providential order of nature. By the 1850s, he was dismissed as an amateur by Armand de Quatrefages (1810–92), who then held the anthropology chair at the Musée d'Histoire Naturelle. Nevertheless, Virey's articles on black

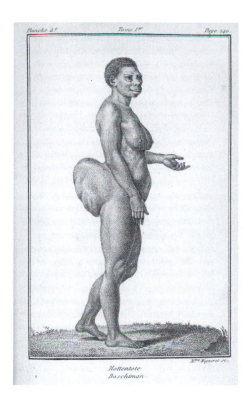

Figure 15.6. Julien Joseph Virey, *Histoire naturelle du genre humain*, 2nd ed., 3 vols. (Paris: Crochard, 1824), book 1, plate 2, 240. Lithograph with Hottentot woman. © British Library Board; Robana

people and humankind, written and published in the 1810s, continued to influence articles dealing with these topics in the Larousse encyclopedia of 1865–90.[32]

Virey was not wedded to a single view and indeed tried to reconcile different positions, sometimes within the space of a few pages or even in the same paragraph. His contempt for black people was particularly sharp, but he did not deal any better with Native Americans when it came to their intelligence or ingenuity, while Mongols were classified as pusillanimous and perfidious, bowing to the eternal demands of despotism. Interestingly, Virey was in favor of miscegenation, thus opposing a cornerstone of prejudice concerning descent. He considered the interpenetration of races an efficient way to reduce hereditary diseases and compensate for defects of intelligence or aesthetics.[33] Furthermore, Virey equated slavery with the social status of women, revealing the complexities of this racialized reasoning. He explicitly stated that slavery began with the enslavement of women—an idea distant from the misogynous writings of contemporary authors, particularly the libertarian socialist Pierre-Joseph Proudhon. Virey praised Peter the Great for enhancing the status of Russian women.

In the second edition of his work, Virey introduced two chapters opposing the slavery of black people.[34] Although he clearly considered black people inferior, Virey insisted on their perfectibility, perhaps influenced by Blumenbach. He suggested that the unfortunate educational situation and political state of Africa were responsible for blacks' condition, reversing previous arguments for natural and innate inferiority. These later positions may be attributed to the reaction of the public, and specifically that of women, who probably made up a significant part of the readership of his works and the encyclopedias he contributed to. Political engagement might have played a role, though, too. Abolitionism was not a powerful movement in France, especially not between the 1800s and 1820s, but Virey was to become a member of the liberal center-left group in the French parliaments of 1831 and 1834, along with Tocqueville. These apparent contradictions match Virey's reconciliation of the vital principle of transformism with a providential vision of the universe, the heredity of acquired characteristics with the limitations of environmentalism, a scientific approach with metaphysical ambitions, immanence with transcendence, and monogenism with polygenism as possible interpretations of empirical phenomena.[35]

In the nineteenth century, research concerning the variety of human beings still reflected aspirations toward universal knowledge. The effort to reconcile the developing disciplines of science with an ethnology taking its first serious steps is well represented by Prichard, a prominent medical doctor, Quaker, and committed British citizen engaged in the abolitionist movement. Between 1813 and 1847, Prichard published three editions of his major work, *Researches into the Physical History of Mankind*. He followed Blumenbach on the essential unity of the human species, clear separation between apes and human beings, and perfectibility of Africans. Prichard's most significant contribution was to depart from Blumenbach's idea of an original classification of races. For Prichard, race was not a rigid causal category. He accepted innate features as well as the appearance of new ones formed by mutation linked to diversification, differentiation, and diffusion, yet he rejected the inheritance of acquired characteristics. Prichard mixed biology, linguistics, and social and political systems in his ethnographic approach to explain human variety. That is why he used the established denominations of tribes, nations, and races indifferently or ambiguously. For him there were no clearly marked races, and he stated that it was impossible to define the "Negro" type and apply it to one single nation in Africa, such was the variety that existed.

As early as 1826, the second edition of *Researches* revealed the extent of the ethnographic material collected. Prichard broke with the idea of a single Native American race, for example, to talk about American races, including more than three hundred American entries in his repertoire concerning what we would nowadays call ethnicities. This catalog of human variety was enormously extended in the third edition, which became a massive encyclopedia of the ethnographic knowledge of Prichard's day, illustrated with engravings of skulls and human types.[36] The ethnographic maps of the world he published in 1843 contributed to this enormous collection of information and attempted to locate the main human groups on each continent.[37] In this enterprise, Prichard was certainly helped by contemporaneous linguists, who had been making significant progress on the origins and evolution of languages from Anquétil Duperron, William Jones, and Friedrich Schlegel onward. An earlier world atlas of languages by Adrien Balbi, published in 1826, reflects the momentum of this new trend, which quickly identified the comparative diversity of Native American languages.[38]

In the first edition of his book, Prichard maintained that the "primitive stock of men were negroes"—an assertion he dropped from the second edition. Prichard was not a transformist, but he systematically applied the idea of progress to human's physical and mental development. Like many other liberals of his time, Prichard accepted the idea of the civilize white man as the standard to be attained—with more capacious skulls, finer and more delicate, in general best fitted for the habits of an improved life—against which he set the black African—tougher and coarser, though more perfect in the sensorial organs and able to improve.

Prichard's scientific and ethnographic conclusions were influenced by his Christian faith along with his conservative evaluation of the French Revolution. He never quoted the main French philosophers—neither those who tended toward deism nor those who tended toward materialism. For the same reasons, he did not even quote the writers of the Scottish Enlightenment, although he had studied in Edinburgh. Prichard explicitly refused the polygenism advanced by Henry Home, Lord Kames, and throughout his life maintained a monogenist stance based on his vision of revealed religion.[39] He never contradicted the main chronological tradition of the Bible, which most scientists of his day had abandoned.[40]

This chapter has investigated plural and sometimes-contradictory theories of races. It has pointed out early challenges to the consistency of such theories, which highlighted blurred and shifting frontiers between categories. Alexander von Humboldt (1769–1859), a disciple of Blumenbach and one of the major scientific authorities of the first half of the nineteenth century, pushed this criticism further. He both developed some of Prichard's main arguments and recovered Herder's vision of language, supported by the extensive, innovative, and more accurate linguistic research of his brother, Wilhelm von Humboldt. Humboldt considered language as intimately associated with the affinity of races, implying the similarity of linguistic structures. He advocated the unity of humankind, citing the many intermediate gradations in skin color and skull forms—gradations that would make it impossible to establish a clear distinction between races. He pointed out that the alleged anatomical contrasts among human beings had disappeared in the face of recent research by Friedrich Tiedemann on the brains of black and white people, or by Vrolik and Weber on the form of the pelvis. According to Humboldt, comparisons of the black populations of Africa, South India, and the west Australian archipelagos had shown no connection between skin color, woolly hair, and cast of countenance.

Humboldt reasserted Buffon's old assertion concerning fertility and reproduction: different races were variations within a single species, not different species of a genus, since in the latter case hybrid descendants would remain sterile. Humboldt went further than previous authors, denouncing the lack of clear definition in the noun races and instead proposing the use of the expression varieties of human beings. He mentioned the five races identified by Blumenbach and seven races suggested by Prichard, but stated that "we fail to recognise any typical sharpness of definition, or any general or well-established principle, in the division of these groups." Humboldt also observed that several groups could not be included in any category, and that geographic areas could not serve as points of departure for races in any precise way, since several regions had been inhabited at different periods by different groups. In his view, to search for the "cradle of the human race" was to pursue a myth. Finally, Humboldt explicitly refused "the depressing assumption of superior and inferior races of men," and the unhappy Aristotelian doctrine of slavery as an institution condoned by a nature that bestowed unequal rights to freedom on human beings. Humboldt considered that all nations were destined for freedom and (quoting his brother) denounced the erection of barriers among humans to prevent natural perfectibility—the result of prejudice.[41]

The methodological problems of racial construction, shifting conceptual content of the noun race, background of prejudice responsible for the hierarchy of human types, and political meaning of the theories of races were therefore boldly exposed. This critical view did not, however, sever the main lines of experiment and search for an explanation for the variety of human beings. The debate over typologies of races would continue, based on the long inquiry from Linnaeus to Prichard that this chapter has attempted to characterize. The relation between humans and other animals, discussed on a scientific basis since Linnaeus (we have seen how Cuvier's typology was challenged by Lamarck's transformism and Saint Hilaire's unique plan of animals), would thrive in this new environment. The measurement of human beings, inspired by Camper's interest in the facial angle and Cuvier's comparative anatomy, would be further developed in the following decades. As this chapter has mainly focused on scientific developments in the concept of human variety from the 1730s to 1840s, I now need to chart how the enormous political change of the mid-nineteenth century had an impact on research. After a long period of structural and multiple changes, the 1840s and 1850s presented a turning point in which scientific research on the variety of human beings became much more assertive, ideologically aggressive, and politically engaged. I call this new development scientific racialism, as it presented a scientific effort to justify and reify divisions as well as hierarchies of races, supposed to be innate, immutable, and perpetual.

CHAPTER 16

Scientific Racialism

The revolutions of 1848 disrupted the new conservative order that had established itself across Europe after Napoléon. They were the outcome of internal conflicts due to the processes of industrialization, urbanization, intense migration, political recognition of the middle class, and the political demands of the new working class, whose miserable conditions were aggravated by poor harvests and agricultural crisis. The resilient political, social, and economic structures of the ancien régime, which had survived or been partly reconstituted after the first impact of the French Revolution, were rocked to the core. Major riots, particularly in Paris, Vienna, and Berlin, spread through the kingdom of France, Austrian

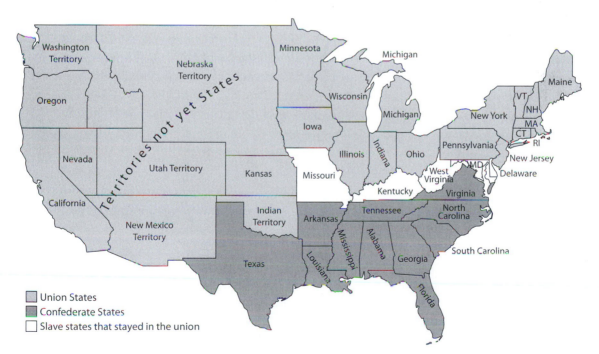

Map 16.1. Union and Confederate states during the Civil War (1861–65).
Source: Geoffrey Barraclough, ed., *The Times Atlas of World History* (London: Times Books, 1990), 222

Empire, and kingdom of Prussia. The revolt swept across Europe through both urban areas and the countryside, crossing nearly all borders except those of the Iberian Peninsula, Scandinavia, and Russia. It triggered national projects of independence, mainly in Hungary, but also in Bohemia and the Balkans. The German project of unification was promoted by the liberal movement, which managed to create a general parliament in Frankfurt. The project was blocked in Prussia and Austria by the rooted interests of traditional elites, who felt that they were unable to control the process. In Italy, the Milanese liberal revolt against the Austrian Empire was unsuccessful, despite military intervention by the kingdom of Piedmont, and the republican experiment in Venice met the same fate. In Rome, the republic created in opposition to Pius IX's compromise with Vienna was militarily suppressed by the French under their new leader, Napoléon III, who was eager to forestall the arrival of Austrian troops, while the liberal revolt in Sicily was quelled by the kingdom of Naples.

In all these movements, liberal monarchists had to compete with republicans, socialists, and communists. The social issue was on the table: working-class misery, dispossession, and political exclusion had triggered egalitarian ideologies that questioned the legitimacy of private property, and these ideologies received public support. National ideology based on the notion of ethnic communities of citizens sharing the same language and culture disrupted decades of international liberalism. The republic of Hungary, suppressed by the combined forces of Austria and Russia, had to face military opposition from Croats, Serbs, and Romanians. The clash between Czechs and Germans in Bohemia also showed the limits of national projects, and worked in favor of the composite Habsburg monarchy. Conservative victory all over Europe in 1849–51 did not mean that things stayed as they were: the last traces of serfdom and feudal rights as well as duties were removed; constitutions more or less centralized by the sovereign were instituted; and the seeds of national projects were sown in an environment of compromise in which international liberalism and cosmopolitanism lost their appeal.[1] The extraordinary spread of the revolt had presented new social and political challenges: while merit still struggled to assert itself against privilege in the new system of values, the struggle for equality against inequality (notions naturally permeated by multiple points of view) became an important issue in the conceptual separation of the new and old social orders. In Europe, reflection on race and the scientific quest for the origins of human variety became a major tool for proving the supposedly inherent, rooted origins of inequality, in order to undermine the powerful movement for equality as artificial and antinatural.

In the United States, there was no particular event that spurred on scientific racialism; it resulted from an accumulation of social and political tensions coupled with conflicts that had been building up since the American Revolution. The issue of slavery was obviously on the table from the moment of the Declaration of the Independence in 1776: under pressure from the southern delegates, Jefferson sought to suppress a passage condemning King George III for stimulating the slave trade. The egalitarian spirit of the declaration was famously defined by the second paragraph—"We hold these truths to be self-evident, that all men are created equal, that they are endowed by their Creator with certain unalienable

Rights, that among these, are Life, Liberty and the pursuit of Happiness"—but it concerned only white men.[2] The discussion of the constitution was based on a compromise: the issue of slavery would be dealt with at the level of each state, not at the federal level. The main debate was about the white representation of slaves, since the southern states claimed that they had duties concerning this population that should be politically acknowledged in the House of Representatives. The decision was to count each slave as three-fifths of a person for the purposes of electoral calculation, a significant metaphor for the worth of humans as commodities.[3] Between 1780 and 1804, the states north of Maryland decided to abolish slavery, although in a gradual way—with the exception of the radical case of Massachusetts—and without providing political rights for the freed population. The prohibition of the slave trade in 1807 put further pressure on the southern states, increasing prices, and promoting the kidnapping and smuggling of free black men.

It was the expansion of the United States to the west, and the dispute between the supporters of free soil and those of slave soil, however, that was immediately identified as a potential threat to the Union. In 1787, the Northwest Ordinance forbade slavery in the territories northwest of the Ohio River. In 1820, the congressional debate on the Tallmadge Amendment to limit slavery in Missouri failed, although it was agreed that slavery would be forbidden in territories established north of the thirty-six degree, thirty-three minutes latitude parallel. The consequences of this decision proved to be significant: in 1845–48, the annexation of Texas along with the conquest of New Mexico and California from Mexico raised new tensions with the creation of slave soil in territories where slavery had previously been illegal. These tensions were further fueled during the following year by the Californian decision to reject slavery and create a state based on free soil. The southern states obviously felt a need to extend slavery into the new states in order to maintain a political balance, but the struggle struck a chord with the northern antislavery movements, which were increasingly supported by the massive number of European immigrants, who logically chose free soil states. The compromise created in 1850 reinforced the status quo with the Fugitive Slave Act, according to which all runaway slaves were to be returned to their owners in the South. This act was vigorously denounced by the antislavery movements, in which new figures like the former slaves Sojourner Truth and Frederick Douglass played a major role.

It was arguably the Nebraska-Kansas Act, enacted by Congress in 1854, along with an amendment to repeal the Missouri Compromise and open the possibility of slave soil north of the thirty-six degree, thirty-three minutes latitude parallel, that triggered vigorous opposition in the northern states, whose inhabitants started to boycott the Fugitive Slave Act. Over the following years, the rigged Kansas vote for slave soil exposed the constant southern push for the extension of slave soil. Slavery had been placed center stage in the political debate. In the meantime, the ambiguities of the northern states—free soil was accompanied by the idea of white homogeneity, and the abolition of slavery was equated not so much with the dignity of humans as with the total exclusion of black people, who had been blatantly removed from Vermont in 1777—had been only partly and temporarily overcome. In the 1820s and 1830s, the antislavery movement gained momentum in the northern states,

Figure 16.1. Anonymous photograph of Frederick Douglass, age thirty-eight (1856).
© Smithsonian Institution, Washington, DC; Corbis

following the campaign for immediate emancipation launched by the journalist William Lloyd Garrison, who created the American Anti-Slavery Society in 1833 with Theodore Weld, an evangelical minister, and Robert Purvis, a free African American. This movement prepared public opinion in the northern states to move against the secession decided on by the southern states in 1860, after the election of Abraham Lincoln on a moderate antislavery platform as president of the United States.[4] It is in this political and social context that we need to analyze scientific racialism and its complex ramifications, particularly the debate between monogenists and polygenists, which cut across north-south boundaries.

Finally, the expansion of the British Empire in Asia raised new issues of ideological justification and assertion at different administrative levels (local, regional, and central). The conquest of India and spread of the British Empire in Asia from the 1750s onward established an entirely new relationship between conquerors and dependents, due not only to the scale of the enterprise—much wider than the previous Portuguese and Dutch dominion over intercontinental maritime trade and scattered territories—but also to the system of indirect rule, which excluded the creation of a mixed-race elite after the 1790s. This situation contrasted with previous European imperial experiences in the area, requiring new ideological ground in order to involve local elites and populations. While the Portuguese had used religion and the social promotion of mixed-race people to establish bridges with local populations in Asia, the British used the translation of the Vedas to find a common ancestor. The consequences of this linguistic and anthropological construction were vast: in the process of nation building, which liberalism spread worldwide, the identification of the ancestors or founders of a nation became crucial.[5] Aryanism was used in Europe to promote the idea of a supposedly white imprint stamped on the major civilizations, making sense of contemporary imperial projects, but it was also utilized in Asia by both European and local elites to find a common ground for understanding as well as interaction. The challenge here, as Tony Ballantyne indicates, is to overcome a traditional Eurocentric approach and include the appropriation of this ideological construction by local elites, either by loyalist natives eager to reinforce their position in the colonial system, or by militant natives interested in asserting their own identities based on noble, virile, and warrior ancestry.[6]

These three distinct historical contexts—new challenges to social inequality in Europe, racial inequality in the United States, and European imperial dominion in Asia—have never been perceived as together influencing the development of scientific racialism. This chapter aims to do so.

HISTORY AS RACIAL COMPETITION

The book *Races of Man*, published in 1850 by Robert Knox (1791–1862), offers a useful introduction to the scientific racialism that emerged in the 1840s and 1850s in opposition to the humanism of Blumenbach, Prichard, and Humboldt.[7] For Knox, races were everything in human history: they were not the result of accident; they were not interchangeable; they represented the laws of hereditary descent in combination with the effects of soil and climate. This essentialist approach—which held that the physical and mental attributes of race were unalterable—led Knox to mock the idea of progress in human civilization, and refuse the notion of improvement brought about by education or government.[8] His message included a criticism of Humboldt: "Is Ireland civilised?" he asked, ironically, two years after popular revolt had broken out there.[9] Religion did not matter much either: Christianity had left no significant imprint, since its different forms—Greek, Roman, or Lutheran—had only expressed the essential features of different races: Sarmatians (or Russians), Celts, and Saxons. He criticized the historian and politician Thomas Babington Macaulay for pointing to religion as the main agent of historical change and asked sarcastically: "Is the Caledonian Celt [Protestant] better off than the Hibernian [Catholic]?"[10] For him, empires, monarchies and nations were all humanly contrived, often held together by fraud and violence. As a self-appointed Saxon from the Scottish Lowlands, Knox resented the government in London as being created by the Normans, dominated by the Flemish of the southeast, and opposed to the Celts and Saxons in the rest of the country. He offered the example of a Negro or a Tasmanian accidentally born in England: they would be English, but could not become a Saxon.

Knox naturally questioned the big shift represented by Prichard's efforts to build an encyclopedia of human variety; for him, all significant races were to be found in Europe, not in Tasmania or the lands of the Hottentots. He mocked Blumenbach for his idea of a Caucasian race, and François Guizot for having written about a European civilization, "an abstraction which does not exist."[11] The object of Knox's work was to show that European races differed from each other as widely as the Negro from the Bushman, the Kaffir from the Hottentot, or the Red Indian from the Eskimo. This suggests that preparations for the new stage of European imperialism, defined by the territorial occupation of Asia and scramble for Africa, had unleashed an internal, Eurocentric dispute over which were the most capable races. Yet

Knox criticized the European imperial projects, deriding their claims to convert or civilize people, which according to him were a pretext for robbery and enslavement. He considered that races expressed the relationship between hereditary descent and the environment, and that migration would expose Europeans to local corruption, making a future degeneration inevitable. This assertion was applied to the United States: "The social condition of the Saxon can only be seen in the free states of America . . . in Britain he was enslaved by a Norman dynasty, antagonist of his race."[12] But the Saxon would degenerate to the Indian level in the end—and Knox cites the example of the barbarian European in South Africa, where he served with British troops. Only the best races, which remained in their original environment, would prevail, he asserted, in an echo of de Pauw. The crucial contemporary political debate on nationhood hence had been subsumed under a simultaneously intranational and supranational debate on race. Still, the theory of races would be reinterpreted and reused under national political paradigms and projects. Knox himself made the link twelve years later; the second edition of his book in 1862 was subtitled *A Philosophical Enquiry on the Influence of Race over the Destiny of Nations*.

The major difficulty of Knox's work was to establish the borders between the different races in Europe. The superior Saxon was to be found in Scandinavia, north and east of the Rhine, eastern Scotland and eastern England, northern and eastern Ireland, parts of Switzerland (among Protestants, naturally), and among the noblest people in classical Greece, although the Saxon had by then disappeared from southern Europe and France. This Saxon was supposed to be tall, powerful, and athletic, with fair hair, blue eyes, a fine complexion (the only fair race in the world), but not well proportioned, because their torso was too large. They were considered a lover of work, order and cleanliness, profit, and punctuality in business. Yet the Saxon was not seen as an inventor or theoretician, and had the lowest taste in art and music. The Saxon was the only natural democrat on earth—the only human being who truly understood the meaning of the word liberty—and was tolerant, with an abstract sense of justice, an inordinate self-esteem (and thus a hatred of genius), a love of independence and fair play, and a hatred of dynasties and governments. Knox politically advocated a republican confederation of Saxons in Europe.[13]

The Celt was to be found in southern Europe, France, western Ireland, parts of Wales, and the Scottish highlands. They were depicted as a furious fanatic (Roman Catholic), indolent, mentally a slave, without self-reliance or self-confidence, incapable of understanding the word liberty, a lover of war, an antagonist of order and patient industry, without accumulative habits, restless, treacherous, and undecided. Celts were condemned to decline, and Knox relaunched the old idea, which Hume had demolished, of the decreasing population in Spain and Portugal, where there were fewer people than in Roman times. Nonetheless, Knox underlined several times his admiration for France as the best expression of the Celtic talent for music and literature, and for its greatest leader, Napoléon, whose dreams of world sovereignty had been betrayed by his own race.[14]

The Slavonian, also denominated as Flemish, was to be found in Poland, Austria, south Germany, and Belgium. This race lacked the main attributes of the Saxons and showed the seeds of despotism, as in Austria. Knox contradicted himself in various parts of the book, first considering that the Slavonians were the most intellectual of all races, then attributing that quality to the Saxon-Germans, and finally declaring that Slavonians (Slavs) and Russians had shorter skulls than the Saxons. The Sarmatians (or Russians) were described as having occupied part of eastern Europe, but in this case the author did not develop his stereotypes. Obvious hesitations as to nomenclature for and geographic identification of the European races can be further observed when Knox considered the intersecting regions: the Celts interacted with the Saxons and Flemish/Slavonians in the south of England and Switzerland, while the Saxons mingled with the Slavonians in Austria and on the Rhine, and with the Slavonians and Sarmatians in eastern Europe.[15]

Knox expressed the utmost contempt for mixed-race people, deliberately ignoring empirical data already made available by Buffon, Blumenbach, and Prichard, who had opposed the traditional view that hybrid beings were infertile. Knox reproduced all the stereotypes accumulated since classical antiquity. When mules or hybrids accidentally appear in nature, they cease to be, since they are either nonproductive or the weaker strain disappears. In his words, mulattoes were "a worthless race" that could not survive beyond the third or fourth generation, "because of the law of specialization, the law of hereditary descent and the law of deformation." He used the example of the Spaniards in America, who intermixed with the native population, while the resulting mulattoes degenerated into Indians. According to his view, indigenous people would always prevail, so the vital energy of the Spaniards (although they were not of pure stock) was destined for extinction. Knox also pointed to the French Celts in Canada and British Saxons in America as supposedly being in physical decline, although the Saxon's natural antipathy toward the dark races and a lack of intermixing would delay the process. The most contemptuous phrase is reserved for "the mixed barbarian and savage race of slaves, now called Egyptians [Gypsies]."[16]

If mixed-race people were a disaster for Knox, he reserved no greater respect for the non-European races. The book is a catalog of all the accumulated prejudices and verbal abuses relating to human beings that against all evidence, would continue to be reproduced until the Holocaust and beyond. It is useful to highlight some of Knox's passages, since they make widespread prejudices explicit:

The Gypsy has made up his mind, like the Jews, to do no work, but to live by the industry of others . . . begging and telling fortunes.[17] . . . Has he no ingenuity, no inventive power, no mechanical or scientific turn of mind? . . . The real Jew has no ear for music as a race, no love of science or literature. . . . [H]e invents nothing, pursues no enquiry. . . . Their sole occupation is to secure a good bargain, to . . . sell again at a high price. Their infamous life is spent between these two lies.[18] . . . The inhabitants of Central Africa have no history. . . . [W]ere Central Africa . . . sunk under the Ocean wave, and with it the black race, what would we lose? . . . [N]o inventions, no discoveries, no fine arts, no sublime thoughts, nothing to distinguish man from the brute.[19] . . . Hindus and Chinese will work as slaves for ten centuries.[20] . . . So profound was their ignorance that they [the Chinese] could not send a single person to

Europe so as to give any information about the armament which ultimately overthrew and plundered them.[21]

Knox also reflected on the Copts, who allegedly had created the pyramids, and perhaps migrated to West Africa and Central America, then declined due to intermixing with the African race.[22] The main idea was that races were unchangeable. African and American races could not be civilized: "the dark races stand still, the fair progress."[23]

Knox was a Scottish surgeon, anatomist, and zoologist, a fellow of the Royal Society of Edinburgh, and member of the Royal College of Surgeons of Edinburgh, where he created the Museum of Comparative Anatomy. He had studied at the University of Edinburgh and served in the army from 1814 to 1820, first in Brussels, where he treated the wounded from the battle of Waterloo, and then in South Africa. He also worked and studied in Paris with Cuvier and Saint Hilaire. In his approach to race, Knox was close to the compartmentalized vision of Cuvier, who separated zoological types linked to specific environments and subject to extinction. Indeed, he went even further, considering races at the level of species, successively created on Earth, which placed him close to polygenism.[24] He created a curious blend of republicanism, anticlericalism, freethinking, and scientific racialism alien to creationism, which would influence other authors. Knox also engaged in ethnological research, claiming stereotyped observations that he made of a community of Gypsies (Roms) temporarily in Scotland and the Jewish community in London as his fieldwork. Knox was dismissed from the School of Anatomy at Edinburgh for accepting bodies of tramps and drunks from a gang of murderers—the Burke and Hare case that so revolted the city. This scandal deeply affected Knox's reputation, but his essentialist vision

[The Jew.]

Figure 16.2. Robert Knox, *The Races of Man: A Philosophical Enquiry into the Influence of Race over the Destinies of Nations* (London: Henry Renshaw, 1862), 193. Representation of Jews. Cambridge University Library V.20.24
Reproduced by kind permission of the Syndics of Cambridge University Library

of races as immutable, hierarchical, and naturally averse to intermixing made an impact, as we will see.

The extent of Knox's influence has been disputed. Scholar Nancy Stepan argues that Knox represented a turning point in the fully biologized understanding of race in Britain, breaking away from the Enlightenment and universal Christian values.[25] This image of a new racialized and strictly hierarchical British way of thinking has been taken up by scholars Catherine Hall and then Robert Young, who extensively quote Knox in their works.[26] Peter Mandler, by contrast, has contested the influence of Knox, pointing out that the reception of Knox's book in the general and specialized press has been overrated.[27] Mandler shows that only one of three book reviews was positive. He challenges the idea that biological racism had become a main intellectual trend, and quotes Robert Latham as a contemporary of Knox with an opposing perspective who had been a successful and popular author on human variety.

I would contest the idea of Knox as a biological racist. He did not add any significant biological facts or arguments to the basic framework established by his master, Cuvier, in the 1810s. Moreover, he included all the linguistic, ethnographic, and historical stereotypes that had accumulated through the centuries, and been transformed by the Enlightenment and early nineteenth century natural history into definitions of races. Knox also added new stereotypes resulting from his alleged fieldwork. What is new is the intellectual framework blending the reassertion of the immutability of races, inevitable failure of intermixing, breakaway from biblical creationism, and irreligious overall vision. Knox's book was cited by polygenists in North America because of its praise of Anglo-Saxons as a superior race and contempt for nonwhite races, but they did not share its materialism. Yet Knox was widely read by nearly all the authors interested in human variety in the 1850s and 1860s; even Darwin quoted him. It is not sufficient to analyze an author's reception through newspapers reviews as Mandler does; books could be widely read and drawn on, despite receiving few or even negative reviews. James Hunt, secretary of the Ethnological and then Anthropological Society of London shared many of Knox's ideas. Catherine Hall has rightly underlined the new ideological atmosphere of the mid-nineteenth century, but Knox's views did not represent mainstream racialism in Britain.

We need to look beyond national frontiers to understand that Knox was crucial on the other side of the Atlantic. Mandler's reference to Latham as a popular counterpoint to Knox is important: Latham was the curator of the exhibition on human variety created for the opening of the Chrystal Palace in Sydenham in 1854—an exhibition defined by the same hierarchy of races proposed by Cuvier, but smoothed out by the succession of different stages in human lifestyles, such as hunting, pastoral, agricultural, and commercial, along with the ideas of diffusion and progress.[28] Latham kept the connection with previous humanist ethnology in the face of Knox's and Hunt's ideas. He published widely on the ethnology of the world as well as European and British peoples. He contested the notion of the purity of races, highlighting the continuous intermixing, in various combinations and to various degrees, particularly on the British Isles. Latham expected that this trend would only gather pace in the future.[29]

Arthur Gobineau (1816–82), who styled himself Comte de Gobineau, published his long *Essai sur l'inégalité des races humaines* in 1853–55, reinforcing the vision of innate and immutable races.[30] This book was to have little impact on contemporary France, but was immediately translated and reinterpreted, in 1856, in the United States by Josiah Nott (the first volume), and in 1898–1901, in Germany, by Ludwig Schemann, a disciple of Richard Wagner. Serious studies on Gobineau were first published in France by Ernest Seillière in 1903 and Robert Dreyfus in 1905, followed by a new edition of his works produced by Clément Serpeille in the 1920s, which finally attracted public attention. But it was Nazi propaganda in the 1930s that decisively contributed to the creation of a particular vision of the author. Gobineau in fact was not anti-Semitic: he praised Hebrews as ingenious, strong, capable, and intelligent people, warriors, farmers, traders, doctors, state builders, and successful migrants.[31] Nor did he praise the "highly intermixed" contemporary Germans as representatives of pure Aryan blood, which he thought had left its last traces, although these were declining, in Scandinavia, England, and North America.[32] Nor did he describe all blacks as inept, because this in turn would have forced him to state that all Europeans were intelligent, which was far from his elitist reasoning.[33]

Gobineau was obsessed with the new popular trend of equality; it is not by chance that inequality is at the center of his book's title. He wanted to prove that inequality was deeply rooted in nature. His project was a history of the world in which the impact of the hierarchy of races would show that some were essentially much more capable than others, countering the "liberal dogma of fraternity," which assumed "absolute equality of races."[34] Gobineau constructed an erudite framework, demonstrating an impressive ability to collect archaeological, linguistic, historical, ethnological, and scientific data that could feed his argument. The direct impact of the 1848 revolutions shaped his life: although a royalist and *légitimiste* (supporter of the Bourbons), in 1849 Gobineau became secretary to Tocqueville, minister for foreign affairs in the Napoléon III administration—a position that opened the way for his diplomatic career. In contrast to Tocqueville, a moderate liberal aristocrat who accepted the rise of the masses, future of democratic principles, and suppression of the privilege of birth as inevitable, Gobineau maintained an elitist outlook and contempt for the principle of promotion by merit. This is why the wise Tocqueville kept his distance from Gobineau after the publication of the book, which Tocqueville described as the product of a horse dealer (*maquignon*) who wanted to explain everything through differences of race, and criticized as a fatalist view that birth and blood affected entire peoples, comparing it to doctrines of materialism and predestination.[35]

Gobineau did not quote Knox, and his project was not strictly centered on Europe; rather it had a worldwide scope, based on the promotion of Aryans as the white race from central Asia that had supposedly left its imprint on all major civilizations—Hindu, Egyptian, Assyrian, Chinese, Greek, Roman, German, Algonquian, Aztec, and Inca—before retreating to Europe and exerting what was left of its influence in the Anglo-Saxon countries.[36] He contended (as Knox did), however, that the spread of Christianity did not change the way of life, political configuration, or capacity for civilization of the various races and peoples converted.[37] Gobineau also postulated the degeneration of all races due to intermixing and consequent reduction of populations since antiquity, though without compiling any serious data to prove his point.[38] He decided not to take a position between the monogenists and polygenists, pointing out the flaws in both assertions. Yet he clearly valued Cuvier's notion of specific environments for the location of species, refused the argument of climate as a justification for variety, and maintained that white peoples had experienced an isolated development—all of which placed him close to polygenism.[39] In addition, he drew from Cuvier's system of three basic races—white, black, and yellow—considered pure and original, thus refusing the hybrid varieties integrated by Blumenbach and Prichard into their classifications.[40]

Gobineau criticized all criteria for skull measurement: first those of Camper (facial angle); then those of Blumenbach (vertical measurement from the top), Richard Owen (vertical measurement from below), and Samuel George Morton (1799–1851; capacity of the skull or the brain size), pointing out the absence of identical criteria of age along with economic and social position for the skulls measured.[41] He did not challenge biblical creationists, accommodating post biblical genealogies in his narrative, although his convictions about the original purity of races, as linked to specific environments, and contempt for Christian morality, which he equated with the ethos of slaves, and held responsible for democratic and egalitarian ideas, made him attractive to southern thinkers in the United States. The idea of a basic antipathy between races and antagonism between their intellectual capacities was at the heart of his book: "The European cannot pretend to civilise the Negro, as he can only transmit to the mulatto a fragment of his aptitudes. . . . [M]ixed culture is only a degree more advanced towards the white culture; the inequality of intelligence between different races is well established."[42] The idea of decadence was crucial: Gobineau contended that the golden age of racial purity was long gone. For him, the history of the world involved a constant intermixing of peoples, with the most capable elements always providing the initial drive, until they were overwhelmed by the lower elements in the mixture, leading to inevitable decline. But he believed in some permanence of physical features, and held them responsible for radical differences in appearance and ability.[43]

Stereotypes concerning the different races were part of Gobineau's account: there was an inequality in strength due to the inferior capacity of American "savages," Hindus, Australians, and black peoples in general; and there was intellectual inequality among different peoples across time and place, which was used to contest the idea of the perfectibility of all races, and was a cornerstone of Gobineau's reasoning against egalitarian ideas.[44] In the classical Hindu, Greek, and Roman worlds he found some summits of rhetoric, literature, and philosophy that had been unchallenged since. He did not believe in progress: humans do things differently; new technologies do not seriously change basic ways of thinking; and what has been gained in material conditions as well as political complexity has been lost in spiritual capability and ethical outlook.[45] This constant charting of gains and losses defined Gobineau's reasoning, since the intermixing of races facilitated the diffusion of civilization from the stronger to the weaker, but at the same time contained the seeds of degeneration due to the inevitable submersion of elites (or higher races) in the more base standards of the masses (or low races). He even recognized that artistic and literary genius along with manners and beliefs improved with miscegenation, yet these transitory benefits would not prevent the ultimate decline into disorder.[46]

Savage races, from Gobineau's point of view, had always been savages and would remain so until they disappear.[47] He repeated the idea of black races' bestiality, reproducing Cuvier's "evidence" of the apish pelvis, which had already been proven wrong, and the supposedly narrow forehead and inferior intelligence, dominated by the passions and senses, plus the unstable humor and uncontrollable emotions of peoples who were simultaneously cowards and murderers.[48] The yellow race was assigned the opposite features: a large forehead, a tendency to obesity, low physical vigor, apathy, weak desires, an obstinate will, a taste for material pleasure, selective gluttony, a superficial understanding of problems, and a love of practical usefulness. They were a pragmatic people, but not inventors. The white race was characterized as having intelligent energy, a more elevated sense of utility than that of the yellow race, perseverance coupled with physical strength, an extraordinary instinct for order, a pronounced sense of freedom, and honor as well as sense of proportion. Yet they were inferior as regards the development of their senses.[49]

The only original idea here was that the yellow race had its origins in America and migrated to Asia, rather than the other way around, which gave more space to the Aryans and explained the blossoming of white civilizations in Eurasia.[50] From Gobineau's perspective, all civilizations had developed from the white race, which had been settled and politically organized from the start.[51] The aristocratic, elitist, and peer rule of superior intelligence, strength, honor, and beauty, which he identified with the Aryans as well as the whiter segments of the Semitic and Celtic populations, were qualities constantly challenged by intermixing and inevitable decline, as the darker races carried within them the seeds of democracy and egalitarianism that flourished because of their low standards. Gobineau's vision of world history obsessively tried to identify progress and innovation as related to white races with noble and feudal ideals, followed by degeneration and decline through intermixing with dark races shaped by communitarian habits.[52] Wise, temperate royal rule was thus threatened by the absolute regime of the republic.[53] Hence Gobineau's vision of the European Middle Ages opposed the nobility to the mixed-race bourgeoisie, with the former still close to the Aryan principles, while the people below were equated with slaves, blacks in southern Europe, and Finns in the north.[54] Normans were considered Aryans on the same level as Anglo-Saxons, which corresponded to the then-popular evaluation of the Vikings and their migrations missed by Knox.[55]

This view was based on the systematic, arbitrary identification of sections of Aryans or white Semites in intermixed populations, defined by hierarchies of evolving proportions of blood.[56] Here's just one example of this arbitrariness: the Egyptian of 2000 BC supposedly had one-third Aryan blood, one-third white blood as descendants of Shem, and one-third black blood, while in 700 BC the proportion of black blood had reached half, and Aryan blood declined to one-tenth.[57] Gobineau used comparative mythology and linguistics to establish fabulous genealogies linking Hindus and Egyptians as well as Hindus and Chinese, and linking Aryans, Celts, and Semites to produce the Romans; he also elaborated on the original Egyptian and Arab elements of the Abyssinians, and the caste-based society handed down from the Hindus to the German tribes.[58] The analysis of the supposed racial background of the main religions and civilizations is generally based on imagined principles and deductive reasoning. Finally, Gobineau asserted the resistance of the main races to change, offering the case of the Hindus and Chinese, who could be conquered but would never modify their ways of thinking and doing.[59] The continuity of basic stereotypes needs to be stressed. Gobineau developed the refrain, adding praise for feudal nobility as the supreme expression of the supposed virtues of natural inequality and the notion of the inevitable decline of humankind due to the widespread process of miscegenation.

IMMUTABLE RACIAL HIERARCHIES

In the meantime, in the United States, the measurement of human skulls had been driven by the collection of hundreds of specimens and a new method, now based on cubic capacity, of calculating brain size. The first attempts at identifying the different races by the form of their brain had been disputed, and the obvious underlying idea of this latest operation was that intelligence resulted from brain magnitude. But the new criterion, promoted by Morton, required a large sample to establish its scientific credentials. Hundreds of skulls were collected from all over the world, but for practical reasons Morton concentrated his studies on two peoples, the American Indians and Egyptians, since he had been generously provided with a considerable number of mummified skulls by George Robins Gliddon (1809–57), vice-consul of the United States in Cairo (see below). A natural scientist with significant publications on geology, hybridity in animals and plants, and the anatomy of human beings, Morton used the measurement of skulls for his project on human variety.

In his book *Crania Americana*, published in 1839, Morton distinguished five main categories of human beings—Caucasians, Mongolians, Malays, Americans, and Ethiopians—subdivided into twenty-two families, following an approach close to Blumenbach's. Curiously the volume was dedicated to Prichard, whose monogenist views would be targeted some years later by this generation of natural historians. The attribution of specific features to each human variety was in line with previous stereotypes, although Morton believed that the Mongolians were ingenious and highly susceptible to improvement, while the Malays were active and able migrants and maritime people. The American Indians were alleged to be incapable of any improvement: slow to acquire knowledge, restless, vengeful, and fond of war, but wholly lacking a spirit of maritime adventure. The Ethiopians (or African people) were considered the lowest grade of humanity, and the Hottentots were the nearest approximation to lower animals.[60] Morton's research confirmed that the Caucasian brain was the biggest, with an average of eighty-seven cubic inches; the American Indian brain reached eighty-two cubic inches; and the African brain measured seventy-eight cubic inches.[61] Ironically, Gobineau was the first to expose the methodological flaws in Morton's method.

The twist came from the polygenist approach. The physical and mental features of different people, Morton explained in his introduction, mentioning the Arabs, Hindus, and Jews, were the same as thousands of years ago—an idea based on reproductions of the images found by archaeologists in the pyramids. Hence, differences were independent of external causes; each race was adapted from the very beginning to its peculiar local destination.[62] Morton did not reject creationism but on the contrary, built on it: his idea was that multiple creations expressed God's perfect purpose, fitting human varieties for the specific moral and physical circumstances in which they were supposed to live—an opinion formulated in 1830 by the US polygenist and prominent medical doctor Charles Caldwell, who echoed previous polygenists such as Lord Kames and White. The second book published by Morton, in 1844, *Crania Aegyptiaca*, further unveiled his political program: the Egyptians who had built the pyramids were naturally white—an assertion proved by facial angle and skull size. Morton divided the skulls between the Caucasian and Negro races, with the former subdivided into Pelagians (Greek ancestors), Semitic (receding forehead; long, arched, and prominent nose; and marked distance between the eyes), and Egyptian (narrower and receding forehead; face more prominent, with smaller facial angle; aquiline nose, angular face, and sharp features; and long, soft, and curling hair). These structural features, which supposedly had divided black and white people since before 2000 BC, confirmed his opinion concerning immutable differences among races, which therefore were close to species. Morton also discussed hybridity, projecting the general assumptions of the time onto the Copts, considered a mixed race of Caucasian and black ancestry.[63] It was exactly this weakness in his system that was targeted by the monogenist John Bachman—a Lutheran minister, social reformer, and naturalist who sustained the unity of human species—in a polemic launched against Morton.

Morton's influence was considerable. He was born in Philadelphia, graduated in medicine from the University of Pennsylvania, and earned an advanced degree from the University of Edinburgh. Morton worked his entire life in Philadelphia, becoming a professor of anatomy at the University of Pennsylvania and president of the Academy of Natural Sciences of Philadelphia. He played a major role in convincing Louis Agassiz (1807–73), discussed below, to shift his views from monogenism to polygenism in 1846. Brought up a Quaker, Morton became an Episcopalian later in life, and although a scientist, he became known as the founder of American ethnology. He significantly demonstrates how the new scientific racialism crossed cultural borders: Morton was a distinguished citizen in the first North American state to abolish slavery, but like many other northern people he supported the idea of a hierarchy of races. The role of Philadelphia in these years as the center of institutionalized racial debate has not been sufficiently highlighted. Groups, particularly the Social Improvement Society, frequently organized conferences and public discussions, while the city's high concentration of printing presses reproduced the debates between abolitionists and antiabolitionists, which were permeated by ideals of white equality that cut across cultural boundaries reinforced by black exclusion.[64]

This tension between the egalitarian aspirations of white people and their ideas about the supposed inferiority of black people distinguishes the US authors of scientific racialism from European writers, who were more interested in justifying inequality among white people. The most pertinent case of this American trend is John Campbell (1810–74), who in 1848 published *A Theory of Equality* based on lectures he gave on the French Revolution, followed in 1851 by *Negro-Mania: Being an Examination of the Fabulous Assumed Equality of the Various Races of Men*, and in 1861, *Unionists versus Traitors*, showing how strongly opposed racialist thought could be to Southern secession. He labeled those who defended equality between white, red, and black people as ignorant fanatics, and specifically targeted Prichard as advocating this vision. He asserted the innate inferiority of black people (and nonwhite people in general), refuted the idea of underdevelopment due to white oppression, and asked the usual questions: What has the black race done in five thousand years? Where are monuments in Africa? Where are the law codes? Where are the writers, politicians, scientists, inventors, explorers, and artists? On hybridism, Campbell quoted Charles Hamilton Smith, who had reinforced the idea of infertility in interracial couples against mounting scientific evidence.[63]

Josiah Clark Nott (1804–73) became the crucial member of this American group of polygenists who worked together or influenced each other. Born in South Carolina, the son of a federalist politician and judge, Abraham Nott, he graduated in medicine from the University of Pennsylvania and completed his studies in Paris. He lived in Mobile, Alabama, where he founded the College of Medicine, where he was a professor of surgery. During the Civil War, he served as a Confederate surgeon and hospital inspector. Nott worked with Gliddon to promote and enlarge Morton's approach to the human races. He was one of the scientists who involved Agassiz in this new theory of races, in which multiple creations (or polygenism), linked to the location of animals, plants, and human beings in their specific environment, were mixed with the measurement of skulls, analysis of old images in pyramids, and reproduction of old stereotypes concerning the attributes of different races and irreversible decline of mixed-race people.

The full title of the book edited by Nott and Gliddon in 1854 reveals their purpose and method: *Types of Mankind or Ethnological Researches, Based upon the Ancient Monuments, Paintings, Sculptures, and Cranes of Races, and upon Their Natural, Geographical, and Biblical History*. The idea was to demonstrate the innate and immutable physical as well as mental features of the different races, based on analyses of mummified skulls and thousand-year-old images. The purpose of the volume was clearly defined by one of its contributors, Henry S. Patterson, who indicated the central role played by America in the adaptation of three different races—white, red, and black—now confronted with the immigration of a fourth one (Chinese and Indians). In Patterson's opinion, the relationships between and management of all these people depended on their intrinsic racial characters. Patterson's main target was Humboldt and his critical vision of the hierarchies of races, supposedly based on moral judgment rather than physical reality. Nott contested the perfectibility of races, arguing that they had been immutable for four thousand years. He used the notion of ethnology coined by Luke Burke as the science of mental and physical differences in humankind along with the organic laws on which they depended, which sought to deduce the principles of human organization from these investigations.[66] This practical and political vision of racialized ethnology was fully employed by Nott in his dealings with Calhoun, the famous senator from South Carolina who became secretary of war and the seventh US vice president; Nott provided Calhoun with scientific ammunition for political arguments against the abolition of slavery.

The last key member of this group was Louis Agassiz (1807–73): ichthyologist, glaciologist, zoologist, geologist, and natural historian. Agassiz studied in Zurich, Heidelberg, and Munich before meeting Cuvier and Humboldt in Paris. He received their support to obtain his first job at the University of Neuchatel. In 1846, Agassiz moved to the United States and became a professor of zoology and geology at Harvard, where he founded the Museum of Comparative Zoology. In the same year he met Morton, and shifted from monogenism to polygenism, agreeing to be involved in conferences and publications organized by Nott. He maintained a lifelong allegiance to his master, Cuvier. Agassiz rooted his vision of nature in Cuvier's typology of the animal world, based on the compartmentalized idea that different species had been perfectly created from the beginning and conceived for specific environments, according to a divine order. Agassiz clearly positioned himself against Lamarck's transformism and Saint Hilaire's unique plan of living beings. He opposed the idea that the four great zoological branches were connected. Environmentally related multiple and independent creations (then labeled special creationism) appeared to confirm his previous researches on fish fossils and glaciers, providing new coherence to Cuvier's vision of nature and bringing to a close the systematic assault on the master's order of knowledge by the growing number of transformists.

Agassiz's essay for Nott and Gliddon's *Types of Mankind*, titled "Sketch of the Natural Provinces of the World and Their Relation to the Different Types of Men," was an early work in which connected with conditions of temperature, soil, and vegetation, he selected and placed eight races into nature: Arctic, Mongol, European, American, Negro, Hottentot, Malay, and Australian. In the *Essay on Classification*, published in 1857 as part of the *Contributions to the Natural History of the United States*, and later separately printed in London (1859) and Paris (1869, in a significantly enlarged edition), Agassiz developed all his basic ideas on nature and human races, equating the latter with species, such was the difference he believed to exist between them.[67] His vision of the hierarchy of races did not prevent Agassiz from maintaining a comfortable position at Harvard and backing Unionism, as did many other Northerners who favored the abolition of slavery, but assumed the innate physical, social, and mental inferiority of black people.

It is against this background that we have to analyze Agassiz's expedition to Brazil, from April 1865 to August 1866, immediately after the end of the Civil War. The expedition involved a significant number of experts and young scholars, like William James (1842–1910), the future psychologist and philosopher, who then was at the Lawrence Scientific Institute at Harvard. James found it a terrible trip, catching smallpox and feeling seasick, and his abolitionist family, strong supporters of the Union during the Civil War, did not feel uncomfortable with Agassiz's project, overtly organized for research in the natural sciences, but quite patently looking for evidence to contest Darwin's theory on the origin of species and obtain confirmation of Agassiz's own theory of races.

Agassiz collected, made notes on, and drew illustrations of a large number of species on this journey. In addition, the account of the expedition published by his wife included extracts from his own diary, in which he expressed horror at the vision of a multiracial society. He believed that slavery had even more odious aspects in Brazil than in the United States, due to "the less energetic and powerful race of the Portuguese and Brazilian . . . compared to the Anglo-Saxon." His idea was that "the free blacks compared well in intelligence and activity with the Brazilians and Portuguese," who gave the "singular spectacle of a high race receiving the impress of a lower one, of an educated class adopting the habits and sinking to the level of the savage." The courteous treatment of Indian women by Brazilian gentlemen, for instance, shocked Agassiz. He was also disgusted by the extension of hybridism: "All clearness of type had been blurred, and the result is a vague compound lacking character and expression. . . . [T]he fact, so honourable to Brazil, that the free negro has full access to all privileges of any free citizen, rather tends to increase than diminish the number." Again he compared humans with animals, equating the hybrid qualities of mixed-race people (cafuzo, mameluco, and mulatto) with the qualities of the mule—an ancient topic. The "uninterrupted contact of half-breeds with one another is a class of men in which pure type fades away as completely as do all the good qualities, physical and moral, of the primitive races, engendering a mongrel crowd as repulsive as the mongrel dogs."[68]

The old stereotypes used to abuse mixed-race people are patent in Agassiz, showing how they were the cornerstone of scientific racialism. In Agassiz's vision, Brazil offered a useful example of the sort of mixed-race society that the United States should avoid. This was the clear message of *A Journey in Brazil*. The book reached six editions in one year, and was reprinted several times in the 1870s and again in 1895, which means that it was well received both in the northern and southern United States among white people who were then trying to find a model for their relations with black people. Agassiz used his experience in Brazil to promote the segregation of and discrimination against black people in the United States after the abolition of slavery. We have to relate his intervention to political practices on the ground: the defeat of the Confederacy and victory of abolitionism did not lead to equal rights. After the short period of failed Reconstruction based on the idea of human equality, the Jim Crow laws of segregation imposed from 1876 onward reflected the restoration of political white control of the South through blatant violence and daily intimidation. White mobs regularly lynched black people, instigated by semipublic organizations such as the notorious Ku Klux Klan, first active in 1865–74. Black people were effectively disenfranchised, while segregation pervaded daily life in schools, transportation, and public places, reinforced by law.[69] Agassiz's book encapsulates what scientific racialism in the United States was really about: a politically committed development in the theory of races on behalf of southern policies of exclusion, segregation, and discrimination that lasted until the 1960s under the benevolent gaze of northern white pragmatists who shared the same basic racial prejudices.

ARYANISM

In the meantime, in Asia and Europe, the myth of Aryans as the white ancestors of various populations was being created and diffused, as we have seen through the analysis of Gobineau's main work. Aryanism must be scrutinized in the context of a long-term European trend of deprecation of, but also fascination with, Asian peoples, objects, and ideas.[70] In the 1680s, when Giovanni-Paolo Marana challenged the biblical narrative of time, he imagined Brahman books with a history of the world thirty million years old.[71] The idea that India and China had a much older history than the Jewish one had been suggested by Jesuit missionaries, particularly Martino Martini, in the seventeenth century. The accumulation of Jesuit information on Indian and Chinese texts throughout the eighteenth century had led to renewed interest in Sanskrit and translations of texts dating back thousands of years. The translation of crucial Brahman (and Persian) texts by John Zephaniah Holwell in 1765, Anquetil-Duperron in 1771, Charles Wilkins in 1785, and William Jones in 1796, most of them employees of the East India Company, created a new movement, leading to the creation of schools of Oriental languages in Benares (1791), Paris (1795), Calcutta (1800), and London (1805), followed by the establishment of chairs in the main universities in England, Germany, and France.[72] The extensive work of Friedrich Max Müller (1823–1900), who translated the *Rig-Veda* from 1849 onward, further inspired this movement, although Müller insisted that linguistics should not lead to anthropological speculation.[73] The fascination with the Orient had been fueled by Voltaire, who turned Jesuit texts on their head to undermine the Bible, arguing that it had derived from much older Eastern traditions.[74] The legendary origins of white people shifted from the Caucasus to central Asia. Kant already mentioned white populations in Tibet and northern India in 1775, but in the mid-nineteenth century, it was Gobineau who enshrined the notion that the Aryans were the ancestors of white people all over the world.

The *Rig-Veda* mentioned the migrations of pastoral people called Arya to India and clash of these light-skinned noble invaders with local dark-skinned populations labeled barbarians. This is the source of the myth of Aryanism, since the *Rig-Veda* had probably been composed around 2000 BC. The text was considered to supply the first evidence of conflict between light- and dark-skinned populations. Gobineau equated the main achievements of civilization on different continents, from the Egyptians to the Aztecs and Incas, including the Chinese and Indian, with the presence of Aryans. Mythmaking always has a purpose. In this case, Aryans were handy to promote white supremacy, and also were used to naturalize social inequality around the world. Gobineau apportioned various amounts of Aryan blood among different peoples to justify the original strength of elites followed by inevitable decline due to mixed blood. Aryanism became a convenient ideology for British imperialism in Asia, since it emphasized the common white ancestry of British and Indian elites.[75] But in order to assert their own social status, Indian groups also used the idea that these white pastoral people from central Asia had conquered India and subjugated the Dravidian population of the south. This ideology of superior origin spread in Asia and Oceania, so that native peoples as faraway as New Zealand used it to enhance their social position and negotiate with the colonizers.[76]

Aryanism would have an extraordinary impact on Europe, too, due to the racialized vision of humankind. In France, Marcelin Berthelot and Hippolyte Taine diffused Gobineau's ideas. Aryanism was accepted as a major reference by Paul Broca, but dismissed by Armand de Quatrefages, both of them leading naturalists. The next generation continued the debate about degrees of Aryan blood, with Paul Topinard accepting its general influence and Vacher de Lapouge lamenting the extinction of the Aryans due to the emergence of mixed-blood people. In Germany, the Aryan myth was spread through different projects and authors: Rudolph Virchow organized an enormous inquiry into physical features among schoolchildren, thereby disproving his ideological stance on pure Aryans, as a significant portion of Jews shared the same supposed distinctive physical features; Richard Andree advocated the strength of Jewish blood, capable of absorbing people from other origins; anthropologist Ludwig Woltman sustained the supremacy of Nordic people, equated with Aryans; the historian Heinrich von Treitschke regarded white people as the aristocracy of the human species against the calamity of the Jews; and Alfred Rosenberg promoted the Aryan mystic.[77]

The diffusion of Aryanism coincided with the idea of Pan-Germanism, which fused nationalism and racial construction. Aryanism, however, was not overwhelmingly present in Europe. In southern Europe it was virtually nonexistent, until it was introduced in Italy during the final stage of the alliance between Benito Mussolini (1883–1945) and Adolf Hitler (1889–1945). In England, despite the reference to it by Darwin, Aryanism never really became rooted and had to compete with other mythical origins, particularly Saxon and Teutonic. The equation of Teutonic with Aryan had some impact on the United States. At the turn of the century, William Z. Ripley, a leading American sociologist and economist, who believed that races crucially explained human differences, used the cephalic index to divide the population of Europe into three groups—Teutonic, Alpine, and Mediterranean.[78] It is against these developments of racial construction, which gained rigidity during the period leading to the Civil War in the United States, aftermath of the European revolutions of 1848, and expansion of the British Empire in Asia, and contributed to the invention of Aryanism, that I need to analyze Darwin's new ideas of and their impact on perceptions of variety in human beings.

CHAPTER 17

Darwin and Social Evolution

The second half of the nineteenth century witnessed a dramatic sequence of economic, political, and social events that directly interlinked with the theories of races. I have already discussed the recomposition of white supremacy in the southern United States through the violent disenfranchising of the emancipated black population. In Europe, the defeat of the revolutionary movements of 1848 was followed by the organization of a new conservative order, which reflected the emergence of a bourgeoisie as well as middle classes mixed with institutional and symbolic elements of the ancien régime, even though the latter had been eroded as a social system. The living conditions of the industrial working class led to the creation of trade unions along with socialist and communist movements. The short life of the Paris Commune became a testimony to the consequences of social and political division, reflected in an atrocious civil war and massive final repression of the revolution. The new national framework of German and Italian processes of unification in the 1860s and 1870s had a further major political impact. Nationalist trends spread all over Europe, and raised the issues of social and ethnic division in a climate of dramatic economic change—a result of industrialization coupled with the abolition of rural feudal privileges, rights, and duties.

From the 1870s onward, anti-Jewish movements in Russia and Germany grew out of different traditions—Jewish exclusion in Russia confronted with the consequences of the assimilation of large communities in Poland; inclusion in central Europe stimulated by Napoleonic laws—but also from the profound shake-up caused by modernity—a new economic structure, migration, and the disruption of local social environments. In the meantime, the new wave of colonial expansion set off by the British conquest of India from the mid-eighteenth century to the 1810s gained momentum in the 1830s and 1840s with the French conquest of Algeria, the British expansion in Canada, Oceania, and Africa, the Dutch occupation of Indonesia, followed by the French expansion in Indochina in the 1860s, and the scramble for Africa in the 1880s and 1890s—the latter with the participation of new European powers, Germany, Italy, and Belgium. From 1830 to 1913, the surface of the world controlled by the Western powers increased sixfold and the subject population more than doubled.[1] This vast European expansion throughout the nineteenth century naturally raised new issues concerning interethnic relations all over the world.

The relationship between political trends and racial constructions, however, cannot be seen as purely instrumental. Certainly there was a specific scientific inquiry into the variety of human beings that was influenced by traditional prejudices, and connected to political issues of colonial legitimacy, interethnic relations, and nation building, but it cannot be reduced to an ideological strategy. The theories of races, as we have seen, were far from coherent, with some reflecting new developments, and others involving areas of resistance. The divide between monogenists and polygenists was the major though not the only one, representing options that were not consistent from a political point of view, cutting across abolitionists and supporters of slavery. New theories of race, on the other hand, could have an impact on the different scientific, political, and ideological frameworks, reshaping general points of reference and providing tools for conflict at the lowest level among different ethnicities in their negotiation of daily life. These theories, as we also have seen, were related to the general scientific concepts concerning the creation of the world, origin of species, and improvement or degeneration of species. The idea of the creation of perfect species by God, which led to the dominant idea of the degeneration of species to explain variety, was not seriously challenged until the late eighteenth century. It was only with Lamarck, who projected the notion of a permanent transformation of nature, and Saint Hilaire, who promoted the idea of a common plan among animals, that the concept of degeneration started to be questioned at its most profound level from a scientific perspective, paving the way for an insistence on improvement as a viable explanation for variety. This idea itself was not alien to the notion of progress built up through the eighteenth century in both the religious and political fields. But it was the evolutionary theory formulated by Darwin during the 1840s and 1850s, and finally published in a comprehensive book in 1859, *On the Origin of Species by Means of Natural Selection, or the Preservation of Favoured Races in the Struggle for Life*, that decisively contributed to the disruption of the order of knowledge promoted by Cuvier and Agassiz. The issue here is to reconstitute the main aspects of this new vision, the impact it had on racial construction, and how prejudices concerning descent adapted to the new scientific framework.

DARWIN'S THEORY OF EVOLUTION

In 1831, Darwin was only twenty-two years old when he set sail for his five-year scientific voyage around the world on board the *Beagle*, following a good education in botany, zoology, and geology. These were to be crucial, formative years, in which Darwin would further develop his powers of observation. The notebooks for and final text of the *Journal of Researches*, published in 1839, which established his reputation as a scientist, show a learned and skillful young researcher, eager to reflect on new findings, confront them with the available knowledge, and look for radically new explanations—for example, in relation to the formation of coral reefs. The observation of nature went hand in hand with the observation of people in different habitats. Ethnology was emerging in dialogue with natural history. Darwin's viewpoint is interesting for more than one reason. First, he benefited from a liberal upbringing: his paternal grandfather, Erasmus Darwin (1731–1802), was visited by the main intellectuals of his time, keen to meet the learned physician who had developed an independent vision of nature alien to biblical creationism and close to Lamarck's ideas of transformism.[2] Charles Darwin married his cousin Emma Wedgwood, who came from the family of the pottery firm; they both had abolitionist ancestors. When he studied medicine in Edinburgh (1825–27), Darwin became friendly with John Edmonstone, a black freedman who taught him how to embalm animals.[3] Darwin was an abolitionist all his life. Both his capacity for observation and abolitionist position make Darwin's remarks on savage peoples even more interesting.

The shock of meeting the natives in Tierra del Fuego was vividly expressed by Darwin: "I could not have believed how wide was the difference between savage and civilised man: it is greater than between a wild and domesticated animal, inasmuch as in man there is a greater power of improvement."[4] Darwin made a favorable comparison between the powerful bodies of three young men he met there who stood six feet high, and the "stunted, miserable wretches farther westwards," but he lamented that their only garment was a mantle made out of guanaco skin with the wool outside, worn over the shoulders and leaving their bodies half exposed (other tribes would have seal or otter skins). His description of their appearance was completed with a reference to the "dirty coppery red colour" of their skin, which was filthy and greasy, the entangled hair, discordant voices, hideous faces, violent gestures, body painting, and feather ornaments, which made the Fuegians closely resemble the devil as represented on the stage in plays. Their attitudes were considered abject, the expression of their countenances distrustful, surprised, and startled. The Fuegian language was considered inarticulate, based on hoarse, guttural, clicking sounds. The various tribes were cannibals when at war, and "when pressed in winter by hunger, they kill and devour their old women before they kill their dogs," because the dogs could catch otters.[5] Darwin depicted natives sleeping on the wet ground coiled up like animals, scarcely protected from the wind and rain. It was his opinion that the natives did not have government or chiefs, and were alien to any sense of having a home, and still less to any domestic affection, "for the husband is to the wife a brutal master to a laborious slave," capable of injuring children for minor misdemeanors.[6] He concluded, "Viewing such men, one can hardly make oneself believe that they are fellow-creatures, and inhabitants of the same world."[7]

Darwin conceded that the natives were excellent mimics: they could imitate any European gesture and reproduce entire phrases. They were also sensitive to Europe music and dance. It was only at this point in the narrative that Darwin disclosed the existence of three young Fuegians on board, captured by Captain Fitz Roy on a previous expedition, educated in England, and brought back to their home. They could speak English and dressed as Europeans. Darwin described each of them: Jemmy Button was his favorite because of his good humor, but they all suffered from uncontrollable emotions. He also highlighted their excellent sight, much better than that of any sailor. Darwin was shocked when Button finally met his mother, who had searched for him, inconsolable, after his disappearance. The meeting was considered less interesting than a horse coming across an old companion:

mother and son stared at each other for a short time without demonstration of affection, and the mother then went off to look after her canoe. The relatively happy encounter of the prodigal son fast declined into dissension within Button's tribe, provoked by the systematic plundering of the Europeans' possessions, with the missionary brought to stay with them being the first target. The narrative focused on the educated Fuegians: first ashamed of the appearance and ways of their fellow tribespeople; then divided between European and native allegiances; and finally abandoning their European patina to become natives again in appearance and actions.[8]

Darwin's final remark on the social system of the Fuegians shows again how reflections on the different stages of humankind and prevailing racial constructions were linked to the issue of inequality, which at the turn of the century was dealt with in a debate between William Godwin and Thomas Robert Malthus that is reflected here through reference to Malthus's assertion that only self-interest motivates humankind.[9] For Darwin, the perfect equality among the individuals composing the Fuegian tribes had retarded their civilization. Peoples governed by hereditary kings were considered most capable of improvement, and among races, the more civilized ones had the more sophisticated governments.[10] Darwin equated equality with baseness: pieces of cloth given to the Fuegians were torn into shreds and distributed; no individual would be richer than the others. Individual property, the notion of superiority, and an accumulation of power were unthinkable in this tribal regime, yet for Darwin they were the sinews of improvement. The comparison between the "savages" and "barbarians" that Darwin met during his voyage around the world highlights his hierarchy. The Fuegians were placed at the bottom of the scale, along with the warlike cannibals and murderous New Zealanders (or Maori), Australian aborigines (skillful with the boomerang, spear, and throwing stick in climbing trees and methods of hunting, but feeble in mental capacity), and "wretched" South African tribes prowling the land in search of roots. They were all contrasted unfavorably with the relatively civilized South Sea islanders—the manners and even tattoos of the Tahitians were praised—and proficient Eskimos, with their subterranean huts and fully equipped canoes.[11]

Darwin possessed an independent and acute mind, although for some of his observations he was indebted to Captain Cook's journals. These observations reveal continuities in the descriptions of the peoples of the world, reminding us of the early accounts of Native Americans by Columbus, Vespucci, or Caminha, even though the detachment (and repugnance) concerning savages sounds even more pronounced after centuries of contact. The divergence was reinforced by the eighteenth-century notion of civilization, and enhanced by the industrial revolution and progress in the comfort of daily life as well as the quality of transportation. The voyage of the *Beagle* was certainly more comfortable and safe than previous circumnavigations of the world, although the second trip made by Cook (1772–75) had been particularly successful in terms of a radical reduction in the loss of human lives.[12] The filthiness of the native body along with the scanty clothes, diabolic body paintings and tattoos, constant warfare driven by revenge, cannibalism, cruelty, and absence of justice as well as the inferior local languages were not new topics; vehement disgust was an expression of the Europeans' projection of their own self-perception. Darwin's descriptions, however, represent the highest level then reached by travel accounts. They were attentive to habitat, housing, material culture, family structure, division of labor, and political specialization.

The claim that inequality was a source of social improvement lay at the core of contemporary debates between socialists and liberals; it shows that Darwin was aware of the major social and political discussions of his time. Nevertheless, Darwin's lack of empathy concerning the savages did not shake his abolitionist convictions. Darwin expressed his indignation when confronted with the daily cruelty toward slaves in Rio de Janeiro, where he saw instruments for their torture, heard the cries of slaves being punished, and intervened on various occasions to stop further suffering. He equated slavery with the moral debasement of a whole society; he protested against the idea of slavery as a tolerable evil, denouncing the way in which people were "blind[ed] by the constitutional gaiety of the negro"; and he refused the attempt to "palliate slavery by comparing the state of slaves with our poorer countrymen." Darwin raised a crucial issue that could be related to many other situations of oppression: "Those who look tenderly at the slave owner and with a cold heart at the slave, never seem to put themselves into the position of the latter," concluding emotionally, "It makes one's blood boil, yet heart tremble, to think that we Englishmen and our American descendants, with their boastful cry of liberty, have been and are so guilty: but it is a consolation to reflect, that we at least have made a greater sacrifice, than ever made by any nation, to expiate our sins."[13]

Darwin's early writings did not provoke any major stir, but they are interesting as a testimony of his reflections on topics close to my inquiry. It was his systematic reflection and conclusions on the origin of species that created a new framework of scientific reasoning, with an undeniable impact on the perception of natural human beings and racial construction. The book *On the Origin of Species by Means of Natural Selection* was published when Darwin was fifty years old, after he had dedicated the greater part of his life to the systematic observation of nature and collection of information through an extraordinary network of correspondents around the world. The book criticized the two main assumptions of scientific racialism: the idea of the independent creation of species, and the notion of the immutable character of the surviving species. The critique of this second assumption was nuanced, since naturalists had accepted variation due to external conditions, particularly climate and food, but Darwin maintained that this theory would not explain the process of internal organic modification. Darwin also criticized the Lamarckian conception of the transformation of nature, which had been popularized in England by Robert Chambers in an anonymous book, *Vestiges of the Natural History of Creation*, published in 1844, because it did not explain the means of the modification and adaptation of organic beings.[14]

The two main inspirations for Darwin's new approach were Charles Lyell on geology and Malthus on demography. Lyell provided the notion that the formation of Earth's crust took many millions of years.[15] The obvious consequence to Darwin (not to Lyell himself) was that the evolution of species could not be contained within the traditional biblical narrative of several thousands of years. This enlarged time frame, already hinted at by eighteenth-century naturalists, opened an epistemological space for considering extremely slow processes of variation in organisms—a reflection fueled by the discussion, widely entertained since the seventeenth century, of the nature of fossils. Malthus established the principles of demography on the basis of a geometric increase in populations confronted with an arithmetic increase in resources. Although Malthus raised other critical issues of demography, such as the mortality rate and control of the birthrate through the age of marriage, it was the idea of a permanent scarcity of food supply and competition for this resource that caught Darwin's attention.[16] The projection of the struggle for survival onto the animal and vegetable world created the setting for the crucial new idea of natural selection through the extinction of less improved forms of life along with the success of those better fitted to life in their environment through successive, improved variations.[17]

Darwin's demonstration of the process of natural selection was fundamental to the success of his book: he started with the variation of species through domestication, based on recognizable experience, and moved on to the struggle for existence in nature, addressing both the vegetable and animal worlds in a comprehensive and interdependent way. Darwin highlighted destruction in nature as a result of changes in life conditions—climate, food, and migration—which in turn explained why variation in species was key for adaptation and survival in a world of limited resources. The long, slow process of slight modification to species provided some with advantages over others, reinforced by further modification, and expressed through successive diversification, specialization, and the perfection of organs and structure linked to specific functions in order to adapt to different environments. The strength of Darwin's book lies in the wealth of examples put together and thorough analysis of each case, always connected to the demonstration of the main thesis, and reinforced by a diagram of the tree of life representing imperceptibly fine gradations through millions of generations during millions of years, with massive extinction of intermediate and less improved forms. The theory of interrelated animals developing from different species was explained through the transition of organic beings from an aquatic to a land environment, and from aquatic and land environments to the air with the development of flight. Through these transitions, Darwin underscored the modification of structure, changing functions of organs, and presence of residual, now-useless organs as the only remaining physical reminder of previous functions. He dismissed the idea of the independent creation of species related to specific forms of environment, as different species existed in similar habitats and species migrated from one habitat to another. The idea of a cataclysm overwhelming the whole world (Noah's flood) was also dismissed, as there had been an unbroken succession of generations. Embryology testified to the real affinities of all organic beings, since the embryos of mammals, birds, reptiles, and fish were so similar to each other as well as so unlike their adult forms, clearly indicating a community of descent. Darwin concluded that all animals and plants descended from shared prototypes, and that "all living things have much in common in their chemical composition, their germinal vesicles, their cellular structure, and their laws of growth and reproduction."[18]

The demolition of biblical creationism changed the paradigm of natural history, clearing the way for a long view of the evolution of all vegetable and animal species on Earth.

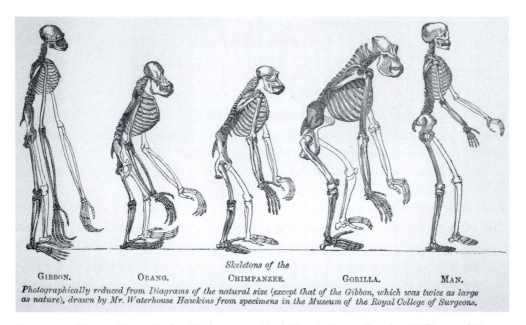

GIBBON.   ORANG.   CHIMPANZEE.   GORILLA.   MAN.

Skeletons of the

Photographically reduced from Diagrams of the natural size (except that of the Gibbon, which was twice as large as nature), drawn by Mr. Waterhouse Hawkins from specimens in the Museum of the Royal College of Surgeons.

Figure 17.1. Thomas Henry Huxley, *Evidence as to Man's Place in Nature* (London: William and Norgate, 1863), table before the title page with the evolutionary comparison of the skeletons of apes and humans. Reprinted with permission from Paul D. Stewart; Science Photo Library

Although Darwin decided not to publish the chapters on humankind to avoid unnecessary religious debate centered on the place of human beings in the Creation, the consequences of his theory were obvious to all readers. One of the most faithful followers of Darwin, Thomas Henry Huxley, published the essay *Evidence as to Man's Place in Nature* in 1863.[19] The first Neanderthal skull had been found, and Huxley reflected the general feeling of the new generation of naturalists attracted by Darwin's ideas: the relationship of human beings with other mammals, mainly with apes on the tree of life, sharing the same ancestors, received new impetus. Darwin's only concession to the religious establishment was the deist reference, at the end of the book *On the Origin*, to "the laws impressed on matter by the Creator," slightly enlarged in later editions to "[life] originally breathed by the Creator."[20] It did not protect him from the fury of some dignitaries of the Anglican and Catholic churches, but the ecclesiastical reaction was useless; the cultivated public and most naturalists, already involved in Darwin's extensive correspondence, were largely receptive. Alfred Wallace, who in 1858 produced an essay with a similar theory of evolution, triggering Darwin's rush to complete the book *On the Origin*, trusted Darwin's skills to organize the evolutionary troops in the style of a general. Later they diverged over sexual selection (Wallace's socialist upbringing meant that he was not convinced of aristocratic good looks and aesthetic models) and the limits of evolutionary thought (Wallace became a spiritualist, leaving humans aside from the general scheme of nature). But Darwin did show perseverance and strategic shrewdness, constantly contacting, involving, or neutralizing naturalists all over the world, and cautiously waiting for others to open up new fields, as in the cases of Huxley in paleontology and Ernst Häckel in embryology, to diffuse his own theories in more radical terms, until he felt it was time to publish his own book, painfully produced in the face of doubts and psychosomatic crises.

The Descent of Man, and Selection in Relation to Sex was published in 1871, twelve years after *On the Origin*, when the debate was widespread and Darwin's ideas could not come as a shock.[21] In any case, Darwin knew that the religious establishment, which remained extremely powerful, would react violently against a total abandonment of creationism now that evolution by means of natural selection included humans—an issue only implicit in *On the Origin*. The fright over the "red" commune in Paris in the same year and Irish Fenian rising in 1867—the latter spreading through bombing activities to the English mainland— did not help to soothe the moral indignation against this new attack on biblical creationism, portrayed by most of the religious establishment as protection against savagery, criminality, and social and political upheaval. *The Descent of Man* was criticized for spreading irreligious visions and further corrupting society. But the book sold many thousands of copies in 1871 alone and was immediately translated into five languages. It was a major scientific and popular success.

The Descent of Man was written to show that humans (always designated as man) originated from preexisting forms of life, like other species, and that humans had been formed over a long period of time and had evolved into different races. This posited that humans and all varieties of human beings were to be situated in nature; that there was space neither for biblical creationism as the origin of humankind nor for lower races close to apes; and that all varieties were descended from previous forms. That human beings were the product of evolution from common ancestors created an entirely different framework for considering past and future possibilities, which had an undeniable impact on how races were perceived. That is why we need to follow the stages of Darwin's thinking. He started by comparing humans with other mammals, showing the similarities of bones and brain structure, muscles, tissues and blood, reproductive functions, diseases, embryonic development, and residual organs no longer in use. The importance of the hand, shared with apes but more sophisticated in humans, impact of an erect body on the functioning of the senses, adaptation of humans to all climates, and development of the brain—all these were attributed to natural selection and led to the refusal of separate creations. Darwin also contested the volume of the brain as an adequate measure of intelligence, and asserted that there was "no fundamental difference between man and the higher mammals in their mental faculties."[22] He pointed out that humans shared senses and emotions with other animals as well as a capacity for imitation and memory, although humans alone excelled in imagination and reason, having developed language as a major tool for reflection and conceptualization. Humans as social animals distinguished themselves by their moral sense, although savages were considered to have it to only a limited degree, as evidenced by supposedly restricted sympathy toward their own tribe, insufficient powers of reasoning concerning the common good, and weak powers of self-command.

Scholars James Moore and Adrian Desmond attribute Darwin's more conservative stance in this book to the hardening of attitudes in the 1860s.[23] But if we take one significant example, Darwin's remark concerning the immorality of savages, used to counter the Irish historian William Lecky's benevolent arguments, was in line with his observations of savages during his voyage on the *Beagle*.[24] In terms of eugenics, though, I would agree with Moore and Desmond: Darwin quoted William Greg, Wallace, and Francis Galton on the failure of natural selection in civilized nations, as a result of vaccinations, poor laws, and asylums—medical care and social assistance for the less fortunate, which promoted the survival and propagation of the weaker members of society, leading to a "deterioration in the noblest part of our nature."[25] Darwin blended eugenics with an essentialist approach to nations. He drew attention to another process of negative selection, produced by the Spanish Inquisition over centuries, which systematically excluded those people most ambitious in thought and action, and thus was responsible for long-term decline, while the emigration of the most energetic people to British America had produced the opposite outcome.[26] But Darwin acknowledged that all civilized nations descended from barbarians, showing the possible improvement of savages through independent steps along the scale of civilization. He quoted anthropologist Edward Tylor, who in 1865 had published *Researches into the Early History of Mankind and Development of Civilization*, based on the idea of intellectual abilities shared by all groups of people and differences in social evolution resulting from education.[27] Darwin explicitly rejected the idea of human being's decline: "To believe that man was aboriginally civilised and then suffered utter degradation in so many regions, is to take a pitiably low view of human nature," maintaining instead "that progress has been much more general than retrogression; that man has risen, though by slow and interrupted steps, from a lowly condition to the highest standards as yet attained by him in knowledge, morals and religion."[28]

In comparison with the attempts by Blumenbach and Cuvier to place human beings in a separate order, Linnaeus's classification of humans among the primates was praised. Here Darwin follows Huxley, who considered the differences between humans and the higher apes to be less significant than those between higher and lower apes. Darwin formulated the hypothesis of a common ancestor of human beings and higher apes, probably in Africa. The chapter on the races of humans reasserted a common ancestry, although Darwin considered that races differed in physical (even in the convolutions of the brain), mental, and intellectual characteristics. He explicitly contradicted Agassiz, pointing out that different human races were distributed over the world across varying conditions of soil and climate. Ambiguity concerning hybridism and fertility was ruled out by the extreme cases of racial mixture in Brazil and Chile, while in describing the extreme variability in the distinctive features of all races, Darwin echoed Prichard in denouncing artificial divisions and classification. Darwin explicitly refused to classify different human groups as species, and engaged in a long argument about similarities among them to conclude that modifications were either the direct result of exposure to different conditions or the indirect result of some form of selection.[29]

Social evolution was hinted at in the final sections of part I, where Darwin addressed the issue of the extinction of races due to war, slaughter, cannibalism, slavery, and absorption, focusing on the recent instances of colonization in New Zealand and Australia, with the consequent spread of diseases and changes in the conditions of everyday life resulting in a dramatic decline of the native population. Darwin pointed out that the joint offspring of English and Tahitian parents were more resistant to disease, and that they increased in numbers when they settled on the Pitcairn Islands, which suggests that he did not share the common prejudice against mixed-race people.[30] When he addressed the formation of the races of humans, Darwin held that in some cases, the crossing of distinct races had led to the formation of a new race—another echo of Prichard's denial of unalterable racial identity. He also highlighted the blurred frontiers between races, citing Broca, then a leading French physician and physical anthropologist: "European and Hindoos, who belong to the same Aryan stock, and speak a language fundamentally the same, differ widely in appearance, whilst Europeans differ but little from Jews, who belong to the Semitic stock, and speak quite another language."[31]

Darwin shifted the discussion on human variety from divine plan to natural origin, from separate creations to a tree of life, from degeneration to evolution. He refused to classify varieties of human beings, although he shared his contemporaries' stereotypes about savages and clearly believed in the superior qualities of whites, but remained an abolitionist all his life, and believed in the possibility of improvement of all human beings. The impact of Darwin's work on the explanation of human variety can perhaps be summarized in this way: it placed all humans in nature; it broke from the idea of innate and unchangeable features; and it promoted the concept of evolution by means of natural selection. Darwin certainly contributed to the creation of a new scientific framework—one in which evolution implied a struggle for survival, meaning the decline and massive destruction of the unfit, yet also presupposed the constant improvement of the fittest. This scientific framework imposed an adaptation of prejudices concerning descent and racial constructions. Traditional ideas, such as those of natural slaves along with unchangeable physical and mental features, could no longer be sustained, although ideas of evolving hierarchy, the inferiority of the unfit, and the gap in civilization between sophisticated and rudimentary groups found their way through the new evolutionary system into public discourse. The best example is Nott (see above), a physician and naturalist involved in promoting racial constructions based on the idea of separate creations in order to feed political intervention in favor of slavery in the southern United States. Nott had little trouble in accommodating Darwin's ideas of evolution by means of natural selection in his vision of the hierarchy of human races. In the meantime, Darwin's view of nature was exposed to radical social criticism. Karl Marx (1818–83) wrote ironically to his friend Friedrich Engels that "Darwin rediscovers, among the beasts and plants, the society of England with its division of labour, competition, opening up of new markets, 'inventions' and Malthusian 'struggle for existence.' This vision is Hobbes's *bellum omnium contra omnes* and is reminiscent of Hegel's *Phenomenology*, in which civil society figures as an 'intellectual animal kingdom,' whereas in Darwin the animal kingdom figures as 'civil society.'"[32] Marx liked Darwin's "materialism," but he was opposed to the liberal ideas adopted by the naturalist.

SOCIAL EVOLUTION

Marx was a Lamarckian, like Auguste Comte (1798–1857), who died before the publication of *On the Origin*, and Herbert Spencer (1820–1903). For these three crucial nineteenth-century social thinkers, the idea of transformism in nature supported their notion of progress and social change; Darwinism did not (or would not) have a major impact on their ideas. The three stages of humankind defined by Comte—religious, metaphysical, and positive or scientific—had as their explicit purpose the projection of scientific thought onto society and discovery of its laws of progress. Positivism was a system clearly built on the Western tradition. Comte only mentioned people from other areas of the world when he considered them useful to demonstrate his ideas about the different stages of humankind—in particular fetishism, polytheism, and the caste system. He explicitly excluded the history of the Indians and Chinese because they had not been influential, by which he meant that they had not contributed to progress. In his view, their inclusion would be misleading, creating an obstacle to understanding the laws of "social evolution" (his exact terms). Comte stated, "Our historical exploration must be reduced to the elite or avant-garde of humankind, which consists of the majority of the white race or the European nations."[33]

Marx too had as his goal the discovery of laws of social evolution, although—unlike Comte and Spencer—he did not engage in long reflections on developments in science. He was inspired by the German philosophical tradition (Hegel and Ludwig Feuerbach) and British tradition of economic thought (David Ricardo), but built up his own perspective, based on the dialectical progression of modes of production and a succession of struggling social classes, each connected to a new economic system, which would result in the working class resolving class conflict and liberating humankind through revolution, breaking with declining capitalism and the bourgeois state to establish the advent of communism, a final, harmonious global community, meaning the end of history. The interesting side of Marx's theory was his denial of the superiority of the upper classes, which he saw condemned to inevitable decline, and praise of the virtues of the working class. The break with (and reversal of) hierarchical prejudices would have important consequences later, particularly for the debate on racial construction. Yet "scientific socialism" was entirely based on the analysis of Western capitalism; the references to other economic cases just fed into the main argument. Marx replicated Comte's idea of a Western avant-garde, and his reflections on Asia were rooted in Oriental despotism. The issue of races was secondary to that of classes, even if Marx dedicated an essay to the "Jewish Question," shaped by stereotypes against his own ancestors.[34]

Social Darwinism has been defined as the social and political use made of Darwin's evolutionary ideas from 1859 to the Second World War.[35] Although the label was first used in the late 1870s and early 1880s, it only became widely recognized after the publication in

1944 of Richard Hofstadter's *Social Darwinism in American Political Thought, 1860–1915*, influenced by Talcott Parsons.[36] The book was criticized for applying the label to several American social scientists, such as William Graham Sumner (1840–1910), who were open to other influences and worked on a wider range of theoretical issues. Scholar Robert Young has reinforced the idea that Darwinism is social, since science is never separated from social, economic, and ideological issues; in this instance, the theory of evolution by natural selection is interpreted through the Marxist view of industrial and social change along with the Victorian competitive ethos.[37] Another scholar, Mike Hawkins, even makes a case against the revisionist denial of the existence of social Darwinism; he defines it as a set of interlinked ideas—natural selection, struggle for existence, and survival of the fittest—subject to change over time.[38] The research was extended to the influence of social Darwinism in France, mainly based on Gustave Le Bon.[39] But Spencer's intervention makes the argument more complicated.

There may be good reasons for maintaining the designation social Darwinism, since Darwin's ideas influenced social analysis. Yet the link between the transformation of nature and transformation of society preceded Darwin. The notion of social evolution was coined by Comte and developed in a parallel way by Spencer. The influence of Lamarck's idea of the inheritance of acquired characteristics had been accommodated by Darwin in his system of thought and accepted by contemporary social thinkers until August Weissmann (1834–1914) debunked its principles in 1883 with the discovery that the germ cells (egg and sperm cells) are independent from the somatic body cells and unaffected by experience, underlining the importance of Darwin's idea of natural selection. Lamark's ideas, however, were crucial for the new social thinking of the nineteenth century. This is why I prefer the notion of social evolution in order to include the various authors who reflected on transformism, natural selection, or/and the struggle for existence applied to society under the large umbrella of individual as well as collective improvement.

Spencer shared Comte's interest in universal laws and synthetic philosophy, accepted the notion of sociology as a new discipline, and coined the concept of society as a social organism. He engaged in a dialogue with Darwin. Spencer's system of thought was clearly based on the idea of progressive evolution, meaning the division of labor and differentiation of society from simple to complex forms, but also on liberal principles, particularly economic laissez-faire and the social survival of the fittest, refusing the intervention of the coercive state (in which he was close to Godwin's views), imperialism, and militarism.[40] This antimilitarist and anti-imperialist stance, in line with the tradition of liberal thinkers such as Smith and Edmund Burke, had a tremendous impact on American liberal conservative thought, particularly on Sumner. Spencer tried to include all human groups in his approach to evolution. In the *Principles of Sociology*, for example, he posited a link between physical and mental backwardness in savages, who he supposed to have deficient features even at the level of the nervous system.[41] This persistent vision of entangled physical and mental differences contrasted with the idea of exclusively cultural differences sustained by Tylor (see above) in his *Researches into the Early History of Mankind and the Development of Civilization.* Besides carrying out an astonishing program of research involving gesture, art, mapmaking, nomenclature, writing (including the quipus used by the Incas), myths, fire, and cooking, Tylor stated that differences in the civilization and mental state of peoples were differences of development not origin, of degree rather than kind, related to the stages of progress shared by all humankind.[42]

Spencer's program of sociological research was certainly more complex than suggested above. He engaged in a collective research project, and set out to acquire data on each human group in order to complete a uniform, comparable set of tables offering structural and functional descriptions of peoples (physical and mental features), and divided by operative and regulative mechanisms comprehending political, ecclesiastical and family structures, customs, sentiments, ideas and language, land and crafts, tools, housing, food, clothing, and weapons. Spencer included the races of Oceania, Africa, Asia, and America. He distinguished the old civilizations of Mexico, Central America, and Peru, and those of the Hebrews and Phoenicians as well as those of the French and English, and described both from a historical point of view.[43] The project included information on the Chinese, Greeks, ancient Egyptians, Assyrians, Romans, and Arabs, showing an implicit division between peoples with history and peoples without history—a widely shared assumption. The basic stereotypes concerning savages or primitive people were apparent, even if presented in a much more descriptive and comprehensive way, reminding us of the previous efforts of Prichard's encyclopedia of human variety. The references to the Chinese (a rigid and obedient society), Ottomans, and Incas (both military societies, vulnerable to external shocks) reproduced old assumptions, denigrating mixed-race people, such as the half caste of the new Hispanic republics of America, as unable to create stable institutions, although Spencer acknowledged the benefits of upward mixing, like that of the Hebrews with other Semitic races, or that of the Athenians, Romans, and British with "Aryan" races.[44]

The following generation of social evolutionists broke from the secular and materialist trend of the first generation, reintroducing religion and its merits into the general picture. Benjamin Kidd (1858–1916) presents the most interesting example of this line of thought. His book *Social Evolution* (1894) acknowledged the importance of religion in the evolution of society and credited Christianity with providing the basic principles of Western civilization.[45] He criticized cruelty, fraud, violence, and intimidation as practices that had led to the extermination of the native peoples of Australia and New Zealand. Although he lamented discrimination against black people, discussed the English Poor Law, and addressed the "social question," coming out in favor of humanizing the conditions of the "lowest and lightest types of humankind," he contended there was no power that could change the basic laws of competition and selection. The inferiority of black people after abolition in the United States is a case in point: Kidd acknowledged the use of ostracism and prejudice, intimidation and violence by white people to maintain power; he criticized the indifference to or even support for those practices by "many honourable citizens of the North" against the ideals of liberty, religion, and government. At the same time, he believed that all this was part of an inevitable process in which the masses were being slowly raised, and the barriers of birth, class, and privilege broken down, propelled by the most successful types of human being.

Despite his (rhetorical) humanitarian stance, Kidd considered violence to be an expression of rivalry and natural selection in a society that was increasingly competitive, and subject to stress and a fast pace of change, in which the less suitable forms disappear. Progressive people were energetic, vigorous, and virile; the absence of these qualities left nations, groups, and individuals behind, like the "careless, shiftless, easily satisfied negro of the United States and the West Indies."[46] The struggle for progress was, in Kidd's words, a fact of human life, carried out by the Anglo-Saxons at the cost of other races (external and internal) in order to achieve the highest civilization. It was not an accident of history or innate depravity; it resulted from "deep-seated physiological causes, the operation of which we must always remain powerless to escape."[47] Kidd naturalized political and social power, viewing white supremacy as a fact of social evolution, such as the extermination of the red Indians or Maoris. The application of evolutionary principles was used to explain the decline of weaker people before those who were stronger as well as the subordination and exclusion of the least efficient (another key word). He opposed socialist solutions since they were against nature, thus promoting the explicit naturalization of social and material inequality. In his vision, the future was left to take care of itself; the sacrifices caused by rivalry and competition were necessary ones for the progress of the whole social organism.

Not all social evolutionists shared this zeal for an ideological justification of violence and abuse under the cover of charitable rhetoric. Sumner, a professor of sociology at Yale, was a classic liberal who advocated free trade and the gold standard, declaring himself against state intervention and socialism. Consistent with his principles, he questioned the imperialist expansion of the United States (the Spanish-American War and the war against insurgence in the Philippines), mocked as "the conquest of the United States by Spain"—that is, the absorption of Hispanic principles of conquest and subjugation of peoples that would lead to decay as well as control of the country by bankers and businesspeople dependent on government subsidies and contracts.[48] In his reflections on imperialism, Sumner coined the important notion of ethnocentrism. Folkways are another of Sumner's concepts. These notions were meant to further promote the sociological analysis of moral behavior shaped by various customs and institutions in past and present societies around the world.[49] Sumner rejected the aim of social equality, and affirmed the idea of competition and the struggle for life as principles of social evolution. He opposed poor laws, and accepted the idea that the gap between poverty and wealth increased in higher civilizations. At the same time, he expressed a clear revulsion against the practice of lynching black people in the South as an assault on law and a violation of basic rights.[50]

Social evolutionists embraced both traditional and new stereotypes used in relation to savages and primitive peoples, with the latter seen as a new designation that reflected the idea of successive steps in the progress of the whole of humankind. Evolutionary theories did not smooth out the tangled vision of mental and physical hierarchies of groups of human beings, but they started the shift from biological to historical explanations of human cultural diversity, renewing the tradition of Acosta and Lafitau.[51] Theories of social evolution offered a diversity of forms and meanings that could include the reversal of progressive principles of natural selection, thereby allowing for the idea of primordial and superior Aryanism destined to decline. G. Vacher de Lapouge's late-nineteenth-century book opposing the "sentimental policies" inspired by Christianity is a case in point. He labeled the main ideals of the French Revolution (liberty, equality, and fraternity) fictions, since reality, in his view, was shaped by the strength of natural laws, races, and evolution, all pushing for growing specialization, inequality, and interdependence, and leading to ever-reduced freedom for the individual, squeezed by environmental changes and the laws of descent. Lapouge's vision fed racialist and extremist movements, and reversed Spencer's principles, drawing on Gobineau's pessimism about the decline of Aryan influence: social selection would eliminate the best through war and the power of the masses, with the latter encompassing Lapouge's negative vision of trade unions, feminists, and socialist movements.[52]

Aryanism was very much alive at the turn of the twentieth century (see chapter 16), despite a dismissive reference to the Aryan myth by Ripley. But this same author's vision of the Teutonic race provided an equivalent definition of the superior white race, as tall, fair skinned, blond, light eyed, and endowed with a superior cephalic index of skull capacity.[53]

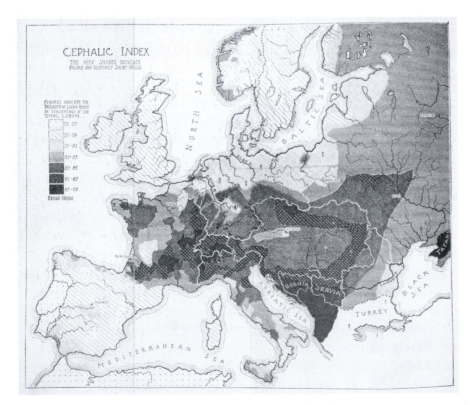

Figure 17.2. William Z. Ripley, *The Races of Europe: A Sociological Study* (London: Kegan Paul, 1899), map of races in Europe based on the cephalic index.
© British Library Board; Robana

Madison Grant, who played a significant role in the 1910s and 1920s, and influenced policies of immigration in the United States, was inspired by not only Ripley's theory of races but also Galton's eugenics. Eugenicists sought to improve races through charting inherited intelligence and working out policies to exclude "dysgenic" mixtures or less able human beings from reproduction. For Grant, history was driven by racial conflict. Inherited physical and psychological features explained social cleavage; classes were equated with old races. Grant clearly opposed the notion not only of equality but also of democracy, and asserted that the Declaration of Independence addressed only white men. He promoted the idea that the United States had been created by Protestant and Nordic men, and criticized the absence of dignity of race among Spaniards, Portuguese, and French, who had mixed with other races in line with teachings of the Catholic Church. Grant was anxious about the decline of the white race and return to barbarism in the Caribbean. He opposed Irish, southern European, Mexican, and Asian immigration. Finally, he considered President Woodrow Wilson's policy in favor of self-determination in the world as suicidal for the white man.[54]

Lothrop Stoddard further developed these ideas, raising the specter of social revolution and threat of future independence of the colonial world, which would submerge the civilized world. This was phrased, according to Stoddard, exactly at the high point of Western supremacy in the world, which was already challenged by Japanese military skills, pan-Islamism, black solidarity, and the Indian independence movement.[55] Karl Brandt, major general of the SS, Hitler's personal physician, and the most important medical authority in Nazi Germany, when accused of mass murder after the Second World War at the Nuremberg tribunal, argued that Grant had justified the elimination of inferior people.[56]

To sum up, theories of social evolution rendered obsolete creationism and the vision of immutable races with innate characteristics, but reinforced the ideas of hierarchy and different rhythms of human progress, or access to higher forms of civilization. Although physical features did not disappear from explanations of human variety, cultural features became increasingly important in the second half of the nineteenth century. In the meantime, the extraordinary boom in European colonial expansion in Africa and Asia inspired new public curiosity about human differences. From the 1870s to 1930s, the exhibition of human types from different continents was part of the program of universal and colonial exhibitions in Europe and America, along with the products of different lands. Darwin's naturalization of all humans (generally conceptualized as male) did not disrupt the traditional view of savages in nature. Human zoos became extremely successful.[57] The fact that Africans, Asians, and Native Americans were subjected to the European or North American white gaze defined a clear hierarchy between subject and object that comforted the white working and middle classes in a world of enormous social change. Anthropologists diffused ideas of the perfectibility of all human beings and possibility of progress, but the inhabitants of the Western world simultaneously felt that they were already part of a higher civilization, looking down on the savages, primitives, and barbarians lagging behind, subject to colonial rule and brought to be exhibited at the center of civilization (the metropolis) as exotic creatures akin to the wild animals on view in zoos such as the Jardin d'acclimation in Paris. Theories of social evolution displaced hierarchies based on immutable races, yet these theories accepted hierarchies based on different stages of civilization, thereby naturalizing social competition and colonial exploitation. This new theoretical framework did not reduce prejudices against peoples from other continents, expressed, for example, in the ubiquitous publicity for colonial products—also on display at the numerous colonial and universal exhibitions. Theories of social evolution would also be used against racialized minorities in different countries of the Western world.

✷✷✷

The scientific framework for the classification of human beings started with Linnaeus, who placed humans among the mammals. Linnaeus developed the concept of subdivisions, based on phenotype and mental features. He integrated the allegories of continents and stereotypes concerning different peoples of the world that had resulted from the European oceanic expansion. Succeeding generations of naturalists enlarged the scope of the research, integrating new findings and extraordinary advances in ethnographic information. The debate between unique and plural creation, or between monogenists and polygenists, developed from the seventeenth to nineteenth century. The notion of a common ancestry explained variation through climate, food, and migration, while the concept of different ancestry located in specific environments explained variation through original design and innate, immutable features. Racial constructions reflected this debate. Variable definitions of the number and location of races, however, raised doubts about the validity of the procedure—skepticism that was particularly expressed by Prichard and Humboldt.

In the meantime, notions of degeneration from a perfect Creation were confronted by ideas of progress and improvement, transferred into the field of naturalism through the notions of transformism (Lamarck) and a unique plan among animals (Saint Hilaire). Comparative anatomy, which had led to Cuvier's compartmentalized vision, could also open up the recognition of connections between different species, based on the idea of change and the inheritance of acquired features. While Agassiz developed Cuvier's hierarchical, innate, and immutable view of human races, Darwin disrupted previous debates with the idea of evolution by means of natural selection. The degeneration of perfect Creation was replaced by slow modification, variation, and extinction of species through millions of years. Innate and immutable vision of races, so crucial in the United States before and during the Civil War to justify slavery, adapted to the impact of evolutionary theories, but did not evacuate the political field. Theories of social evolution inspired by Lamarck and Darwin substituted different stages of the civilizing process for innate hierarchies, reintroduced culture and history into the picture, and created a flexible framework to justify new colonial Western expansion. Aryanism could be absorbed by these different frameworks: it played a more ambiguous role, enabling various peoples throughout the world to claim white ancestors from central Asia, and thus establishing a recognizable background for specific political projects.

PART V

NATIONALISM AND BEYOND

Prejudices concerning ethnic descent coupled with discriminatory action significantly increased as nationalism expanded in the nineteenth and twentieth centuries. This new ideological setting affected Europe and the Middle East first, although it quickly spread to other areas of the world. Nationalism stimulated new political projects, which carried with them the reinvention or assertion of identities along with the division or merging of previous polities organized by imperial logic or local tradition. The enormous political and social reorganization of this period had an impact on prejudices. The definition of the enemy or enemies was based on national divides, which included assumptions about religion and race. Religious identity gained renewed importance, mainly in relation to minorities, even if the new political framework was largely premised on language in common and assumptions about shared descent. Therefore, the idea of a medieval religious racial divide replaced by the modern naturalization of the racial divide proposed by Fredrickson seems schematic and anachronistic.

As nations asserted themselves against empires (the Ottoman, Austrian, and Russian—all by nature multiethnic), or reinvented national polities against fragmented local and regional interests, as in Germany and Italy, disputed territories were at the center of political debates. Policies of exclusion became paramount as frontiers were reshuffled, and this had a major impact on central and eastern Europe. The debate on human rights stimulated by the American Declaration of Independence and, decisively, French Revolution reverted to the question of who should be entitled to or excluded from citizenship and civil rights. The emergence of democracy, which pushed the decline of multiethnic empires, also had its dark side, since it unleashed intercommunity and international rivalry for the control of territory.[1] Theories of races were all too present in this period. How did European nationalism integrate notions of race that had previously focused on the peoples of the world? Was there a fusion between race and nation due to their common stress on descent? Where and how did this fusion occur, and why was it eschewed in other places? Was genocide the extreme outcome of ideologies of racial nation? These are the issues that structure the chapter on nationalism.

Nationalism had an impact beyond Europe. It was integrated in Iberian America, extended to Asia, and penetrated Africa. The national ideal, transmitted by old and new European colonial powers, defined a new setting for rooted interethnic perceptions on these different continents. The elites of independent Iberian America, usually related to oligarchies dating back to colonial time, had to deal with the diversity of ethnic formation on the ground, from Mexico with its majority of Native Americans, to Brazil with its vast majority population of African descent. The formulation of origin myths became part of new national constructions—linked in the Mexican case to the Aztec confederation and in the Brazilian case to the Tupinamba, although the presence of Native Americans in the latter instance was remote. These national foundation myths revealed the new need of elites to negotiate power with populations that had been significantly involved in the process of independence or wars after independence. Multiethnic realities defined the possibilities (and limits) for the acceptance of national ideologies of common descent.

In Asia, national ideologies boosted old ethnocentric beliefs of superiority, particularly among the Yamato in Japan or Han in China—both considered the central ethnicities in their countries. The decline of the Qing Dynasty fueled new political projects by the Han, while in Japan national ideology helped to reform and modernize the Yamato's political control. In these cases, the perception of Western imperial designs played a key role in diffusing the national framework and formulating imperial projects, especially in Japan. In India, national projects struggled with the caste system and religious divide between Hindus and Muslims, but played a major part in resisting Western imperialism. After the partition between Pakistan and India, a national framework was asserted through the notion of descent linked to religious allegiance, specifically in Pakistan. In Africa, old patterns of ethnic divide had been influenced by racial constructions, particularly in the Sahel. Colonial powers significantly influenced racial construction further south in the lakes region, but also in other regions, such as South Africa, where a formally segregated society came into being in 1948. The issue here is to understand the real influence of racial constructions and complicated relation with national projects. This provides the background for the last comparative chapter.

CHAPTER 18

The Impact of Nationalism

Nations and Races

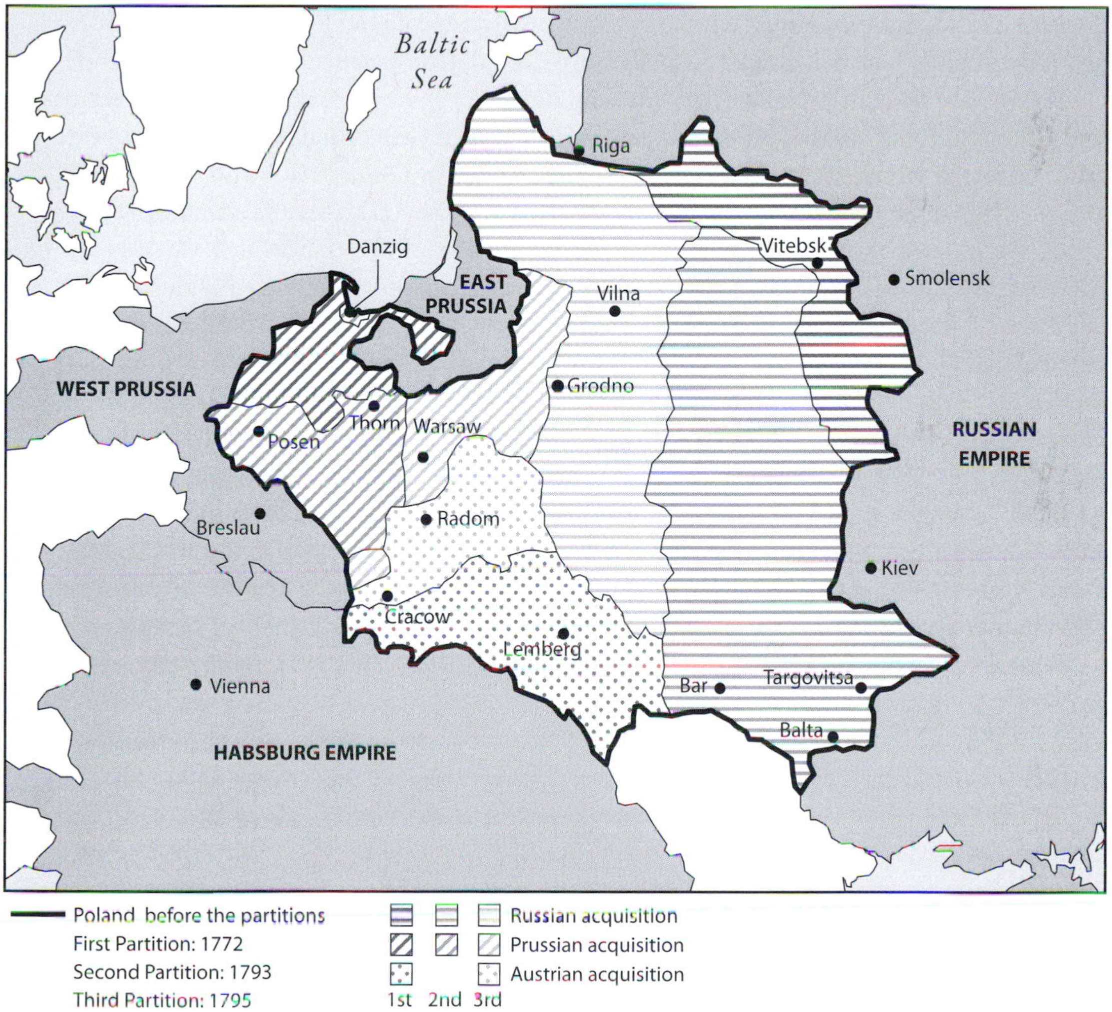

Map 18.1. The partition of Poland, 1772–95.
Source: Geoffrey Barraclough, ed., *The Times Atlas of World History* (London: Times Books, 1990), 197

Political development in Europe and the Middle East during the second half of the nineteenth and first half of the twentieth centuries dramatically changed the debate about variety in human beings. European internal ethnic diversity had largely been ignored by Darwin and the social evolutionists, while the religious contribution to that diversity had virtually disappeared from the picture. Global variety had monopolized reflection on this topic. Now the rise of nationalism in Europe, combined with the expansionism of the three great powers—the Russian, Austro-Hungarian, and German empires—placed relations between different ethnicities at the center of the political action.[1] The issue had already been raised during the revolutions of 1848, when Hungarians and Czechs revolted against Vienna, only to be confronted by the political ambitions of the Romanians, Croats, and Serbs in the former case, and ambitions of a significant German minority in the latter. In the 1850s and 1860s, the new order established in Europe after the defeat of revolution slowly integrated the political dreams of German or Italian unity previously favored by liberals. The process of Italian unification contributed to redefining the political balance of power in Europe, since Italy now had to be taken into consideration. Yet the unification did not have any significant ethnic impact, as ethnic minorities such as the Greeks and Albanians had been more or less assimilated over time. The only identifiable minority, the Jewish community, was small and not particularly targeted, even if there were several cases of conflict triggered by the Catholic Church.[2]

By contrast, the German unification, in which Prussia played a leading role, had a major impact on Europe.[3] Germany did not have to deal with significant internal ethnic minorities, except for the Slavs in the East—the result of the partition of Poland between Prussia, Russia, and Austria in 1772–95—and the Jewish community. But the process of unification had consequences outside Germany, due to its impact on German minorities in the Austro-Hungarian and Russian empires. The multinational composition of the Habsburg monarchy favored a balance between different ethnicities, expressed in the elevation of Hungary to the status of a joint monarchy with Austria (1867), thereby transforming the empire into a dual monarchy, while Croatia obtained its autonomy (1868). The unrest of other nationalities was not appeased by the male universal suffrage established in Cisleithania, the Austrian part of the Austro-Hungarian Empire, in 1907. The increased Slav presence in the Parliament in Vienna only exacerbated the resentment of the privileged German minority—a resentment already expressed by the Pan-German Party created by Georg Ritter von Schönerer in 1879, and (partly) by the Christian Social Party created in 1893 by the future mayor of Vienna, Karl Lueger. Austria's participation in the partition of Poland had enlarged its Slavic regions, while the intervention in the nineteenth-century Balkan wars with the Ottoman and Russian empires had further increased ethnic diversity.[4]

The national issue, in the meantime, had set off a general crisis in the Ottoman territories of Europe. The Greek revolution in 1821, supported by British, French, and Russian intervention, led to independence in 1830. This had been preceded by Serbian revolts in 1804–17, leading to an autonomous status for Serbia. The revolts of Romanians, Bulgarians, and Serbs in the 1860s and 1870s created a new trend toward national independence, which

Map 18.2. The process of German unification (1815–71).
Source: Geoffrey Barraclough, ed., *The Times Atlas of World History* (London: Times Books, 1990), 216

was partly recognized in 1878 by the Treaty of Berlin after years of warfare involving ethnic slaughter and massive migration. The Skull Tower built by the Ottomans in Niš with murdered Serbian revolutionaries' skulls aptly symbolizes the level of atrocities. The new states and autonomous political entities expanded over the following decades until the Balkan War (1912–13) reduced the Ottoman territories in Europe to East Thrace.[5]

In the Ottoman Empire, the refugees from the west had been preceded by the refugees from the east; the successive expansion of the Russian Empire in the eighteenth and nineteenth centuries resulted in Russia's total control of the northern and eastern boundaries of the Black Sea, leading to a massive migration of Tatars (the Crimean Khanate fell in 1783) and Circassians (their independent polity in the northwest Caucasus fell in 1864, after thirty years of war). During this long period, the Russian policy of imposing Orthodox Christianity prompted further Muslim migration to the Ottoman Empire. As a result of all these events, the territory of the Ottoman Empire shrank from 3 million square kilometers in 1800 to 1.3 million square kilometers in 1913. The estimate of Muslim refugees entering Ottoman lands up to this date is between six and seven million, of which probably four million arrived from the Caucasus and Crimea.[6] Meanwhile, the Russian expansion in eastern Europe in the eighteenth century had meant the integration of the vast majority of Europe's Jewish population, previously living in Polane and Ukraine, into the Russian Empire. This expansion challenged the Russian authorities' traditional policy of excluding Jews from their territory. Now they had to accommodate four million Jews—a significant minority in their newly acquired territories.

I agree with Ernest Gellner and Eric Hobsbawm's idea that nationalism in general preceded the nation, although there was often some kind of ethnic collective feeling that could sustain nationalist projects.[7] In western Europe, the ethnic origin of nations—in England, Portugal, and France—is arguably more observable than elsewhere, even though the complicated case of Spain shows the limits of a strict western/eastern divide. Racial constructs should be introduced into the picture, since the equation of nation with race in the late nineteenth and early twentieth centuries reinforced perceptions of shared blood, common descent, and superior attributes. The existence of nationalism before the existence of nations is observable in eastern Europe, the Balkans, and the Middle East, where political projects in many instances anticipated the actual creation of nations as communities of citizens with equal rights and obligations.

The right to citizenship at birth expresses an important divide established in the late eighteenth and early nineteenth centuries: jus soli was pushed by the American and French revolutions, and meant the right to citizenship for all children born in their territories, while Germany and the eastern European countries established jus sanguinis, limiting the right to citizenship to the children of existing citizens. The notion of descent therefore was crucial in the essentialized vision of nation represented by jus sanguinis, while jus soli represented a more open and flexible understanding of citizenship. The divide between western and eastern Europe on this issue has since been blurred by more restrictive measures during the past thirty years in western Europe, but all the Americas still follow the rule of jus soli, linked to their strong historical tradition of immigration.

Secularization did not have a major impact on central and eastern Europe in the nineteenth century. In an area shaped by state formations based on multiple ethnicities, religion still proved to be significant in the definition of nations and international political alliances. Austria opposed Greek independence, viewed as a threat to the political balance of the Balkans, while conservative Russia brought its military weight to support the liberal national movement, partly due to a shared religious allegiance. The same logic applied to the independence movements of Serbia, Romania, and Bulgaria, since these nations shared Orthodox Christianity. Ottoman reaction likewise had a religious base: political elites were trying to balance traditional Islamic dominion with new rights for Christian minorities, although Albanian independence in 1912, promoted by Muslims with the support of Christian (Orthodox and Catholic) minorities, created a new divide within the empire. The crisis in the Ottoman Empire led to Turkish nationalism. The Committee of Union and Progress (CUP, or Young Turks), created in 1889, played a major role in the last phase of Ottoman rule (1908–18), shaping a new policy centered on Turkish Anatolia and Thrace that meant ruthless ethnic cleansing. The loss of extensive territories in the Middle East during the First World War broke down the institutional framework of the Ottoman Empire; the Greek and Allied invasion of Anatolia in 1919–22 triggered a military rebirth of resistant forces led by Mustafa Kemal, who defeated foreign intervention and finally declared the Republic of Turkey in 1923.[8]

The First World War also engulfed the other two empires. The Austro-Hungarian Empire did not survive military defeat and broke down, with the secession of Hungary, independence of Yugoslavia, and creation of Czechoslovakia, plus the loss of South Tyrol, Trieste, and Istria. The Russian Empire, disrupted by the democratic revolution of February 1917 and radicalized by the Communist revolution in November of that year, saw the creation of the new states of Finland, Estonia, Latvia, and Lithuania. The re-creation of Poland affected the three previously existing central and eastern European empires. While the Austro-Hungarian political entity was never reconstituted, the Soviet Union managed to recover most of the territory of the former Russian Empire, although within an entirely different ideological and national framework.[9] The main contribution of the Soviets to the new world order was to promote an anticolonialist stance and national emancipation, which had been looming since the 1880s, in Asia and Africa. Christian solidarity entirely broke down: Soviet Russia actively supported Turkish resistance in 1920–22 with guns and money; and the treaty of Kars in 1921 gave Turkey a favorable northeastern settlement of frontiers. The humiliation of Germany after fifty years of development, military victories, and growing national pride would have the most serious consequences.[10] Among other conditions, Germany had to return Alsace and Lorraine to France plus pay heavy war compensation, while its union with a territorially reduced Austria was opposed. It is against this background that we can evaluate the new conditions for the expression of prejudice concerning ethnic descent coupled with discriminatory action. Basically, what we need to understand is the new configuration of racial prejudice and its role in political projects.

The American and French revolutions contributed decisively to placing the notion of civil rights at the center of the new system of values. The gap between promises and realities became patent: in the American case, civil rights only concerned white people, while in both instances women were not included. The debate over civil rights, however, used historical cases of oppressed minorities to reflect on boundaries (see chapter 9). The "Jewish question" was thus used as a test for universal secularism and national citizenship.[11] The United States in 1788 and France in 1791 had been the first countries to recognize civil rights and equal citizenship for Jews. The practice of granting citizenship to Jews spread to other European countries during the nineteenth century, as liberal ideology was diffused, mainly in central Europe, reaching the Austro-Hungarian Empire (1867), North Germany Confederation (1869), and German Empire (1871). This was not a special concession but rather the result of the emergence of notions of citizenship and civil rights, which gathered momentum against the traditional patchwork of noble privileges and exemptions from taxes, feudal obligations and duties of serfdom, and rights attributed to specific estates and communities—in sum, against the principle of legal inequality that had defined the ancien régime. The notion of equal status for all strata and communities simply included the Jews, liberating them from the secular oppression of tax burdens as well as exclusion from professions and offices.

The success of the Jews was undeniable, particularly in finance and the liberal professions, although many of their artisans (the majority of the community) were affected—as were those of all the other ethnicities—by the Industrial Revolution. The ascent of Jewish communities from a traditional situation of oppression did not go unnoticed. In this long period of difficult transition from feudal and seigneurial privileges to modernity, economic difficulties and radical changes in lifestyle imposed by the twin processes of industrialization and urbanization carried with them the seeds of revolt. Jews became an easy target for discontent, which could build on historical precedents. The extension of civil rights to Jews was opposed at its beginning in all countries: in 1757 in England, a Whig proposal for the naturalization of resident Jews was blocked by strong opposition; in 1808, Napoléon limited Jewish rights for ten years; in 1819, anti-Jewish riots spread through various parts of Germany; in 1870 in Alsace, there were riots with assaults on property in protest against the naturalization of 35,000 Jews; in 1881–82, there were anti-Jewish riots in West Prussia, Romania, and the Austro-Hungarian Empire; in 1893 and 1899, riots occurred in Bohemia; in 1898, in connection with the Dreyfus affair, riots were reported in fifty-five localities in France, but without any killings; the same year witnessed pogroms in west Galicia; in 1907, pogroms occurred in Romania; in 1918 in Poland, the Jews were targeted by the new republic; and in 1919, the defeat of the Communist revolution in Hungary was followed by pogroms.[12]

Anti-Jewish discriminatory action, based on traditional Christian prejudices, became the main expression of social and political tensions in the western regions of the Russian Empire (basically, what had been Poland and Ukraine) throughout the nineteenth century. By the end of the nineteenth century there were 5.2 million Jews in those regions. Pogrom, a Russian word, was coined in this period to designate riot or assault against a Jewish community followed by plunder and massacre. Such activities had occurred in the past, mainly in Ukraine—in Odessa, for instance, pogroms were recorded in 1821, 1849, 1859, and 1871, before the major massacres of 1881 and 1905—but political instability after the assassination of Czar Alexander II in 1881 created conditions for the spread of acts of hatred on a large scale, affecting different regions and involving dozens of towns. Anti-Jewish legislation was passed that same year, although only one of the conspirators had been identified as a Jew. Political instability increased during the last decades of the Russian Empire—a situation reflected in three major waves of pogroms: 1881–84, 1903–6 (peaking after the revolution of 1905), and 1919–20, which killed many thousands of Jews and extensively destroyed property (houses, shops, and factories).[13] The first two waves were not directed by the state, even though it did little to stop them, while the secret police diffused inflammatory anti-Jewish propaganda, particularly in 1903, in the infamous forgery known as *The Protocols of the Elders of Zion*, attributing plans for world domination to the Jews. Socialist movements, here and elsewhere, condemned anti-Semitism as a backward and biased perception of conflicts, but their adherents were accused by the conservative order of being manipulated by the Jews, which was a way of racializing and thus containing political opposition.

The revolution of February 1917 was faithful to its liberal standards and abolished all legal restrictions on Jews, who became citizens with equal rights—a status naturally maintained by the Bolshevik revolution, in principle alien to racial prejudice. These liberties further ignited anti-Jewish feelings among old-order elites and economically embattled local populations. The White Russian Army and anti-Bolshevik Volunteer Army directly promoted the last wave of pogroms during the period of civil war in Russia and Ukraine; anti-Jewish persecution was then clearly used as a device to mobilize the population against the Red Army. The devastation in Ukraine was incomparably higher than in previews pogroms, because the Volunteer Army used military techniques of assault and mass murder on a large scale; the death toll is estimated at 160,000 to 200,000 people in a population of 1.6 million Jews in the region.[14] The link between the second and third waves of anti-Jewish pogroms is well expressed in the battle cry shared by the Black Hundred militias and White Army: "Beat the Yids and Save Russia!"

The pogroms were generally provoked during Holy Week under a pretext familiar since medieval riots: alleged Jewish contempt for the sacred celebration of the sacrifice of Christ. But these complaints were coupled with the political accusation that Jews exploited the common people. Although the catastrophic effects of industrialization in the western territories of imperial Russia impacted on both Jews and Christians, the hatred of Jews was further increased by their successful social integration. Jews had been involved in military service since 1827, and access to the education system had led to extraordinary advances in their standing in all areas of knowledge, including the main professions and public offices. Racial hatred, in this case, was not a justification of hierarchy and dominion. It was the opposite: a reaction against the integration of a previously oppressed ethnicity, coupled with diminished competitive skills among the Christian majority of the population. In the context of the difficult transition to modern society, the Russian racial terror of the civil war, which targeted Jews and accused them of exploitation as well as complicity with the Communist regime, sowed the seeds of much more lethal violence elsewhere, once totalitarian states decided to use Jews as scapegoats.

The Russian anti-Jewish pogroms, as we have seen, were not unique, although their extent and ferocity were unparalleled. In the period between 1870 and 1920, the worst forms of racial terrorism came from the Ottoman Empire. Squeezed between the Russian expansion in the east and emergence of national states in the Balkans, involved in bloody ethnic fighting and revenge, flooded throughout the nineteenth century from both sides by millions of Muslim refugees, who carried with them resentment and anti-Christian feelings, traumatized by constant defeat and loss of huge parts of its territory, blocked by a fossilized political and cultural system, the Ottoman Empire found its attempts at reform, particularly the liberal constitution of 1876, to be inconsequential and short lived. In 1878, the treaty of Berlin placed the protection of the religious minorities under international supervision. The duty of care for minorities was for the first time formally included in international law, yet it was felt as an intrusion by the Ottoman Muslim population.

THE ARMENIAN GENOCIDE

The Ottoman state, which had tried to reduce inequality among ethnicities during the period of reorganization (Tanzimat) of 1839–76, obtained slightly better integration in the

Map 18.3. New states in the Balkans, 1800–1913.
Source: Geoffrey Barraclough, ed., *The Times Atlas of World History* (London: Times Books, 1990), 215

short term, but also increased rivalry. In the last decades of the nineteenth century, it ceased to protect its multiethnic and multireligious population of subjects who were differentiated by tax systems along with unequal access to professions and offices, accepting or even promoting ethnic persecution. In 1894–96, the massacres of the Christian Armenian populations reached 100,000 to 250,000 deaths—far higher than that of all the Russian pogroms against Jews up to that date. Like other ethnicities, the Armenians created their own nationalist movements in the last decades of the nineteenth century. Some of them were armed for self-defense, since local communities had regularly been targeted by Muslim refugees and nomadic Kurdish tribes. The majority of Armenians had traditionally lived in the southeastern and eastern provinces of Anatolia, close to the new borders with the Russian Empire, placing them under constant suspicion. It should be pointed out, though, that under the Russian Empire, the Armenians also had a strong presence in the Caucasus, where they competed with the Muslim populations. During a general movement of nationalistic divisions, the Armenians' conflict of allegiances (and interests) between the two empires was constantly pointed out by their rivals.

The creation of the Turkish nationalist movement in 1889 represented a major shift in political perceptions and practices for the late Ottoman Empire. The Young Turks considered Anatolia (and Thrace) the territorial core of an Ottoman Empire based on Turkish nationality. Despite huge war losses and constant emigration, which peaked in the 1890s and 1900s, and mainly affected the Christian population, the Ottoman Empire then numbered 17.4 million people, according to the census of 1881–93; of those, 4.5 million were Christians, half were Armenians, and nearly half were Greeks.[15] The population concentrated precisely in the core territories, with the Greeks in the west and Armenians in the east, while Istanbul registered 56 percent Christians out of a population of 900,000. The major part of the Armenian population was rural and considered more "modern" than the dominant Muslim populations.

Like the Jews under the Russian Empire, the Armenians were not targeted to justify social hierarchy; the main persecutions came with better integration and liberal attempts at reform toward equal rights—again constituting a case of relative success and increasing competitiveness. Armenians were systematically accused of profiteering and usury, offering another parallel with the Jewish situation. In the Ottoman Empire, nations were generally related to religion, but in the European atmosphere of the early twentieth century, nations were also interpreted as races. Although no program of ethnic cleansing was publicly defended, the vision of a homogeneous Turkish nation-state defined the Armenians as an internal enemy that needed to be removed. They were considered a fifth column of Russian expansion and Russia's projects for the partition of Anatolia. The process of transition from the Ottoman Empire to a Turkish state was complex, since the Young Turks preferred the modernization and liberalization of Ottoman society. The Young Turks engaged in dialogue with various Armenian organizations, and established regular channels of communication with them during the constitutional period (1908–15), although this process was disrupted during the massacre of 25,000 Armenians in Cilicia in April 1909. This massacre coincided with an attempted conservative coup against the Young Turks, which during its temporary weakness did not oppose violence against the Armenians, thus defining its future position.

The participation of the Ottoman Empire in the First World War, in alliance with the Germans and Austro-Hungarians against the Russians, was the final blow to precarious relations between communities. Even though Armenians were engaged in military service and performed as well as the Turks, defeats transformed them into an ideal scapegoat, accused of desertion and spying on behalf of the Russians. Regular abuse and plunder of Armenian villages had not been controlled after 1909, and increased during the war. On July 16, 1914, the leaders of the social democratic Hunchakian Party were detained and accused of separatism (eleven would be hanged in May 1915). Even so, the detention of hundreds of political and intellectual Armenian leaders in April 1915 in Istanbul, and immediate implementation of a vast program of deportation of the Armenian community, took the Armenian political elite by surprise. The very survival of the community was at stake, with total annihilation organized by the state and implemented by the Special Organization composed of tens of thousands of criminals specially liberated from the prisons, controlled by a top layer of military and political agents, and helped by the local structures of government. The deportations included the plunder and systematic massacre of the involved populations, specifically those of the eastern provinces. Sections of the Armenian populations deported from Cilicia (southeast Anatolia) and the western regions of Anatolia managed to arrive at their destination (Syria and Iraq). The Armenian parliamentarians and leaders who did not manage to escape were killed in cold blood. The agreed-on estimate of the Armenian death toll in 1915–16 is around a million people, which probably accounted for half the total population of Armenians still living in Anatolia. The other half managed to take refuge in the Russian Empire, from where some of them reemigrated, particularly to France and the United States. A tiny minority returned after the First World War, only to be targeted again during the war of 1919–22.[16]

This was the first example of a programmed genocide committed against a specific national minority by a state. It was no longer a case of vulnerable communities let down by a state that could not (or as in the instance of Russia, would not) guarantee protection and security. The deportations were organized by state agencies responsible for the identification of people to be arrested, formation of convoys, and seizure of property. Local government was directly involved, particularly in the plunder and confiscation of property. Deportations were simply a pretext for mass murder, either directly conducted by the Special Organization or outsourced to Kurdish nomadic tribes invited to plunder the convoys. Women and children were the major victims of these massacres; adult males were at war or had already escaped, since the Turkish and Kurdish practice was first to disarm and execute the male population of a village since they might resist. Some Armenian women and children were violently converted to Islam and integrated into local communities. Although the Young Turks destroyed massive amounts of archival records in 1918, testimonies, local reports, and central orders for the murder of innocent civilians were nevertheless retrieved and presented at the (aborted) trials that followed in 1919.

This was a clear case of the creation of a scapegoat for the decline and defeat of the state to justify ethnic cleansing, mobilize the core population of Turks, and involve the Kurds in criminal action, since their leaders had been tempted by an alliance with the Armenians. It also served as a program for the Turkification of the Muslim populations. The extermination of the Armenians was meant to send a message to other non-Turkish communities, some of them under suspicion as well due to the previous secession of Muslim Albanians. Kurdish nomadic tribes might be useful to perpetrate plunder and massacre on certain occasions, but they were also under threat, since settled Kurds had normal relations with the Armenians and in many situations helped them. Seven hundred thousand Kurds were deported after the removal of the Armenians, this time to be assimilated in small groups, while Kurdish communal life came under pressure, mainly after 1923.[17] The rules of the game suddenly changed when Kemal's secular and republican policies precipitated conflict. In 1924, the rebellion of the Alevi Kurds, followed the year after by the rebellion of the Kurd Sheik Said Piran against the abolition of the Caliphate and projected judicial reforms, particularly the replacement of Islamic courts by secular courts and the sharia by a Western-inspired civil and penal code, marked the beginning of a long sequence of Turkish military engagements against the Kurds that continue to the present day.[18]

The persecution of Christian communities in the final years of the Ottoman Empire did not exclusively target Armenians. Syriac Christians also suffered extensive persecution, including plunder and massacre, almost at the same level as the Armenians, although the case is less well known because of the smaller size of their community. The Greek community, extremely important in western Anatolia, was obviously also under suspicion, even though the fact that the Greek state existed meant the threat of reprisals and contributed to keeping daily abuse at a low level—as Arnold Toynbee immediately observed.[19] Still, it is estimated that 500,000 Greeks in the Pontus region were massacred at the end of the First World War. In 1923, the exchange between the two states of 1.5 million Greeks for 500,000 Turks brought ethnic cleansing to a close on both sides. This explains why the Ottoman Empire did all it could to prevent the creation of an Armenian state in the Caucasus, extending war to the region after the Russian Army fell apart following the revolution of 1917. In 1915, Russia had occupied part of eastern Anatolia, making the Ottoman nightmare of partition of their core territory a probable reality. The Armenian state's project was limited by the Turkish-Armenian War in 1920, shaped by Bolshevik intervention, when the Red Army obtained control of the Caucasus at the end of the civil war and placed it under the Soviet Union.

The Armenian question, far from being erased, as Talât Pasha, leader of the Young Turks, and grand vizier between February 1917 and October 1918, predicted, was to surface in the collective memory and become a major issue of debate in the second half of the twentieth century. Talât Pasha could not have anticipated the tricks that history would play when he declared to Western ambassadors that the Armenians had been eradicated from Anatolia; allegedly he even boasted that he had done more to "solve" the Armenian question in three months than Sultan Abdul Hamid II had in thirty years. Henry Morgenthau, US ambassador in Istanbul in 1915–16, reported his reaction to the first of three justifications (profiteering at the expense of the Turks, separatism, and collusion with a foreign power) that Talât Pasha gave for the deportations: "massacre as a means of destroying business competitors is certainly an original concept."[20] The Young Turks in many ways set a precedent for Nazi Germany, based on a fusion of the concepts of nation and race, when they targeted for deportation and physical exclusion an entire ethnicity considered a rival nation that should not share the same territory.[21] The Nazis would replace the archaic methods of plundering and massacring Armenians on the road, leaving corpses by the thousand in the open air for weeks and months, with modern, efficiently organized mass murder. There was a further important difference: in the Turkish case, traditional religious rivalry did not exclude instances of abduction of women and children for forced conversion and adoption. Finally, the Armenian example brought with it a crucial innovation in international law: on May 24, 1915, the Triple Entente declared that its signatories would hold the members of the Ottoman government and civil servants who participated in the massacres personally responsible for crimes against humanity.

THE HOLOCAUST

Between 1870 and 1920, nothing of this kind occurred elsewhere in Europe, with the exception of the Russian Empire, although anti-Jewish propaganda proliferated in France and Germany. In the 1870s, the generally calm and respectful French attitude toward the Jews changed, perhaps stimulated by economic depression, the disaster of the Franco-Prussian War, and the disruption provoked by the commune. A new anti-Jewish campaign was unleashed not only in the press but also through second-rate literature. Yet it was the scandal of the conviction in 1894 of Alfred Dreyfus (1859–1955), an artillery officer of Jewish and Alsatian origin accused of spying on behalf of the Germans, that triggered the major eruption of anti-Jewish propaganda in France. It soon emerged that the officer had been maliciously accused without convincing proof, raising the issue of racial discrimination. Two years later evidence came to light that pointed to another officer, Ferdinand Esterhazy, as the real culprit, but the French military establishment absolved him and accepted new forged documents against Dreyfus. Public opinion was divided between pro- and anti-Dreyfusards. Writers such as Émile Zola put their weight behind the condemned innocent, who was also supported by Anatole France, Henri Poincaré, and Georges Clémenceau. Dreyfus was exonerated in 1906, reinstated in the army with the rank of major, and served during the First World War.[22] The extreme right-wing movement, Action Française, led by Charles Maurras, intervened heavily in this affair, although the outcome shows that French society had defenses against anti-Jewish propaganda and decency finally prevailed.

The campaign against the Jews was more structured in Germany, where soon after the unification authors such as Wilhelm Marr (1819–1904) denounced the supposed Jewish control of finance and industry, exploiting the state and common people. In 1879, Marr published a long pamphlet, *Der Sieg des Judenthums über das Germanenthums* (The way of Judaism over

Germanicism), in which for the first time the conflict between the two races was considered crucial for the future of the country. In this vision, there was no space for integration or accommodation, just a deadly struggle to prevent Germany's end under the increasing control of all spheres of life by Jews.[23] In the same year, Marr created the Anti-Semitic League (he coined the expression anti-Semitic) to promote the expulsion of Jews from the country. In the meantime, old and new anti-Jewish stereotypes of greed, outrageous interest rates, speculation in times of scarcity, monopolization of trade, manipulation of prices following poor harvests, and inhuman industrial conditions were part of the cocktail of accusations disseminated by the press, as if all the problems of industrial capitalism were due to Jewish machinations. Hermann Ahlwardt, condemned in court for forging Jewish documents, which did not prevent him from being elected to Parliament and hence gain immunity from prosecution, published a string of long anti-Jewish pamphlets, some of them with revealing titles, such as, in 1891, *Die Gipfel Jüdischer Frechheit* (The summit of Jewish boldness), or in 1892, *Der Verzweiflungskampf der Arischen Völker mit dem Judenthum* (The desperate struggle of the Aryan people against the Jews). The clash between the two races predicated by Marr was developed by these works, contributing to raise the level of anti-Judaism. Nor were intellectuals immune from these propagandist efforts; the historian Heinrich von Treitschke, for example, infamously labeled the Jews materialist and dishonest.[24]

Meanwhile, racial ideology was becoming a general explanation for the variety of human societies. Praise of Teutons or Aryans as responsible for human evolution was bestowed by many authors under the spell of German virtue unleashed by the process of unification. The popular and traditional side of this trend was well represented by Lanz von Liebenfels's newspaper for blond people, but the anthropologist Ludwig Woltmann was more serious, since his work combined Aryan pride with a discussion of Marxism.[25] He opposed the Marxist vision of class struggle with a racial vision of struggle based on the essential qualities of different peoples, then equated with nations. Contrary to current assumptions of modern historiography, social Darwinism scarcely, if at all, informed such views, as it conceptualized the attributes of peoples as changeable; the pattern of immutable, perpetual qualities related to climate and soil had been established by scientific racialism in the mid-nineteenth century (see chapter 16). It was this body of ideas, disseminated by various authors, that would influence Hitler and the Nazis, while social Darwinism played a subordinate role.

The book by Houston Stewart Chamberlain (1855–1927), *Die Grundlagen des Neunzehnten Jarhundert* (Foundations of the nineteenth century), published in 1899, expressed anti-Jewish feelings fueled by German nationalist intellectuals involved with the Bayreuth circle of admirers of Wagner (Chamberlain was to marry Eva Wagner, the composer's daughter, in 1908).[26] Chamberlain's book sold a hundred thousand copies before 1914. The author, a Briton who took German nationality, and during the First World War published pamphlets of German propaganda against Britain, became a friend of the emperor. His book promoted the idea of Teutonic supremacy in world history, mediated by the vision of Aryanism. Müller was cited, even though he had been careful to warn against the misuse of Aryan references in any sense beyond the linguistic. Gobineau was extensively quoted on Aryan superiority in the world, but as we have seen, the French author had not been anti-Jewish and considered the Germans a mixed race. Chamberlain categorized the leading Nordic and Teutonic people as Aryans, yet did the same with the Greeks, Romans, Celts, and Slavs, although he suggested that these had lost their Aryan element over time, unlike the Nordic people. He clearly integrated Marr's view of the crucial clash between Jewish and German races. Indeed, he disputed Leopold von Ranke's idea of the nineteenth century as the century of nationalities. For Chamberlain it was the century of races, threatened by their increasing mixture, and the entire future would depend on this life-and-death racial struggle.[27] Northern Europeans had become the makers of world history through state building, innovative thought, and original art.[28] Major steps forward in civilization in southern Europe had been pushed further by the Gothic (or Aryan) influence, particularly that of what Chamberlain called the German-Hellenics along with Lombard Goths and Spanish Visigoths.

Chamberlain acknowledged that all great races had become mixed to a certain degree, but he maintained that Jews were the furthest away from being a pure race, as they were likely to be 50 percent Syrian, 5 percent Semitic, 10 percent Indo-European (Amorite), and 35 percent mixed descent, making them a race he classified as mongrel due to the gap between its constituent elements, and considered worse than the products of interbreeding between the Spanish and South Americans.[29] One might wonder how such baseness could represent a "danger to Europe," yet Chamberlain stated that the Israelite nation existed only as an idea and a will, based on a special way of thinking and feeling, held together by the pecuniary interest of its priestly noble caste, working through permanent machinations toward universal empire.[30] The recent blossoming of Jewish culture was attributed to their imitative skills, directed at controlling European civilization, which would lead to the destruction of the latter through the imposition of Oriental customs and modes of thought, just as the Islamic (labeled Mohammedan) fatalist vision of the world had reduced an energetic nation, the Turks, to complete passivity.[31] Chamberlain condemned the emancipation of the Jews along with the bestowing on them of equal civil rights and the right to marry non-Jewish people, all bought by Jewish financial leaders, who would marry their daughters outside the community, though the offspring would still be Jews, while the sons would only marry inside the community.[32] He mocked the eighteenth-century vision of the fraternity of nations as sentimental, and regarded both liberal and socialist ideas of reform as abject.[33] Chamberlain harked back to the idea of polygenism (the theory of multiple creations; see chapter 16) to claim that only Jews were descendants of Adam and Eve, while the rest of humankind was of a much older origin—another indication of the importance of scientific racialism in the representation of Teutonic supremacy.[34] He also expunged religion from the picture: Judaism was materialist, void of contemplative wonder, without mysteries, based on ritual and precept, not on revelation, and a "monolatry," not monotheism.[35] The preservation of Judaism had been primarily the work of Christianity: "though Christ was the builder, we got the architecture from the Jews," since an un-Aryan spirit (meaning nonwarrior, noncreative, and nonenergetic) was instilled in Christianity by Jews.[36] As others were to put it more clearly, Christianity was considered the religion of slaves.

This antihumanist and anticompassionate stance was very much in line with the spirit of the times. Throughout the nineteenth century, liberalism had created a secular system of values that placed respect for the individual and civil rights at the center of its ideology, independent of all reference to God or obedience to churches of different confessions. Perceived de-Christianization had led to successive papal interventions against liberal thought, such as the *Syllabus Errorum*, published by Pius IX on December 8, 1864, as a list of propositions condemned by the church.[37] By the end of the nineteenth century, right-wing nationalist movements were considered to more or less favor Catholic restoration, although in several cases the new ideologies had obliterated religious traditions as useless and anachronistic. As a consequence of this turn, the agents involved were not deterred by basic religious principles of charity or respect for human beings; the commandment "thou shall not kill" simply became ignored as obsolete. The dehumanization of political enemies or racial targets, as we have seen with the persecution of Jews in Russia or the Armenian genocide in Turkey, were part of a general shift toward indifference in the face of human suffering on the part of people who did not belong to the right nation or race.

This background is present in Chamberlain's book as a specific blend of stereotypes with traditional and modern ideas. There is a noticeable reinstatement of polygenism forty years after Darwin; Chamberlain praised the man, but rejected his theories, partly influenced by his professor, Karl Vogt, a disciple of Agassiz who tried to reconcile polygenism with evolutionary theories.[38] The promotion of the significance of races, and the struggle between them, in defining the future of humankind was in line with the polygenist authors of the 1840s and 1850s. Neither the claims about the imitative skills of the Jews nor those about their project of universal empire were new. The major innovation was to completely deny the immutable physical features and sublime religious ideals of the Jewish race, which thus was reduced to a repository of interest and greed, while at the same time Christianity was criticized as a useless delusion of charity, an obstacle to forceful Aryan policies. The French Revolution was considered a catastrophe and the idea of progress questioned in keeping with Gobineau's theories.[39] Antiliberal and antisocialist ideas were the cornerstone of this praise of racial struggle, which was in accord with the North American current defined by Ripley and Grant (see chapter 17).

It was this antihumanist and ruthless narrative of the Aryans' (Teutonic) struggle for their future and the future of humankind that would be taken up in the context of a defeated, resentful Germany. Adolf Hitler (1889–1945), born in Austria of German parents, lived in Vienna and then Munich, where he volunteered for military service in the First World War. Involved in propaganda and intelligence among military units at the end of war, he became a member of the German Workers' Party, which under his leadership was renamed the National Socialist German Workers' Party in 1920. Hitler was detained as a promoter of the Munich putsch of 1923. He used the trial to diffuse his nationalist ideas, spending his time in prison writing *Mein Kampf*, which was published in 1925.[40] He made extensive use of Chamberlain's book. Hitler visited Chamberlain in Bayreuth, paid public homage to him as an ideological mentor, corresponded with him, made him a member of the National Socialist Party, and attended his funeral. Hitler did not explicitly quote any author, appropriating all he could from others for his own particular blend of ideas, but Chamberlain was obviously the origin of the notion of an absence of real religion and pure ancestors in the Jewish race, and the accusation of the Jewish pursuit of universal empire, this time supported by *The Protocols of the Elders of Zion*, taken as a serious document and considered proven by major Jewish achievements.[41] The supposed strategic matrimonial alliances of the Jews were also directly quoted, although with a sarcastic twist: "If the worst came to the worst, a few drops of baptismal water would settle the matter, whereupon the Jew could carry on his business safely."[42]

Chamberlain had never devised a political program, whereas the one in *Mein Kampf* was vast and coherent, giving a central negative role to the Jews. Hitler analyzed the policies of the main German parties in Austria, explaining their failures. Schönerer was elitist and did not address the problems of the working class, which Hitler claimed to know, since he had worked as a manual laborer in Vienna for five years. The upper classes' hold on political power was seen as insignificant. Schönerer's conflict with the Catholic Church had been a major mistake, for the support of such institutions was important for the success of any political project. Lueger, in Hitler's view, based his anti-Semitism on religion, not on race; it was a proselytizing enterprise that did not upset the Jews. The Christian Socialists had collapsed because "the movement was deprived of the only source of energy from which a political party can draw the necessary driving force."[43] Anti-Judaism therefore was explicitly understood as a driving force of Hitler's political project.

Jews were seen as controlling finance and industry, depersonalizing business through stock exchange, manipulating the press, bringing about degeneration in art, literature, and theater, and influencing all spheres of public life.[44] They were liberals but also Marxists, capitalists yet at the same time socialists, exploiters of the working class and organizers of trade unions. Later, Hitler would state that the Jews had killed or attacked thirty million people in Russia, that the Communist commissars in Soviet Russia were Jews, and that they expropriated the wealth of capitalists, but were at the receiving end of the process too.[45] Jews had invented civil rights and democracy to promote their own interests, since equality allowed them to control the system, while power based on numerical representation debased the Germans as a race.[46] Here Hitler was probably thinking about Austria and the "Slavification" of the empire through universal suffrage. Cosmopolitanism and international capitalism were equated with Jewish interests as opposed to those of the nation. Jews, then, were made responsible for all economic, social, and political failures, particularly the war defeat; they were responsible for both capitalist exploitation and its false Marxist alternative. Jews were accused of despising manual work and having created the label proletariat in order to diminish the pride of the working class, while they, as parasites, lived off the work of others. They were also accused of artificially separating the categories of nation and social good, which in Hitler's view were naturally integrated (hence National Socialism). As a motor of Hitler's political project, anti-Judaism ticked all the boxes of discontent.

Hitler inserted a totalitarian critique of liberalism into his onslaught: the parliamentary regime was as corrupt and false as the Jews. Democracy, in his view, was just a forerunner of Marxism, labeled a bacillus and pest, as were the Jews, debased as human beings. The critique of Marxism, considered a Jewish doctrine, was reminiscent of nineteenth-century racial theories, with a flavor of Gobineau's praise of inequality: "[It] repudiates the aristocratic principle of nature and substitutes for it the eternal principle of force and energy, of numerical mass and its dead weight"; it denies the individual worth of the human personality, contradicts the primary significance of nationhood and race, takes away the very foundations of human civilization.[47] The only genuine democracy had been the traditional German one, based on the choice of a leader (Hitler does not explain how) obliged to accept full responsibility for all their actions and omissions. Control of and accountability for the leader's acts obviously went unmentioned. The dismissive reference to public opinion as always subject to manipulation indicates the roots of Hitler's contempt for democracy.[48] According to this vision, the masses were only capable of achieving anything when they were placed under the control of a leader.

But what would Hitler give the working class? Pride of race, equated with nation; renewed spirit with a civilizing mission; and territorial expansion in Europe. Cleansing the nation of Jewish influence ("moral pestilence") was the main program. Party members were to recover their dignity through the wearing of uniforms and participation in the storm troops, launching terrorist attacks and brutal intimidation against Jews as well as political adversaries. Hitler pinned his hopes of fulfilling his military dreams (revenge for defeat and the extraction of compensations that had followed) on the masses, since the "German bourgeoisie, especially in its upper circles, is pacifist even to the point of complete self-abnegation."[49] In his mind, the integration of Austria would be the first step toward the emancipation of the German nation.[50] Territorial expansion would follow, since Germany did not have sufficient space to increase its population.

The competition between races was considered limited by territorial boundaries; culturally superior races that were less ruthless would be dominated by inferior races. Hitler rejected colonial adventures on other continents. Territorial expansion should take place exclusively in Europe, not in the Cameroons.[51] The influence of the nineteenth-century polygenist vision of immutable races connected to soil and climate is visible here: Hitler posited that Germans could only maintain their character in Europe. He obviously coveted eastern Europe, seen as underpopulated at the time. *Mein Kampf* repeatedly expressed contempt for Slavic populations. Hitler rejoiced at the Japanese victory over the Russians in 1905, for instance, which he considered a blow to the Austrian slavism.[52] Superior races were limited to the Germans, Scandinavians, Dutch, British, and North Americans. Hitler criticized Vienna as a Babylon of races. Aryanism was used according to Gobineau and Chamberlain, ignoring the previous deconstruction of its legend by Salomon Reinach in 1892 and Siegmunt Feist in 1915.[53] Hitler reproduced all the stereotypes of miscegenation as degeneration and chaos. The motif of the book was that the German state was a German nation, and the program to mobilize the masses was based on the definition of Jews as internal enemy; defeat in the First World War was attributed to ignoring this internal enemy.[54] The ultimate goal was defined in the epilogue: "A state which, in an epoch of racial adulteration, devotes itself to the duty of preserving the best elements of its racial stock must one day become the ruler of the world"—an ambition of universal dominion that Hitler had repeatedly attributed to the Jews.[55]

In *Mein Kampf*, Hitler defined the foundations of his thought, his vision for Germany, and his party's political program. The book's message was crystal clear: there was no dissimulation. All reasoning was based on the eradication of the Jews (exactly when Hitler shifted from forced emigration to total extermination is a matter of dispute), territorial expansion, and world supremacy of the German nation. Antiliberal, antidemocratic, and anti-Marxist principles were patently argued. The influence of scientific racialism was overwhelming. Although Hitler saw the potential of targeting Jews to mobilize the masses and at the same time threaten political enemies through a display of terror toward a defenseless minority of the population, he obviously believed in immutable racial features as the explanation for historical, social, and political trends as well as possibilities. The translation of this theory of races into political action would be lethal. The genocide of the Jews and Roma, as we will see, reached an unprecedented scale of systematic atrocity. The elimination of all political adversaries was also part of the program. In his crude style, Hitler had already defined his great objective: the extermination of Marxism (he never bothered to distinguish between social democrats and Communists, though the latter's distinct policies had been apparent since the turn of the century in a divide sealed by the Bolshevik revolution). The antihumanist stance was also put forward in *Mein Kampf*: "When nations are fighting for their existence . . . all humane and aesthetic considerations must be put aside."[56] Hitler spoke loudly and clearly against the pacifist and humanitarian ideal, which would only be useful "when the most superior type of mankind has succeeded in subjugating the world"—in other words, when this type was in control of conquered nations.[57]

The policies of Nazi Germany were consistent with this program that Hitler defined so early on. What is surprising is how quickly the German state was shaped by racial prejudice and discriminatory action. Nazi Germany presents the most complete case of political application of racial theories.[58] It is also the most disconcerting and apparently illogical instance, since the reality was surprisingly different from the image of danger and threat propagated by Hitler and his supporters. Jews represented less than 1 percent of the total German population; according to the official estimate of 1928, there were 564,000 Jews in a population of 65 million. Moreover, Jews were far from being an isolated community. The process of integration had increased dramatically in the previous century, from the economic, social, professional, and physical points of view, expressed by 60 percent Jewish intermarriage with Christians in 1932.[59]

Racial exclusion nevertheless prevailed as state policy, systematically pushed through paramilitary action. The Nazi storm troops, numbering 700,000, contributed significantly to eroding democracy through constant street battles against Communists, particularly the provocative "Bloody Sunday" in Altona (Hamburg) on July 17, 1932. As the Nazis rose to power—Hitler was invested as the German chancellor on January 30, 1933—the storm troops were immediately used to annihilate the property rights, personal security, professional standing, and basic legal rights of the Jewish community, underlining the downgrading of their citizenship with aggressive action backed by the law. On April 1, 1933, a general boycott against Jews represented the disruption of their civil rights; shops were stormed and closed down, access to work was blocked, and people were arrested. This violent, intimidating attack preceded the legal removal of Jews from the judicial system (as judges, prosecutors, lawyers, and notaries), civil service (including hospitals and universities), and arts, culture, and sciences. Non-Aryan subjects were legally defined during the same month based on genealogy: a single Jewish parent or grandparent would be sufficient to exclude a person from citizenship. Birth certificates, marriage licenses for parents, and military documents could be used as proof. Hitler believed that race was spiritual (meaning willed or an ideal) and physical, not religious, but again there were, paradoxically, neither spiritual nor physical objective criteria to define it. When it came to policies of exclusion, the criteria for identification were the traditional ones, based on genealogical inquiry and reputation.

State policy impacted on all levels of society, generating segregation in restaurants, hotels, and clubs, severing public contracts, and disrupting private relationships. The confiscation of the property of Jewish or political émigrés was the next step. In July 1935, an anti-Jewish riot in Berlin prepared public opinion for the Nuremberg Laws, which completed the legal framework of the racial state with this definition of citizenship: "A Reich citizen is a subject of the state who is German or of related blood, who proves by his conduct that he is willing and fit faithfully to serve the German people and the Reich." This meant that all Jews were excluded, but also all opponents of the Nazi regime. Socialists and Communists had been banned in March 1933; now they were excluded from citizenship and implicitly equated with Jews—an operation consistent with Hitler's ideology. The laws forbade marriage and extramarital intercourse between Jews and Germans. Jews were explicitly excluded from Reich citizenship, voting rights, and public office. The definition of a Jew once more reveals the weak basis of the racial state: "A Jew is a person descended from at least three grandparents who are full Jews by race. . . . A *Mischling* [mestizo or mixed race] who is a subject of the state is also considered a Jew if he is descended from two full Jewish grandparents." The law also labeled people as Jews if they were members of the Jewish religious community, married to Jews, and born of a marriage that included a Jew or born of extramarital intercourse with a Jew.[60] These artificial categories remind us of the inquisitorial definition of New Christians with full, half, one-quarter, or one-eighth Jewish blood. Such categorization was all based on genealogy, even after two centuries of scientific discussion of race; except for the traditional criterion of kinship, there was nothing objective that could define a Jew. And rightly so, given that extensive research carried out in Germany in 1875–76 by Rudolph Virchow—research that had involved millions of schoolchildren—had shown that around 32 percent of Jews had fair hair and 19 percent blue eyes; research in New York by Maurice Fishberg, published in 1911, had rejected the stereotype of the Jewish hooked nose;

Figure 18.1. Anonymous photograph after Kristallnacht, November 1938. Ridicule and humiliation of the Jewish inhabitants of Baden-Baden, escorted by the SS to the streets with a sign that reads "God does not abandon us."
© 2013. Photo: Scala, Florence; BPK Bildagentur für Kunst, Kultur, und Geschichte, Berlin

and research developed during the First World War had demonstrated that even blood groups, whose existence had recently been discovered, could not identify Jewish people.[61]

The invasion and annexation of Austria by Nazi Germany in March 1938 was euphorically received by local Nazi supporters, who launched anti-Jewish riots and occupied Jewish property. The Nazi Order for the Declaration of Jewish Property followed the obliteration of Jewish rights, offering "legal" expropriation as compensation for alleged damage caused by Jews to the German people. The expulsion of Polish Jews from Germany and Austria was the next step to liberate German territorial space from non-Aryan elements. In November 1938, the murder of a German diplomat by a tormented Polish Jew in Paris created a pretext for the worst set of pogroms in the history of Germany and Austria—the Kristallnacht pogroms, during which Nazi storm troops destroyed more than 400 synagogues by setting fire to them, ransacked 7,500 Jewish businesses, looted thousands of Jewish homes, and arrested and sent 34,000 Jews to concentration camps. The Nazi state duly confiscated the insurance for the devastation it had promoted. To expiate the diplomat's death, a fine of 1 million Reich marks was imposed on the Jewish community, while all its property was confiscated by the state (an estimated total of 6 billion Reich marks). This was the concluding piece of the program of the Aryanization of the economy, forcing out Jews physically and legally. By fall 1938, only 150,000 to 170,000 Jews had left Germany; the Kristallnacht pogrom led to the instant emigration of many more, despite the strikingly small opportunities offered by other countries as well as the scarce financial resources left to a community that had been successively plundered, expelled from work, and terrorized. The remaining Jews were sent to concentration camps, rounded in ghettos, and confined to forced labor.[62]

During the Second World War, Nazi efforts at racial exclusion, just like those of the Ottoman Empire during the First World War, did not abate; on the contrary, these efforts were upgraded to total extermination.[63] One might think that the constraints on military

Figure 18.2. Anonymous photograph after Kristallnacht, November 1938. A woman is humiliated on the streets with a sign that reads "I am a Christian pig and buy from Jews." © 2013. Photo: Scala, Florence; BPK Bildagentur für Kunst, Kultur, und Geschichte, Berlin

resources and difficulties of the war economy would have sidelined anti-Jewish policies, but the opposite occurred, involving many thousands of special troops along with significant expenditure on arms, fuel, transport, and the building of extermination camps with gas chambers and crematoriums. In a speech on January 30, 1939, Hitler had already promised to annihilate the Jewish race in Europe, perversely making Jews responsible for the war, even though the Third Reich had already occupied Austria and Czechoslovakia. The conquest of Poland, Belgium, the Netherlands, France, and part of the Balkans violently extended the eradication of Jewish rights and expropriation of Jewish property as well as proliferation of concentration camps and forced labor. But it was during the first stages of the war with Russia (summer–fall 1941) that the extermination program for all Jews in Europe was defined. Here the Nazis were working on an entirely different scale. Before the conquest of Poland, 3 million Jews lived there; the Soviet Union had around 5 million Jews, although a significant number had been added in the previous two years through annexations and Polish refugees. On January 20, 1942, the protocol of the Wannsee Conference attended by the top ministers and SS leaders responsible for the "final solution" inventoried 11 million Jews in Europe.[64] The explicit purpose was to clear areas required for the German people.

The conquest of Eastern Europe represented for Hitler the "vital space" for German colonization and expansion—space in which the local Slav populations were to be reduced to a subordinate status, and "racially valuable" children were to be abducted from their parents and Germanized. The extermination of Jews was the crucial part of this vast project of racial purging and replacement. Terror against the Jews played an obvious role in neutralizing

Map 18.4. Nazi expansion in Europe, 1942.
Source: Geoffrey Barraclough, ed., *The Times Atlas of World History* (London: Times Books, 1990), 272

possible political opponents, yet it is undeniable that Hitler believed in his racial policies, since he ordered the killing of all Jews in concentration camps in case of civil uprising to eradicate possible leaders. He also extended his program of Jewish extermination to all areas occupied by Germany or under German influence. Vichy France replicated Nazi laws and collaborated in the deportation of tens of thousands of Jews to concentration camps. In July 1938, the Italian fascist state asserted the Aryan origin of its population and called for the removal of the Jewish population, expelling all refugees who had arrived after 1919, and excluding all other Jews from the civil service and liberal professions. Deportation started when the Italian fascist regime broke down and the Nazis took over. In Hungary, during the last stages of the war, more than half of the 725,000 Jews were deported, and the others were concentrated in ghettos. In Bulgaria, Jews from the new territories were deported. In Yugo-slavia, the fascist Croatian Ustaša militia, which in 1941 controlled a Nazi protected state, murdered 300,000 Serbs, Jews, and Roma. The deportation of Jews from Nazi-occupied Greece was devastating. In Salonika alone, 48,000 were deported and killed from a community that had numbered 56,000 in 1940. But the extermination in those parts of Eastern Europe occupied by the Nazis reached unparalleled numbers.

Local populations in some cases refused to collaborate with the Nazis. In France, the majority of the Jewish community survived, while only a small percentage of confiscated Jewish businesses were taken over. In Italy, deportation remained relatively limited, as it was met with organized resistance and local protection by Catholic institutions and even top figures in its hierarchy. The most successful instance was in Denmark, which steadfastly resisted handing over the Jews while the authorities ferried nearly the whole community, 7,000 people, to Sweden, a neutral country.[65] The result of Hitler's systematic policy of ex-termination, ruthlessly pursued right up to the end of the war, even with defeat clearly in sight, meant a total of 6 million Jews killed by the Nazis; two-thirds were the victims of mass murder by mobile armed units in Poland and the Soviet Union, and one-third were exterminated in concentration camps.[66]

The Jews were the central target of Nazi racial purification, but they were not the only ones. On October 15, 1935, the Law for the Protection of the Hereditary Health of the Ger-man People prohibited marriage and sexual intercourse with "alien races" and "less valuable groups," particularly Gypsies, blacks, and their "bastards." On December 8, 1939, Gypsies (Roma and Sinti) were defined as criminal and asocial, a nuisance that the state had to get rid of, and they were targeted by the racial purification program. It is estimated that over 500,000 were killed in Nazi-occupied Europe.[67] Eugenics was part of the Nazi project, although in this field, unfortunately, Germany was not alone.[68] Race was obviously part of the program of

Figure 18.3. Liberation of Bergen-Belsen camp by British troops on April 15, 1945. Franz Hoessler, first lieutenant of the SS, former commander of the women's camp Auschwitz-Birkenau, posing in front of a lorry with bodies for a British newsreel. Photo 24.4.1945. Reprinted with permission from AKG-images, Berlin; Ullstein bild

purification of the German population, which included the sterilization of significant groups, especially mixed-race people, but also involved the elimination of 70,000 people considered physically or mentally handicapped, including homosexuals. The bishop of Münster wrote a letter in protest. It was one of the few cases of public protest by the Catholic Church against Nazi policies. Socialists and Communists were also targeted after they were banned, in March 1933, and they too were sent to concentration camps. On July 17, 1941, the war directive concerning the invasion of Russia explicitly required the elimination of all Communists and Jews. The Bolsheviks and Communist intelligentsia had already been singled out before the war for future extermination in order to decapitate organized resistance. In the concentration and extermination camps, Jews remained the vast majority of victims, yet they shared their fate with Communists, socialists, and active liberal democrats from Germany and the occupied countries. The Polish political elite, army, and aristocracy were also targeted to prevent resistance. Contempt for Slav populations, considered subhuman, was expressed by the neglect and mass murder of prisoners of war. A stunning total of 3.5 million Red Army soldiers, captured in the first months of the invasion of Russia, were slaughtered. In March 1941, Heinrich Himmler estimated that 20 to 30 million people would have to be exterminated in the Soviet Union.[69] Germany's ultimate defeat meant that this figure "only" reached the lower mark, revealing that the Nazis knew exactly the scale of their operation.

Hitler's ideology of races did not change during twelve years of power, of which six consisted of war and direct confrontation with many other peoples. Successive concentrations of power allowed Hitler to transform his ideas into increasingly lethal policies, from forced emigration to extermination. The "table talks" or monologues with his inner circle of collaborators were recorded, and constitute interesting testimonies to his reflections and intentions. In the first months of the victorious invasion of Russia, a euphoric Hitler voiced contempt for the Eastern peoples: "the Hungarian is as lazy as the Russian"; "the Russian territory is our India"; "we shall rule it with a handful of men"; and "if other people, beginning with the Vikings, had not imported the rudiments of organization into Russian humanity, the Russians would still be living like rabbits." Hitler's project for Russia would prevent a return to Christianity, because Christianity would give the Eastern Europeans an element of organization. The Eastern Europeans' lands would be taken away, and given to Germans, Danes, Dutch, Norwegians, and Swedes.[70] In these monologues, Christianity was to be left to die a natural death (an idea repeated several times), since it functioned as a prototype for the Bolsheviks and the empowerment of slaves. The decline of Christianity was attributed to democratic recruitment.[71] The "inferior race" certainly surprised Hitler with a reaction and military capacity he obviously had not predicted.

Living in a bunker in the final months of withdrawal and defeat, Hitler reflected on racial ideology. He rejected colonialism, because the white race had been unable to impose any changes: "The Hindus have remained Hindus, the Chinese have remained Chinese, and the Moslems are still Moslems. . . . [T]hey have remained essentially unchanged."[72] In these phrases one can see the essentialism of scientific racialism, although there is more, related to the same vision of races connected to soil and climate. Hitler declared himself distressed at the "thought of those millions of Germans . . . who emigrated to the United States, and who are now the backbone of the country." He considered them not only lost to the homeland but also enemies, "more implacably hostile than any others. . . . The German emigrant retains, it is true, his qualities of industry and hard work, but he very quickly loses his soul. There is nothing more unnatural than a German who has become an expatriate."[73] Moreover, "a race of the mind is something more solid, more durable than just a race, pure and simple. Transplant a German to the United States and you turn him into an American. But the Jew remains a Jew wherever he goes, a creature which no environment can assimilate."[74] He still thought that "never before has there been a war so typically and at the same time so exclusively Jewish."[75]

Until the end Hitler believed, or pretended to believe, in his own propaganda that Russians, British, and Americans were Jews or Jew ridden. He regretted not having been bolder in fighting against colonialism due to the alliance with Mussolini. Such a stance, he claimed, would have spread credibility among colonized people, particularly the Muslims, and mobilized them against the British. He dismissed the Aryan pretense of the Latin peoples. He also regretted that "pride of race is a quality which the German, fundamentally, does not possess." Germans had been torn by internal dissension and religious wars, subjected to foreign influences. "Christianity is not a natural religion for the Germans, but a religion that has been imported, which strikes no responsive chord in their hearts and is foreign to the inherent genius of the race." Hitler singled out the Prussians and Austrians for their pride of race, as peoples who had never been dominated by another race (an echo of Tacitus and the unbeatable Germans), possessing the accumulated experience of domination and power, while he lamented "the inferiority complex from which so many Germans suffer," which he implicitly regarded as responsible for the disasters of war.[76]

The fusion of nation and race was already evident in the Turkish case, which led to the Armenian genocide, combined with repeated massacres and exclusions of many hundreds of thousands of Greeks and Kurds. Religion was the main marker for ethnic cleansing, but the Kurds were also Muslim. This was the first extreme case of targeting other communities (also labeled as races) to clear an area considered the core territory—in this instance, for the Turkish nation. The idea that a homogeneous nation should rule a homogeneous territory was behind these events. Only Kurdish cultural and political resistance prevented the full implementation of plans to make the whole population Turkish. The fusion of nation and race was pushed even further by the Nazi German racial state, where the idea of pure Germans defined citizenship without compromise, excluding minorities that had fought for the country in previous wars. The Nazi political project of empire in Europe and dominion over the world required the extermination of the Jews, defined as the main enemy, and subordination of inferior races, such as the Slavs, targeted for dispossession of their lands and as a source of servile labor. Racism reached unprecedented levels, based on national or expansionist political projects. The expulsion of minorities was replaced by extermination in a secularized society in which political struggle had displaced all major deterrents to the complete debasement of human beings. This model of the nation-race was followed in parts of Europe where Nazi or fascist movements and governments spread. Mussolini's Italy and

Vichy France complied with Nazi requirements for Jewish persecution. But it is important, before I conclude this chapter, to analyze exceptions to this phenomenon.

The absence of persecution of Jews in modern Spain and Portugal remains a relatively neglected issue.[77] The issue is significant, as Iberia in previous ages had violently converted and expelled Jews and Muslims, becoming the most striking early modern case of discrimination against and segregation of minorities. The distinction between New and Old Christians that structured these societies based on purity of blood was abolished in 1773 in Portugal, and only between 1835 and 1870 in Spain, illustrating the resilience of the ethnic divide (see chapter 9). During the Second World War, Spain and Portugal maintained their neutrality, despite the direct intervention of Germany in the Spanish Civil War. In his novel *Raza*, the dictator Francisco Franco dismissed the importance of the historical issue of conflictive races, instead praising the relation to the land and common idea of *hispanidad*.[78] The Falangistas (Spanish fascist movement) and Franco himself praised the expulsion of Jews by the Catholic kings, never criticized Hitler's racial policies, and equated Jews with Freemasons and Communists. Yet no political action was taken against the Jews. The extension of citizenship to Sephardic communities granted in the mid-nineteenth century was maintained. Antonio de Oliveira Salazar's regime in Portugal was even more discrete, and the small Jewish community was never disturbed. The key issue was to what extent Jewish refugees from Europe were to be accepted.[79]

This absence of persecution can only be explained in historical, sociological, and political terms. Collective memory is important here: the fierce debate between liberals and absolutists in the nineteenth century concerning the historical past left sequels for the twentieth century. In Portugal, the absolutists dropped the issues of the Inquisition and purity of blood immediately after the liberal revolution of 1820, while Spanish conservative resilience never involved more than nostalgic reference to the pure Catholic past. Nobody wanted to reactivate disputed projects that had left so many wounds. Conservative Catholicism in the twentieth century wanted to avoid new ethnic divisions, and this contributed to preventing Franco and Salazar from adopting a secular racialist stance. Hitler blamed Spanish neutrality during the war on Franco's "Jesuit" brother-in-law.[80] Besides, Spain had lost almost all its colonies by the end of the nineteenth century and was confronted with the autonomous projects of its rich industrialized peripheries, Catalonia and the Basque country—what José Ortega y Gasset called "invertebrate Spain."[81] In Portugal, the survival of the colonies until 1975 left ample space for racial discourses and racist policies, but the Jews were never targeted.[82] The liberal constitutional monarchy (1834–1910) and republic (1910–26) had left undeniable imprints. The issue is also sociological: Jews had returned to Portugal from North Africa and France in the mid-nineteenth century, while in Spain most Jews returned after Moroccan independence in 1956. They numbered less than 10,000 people by the mid-twentieth century. This meant that Jewish communities in Portugal and Spain were residual; they did not have weight or visibility in any field. Without direct foreign intervention, there were no grounds for any political project seeking their discrimination, segregation, expulsion, or extermination.

|||||||||||||||||||||||||||||||||||||||||||||||||||||||||||||||||||||||||||||||||||||||||||||||||||||||||||||||||||||||||||||||

CHAPTER 19

Global Comparisons

EUROPE: DEPORTATIONS, FORCED MIGRATIONS, AND SLAVE LABOR

In Europe, racial supremacy was opposed by working-class virtue in the clash between the two totalitarian regimes (fascist-Nazi and Communist) in the Second World War. The transformation of Germany into a racial state meant that non-Germans were classified into a racial hierarchy. Gypsies were at the bottom of the scale, typified as criminal and asocial; blacks were considered of little value; Jews were targeted as the internal enemy; and Slavs were labeled an inferior race. Jews were marked for extermination since they were defined as a social and political danger. Slavs were portrayed as subhuman in order to target them for forced labor. Classification was thus motivated by political projects and social context. Asians were considered immutable and locked in their traditions, but it was unnecessary for the Nazis to include them in their racial system, at least until they had achieved dominion over Europe. The project of a huge reversion to forced labor (slavery) became a growing reality under war conditions, although one wonders how a racial system in which the vast majority of the population would explicitly be considered inferior might have been imposed on a whole continent. The Soviet system's refusal of a racial divide, which was considered a capitalist justification of a world division of labor, proved to be limited: some ethnicities were seen as more resistant than others to anti-working-class (meaning anti-Communist) political action. Internationalism served to enlarge the Soviet Union's influence and create a community of interests among the organic agents of the working class (the new international elite promoted by the Soviet political project). A class divide, for a while, proved to be more inclusive than a racial divide. Still, the ploys of nationalism played a major role in the political logic of Joseph Stalin's Soviet Union. Russian nationalism proved to be the most efficient ideological weapon when it came to mobilizing the population against Nazi German invasion.

The deportation of national minorities did not stop in Europe with the end of the Second World War. It is true that the seeds of conflict had been sown by Nazi invasions, massacres, deportations, and the colonization of conquered territories by Germans. The horrors of war and its racial foundations had left vivid memories in the occupied territories, but peace might have healed wounds and imposed civil methods for integrating minorities. Yet this

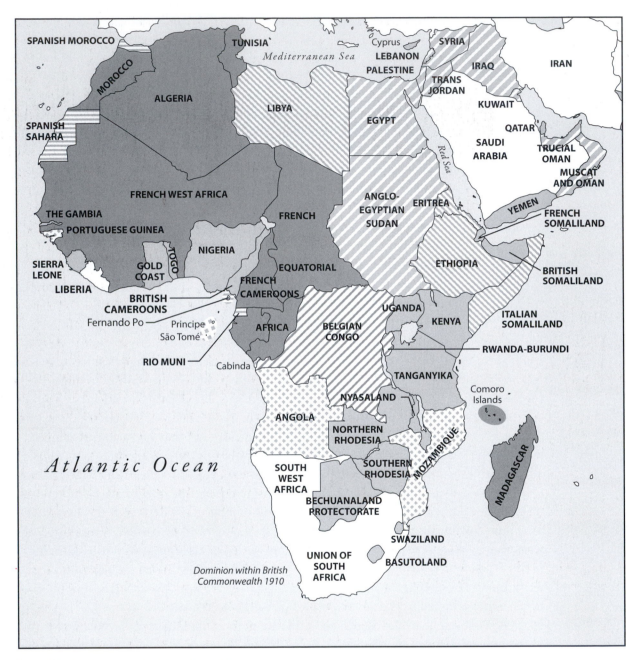

Map 19.1. The Western colonial world in 1939.

is not what happened: in the Soviet Union, Stalin deported ethnic Germans who had historically lived along the Volga and those living in Königsberg (Kaliningrad), while Poland, Czechoslovakia, and Hungary proceeded with massive expulsions of German communities. It is estimated that 12 million Germans were uprooted between 1945 and 1948, with probably 500,000 dying in the process.[1] National loyalty had become a crucial issue after the war.

Source: Geoffrey Barraclough, ed., *The Times Atlas of World History* (London: Times Books, 1990), 276–77.

The concept of the nation-state, combined with political allegiance, became important even in the Communist regimes of Eastern Europe that were now under Soviet influence, despite claims of working-class internationalism. The issue of national minorities affected states that were theoretically friends. The Hungarian minority in Romania, for example, continued to be the object of projects of Romanization until the fall of the Communist regime. The

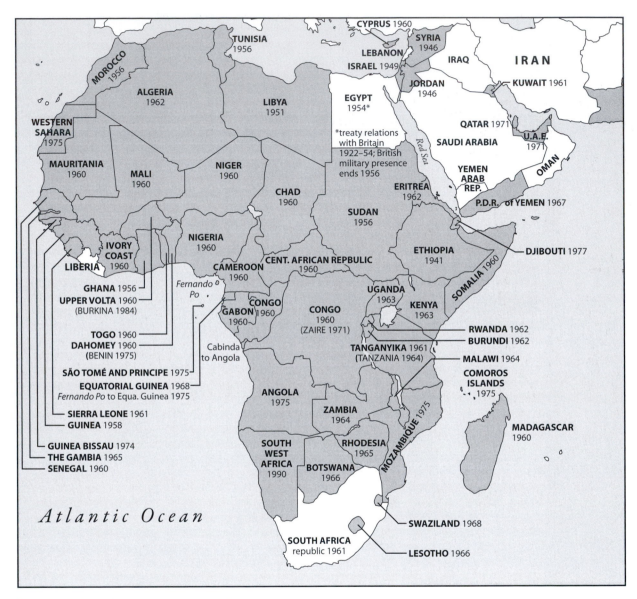

Map 19.2. Independent territories since 1947.

reconstitution of Yugoslavia after the Second World War under the leadership of the anti-Nazi resistance leader Josip Broz Tito, a Communist Croat, postponed major outbreaks of ethnic and national revenge until the fall of Communism in Eastern Europe. The war between Serbs, Croats, and Bosnian or Albanian Muslims between 1991 and 1995 over the creation of new states unleashed new political projects, mainly for a Greater Serbia, which led to ethnic atrocities in the whole region, dividing populations that had experienced a significant level of intermarriage. The religious division was coupled with national and ethnic divides, reinstating late nineteenth-century lines of allegiance. But this is not all: in 1955,

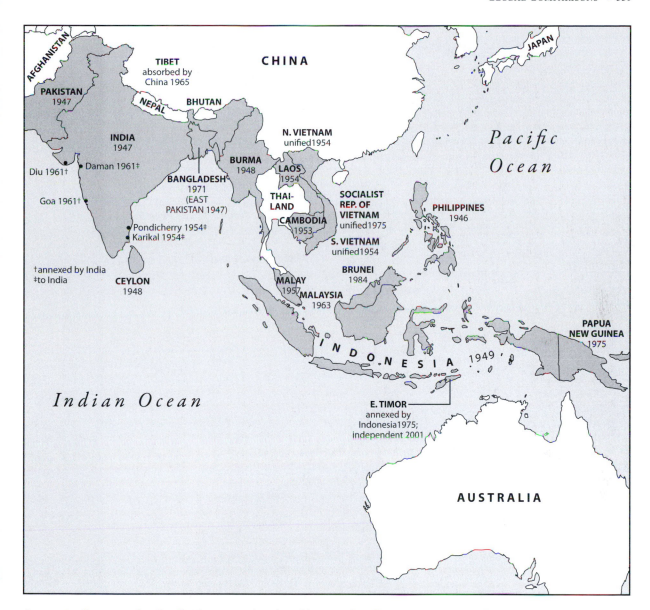

Source: Geoffrey Barraclough, ed., *The Times Atlas of World History* (London: Times Books, 1990), 276–77

in Istanbul, the memory of genocide and massacres was not sufficient to deter a major riot against the Greek community, which triggered the final migration of 200,000 Greeks who had been allowed to stay in Turkey by the Treaty of Lausanne.[2]

The Soviet Union rejected racial theory as archaic and capitalist oriented, but the Jews, who had been relatively protected during the civil war, were under suspicion of being class traitors during the Second World War. They had to deal with the daily threat of being sent to the gulag—an atmosphere skillfully re-created in *Life and Fate* by Vasily Grossman.[3] Deportation of suspected ethnic groups started in the late 1920s, with the Ingrian Finns, to

Map 19.3. Territorial changes and population movements in Europe, 1945–49.

Source: Geoffrey Barraclough, ed., *The Times Atlas of World History* (London: Times Books, 1990), 274

be followed by Crimean Tatars, Greeks, Kalmyks, Balkars, Karachays, Turks, Far Eastern Koreans, Poles, Romanians, Lithuanians, Estonians, Chechens, and Ingush. It is estimated that 5.9 million people were subjected to such internal forced migration, while another 6 million were affected by forced migration from neighboring countries.[4] Suspected ethnicities were often put together in forced labor camps with the class enemy, the urban upper class and rural kulaks, on the pretext of their "reeducation through work." The Soviet gulag grew steadily to account for between 2.1 and 2.5 million people in the 1940s and 1950s, until the disruption produced by Nikita Khrushchev in 1956. In the twentieth century, the emancipation of the working class ironically led to the creation of massive modern slavery under Stalin. The Soviet Union's ethnic map was reshaped, although Khrushchev allowed the return of several ethnic groups to their former homelands. The economic contribution of forced labor, meanwhile, was much less efficient than in Nazi Germany, where it had been outsourced to private companies.[5]

The situation in Germany was different. In 1938, full employment had been reached and the war mobilization made the need for immigrant work acute. Conquests brought prisoners of war—a resource that had already been massively mobilized for forced labor during the First World War. Racial categorization guided the segregation, selection, and forced migration of Slavs. During the Second World War, approximately 13.5 million foreigners worked in Germany, with 12 million of them as forced labor. In fall 1944, out of a total of 8.1 million people subjected to forced labor, 2 million of them were prisoners of war. Historian Seymour Drescher has rightly pointed out that these numbers are comparable with the transatlantic slave trade: Germany managed to absorb as much forced labor in six years as did all the European colonies in America over a period of 350 years.[6] Racist hatred and intended racial extermination, however, created much higher wastage in the German case: nearly 7 million potential workers were lost to the German war effort through work exhaustion, starvation, and mass murder. As the death toll of young Germans on the battlefield dramatically increased—2.6 million Germans died unnecessarily in the last ten months of the war due to the Nazis' persistent denial of defeat—the Nazi leaders intended to develop a steady slave economy for the future that would follow victory—an aim voiced by Himmler.[7] This is the clearest case of a political project and practice of a slave system based on racial theories in twentieth-century Europe.

DISCRIMINATION AND SEGREGATION IN THE AMERICAS

In the Americas, racial policies shaped extensive discrimination and segregation, but they did not reach the twentieth-century European level of enslavement and extermination. The expulsion of Native Americans from their land was a long process more or less concluded during the nineteenth century. The processes of independence from Spanish rule extended individual rights and curbed communal rights over land, since liberal politicians privileged individual access to land over collective possession, and this development affected the Indians' traditional rights. In certain cases, like the Mapuche in Chile and Argentina, the expropriation of Indian land was prolonged throughout the nineteenth and twentieth centuries as a result of local resistance. In 1884, in Chile, the Mapuche were forced on to reservations. The reservation boundaries were repeatedly reduced between 1927 and 1961, until the reservations themselves were abolished in 1962.[8] The consequence of this process was that Native Americans were largely uprooted, lost much of their connection with their traditional environment, and became increasingly assimilated. In Brazil, the late occupation of a vast territory claimed by the state left peripheral regions, mainly in the Amazon basin, under the relative control of Native American tribes, but in a scattered way due to the nineteenth-century patterns of concentration and dispossession of populations. Native control of land did become regulated in time, largely after the creation of the Indian Protection Service in 1910; liberal policies were revived in the early 1960s, and again in the late 1980s. In 1961, the creation of the Indigenous Park of Xingu, an area of 26,420 square kilometers in Mato Grosso, Brazil, was designed to preserve the lands of fourteen ethnic groups and provide them with a special environment, initiating a movement toward the concentration of lands for Native protection.[9] Yet the discovery of precious minerals, exploitation of valuable timber, and more recently, development of soya plantations all have been reducing the boundaries of relatively autonomous Indian territories not formally protected. Some cases of atrocious criminality against Native Indians have been reported in various areas, showing that racist prejudices are still alive among people who equate Indian nomadic habits with vagrancy.

In North America, the British colonial legacy meant permanent conflict between local Native tribes and Europeans who arrived in search of land. These wars involved wide-scale destruction of Indian settlements along with standing crops and livestock and the displacement of populations, which sometimes led to the annihilation of whole tribes. The concept of the Indian reservation was invented by the British in Virginia in 1646, and spread during the nineteenth-century conquest of the West by the United States. The idea of confinement was the main motive for the hundreds of treaties imposed on nearly all the tribes after years of war. These treaties were rarely respected, since precious metals were found or new waves of migrants targeted previously reserved lands. The policy of transforming Native Americans into full-time farmers, formulated by President Jefferson, met natural resistance. The purchase of Louisiana, including the Midwest, from the French (1803) and seizure of Florida from the Spaniards (1810–19), followed by the annexation of Texas (1845), integration of Oregon, previously shared with the British (1846), and conquest of New Mexico, Arizona, and California from Mexico (1846–48) drove many of the local tribes into war. The conflicts between Euramericans and Native Americans increased after gold was discovered in California in 1848.

The Indian Act Removal of 1830 implied vast transfers of Native populations. Indian wars in all territories were prolonged until 1890, including major campaigns in 1848–61 and 1866–90. From a legal point of view, Native Americans were always considered as foreign nations, and thus British or US authorities signed treaties with them. They could be integrated as individuals, since intermarriage, informal unions, and adoptions always occurred, but not as collective entities, since they supposedly had their own sovereignty. This policy, questioned in 1831 by the Supreme Court in a judgment on a petition presented by the Cherokees, was terminated in 1871: Native Americans ceased to be recognized as foreign nations; they were treated as domestic dependent nations, wards of the government, without full sovereignty. Since then there have been agreements, but not treaties. Citizenship was only conferred on all Indians by the Indians Citizenship Act in 1924.[10] This created a peculiar situation—still true today—in which a Native American who was a member of a tribe had triple citizenship: of the United States, the state where they lived, and their tribe.

Until the 1920s and 1930s, Native Americans in North America were consistently considered an inferior race by Europeans or their descendants; compassion finally started to replace hostility. Persistent memories of their traditional ways of life helped American Indians to resist the long forced transition to modern society in which they were at a permanent disadvantage. They also represent a significant case of increasing miscegenation: eight out of ten Native Americans are of mixed descent, which once more raises the issue of racial definition based on people's own perceptions and self-identification. The US census of 2010 identified roughly 2.8 million Indians in a population of 308.7 million people (0.9 percent).[11] The Bureau of Indian Affairs supervises 225,000 square kilometers of land held in trust by the United States for the Native Americans, despite dramatic losses of land designated for reservations between 1880 and 1934. It serves 1.9 million Native Americans and Alaskan Natives; 400,000 people are currently the subjects of 565 federally recognized tribal governments.[12] Native Americans benefited from African Americans' civil rights campaign in the 1960s, although they always had their own agency, and their own political representation was responsible for the Indian Reorganization Act of 1934 (reinstitution of self-organization and self-government) and Indian Claim Commission Act of 1946 (monetary compensation for treaty violations and the mismanagement of resources). The improved image of Indians at all levels of education, development of specific Indian heritage museums, and reevaluation of Indian culture and history have changed white perceptions during the past fifty years.[13]

The same movement toward a reevaluation of Indian culture became widespread in Latin America in the 1980s and 1990s. At the same time, the development of favorable policies at the highest level of agencies dealing with natives coupled with increasing relations between the museum services and Native populations has not squared with realities on the ground, due to the economic interests of miners, farmers, and those who exploit equatorial forests. In Brazil, the latest census in 2010 identified around 818,000 indigenous people out of a population of 190.7 million (0.4 percent).[14] The inclusion of mixed-race descendants of Native Americans would produce a much higher number. Native Americans, who live within their traditional culture on specific reservations, have been better protected over the past decades, favored by environmental policies implemented in the Amazon, but the overall situation is far from satisfactory. In other Latin American countries, mainly Mexico or Peru, Native American descendants represent a significant portion of the population, generally coinciding with the lowest strata. Improved civil rights have reduced expressions of racism by the dominant strata, although economic and social problems have mounted in different regions, particularly in Chiapas, Mexico. In Latin America as a whole, an ethnic mix is generally the rule, although proportions vary.[15]

The Civil Rights Law of 1866 along with the Fourteenth and Fifteenth amendments of the US Constitution (1868 and 1870) granted citizenship to all people born or naturalized in the United States, guaranteeing equal voting rights to all citizens, no matter what their "race, color, or previous condition of servitude," and the Civil Rights Act of 1875 forbade racial segregation.[16] Yet significant white resistance in the southern states prevented the full implementation of these laws. The ideology of white supremacy was reinforced through paramilitary groups like the Ku Klux Klan, which exercised systematic violent intimidation against the black population. Segregation laws in schools, public transportation, public facilities, restaurants, hotels, theaters, and all places in the public sphere were published in the southern states from 1876 onward. The Supreme Court and US government accepted these policies, eager to heal the North/South divide after the rule of president and former general Ulysses Grant (1869–77). Segregation laws also forbade interracial marriage or sexual intercourse. Black migration to the northern states was followed by informal segregation there, especially in access to education, finance, and housing, but in the southern states, law formally reinforced segregation. The black population was effectively disenfranchised in the South; the poll tax and literacy qualifications excluded the vast majority of blacks from voting. The abolition of slavery imposed on the South at the end of the Civil War was not followed by real emancipation, contrary to what might have been predicted.[17] Blacks henceforth were subject to arbitrary violence without restraint, since they no longer represented the property (or capital) of slave owners, culminating in the extreme practice of lynching. While lynching was originally part of the general "Wild West" experience of expedient "justice," it became increasingly used in the southern states to intimidate black people who proved to be independent, bold, upwardly inclined farmers, claiming their rights or not being sufficiently submissive.

Sam Hose was a black plantation worker near Newman, Georgia. In April 1899, he went to collect his wages from a planter, Alfred Crawford. According to some versions of this story, Hose asked for a pay rise; according to others, he asked for wages that the planter owed him or permission to see his mother. Whatever it was that Hose requested, Crawford refused, and a harsh exchange of words followed. The next day, while Hose was chopping wood, the planter arrived and resumed the argument, threatening him with a pistol. Hose flung the ax in Crawford's direction, struck him on the head, and killed him instantly. Other versions place the event in Crawford's house. Hose was soon detained by a mob, which accused him of murdering the planter, pillaging his house, and raping Crawford's wife—an allegation she denied to a white detective. More than 2,000 people came out for the lynching, some on a special train from Atlanta. Hose was stripped of his clothes and chained to a tree. The self-appointed executioners cut off his fingers, ears, and genitals. They also skinned his face, and some people plunged knives into the victim's flesh. Then

Figure 19.1. Anonymous photograph of lynching W. C. Williams, October 15, 1938 in Ruston, Louisiana, US. Reprinted with permission from Bettman / Corbis.

they soaked Hose with kerosene and set fire to him with a torch. The mob watched the contortions of the body, distortion of Hose's features, and his eyes bulging out of their sockets. While Hose was still alive he cried only "Oh my God!" and "Oh Jesus!" When his body cooled down, the rest of his heart, liver, and bones were cut into small pieces and divided by the crowd.[18]

In this case there was a homicide, apparently in self-defense. In many other instances there was scarcely any evidence, while lynching on the basis of mistaken identities increased. But this did not matter, as long as lynchings fulfilled the purpose of terrorizing black people and keeping them "in their place." Hose's torture was standard; it matches many other descriptions. Lynching photos were sometimes transformed into "tourist-style" postcards of Southern white pride. It is especially striking that the participants posed next to the executed; nobody hid their face. The photographs functioned as proof of the validity of the act.[19] Yet they also compromised and involved the community, underlining cohesion and normality against transgression. Obviously white people did not consider lynching a crime. In the few cases that came to trial, all-white juries acquitted the accused. Respected citizens, local authorities, and even senators joined the lynching. They were religious people, who would go to church without feeling a shadow of guilt. It was openly argued that lynching represented justice, despite the fact that it was far more sadistic than early modern executions (except under riot conditions). Whole families turned out for the occasion, and parents asked that schools close down for the children to join in. In the photos, some people smile at the burned bodies. At home, white people hung photos of the event on their walls, with "relics" (trophies) of the victim. This regular practice of illegal executions continued until the 1940s, with several cases still being registered in the 1950s and 1960s. An estimated 4,742 blacks were lynched between 1882 and 1968.[20]

Contempt, debasement, and dehumanization were present in this extraordinarily prolonged white racial hate in the southern United States as a response to emancipation. Segregation, as we have seen, was not exclusive to the South; the participation of black people in the US armed forces in the First World War was still defined by segregation, only attenuated in the Second World War. It was the experience of black sacrifice that in 1948, brought about President Truman's Executive Order 9981, which established equal treatment for all races in the army. It took a courageous and long struggle for civil rights, led by black movements, associations, and respected church figures such as Martin Luther King Jr., to challenge segregation laws and force federal intervention. Civil rights advocates had to withstand murder, detention, permanent vilification, and abuse, all with dignity to attract support and reverse white hostility. The radicalization of the movement played a role in the changing mood of the 1960s. As the Cold War was on the doorstep through the Cuban missile crisis, the shameful segregation of a significant portion of the American population could not be squared with the United States' claims to lead the "Free World."

During the Second World War, other sections of the US population, such as citizens of Japanese origin, were targeted and detained in internment camps (more than 100,000), but the regular segregation of the black population persisted for a long time. The turning point came in 1954, when the Supreme Court finally recognized that segregation in public (state) schools was unconstitutional—a decision forcefully implemented in the face of southern white resistance. Desegregation was further advanced in 1964 with the Civil Rights Act, which prohibited discrimination of any kind, followed in 1965 by the Voting Rights Act, which made all restrictions on black people's right to vote illegal and created conditions for wide voter registration. In the same year, President Lyndon Johnson issued Executive Order 11246, which required government contractors to take affirmative action concerning minority employment. In 1968, the Civil Rights Act forbade discrimination in the sale, rental, and financing of housing. Desegregation went further with the new Civil Rights Acts of 1988 and 1991, which banned employment discrimination by private institutions receiving federal funds.[21] Informal segregation still persists, being particularly evident in neighborhood composition, but it is not hidden anymore; it has become a major political issue. Racism did not evaporate, and yet it ceased to be backed by the law. Moreover, the civil rights movement in the United States created an example that influenced the struggle for reform elsewhere, contributing to the antiracist norm that has spread across the world in the past fifty years.

The struggle for the abolition of slavery followed by segregation influenced the classification of races. Even though until the beginning of the nineteenth century there had been some space for mixed-race people, by the end of the century the opposition of whites and blacks was paramount; mixed-race people disappeared from classifications of race; an element of black ancestry classified a person as black. White purity of race was the criterion for high status, favoring poor whites at the expense of black people. African Americans benefited in time from the civil rights movement. They acquired access to better conditions of work, finance, and housing. Many problems of economic and social exclusion still persist, though. Black individuals can climb the social ladder, but they will still be identified by their racial background. In the meantime, a self-defensive logic of identity turned the historical classification of races based on white perceptions of hierarchy on its head: African American communities became naturally proud of their descent, and started to use the noun race to promote their shared inheritance with the civil rights movement. The desire for race replaced and defied contempt for race.[22]

The opposite occurs in Brazil, where mixed-race people can become white. Three principal reasons explain this phenomenon. First, the frontiers between the white and black populations became blurred over time, with the proportion of mixed-race people reaching a significant level early on. Second, the management of a slave society by a white elite of 20 to 30 percent of the population was historically based on significant manumission, depending on a buffer of skilled mixed-race workers and supervisors. Third, Brazil is situated in Iberian America, where mixed-race populations were the rule, although the mix was based much more on Native Americans in the Spanish colonies of Mexico and Peru. Mexican José Vasconcelos, who in 1929 published the crucial book *The Cosmic Race*, was the first to voice pride about being of mixed race.[23] In Brazil, the ideology of white supremacy, which had played a major role in attracting massive European migration between 1880 and 1930, was decisively challenged by Gilberto Freyre's book, *Casa Grande e Senzala*, published in 1933 and translated into English as *The Masters and the Slaves*.[24] Freyre refounded Brazilian national mythology and national pride based on the virtues of mixing.[25] He virtually ignored Natives, but stressed African and European cultural, economic, and social inputs. The consequences of this turning point were vast: racial classifications in Brazil are still complex, as several categories are used for mixed-race people's self-identification in the census, and individual social mobility is generally equated with racial mobility, so that successful mixed-race people will perceive themselves as white. The Brazilian problem remains that social exclusion is generally connected with blackness. In the 1950s and 1960s, Marvin Harris, Fernando Henrique Cardoso, and Octávio Ianni challenged the myth of relative racial harmony through research that identified deep-rooted racism in everyday life.[26] Since then, black movements have been increasing their political influence, and the restoration of democracy in 1985 was followed by affirmative action aimed at mitigating social exclusion.[27] The North American model is now firmly based on desegregation legislation. The Brazilian model is less efficient in terms of antiracist legislation, particularly when it comes to discrimination in the job market, but it benefits from the tradition of individual racial

mobility and acceptance of an extended gradation in skin color that make race less dominant as a social marker.

APARTHEID AND GENOCIDE IN AFRICA

Africa showed more resistance than the Americas to European culture and its legacies. This
can be explained by not just political and economic structures but up to the late nineteenth
century, the natural effect of diseases: in Africa, it was the European immune system that
could not cope with malaria, cholera, or yellow fever. Racism is largely a colonial legacy,
although the idea of an exclusive European input has been challenged by drawing attention to Muslim interaction, particularly in the Sahel, West Africa, as well as the historical
antagonism of African ethnicities fueled by territorial disputes.[28] Even if the transatlantic
slave trade was built on previous African and Muslim practices, its extraordinary impact is
undeniable, both on perceptions of African people and the regulation of colonial societies.
In most of Africa, European colonialism was only effective between the 1880s and 1950s,
which means for a much shorter period of time than in the Americas. Even in the Portuguese case, territorial domain was reduced between the fifteenth and nineteenth centuries
to coastal enclaves, with the exceptions of Mozambique, where the Portuguese presence was
significant in the Zambezi valley, and Angola, where they exerted great influence along the
Cuanza River, and through the relatively stable alliance they maintained with the kingdom
of Congo for nearly two centuries. Miscegenation remained extremely limited in Portuguese Africa. In 1959 (the last year of a racial census), less than 1 percent of the population in Angola and Mozambique was classified as mixed race, while on the islands of São
Tomé and Príncipe mixed-race people rose to 7 percent. Only on the Cape Verdean islands,
where the figure was 70 percent, was there a mixed society comparable to that of Brazil,
although not based on a plantation economy. The transition from slavery and later forced
labor to free labor was hindered by late industrialization, but gained impetus in the 1960s
during the colonial wars when Angola and Mozambique registered extraordinary economic
growth. The colonial system was naturally based on racial discrimination and, in the case
of Mozambique, informal segregation influenced by the South African experience. In all
cases, independence meant the political repossession of these territories by Africans. Racial prejudices did not entirely disappear, however; the connection of the ruling party (the
MPLA) to the significant mixed-race elite of Luanda was used in the 1980s and 1990s by
opponents of the regime, who tried to assert their political credentials based on blackness.
In the instances of the French, Belgian, and English colonies, the late arrival of colonial
rule was marked by the distance that colonial elites adopted based on racial prejudice and
discriminatory action. The atmosphere in these colonies can best be glimpsed in journals
such as the famous *L'Afrique fantôme* by Michel Leiris, published the year after the return
of the French ethnographic mission from Dakar to Djibouti (1931–33).[29] Racial hierarchy,
prejudice, paternalism, derision, problems of colonial administration, the plunder of local

cultures under the guise of protection, and flaws of anthropological research were recorded in a candid and reflective way.

The Germans' colonial presence in Namibia was limited in its time span (1886–1914), but surprisingly devastating. The Herero, a seminomadic population of shepherds and farmers, occupied a fertile part of the central lands of Namibia coveted by German colonists since most of the country was a desert. The colonists' pressure naturally triggered native resistance, which led to incidents in January 1904, in turn serving as a pretext for a vast military operation led by General Lothar von Trotha. The general conducted an implacable pursuit of the Herero through the desert, with the latter suffering a massive death toll, while their cattle disappeared due to hunger and thirst. Von Trotha aimed to expel the Herero from Namibia and exterminate those who tried to stay, explicitly including women and children. His decision was taken locally, but backed by the government in Berlin. In early 1905, the German Parliament revoked von Trotha's policy of extermination and ordered the detention of the surviving Herero, who were placed in concentration camps and used as forced labor until 1908.[30] Demographic estimates vary, but from an estimated population of eighty thousand, only fifteen thousand Herero survived. They were forbidden to own land or cattle—the two basic conditions for their subsistence. They were not the only ethnic group targeted. The Nama were slaughtered at the same time, although their population did not decline to such a low level.

In 1948, the UN Convention on the Prevention and Punishment of the Crime of Genocide listed the following as significant acts: killing members of the targeted group, causing serious bodily or mental harm, deliberately inflicting conditions of life that will bring about the physical destruction of the group, imposing measures intended to prevent births within the group, and forcibly transferring children from one group to another.[31] The Namibian case clearly fulfills the first three criteria: the first year of brutal eradication and the vulnerable position in which the Herero were left did not require the other two, even though the change of policy probably spared the remaining 20 percent of the population. It is a clear case of genocide of an ethnic group, with publicly defined intent and the corresponding practice of extermination. Racial prejudice played an undeniable role based on contempt for African ethnicities and irritation at the resistance of this ethnic group. The genocide was linked to the political project of the colonists: to occupy the best lands and expel the natives.

The South African case is much more complex, never reaching the level of genocide, yet establishing a succession of forms of segregation until the apartheid era (1948–94). It also reveals the inheritance of the colonial period, in which the occupation of the hinterland was radically extended during the eighteenth and nineteenth centuries. The British took over what had been a Dutch colony during the Napoleonic Wars, and their main impact was the abolition of slavery in 1833. People living on the frontiers were believed to make much more use of segregation in their later push into the interior than in the first stage of the colonial period, which was defined by extensive sexual intercourse and intermarriage with the Khoikhoi. The new Boer republics—Natal, Orange, and South African—excluded nonwhites from voting, offering a contrast with relatively liberal practices in Cape Town for most of the nineteenth century. In 1854, the Refugee Law in Natal stipulated that black immigrants must serve for three years at official wages. This issue of native labor proved to be crucial in the new trend toward segregation. In the 1860s, indentured labor was imported from India to work in the sugar plantations, but free Indians who followed as traders were discriminated against through taxes and political exclusion; the Boer republics simply barred them from owning or renting fixed property, and in 1907 Indian immigration was limited. In 1877, corporal punishment for work infractions was legalized, while native mobility became restricted and reserves were created, followed by the forced transfer of populations. In 1913, the Native Land Act forbade natives to occupy land outside their reserves, except as labor-tenants, thus completely depriving native people of land. Territorial segregation was reinforced in 1920 by the Native Affairs Act. Over time, the exclusion of native people from access to prime land meant that land was released for white business activity.[32]

Economic change played a major role in this process: the discovery of diamonds in 1871 in Kimberley and gold in 1886 in Transvaal attracted extraordinary migration, led to two wars that integrated the Boer republics into South Africa, and created an industrialization based on the racial division of labor, limiting black employment to unskilled work. The impact of the mining industry was visible in the organization of its workforce along racial lines; the law of 1894 restricted craft apprenticeships to whites, thereby excluding black people from skilled labor. Urban residential segregation hardened in the 1890s, but it was during the twentieth century that it became a widespread reality, advanced in particular by the Natives Act of 1923. The division of religious services for whites and blacks, separation of hospitals and prisons, and informal segregation of train wagons (third class for black people) had already been established during the second half of the nineteenth century. Institutionalized segregation in education started with the School Boards Act of 1905, firmed up in 1923. In the meantime, hotels, sports, theater, and other leisure facilities were all touched by segregation procedures reinforced during the 1930s and 1940s.

British policies of assimilation had given way to policies of segregation in the 1890s; successive wars with resistant native ethnic groups and integration of the Boer republics explain this new development, in line with the segregation laws of the southern United States. Indeed, South Africa and the southern United States offer a telling comparison.[33] In 1936, the African franchise in Cape Town was abolished, while more land was allocated to reserves to suit the segregationist vision developed by the white political parties. Thus the establishment of apartheid in 1948 was built on strong foundations. Territorial segregation was pushed to the limits: in 1951, the Bantu Authorities Act defined a political process of retribalization of the reserves; in 1959, the Bantu Self-Government Act reinforced the fiction of African independent entities, supposedly distinct from an ethnic point of view; in 1970, the Bantu Homeland Citizenship Act compelled all Africans to become citizens of a Bantustan, even if they lived in a white area, in an attempt to deny them full South African citizenship. Between 1960 and 1985, 3.5 million people were forced to relocate. In 1949, mixed marriages were forbidden, and the following year sexual relations between white and black people became a crime. Separate amenities for white and black people developed in the 1950s.

Scientific racialism once more proved critical to the ideological justification of apartheid a century after the (relative) success of the same process in the United States. The idea of God's plan for the world, or God as "great divider," was adapted to the conditions of South Africa, now at a microlevel of white and black territorial segregation that had nothing to do with Agassiz's idea of connection between race and environment. Immutable racial differences, supposed black inferiority and white superiority, were again claimed in the face of international scrutiny, also carried out in the late 1940s and 1950s, by numerous international forums dedicated to discussions of the racist background of the Second World War. A strong African movement and international criticism brought about the progressive isolation of the apartheid regime, triggering ideological shifts, especially the idea of the "separate development" of different races and unsustainable argument that segregated facilities were of similar quality. The system declined in the 1970s with the crisis of the unviable Bantustans, legalization of black trade unions, and breakdown of segregation. Mixed marriages were now permitted under certain circumstances and multiracial access to universities followed as well as the attempt to integrate colored people and Indians into a political tricameral system established in 1984. In 1989, the fall of the Berlin Wall provided the final blow to the apartheid regime, which had claimed to be a bulwark against Communism. In 1994, Africans were finally free to vote in the first serious elections ever held. This was a major outcome of the process of desegregation, but there is still a long way to go to overcome the massive inequality introduced by the systematic dispossession of Africans by white settlers.[34]

The genocide of the Tutsi by the Hutu in Rwanda could be interpreted as a classic interethnic feud, but it falls into the definition of racism as prejudice and discriminatory action against a group believed to share specific attributes inherited from generation to generation. The evaluation of people according to skin color is just one prejudice among others—an often-absent one, as we have seen in relation to the racial divide in the Ottoman Empire and Nazi Germany. In Rwanda, the European racial classifications became interlinked with a traditional political practice of ethnic distinction and division. European ideals of beauty and racial divide were projected onto the region that is now Rwanda and Burundi: the Tutsi (15 percent of the population, traditionally shepherds controlling most of the land and political power) were considered closer to the classical beauty ideal, due to their long thin noses, tallness, and allegedly lighter skin color. The legend of biblical Ham's descent was once more invoked to place the Tutsi close to the Cushites and Ethiosemites. But in the 1980s, this assumption was replaced by the genetic absence in the Tutsi of the sickle cell (found in other peoples in the region, and responsible for the latter's long-term resistance to malaria) and the Tutsi's ability to digest milk (much higher than among the Hutus). In the late colonial period, the Belgians gave different identity cards to the Tutsi and Hutu, contributing to the separation between the ethnicities, even though the two already had a significant level of intermarriage, increased in the 1970s and 1980s. The Tutsi were first privileged over the Hutu, due to the historical political dominion of herders over cultivators, but eventually the Belgians accepted a Hutu political revolution in the late 1950s, which had a profound effect on the independence process, overthrowing the Tutsi monarchy and creating a republic.

Violence between the two ethnic groups, racialized through the process of conflict over power and resources, mainly access to land, started during the process of independence. Thousands of Tutsi refugees escaped from Rwanda and Burundi, primarily to Uganda, and then thousands of Hutu refugees fled, mainly to Congo. In 1972, the mass killings that the Tutsi-controlled army of Burundi carried out were responsible for Hutu flight; Tutsi refugees fled during the Hutu uprisings in 1993. Refugees from both ethnicities performed an important political role in other countries, particularly the Tutsi in Uganda, where they fought under the National Resistance Movement, and became part of the government and army elite until evicted from power. Created mainly by Tutsi in 1979, the Rwandese Alliance for National Unity was replaced by the Rwandan Patriotic Front in 1986, and the latter decided to invade Rwanda in 1990 with former Tutsi commanders and soldiers of the Uganda National Resistance Movement. Civil war followed, only to be suspended in 1993 by a precarious UN-mediated peace agreement, which collapsed on April 6, 1994 when President Juvénal Habyarimana's plane was shot down near Kigala's airport, killing him along with the president of Burundi, Cyprien Ntaryamira. Civil war immediately broke out again—the Rwandan Patriot Front battalion stationed near Kigali had to fight its way back into the northern mountains—but at the same time a vast operation of genocide of the Tutsi and moderate Hutus, who were considered traitors, was launched by the government and Hutu militias all over the territory, indicating central planning and coordination. It is estimated that a half million people died. This genocide only stopped with the final victory of the Rwandan Patriotic Front in early July 1994. The dehumanization of the Tutsi preceded the killings: Hutu newspapers condemned the Tutsi as cockroaches to be eliminated, opposed intermarriage, and denounced normal relationships between the two ethnicities as treason.[35]

OUTCASTS AND DISCRIMINATION IN ASIA

A comparison of the situations described above with Asia becomes more significant when we consider that the continent was less touched than others by the European expansion. It is important to explore whether the peoples of Asia experienced prejudices that went beyond ethnocentrism to define hierarchies as well as propose a racial construct that justified political dominion or enhanced political projects. The following brief sketch will concentrate on the three main Asian civilizations: Chinese, Japanese, and Hindu. The classic texts of Confucianism set out the division between the core Han culture and barbarians.[36] Chinese ways or manners were defined as the standard against which the behavior of people outside the empire was evaluated. The cultural definition of barbarian could be compared to the Greek one: theoretically, the barbarian could be culturally assimilated, becoming Chinese. Physical features and cultural dispositions, though, were often blurred: lineage and descent played an important role in the construction of identity, and the idea of the immutable "nature" of different peoples is present in the Chinese tradition. The opposition between humans and animals, which we already saw in Europe and America, used to denigrate people when they are equated with animals was also crucial in the representation of "savages" or tribal minorities living on the peripheries of the empire, particularly in mountainous regions. The Rong were compared to birds, the Di (a northern tribe) to dogs, the Man and Min (southern tribes) to reptiles, and the Qiang to sheep. The separation of common and fine people from mean people (servants, attendants, entertainers, prostitutes, actors, beggars, boat people, fisherfolk, and slaves) was legally abolished by Emperor Yongzheng in 1723, but prejudices and discrimination persisted, especially concerning intermarriage.

The Book of Rites (third century BC) divided the world into five parts, naturally making the imperial center the hub of civilization, surrounded by the royal domain and lands of the feudal princes, beyond which lay a zone of pacification separating the two central zones from the outer two, which were inhabited by barbarians and savages. Color symbolism was used in the representation of the cardinal points of the compass: black for the north, white for the west, red for the east, blue for the south, and yellow (the color of the emperor, glory, and advancement) at the center. The myth of the Yellow Emperor Huang Di, purportedly born in 2704 BC, considered the ancestor of all Han, certainly played a part in the tradition of yellow race, which was introduced in Europe at the end of the seventeenth century and assumed by Chinese reformers in the nineteenth century. The division between raw and cooked barbarians (savage and submissive) reflects the projection of an archaic opposition of food habits onto the hierarchy of peoples of the world. The Chinese discovered African people late, but from the twelfth century on, black skin, curly hair, and the habit of eating raw food were equated with devil slaves. The opposition of white and black can be observed in China from early times, as in other Asian cultures: the praise of "white jade" skin is found in the earliest poetry, and gradations of color not only separated the Chinese from the other peoples of the world but also distinguished the "black-headed" laborers, showing the relationship between external and internal (social) divisions, as in Europe.[37] Hair was another important physical marker due to the Chinese lack of facial and body hair. Hairy people were necessarily barbarians, like the black peoples of the Nam-Viet Cham Empire, Khmers, or wavy-haired peoples of the mountains, not to mention the distant people of the Andaman Islands (the Bay of Bengal), believed to be anthropophagi (a fearful perception of boundaries to civilization shared with Europeans). Successive contacts with Europeans confirmed the equation of hairy people with barbarians, while white skin color developed connotations of an ash-white devilish nature. Black skin color was perceived as ugly and dirty, like coal, while black people were considered slaves.

The rule of dynasties of foreign origin, particularly the Mongols (Yuan, 1271–1368) and Manchu (Qing, 1644–1911), contributed both to keeping the system relatively open and asserting the Han as the main ethnicity. During the eighteenth century the idea of descent took root politically, and the Chinese Empire turned toward a rigid classification and hierarchy of ethnicities. The refusal of marriage with foreign people and perception of mixed ethnicities as mongrel races became more widespread. But it was the erosion of the Qing

Dynasty throughout the nineteenth century that unleashed ideas close to those of racial purity, fueled by growing opposition to the dynasty and ethnic rebellions: the Taiping Rebellion, led by the Hakka (Han minority) in Guangxi, Jiangxi, Zhejiang, Anhui, and Jiangsu (1850–64); the Panthai Rebellion of the Hui Minority in Yunan (1856–73); the Dungan Revolt, partly Muslim, in Shaanxi, Gansu, Ningxia, and Xinjiang (1862–77); and the Hakka-Punti (both Han minorities) Clan Wars in Guangdong (1855–67). The Taiping Rebellion alone resulted in an estimated twenty million dead—the worst civil war of the nineteenth century anywhere in the world. Although these rebellions involved ethnic allegiances and enmity, racial divide was not their main motivation.

Defeat by the British (the Opium Wars, 1839–42, 1856–60) and Japanese (1894–95) marked the transition to nationalism blended with notions of race, coinciding with similar developments in Europe. Old ideas of aliens as devils, subhuman, animals, hairy, and stinking were combined with the belief that these people wanted to enslave the Chinese. The Japanese, still considered vassals of the empire, were denigrated as dwarf slaves. Although the opening of China to the Western world was slower than that of Japan, with the translation of scientific authors occurring later, Chinese missions in Europe and the United States in the last decades of the nineteenth and early decades of the twentieth century, followed by a significant number of Chinese scholars in Western and Japanese universities, ensured the spread of the ideas of Lamarck, Darwin, and Spencer. Cultural borrowing, as usual, was creative and diversified; it is difficult to define a mainstream trend. Tan Sitong (1865–98) established a hierarchy of peoples of the world dominated by the Chinese states (China, Korea, Tibet, Vietnam, and Burma), followed by the barbarian states (Japan, Russia, Europe, and North America), and the States of the Beasts (Africa, South America, and Australia). This classification blended race and political geography, which had recently been introduced in China, to define the core of the Chinese universe. Yan Fu (1853–1923), who spread the ideas of Darwin, Huxley, and Spencer in China, abandoned cultural divisions in favor of a racial construction based on physical features and lineage. Color symbolism established a common ground between the East and West: the four races identified by Yan Fu were yellow (in most of Asia), white (in Europe), brown (on the islands from the Philippines to India), and black (in Africa and tropical areas). Liang Qichao (1873–1929), who created modern journalism in China and toured the United States, introduced a fifth race, the red American Indians, adapting the hierarchy to fit in the symbolic importance of the number five for the Chinese. Other reformers developed the intellectual divide between the yellow and white races as well as races that were red, brown, and black. The definition of the four or five races drew both from scientific racialism and Darwinism: they were immutable and connected to specific environments; and the idea of the survival of the fittest justified the progressive extinction of the red, brown, and black races as white ones expanded. Reformers who credited the Han with the ability to react and face the Western challenge advanced the same sense of threat at the idea of sharing the destiny of the lower races.

The idea of national racial homogeneity became crucial in the early decades of the twentieth century, shared by reformers and revolutionaries alike, and was quickly adopted by the republican intellectual elite under Sun Yat-sen (1866–1925), who praised the Chinese (Han) race as four hundred million strong against the mingled races of Mongolians (a few million), Manchu (one million), Tibetans (a few million), and Turks (over a million). The Chinese perception of India in this period is revealing: the British had conquered India due to the internal divisions of the caste system, which prevented racial and national cohesion. Meanwhile, North American prejudices against black people had seeped into Chinese reasoning, while German prejudices against Jews were also reproduced; Africans and Australian aborigines were supposed to have small brains; black slaves were related to gorillas and Malays to the orangutan, while the Burmese were described as lazy, the Thais as cowards, and the Vietnamese as frivolous and dishonest. Measurement of skulls, bodies, and noses followed, together with the discovery of blood types during the First World War; the prevalent Han racial type was defined by Li Chi as brachycephalic-leptorrhine (small nosed) with blood type O, although the IQ tests were largely dismissed as culturally biased. Eugenics also had its Chinese promoters, even though people like Zhang Junjun, who worried about the decline of the race and need to improve it, never managed to create any significant institutional framework for their ideas. A political need to integrate other ethnicities damped down claims about racial purity; several intellectuals in the 1930s underlined the contribution of other ethnicities, praising cultural mixing and the infusion of new blood. White color ceased to be viewed as superior, while scant body hair was considered a crucial sign of an advanced race.

Pan-Asianism emerged in different periods as a political project of coalition against white expansion, only to be knocked back by Japanese imperialism; the anti-Japanese caricatures of the 1930s defined the invaders as hairy, beastly midgets. Naturally, the Communist revolution abolished the discourse on race to instead stress the unity of the working class along with the struggle against the bourgeoisie and remaining feudal elements. The conflict with Russia in the 1960s nevertheless created some ambiguity, sparked by China's claim to leadership of the nonaligned developing countries. The modern image of China as a pluralistic, multiethnic state cannot be dismissed, since it represents an extraordinary step forward, even if the autonomous status of fifty-five recognized ethnic minorities or the management of the politically controversial (re)integration of Tibet represent major challenges. The policy of forced internal migrations was followed in the 1970s and 1980s by the recognition of ethnicities, but in the meantime the ethnic landscape has been entirely transformed—for instance, in Xinjiang, where the autochthonous Uyghur, who were dominant, are about to become a minority, overwhelmed by the migrant Han. The Han in various parts of China see the Uyghur as primitive, religious (Muslim), and criminal, unable to speak Mandarin or adjust to development, and able to make a living only by selling food.[38] Internal and seasonal migrations have produced new tensions against the background of enormous industrialization, while ethnicities are defined in terms of descent, religion, language, and cultural proximity to the Han.[39] Internal divisions traditionally label tribal people, particularly the Zou, mountain aborigines of Taiwan, Yi, Miao, and Yao of the mountains of southwest China, as primitive and backward.[40] Even the Han, who constitute

92 percent of the 1.3 billion Chinese, are not immune to internal feuds, as revealed by the nineteenth-century conflicts between the Hakka and Punti, or divergent experiences of the Hakka diaspora in different regions and countries.[41]

To sum up, in China there has been a traditional idea of descent, cultural difference, and hierarchy concerning peripheral people, although the need to assimilate other peoples culturally has prevented extreme forms of discriminatory action. Conquest and rule by dynasties of foreign origin kept the system relatively open, with the selection of administrative and political groups through exams, and their promotion by performance, producing a situation in which hierarchy was theoretically based on merit and not on heredity, on individual mobility and not on immutable lineage. Even so, the centrality of the Han people became progressively linked to the idea of pure race throughout the eighteenth and nineteenth centuries, following the impact of the Western divisions of humankind. Nationalism combined with theories of race was introduced at the turn of the twentieth century as a response to the general crisis of the Qing Dynasty. This racist trend was generally interrupted by the Communist conquest of power, although prejudices against minorities are still visible and active.

Japan differs from China in four key ways. Its territory is made up of islands, which long prevented a comprehensive vision of the world, although the traditional mythology of the divine origin of the emperor and their subjects or descendants supported the idea that the Japanese were a superior people (a concept still taught by Hirata Atsutane, 1776–1843). The Meiji Restoration in 1868 as a reaction to Western intrusion and the forced opening of Japanese ports produced an extraordinarily fast industrialization and modernization, much in advance of China; while China had expanded its borders up to the eighteenth century by integrating contiguous territories, Japan's scattered colonial experience came in the late nineteenth and early twentieth centuries, and was developed during the Second World War under the spell of Western imperialism. Finally, the polarized notions of purity and impurity of occupations made their way into Japan early, at least from the sixth through eighth centuries onward, producing a caste of untouchables segregated by law until the nineteenth century—the impact of which is still felt today. The Japanese missions to the United States and Europe in 1860 and 1871–73 absorbed racial constructs concerning not only other peoples of the world but also internal minorities in the Western world, such as African Americans and Jews. Historian Kuma Kunitake assimilated the idea of the inevitable decline of the red Indian population, and expressed concern for the Asian population. Takahashi Yoshio proposed improving the Japanese stock through intermarriage with Europeans. The idea was so widespread that Prime Minister Itō Hirobumi (1841–1909) consulted Spencer on this issue, though Spencer's response was negative.[42]

The Japanese shared the Chinese revulsion toward hairy people, only this time the negative stereotype was projected onto their own indigenous people, the Ainu. They used Western prejudices against the Chinese to depict the Sino-Japanese War of 1894–95 as a conflict between civilization and decadent Oriental despotism.[43] Darwin and Spencer were widely translated between the 1870s and 1890s, and social Darwinism became an important

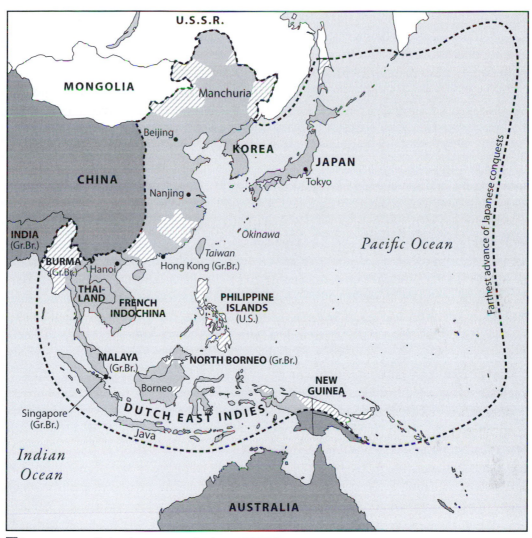

Japanese-controlled territory at surrender, August 14, 1945

Area occupied by Japanese and regained by Allies before August 1945

Allied-controlled territory

Map 19.4. Japanese expansion, 1894–1945.
Source: Jane Burbank and Frederick Cooper, *Empires in World History: Power and the Politics of Difference* (Princeton, NJ: Princeton University Press, 2010), 401

theoretical framework, with Katō Hiroyuki advocating constitutional monarchy and representative democracy as required by social and natural evolution.[44] The Japanese greatly impressed the Western powers with their victories against the Chinese and Russians; they were the only Asian power invited to the negotiations for the Treaty of Versailles after the First World War. The Japanese government and diplomats were so aware of Western racial prejudices that they tried to introduce the principle of racial equality into the treaty. The

British and North Americans refused this request, not wanting to abolish their restrictions on Asian (and Japanese) immigration into Australia and the United States. The French were the only ones to support racial equality as a universal principle, clearly spotting Wilson's contradictory ideas on self-determination and racial inequality.[45]

The idea of a homogeneous population is regarded similarly in Japan and China: the Yamato constitute around 96 percent of the total population of 128 million people recorded in the Japanese census of 2010.[46] Estimates of the real size of minorities—Chinese, Koreans, Brazilians, Filipinos, and Ainu (natives of Hokkaido and the Kuril Islands)—vary significantly; there are also 2 million foreigners, including a significant number of Muslim workers from Pakistan, Bangladesh, and Iran (probably 100,000). Moreover, the 1.6 million Ryukyuans, southern islanders categorized as Yamato, were only integrated into Japan in 1872 after a long period during which they had been a tributary people both of China (from 1372) and Japan (from 1609). They were not considered pure Japanese; their language and culture were suppressed for decades. Suspicion concerning their loyalty emerged during the Second World War, and the Japanese slaughtered the Ryukyuans during the battle of Okinawa against the North Americans. The Ryukyu Islands remained under US administration until they were returned to Japan in 1972. The indigenous Ainu, who lived in the northern areas of Hokkaido and on the Kuril Islands, saw their territories effectively integrated only after the Meiji Restoration of 1868 (the occupation of the Kuril Islands came with the Treaty of Saint Petersburg negotiated with Russia in 1875). The Japanese (Wajin) quickly outnumbered the Ainu, expelling them from the more productive agricultural lands. The Ainu were reduced to a minority, considered primitive, and stuck in their traditional way of life: they were exhibited in a "native village" at the Industrial Exposition of Osaka in 1903, along with Taiwanese aborigines as well as Malay and Javanese people. This display was modeled on the Universal Exposition in Paris in 1889, in which colonial peoples had been exhibited as "products of the land." The Exposition in Osaka was attended by 4.3 million people, which meant that a racial construction and contempt for colonial peoples were shared by a significant percentage of the population.[47] The Japanese government only started to seriously address the situation of the Ainu in the 1960s and 1970s, after a long period of discrimination and segregation.

The Japanese colonial experience, mainly in Taiwan (conquered in 1895) and Korea (annexed in 1910), led to forced movements of population and the introduction of a cheap labor force in Japan, particularly in the 1920s and 1930s, due to the swift absorption of working-age people into employment, and involvement of Japan in war with China (1937–45) and later the Second World War (1941–45), which meant an increasing need for labor not only for military-industrial development but also for the basic needs of the population. The number of Koreans in Japan increased from 14,000 in 1917 to 1 million in 1939 and 2.1 million in 1945.[48] The Koreans were employed in mines and factories, systematically receiving much lower salaries than their Japanese colleagues in the same jobs. During the colonial period, the Koreans enjoyed Japanese citizenship and access to welfare, but this ended with Korean independence. The Koreans who stayed in Japan (now probably 800,000 people, depending on the criteria for inclusion of naturalized people) had to cope not only with a lack of citizenship but also with widespread discrimination in relation to work and housing. The problem only started to be addressed in the 1960s and 1970s, when the Japanese signed international treaties that directly or indirectly concerned the rights of the Koreans.[49] The process of naturalization became more open in the 1990s, but prejudices against an inferior race, due to its colonial background and the division of modern Korea, still put a strain on the community's identity.

The situation of the Chinese in Japan (probably 600,000 people), partly descended from migrants from colonial Taiwan, is by comparison better due to diplomatic relations with China and public recognition of the tremendous economic growth in their country of origin. The status of the Chinese is also different: they are more affluent, based on their occupations as merchants and artisans. The example of Kobe's Chinatown, promoted as a major tourist venue since 1985, favors the perception of the community, although prejudices have not vanished. The Brazilian community (more than 300,000 people), which took advantage of the opening of Japanese frontiers in 1991 to the Nikkei, descendants of Japanese abroad, is perceived as a noisy population whose relaxed and expressive manners, acquired through four generations in Brazil, do not fit into the reserved and controlled local culture. The Filipino community (around 300,000 people) is quite recent—the result of a boom in tourism and domestic service. The Japanese perception of the Filipinos as mostly prostitutes and entertainers is pervasive, and affects mixed marriages with the Japanese (a significant percentage of the total).[50]

The existence of outcasts (untouchable people) most strongly differentiates Japan from China in the area of prejudice and discriminatory action against specific population groups. Shinto and Buddhism converged to define the spiritual and physical notion of pollution connected to specific occupations, especially the removal of dead bodies (human or animal), slaughter of animals (Buddhism explicitly condemns interference with the cycle of life), and preparation or use of animal products. Wounds, blood, death, and dirt all come under the same notion of impurity, which not only stigmatizes particular professions—for example, butchers, grave diggers, and executioners—but also women who are menstruating or approaching childbirth. Women had to carry the stigma of impurity in specific, recurrent moments of their lives not only in Japan but also in many other cultures, including European ones. The untouchable caste in traditional Japanese society included two different types of people: the settled and the vagrant. The first group, the Eta (meaning literally, much filthy), were untouchable as a result of their polluted occupations: dealing with leather, bone, gut, or fur; slaughtering animals and butchery; taming animals; manufacturing saddles, armor, bowstrings, and musical instrument strings; employment as village guards, executioners, and providers of mortuary services; work in the soil fertilizer trade; making baskets and straw sandals; and textile dying. Such people were locked in the same occupations from generation to generation, carrying with them a hereditary stigma. The second group, called Hinin (or nonpeople), were beggars, prostitutes, entertainers, and fugitives from justice, but these people could settle down in normal communities—meaning that their status was neither acquired nor reproduced by descent. The Eta could own land, and specialize in trades such as weaving and leather production, achieving significant wealth at times; they even had local self-government, and could enter into contracts with "normal" communities to perform work traditionally considered inferior. Yet all untouchable people were segregated: they had to address so-called normal people through the backdoor, avoid touching these people, and could certainly not marry them.

The terms Eta and Hinin were abolished in 1870, when these people were recognized as Yamato and legally cleared of any defect. Later they were designated Burakumin, meaning citizens of special communities. The problem is that discrimination did not vanish with the abolition of their lowly status, while they ceased to hold a monopoly on their traditional occupations, even leather production—a negative consequence of the process of desegregation. Physically, the Burakumin are totally unidentifiable; they are Yamato, living in the traditional core regions of Japanese civilization, although ancient prejudices attributed an alien or less than human origin to them. Intermarriage was avoided, since the traditional ghettos of the Burakumin were well identified. Segregation in the classroom, for instance, was only abolished in 1930 (the Civil Rights Bill enacted by the Parliament also addressed discrimination in public offices) after decades of political action, but discrimination in the media, particularly in comic books, continued (for the Burakumin and colonial peoples). The constitution of 1946 specified equal rights for all citizens, and ten Burakumin were elected to Parliament, while Matsumoto Jiichiro became vice president of the House of Councilors, and some of the Burakumin benefited from land reform. Institutional inequality was thus disrupted.

The possibility of Burakumin crossing the divide and mingling with society as a whole has increased in recent decades. Estimates of the Burakumin population vary from 1 to 2 million people, meaning that it is a significant minority. Even though Japan is not a society structured according to a caste system, the existence of segregated untouchables, based on the notion of impurity but not on economic functionality, raises the issue of how old classifications and prejudices that are close to racial constructs are perpetuated. This is an interesting case study from a theoretical point of view because it forces us to reflect further on the concepts of racism and race. George De Vos has underlined the similarities between psychological attitudes linked to caste and racial prejudices, although he recognized that "racism is usually based on a secularised pseudo-scientific biological mythology, whereas caste . . . is often based on a pseudo-historical religious mythology."[51] Castes are not necessarily based on religious ideas, nor are races necessarily justified using scientific ideas, but De Vos is right to point out the shared psychological attitudes structured by the ideas of social hierarchy, definitions of inferiority, and exclusion of groups of particular lineage. This leads us to consider other societies permeated by the concept of contamination, caste barriers, and formally inherited social positions.

In Tibet, the untouchables are known as Ragyabpu; they are responsible for disposing of corpses, clearing away the carcasses of dead animals, and searching criminals and vagabonds. In Korea the principal untouchable groups are the Parkchong—slaughters, butchers, and tanners—and Chiain—petty criminals, prostitutes, diviners, beggars, and itinerant peddlers, who are believed to descend from an alien wandering group sometimes identified with the Tartars. These people have been forced to live in segregated communities. The parallel with Japan is obvious, with a similar divide between settled communities and vagrants, but while Japan untouchables are placed outside society, in Korea they are identified as lower castes. These categories, however, have always been applied to a small minority of society.[52]

The case of India is totally different. Here the caste system permeates all levels of society based on notions of purity and impurity, cleanliness and pollution, protection and contamination, superiority and inferiority, endogamy and occupational inheritance, and spatial segregation and shared rules of hierarchical behavior. The logic that filthy jobs are connected to social degradation is at the heart of the system; ritual contamination leads to expulsion (casting out) from superior groups. The size of the untouchable castes is much higher in India than in Japan; in 2011, the total population of India reached 1.21 billion.[53] A projection based on previous percentages, which had been stable for several decades, would mean around 170 million untouchable people. This is why the untouchables have been at the center of political action in India both during the process of independence and ever since. As early as 1923 the British published antidiscriminatory laws concerning education, and in 1935 labeled the untouchables "scheduled castes." These castes are still designated in the same way.

The Indian Constitution of 1949 abolished the notion of untouchables and criminalized the practice of their exclusion; it also declared the state's duty to protect the interests of these groups. This decisive political action was followed by the Untouchability Offenses Act of 1954, which prohibited restrictions on the use of public spaces and equipment. Mohandas Karamchand Gandhi (1869–1948) did not contest the Varna system, based on four functions (spiritual—the Brahman priests; political—the noble Kshatriyas; trade and farming—the Vayshias; and servile—the Shudras), but he held that untouchability was not part of Hinduism. Despite political efforts, the reality of the untouchable stigma persists. The politician B. R. Ambedkar, an untouchable and a contemporary of Gandhi, always maintained that the stigma could only be eradicated together with the caste system. The belief in reincarnation certainly provides flexibility to the system, since actions in one's lifetime define one's place in the next life that will be lived; but mobility through reward (or punishment) is deferred to another life, which helps maintain the hierarchy of the system. In recent decades, the explosion of industrialization and urbanization has redefined the organization of as well as possibilities for occupations in India, drastically increasing social mobility. In this context, untouchability theoretically becomes meaningless. Yet as we have seen in Japan, the absence of an economic rationale does not prevent prejudice and segregation from being prolonged. India's extensive rural areas, which still occupy 50 percent of the total workforce, contribute to perpetuating the traditional logic of untouchability.

The debate around the caste system and the European construction of a hierarchical vision of complex Indian society has evolved from Louis Dumont's structural vision, although Dumont acknowledged the transition from a system of relations to one of elements, or from structure to substance.[54] Basically, scholars have accepted his definition of a relational caste system as operational, while the initial idea of a linear top-down gradation in a hierarchy of castes has been rejected as rigid and distant from reality. The oppositional pairings of caste versus class, holism versus individualism, hierarchy versus equality, and stability versus transformation have been dismissed as part of an essentialist approach.[55] The evolution of castes, creation of new status groups, and continual process of systemic change are subjects highlighted by recent research. The connections between castes and occupations have frequently been debated, since they do not coincide in the different regions of India. The comparative place of castes in the hierarchy of the system also varies. Gnana Prakasam's work exploring the changing status of the Satnami movement, initiated by Ghasi Das among the Satnamis of Chhattisgarh and inspired by the Bhakti tradition of a specific devotional path within Hinduism, shows how this new sect managed to break their traditional link with a caste-dictated occupation, oppose the caste system, and develop an egalitarian ideology. Satnamis finally transformed themselves into a politicized regional community with a strong sense of identity open to competition and collective action. They successfully removed the spatial isolation and caste segregation associated with untouchables, breaking the barriers against caste cohabitation. This presents an interesting example of change to the caste system at a regional level.[56]

The top-down approach to castes has also been questioned because it does not allow for an adequate understanding of the system's flexibility along with different perceptions of the lower castes, their own forms of identity, and the articulation between material and spiritual dimensions. Rosa Maria Perez's study of the Vankar from Valthara (Gujarat) suggests the ambiguity of the division between purity and impurity, and the need to reassess the logic of pollution, since the untouchables feel polluted by the presence of a member of a superior caste in their own facilities, themselves performing rituals of purification after the event. The reversible logic of the system was further exposed by a long drought during which the superior castes begged the Vankhar to perform rainmaking rituals: the untouchables might have been at the bottom of the system, but they supposedly controlled the process of inducing rain. Moreover, the Vankhar had their own mythical background, according to which they descended from kings.[57] The complementary and reversible logics of the caste system were revealed by this approach from below, although it should be pointed out that the Vankhar have only benefited from a symbolic level of compensation, far removed from access to political and economic resources.

✶✶✶

The persecution of Jews in nineteenth- and early twentieth-century Russia presented the first case of modern racial hatred premised on religious and ethnic divisions linked to political and national projects. The integration of an old minority into the emerging liberal order, based on the notion of equal rights and citizenship, tested the limits of secular universalism in the troubled transition to urban and industrial society in several European countries. In the meantime, the Ottoman Empire broke down under the rivalry of nationalist and imperialist projects, which promoted the fusion of the notions of nation, religion, and race. The genocide of the Armenian population in Anatolia was the most disastrous outcome of a century of forced migrations, massacres, and ethnic cleansing, triggered by the political project of the Young Turks to clear Anatolia and East Thrace for its own nation. Massive enslavement of populations by Nazi Germany was motivated by racial ideology connected to political projects of empire, in which the extermination of supposedly dangerous Jews was combined with the dispossession and subordination of Slavs.

The Soviet Union registered a process of enslavement on almost the same scale motivated by class reeducation, although suspicious ethnicities were also targeted. A vast process of expulsion of national minorities after the Second World War in Eastern Europe reflected the consequences of previous massacres and forced migrations, largely catalyzed by the idea of nation as shared descent. The last wars in Europe reflecting a renewed process of national, religious, and ethnic divide occurred in Yugoslavia in 1991–95 and 1998–99. In the meantime, dispossession, segregation, or forced assimilation of Native Americans was concluded by the early twentieth century. Compassion only started to replace hostility in the 1910s and 1920s in the Americas. Segregation of African Americans in the United States became institutionalized in the southern states after the Civil War and failure of Reconstruction. It took a long movement of civil rights to demolish institutional racism from the 1960s onward. Informal racism is still powerful in the Western world, but over the past fifty years antiracism has become the norm.

In Africa, colonial projects to dispossess natives of their land led to the first case of the racial persecution and genocide of an entire population—the Herero in Namibia in 1904. In South Africa, the apartheid regime between 1948 and 1994 was preceded by policies of discrimination against the native population, dispossessed of its land and excluded from skilled jobs. Segregation became systematic during apartheid, with the native population forced into massive migration and partly rounded into Bantustans. Black Africans were denied full citizenship as well as political and civil rights, until the transition to democracy was imposed by freedom fights and international pressure. The genocide of Tutsi by Hutu in Rwanda in 1994 represents a case of prejudice concerning descent that had been looming in the region since the colonial period. The fight for land and political resources caused a long-term conflict between the majority Hutu cultivators and minority Tutsi herders, who controlled most land up to the colonial period. Racial constructs in Africa due to Muslim intervention in the Sahel or ethnic rivalry in the lakes region show some similarities: the conflict between the Tuareg and black Africans, or herders against cultivators in Mali and Niger, might be considered equivalent to the conflict in Rwanda and Burundi.

In Asia, prejudice concerning descent has been related to the definition of central ethnicities in China and Japan. In China, the tradition of promotion by merit did not encourage long-term divides; the descendants of conquerors had to cope with cultural assimilation into the Han system. Peripheral peoples were discriminated against and the breakdown of the Qing Dynasty favored new Han pride as a central race, but there were no major massacres motivated by race. The existence of untouchable people in Japan, Korea, and Tibet is an indicator of long-term discrimination and segregation based on the notion of impure occupations. Racial constructs influenced Japanese late colonial projects in Korea, China, and Southeast Asia, leaving traces of discrimination against Koreans. In India, the caste system reveals a vast and rooted segregation of the untouchables, who represent about 15 percent of the population. The untouchables are formally protected by the constitution of 1949, although practices resulting from the notion of impurity and contamination persist.

Conclusions

This book has demonstrated my initial hypothesis that racism has historically been motivated by political projects. The only possible exception concerns the exclusion of Romanies (or Gypsies), since persecution of this nomadic minority expressed fears from settled communities against other ways of life. What was at stake here, however, was the monopoly of resources against a minority that wanted to retain its independence even as it moved across borders without integrating a specific economic, social, and political order. Gypsies converted to Christianity, but they were generally seen as outsiders. The role of specific economic conditions, included in my initial hypothesis, proved to be relatively important in the process of transition to modernity, channeled by or subordinated to political projects involving interethnic or international struggles for territory.

For the first time, discrimination and segregation against converted Muslims and Jews in Iberia created a dividing line within the Christian community against the universal principles of Saint Paul, since they were inside the same social formation. This new separation showed that religious conflict between the three religions of the book had been coupled with prejudice concerning ethnic descent: violent or forced conversion was not followed by complete integration. Competition for the control of cities, neighborhoods, economic activities, and access to political and ecclesiastical positions largely motivated status distinction between Old and New Christians. The tension between forced religious integration coupled with discrimination and segregation can be interpreted as an uprooting of religious beliefs followed by subordinated status within the Christian community. Dispossession of the main features of collective identity for better political control aimed at transforming majorities—Muslims in the south—into minorities, breaking down their main tool of resistance.

Reality nonetheless proved to be more complex: discrimination and segregation was opposed by upper segments of Old Christians, mainly the aristocratic landlords of the countryside, who depended on the work and knowledge of the Moriscos, while the ecclesiastical hierarchy was far from united in this project, since from the beginning the pope, the cardinals, and some bishops saw the dangers of disrupting the Christian community. A movement of lower, middle, and upper segments of urban Old Christians, who created a block of interests providing poor strata of the population with distinguished status, implemented the statutes of purity of blood. This consolidation of social interests promoting lower segments of the population coupled with discrimination and segregation of ethnic communities would be replicated later in entirely different social contexts, particularly in South Africa and the southern United States.

The establishment of the Inquisition against violently converted ethnic communities played a major role in Iberia. The tribunal contributed to diffusing the notion of purity of blood through systematic genealogical inquiry, and the exclusion of those condemned and their descents from certain professions. The explicit purpose of the Holy Office was to prosecute heresy among New Christians and Moriscos, although it also dealt with the heresies of Old Christians. The degree of penalties was ethnically differentiated. The tribunal kept productive and competitive ethnic populations under pressure through constant scrutiny. It contributed to institutionalizing racism. In 1492, it inspired the first royal decision in Castile and Aragon to expel the Jews, supposedly to protect the converted community from reverting to the old faith. The tribunal struggled to support the expulsion of Moriscos from Spain in 1609–10, since it would wipe out their main clients in certain regions. The expulsion involved around three hundred thousand people, but many others had been integrated, especially in the countryside. This meant that the policy of integration and subordination partly failed in the long run. The New Christians of Jewish origin presented a more complex situation since they either escaped to the Ottoman Empire, North Africa, and other European states, or integrated in the long run—a movement facilitated by their urban environment. In any case, Iberia presents a clear case of early prejudice concerning ethnic descent coupled with institutionalized discriminatory action.

The Christian reconquest of Sicily and the Latin Kingdom of Jerusalem are interesting counterexamples, since converted Muslims were also discriminated against, but on an individual basis, probably because the numbers involved were inferior to those of the Iberian Peninsula, where Muslims had become rooted throughout five to eight centuries of steady political dominion. Non-Latin Christians were also object of discrimination. The Orthodox Church's hierarchy was wiped out by the Norman Conquest of Sicily and south Italy, as it took place during the Latin Kingdom of Jerusalem, although in the latter case political weakness before major Muslim powers in the region imposed restrictions, allowing for the survival of some bishoprics and maintenance of the convent network. The same policy of discrimination was developed against other Christian minorities in the region, particularly Jacobites and Syriacs; only Armenians and Maronites became allies through their recognition of the pope. The major case of treating the Greeks as an inferior ethnicity came with their enslavement by Catalans of the duchy of Athens, who sold them in the western Mediterranean until the Aragonese king forbade this practice. A similar situation occurred in Iberia with Christians enslaving mozárabes while raiding Muslim territories, but that practice did not last either. Internal colonialism in Europe replicated discrimination of peripheral ethnicities Christianized from the beginning (as the Irish) or at a later stage (as the Saami or Lapps). Yet all these cases configure ethnic rivalry within the Christian community or religious rivalry between Christian churches that did not lead to racism: the integration of Christians into the Latin ritual or main communities was not followed by discrimination or segregation based on prejudices concerning ethnic descent.

Native Americans were considered alien nations until the nineteenth century in British America and the United States. In the 1630s in New England, the attempt to convert them and promote their first stage of integration through specific villages under control of preachers was not successful. They could integrate individually, but not collectively. The status of alien nations was only changed in 1871 into domestic dependent nations; citizenship was only granted in 1924. Converted natives in Spanish America were successfully integrated, although they suffered constant discrimination based on prejudices related to ethnic descent. They became vassals of the king with a recognized political position, but were subordinated citizens. The creation of the Repúblicas de Indios with a certain degree of autonomy meant positive segregation to avoid further disruption of local communities and agricultural output. Natives were recognized as the first occupiers of the land; elites had access to colleges and universities, although they were excluded for a long time from ecclesiastical positions and access to religious orders. In the Brazilian case, war and European diseases also decimated Native Americans, but their nomadic and seminomadic condition made them even more vulnerable than in Spanish America. Some were integrated into the white population, but the great difference between Portuguese and Spanish America in the long run was the overwhelming presence of African slaves in the former case.

Slavery led to the reinforcement of previous prejudices against sub-Saharan African people. The extensive mixing of different ethnicities in Iberian America coupled with the systematic conversion of natives and slaves led to the formation of a complex relational framework of social prejudices, which in the Mexican case were expressed by the castas paintings. The debasement of inferior castas via animal metaphors was a crucial feature of these classifications. The hierarchy of castas, however, did not lead to a closed system of descent: significant individual social mobility expressed openness. In Brazil, the bestowing of white status on successful mixed-race people became the norm, while over the past twenty years the equation of poverty with blackness has led to policies of affirmative action to reduce social and political inequality. Long-standing social inequality in Iberian America is linked to the rights of conquest, dispossession of Native Americans, slavery as a social system, and a tradition of rule by tiny elites of white descent. Increasing access to civil rights by the lower strata of the population and changes in the power elites have redressed this situation to some extent, but racism has not disappeared.

By contrast, mixed descent in British America was targeted by permanent discrimination and segregation. The existence of mixed-race people was acknowledged from the seventeenth to the mid-nineteenth century, although segregationist laws after the Civil War institutionalized the rule of one drop of black blood defining blackness. Blacks were not only dispossessed from civil rights acquired with the abolition of slavery in 1865; they were submitted to formal segregation and violent daily intimidation including regular acts of lynching. It took a century of civil campaigns and the black movement of the 1960s to terminate formal segregation. Antisegregation laws and changes in the power elite during the past forty years disrupted institutional racism. In the Caribbean, the division between black and white has been complicated by the existence of colored people, meaning that mixed-race people achieved some form of recognition due to the low numbers of white people. Political developments in different countries disrupted the colonial tradition of white supremacy, although inequality and racism persist to different degrees.

The American experience of European colonialism created the first experimental environment for the extension of prejudices concerning ethnic descent coupled with discriminatory action to other continents and other peoples of the world. The notion of blackness, or "blacks of the land," was applied to Native Americans and Asians, first by the Portuguese, and then by the Spaniards, British, and Dutch, in order to justify domination and hierarchy. Mixed-race communities were crucial for the Portuguese in Asia, since they depended on them, but the fiction of local elites constituted by pure Old Christians (meaning Europeans) was maintained until the nineteenth century. Dutch and British East India companies had better access to European (male) labor power, which significantly mixed with native populations until the late eighteenth century, when the British started to exclude mixed-race people from jobs at the East India Company and the Dutch in South Africa began to create white militias.

Early hierarchies of peoples of the world were directly influenced by the colonial experience. In 1570, the allegorical four types of humankind identified with continents, represented by Ortelius on the title page of his famous atlas, synthesized seventy years of iconographic experiments related to the European expansion and universal ambitions of the Holy Roman Empire. The enormous impact of this title page is visible in hundreds of drawings, engravings, paintings, and sculptures produced in early modern Europe. Visual culture expressed hierarchies of peoples of the world defined by physical and mental attributes better than written culture. Such visual acts were fed by ethnic prejudices made increasingly complex by travel accounts and geographic treatises. They were complemented by other criteria of hierarchies of peoples of the world cutting across continents, as suggested by Acosta. But it was the synthetic vision of Ortelius's typology that proved most successful and finally was inscribed into the new classification of nature created by Linnaeus in the eighteenth century.

Racism preceded theories of races, yet the inclusion of old and new prejudices related to ethnic descent into a scientific framework enhanced discriminatory action, since it crystallized ethnic prejudices, giving them a superior status of knowledge. Theories of races had an extraordinary impact not only on the Western world but also on other continents, where they were adapted to local needs. Even so, typologies of the variety of human beings remained precarious and changeable: monogenism (unique creation) was confronted since the seventeenth century with polygenism (multiple creations), which reinforced the idea of inequality inscribed in nature since the beginning of time. The first generations of monogenist natural historians (Buffon, Camper, and Blumenbach) acknowledged the improvement of humankind, thus disrupting the old principle of a perfect creation followed by degeneration. Their classification varied and was not rigid, cutting across continents. Nevertheless, polygenists such as White quickly integrated the first measurement of the human skull through the facial angle suggested by Camper to prove multiple creations and the closeness of Africans to apes. Rigid typologies proposed by Cuvier, reducing human variety to white, yellow, and black races, contributed to reinforcing the polygenist trend, even unintentionally. Lamarck and Saint Hilaire challenged Cuvier's system of nature, instead promoting ideas of transformation and connection between different classes of animals. Prichard and Humboldt further demolished a compartmentalized notion of races, but this critical stance was immediately opposed by the immutable vision of races promoted by North American polygenists engaged in the abolitionist debate of the mid-nineteenth century, particularly Morton, Nott, and Agassiz. New measurements (or mismeasurements) of human skulls supported this perspective. These scientific racialists became extremely influential in defining right-wing nationalist and totalitarian policies until the Second World War. They inspired segregationist laws in the United States and South Africa. In the meantime, Gobineau promoted the vision of Aryans as superior white people responsible for all gains of civilization in the world and equated miscegenation with degeneration. While Aryanism was used in the Western world to promote white supremacy and in Europe to justify internal expansionist projects, Asian and Oceania peoples saw the advantage of claiming noble white ancestors to reinforce their position within the British Empire, or claim autonomy and independence.

The notion of evolution by means of natural selection promoted by Darwin finally rendered the debate between monogenists and polygenists irrelevant, asserting the idea of humankind as one single species. The paradigm of species slowly being modified over millions of years provided the context for the variation of human beings within the general scheme of evolution. Theories of social evolution inspired by Lamarck and Darwin substituted different stages of the civilizing process for innate hierarchies. The naturalization of hierarchies was reintroduced under evolutionary premises; improvement and perfectibility were accepted, but so also was the possibility of decline linked to competition for resources along with an inability to adapt to new economic, social, and political conditions. The long-term impact of abolitionism from the 1770s in England to the 1860s in the United States reflected the ambiguity of this theoretical background. The idea of respect for human dignity strengthened the movement for the abolition of the slave trade and slavery, although black people were not necessarily considered equal or ready for access to all civil rights, especially the basic right to property, which is the lever of social structures.

Nationalism brought with it the fusion of nation and race, with collective identity based on the idea of a shared language and descent. The impact of this political movement was felt first in multiethnic empires, mainly the Ottoman and Austrian. The emergence of nationalism in the Balkans and the Caucasus dramatically reduced the territory of the Ottoman Empire, where long-standing antagonism between Muslims and Christians was transformed into a racialized persecution of Armenians and Greeks, as the Young Turks tried to create a homogeneous state. The first genocide in Europe—as the premeditated extermination of an ethnic, national, or religious group—occurred in 1915 against the Armenians in the Ottoman Empire. Massive deportations were followed by massacres organized by the state, which resulted in the death of a million people. The purpose was to cleanse the territory as well as exterminate a nation-race accused of being overly competitive and profiteering from the Muslim population. The large-scale persecution and massacres of the Greek population did not reach the same level, due to the existence of a Greek state. Prejudice concerning descent led to extermination, massacre, and expulsion, driven by a clear political project of creating a racial state exclusively based on Turkish identity. The dislike of people considered to have negative features transmitted from generation to generation was based on religious antagonism. The Kurds could not be submitted to the same level of atrocities since they were Muslims, but they suffered deportation, transfer of populations, and systematic attempts to assimilate them into a Turkish identity. Religion and a particular concept of nature were strongly implicated in this modern case of racism leading to genocide.

The transformation of Jews into a scapegoat for the problems of the transition to modernity began with the French Revolution and its impact on Europe. Universal claims for civil rights disrupted old privileges and shook the foundations of the ancien régime; the promotion of this traditionally oppressed religious community was seen as a test of the limits of these assertions. Opposition to the integration of Jewish communities was voiced in various countries, fueled by the increasingly successful presence of Jews in education, business, and politics. The economic crisis of the 1870s brought with it new anti-Jewish tendencies that became especially important in Germany. In the meantime, there were repeated pogroms in the western territories of Russia throughout the nineteenth and early twentieth century. The striking point here is that the theories of races had not dealt with Jews because many authors were interested in classifying major varieties of humankind across the world. Knox had targeted Jews, mobilizing old prejudices, but at the turn of the twentieth century it was Chamberlain who placed the Jewish threat at the center of a German struggle for the future, building on previous anti-Semitic tendencies. According to this vision, the racial struggle was placed in opposition to the class struggle. Competition for space and resources was dramatized as a struggle for survival inspired by both scientific racialism (which predominated with its ideas of innate and immutable racial characteristics) and social Darwinism. Hitler followed Chamberlain's ideas and turned them into political action, transforming the Jews into the internal enemy that needed to be expelled (later exterminated) if German supremacy in Europe was to be achieved. Socialists and Communists were equated with Jews, or stigmatized as Jew ridden.

Germany became a racial state driven by prejudices relating to ethnic descent coupled with discriminatory actions. Jewish communities lost their citizenship and civil rights; they were deported, rounded up in concentration camps, compelled to forced labor, and exterminated. This genocide led to six million deaths. Religion was absent from the picture, since Jews were stripped of their beliefs in order to present them as opportunistic businesspeople. Yet without the traditional religious divide and set of prejudices, political action would not have been possible. This is why the idea of two different kinds of racism—modern natural racism and premodern religious racism—is untenable. Despite laboratorial efforts, Nazi Germany never managed to identify natural features specific to the Jewish population; these were identified through the traditional methods of reputation and genealogy used by the Inquisition in the past. In addition, the traditional antagonism between Germans and

Slavs was racialized, since Hitler wanted to transform "inferior" Slavs into forced labor dispossessed of property. Twenty million Russians were killed during the Second World War, while twelve million Slavs were enslaved and sent to work in labor camps. Racism again served political projects—in this case, Nazi policies of German supremacy and expansion. Eugenics, which promoted the idea that social and biological engineering could improve the qualities of a race, was implemented against people with disabilities, Jews, Gypsies, and black people. Gypsies also suffered an extensive process of extermination.

The Soviet Union favored class struggle, but deported, both before and after the Second World War, several ethnicities suspected of being disloyal to the regime, while enslaving millions of political and social opponents in concentration camps for forced labor. Germans were massively deported from various Eastern European countries after the war, while ethnic cleansing was practiced or attempted in and between Communist countries that theoretically were comrades in arms. In Yugoslavia, a country reconstituted after the Second World War, ethnic hatred was contained until the fall of the Soviet bloc. In 1991, the creation of new states in the old Yugoslav federation led to war based on religious and national divides, followed by processes of ethnic cleansing.

The old conflict between Greeks and Ottomans, translated into the War of Independence (1821–30), Balkan Wars (1912–13), and Greco-Turkish War (1919–22), saw extensive massacres of civil populations and finally the exchange of expelled minorities from both countries. The sequels of this hatred in which nation was equated with religion and race were long lasting: anti-Greek riots were perpetrated by the mob in Istanbul in 1955, while the independence of Cyprus in 1960 was followed by massacres, and the Turkish invasion in 1974 led to the partition of the island and increased ethnic cleansing. Local projects of integration with Greece opposed by political projects of Turkish expansion were at stake in this process.

The absence of an anti-Jewish attitude in modern Iberia is the counterpoint to these trends: despite the long-term obsession with purity of blood between the late fifteenth and early nineteenth centuries, there was no real movement against Jews during the twentieth century. The reason lies in the residual numbers of the community and memory of the debate on this historical issue that pervaded the whole of the nineteenth century. There were no grounds for targeting Jews in pursuit of political projects.

Prejudice concerning descent was visible in colonial Africa, leading to varied forms of discrimination and segregation. In 1904, the Hereros in German Namibia were targeted for a massive process of persecution and extermination, presenting the first case of modern genocide. The tardy intervention of the German Parliament meant that as few as 20 percent of the population may have survived. This case was clearly linked to the ethnic cleansing of people on the central lands coveted by colonial farmers; it was a project to dispossess people of their communal lands. The case of South Africa never reached the same proportions, but segregation of the African populations became formally framed by legislation throughout the nineteenth century, particularly in the new Boer republics after the British abolition of slavery in 1833. The emergence of a mining industry in the last decades of the nineteenth century reinforced the division of labor along racial lines based on white supremacy and the exclusion of black people from skilled work. Indian migrants were also targeted as white supremacy was asserted.

The establishment of apartheid between 1948 and 1994 institutionalized racial segregation at all levels—education, leisure, public spaces, and political participation—and was followed by the significant transfer of African populations and creation of white-sponsored polities, Bantustans, in order to dispossess native populations of their land and civil rights. Political opposition and the end of the Cold War brought the end to apartheid. In other regions of Africa, specifically in the Great Lakes, in which the genocide of the Tutsi took place in 1994, or the region of Sahel, West Africa, where the Tuareg have been revolting against African ethnic majorities during the past decades, it has been disputed whether major ethnic hatred was sparked by colonial divisions and theories of races, or by local perceptions of descent. The example of the Tuareg may show the imprint of old Muslim prejudices against African people shared with Europeans, although long-standing conflict between pastoralists and agriculturalists may have catalyzed an old idea of descent. This line of division is also visible in Rwanda and Burundi between Tutsi and Hutu, although in this case colonial divisions and European racist examples played an undeniable role.

Racism is not exclusive to the Western world. We have seen how the idea of descent was already present in African notions of lineage and kinship. Racial prejudices in various areas were coupled with discriminatory action that led to genocide during and after the colonial period. In Asia, the notion of descent has been well rooted for millennia. In China, the Han were considered the central ethnicity that embraced other ethnicities in the process of their expansion; they imposed their own cultural and political criteria on foreign rulers. Prejudices and discrimination against peoples from the peripheries—the mountain dwellers of the southwest or Muslims of central Asia—are still observable today, which explains the migration of people from the center in order to change the ethnic composition of contested peripheral areas. A lack of powerful feudal elites, however, prevented the justification of social dominion by blood, while the practice of recruiting administrative and political elites through exams perpetuated an ideal of promotion by merit. The Communist regime has formally refused the racial vision of the world, but again some ethnicities are still treated as more suspicious than others.

In Japan, social and ethnic hierarchies have an entirely different history. The emperor claimed divine origin, while the Yamato, the central ethnicity representing the vast majority of the population, was considered to be under the emperor's influence. The acceptance of Confucianism did not lead to promotion by merit through exams. The Daimyo (a military caste controlling land) were reorganized under the Tokugawa system of centralized feudalism, while the Samurai were assigned to administrative functions. The notion of blood and descent was only too present. Japan has untouchable people, the Burakumin, who were segregated because of their traditional polluted occupations: working with animal parts and products, dealing with death, and taking care of waste matter. Institutionalized segregation was prohibited in 1870, 1930, and 1946, but informal discrimination persists. The

Ainu from the northern island of Hokkaido were considered barbarians and colonization followed, dispossessing the natives of their best land. Late Japanese colonial expansion triggered Chinese caricatures of "hairy dwarfs," while the Koreans brought to Japan as cheap labor from the 1920s to 1940s lost their citizenship after their country's independence.

In India, the caste system permeates all levels of society based on notions of purity and impurity, cleanliness and pollution, protection and contamination, endogamy and occupational inheritance, spatial segregation and shared rules of hierarchical behavior. The untouchable castes are much more important here than elsewhere, representing around 15 percent of the total population. Recent studies have challenged the idea of this system as immutable, showing that new castes have been created, collective statuses can shift, notions of integrity can be reversed, and ritual compensation for outcasts may occur. Yet the notion of caste descent is deeply rooted in this society, and continues to structure forms of discrimination.

As early as the 1870s, scientific research in Germany had abandoned the idea of finding particular physical features that could distinguish the Jewish population. The discovery of blood groups during the First World War did not lead to distinctive links to previously defined racial groups. The sequencing and mapping of the human genome in 2000 has been followed by renewed debate on race. Some genes and mutations are related to specific ethnic groups, and can increase immunity or propensity for particular diseases, but they do not coincide with large conceptions of races. Genetic differences within what were formerly defined as racial groups are considered more important than the differences between those groups. The definition of boundaries remains a riddle for scientists interested in the variety of human beings. The Holocaust certainly demonstrated the extreme dangers of any vision of future societies based on race struggle. Immediately after the war, the UN Educational, Scientific, and Cultural Organization launched a debate on the theories of races in order to illuminate their precarious foundations. This was followed by the black civil rights movement of the 1960s in the United States, which contributed to the widespread rejection of discrimination based on the idea of natural inferiority. The perception of race has been turned on its head, and the term is now used to express collective identity and protect minorities in accordance with notions developed by bioethics.

The main idea developed by my research is that racism assumed different forms shaped by specific conjunctures. There is no cumulative and linear racism. In all the significant cases I have studied, prejudices concerning ethnic descent coupled with discriminatory actions have been motivated by political projects. Specific conjunctures of economic or political crisis have proved to be crucial in explaining the mobilization of prejudices and their transformation into political action, serving specific social interests. Discrimination against and the segregation of Jews and Muslims in medieval Europe were followed by similar actions against New Christians and Moriscos, showing the transfer of the existing prejudices despite religious integration. The monopolization of economic, political, and social resources was at stake as these practices were renewed within different religious frameworks. Prejudice and discrimination could perpetuate subordinate social and ethnic positions, particularly in the case of black slaves and freedpersons in the New World, but they could also undermine successful competitors, such as Armenians in the Ottoman Empire, or Jews in Russia and Germany. Although theories of races have lent a scientific framework to classifications of humankind, religion has been entangled with perceptions of descent in medieval, early modern, and modern forms of ethnic hatred. In the meantime, colonial divisions of labor have fueled racial forms of discrimination. Equating nationhood with race (and in many instances religion) brought with it new forms of dispute over territory. The violence of ethnic cleansing reached unprecedented levels in the twentieth century through forms of enslavement and genocide never seen before, spreading from Europe to other continents where specific dynamics of ethnic conflict had been looming.

An antiracist norm of behavior now prevails in most parts of the world. Racism has not disappeared, though. It has abandoned its claims of physical differences, and replaced this with cultural incapacity. Migration is not opposed by physical arguments but instead through the idea of cultural backwardness and people's inability to adapt. The argument of inferiority has been abandoned in the political debate; rather, immigrants are accused of benefiting from social assistance not designed for them. Contentions about identity and exclusion are still on the table; the criteria for the attribution of citizenship are still the main tool to define belonging. Identities nevertheless do not always coincide with formal citizenship, as informal forms of discrimination can be extremely powerful without institutional frameworks or state enforcement. If this is the state of the discussion in the Western world, it does not mean that old problems have been resolved, there and elsewhere. Daily violence between ethnicities is visible in different parts of the world, as is slavery and enslavement, frequently based on prejudices related to ethnic descent. In sum, there is still a considerable way to go to realize the dream of human dignity and the real implementation of human rights.

NOTES |||||||||||||||||||||||||||||||||||||||||||||||||||||||||||||||||||||||||||||||||||||||||||||||||||||||||||||||||||||||||||||||||||||||||||||||||||||

INTRODUCTION

1. I have used, among other sources, the Le Menil collection of images of black people now at the Warburg Institute, University of London, and the W.E.B. Du Bois Institute for African and African American Research, Harvard University. For the outcome of that project, see David Bindman and Henry Louis Gates, eds., *The Image of the Black in Western Art*, 8 vols. (Cambridge, MA: Belknap Press, 2010–12).

2. Pierre van den Berghe, *Race and Racism: A Comparative Perspective*, 2nd ed. (New York: Wiley, 1978); Carl N. Degler, *Neither Black nor White: Slavery and Race Relations in Brazil and the United States* (New York: Macmillan, 1971); George M. Fredrickson, *Diverse Nations: Explorations in the History of Racial and Ethnic Pluralism* (Boulder, CO: Paradigm, 2008). Other books deal with this comparison; see especially Charles V. Hamilton, Lynn Huntley, Neville Alexander, Antonio Sérgio Alfredo Guimarães, and Wilmot James, eds., *Beyond Racism: Race and Inequality in Brazil, South Africa, and the United States* (Boulder, CO: Lynne Rienner, 2001).

3. See David Bindman, *Ape to Apollo: Aesthetics and the Idea of Race in the 18th Century* (London: Reaktion Books, 2002).

4. Lucien Fèbvre, *Pour une Histoire à part entière* (1962; repr., Paris: École des Hautes Études en Sciences Sociales, 1982), 15.

5. Benjamin Isaac, *The Invention of Racism in Classical Antiquity* (Princeton, NJ: Princeton University Press, 2006).

6. Frank M. Snowden, *Before Color Prejudices: The Ancient View of Blacks* (Cambridge, MA: Harvard University Press, 1983).

7. George M. Fredrickson, *Racism: A Short History* (Princeton, NJ: Princeton University Press, 2002).

8. Claude Lévi-Strauss, *L'anthropologie face aux problèmes du monde moderne* (Paris: Seuil, 2011), 105–46. The same reasoning is implicit in Claude Lévi-Strauss, *L'autre face de la lune: Écrits sur le Japon* (Paris: Seuil, 2011).

9. Peter Wade, *Race, Nature, and Culture: An Anthropological Perspective* (London: Pluto, 2002); Peter Wade, *Race and Ethnicity in Latin America*, 2nd ed. (London: Pluto, 2010).

10. Arthur Keith, *Ethnos or the Problem of Race considered from a New Point of View* (London: Kegan Paul, 1931), 26, 73–74.

11. See Stuart Hall, "Race, Articulation, and Societies Structured in Dominance," in *Race Critical Theories: Text and Context*, ed. Philomena Essed and David Theo Goldberg (Oxford: Blackwell, 2002), 38–68.

12. Etienne Balibar and Immanuel Wallerstein, *Race, Nation, Class: Ambiguous Identities* (London: Verso, 1991).

13. Michael Omi and Howard Winant, *Racial Formation in the United States from the 1960s to the 1990s*, 2nd ed. (London: Routledge, 1994).

14. Max Weber, *Economy and Society*, trans. Guenther Roth and Claus Wittich, 2 vols. (Berkeley: University of California Press, 1978), 385–98, 932–35. For the relevant passage, see ibid., 386.

15. Alain Rey, ed., *Dictionnaire historique de la langue française* (Paris: Le Robert, 1998), 3:3056–57. The appearance of the nouns in English followed a similar course. See John A. Simpson and Edmund S. C. Weiner, eds., *Oxford English Dictionary*, 20 vols. (Oxford: Clarendon, 1989).

16. Simpson and Weiner, *Oxford English Dictionary*, 13:69–70; *Grande Dizionario della Lingua Italiana* (Turin: Unione Tipografica Editrice Torinese, 1990), 15:586–88; Arlette Jouana, *L'idée de race en France au XVIe siècle et début du XVIIe*, 2nd ed., 2 vols. (Montpellier: Université Paul Valéry, 1981); Joan Corominas,

Diccionario crítico etimológico castellano e hispánico, 7 vols. (Madrid: Gredos, 1981); Rafael Bluteau, *Vocabulario Portuguez e Latino*, 10 vols. (Coimbra, Portugal: Colégio das Artes, 1712–28); Antônio Houaiss, ed., *Dicionário Houaiss da Língua Portuguesa* (Rio de Janeiro: Objectiva/Instituto Houaiss, 2001).

17. See Claudio Pogliano, *L'ossessione della razza: Antropologia e genetica nel XX secolo* (Pisa: Edizioni della Normale, 2005); Sheldon Krimsky and Kathleen Sloan, eds., *Race and the Genetic Revolution: Science, Myth, and Culture* (New York: Columbia University Press, 2011).

18. Michael J. Bamshed and Steve C. Olson, "Does Race Exist?" *Scientific American* 289, no. 6 (December 2003): 78–85; Race, Ethnicity, and Genetic Working Group, "The Use of Racial, Ethnic, and Ancestral Categories in Human Genetic Research," *American Journal of Human Genesis* 77, no. 4 (October 2005): 519–32; David B. Goldstein and Joel N. Hirschhorn, "In Genetic Control of Disease, Does 'Race' Matter?" *Nature Genetics* 36, no. 12 (December 2004): 1243–44.

19. Sarah Daynes and Orville Lee, eds., *Desire for Race* (Cambridge: Cambridge University Press, 2008). The issue had been raised for the colonial context. See Ann Laura Stoler, *Race and the Education of Desire: Foucault's "History of Sexuality" and the Colonial Order of Things* (Durham, NC: Duke University Press, 1995).

20. See Henri Tajfel, ed., *Social Identity and Intergroup Relations* (Cambridge: Cambridge University Press, 1982); Craig Calhoun, ed., *Social Theory and the Politics of Identity* (Oxford: Blackwell, 1994).

21. Frank Dikötter, ed., *The Construction of Racial Identities in China and Japan* (London: Hurst and Co., 1997); Peter Robb, *The Concept of Race in South Asia* (Oxford: Oxford University Press, 1997).

22. Bruce S. Hall, *A History of Racism in Muslim West Africa, 1600–1960* (Cambridge: Cambridge University Press, 2011).

23. Rey, *Dictionnaire historique de la langue française*, 1:1325–26; *Thesaurus Linguæ Latinæ* (Leipzig: E. B. Teubneri, 1931–53), 5:923–94; J. C. Niermeyer and C. van De Kieft, *Mediæ Latinitatis Lexicon Minus*, 2nd ed. (Leiden: Brill, 2002), 1:502.

24. James M. Jones, *Prejudice and Racism*, 2nd ed. (New York: McGraw-Hill, 1997); Simpson and Weiner, *Oxford English Dictionary*.

25. Convention on the Prevention and Punishment of the Crime of Genocide, Resolution 260(III)A, UN General Assembly, December 9, 1948, http://www.hrweb.org/legal/genocide.hmt (accessed September 3, 2011).

26. Michael Adas, *Machines as the Measure of Men: Science, Technology, and Ideologies of Western Dominance* (Ithaca, NY: Cornell University Press, 1989).

27. Marc Bloch, *The Historian's Craft*, trans. Peter Putnam (Manchester: Manchester University Press, 1954).

Chapter 1: From Greek to Muslim Perceptions

1. I am guided here by Benjamin Isaac, *The Invention of Racism in Classical Antiquity* (Princeton, NJ: Princeton University Press, 2006).

2. Marcel Detienne, *Comment devenir autochtone: Du pur Athénien au Français raciné* (Paris: Seuil, 2003).

3. Frank Snowden (*Before Color Prejudice: The Ancient View of Blacks* [Cambridge, MA: Harvard University Press, 1983]) rejects prejudice concerning descent for this period.

4. P. D. King, "The Barbarian Kingdoms," in *The Cambridge History of Medieval Thought, c. 350–c.1450*, ed. J. H. Burns (Cambridge: Cambridge University Press, 1988), 137.

5. Herwig Wolfram and Walter Pohl, eds., *Typen der Ethogenese unter besonderer Berücksichtigung der Bayern*, 2 vols. (Vienna: Österreichischen Akademie der Wissenschaften, 1990); Andrew Gillett, ed., *On Barbarian Identity: Critical Approaches to Ethnicity in the Early Middle Ages* (Turnhout, Belgium: Brepols, 2002); Thomas F. X. Noble, ed., *From Roman Provinces to Medieval Kingdoms* (London: Routledge, 2006); Peter Heather, *Empires and Barbarians* (London: Macmillan, 2009).

6. I am not going to discuss here the fiction of the *translatio imperii* promoted by the Byzantine rulers. See D. M. Nicol, "Byzantine Political Thought," in *The Cambridge History of Medieval Thought, c. 350–c.1450*, ed. J. H. Burns (Cambridge: Cambridge University Press, 1988), 59.

7. Victor of Vita, *History of the Vandal Persecution*, trans. John Moorhead (Liverpool: Liverpool University Press, 1990). The original *Historia persecutionis vandalorum*, written by a Catholic bishop who was an eyewitness, was widely printed in the sixteenth, seventeenth, and eighteenth centuries. For the original historical context, see

Chris Wickham, *The Inheritance of Rome: A History of Europe from 400 to 1000* (London: Penguin Books, 2009), 76–82. The negative perceptions of Vandals through history are collected in *Shorter Oxford English Dictionary on Historical Principles*, 5th ed. (Oxford: Oxford University Press, 2002), 2:3502. Limited devastation and distortion by the official church against Arian Vandals was pointed out in Yitzhak Hen, *Roman Barbarians: The Royal Court and Culture in the Early Medieval West* (Basingstoke, UK: Palgrave, 2007), chapter 3.

8. On the conversion of the barbarian kingdoms and relations between Christians and Jews, see Peter Brown, *The Rise of Western Christendom* (Princeton, NJ: Princeton University Press, 1996); Bruno Dumézil, *Les racines chrétiennes de l'Europe: Conversion et liberté dans les royaumes barbares Ve–VIIIe siècle* (Paris: Fayard, 2005).

9. On the complex process of their expansion and sedentarization, see Halil Inalcik, *An Economic and Social History of the Ottoman Empire,* vol. 1, *1300–1600* (Cambridge: Cambridge University Press, 1994); David J. Roxburgh, ed., *Turks: A Journey of a Thousand Years, 600–1600* (London: Royal Academy of Arts, 2005).

10. Fernand Braudel, *Grammaire des Civilisations* (1963; repr., Paris: Flammarion, 1993), 71–124; Albert Hourani, *A History of the Arab Peoples* (Cambridge, MA: Belknap, 1991), 7–208.

11. Al-Muqaddasī, *Ahsan at-Taqāsīm fī Ma'rifat al-aqālīm (La meilleure répartition pour la connaissance des provinces)*, ed. and trans. André Miquel (Damascus: Institut Français de Damas, 1963), 75–78.

12. André Miquel, *La géographie humaine du monde musulman jusqu'au milieu du XIe siècle* (Paris: Mouton, 1975), 2:65–66, 101, 141–43, 195; Bernard Lewis, *Race and Slavery in the Middle East: An Historical Enquiry* (Oxford: Oxford University Press, 1990), 31–32.

13. *Shorter Oxford English Dictionary*, 2:2669; Alain Rey, ed., *Dictionnaire historique de la langue française* (Paris: Le Robert, 1998), 3:3386–7.

14. *Diccionario de la Lengua Española*, 22nd ed. (Madrid: Real Academia Española, 2001), 1043, 1379; Antônio Houaiss, ed., *Dicionário Houaiss da Língua Portuguesa* (Rio de Janeiro: Objectiva/Instituto Houaiss, 2001), 1969, 2523; *Dizionario Italiano* (Milan: Rizzoli, 1988), 616, 900; *Shorter Oxford English Dictionary*, 1:1828, 2:2669; Rey, *Dictionnaire historique de la langue française*, 2:2168.

Chapter 2: Christian Reconquest

1. In his edited sixteen-volume *Monumenta Cartographica Africæ et Ægypti* ([Cairo, 1926–51], especially part 2, vol. 2 [1932]), Yossouf Kamal publishes a list of 466 North African dioceses in the years 482 to 484 (fl. 329r–v). On this apocalyptic literature, see Jean Flori, *L'Islam et la fin des temps: L'interprétation prophétique des invasions musulmanes dans la chrétienté médiévale* (Paris: Seuil, 2007).

2. Jihad as a personal and collective duty is an idea well documented since early on, particularly during the eighth, ninth, and tenth centuries; see, for instance, Ibn Hawqal and Ibn Ahmad, in *Biblioteca Arabo-Sicula*, ed. Michele Amari (1880–81; repr., Bologna: Arnaldo Forni, 1981), 1:24, 392. On the Christian tradition and Islam, see Benjamin Z. Kedar, *Crusade and Mission: European Approaches toward the Muslims* (Princeton, NJ: Princeton University Press, 1984); James M. Powell, *The Crusades, the Kingdom of Sicily, and the Mediterranean* (Aldershot, UK: Ashgate, 2007).

3. Kedar, *Crusade and Mission*, 23.

4. See Jonathan Riley-Smith, *The First Crusade and the Idea of Crusading* (London: Athlone Press, 1986).

5. It is here that I disagree with Paul Alphandéry and Alphonse Dupront (*La Chrétienté et l'idée de Croisade* [1954–59; repr., Paris: Albin Michel, 1995]), who limit the notion of the Crusade to the expeditions to conquer or protect Jerusalem, although they acknowledge the fact that the launch of the First Crusade did not mention the Holy City or holy places. They also refuse to consider the Norman Conquest of Sicily or Christian reconquest of Iberia as coming within the spirit or being precursors of the Crusades (ibid., 29–30). This position was later, ironically, nuanced in Alphonse Dupront, *Le mythe de croisade* (Paris: Gallimard, 1997), 1:367: "L'Espagne a sa croisade à elle. Jusqu'où celle de la Chrétienté lui importe-t-elle?" For a broader vision of the Crusades, see Jonathan Riley-Smith, *The Crusades: A Short History* (London: Athlone Press, 1987).

6. Judith Herrin demonstrates the absence of a formal split to sustain the idea of "great schism" in her *Byzantium: The Surprising Life of a Medieval Empire* (London: Penguin, 2008), 47–48.

7. See Michel Balard, *Les latins en Orient (Xe–XVe siècle)* (Paris: Presses Universitaires de France, 2006), 382–90.

8. See J. B. Harvey and David Woodward, eds., *Cartography in Prehistoric, Ancient, and Medieval Europe and the Mediterranean* (Chicago: University of Chicago Press, 1987).

9. I have followed here the reconstruction of events proposed in Josef Deér, *The Dynastic Porphyry Tombs of the Norman Period in Sicily*, trans. G. A. Gillhof (Cambridge, MA: Harvard University Press, 1959). I also agree with the main aspects of this artistic interpretation of the funerary monuments, although Deér does not analyze the supports of the sarcophagi.

10. It is essential to say that Roger II emulated Byzantine emperors and adopted imperial symbols, as Deér (ibid.) points out. It is known that the preacher at the Capela Palatina in Palermo addressed Roger II as basileus. See Hubert Houben, *Roger II of Sicily: A Ruler between East and West*, trans. Graham A. Lord and Diana Milburn (Cambridge: Cambridge University Press, 2002), 133.

11. The lion was used in medieval heraldry as a symbol of strength and power, mainly after the twelfth and thirteenth centuries. See Michel Pastoureau, *Figures de l'héraldique* (Paris: Galimard, 1996), 58–61; Michel Pastoureau, *Une histoire symbolique du Moyen Âge occidental* (Paris: Seuil, 2004), 49–64. The image of the lion as a symbol of sovereignty and justice is evident in medieval bestiaries, and later included in books of emblems.

12. The goat as a symbol of lust in pagan antiquity was transformed into a symbol of the damned at the last judgment (Matt. 25:32–33). See James Hall, *Dictionary of Subjects and Symbols in Art* (London: John Murray, 1979), 139–40. The goat was also used during the Middle Ages to depict the devil. See Jean Chevalier and Alain Gheerbrant, *Dictionnaires des symboles* (Paris: Seghers, 1973), 1:221–24.

13. Roger II conquered the rich island of Djerba in 1135, launched successive attacks until the Zirid kingdom became his tributary in 1142, destroyed Djidjelli in 1143, and conquered Bresk, Cherchell, and the islands of Kerkenne in 1144–45, immediately before the donation of the sarcophagus. The conquest went on: Tripoli fell in 1146; Mahdia, Susa, Sfax, and Gabes were defeated in 1148; and Bone followed in 1153. See Hubert Houben, *Roger II of Sicily*, 77–80. William I lost these territories in 1156–60.

14. See Michael McCormick, *Eternal Victory: Triumphal Rulership in Late Antiquity, Byzantium, and the Early Medieval West* (Cambridge: Cambridge University Press, 1986), 162. In 956, in Constantinople, Byzantine soldiers turned the Islamic standards on their heads during the ritual humiliation of Abu'l Asā'ia, the cousin of the emir of Aleppo. There is a sixteenth-century literary account of this tradition reenacted in Constantinople under the Turks, who performed it against the defeated Christians. See Juan de Ulloa Pereira, *Viaje de Turquia*, ed. Fernando G. Salinero (Madrid: Catedra, 2000), ms. 1557–58, 154–55.

15. Roberto Salvini ("Monuments of Norman Art in Sicily and Southern Italy," in *The Normans in Sicily and Southern Italy*, ed. C.N.L. Bruke [London: British Academy, 1977], 64–92) suggests that one Arab, one Greek, one Norman, and one "Latin" [*sic*] are all represented in this setting, but the figures are not clearly identified.

16. This was the standard clothing in western Europe at this time, lasting until the turn of the thirteenth to the fourteenth centuries. See Françoise Piponnier and Perrine Mane, *Dress in the Middle Ages*, trans. Caroline Beamish (New Haven, CT: Yale University Press, 1997), 40–41.

17. There is a later example of this typology on the base of the Paschal Candelabrum at Capela Palatina, carved in the 1180s, in which four lions hold two animals and two human beings. See William Tronzo, *The Cultures of His Kingdom: Roger II and the Capela Palatina in Palermo* (Princeton, NJ: Princeton University Press, 1997), 84.

18. The issue of the title of the kings of Sicily is raised in Houben, *Roger II of Sicily*, 131–32.

19. David Abulafia, *The Two Italies: Economic Relations between the Norman Kingdom of Sicily and the Northern Communes* (Cambridge: Cambridge University Press, 1997).

20. Charles Verlinden, *L'esclavage dans l'Europe médiévale* (Gent: Rijksuniversiteit te Gent, 1977), 2:196–208.

21. Aziz Ahmad, *A History of Islamic Sicily* (Edinburgh: Edinburgh University Press, 1975).

22. Henri Bresc, *Politique et société en Sicile, XIIe–XVe siècle* (Aldershot, UK: Variorum, 1990), text 1.

23. Ibid.

24. Reported by the *Chronicon* of Romualdo II, archbishop of Palermo, and mainly, (disputably) Hugo Falcando, *Historia*, in *Cronisti e Scrittori sincroni della dominazione normanna nel Regno di Puglia e Sicilia*, ed. Giuseppe del Re (Naples: Stamperia dell'Iride, 1845), 1:33, 382–83.

25. Francesco Giunta, *Bizantini e Bizantinismo nella Sicilia Normanna* (Palermo: Priulla, 1950), 89.

26. There is no reference to this ruler in the Arabic chronicles, and Michele Amari (*Storia dei musulmani di Sicilia* [Florence: Felice Le Monnier, 1868)], 3:149) rejects the suggestion of Ibn-el-Wardi as the original name.

27. Geoffrey Malaterra, *The Deeds of Count Roger of Calabria and Sicily and of His Brother Robert Guiscard*, trans. Kenneth Baxter Wolf (Ann Arbor: University of Michigan Press, 2005), 177 (4.1.).

28. Steven Runciman, *The Sicilian Vespers: A History of the Mediterranean World in the Later Thirteenth Century* (Cambridge: Cambridge University Press, 1958). The main sources are Saba Malespina, *Rerum sicularum historia,* in vol. 2, *Cronisti e Scrittori sincroni della dominazione normanna nel Regno di Puglia e Sicilia,* ed. Giuseppe del Re (Naples: Stamperia dell'Iride, 1845); Nicolo Jamsilla, *De rebus gestis Frederici II imperatoris ejusque filiorum Conradi et Manfredi Apuliæ et Siciliæ Regum,* in vol. 2, *Cronisti e Scrittori sincroni della dominazione normanna nel Regno di Puglia e Sicilia,* ed. Giuseppe del Re (Naples: Stamperia dell'Iride, 1845).

29. Verlinden, *L'esclavage dans l'Europe médiévale*, 2:287–90.

30. See the chapters by Pierre Bonnassie, Pierre Guichard, and Marie-Claude Gerbet in Bartolomé Bennassar, ed., *Histoire des espagnols, VIe–XXe siècles*, 2nd rev. ed. (Paris: Robert Laffont, 1992), 11–285; Vicente A. Alvárez Palenzuela and Luís Suárez Fernández, *Historia de España: La España musulmana y los inícios de los reinos cristianos (711–1157)* (Madrid: Gredos, 1991); Vicente A. Alvárez Palenzuela and Luís Suárez Fernández, *Historia de España: La consolidación de los reinos hispânicos (1157–1369)* (Madrid: Gredos, 1988); E. Levi-Provençal, *Histoire de l'Espagne Musulmane*, 4 vols. (Paris: Maisonneuve, 1950).

31. See José Orlandis, *Historia de España: Época visigoda (409–711)* (Madrid: Gredos, 1987); José Angel de García Cortázar, *Historia de España Alfaguara: La época medieval* (Madrid: Alianza, 1983); Miguel Ángel Ladero Quesada, ed., *La reconquista y el proceso de diferenciación política (1035–1217)* (Madrid: Espasa-Calpe, 1998); Maria Helena Cruz Coelho and Armando Luís Carvalho Homem, eds., *Portugal em definição de fronteiras (1096–1325)* (Lisbon: Estampa, 1996).

32. See also Maria Filomena Lopes de Barros, *Tempos e espaços de mouros: A minoria muçulmana no reino português (séculos XII a XV)* (Lisbon: Fundação Calouste Gulbenkian, 2007); James M. Powell, ed., *Muslims under Latin Rule, 1100–1300* (Princeton, NJ: Princeton University Press, 1990); Pierre Guichard, *Les musulmans de Valence et la reconquête*, 2 vols. (Damascus: Institut Français, 1990–91); Robert I. Burns, *Islam under the Crusaders: Colonial Survival in the Thirteenth Century Kingdom of Valencia* (Princeton, NJ: Princeton University Press, 1973).

33. See also Maria Luísa Ledesma, *Estudios sobre los mudéjares en Aragon* (Teruel, Spain, 1996), Miguel Angel Ladero Quesada, *Los mudéjares de Castilla en tiempos de Isabel I* (Valladolid, Spain: Instituto Isabel la Catolica, 1969); Mark D. Meyerson, *The Muslims of Valencia in the Age of Fernando and Isabel: Between Coexistence and Crusade* (Berkeley: University of California Press, 1991); José Hinojosa Montalvo, *Los mudéjares: La voz del Islam en la España cristiana*, 2 vols. (Teruel, Spain: Centro de Estudios Mudéjares, 2002).

34. There is still work to be done on the history of the mozárabes. See Diego Adrián Olstein, *La era del mozárabe: Los mozárabes de Toledo (siglos XII y XIII)* (Salamanca: Universidad de Salamanca, 2006). Still useful is Francisco Javier Simonet, *Historia de los mozárabes de España*, 2 vols. (1897–1903; repr., Valladolid, Spain: Maxtor, 2005).

35. Aires A. do Nascimento, ed. and trans., *Hagiografia de Santa Cruz de Coimbra: Vida de D. Telo, Vida de D. Teotónio, Vida de Martinho de Soure* (Lisbon: Colibri, 1998), 117. For a reference to the episode, see José Mattoso, *D. Afonso Henriques* (Lisbon: Temas e Debates, 2007), 163.

36. Aires A. do Nascimento, ed. and trans., *De expugnatione lixbonensi: Conquista de Lisboa aos Mouros; Relato de um cruzado* (Lisbon: Vega, 2001). Also mentioned in Mattoso, *D. Afonso Henriques*, 247.

37. Fortunato de Almeida, *História da Igreja em Portugal* (1930; repr., Porto, Portugal: Portucalense Editora, 1967), 1:274.

38. For a translated version of the poetic lament of Rabbi Abraham ibn Ezra, see S. Schwartz, "Elegia de Rabi Abraham ibn Ezera (1092–1167) sobre a tomada de Lisboa," *Revista Municipal* (Lisbon) (1952): 55.

39. Orlandis, *Época Visigoda*, 262–64.

40. McCormick, *Eternal Victory*, 312.

41. Luís Suárez Fernández, *Judíos españoles en la Edad Media* (Madrid: Rialp, 1980); Luís Suárez Fernández, *Los Judíos* (Barcelona: Ariel, 2005); Maria José Ferro Tavares, *Os judeus em Portugal no século XIV*, 2nd ed. (Lisbon: Guimarães, 2000).

42. David Nirenberg, *Communities of Violence: Persecution of Minorities in the Middle Ages* (Princeton, NJ: Princeton University Press, 1996); Maria José Ferro Tavaraes, *Os judeus em Portugal no século XV*, 2 vols. (Lisbon: Universidade Nova de Lisboa, 1982–84).

43. Albert A. Sicroff, *Les controversies du statut de pureté de sang en Espagne, XVe–XVIIe siècle* (Paris: Marcel Dicher, 1960). On the caste divide, see Francisco Bethencourt, *The Inquisition: A Global History, 1478–1834* (Cambridge: Cambridge University Press, 2009), 323–30.

44. Jaime Contreras et al., *La expusión de los judíos de España* (Madrid: Información y Historia, 1997); Angel Alcalá Galve, ed., *Judios, sefarditas y conversos: Las consequencias de la expulsion de 1492* (Valladolid, Spain: Ambito, 1995); François Soyer, *The Persecution of the Jews and Muslims of Portugal: King Manuel I and the End of Religious Tolerance (1496–7)* (Leiden: Brill, 2007).

45. Léon Poliakov, *Histoire de l'antisémitisme*, vol. 1, *L'âge de la foi* (1956; repr., Paris: Calmann-Lévy, 1981), 241–66. For the theological debate, see Jeremy Cohen, *The Friars and the Jews: The Evolution of Medieval Anti-Judaism* (Ithaca, NY: Cornell University Press, 1982); Jeremy Cohen, *Living Letters of the Law: Ideas of the Jew in Medieval Christianity* (Berkeley: University of California Press, 1999).

46. Ronnie Po-chia Hsia and Harmut Lehmann, eds., *In and Out of the Ghetto: Jewish-Gentile Relations in Late Medieval and Early Modern Germany* (Cambridge: Cambridge University Press, 2002); Miri Rubin, *Gentile Tales: The Narrative Assault on Late Medieval Jews* (New Haven, NJ: Yale University Press, 1999). On accusations of anthropophagi and ritual murder, see Gavin I. Langmuir, *Toward a Definition of Antisemitism* (Berkeley: University of California Press, 1990).

47. Mark R. Cohen and Abraham L. Udovitch, eds., *Jews among Arabs: Contacts and Boundaries* (Princeton, NJ: Darwin Press, 1989); Mark R. Cohen, *Under Crescent and Cross: The Jews in the Middle Ages*, 2nd ed. (Princeton, NJ: Princeton University Press, 2008).

48. See Poliakov, *Histoire de l'antisémitisme*, 1:60.

49. Yedida Kalfon Stillman, *Arab Dress from the Dawn of Islam to Modern Times* (Leiden: Brill, 2000), 101–19.

50. Poliakov, *Histoire de l'antisémitisme*, 1:85.

51. Joshua Prawer, *The Crusaders' Kingdom: European Colonialism in the Middle Ages* (1972; repr., London: Phoenix Press, 2001), 57–59, 233–51; Joshua Prawer, *The History of the Jews in the Latin Kingdom of Jerusalem* (Oxford: Clarendon Press, 1988), chapter 5.

52. Ronnie Ellenblum (*Frankish Rural Settlement in the Latin Kingdom of Jerusalem* [Cambridge: Cambridge University Press, 1998]) shows the existence of a significant Latin minority with more ties with the Muslim world than had been acknowledged by the previous generations of scholars.

53. Ludolph of Sudheim, "Le chemin de la terra sainte," trans. Christiane Deluz, in *Croisades et pèlérinages: Récits, chroniques et voyages en Terre Sainte, XIIe–XVIe siècle*, ed. Danielle Régnier-Bohler (Paris: Robert Laffont, 1997), 1035.

54. Usama Ibn Munqidh (*The Book of Contemplation: Islam and the Crusades*, trans., intro., and notes Paul M. Cobb [London: Penguin, 2008]) mentions frequent plunder and military engagement between Christians and Muslims, but also pacific relations.

55. Benjamin Z. Kedar, "The Subjected Muslims of the Frankish Levant," in *Muslims under Latin Rule, 1100–1300*, ed. James M. Powell (Princeton, NJ: Princeton University Press, 1990), 135–74.

56. Thomas S. Asbridge, *The Creation of the Principality of Antioch, 1098–1130* (Woodsbridge, UK: Boydell Press, 2000).

57. See Gabriella Uluhogian, Boghos L. Zekiyan, and Vartan Karapetian, eds., *Armenia: Impronte di una civiltà* (Milan: Skira, 2012).

58. Prawer, *The Crusaders' Kingdom*, 52–55. It is fascinating to compare the descriptions of the Oriental Christian churches by Louis de Rochechouart in 1461 and Guy de Toureste in 1486; see Danielle Régnier-Bohler, ed., *Croisades et pélérinages: Récits, chroniques et voyages en Terre Sainte, XIIe–XVIe siècle* (Paris: Robert Laffont, 1997), 1151–54, 1187–92.

59. Bernard Hamilton, *The Latin Church in the Crusaders States: The Secular Church* (London: Variorum, 1980), chapter 7.

60. Bernard Hamilton, *Crusader, Cathars, and the Holy Places* (Ashgate, UK: Variorum, 1999).

61. Ibid.

62. Hamilton, *The Latin Church*, chapter 8.

63. Prawer, *The Crusaders' Kingdom*, 159–91, 214–32.

Chapter 3: Universalism: Integration and Classification

1. Luca D'Ascia, *Il Corano e la tiara: L'Epistola a Maometto II di Enea Sílvio Piccolomini (papa Pio II)* (Bologna: Pendragon, 2001). The letter is translated into Italian and transcribed in the original Latin, preceded by an extensive introduction.

2. Pius II, *Commentaries*, ed. Margaret Meserve and Marcello Simonetta, 2 vols. (Cambridge, MA: Harvard University Press, Villa I Tatti Renaissance Library, 2003–7).

3. Luca D'Ascia, *Il Corano e la tiara*, 236 (Latin transcription of the letter).

4. Ibid., 238, 269–70.

5. *The Holy Bible* (King James version): Acts 10:34–35, 10:44–48, 11:1–18, 11:26, 13:26, 13:47, 14:27, 15:3, 15:9–11, 18:6; Romans 2:26, 9:30, 11:11, 15:7–12; I Corinthians 12:12–13; Galatians 2:14–21, 5:11–12; Ephesians 1:22–23, 2:11–22; Hebrews 9:26–28, 10:9–12.

6. Thomas Aquinas, *Political Writings*, ed. R. W. Dyson (Cambridge: Cambridge University Press, 2002), 85–89, 114–26, 158–65; Anthony Pagden, *The Fall of Natural Man: The American Indian and the Origin of Comparative Ethnology* (Cambridge: Cambridge University Press, 1982), 63–64.

7. Aquinus, *Political Writings*, 233–34, 267–73.

8. James M. Powell, "The Papacy and the Muslim Frontier," in *Muslims under Latin Rule, 1100–1300*, ed. James M. Powell (Princeton, NJ: Princeton University Press, 1990), 175–203; Benjamin Z. Kedar, *Crusade and Mission: European Approaches toward the Muslims* (Princeton, NJ: Princeton University Press, 1984), particularly 73.

9. Dante Alighieri, *Monarchia*, ed. and trans. Federico Sanguineti (Milan: Garzanti, 1985), 124–28; Lorenzo Valla, *La falsa donazione de Costantino*, ed. and trans. Olga Pugliese (Milan: Rizzoli, 2001).

10. James Muldoon, *Popes, Lawyers, and Infidels* (Philadelphia: University of Pennsylvania Press, 1979).

11. Jean Devisse, *L'image du noir dans l'art occidental*, vol. 2, *Des premiers siècles chrétiens aux 'grandes découvertes'*, book 1, *De la menace démoniaque à l'incarnation de sainteté* (Freiburg: Office du Livre/Le Ménil Foundation, 1979), 230.

12. Devisse, *L'image du noir dans l'art occidental*, 2:1:129–31. See also ibid., *Les Africans dans l'ordonnance Chrétien du monde (XIVe–XVIe siècle)*, by Jean Devisse and Michel Mollat (Freiburg: Office du Livre/Le Menil Foundation, 1979), 2:2:34, 44.

13. Devisse, *L'image du noir dans l'art occidental*, 2:1:135–39. I have not followed all of Devisse's interpretations; he did not make the obvious connection of the wise kings with the three continents. See also ibid., 2:2:28–30.

14. Devisse, *L'image du noir dans l'art occidental*, 2:1:149–204.

15. Dante, *Monarchia*, 138.

16. Robert Bartlett, "Illustrating Ethnicity in the Middle Ages," in *The Origins of Racism in the West*, ed. Miriam Eliav-Feldon, Benjamin Isaac, and Joseph Ziegler (Cambridge: Cambridge University Press, 2009), 132–56 (especially 137–39).

17. Devisse and Mollat, *Les Africans dans l'ordonnace Chrétien du monde (XIVe–XVIe siècle)*, 2:2:237–41.

18. Ibid., 2:2:73, 156. See the complete analysis of this legend in David M. Goldenberg, *The Curse of Ham: Race and Slavery in Early Judaism, Christianity, and Islam* (Princeton, NJ: Princeton University Press, 2003).

19. Michael Hechter, *Internal Colonialism: The Celtic Fringe in British National Development, 1536–1966* (Berkeley: University of California Press, 1975).

20. Régis Boyer, *Les Vikings: Histoire, mythes, dictionnaire* (Paris: Robert Laffont, 2008).

21. Bartlett, "Illustrating Ethnicity in the Middle Ages," especially 143–45.

22. Eric Christiansen, *The Northern Crusades*, 2nd ed. (London: Penguin, 1997).

23. Muldoon, *Popes, Lawyers, and Infidels*, 57.

24. John MacKenzie, ed., *Peoples, Nations, and Cultures: An A-Z of the Peoples of the World* (London: Weidenfeld and Nicholson, 2005), 399–400.

25. Nora Berend, *At the Gates of Christendom: Jews, Muslims, and "Pagans" in Medieval Hungary, c. 1000–c.1300* (Cambridge: Cambridge University Press, 2001), chapters 5–6.

26. Robert Bartlett, *The Making of Europe: Conquest, Colonization, and Cultural Change, 950–1350* (London: Penguin, 1994).

27. Charles Verlinden, *L'esclavage dans l'Europe médiévale* (Gent: Rijksuniversiteit te Gent, 1977), 1:321–30.

28. David Jacoby, "From Byzantium to Latin Romania: Continuity and Change," in *Latin and Greeks in the Eastern Mediterranean after 1204*, ed. Benjamin Arbel, Bernard Hamilton, and David Jacoby (London: Frank Cass, 1989), 1–44.

29. See Gerard of Wales, *Expugnatio Hibernica: The Conquest of Ireland*, ed. A. Brian Scott and Francis X. Martin (Dublin: Royal Irish Academy, 1978); Gerard of Wales, *Topographia hibernica*, ed. James Dimock, in *Giraldi Cambrensis Opera* (London: Rolls Series, 1861–91), 5:1–204. For a later synthesis of these prejudices, see John Davies, *Discovery of the True Causes Why Ireland Was Never Entirely Subdued* (London: John Jaggard, 1612). For the best analysis, see Bartlett, "Illustrating Ethnicity in the Middle Ages," especially 148–56.

30. A. Cosgrove, "Marriage in Medieval Ireland," in *Marriage in Ireland*, ed. A. Cosgrove (Dublin, 1985); James Lydon, "The Middle Nation," in *The English in Medieval Ireland*, ed. James Lydon (Dublin, 1984).

31. John H. Elliott, *Empires of the Atlantic World: Britain and Spain in America, 1492–1830* (New Haven, CT: Yale University Press, 2006), 79–80.

Chapter 4: Typologies of Humankind and Models of Discrimination

1. Maria Laura Testi Cristiani, "Nicola Pisano nella cupola del Duomo di Siena," *Critica d'Arte* 10 (1986): 30–40, 11 (1986): 28–30.

2. Dante Alighieri, *Monarchia*, ed. and trans. Federico Sanguineti (Milan: Garzanti, 1985), 138.

3. Martin W. Lewis and Kären E. Wigen, *The Myth of Continents: A Critique of Metageography* (Berkeley: University of California Press, 1997).

4. Natalia Lozovsky, *"The Earth Is Our Book": Geographical Knowledge in the Latin West, ca. 400–1000* (Ann Arbor: University of Michigan Press, 2000), 106.

5. I disagree here with Robert Bartlett, who dismissed descent as a relatively insignificant criterion in this period. See Robert Barlett, *The Making of Europe: Conquest, Colonization and Cultural Change, 950–1350* (London: Penguin, 1994).

6. Idrisi, *Il libro di Ruggero*, partly translated in Michele Amari, ed., *Biblioteca Arabo-Sicula* (1880–81; repr., Bologna: Arnaldo Forni, 1981), 1:42.

7. Niketas Choniatēs, *O City of Byzantium: Annals of Niketas Choniatēs*, trans. and intro. Harry J. Magoulias (Detroit: Wayne State University Press, 1984), 50–51. For a reproduction of the portrait of Manuel Komnenos with Maria of Antioch, see ibid., xxxii.

8. See Song of Solomon 1:5 and 1:6 in the authorized King James version: *The Holy Bible Containing the Old and New Testaments* (Cambridge: Cambridge University Press, n.d.). Choniatēs cleverly amalgamated the beginning of two verses.

9. The patristic exegesis of the biblical extracts on blackness is well analyzed in Jean Marie Courtés, "Traitement patristique de la thématique 'Ethiopiennes,'" in *L'image du noir dans l'art occidental*, by Jean Devisse (Freiburg: Office du Livre/Le Ménil Foundation, 1979), 2:1:9–31.

10. *Corpus Christianorum: Continuatio Mediæualis*, vol. 63-A, *Willelmi Tyrensis Archiepiscopi Chronicon*, ed. R.B.C. Huygens, annotated H. E. Mayer and G. Rösch (Turnhout, Belgium: Brepols, 1986), 15–20, 16–20, 18–22. See also the French translation by Monique Zerner in Danielle Régnier-Bohler, ed., *Croisades et Pélérinages: Récits, chroniques et voyages en Terre Sainte XXe–XVIe siècle* (Paris: Robert Laffont, 1997), 604, 623, 650.

11. These examples are taken from Choniatēs's chronicle, but other sources, like the comments of Anna Komnena (1083–1153) on the Crusaders, develop the same idea of the brutal behavior, extraordinary greed, and barbarian manners of the Latin Christians (also named Franks); see Anna Comnena, *The Alexiad*, trans. E.R.A. Sewter (London: Penguin, 1969), 14:438–51.

12. See John of Joinville and Geoffrey of Villehardouin, *Chronicles of the Crusades*, trans. and intro. M.R.B. Shaw (Harmondsworth, UK: Penguin, 1963); Robert de Clari, *La conquête de Constantinople*, ed. and trans. Peter Noble (Edinburgh: Société Rencevals, 2005); Alfred J. Andrea, ed., *Contemporary Sources for the Fourth Crusade* (Leiden: Brill, 2000).

13. *Patrologiæ cursus completus* (Paris: J-P-Migne, 1855), 211:246 (§ 19): "Age, inquit, perfide senex, ostend mihi quas potiores servas reliquias, vel scias te statim mortis supplicio puniendum"; cited and translated in Joshua Prawer, *The Crusaders' Kingdom: European Colonialism in the Middle Ages* (1972; repr., London: Phoenix Press, 2001), 182.

14. Prawer, *The Crusaders' Kingdom*, 214.

15. Alfonso X the Wise, *Libro de los juegos: Ordenamiento de las tafurerias*, ed. Raul Orellana Calderón (Madrid: Fundación José Antônio de Castro, 2007); Matilde Lopez Serrano, ed., *Cantigas de Santa Maria de Alfonso X el Sabio, rey de Castilla* (1979; repr., Madrid: Patrimônio Nacional, 1987).

16. Olivia Remie Constable ("Chess and Courtly Culture in Medieval Castile: The Libro de Ajedrez of Alfonso X, el Sábio," *Speculum* 82, no. 2 [April 2007]: 301–47) contests the idea of chess as an allegory for the whole range of humankind and considers that the variety of human types represented in this book is limited to court society.

17. Ibn Khaldûn, *The Muqaddimah: An Introduction to History*, trans. Frank Rosenthal, ed. N. J. Dawood (Princeton, NJ: Princeton University Press, 1967), 59, 117.

18. Ludolph of Sudheim, "Le chemin de la Terre Sainte," in *Croisades et Pélérinages: Récits, chroniques et voyages en Terre Sainte XXe–XVIe siècle*, ed. Danielle Régnier-Bohler (Paris: Robert Laffont, 1997), 1035.

19. See the facsimile edition, *El Atlas Catalan de Cresques Abraham* (Barcelona: Diaspora, 1975); Evelyn Georges Grosjean, ed., *Mappamundi: The Catalan Atlas for the Year 1375* (Zurich: Urs Graf, 1978); Monique Pelletier et al., *Mappamundi: Une carte du monde au XIVe siècle* (Paris: Montparnasse Multimedia, 1998), a CD-ROM edition with all the captions translated into French; Evelyn Edson, *The World Map, 1300–1492: The Resistance of Tradition and Transformation* (Baltimore: Johns Hopkins University Press, 2007).

20. Felipe Fernández-Armesto, *Before Columbus: Exploration and Colonisation from the Mediterranean to the Atlantic, 1229–1492* (Basingstoke, UK: Macmillan, 1987), 146.

21. For a good French translation of the original Latin, see Guillaume de Rubrouck, *Voyage dans l'empire mongol (1253–1255)*, trans. Claire Kappler and René Kappler (Paris: Payot, 1985). I have used the Latin and English versions; Richard Hakluyt, ed., *The Principal Voyages, Traffiques, and Discoveries of the English Nation* (1589; repr., Glasgow: James MacLehose and Sons, 1903), 227, 291.

22. Robert I. Burns, "Muslims in the Thirteenth Century Realms of Aragon: Interaction and Reaction," in *Muslims under Latin Rule, 1100–1300*, ed. James M. Powell (Princeton, NJ: Princeton University Press, 1990), 79.

23. Francesco Giunta, *Bizantini e Bizantinismo nella Sicilia Normanna* (Palermo: Priulla, 1950), 61.

24. Geoffrey Malaterra, *The Deeds of Count Roger of Calabria and Sicily and of His Brother Duke Robert Guiscard*, trans. Kenneth Baxter Wolf (Ann Arbor: University of Michigan Press, 2005), 60, 65, 71 (1.13, 1.17, 1.28).

25. Hugo Falcando (disputed author), *La Historia*, in *Cronisti e Scrittori sincroni della dominazione normanna nel Regno di Puglia e Sicilia*, ed. Giuseppe del Re (Naples: Stamperia dell'Iride, 1845), 1:279.

26. Ibn Hawqal, travel account partly translated in Amari, *Biblioteca Arabo-Sicula*, 1:24.

27. Abd Allah Yaqût, travel account partly translated in Amari, *Biblioteca Arabo-Sicula*, 1:209–10.

28. Khaldûn, *The Muqaddimah*, 28, 116.

29. P. D. King, "The Barbarian Kingdoms," in *The Cambridge History of Medieval Political Thought, c. 350–c.1450*, ed. J. H. Burns (Cambridge: Cambridge University Press, 1988), 130–31.

30. Joseph F. O'Callaghan, "The Mudéjares of Castile and Portugal in the Twelfth and Thirteenth Centuries," in *Muslims under Latin Rule, 1100–1300*, ed. James M. Powell (Princeton, NJ: Princeton University Press, 1990), 11–56.

31. Benjamin Z. Kedar, "The Subjected Muslims of the Frankish Levant," in *Muslims under Latin Rule, 1100–1300*, ed. James M. Powell (Princeton, NJ: Princeton University Press, 1990), 155.

32. Ibn Jubayr, travel account partly translated in Amari, *Biblioteca Arabo-Sicula*, 1:144, 162.

33. This episode is reported by several Arab writers—for example, Ibn al Atir and Ibn Khaldûn; see ibid., 1:479–80, 2:229. See also the Christian view from the contemporary archbishop of Salerno, Romualdo Guarona, in Giuseppe del Re, ed., *Cronisti e Scrittori sincroni della dominazione normanna nel Regno di Puglia e Sicilia* (Naples: Stamperia dell'Iride, 1845), 1:17–19.

34. See the chroniclers of Romualdo and (supposedly) Falcando in del Re, *Cronisti*, 1:31, 341–49.

35. Falcando in ibid., 1:355–60.

36. Geoffrey Malaterra, *The Deeds of Count Roger*, 182 (4.6).

37. For a description by the contemporary archbishop Romualdo of the 1161 riot and the massacre of the Muslims, see del Re, *Cronisti*, 1:26.

38. Henri Bresc, *Politique et société en Sicile, XIIe–XVe siècle* (Aldershot, UK: Variorum, 1990), chapter 8.

39. Charles Verlinden, *L'esclavage dans l'Europe médiévale* (Gent: Rijksuniversiteit te Gent, 1977), 1:176–78.

40. James M. Powell, "The Papacy and the Muslim Frontier," in *Muslims under Latin Rule, 1100–1300*, ed. James M. Powell (Princeton, NJ: Princeton University Press, 1990), 175–203; James Muldoon, *Popes, Lawyers, and Infidels* (Philadelphia: University of Pennsylvania Press, 1979).

41. Verlinden, *L' esclavage dans l'Europe médiévale*, 1:38–39.

42. Karla Malette, *The Kingdom of Sicily, 1100–1250: A Literary History* (Philadelphia: University of Pennsylvania Press, 2005), 166–67. For the letter of excommunication, see Jean Louis Alphonse Huillard Breholles, *Historia diplomatica Frederici secundi* (1852–61; repr., Turin: Erasmo, 1963), 6:1:325.

43. Burns, "Muslims in the Thirteenth Century Realms of Aragon," 86.

44. I am extending here the notion of the stranger, or the stranger within, elaborated in Georg Simmel, "The Stranger," in *On Individuality and Social Forms*, ed. and intro. Donald N. Levine (Chicago: University of Chicago Press, 1971), 143–49.

PART II: OCEANIC EXPLORATION

1. The geographic notion of continents only became rooted in the nineteenth century, but I will use it as synonym for parts of the world.

2. Isidore of Seville, *Etimologie o origini*, ed. and trans. Angelo Valastro Canale (Turin: UTET, 2004), 1:706–7 (IX, II, 2). On this point Isidore followed Saint Augustine, *The City of God against Pagans*, trans. William M. Green, 7 vols. (Cambridge, MA: Harvard University Press, 1966–72). The significant passage is in ibid., 5:39 (book 16, chapter 6).

3. Armando Cortesão, ed., *The Suma Oriental of Tomé Pires and the Book of Francisco Rodrigues* (London: Hakluyt Society, 1944). Pires's manuscript was first included in Giovanni Battista Ramusio, *Navigazioni e Viaggi*, ed. Marica Milanesi, 6 vols. (1550–59; repr., Turin: Einaudi, 1978–88). It was preceded in this compilation by a text of similar scope, also written in 1512–15, by Duarte Barbosa, a notary at the royal factory of Cannanore in India. For the critical edition, see Maria Augusta da Veiga e Sousa, ed., *O livro de Duarte Barbosa*, 2 vols. (Lisbon: IICT, 1996–2000).

4. Gonzalo Fernández de Oviedo, *Historia General y Natural de las Índias*, ed. Juan Pérez de Tudela Bueso, 5 vols. (Madrid: Atlas, 1959). The first part had been published in Seville in 1535, and the beginning of the second part in Valladolid in 1557. It was translated by Ramusio, although two-thirds of the text remained in manuscript form until the nineteenth century. For the only clear and synthetic history of the manuscript, see Giovanni Battista Ramusio, *Navigazione e Viaggi*, ed. Marica Milanesi (1550–59; repr., Turin: Einaudi, 1978–88), 5:343.

5. This was the first consistent account of the region. Although it remained in manuscript form until 1733 (a bad edition, only corrected in 1841), it reveals a new capacity for protoethnographic description: António Brásio, ed., *Tratado breve dos rios de Guiné e Cabo Verde* (Lisbon: LIAM, 1964).

6. Giovanni Botero, *Relationi universali*, rev. ed., 4 parts (Vicenza: Heredi di Perin, 1595). He never left Europe (he knew Italy, France, and Spain well), but he could read several languages, including Portuguese and Spanish, and made good use of the most recent accounts.

7. See Nell Irvin Painter, *The History of White People* (New York: W. W. Norton, 2010).

8. Martin W. Lewis and Kären E. Wigen, *The Myth of Continents: A Critique of Metageography* (Berkeley: University of California Press, 1997).

CHAPTER 5: HIERARCHIES OF CONTINENTS AND PEOPLES

1. Abraham Ortelius, *Theatrum Orbis Terrarum*, 1st ed. (Antwerp, 1570); C. Koeman, *The History of Abraham Ortelius and His Theatrum Orbis Terrarum* (Lausanne: Sequoia, 1964); L. Voet, *The Plantin Press, 1555–1589*,

vol. 4 (Amsterdam: van Hoeve, 1982); M.P.R. van den Broeke, "Unstable Editions of Ortelius' Atlas," *Map Collector* 70, (1995): 2–8.

2. For the best introduction to this subject, see Elizabeth McGrath, "Humanism, Allegorical Invention, and the Personification of the Continents," in *Rubenianum. Concept, Design, and Execution in Flemish Printing (1550–1700)*, ed. Hans Vlieghe, Arnout Belis, and Carl van de Velde (Turnhout: Brepols, 2000), 43–71. For the iconographic explanations already introduced into the *Atlas* by the verses of Adolphus Mekerkus and extended by Peter Heyns in the translation into Dutch, see Werner Waterschoot, "The Title Page of Ortelius' Theatrum Orbis Terrarum," *Quaerendo* 9, no. 1 (1979): 43–68.

3. Sebastian Münster, *Cosmographei, oder beschreibung aller länder* (1544) (Basel: Henrichum Petri, 1550).

4. See Nicholas Crane, *Mercator: The Man Who Mapped the Planet* (London: Weidenfeld and Nicolson, 2002).

5. See the reproduction in Yussuf Kāmal, *Monumenta Cartographica Africae et Aegypti* (Cairo, 1926–51), vol. 2, part 2, plate 321.

6. See McGrath, "Humanism," 57.

7. Kāmal, *Monumenta Cartographica Africae et Aegypt*, vol. 2, part 4, plate AA2. Ortelius again used the personification of Egypt in his second map of ancient Egypt printed in 1584 (ibid., plate AA4).

8. This and other references in this paragraph were taken from Friedrich Polleross, Andrea Sommer-Mathis, and Christopher Laferl, *Federschmuck und Kaiserkrone: Das barocke Amerikabild in den habsburgischen Ländern*, catalog for the exhibition at Schloss im Marchfeld (Vienna: Bundesministerium für Wissenschaft und Forschung, 1992), 21–23, 128.

9. Burgkmair recycled his first woodcuts of African peoples from Guinea and South Africa printed in 1508 for Balthasar Springer's account of his journey to India with the fleet of the first Portuguese viceroy of India, Francisco de Almeida. Albrecht Dürer, who shared Burgkmair's fascination with exotic artifacts, also participated in the project of Maximilian's triumph with other artists. See Jean Michel Massing, *Studies in Imagery*, vol. 2, *The World Discovered* (London: Pindar, 2007), 114–40.

10. Besides Polleross, see C. A. Marsden, "Entrées et fêtes espagnoles au XVIe siècle," in *Les fêtes de la Renaissance*, ed. Jean Jacquot (Paris: CNRS, 1960), 2:389–411 (for the specific case, see ibid., 402).

11. Fernando Checa Cremades, *Carlos V y la imagen del héroe en el Renacimiento* (Madrid: Taurus, 1987), 268.

12. Sheila Williams, "Les ommegangs d'Anvers et les cortèges du lord-maire de Londres," in *Les fêtes de la Renaissance*, ed. Jean Jacquot (Paris: CNRS, 1960), 2:349–57.

13. Immanuel Wallerstein, *The Modern World-System: Capitalist Agriculture and the Origins of the European World-Economy in the Sixteenth Century* (San Diego: Academic Press, 1974), 1:165–221; Fernand Braudel, *Civilisation matérielle, économie et capitalisme, XVe–XVIIIe siècle*, vol. 3, *Le temps du monde* (Paris: Armand Colin, 1979), 99–200.

14. Hugo Soly, ed., *Charles V and His Time, 1500–1558* (Antwerp: Mercatorfonds, 1999).

15. Leon Voet, *L' âge d'or d'Anvers: Essor et gloire de la Metropole au seizième siècle*, trans. Anne Fillon (Antwerp: Mercatorfonds, 1976); Peter Burke, *Antwerp: A Metropolis in Comparative Perspective* (Antwerp: Martial and Snoeck, 1993).

16. More than 40 percent of the Low Countries population already lived in urban areas around 1500. See Jan de Vries, *The Dutch Rural Economy in the Golden Age, 1500–1700* (New Haven, CT: Yale University Press, 1974), 83.

17. Giorgio Mangani, *Il "mondo" di Abramo Ortelio: Misticismo, geografia e collezionismo nel Rinascimento dei Paesi Bassi* (Ferrara, Italy: Franco Cosimo Panini, 1998); Marcel van den Broecke, Peter van der Krogt, and Peter Meurer, eds., *Abraham Ortelius and the First Atlas: Essays Commemorating the Quadricentennial of His Death, 1598–1998)* (Houten, Netherlands: HES, 1998). The *Album Amicorum*, organized by Ortelius from 1573 onward, recorded around 130 friends from different European countries, including the main humanists of the time.

18. For an inventory, see Susi Colin, "Woodcutters and Cannibals: Brazilian Indians as Seen in Early Maps," in *America: Early Maps of the New World*, ed. Hans Wolff (Munich: Prestel, 1992), 175–83. See also Stephanie Leitch, *Mapping Ethnography in Early Modern Germany: New Worlds in Print Culture* (Basingstoke, UK: Palgrave, 2010).

19. Georg Braun and Frans Hogenberg, *Civitates Orbis Terrarum*, ed. and intro. D. A. Skelton, 3 vols. (1572–1618; repr., Cleveland: World Publishing Company, 1966).

20. Hans Weigel, *Habitus praecipuorum populorum . . . Trachtenbuch* (Nuremberg, 1577). The artist was Jost Amman. See Sabine Poeschel, *Studien zur Ikonographie der Erdteile in der Kunst des 16.–18.: Jahrhunderts* (Munich: Scaneg, 1985), 384.

21. This is still the main thesis in Fernand Braudel, *Civilisation matérielle, économie et capitalisme, XVe–XVIIIe siècle*, vol. 1, *Les structures du quotidien* (Paris: Armand Colin, 1979), 351–69. Carlo Mario Belfanti, "Was Fashion a European Invention?" *Journal of Global History* 3 (2008): 419–43; Ulinka Rublack, *Dressing Up: Cultural Identity in Renaissance Europe* (Oxford: Oxford University Press, 2010), 1–32, 259–85.

22. Abraham de Bruyn, *Omnium pene Europae, Asiae, Aphricae atque Americae gentium habitus* (Antwerp, 1581).

23. For reproductions of these images, see MacGrath, "Humanism," 44–53.

24. Günther Schilder, ed., *Monumenta Cartographica Neerlandica*, 8 vols., (Alphen ann den Rijn, Netherlands: Vitgeverij Canaletto, 1986–2007). This collection includes eight folders with reproductions of the maps. The plates reproducing the world maps of Visscher and Plancius are in the folders for volume 6 (plate 6) and volume 7 (plate 18).

25. See Cesare Ripa, *Iconologia*, ed. Piero Buscaroli, preface Mario Praz (Milan: TEA, 1992); based on the 1618 Tozzi edition.

26. For an analysis of Francken's paintings, McGrath, "Humanism," 59–64. For an inventory of all these cases, see Poeschel, *Studien zur Ikonographie der Erdteile*, 312–431.

27. Carel Allard, *Orbis habitabilis oppida et vestitus*, ed. and intro. R. K. Skelton (1695; repr., Cleveland: World Publishing Company, 1966).

28. Poeschel, *Studien zur Ikonographie der Erdteile*, 312–431. John Marino ("The Invention of Europe," in *The Renaissance World*, ed. John Jeffries Martin [New York: Routledge, 2007], 155) estimated the number of works dedicated to the personification of Europe in this period as 84 in Italy, 39 in the Netherlands, 47 in France, and 15 in Germany. This last case is clearly underestimated, but Marino's figures (without inventory) suggest a reevaluation of the situation in France and the Low Countries.

29. Svetlana Alpers and Michael Baxandall, *Tiepolo and the Pictorial Intelligence* (New Haven, CT: Yale University Press, 1994).

30. Peter Mason, *Infelicities: Representations of the Exotic* (Baltimore: Johns Hopkins University Press, 1998).

31. The issue of Orientalism should be studied in a much wider historical context than that suggested by Edward Said in his *Orientalism* (1978; repr., New York: Vintage Books, 1994). I also think that art had played a much more important role in this strand of thought since the Middle Ages.

32. Anne Middleton Wagner, *Jean-Baptiste Carpeaux: Sculptor of the Second Empire* (New Haven, CT: Yale University Press, 1986); Elizabeth McGrath, "Caryatids, Page Boys, and African Fetters: Themes of Slavery in European Art," in *The Slave in European Art: From Renaissance Trophy to Abolitionist Emblem*, ed. Elizabeth McGrath and Jean Michel Massing (London: Warburg Institute, 2012), 3–38.

33. For the extraordinary increase in territories and populations controlled by Europeans between 1880 and 1938, see Bouda Etemad, *La possession du monde: Poids et measures de la colonisation* (Bruxelles: Complexe, 2000), 229–59.

34. For this notion, see Anthony Pagden, *The Fall of Natural Man: The American Indian and the Origins of Comparative Ethnology* (Cambridge: Cambridge University Press, 1982), 146–97.

35. Bernardino de Sahagun, *Florentine Codex: General History of the Things of New Spain*, ed. and trans. Carles Dibble and Arthur J. O. Anderson, 12 vols. (Santa Fe: School of American Research, 1950–70). See also the integral edition of the Spanish text, Bernardino de Sahagun, *Historia general de las cosas de Nueva España*, ed. Alfredo López Austin and Josefina García Quintana, 2 vols. (Madrid: Alianza, 1988).

36. Bartolomé de Las Casas, *Historia de las Indias*, ed. Agustín Millares Carlo, intro. Lewis Hanke (Mexico City: Fondo de Cultura Económica, 1951); Bartolomé de Las Casas, *Apologética Historia Sumaria*, ed. Eduardo O'Gorman, preface M. León-Portilla (Mexico City, 1967); Bartolomé de Las Casas, *Obra indigenista*, ed. José Alcina Franch (Madrid: Alianza, 1985).

37. Pagden, *The Fall of Natural Men*, 27–119.

38. Besides the references in ibid. (97–98, 161), see Adriano Prosperi, "'Otras Indias': Missionari della Controriforma tra contadini e selvaggi" (1982), in *America e Apocalisse e altri saggi* (Pisa: Istituti Editoriali e Poligrafici Internazionali, 1999), 65–87.

39. José de Acosta, *De procuranda indorum salute*, ed. L. Pereña, V. Abril, C. Baciero, A. Garcia, D. Ramos, J. Barrientos, and F. Maseda (1588; repr., Madrid, CSIC, 1984), 1:60–71.

40. José de Acosta, *Historia Natural y Moral de las Índias*, ed. Edmundo O'Gorman (1590; repr., Mexico City: Fondo de Cultura Económica, 1962), book 6, chapter 19. I have also used the edition by José Alcina Franch with a useful introduction, although the O'Gorman edition is cited below: José de Acosta, *Historia Natural y Moral de las Índias* (Madrid: Historia 16, 1987), 419 (6:19).

41. Acosta, *Historia Natural y Moral de las Índias*, book 7, chapters 1–3.

42. Ibid., book 7, chapter 3.

43. Ibid., book 5.

44. Ibid., book 6, chapters 4–9. The anecdote about Acosta's name is in ibid., chapter 5; the other references are in ibid., chapters 5–6. For an earlier mention of Acosta's prejudices concerning the Chinese characters, see John H. Elliott, "The Discovery of America and the Discovery of Man," *Proceedings of the British Academy* 58 (1972): 102–25.

45. Las Casas, *Obra Indigenista*, 194–95. This is the summary by Domingo de Soto of the first critique addressed by Las Casas to the theories of Juan Ginés de Sepúlveda in Valladolid in 1552.

Chapter 6: Africans

1. Rui de Pina, *Chronica d'el rei D. João II*, in *Crónicas*, ed. M. Lopes de Almeida (Porto, Portugal: Lello, 1977), chapter 37.

2. For a good definition of this ambiguous social type, which pervaded the Portuguese expansion, see Vitorino Magalhães Godinho, *A expansão quatrocentista portuguesa*, rev. and enlarged ed. (1962; repr., Lisbon: Dom Quixote, 2008).

3. This image is inscribed, for instance, in the first systematic description of the kingdom of Congo, translated into Latin, Dutch, English, German, and French, and drawing on the direct testimony of Duarte Lopes, who had lived there for a long time: Filippo Pigafetta, *Relatione del reame di Congo et delle circonvicine contrade* (Rome: Bartolomeo Grassi, 1591), book 2, chapter 5. There is a facsimile of the Italian edition with a Portuguese translation: Rosa Capeans, *Relação do Reino do Congo e das Terras Circunvizinhas*, 2 vols. (Lisbon: Agência Geral do Ultramar, 1951).

4. Pina, *Chronica d'el rei D. João II*, chapter 57.

5. For significant extracts of the different chronicles, see António Brásio, ed., *Monumenta Missionaria Africana: África Ocidental*, vol. 1 (Lisbon: Agência Geral do Ultramar, 1952). See also the important documents in Visconde de Paiva Manso, *História do Congo: Documentos* (Lisbon: Academia Real das Sciencias, 1877). See also W.G.L. Randles, *L'ancien royaume du Congo des origines à la fin du XIXe siècle* (Paris: Mouton, 1968), chapters 7–8; Jan Vansina, *Kingdoms of the Savana* (Madison: University of Wisconsin Press, 1966), 37–69, 98–123; Luc de Heusch, *Le roi de Kongo et les monsters sacrés* (Paris: Gallimard, 2000); Linda M. Heywood and John K. Thornton, *Central Africans and the Foundation of the Américas, 1585–1660* (Cambridge: Cambridge University Press, 2007), 49–108.

6. This sustained process of indoctrination concerned people from different areas: there is a receipt for expenses, from 1538 to 1543, for black and Indian students placed in Lisbon, in two convents of the Secular Canons of St. John Evangelist. See Brásio, *Monumenta Missionaria Africana*, 2:66–69. The most significant documents by the Portuguese king, Manuel, on this issue are from 1512, and concern the embassy of Simão da Silva to Congo. See ibid., Brásio, 1:222–53.

7. Pigafetta, *Relatione del reame di Congo et delle circonvicine contrade*, book 2, chapter 1.

8. Brásio, *Monumenta Missionaria Africana*, 1:414–47. Henrique was elected bishop of Utica

9. Charles Ralph Boxer, *Race Relations in the Portuguese Colonial Empire, 1415–1825* (Oxford: Oxford University Press, 1963), chapter 1; C. R. Boxer, *The Church Militant and Iberian Expansion* (Baltimore: Johns Hopkins University Press, 1978), chapter 1; Heywood and Thornton, *Central Africa*, 103.

10. Randles, *L'ancien royaume du Congo*, 95.

11. Giovanni Antonio Cavazzi, *Istorica descrizione de' tre regni Congo, Matamba et Angola* (Bologna: Giacomo Monti, 1687), book 1, 26, 62–69. For a Portuguese translation, although not a reliable one, see Graziano Maria de Leguzzano, *Descrição histórica dos três reinos do Congo, Matamba e Angola*, 2 vols. (Lisbon: Junta de investigações do Ultramar, 1965).

12. Cavazzi, *Istorica descrizione*, book 5, 601–29. The author was responsible for the late (re)conversion to Catholicism of Queen Njinga, who he assisted until her death and whose funeral he organized. A scene of cannibalism not related to the Jagas was presented at the beginning of the book in an illustration of a palm tree (ibid., 32).

13. Olfert Dapper, *Description de l'Afrique*, 1st Dutch ed. (1668; repr., Amsterdam: Wolfgang, Waesberge, Boom and van Someren, 1686), 94, 117.

14. Ibid., 99.

15. Ibid., 320.

16. Ibid., 348, 356.

17. Ibid., 385.

18. Ibid., 465.

19. Ibid., 395.

20. Ibid., 410, 422.

21. Ibid., 98.

22. Fernand Braudel's refusal of the dynamics of appearance in other continents replicated a rooted European perception expressed by many sources. See Fernand Braudel, *Civilisation matérielle, économie et capitalisme, XVe–XVIIIe siècle* (Paris: Armand Colin, 1979), 1:351–76.

23. Hugh Barnes, *Gannibal: The Moor of Petersburg* (London: Profile, 2005).

24. A. C. De C. M. Saunders, "The Life and Humour of João de Sá Panasco, o Negro, Former Slave, Court, and Gentleman of the Portuguese Royal House (fl. 1524–1567)," in *Medieval and Renaissance Studies in Spain and Portugal in Honour of P. C. Russell*, ed. F. W. Hodcraft, D. G. Pattison, R.D.F. Pring-Mill, and R. W. Truman (Oxford: Society for the Study of Medieval Languages and Literature, 1981), 180–91; Francisco Bethencourt, "Anedotas e racismo em Portugal no século XVI," in *A primavera toda para ti: Homenagem a Helder Macedo*, ed. M. C. Ribeiro, T. C. Cerdeira, J. Perkins, and P. Rothwell (Lisbon: Presença, 2004), 129–42.

25. José Hermano Saraiva, ed., *Ditos portugueses dignos de memória. História íntima do século XVI*, 3rd ed. (Lisbon: Publicações Europa-América, 1997).

26. I follow here the reconstruction of this case in Roberto Zapperi, *Il selvaggio gentiluomo: L'incredibile storia di Pedro Gonzalez e dei suoi figli* (Rome: Donzelli, 2005).

27. Richard Bernheimer, *Wild Men in the Middle Ages* (Cambridge, MA: Harvard University Press, 1952); Timothy Husband, *The Wild Man: Medieval Myth and Symbolism* (New York: Metropolitan Museum of Art, 1980); Roger Bartra, *Wild Men in the Looking Glass: The Mythic Origins of European Otherness*, trans. Carl T. Berrinford (Ann Arbor: University of Michigan Press, 1994).

28. Merry Wiesner, *The Marvellous Hairy Girls: The Gonzales Sisters and Their Worlds* (New Haven, CT: Yale University Press, 2009).

29. For a colored reproduction of the painting, see Nicola Spinosa, ed., *Museo Nazionale di Capodimonte* (Naples: Electa, 1994), 102 (inventory number Q369). As Zapperi (*Il selvaggio gentiluomo*) rightly pointed out, Carracci managed to subvert the iconographic program, showing the harmony between animals (and perhaps their superiority).

30. Jean Michel Massing, "Hans Burgkmair's Depiction of Native Africans" (1995), in *Studies in Imagery* (London: Pindar, 2007), 2:114–40.

31. Francisco Bethencourt, "Race Relations in the Portuguese Empire," in *Encompassing the Globe: Portugal and the World in the 16th and 17th Centuries; Essays*, ed. Jay Levenson (Washington, DC: Smithsonian Institution, 2007), 45–53, 263–65.

32. Nicholas Cleynaert, *Correspondence*, ed. Alphonse Roersch (Brussels: Palais des Académies, 1940), 1:111; Jorge Fonseca, "Black Africans in Portugal during Cleynaerts's visit (1533–8)," in *Black Africans in Renaissance Europe*, ed. T. F. Earle and Kate Lowe (Cambridge: Cambridge University Press, 2005), 113–21.

33. Jean Michel Massing, "The Quest for the Exotic: Albrecht Dürer in the Netherlands" (1992), in *Studies in Imagery* (London: Pindar, 2007), 2:359–75.

34. Anthea Brook, *Pietro Tacca a Livorno: Il monumento a Ferdinando I de' Medici* (Livorno: Commune di Livorno, 2008).

35. The painting is in Dresden at the Gemäldegalerie Alte Meister der staatlichen Kunstsammlungen (inventory 1017). See Christopher Brown and Hans Vlieghe, eds., *Van Dick, 1599–1641* (Antwerp: Antwerpen Open, 1999), 142–43. For a good analysis of the painting and the engravings it inspired, see Carl Depauw and Ger Luijten, eds., *Antoine Van Dick et l'estampe* (Antwerp: Antwerpen Open, 1999), 280–83.

36. Trustees of the Barber Institute of Fine Arts, University of Birmingham. For a reference, see Brown and Hans Vlieghe, *Van Dick*, 180–81.

37. The portrait of Juan de Pareja by Velázquez is in New York City at the Metropolitan Museum of Art. See Antonio Dominguez Ortiz, Alfonso E. Pérez Sánchez, and Julián Gallego, eds., *Velázquez* (Madrid: Museo del Prado, 1990), 384–91.

38. Voltaire, *La princesse de Babylone* (Geneva, 1768); Aphra Behn, *Oroonoko ou le prince nègre*, trans. La Place (Paris, 1769).

39. Museo del Prado, Madrid. The object exists in the Bayerische Nationalmuseum, Munich.

40. Palazzo Venier, Venice.

41. It is the depiction of the story by A.H.J. Lafontaine, *Quinctius Heymeran von Fleming* (Berlin, 1798), sculpted by Friedrich Christina Gotlieb Geyser and published as an engraving in the *Goth Almanac*.

42. See Baltasar Fra Molinero, *La imagen de los negros en el teatro del Siglo de Oro* (Madrid: Siglo XXI, 1995); E. Martínez López, *Tablero de Ajedrez: Imágenes del negro heroico en la comedia española y en la literatura e iconografía sacra del Brasil esclavista* (Paris: Fundação Calouste Gulbenkian, 1998).

43. Lope de Vega, *El prodigio de Etiopia*, in *Obras*, vol. 9, *Comedias de Vidas de Santos*, ed. Menendez Pelayo (Madrid: Atlas, 1964), 113–206.

44. Juan Bautista Diamante, *Comedia famosa: El negro más prodigioso* (Salamanca: Imprenta de la Santa Cruz, n.d.).

45. Lope de Vega, *El negro del major amo*, in *Obras completas*, vol. 11, *Comedias*, ed. Manuel Arroyo Stephens (Madrid: Fundación José António de Castro, 1995), 433–513. The original quote is "La negra soy yo, que vos / ya sois blanco."

46. Andres de Claramonte y Corroy, *El valiente negro de Flandres*, ed. Nelson López (Kassel: Reichenberg, 2007). This is an impressive edition presented as a play script. The original quote is "solo la región o el clima / los diferencia; y si exceden / los blancos en perfección / a los negros es por ser / desdichados y tener / sobre ellos jursidición; / Y del mismo modo fueran / abatidos y imperfetos / los blancos, como sujetos / entre los negros se vieran."

47. Antonio Enriquez Gómez, "Las misas de San Vicente Ferrer," in *Comedias famosas* (Seville: Joseph Padriño, n.d.). There is also a printed fragment of the play at the Biblioteca Nacional de España, *Relación el barbaro convertido y renegado pirata* (n.l., n.d.), R2334734. Gómez fled to France but went back to Spain, lived in Seville under his pseudonym, Fernando de Zárate, published a significant number of plays, saw his execution in effigy by the Inquisition in 1660, and was finally denounced and died in the jail of the tribunal of the faith in 1663. See I. S. Révah, *Antonio Enriquez Gómez, un ecrivain marrane (v.1600–1663)*, ed. Carsten L. Wilke (Paris: Chandeigne, 2003). Gómez wrote an extraordinary play against the Inquisition: *La Inquisición de Lucifer y visita de todos los diablos*, ed. Constance Hubbard Rose and Maxim Kierkhof (Amsterdam: Rodopi, 1992).

48. Lope de Vega, *El santo negro Rosambuco de la ciudad de Palermo*, ed. Luigi Giuliani, in *Comedias*, ed. Albert Blecua and Guillermo Seres (Lleida, Spain: Milenio, 2002), 3:397–498.

49. Luís Vélez de Guevara, *El negro del serafin*, in *Comedias famosas* (ms. 1640–42), fl. 167r–87v, Biblioteca Nacional de España, Mss/14824. On Rodrigo Alvares Pacheco, see López, *Tablero de Ajedrez*, 15, 24.

50. Diego Jiménez de Enciso, *Juan Latino*, in *Segunda Parte de Comedias, escogidas de las mejores de España* (Madrid: Imprenta Real, 1652), fl. 33–63.

51. Aphra Behn, *Oroonoko and Other Writings*, ed. Paul Salzman (Oxford: Oxford University Press, 1994).

52. Bridget Orr, *Empire on the English Stage, 1660–1714* (Cambridge: Cambridge University Press, 2001); Kim F. Hall, *Things of Darkness: Economies of Race and Gender in Early Modern England* (Ithaca, NY: Cornell University Press, 1995).

Chapter 7: Americans

1. Christopher Columbus (in Spanish Cristóbal Colón), *Textos y documentos completos: Nuevas cartas*, ed. Consuelo Varela and Juan Gil (Madrid: Alianza, 1992), 152, 194–97.

2. Ibid., 224–25.

3. See Juan Gil and Consuelo Varela, eds., *Cartas de particulares a Colón y relaciones coetâneas* (Madrid: Alianza, 1984); Francisco Moráles Padrón, ed., *Primeras cartas sobre América (1493–1503)* (Seville: Universidad de Sevilla, 1990); Pedro Mártir de Anglería (Italian original name Pietro Martire d'Anghiera), *Cartas sobre el Nuevo Mundo* trans. Júlio Bauzano, intro. Ramón Alba (Madrid: Polifemo, 1990). These letters reveal the extent of Columbus's network of relations, impact of his own letters, and circulation of a great deal more information that came from oral sources.

4. Columbus, *Textos y documentos completos*, 234, 237, 250, 259–61, 304–5, 308, 313–15, 398.

5. Ibid., 250.

6. Ibid., 260–61.

7. Ibid., 329.

8. Ibid., 290.

9. See António Carreira, *Cabo Verde: Formação e extinção de uma sociedade escravocrata (1460–1878)* (Bissau: Centro de Estudos da Guiné Portuguesa, 1972); J. Bato'ora Ballong-Wen-Mewuda, *São Jorge da Mina, 1482–1637*, 2 vols. (Paris: Fondation Calouste Gulbenkian, 1993).

10. Columbus, *Textos y documentos completos*, 315n3.

11. Ibid., 408.

12. Ibid., 160, 163, 373–74, 378, 398.

13. Ibid., 299–300.

14. Martin Waldseemüller, *Cosmographiae Introductio*, trans. Pierre Monat, intro. Albert Ronsin (1507; repr., Grenoble: Jerôme Millon, 1991); Christine R. Johnson, "Renaissance German Cosmographers and the Naming of America," *Past and Present* 191, no. 1 (May 2009): 3–43.

15. Amerigo Vespucci, *Il Mondo Nuovo*, ed. Mario Pozzi (Alessandria: Edizione dell'Orso, 1993), 70, 155–56. In fact, the book contains four manuscripts (letters), plus the two texts *Mundus Novus* (c. 1502) and *Lettera delle isole nuovamente trovate* (1504, also produced in facsimile).

16. Vespucci, *Il Mondo Nuovo*, 63, 65, 87, 89, 114–16, 146, 167.

17. Ibid., 87–89, 111–19, 141–64, 167.

18. Hans Staden, *Warhaftige historia und beschreibung eyner Landtschaffe der Wilden, Nacketen, Grimmttigen Menschfressen Leuthen in der Newenwelt America* (Marburg, 1557). In the Portuguese translation by Alfredo Löfgren there is a good analysis of the Tupi words used by the author: *Viagem ao Brasil* (Salvador da Bahia: Progresso, 1956). See also the English translation by Neil L. Whitehead and Michael Harbameier: *Hans Staden's True History* (Durham, NC: Duke University Press, 2008). The title clearly indicates the purpose of the book: a "true description of a country of naked, ferocious and cannibal savages in the New World."

19. Alfred Métraux used Staden's book to reconstitute the Tupinamba shamanistic system. See Alfred Métraux, *Religions et magies indiennes d'Amérique du Sud* (Paris: Gallimard, 1967), 43–78.

20. André Thevet, *Les singularités de la France Antarctique*, ed. and intro. Frank Lestringant (1557; repr., Paris: Chandeigne, 1997), 160–64 (chapter 40). Jean de Léry, *Histoire d'un voyage fait en terre du Brésil*, ed., intro., and epilogue Frank Lestringant (1578; repr., Montpellier: Max Chaleil, 1992), 143–50 (chapter 15); for the English translation from the 1580 edition, see Janet Whaley, *History of a Voyage to the Land of Brazil* (Berkeley: University of California Press, 1990).

21. Michel de Montaigne, *Essais*, ed. Albert Thibaudet and Maurice Rat (Paris: Gallimard, 1962), chapter 31.

22. Michel de Certeau, "Ethno-Graphy: Speech, or the Space of the Other," in *The Writing of History*, trans. Tom Conley (New York: Columbia University Press, 1988), 209–43; Michel de Certeau, "Montaigne's 'Of Cannibals,' the Savage I," in *Heterologies: Discourse on the Other*, trans. Brian Massumi (Manchester: Manchester University Press, 1986), 67–79.

23. Joaquim Romero Magalhães and Susana Münch Miranda, eds., *Os primeiros 14 documentos relativos à armada de Pedro Álvares Cabral* (Lisbon: CNCDP, 1999), 95–121.

24. For a reproduction, see Pedro Dias and Dalila Rodrigues, eds., *Grão Vasco e a pintura do Renascimento* (Lisbon: CNCDP, 1992), 10, 93.

25. The painting is in the Museu Nacional de Arte Antiga, Lisbon.

26. For a good summary of this mythology, see Carmen Bernand and Serge Gruzinski, *Histoire du Nouveau Monde* (Paris: Fayard, 1991), 1:21–24. These authors pieced together the story of the Avaporu (eaters of human flesh from the community of the Ava) in the region of Chaco, in the swamps of Izozog in what is now Bolivia. For a more complex analysis, see Métraux, *Religions et magies indiennes*; Hélène Clastres, *La terre sans mal: Le prophétisme tupi-guarani* (Paris: Fayard, 1975).

27. Hernán Cortés, *Letters from Mexico*, trans. and ed. Anthony Pagden, intro. John H. Elliott, rev. ed. (New Haven, CT: Yale University Press, 1986), 35–36, 106–7, 184, 240–41, 256, 164, 363, 457n37 (excellent footnote on ritual), 486n36.

28. For descriptions of human sacrifices, see Fray Toribio de Motolinía, *Historia de los Indios de la Nueva España* (ms. 1542), ed. Georges Baudot (1858; repr., Madrid: Castalia, 1985), book I, chapters 6–10; Francisco López de Gómara, *La conquista de México*, ed. José Luis de Rojas (1552; repr., Madrid: Historia 16, 1987), 466–76; Bernal Díaz del Castillo, *Historia verdadera de la conquista de la Nueva España* (ms. 1575), ed. Luis Sáinz de Medrano (1632; repr., Barcelona: Planeta, 1992), chapter 208; Fray Bernardino de Sahagún, *Historia general de las cosas de Nueva España* (ms. 1558–77), ed. Alfredo López Austin and Josefina Garcia Quintana, 2 vols. (Madrid: Alianza, 1988), book 2, chapters 20–38 (the most extensive descriptions).

29. Carmen Bernand and Serge Gruzinski, *Histoire du Nouveau Monde*, vol. 1., *De la découverte à la conquête* (Paris: Fayard, 1991), 387.

30. Robert Ricard, *La "conquête spirituelle" du Mexique: Essai sur l'apostolat et les méthodes missionnaires des ordres mendiants en Nouvelle-Espagne de 1523–1524 à 1574* (Paris: Institut d'Ethnologie, 1933); James Lockhart, *The Nahuas after the Conquest: A Social and Cultural History of the Indians of Central Mexico, Sixteenth through Eighteenth Century* (Stanford, CA: Stanford University Press, 1992), 203–60, 442–46.

31. Serge Gruzinski, *La colonisation de l'imaginaire: Sociétés indigènes et Occidentalisation dans le Mexique espagnol, XVIe–XVIIIe siècle* (Paris: Gallimard, 1988).

32. On this important topic, although he does not quote Cortés, see David A. Lupher, *Romans in a New World: Classical Models in Sixteenth Century Spanish America* (Ann Arbor: University of Michigan Press, 2006), 235–317. On the context of the Incas, see Sabine MacCormack, *On the Wings of Time: Rome, the Incas, and Peru* (Princeton, NJ: Princeton University Press, 2007).

33. Nancy M. Farriss, *Maya Society under Colonial Rule: The Collective Enterprise of Survival* (Princeton, NJ: Princeton University Press, 1984), 24, 290–91, 312, 340. Cases of human sacrifices were still reported after the conquest.

34. Sabine MacCormack, *Religion in the Andes: Vision and Imagination in Early Colonial Peru* (Princeton, NJ: Princeton University Press, 1991), pp. 85–86, 89, 93–94, 105, 171–72, 200, 414–19. The main sources are Pedro Cieza de León and Guaman Poma de Ayala.

35. Juan de Betanzos, *Suma y narración de los Incas*, ed. María del Carmen Martín Rubio (Madrid: Atlas, 1987), 286.

36. For a study of the traumatized condition of the native population, see Nathan Wachtel, *La vision des vaincus: Les indiens du Pérou devant la conquête espagnole* (Paris: Gallimard, 1971).

37. Walter D. Mignolo, *Local Histories/Global Designs: Coloniality, Subaltern Knowledges, and Border Thinking* (Princeton, NJ: Princeton University Press, 2000); Walter D. Mignolo, *The Idea of Latin America* (Oxford: Blackwell, 2005); Walter D. Mignolo and Arturo Escobar, eds., *Globalisation and the Decolonial Option* (London: Routledge, 2010).

38. Felipe Guaman Poma de Ayala, *Nueva crónica y buen gobierno* (ms. 1615), ed. John V. Murra, Rolena Adorno, and Jorge L. Urioste, 3 vols. (Madrid: Historia 16, 1987), 1:2–19.

39. Inca Garcilaso de la Vega, *Comentarios Reales*, 1609, ed. Mercedes Serna (1609; repr., Madrid: Castalia, 2000).

40. Ayala, *Nueva crónica*, 2:560–68, 3:1072 (or in the original facsimile edition [Paris, 1936], 533–41, 978–96).

41. Garcilaso, *Comentarios reales* 332, 438, 466.

42. Alonso de Ercilla, *La Araucana*, ed. Marcos A. Morínigo and Isaías Lerner, 2 vols. (1560–78; repr., Madrid: Castalia, 1987). Ercilla fought against the fierce Araucanians and then wrote this epic poem. The resistance of the Mapuche was bravely prolonged until as late as 1885.

43. Ulrich Schmidel, *Wahraftige und liebliche beschreibung* (Frankfurt: Feierabend and Hüter, 1567). The text was translated and used by Theodor de Bry in his series of volumes on *America*. The illustrations were particularly good.

44. Gómara, *La conquista de México*, 424.

45. Alvar Núñez Cabeza de Vaca, *Naufrágios*, ed. Trinidad Barrera (1542; repr., Madrid: Alianza, 1985); Perry Vidal, ed., *Relaçam verdadeira dos trabalhos que ho governador dom Fernando Soto e certos fidalgos portugueses passaram no descobrimento da provincia da Frolida* (facsimile) (1557; repr., Lisbon: Agência Geral das Colónias, 1940); Inca Garcilaso de la Vega, *La Florida*, ed. Cármen de Mora (1605; repr., Madrid: Alianza, 1988).

46. On the massacre of the French expedition, see Girolamo Benzoni, *Histoire nouvelle du nouveau monde contenant en somme ce que les espagnols ont fait jusqu'à présent aux Indes Occidentales et le rude traitement qu'ils ont fait à ces pauvres peuples là*, trans. Urbain Chauveton (Geneva: Eustace Vignon, 1579), appendix.

47. For the context, see Kim Sloan, ed., *A New World: England's First View of America* (London: British Museum, 2007).

48. Thomas Harriot, *A Brief and True Report on the New Found Land of Virginia*, intro. Paul Hulton (1590; repr., New York: Dover, 1972), 1.

49. Ibid., 25.

50. Joseph François Lafitau, *Moeurs des sauvages ameriquains, comparées aux mœurs des premiers temps*, 2 vols. (Paris: Charles Estienne Hochereau, 1724).

51. *Spectator* 11 (1711); Richard Ligon, *A True and Exact History of the Island of Barbados*, ed. Kahren Ordhal Kupperman (1657; repr., Indianapolis, IN: Hackett, 2011), 106–7.

52. Jean-Jacques Rousseau, *Discours sur l'origine et les fondements de l'inégalité parmi les hommes*, ed. Jean Starobinski (1755; repr., Paris: Gallimard, 1969), 66, 83–93. Rousseau quotes the other authors in his critique of Hobbes, while Starobinski aptly introduces the reference to Grotius.

53. Voltaire, *L'ingénu* (1767), in *Romans et contes*, ed. René Pomeau (Paris: Flammarion, 1966), 317–81.

54. Robert Bage, *Hermsprong, or Man as He Is Not* (1796), ed. and intro. Stuart Tane (University Park: Pennsylvania State University Press, 1982).

55. Chateaubriand, *Atala* (1801), ed. Armand Weil (Paris: José Corti, 1950); Chateaubriand, *René* (1802), ed. J. M. Gautier (Geneva: Droz, 1970); Chateaubriand, *Voyage en Amérique*, ed. Richard Switzer, 2 vols. (Paris: Marcel Didier, 1964).

Chapter 8: Asians

1. Duarte Barbosa, *O Livro*, ed. Maria Augusta da Veiga e Sousa, 2 vols. (Lisbon: Instituto de Investigação Científica Tropical, 1996–2000).

2. Antônio Houaiss, ed., *Dicionário Houaiss da Língua Portuguesa* (Rio de Janeiro: Objectiva/Instituto Houaiss, 2001), 645; *Diccionario de la Lengua Española*, 22nd ed. (Madrid: Real Academia Española, 2001), 321.

3. Giovanni Battista Ramusio, *Navigazioni e Viaggi*, ed. Marica Milanesi (1550–59; repr., Turin: Einaudi, 1978–88), 2:618–50 (in which the issue of castes is addressed).

4. Barbosa, *O Livro*, 2:200. In the Italian translation we have "Di gente basse e vili si trovano undeci sorti, com le quali alcuna persona onorata non si può impacciar, sotto pena della morte; e in questa cosa fanno grandíssima differenza, e la guardano com gran superstizione": Ramusio, *Navigazioni e Viaggi*, 2:640.

5. For a wider range of examples, see Sebastião Rodolfo Dalgado, *Glossário Luso-Asiático* (facsimile) (1919–21; repr., New Delhi: Asian Educational Services, 1988), 1:225–29.

6. Although the debate on the caste system will never be closed, the analysis suggested by Louis Dumont (*Homo Hierarchicus: Le système des castes et ses implications* [Paris: Gallimard, 1966]) has been challenged—namely, in R. S. Khare, ed., *Caste, Hierarchy, and Individualism: Indian Critiques of Louis Dumont's Contributions* (New Delhi: Oxford University Press, 2006).

7. João de Barros, *Ásia: Década Primeira*, ed. António Baião (1552; repr., Coimbra, Portugal: Imprensa da Universidade, 1932), 354.

8. "O primeiro concílio provincial celebrado em Goa no ano de 1567," in *Archivo Portuguez Oriental*, ed. J. H da Cunha Rivara, fascicle 4 (New Goa, Portugal: Imprensa Nacional, 1862), 1–75; for the relevant passages of the resolution, see ibid., 8–9.

9. Luís Vaz de Camões, *The Lusiads*, trans. Landeg White (Oxford: Oxford University Press, 1997), 146–47.

10. Jean Baptiste Tavernier, *The Six Voyages through Turkey, into Persia and the East Indies by the Space of Forty Years*, trans. J. Phillips, 1st French ed. (1676; repr., London: William Godbid, 1677), part 2, 161.

11. Ines G. Zupanov, *Jesuit Experiments and Behavioural Knowledge in Seventeenth Century India* (Oxford: Oxford University Press, 1999).

12. Gonçalo Fernandes Trancoso, *Tratado sobre o Hinduísmo (Madure 1616)*, ed. José Wicki (Lisbon: Centro de Estudos Históricos Ultramarinos, 1973).

13. "Itinerario di Lodovico Barthema," in Ramusio, *Navigazioni e Viaggi*, 1:824. See Partha Mitter, *Much Maligned Monsters* (Oxford: Clarendon Press, 1977).

14. Tavernier, *The Six Voyages*, part 2, 164, 167, 178.

15. I believe the vision of Orientalism should be studied in the long term, and nuanced, overcoming the schematic but necessary approach laid down in Edward Said, *Orientalism*, 1st ed (1979; repr., New York: Vintage, 1994), 75–79.

16. Francisco Bethencourt, "Political Configuration and Local Powers," in *Portuguese Oceanic Expansion, 1400–1800*, ed. Francisco Bethencourt and Diogo Ramada Curto (Cambridge: Cambridge University Press, 2007), 197–254.

17. *Imagens do Oriente no século XVI: Reprodução do códice português da Biblioteca Casanatense*, ed. Luís de Matos (Lisbon: Imprensa Nacional, 1985). Matos compiled a list of all the significant contemporary European sources for each image.

18. Jan Huygen van Linschoten, *Itinerario, Voyage ofte Schipvaert naer Oost ofte Portugaels Indien* (Amsterdam: Cornelis Claesz, 1596). Linschoten organized an abridged edition of the images with long captions that reproduced the main ideas of the original text: *Icones, habitus gestusque indorum as lusitanorum per indiam viventiam* (Amsterdam: Cornellium Nicolai, 1604). See Ernst van den Boogaart, *Civil and Corrupt Asia: Image and Text in the* Itinerario *and the* Icones *of Jan Huygen van Linschoten* (Chicago: University of Chicago Press, 2003).

19. Bernard Picard, *Cérémonies et coutumes religieuses de tous les peoples du monde* (Amsterdam, 1783).

20. John F. Richards, *The Mughal Empire*, vol. 1.5, *The New Cambridge History of India* (Cambridge: Cambridge University Press, 1993).

21. John Lyly, *Euphues: The Anatomy of Wit* (1578), 2nd ed. (London: Gabriell Cawood, 1580).

22. Nicolas Nicolay, *The Navigations, Peregrinations, and Voyages Made into Turkie*, trans. T. Washington, 1st French ed. (1568; repr., London: Thomas Dawson, 1585); Pierre Belon du Mans, *Voyage au Levant*, ed. by Alexandra Merle (1553; repr., Paris: Chandeigne, 2001); André Thevet, *Cosmographie de Levant* (Lyon: Jean de Tournes, 1554); Guillaume Postel, *La république des turcs* (Poitiers, France: Enguibert de Marnef, 1560). Nicolay was the more "neutral" analyst, while Postel had a clear program of religious and political discussion.

23. Judith Herrin, *Byzantium: The Surprising Life of a Medieval Empire* (London: Penguin, 2008), 98–118.

24. Augier Ghislain de Busbecq, *Travels into Turkey* (London: J. Robinson, 1744), 59 (translated from Latin into English).

25. See Paolo Giovio, *Commentarii delle cose de' turchi* (Venice: Figliuoli di Aldo, 1541). This practice is constantly mentioned by Giovio; see ibid., 4.

26. Busbecq, *Travels into Turkey*, 38.

27. Bernard Lewis, *Istanbul and the Civilization of the Ottoman Empire* (Norman: University of Oklahoma Press, 1963), 47.

28. Tavernier, *The Six Voyages*, part 1, 219.

29. George Sandys, *A Relation of a Journey Begun An. Dom. 1610, Containing a Description of the Turkish Empire of Egypt, of the Holy Land, of the Remote Parts of Italy and Islands Adjoining* (London: W. Barrett, 1615), 47.

30. Belon, *Voyage au Levant*, 404, 437.

31. François Bernier, *Un libertine dans l'Inde Moghole: Les voyages*, ed. Frédérick Tinguely (Paris: Chandeigne, 2008), 218–32.

32. Tavernier, *The Six Voyages*, part 1, 219.

33. Baron Montesquieu, *De l'esprit des lois*, ed. Laurent Versini, 2 vols. (1748; repr., Paris: Gallimard, 1995), 174–81, 198–99, 328, 427–29.

34. Giovio, *Commentarii delle cose de' turchi*, fl. 28.

35. For this set of references, see Postel, *La république des turcs*, 25–26, 46, 52, 106.

36. Busbecq, *Travels*, 34–35, 57, 63, 66–125, 158, 235. But Busbecq also stated that the Greeks were as superstitious as the Turks; ibid., 47.

37. Montesquieu, *De l'esprit des lois*, 180, 459, 939.

38. Postel, *La république des turcs*, 3–7.

39. Sandys, *A Relation*, 58–60.

40. Mary Wortley Montagu, *Letters* (1763), ed. Clare Brant (London: Everyman's Library, 1992), 148–49.

41. See Gilles Veinstein, "L'empire dans sa grandeur," in *Histoire de l'Empire Ottoman*, ed. Robert Mandran (Paris: Fayard, 1989), 129–226 (particularly 169–70).

42. Postel, *La république des turcs*, 46.

43. Marco Polo, *Il Milione*, ed. Marcello Ciccuto (ms. 1295) (Milan: Rizzoli, 1981). For still-useful context, see Donald Lach, *Asia in the Making of Europe*, vol. 1, *The Century of Discovery* (Chicago: University of Chicago Press, 1965), 20–48.

44. Gaspar da Cruz, *Tractado em que se contam muito por estenso as cousas da China* (Évora, Portugal: André de Burgos, 1569). For a modern edition of the book that also contains all the important Portuguese accounts of China written in the sixteenth century, see *Enformação das cousas da China: Textos do século XVI*, ed. Raffaela D'Intino (Lisbon: Imprensa Nacional, 1989). The main quotes are in the prologue and chapters 7–8, 10–11, 16–18, and 26. For an abridged translation of this book and an earlier text by Galiote Pereira, see Samuel Purchas, *Hakluytus Posthumus or Purchas His Pilgrimes*, 1st complete ed., vol. 11 (1625; repr., Glasgow; James MacLehose and Sons, 1906).

45. Bernardino de Escalante, *Discurso de la navegacion que los portugueses hazen à los Reinos y Prouincias del Oriente, y de la noticia que se tiene de las grandezas del Reino de la China* (Seville: Viuda de Alonso Escrivano, 1577). For a facsimile edition published with a useful introduction, see Lourdes Díaz Trechuelo (Laredo: Universidad de Cantabria, 1991). Martin de Rada (O.E.S.A), *Relation of the Things of China*, trans. and ed. Charles Boxer, in *South China in the Sixteenth Century* (London: Hakluyt Society, 1953), 260–310. Juan Gonzalez de Mendoza, *Historia de las cosas más notables, ritos y costumbres del Gran Reyno de China* (Rome: Vicencio Acolfi, 1585). In sixteen years there were thirty-eight editions in Castilian, Italian, English, French, Latin, Dutch, and German. I have used the English edition: Juan Gonzalez de Mendoza, *The History of the Great and Mighty Kingdom of China*, trans. R. Park (London: I. Wolfe, 1588).

46. Mendoza, *The History of the Great and Mighty Kingdom of China*, 19–20.

47. See the Jesuit letters, translated into several languages: *Cartas que os padres e irmãos da Companhia de Jesus escreverão dos Reynos de Japão e China* (1549–89), 2 vols. (Évora, Portugal: Manuel de Lyra, 1598), reproduced in facsimile edition (Maia, Portugal: Castoliva, 1997); Fernão Guerreiro, *Relação anual das coisas que fizeram os padres da Companhia de Jesus nas suas missões . . . nos anos de 1600 a 1609*, ed. Artur Viegas, 3 vols. (Coimbra, Portugal: Imprensa da Universidade, 1930–42).

48. The letter is reproduced in the *Cartas* and many other compilations of Jesuit letters published in different languages, particularly in *Documenta Indica*, and also in *Cartas dos Jesuítas do Oriente e do Brasil, 1549–1551*, of which there is a facsimile edition with an introduction by José Manuel Garcia (Lisbon: Biblioteca Nacional, 1993).

49. Fernão Mendes Pinto, *Peregrinação*, ed. Adolfo Casais Monteiro (1614; repr., Lisbon: Imprensa Nacional, 1983), chapter 34. For the English translation, see Rebecca D. Catz, *The Travels of Fernão Mendes Pinto* (Chicago: University of Chicago Press, 1989).

50. Charles R. Boxer, *The Christian Century in Japan, 1549–1650* (Berkeley: University of California Press, 1951). For the first twenty years of missions, see also Léon Bourdon, *La compagnie de Jésus et le Japon, 1547–1570* (Paris: Fundação Calouste Gulbenkian, 1993).

51. George Bryan Souza, *Survival of the Empire: Portuguese Trade and Society in China and the South China Sea, 1630–1754* (Cambridge: Cambridge University Press, 1986); Liam Brockey, *The Journey to the East: The Jesuit Mission to China, 1579–1724* (Cambridge, MA: Belknap Press, 2007).

52. Jin Guo Ping and Wu Zhiliang, "Desmistificando a 'lenda negra' sobre a 'canibalização dos Portugueses': Seu significado nas relações luso-chinesas das dinastias Ming e Qing," in *Revisitar os primórdios de Macau: Para uma nova abordagem da História* (Macau: Instituto Português do Oriente, 2007), 135–54.

53. Alessandro Valignano, *Historia del principio y progreso de la Compañia de Jesús en las Indias Orientales, 1542–1564*, ed. Josef Wicki (Rome: Institutum Historicum Societatis Iesu, 1944); Alessandro Valignano, *Il cerimoniale per i missionarii del Japone* (original Portuguese text with Italian translation), ed. Josef Franz Schütte (Rome: Edizioni di Storia e Letteratura, 1946); Alessandro Valignano, *Sumario de las cosas de Japón*, ed. José Luís Alvarez-Taldriz (Tokyo: Sophia University, 1954). See also Paolo Aranha, "Gerarchie razziali e adattamento culturale: La 'ipotesis Valignano,'" in *Alessandro Valignano, S. I. Uomo del Rinascimento: Ponte tra Oriente e Occidente*, ed. Adolfo Tamburello, M. Antoni Ücerler, and Marisa di Russo (Rome: Institutum Historicum Societatis Iesu, 2008), 77–98.

54. Matteo Ricci, *Opere storiche*, vol. 2, *Le lettere della Cina*, ed. Pietro Tacchi Ventura (Macerata, Italy, 1913).

55. Jonathan D. Spence, *The Memory Palace of Matteo Ricci* (London: Penguin, 1985), 41–54.

56. Josef Franz Schütte, *Valignano's Mission Principles for Japan*, trans. John J. Coyle (Saint Louis: Institute of Jesuit Sources, 1980), 1:131. Also quoted in Spence, *The Memory Palace*, 41.

57. Pedro Teixeira, *The Travels,* trans. William F. Sinclair (1610; repr., London: Hakluyt Society, 1902), 49, 53, 66, 85, 117. The other authors already quoted share the same vision.

58. Jonathan Spence, *The Chan's Great Continent: China in Western Minds* (New York: W. W. Norton, 1998), 41–61, particularly 43–44. Pimentel also complained about the "baseness" of Chinese table manners.

59. Arnoldus Montanus, *Atlas Chinensis, Being a Second Part of a Relation of Remarkable Passages in Two Embassies from the East India Company of the United Provinces to the Vice-Roy Singlamong and General Taising Lipovi and to Konchi, Emperor of China and East Tartaria*, trans. John Ogilvy (London: Thomas Johnson, 1671), 454.

Chapter 9: Europeans

1. Juan Gonzalez de Mendoza, *History of the Great and Mighty Kingdom of China*, trans. R. Park (London: I. Wolfe, 1588), 19.

2. Jan Huygen van Linschoten, *Itinerario, Voyage ofte Schipvaert naer Oost ofte Portugaels Indien* (Amsterdam: Cornelis Claesz, 1596), chapter 23.

3. John Evelyn, *The Diary*, ed. William Bray (London: J. M. Dent, 1907), 1:370.

4. Ginés Pérez de Hita, *Historia de los bandos de los Zegríes y Abencerrajes*, 2 vols. (Alcalá de Henares, 1601–19), part II, chapters 5 and 14.

5. Samuel Pepys, *The Diary*, ed. Robert Lapham and William Matthews, 11 vols. (London: G. Bell and Sons, 1970–83), quote in vol. 3.

6. Julio Caro Baroja, *Los moriscos del Reino de Granada*, 3rd ed. (1957; repr., Madrid: Istmo, 1985), 37–58, 149–74; Juan Reglà, *Estúdios sobre los moriscos* (1964; repr., Barcelona: Ariel, 1974); L. P. Harvey, *Muslims in Spain, 1500 to 1614* (Chicago: University of Chicago Press, 2005); Rafael Carrasco, *Deportados en nombre de Dios: La expulsión de los moriscos: Cuarto centenário de una ignominia* (Barcelona: Destino, 2009).

7. Louis Cardaillac, *Morisques et Chrétiens: Un affrontement polémique (1492–1640)* (Paris: Klincksieck, 1976); Mikel de Epalza, "Los moriscos frente a la Inquisición, en su visión islámica del cristianismo," in *Historia de la Inquisición en España y América*, ed. Joaquín Pérez Villanueva and Bartolomé Escandell Bonet, vol. 3, *Temas y problemas* (Madrid: Biblioteca de Autores Cristianos, 2000), 737–70.

8. Mercedes Garcia-Arenal, *Inquisición y moriscos: Los procesos del Tribunal de Cuenca* (Madrid: Siglo XXI, 1978); Rafael Benítez Sánchez-Blanco, "La Inquisición ante los moriscos," in *Historia de la Inquisición en España y América*, ed. Joaquín Pérez Villanueva and Bartolomé Escandell Bonet, vol. 3, *Temas y problemas* (Madrid: Biblioteca de Autores Cristianos, 2000), 695–736.

9. Henri Lapeyre (*Géographie de l'Espagne Morisque* [Paris: SEVPEN, 1959]) gave the exact number of 273,000, based on embarcation lists. Here I am citing the round numbers in Carrasco, *Deportados en nombre de Dios*, 292–98—approximations because they were based on incomplete documentation.

10. Fernand Braudel, "Conflicts et refus de civilisation: Espagnols et morisques au XVIe siècle," *Annales ESC*, (1947): 397–410.

11. Samuel P. Huntington, *The Clash of Civilizations and the Remaking of World Order* (New York: Simon and Schuster, 1996).

12. Trevor J. Dadson, *Los moriscos de Villarubia de los Ojos (siglos XV–XVIII): Historia de una minoria asimilada, expulsada y reintegrada* (Madrid: Iberoamericana, 2007).

13. Carrasco, *Deportados en nombre de Dios*, 208–11.

14. Miguel de Cervantes, *El Ingenuoso Hidalgo Don Quijote de la Mancha*, ed. Luis Andrés Murillo, 2nd part (1615; repr., Madrid: Castalia, 1987), 2:525–31.

15. Carrasco, *Deportados en nombre de Dios*, 332.

16. Georg Simmel, *On Individuality and Social Forms*, ed. Donald N. Levine (Chicago: University of Chicago Press, 1971), 143–49; James S. Coleman, *Foundations of Social Theory* (Cambridge, MA: Harvard University Press, 1990), 91–118, 175–96.

17. Joseph Pérez, *Los judíos en España* (Madrid: Marcial Pons, 2005), 164–68.

18. Mark D. Meyerson, *A Jewish Renaissance in Fifteenth Century Valencia* (Princeton, NJ: Princeton University Press, 2004).

19. Pérez, *Los judíos en España*, 172.

20. Maria José Ferro Tavares, *Os judeus em Portugal no século XV* (Lisbon: Universidade Nova de Lisboa, 1982), 74, 256.

21. Francisco Bethencourt, "A expulsão dos judeus," in *O tempo de Vasco da Gama*, ed. Diogo Ramada Curto (Lisbon: Difel, 1998), 271–80.

22. François Soyer, *The Persecution of Jews and Muslims in Portugal: King Manuel I and the End of Religious Tolerance, 1496–7* (Leiden: Brill, 2007).

23. Yosef Hayim Yerushalmi, *The Lisbon Massacre of 1506 and the Royal Image in the Shebet Yehuda* (Cincinnati: Hebrew Union College, 1976).

24. Francisco Bethencourt, *The Inquisition: A Global History (1478–1834)* (Cambridge: Cambridge University Press, 2009), 342–49.

25. Maurice Kriegel, "Un trait de psychologie sociale dans les pays méditerranéens du Bas Moyen Âge: Le juif comme intouchable," *Annales, Economie, Société, Civilisation*, 31, no. 2 (March–April 1976): 326–30; Maurice Kriegel, *Les juifs à la fin du Moyen Âge dans l'Europe méditerranéenne* (Paris: Hachette, 1979); Pérez, *Los judíos en España*, 176.

26. Miri Rubin, *Gentile Tales: The Narrative Assault on Late Medieval Jews* (New Haven, CT: Yale University Press, 1999).

27. Richard Sennett, *Flesh and Stone: The Body and the City in Western Civilization* (New York: W. W. Norton, 1996), 215.

28. Julio Caro Baroja, *Los judíos en la España moderna y contemporánea*, 3rd. ed., 3 vols. (1963; repr., Madrid: Istmo, 1986); Antonio Domínguez Ortiz, *Los Judeoconversos en España y América* (Madrid: Istmo, 1971); Albert Sicroff, *Los estatutos de limpieza de sangre* (original French edition 1960), 2nd rev. ed. (Madrid: Taurus, 1985); Juan Hernández Franco, *Sangre limpia, sangre española: El debate de los estatutos de limpieza (siglos XV–XVIII)* (Madrid: Cátedra, 2011).

29. Bethencourt, *The Inquisition*, 327–30; Fernanda Olival, "Para um estudo da nobilitação no Antigo Regime: Os Cristãos Novos na Ordem de Cristo (1581–1621)," in *As ordens militares em Portugal: Actas do 1° Encontro sobre Ordens Militares* (Palmela, Portugal: Câmara Municipal, 1991), 233–44; Fernanda Olival, *As Ordens Militares e o Estado Moderno* (Lisbon: Estar, 2001), 283–398.

30. For my inspiration here, see Max Gluckman, "Les rites de passage," in *Essays on the Ritual of Social Relations* (Manchester: Manchester University Press, 1962), 1–52; Pierre Bourdieu, "Les rites comme actes d'institution," *Actes de la Recherche en Sciences Sociales* 43 (1986): 130–57.

31. Besides the works of Ortiz and Carrasco already quoted, see Jaime Contreras, ed., *Inquisición española: Nuevas aproximaciones* (Madrid: Centro de Estudios Inquisitoriales, 1987); Jaime Contreras, *Sottos contra*

Riquelmes: Regidores, Inquisidores y Criptojudios (Madrid: Anaya and Mario Muchnik, 1992); David Nirenberg, "Mass Conversion and Genealogical Mentalities: Jews and Christians in Fifteenth-Century Spain," *Past and Present 174 (2002): 3–41*; David Nirenberg, "La generacón de 1391: Conversion masiva y crisis de identidad," in *Furor et rabies: Violencia, conflicto y marginación en la Edad Moderna*, ed. José I. Frea, Juan E. Gelabert, and Tomás A. Montecon (Santander, Spain: Universidad de Camtábria, 2002); David Nirenberg, "Race and the Middle Ages: The Case of Spain and Its Jews," in *Rereading the Black Legend: The Discourses of Religious and Racial Difference in the Renaissance Empires*, ed. Margaret R. Greer, Walter D. Mignolo, and Maureen Quilligan (Chicago: University of Chicago Press, 2007), 71–87; David Nirenberg, "Was There Race before Modernity? The Example of 'Jewish' Blood in Late Medieval Spain," in *The Origins of Racism in the West*, ed. Miriam Eliav-Feldon, Benjamin Isaac, and Joseph Ziegler (Cambridge: Cambridge University Press, 2009), 232–64. The issue is still shaped by the 1950s' debate around racism; the first historians who dealt with this problem wanted to avoid the analogy between persecution of New Christians in Spain and the Holocaust.

32. Jonathan Israel, *Diasporas within the Diaspora: Jews, Crypto-Jews, and the World Maritime Empires (1540–1740)* (Leiden: Brill, 2002); Yosef Kaplan, *An Alternative Path to Modernity: The Sephardi Diaspora in Western Europe* (Leiden: Brill, 2000); Lionel Levy, *La nation juive portugaise: Livourne, Amsterdam, Tunis, 1591–1951* (Paris: L'Harmattan, 1999); Francesca Trivellato, *The Familiarity of Strangers: The Sephardic Diaspora, Livorno, and Cross-Cultural Trade in the Early Modern Period* (New Haven, CT: Yale University Press, 2009); Toby Green, *The Rise of the Trans-Atlantic Slave Trade in Western Africa, 1300–1589* (Cambridge: Cambridge University Press, 2012).

33. Nathan Wachtel, *La foi du souvenir: Labyrinthes marranes* (Paris: Seuil, 2001).

34. Paolo Bernardini and Norman Fiering, eds., *The Jews and the Expansion of Europe to the West, 1450 to 1800* (New York: Berghahn Books, 2001); Bruno Feitler, *Inquisition, juifs et nouveaux chrétiens au Brésil: Le Nordest, XVIIe et XVIIIe siècles* (Leuven: Leuven University Press, 2003).

35. Lucette Valensi, *Ces étrangers familiers: Musulmans en Europe (XVIe–XVIIIe siècles)* (Paris: Payot, 2012).

36. David Hume, "National Characters," in *Selected Essays*, ed. Stephen Copley and Andrew Edgar (Oxford: Oxford University Press, 1993), 117.

37. Anthony Julius, *Trials of Diaspora: A History of Anti-Semitism in England* (Oxford: Oxford University Press, 2010).

38. Ronald Schechter, *Obstinate Hebrews: Representations of Jews in France, 1715–1815* (Berkeley: University of California Press, 2003).

39. Paolo Bernardini and Norman Fiering, eds., *The Jews and the Expansion of Europe to the West, 1450–1800* (New York: Berghan Books, 2001).

40. Marina Caffiero, *Forced Baptism: Histories of Jews Christians and Converts in Papal Rome*, trans. Lydia G. Cochrane (Berkeley: University of California Press, 2012); Kenneth Stow, *Jewish Life in Early Modern Rome: Challenge, Conversion, and Private Life* (Aldershot, UK: Ashgate, 2007); Corrado Vivanti, ed., *Gli Ebrei in Italia. Storia d'Italia: Annali*, vol. 11, 2 books (Turin: Einaudi, 2003), especially the chapters by Renata Segre and Giovanni Micoli.

41. Ronnie Po-chia Hsia and Hartmut Lehmann, eds., *In and Out of the Ghetto: Jewish-Gentile Relations in Late Medieval and Early Modern Germany* (Washington, DC: German Historical Institute, 1995).

42. Léon Poliakov, *Histoire de l'antisémitisme*, vol. 1, *L'âge de la foi* (1956; repr., Paris: Calmann-Lévy, 1981); Gershon David Hundert, ed., *Jews in Early Modern Poland* (London: Littman Library of Jewish Civilization, 1997).

43. Jonathan Karp and Adam Sutcliffe, eds., *Philosemitism in History* (Cambridge: Cambridge University Press, 2011).

44. Laurence Sigal-Klagsbald, ed., *Rembrandt et la Nouvelle Jérusalem: Juifs et Chrétiens à Amsterdam au siècle d'or* (Paris: Musée d'art et d'histoire du Judaïsme, 2007).

45. Jonathan M. Hess, *Germans, Jews, and the Claims of Modernity* (New Haven, CT: Yale University Press, 2002). For the French case, see Schechter, *Obstinate Hebrews*.

46. Angus Fraser, *The Gypsies* (Oxford: Blackwell, 1992); David Mayall, *Gypsie Identities, 1500–2000: From Egyptians and Moon-Men to the Ethnic Romany* (London: Routledge, 2004); Miriam Eliav-Feldon, "Vagrants or Vermin? Attitudes towards Gypsies in Early Modern Europe," in *The Origins of Racism in the West*, ed. Miriam Eliav-Feldon, Benjamijn Isaac, and Joseph Ziegler (Cambridge: Cambridge University Press, 2009), 276–91.

Part III: Colonial Societies

1. David Hume, "Of National Characters" (1741), in *Selected Essays*, ed. Stephen Copley and Andrew Edgar (Oxford: Oxford University Press, 1996), 117–18.

2. Adam Smith, *Wealth of Nations* (1776), ed. Kathryn Sutherland (Oxford: Oxford University Press, 1993), 344.

3. For a critique of this approach, see Jack Goody, *The Theft of History* (Cambridge: Cambridge University Press, 2006).

4. For the most powerful example of an approach centered strictly on the colonizer, see Niall Ferguson, *Empire: How Britain Made the Modern World* (London: Penguin, 2003). Ferguson takes the basic assumptions of "Britishness" for granted in his book.

5. Gilberto Freyre, *The Portuguese and the Tropics* (Lisbon: Commission for the Commemoration of the Vth Centenary of the Death of Henry the Navigator, 1961).

6. Magnus Mörner, *La mezcla de razas en la história de América Latina*, trans. Jorge Pratigowski (Buenos Aires: Paidos, 1969).

7. Lauren Benton, *Law and Colonial Cultures: Legal Regimes in World History, 1400–1900* (Cambridge: Cambridge University Press, 2002).

Chapter 10: Ethnic Classification

1. Maria Concepción García Sáiz, *Las castas mexicanas: Un género pictórico americano* (Milan: Olivetti, 1989); Ilona Katzew, ed., *New World Orders: Casta Painting and Colonial Latin America* (New York: Americas Society Art Gallery, 1996); Ilona Katzew, *Casta Painting: Images of Race in Eighteenth-Century Mexico* (New Haven, CT: Yale University Press, 2004); Pilar Romero de Tejada, ed., *Frutas y castas ilustradas* (Madrid: Museo Nacional de Antropologia, 2004).

2. Katzew, *Casta Painting*, 12–16.

3. Jonathan I. Israel, *Race, Class, and Politics in Colonial Mexico, 1610–1670* (London: Oxford University Press, 1975); R. Douglas Cope, *The Limits of Racial Domination: Plebeian Society in Colonial Mexico City, 1660–1720* (Madison: University of Wisconsin Press, 1994).

4. Anonymous painter (Mexico, eighteenth century), series of sixteen castas, number seven, Museo de America, Spain. The same casta was depicted in many other series, particularly that by José de Páez, c. 1770–80, in this case labeled only "Returns Backwards" and represented as mulatto; see Katzew, *Casta Painting*, 27.

5. Treatise of Friar Diogo de Santa Ana, circa 1632, Manuscritos da Livraria, n. 816, fl. 187r–190v, Arquivo Nacional da Torre do Tombo, Lisbon. There is a discussion in this treatise of the problems of Portuguese India.

6. *Diccionario de la Lengua Española*, 22nd ed. (Madrid: Real Academia Española, 2001). The etymology of the main Spanish racial taxonomy was identified with this dictionary; see also Joan Corominas, *Diccionario crítico etimológico castellano y hispánico*, 7 vols. (Madrid: Gredos, 1981).

7. See E. Wickberg, "The Chinese Mestizos in Philippine History," in *The Chinese Diaspora in the Pacific*, ed. Anthony Reid (Aldershot, UK: Ashgate, 2008), 137–75.

8. For an interpretation of Father José Gumilla, see Maria Concepción García Sáiz, "'Que se tenga por blanco': El mestizaje americano y la pintura de castas," in *Arqueologia, América, Antropologia: José Perez de Barradas, 1897–1981* (Madrid: Museo de los Orígenes, 2008), 351–67.

9. Maria Elena Martínez, *Genealogical Fictions: Limpieza de Sangre, Religion, and Gender in Colonial Mexico* (Stanford, CA: Stanford University Press, 2008).

10. Tejada, *Frutas y castas ilustradas*, 96–135.

11. Katzew, *Casta Painting*, 138.

12. Ibid., 126, 131.

13. Jorge Klor de Alva, "El mestizaje, de Nueva España a Aztlán: Sobre el control y la classificación de las identidades colectivas," in *New World Orders: Casta Painting and Colonial Latin America*, ed. Ilona Katzew (New York: Americas Society Art Gallery, 1996), 132–40; see also the revision of literature in Pilar Romero de Tejada,

"Los quadros de mestizaje del Virrey Amat," in Pilar Romero de Tejada, ed., *Frutas y Castas Ilustradas* (Madrid: Museo Nacional de Antropologia, 2004), 13–23.

14. Tejada, *Frutas y castas ilustradas*; see also Katzew, *Casta Painting*, 148–61. The connection here, however, is made somehow dependent on the European Enlightenment.

15. See Fermín del Pino Díaz, "Historia natural y razas humanas en los 'quadros de castas' hispano-americanos," in *Frutas y castas iustradas*, ed. Pilar Romero de Tejada (Madrid: Museo Nacional de Antropologia, 2004), 45–66.

16. This observation apparently accords with Jorge Cañizares-Esguerra, *Nature, Empire, and Nation: Explorations of the History of Science in the Iberian World* (Stanford, CA: Stanford University Press, 2006). See my divergence below.

17. For research supporting this idea, see Rebecca Earle, *The Body of the Conquistador: Food, Race, and the Colonial Experience in Spanish America, 1492–1700* (Cambridge: Cambridge University Press, 2012), 187–216, especially 215.

18. Raphael Bluteau, *Vocabulario Portuguez e Latino*, 8 vols. (Lisbon, 1712–24).

19. John A. Simpson and Edmund S. C. Weiner, eds., *Oxford English Dictionary*, 20 vols. (Oxford: Clarendon, 1989).

20. Alain Rey, ed., *Dictionnaire historique de la langue française*, 3 vols. (Paris: Le Robert, 1998).

21. Antônio Houaiss, ed., *Dicionário Houaiss da Língua Portuguesa* (Rio de Janeiro: Objectiva/Instituto Houaiss, 2001). I will use this dictionary in all the other references to racial taxonomy in the Portuguese-speaking world.

22. António Sérgio Guimarães, "Colour and Race in Brazil: From Whitening to the Search for Afro-Descent," in *Racism and Ethnic Relations in the Portuguese-Speaking World*, ed. Francisco Bethencourt and Adrian Pearce (London: British Academy, 2012), 17–34.

23. Antonio de Moraes Silva, *Dicionario da lingua portugueza*, 2 vols. (Lisbon: Simão Thaddeo Ferreira, 1789).

24. Stuart B. Schwartz, "Brazilian Ethnogenesis: *mestiços, mamelucos, and pardos*," in *Le nouveau monde, mondes nouveaux: L'expérience américaine*, ed. Serge Gruzinski and Nathan Wachtel (Paris: EHESS, 1996), 7–27 (see the comments by Katia de Queirós Mattoso, ibid., 67–73).

25. Houaiss, *Dicionário Houaiss da Língua Portuguesa*.

26. I checked my first analysis against these useful articles: Dante Martins Teixeira and Elly de Vries, "Exotic Novelties from Overseas," in *Albert Eckhout: A Dutch Artist in Brazil*, ed. Quentin Buvelot (The Hague: Royal Cabinet of Paintings Mauritshuis, 2004), 64–105; Ernst van den Boogaart, "The Population of the Brazilian Plantation Colony Depicted by Albert Eckhout, 1641–1643," in *Albert Eckhout Returns to Brazil, 1644–2002*, ed. Jens Olesen (Copenhagen: Nationalmuseet, 2002), 117–31.

27. Peter Mason, "Eight Large Pictures with East and West Indian Persons: Albert Eckhout's Marvellous Montage," in *Albert Eckhout Returns to Brazil, 1644–2002*, ed. Jens Olesen (Copenhagen: Nationalmuseet, 2002), 147–54.

28. Francisco Bethencourt, "Low Cost Empire: Interaction between Portuguese and Local Societies in Asia," in *Rivalry and Conflict: European Traders and Asian Trading Networks in the 16th and 17th Centuries*, ed. Ernst van Veen and Léonard Blussé (Leiden: CNWS, 2005), 108–30.

29. José Carlos Venâncio, *A economia de Luanda e hinterland no século XVIII: Um estudo de sociologia histórica* (Lisbon: Estampa, 1996), 46; José Carlos Venâncio, *A dominação colonial: Protagonismos e heranças* (Lisbon: Estampa, 2005), 32.

30. Jack D. Forbes, *Africans and Native Americans: The Language of Race and the Evolution of Red-Black Peoples* (Urbana: University of Illinois Press, 1993), 79–83.

31. William George Smith, ed., *The Oxford Dictionary of English Proverbs*, 3rd ed., rev. F. D. Wilson (Oxford: Clarendon Press, 1970), 550.

32. Ibid., 63, 885.

33. Michel Pastoureau, *Black: The History of a Color*, trans. Jody Gladding (Princeton, NJ: Princeton University Press, 2009).

34. It is here that I diverge from David Nirenberg, "Mass Conversion and Genealogical Mentalities: Jews and Christians in Fifteenth-Century Spain," *Past and Present* 174 (2002): 3–41.

Chapter 11: Ethnic Structure

1. A. J. Graham, *Colony and Mother City in Ancient Greece* (Manchester: Manchester University Press, 1964).

2. Peter Burke, *Cultural Hybridity* (Cambridge, UK: Polity Press, 2009).

3. Estimate based on major trends compiled in Linda A. Newson, "The Demographic Impact of Colonization," in *The Cambridge Economic History of Latin America*, vol. 1, *The Colonial Era and the Short Nineteenth Century*, ed. Victor Bulmer-Thomas, John H. Coatsworth, and Roberto Cortés Conde (Cambridge: Cambridge University Press, 2006), 143–84 (for trends, see ibid., 153–54).

4. Peter Boyd-Bowman, *Patterns of Spanish Emigration to the New World, 1493–1580* (Buffalo, NY, 1973); Peter Boyd-Bowman, "Patterns of Spanish Emigration until 1600," *Hispanic American Historical Review* 56 (1976): 580–604.

5. Newson, "The Demographic Impact of Colonization," 143–88, 529–34.

6. Vitorino Magalhães Godinho, "Portuguese Emigration from the Fifteenth to the Twentieth Century: Constants and Changes," in *European Expansion and Migration: Essays on the International Migration from Africa, Asia, and Europe*, ed. P. C. Emmer and M. Mörner (New York: Berg, 1992), 13–48.

7. On the limits of this spread, see Bouda Etemad, *La possession du monde: Poids et mesures de la colonisation* (Brussels: Complexe, 2000), 43–60.

8. Ibid., 38. In the same table, the data on Portuguese India are clearly underestimated.

9. In Goa, 1,861 white people were registered in 1753 and 873 in 1799, but these data apparently do not include the armed forces. See Maria de Jesus dos Mártires Lopes, *Goa Setecentista: Tradição e Modernidade* (Lisbon: Universidade Católica Portuguesa, 1996), 91.

10. On the issue of wastage of emigrants in the British context, see Henry A. Gemery, "Emigration from the British Isles to the New World, 1630–1700," *Research in Economic History* 5 (1980): 179–231. Gemery points out the extraordinary waste in the tropical areas, mainly in the British Caribbean.

11. Alison Games, "Migration," in *The British Atlantic World, 1500–1800*, ed. David Armitage and Michael J. Braddick (Houndmills, UK: Palgrave, 2002), 31–50; James Horn and Philip D. Morgan, "Settlers and Slaves: European and African Migrations to Early Modern British America," in *The Creation of the British Atlantic World*, ed. Elizabeth Mancke and Carole Shammas (Baltimore: Johns Hopkins University Press, 2005), 19–44 (the comparative data on Spanish and Portuguese migration are hugely underestimated); A. N. Porter, ed., *Atlas of British Overseas Expansion* (New York: Simon and Schuster, 1991), 34–36.

12. Nuala Zahedieh, "Economy," in *The British Atlantic World, 1500–1800*, ed. David Armitage and Michael J. Braddick (Houndmills, UK: Palgrave, 2002), 51–68 (table, ibid., 62).

13. It is surprisingly difficult to collect data on the British in Asia before 1800. Consultation of the main monographs on the EIC did not solve the problem. I thank Christopher Bayly for the data I include here.

14. Charles R. Boxer, *The Dutch Seaborne Empire, 1600–1800* (1965; repr., London: Penguin, 1990), 77; Jonathan I. Israel, *The Dutch Republic: Its Rise, Greatness, and Fall, 1477–1806* (Oxford: Clarendon Press, 1995), 930–43; Jan Lucassen, "A Multinational and Its Labor Force: The Dutch East India Company, 1595–1795," *International Labor and Working-Class History* 66 (Fall 2004): 11–39.

15. Jan Lucassen, "The Netherlands, the Dutch, and the Long-Distance Migration in the Late Sixteenth Century to Early Nineteenth Century," in *Europeans on the Move: Studies on European Migration, 1500–1800*, ed. Nicholas Canny (Oxford: Clarendon Press, 1994), 153–91.

16. Filipa Ribeiro da Silva, *Dutch and Portuguese in Western Africa: Empires, Merchants, and the Atlantic System, 1580–1674* (Leiden: Brill, 2011), 98–104.

17. Data published by J. De Laet in 1931 and reproduced in Silva, *Dutch and Portuguese in Western Africa*, 106.

18. Wim Kloster, *The Dutch in the Americas, 1600–1800* (Providence: John Carter Brown Library, 1997), 21–22; Frédéric Mauro, *Le Portugal et l'Atlantique au XVIIe siècle, 1570–1670: Étude économique* (Paris: SEVPEN, 1960), 449.

19. Pierre Pluchon (*Histoire de la colonisation française* [Paris: Fayard, 1991], 307) suggests the lowest estimate of less than 30,000 migrants to New France. For the largest estimate, see Peter Moogk, "Emigration from France to North America before 1760," in *Europeans on the Move: Studies on European Migration, 1500–1800*, ed. Nicholas Canny (Oxford: Clarendon Press, 1994), 153–91.

20. Robert and Marianne Cornevin, *La France et les Français outre-mer* (Paris: Hachette, 1993), 161.

21. Fernand Braudel, *Civilisation matérielle, économie et capitalisme, XVe–XVIIIe soècle*, vol. 3, *Le temps du monde* (Paris: Armand Colin, 1979), 612.

22. For an assessment of the convergent perspectives on this matter between the world system theory developed by Immanuel Wallerstein and the multipolar world theory developed by Ken Pomeranz, see Patrick O'Brien, "A Critical Review of a Tradition of Meta-Narratives from Adam Smith to Ken Pomeranz," in *A Deus Ex Machina Revisited: Atlantic Colonial Trade and European Economic Development*, ed. P. C. Emmer, O. Pétré-Grenouilleau, and J. V. Roitman (Leiden: Brill, 2006), 5–23.

23. Linda Newson, "The Demographic Impact of Colonization," 143 (in this paragraph, I use the data compiled in this crucial article); William M. Denevan, ed., *The Native Population of the Americas in 1492*, 2nd ed. (Madison: University of Wisconsin Press, 1992).

24. António de Almeida Mendes, "Esclavages et traites ibériques entre Méditerranée et Atlantique (XVe–XVIIe siècles): Une histoire globale" (PhD diss., Ecole des Hautes Etudes en Sciences Sociales, 2007).

25. Philip D. Curtin, *The Rise and Fall of the Plantation Complex: Essays in Atlantic History*, 2nd ed. (Cambridge: Cambridge University Press, 1998); Stuart Schwartz, *Sugar Plantations in the Formation of Brazilian Society, 1550–1835* (Cambridge: Cambridge University Press, 1985); Barbara Solow and Stanley L. Engerman, eds., *Caribbean Slavery and British Capitalism* (Cambridge: Cambridge University Press, 1988).

26. All data on the slave trade were collected from the *Trans-Atlantic Slave Trade Data Base*, organized by David Eltis, Stephen D. Behrendt, David Richardson, and Herbert S. Klein: http://www.slavevoyages.org/tast/assessment (accessed June 12, 2009). The figures are disputable, particularly for the earlier periods, but this is the best resource available.

27. See also Johannes Postma, *The Dutch and the Atlantic Slave Trade* (Cambridge: Cambridge University Press, 1990); Johannes Postma, *The Atlantic Slave Trade* (Westport, CT: Greenwod Press, 2003); Pieter Emmer, *The Dutch Slave Trade*, trans. Chris Emery (New York: Berghahn Books, 2006).

28. Jan Rogozinski, *A Brief History of the Caribbean from the Arawak and the Carib to the Present* (New York: Meridian, 1994), 124.

29. Enriqueta Vila Vilar, *Hispanoamérica y el comercio de esclavos* (Seville: Escuela de Estudios Hispano-Americanos, 1977); Elena F. S. de Studer, *La trata de negros en Rio de la Plata durante el siglo XVIII* (Buenos Aires, 1958); Alice Piffer Canabrava, *O comércio português no Rio da Prata (1580–1640)* (1944; repr., São Paulo: Edusp, 1984).

30. Luiz Felipe de Alencastro, *O trato dos viventes: Formação do Brasil no Atlântico Sul* (São Paulo: Companhia das Letras, 2000).

31. Philip D. Morgan, "The Black Experience in the British Empire, 1680–1810," in *The Oxford History of the British Empire*, vol. 2, *The Eighteenth Century*, ed. P. J. Marshall (Oxford: Oxford University Press, 1998), 465–86.

32. Jorge Couto, *A construção do Brasil* (Lisbon: Cosmos, 1997), 276–77; John Manuel Monteiro, *Negros da Terra: Índios e bandeirantes nas origens de São Paulo* (São Paulo: Companhia das Letras, 1994); John Hemming, *Red Gold: The Conquest of the Brazilian Indians*, 2nd ed. (London: Macmillan, 1995).

33. Manuela Carneiro da Cunha, ed., *História dos índios no Brasil*, 2nd ed. (São Paulo: Companhia das Letras, 1998).

34. John M. Monteiro, "Aldeias," in *Dicionário de história da Colonização Portuguesa no Brasil*, ed. Maria Beatriz Nizza da Silva (Lisbon: Verbo, 1994), cols. 35–38.

35. The estimates are based on a wide variety of sources and studies. See Leslie Bethell, ed., *Colonial Brazil* (Cambridge: Cambridge University Press, 1987), mainly the chapters by H. B. Johnson, Frédéric Mauro, and Dauril Alden; Guy Martinière, "O peso do número: Os homens na organização colonial do espaço," in *O império luso-brasileiro, 1620–1750*, ed. Frédéric Mauro (Lisbon: Estampa, 1991), 192–216; Altiva Pilatti Balhana, "A população," in *O império luso-brasileiro, 1750–1822*, ed. Maria Beatriz Nizza da Silva (Lisbon: Estampa, 1986), 19–62; Altiva Pilatti Balhana, "População, composição," in *Dicionário de história da Colonização Portuguesa no Brasil*, ed. Maria Beatriz Nizza da Silva (Lisbon: Verbo, 1994), cols. 649–53.

36. Dauril Alden, "Late Colonial Brazil, 1750–1808," in *Colonial Brazil*, ed. Leslie Bethel, 290, table 4. Alden underestimated the global population—he reduced it to around 2 million—but his partial figures are valid and comparable. The ethnic composition of the population sounds reliable and matches other estimates.

37. See Herbert Klein and Francisco Vidal Luna, *Slavery in Brazil* (Cambridge: Cambridge University Press, 2010), especially 250–94.

38. Caio César Boschi, *Os leigos e o poder: Irmandades leigas e política colonizadora em Minas Gerais* (São Paulo: Ática, 1986); from the same author, see the chapters on confraternities in Francisco Bethencourt and Kirti Chaudhuri, eds., *História da Expansão Portuguesa*, vols. 2 and 3.

39. The book was published under a pseudonym: André João Antonil, *Cultura e opulência do Brasil por suas drogas e minas*, ed. Andrée Mansuy Diniz Silva (1711; repr., Lisbon: CNCDP, 2001), 92–93.

40. Jean-Baptiste Debret, *Voyage historique et pittoresque au Brésil*, 3 vols. (Paris: Firmin Didot, 1834–39). For reproductions of the watercolors and drawings not included in this major work, see *Viagem pitoresca e histórica ao Brasil: Aguarelas e desenhos que não foram reproduzidos na edição de Firmin Didot—1834* (Paris: R. de Castro Maya, 1954). Sérgio Milliet translated the original work into Portuguese under the same title, Jean-Baptiste Debret, *Viagem pitoresca e histórica ao Brasil*, 2nd ed., 2 vols. (São Paulo: Livraria Martins, 1949).

41. Luiz Felipe de Alencastro, "La plume et le pinceau," in *Rio de Janeiro la ville métisse: Illustrations de Jean-Baptiste Debret*, ed. P. Straumann, L. F. de Alencastro, S. Gruzinski, and T. Monénembo (Paris: Chandeigne, 2001), 133–62.

42. Georg Wilhelm Friedrich Hegel, *Lectures on the Philosophy of World History, Introduction: Reason and History* (Cambridge: Cambridge University Press, 1975), 165.

43. Johann Moritz Rugendas, *Malerische Reise in Brasilie* (Paris: Engelman, 1835). There is a facsimile edition published in Stuttgart by Daco Verlag (1986) and a translation into Portuguese by Sergio Milliet (São Paulo: Livraria Martins, 1949); see also the images collected in Boris Kossoy and Maria Luiza Tucci Carneiro, eds., *O olhar europeu: O negro na iconografia brasileira do século XIX* (São Paulo: Edusp, 1994). On other representations, see Serge Gruzinski, "Les nouvelles images de l'Amérique," in *Rio de Janeiro la ville métisse: Illustrations de Jean-Baptiste Debret*, ed. Patrick Straumann et al. (Paris: Chandeigne, 2001), 165–91.

44. Léonce Angrand, *Imagen del Peru en el siglo XIX* (Lima: Carlos Milla Battres, 1972); Miguel Solá and Ricardo Gutierrez, eds., *Raymond Quinsac Monvoisin, su vida y su obra en America* (Buenos Aires, 1948); Claudio Linati, *Costumes et moeurs du Mexique* (London: Engelman, 1830); Carl Christian Sartorius, *Mexico und die Mexikaner*, illus. Johann Rugendas (Darmstadt, 1852; translated into English, and printed in London and New York).

45. Richard Morse, "Urban Development," in *Colonal Spanish America*, ed. Leslie Bethell (ed.) (Cambridge: Cambridge University Press, 1987), 165–202 (table 1, 187); data based on C. Esteva Fabregat, "Población y mestizage en las ciudades de Iberoamérica: siglo XVIII," in *Estudios sobre la ciudad iberoamericana*, ed. Francisco de Solano (Madrid, 1975). For a still-useful resource, see A. Rosenblat, *La población indígena y el mestizaje en América*, 2 vols. (Buenos Aires, 1954).

46. Here I am using the most reliable data, which is that produced in Newson, "The Demographic Impact of Colonization," 160.

47. Rogozinski, *A Brief History of the Caribbean Islands*, 120, 201. This evolution is confirmed by the data for 1750 and 1830 published in Stanley L. Engerman and B. W. Higman, "The Demographic Structure of the Caribbean Slave Societies in the Eighteenth and Nineteenth Centuries," in *General History of the Caribbean*, vol. 3, *The Slave Societies of the Caribbean*, ed. Franklin W. Knight (London: UNESCO, 1997), 45–101.

48. Serge Gruzinski, *The Mestizo Mind: The Intellectual Dynamics of Colonization and Globalization*, trans. Deke Dusinberre (London: Routledge, 2002); Serge Gruzinski, *Les quatre parties du monde: Histoire d'une mondialisation* (Paris: La Martinière, 2004).

49. Jack P. Greene, *Pursuits of Happiness: The Social Development of Early Modern British Colonies and the Formation of American Culture* (Chapel Hill, NC: University of North Carolina Press, 1988), 178–79; Jim Potter, "Demographic Development and Family Structure," in *Colonial British America: Essays in the New History of the Early Modern Era*, ed. Jack P. Greene and J. R. Pole (Baltimore: Johns Hopkins University Press, 1984), 123–56 (see table, ibid., 138).

50. Walter Raleigh, *The Discovery of Guiana*, ed. V. T. Harlow (1596; repr., London: Argonaut Press, 1928), 44, 46–47.

51. Greene, *Pursuits of Happiness*, 84; John H. Elliott, *Empires of the Atantic World: Britain and Spain in America, 1492–1830* (New Haven, CT: Yale University Press, 2006), 168.

52. Morgan, "The Black Experience in the British Empire," 477–78.

53. Jerome S. Handler and Arnold A. Sio, "Barbados," in *Neither Slave nor Free: The Freedmen of African Descent in the Slave Societies of the New World*, ed. David W. Cohen and Jack P. Greene (Baltimore: Johns Hopkins University Press, 1972), 218–19.

54. Orlando Patterson, *Slavery and Social Death: A Comparative Study* (Cambridge, MA: Harvard University Press, 1982), 477.

55. Winthrop D. Jordan, "American Chiaroscuro: The Status and Definition of Mulattoes in the British Colonies," *William and Mary Quarterly* 19 (1962): 183–200; Joel Williamson, *New People: Miscegenation and Mulattoes in the United States* (New York: Free Press, 1980); Walter Rodney, *A History of the Upper Guinea Coast, 1545–1800* (Oxford: Clarendon Press, 1970), 200–22; Margaret Priestley, *West African Trade and Coast Society: A Family Study* (London: Oxford University Press, 1969).

56. Gilles Harvard and Cécile Vidal, *Histoire de l'Amérique Française* (Paris: Flammarion, 2003).

57. Marcel Trudel, *L'esclavage au Canada Français* (Quebec City: Presses Universitaires Laval, 1960). For an updated edition, complemented by an index of slaves and owners on CD-ROM, see Marcel Trudel and Micheline d'Allaire, *Deux siècles d'esclavage au Canada* (Montreal: Hurtubise HMH, 2004).

58. Harvard and Vidal, *Histoire de l'Amérique Française*, 167.

59. Pierre Pluchon, *Histoires de la colonisation Française* (Paris: Fayard, 1991), 1:348.

60. Harvard and Vidal, *Histoire de l'Amérique Française*, 167.

61. Rogozinski, *A Brief History of the Caribbean*, 163.

62. Jean Boulègue, *Les Luso-africains de Senegambie, XVIe–XIXe siècles* (Lisbon: Instituto de Investigação Científica Tropical, 1989); Peter Mark and José da Silva Horta, *The Forgotten Diaspora: Jewish Communities in West Africa and the Making of the Atlantic World* (Cambridge: Cambridge University Press, 2011); Toby Green, *The Rise of the Trans-Atlantic Slave Trade in Western Africa, 1300–1589* (Cambridge: Cambridge University Press, 2012).

63. António Carreira, *Cabo Verde: Formação e extinção de uma sociedade escravocrata (1460–1878)* (Bissau, Guinea-Bissau: Centro de Estudos da Guiné Portuguesa, 1972), 287; António Leão Correia e Silva, "Dinâmicas de decomposição e recomposição de espaços e sociedades," in *História Geral de Cabo Verde*, ed. Maria Emília Madeira Santos (Lisbon: IICT, 2002), 3:1–66.

64. Arlindo Manuel Caldeira, *Mulheres, sexualidade e casamento no arquipélago de S. Tomé e Príncipe (séculos XV a XVIII)* (Lisbon: Ministério da Educação, 1997).

65. Isabel Castro Henriques, *São Tomé e Príncipe: A invenção de uma sociedade* (Lisbon: Veja, 2000).

66. Luc de Heusch, *Le roi de Kongo et les monstres sacrés* (Paris: Gallimard, 2000).

67. Anne Hilton, *The Kingdom of Kongo* (Oxford: Clarendon Press, 1985); Wyatt MacGaffey, *Religion and Society in Central Africa: The Bakongo of Lower Zaire* (Chicago: University of Chicago Press, 1986); Georges Balandier, *Daily Life in the Kingdom of Kongo from the Sixteenth to the Eighteenth Century*, trans. Helen Weaver (London: Allen and Unwin, 1968). For a challenge to the importance of the battle of Mbwila, see John K. Thornton, *The Kingdom of Kongo: Civil War and Transition, 1641–1718* (Madison: University of Wisconsin Press, 1983, 76.

68. Silva, *Dutch and Portuguese in West Africa*, 125.

69. José Carlos Venâncio, *A economia de Luanda e hinterland no século XVIII: Um estudo de sociologia histórica* (Lisbon: Estampa, 1996), 211.

70. *Anuário Estatístico do Ultramar* (Lisbon: INE, 1959).

71. For works that first highlighted ethnic or racial differences, see Marvin Harris, *Town and Country in Brazil* (New York: Columbia University Press, 1956); Marvin Harris, *Portugal's African "Wards": A First Hand Report on Labor and Education in Mozambique* (New York: American Committee on Africa, 1958); Marvin Harris, *Patterns of Race in the Americas* (New York: Walker, 1964). Harris showed that the extremely limited number of mixed-race people recorded in Mozambique contradicted Gilberto Freyre's sweeping notion of Lusotropicalism. For a look at the idea of structural differences between mixed-race groups in Africa and Brazil, see Luiz Felipe de Alencastro, "Geopolitique du métissage," *Encyclopaedia Universalis*, vol. *Symposium* (Paris, 1985), 969–77. For a exploration on a much larger scale and set within a solid historical framework, see Luiz Felipe de Alencastro, "*Mulattos* in Brazil and Angola: A Comparative Approach, from the Seventeenth to the Twenty-First Century," in *Racism and Ethnic Relations in the Portuguese-Speaking World*, ed. Francisco Bethencourt and Adrian Pearce (London: British Academy, 2012), 71–96.

72. Patrick Chabal rightly insists on the historical significance of the mixed-race cosmopolitan population of Luanda. See Patrick Chabal, introduction to *The Postcolonial Literature of Lusophone Africa* (Evanston, IL: Northwestern University Press, 1996).

73. Francisco Bethencourt, "The Political Correspondence of Albuquerque and Cortés," in *Correspondence and Cultural Exchange in Europe, 1400–1700*, ed. Francisco Bethencourt and Florike Egmond (Cambridge: Cambridge University Press, 2007), 219–73.

74. António Bocarro, *Livro das plantas de todas as fortalezas, cidades e povoações do Estado da Índia Oriental*, ed. Isabel Cid, 3 vols. (Lisbon: Imprensa Nacional, 1992). For a discussion of the data, see Francisco Bethencourt, "Low Cost Empire: Interaction between the Portuguese and Local Societies in India," in *Rivalry and Conflict: European Traders and Asian Trading Networks in the 16th and 17th Centuries*, ed. Ernst van Veen and Leonard Blussé (Leiden: CNWS, 2005), 108–30.

75. Vicente L. Rafael, *Contracting Colonialism: Translation and Christian Conversion in Tagalog Society under Early Spanish Rule* (Durham, NC: Duke University Press, 1993).

76. Linda A. Newson, "Conquest, Pestilence, and Demographic Collapse in the Early Spanish Philippines," *Journal of Historical Geography* 32 (2006): 3–20; Linda A. Newson, *Conquest and Pestilence in the Early Spanish Philippines* (Honolulu: University of Hawai'i Press, 2009), especially 254–59.

77. Boxer, *The Dutch Seaborne Empire*, 248.

78. Jean Gelman Taylor, *The Social World of Batavia: European and Eurasian in Dutch Asia* (Madison: University of Wisconsin Press, 1983); Leonard Blussé, *Strange Company: Chinese Settlers, Mestizo Women, and the Dutch in VOC Batavia* (Leiden: KITLV Press, 1986).

79. Leonard Blussé, *Bitter Bonds: A Colonial Divorce Drama of the Seventeenth Century* (Princeton, NJ: Markus Wiener, 2002).

80. William Dalrymple, *White Mughals: Love and Betrayal in Eighteenth Century India* (London: HarperCollins, 2002).

81. Boxer, *The Dutch Seaborne Empire*, 241–72.

82. Silva, *Dutch and Portuguese in Western Africa*, 107.

83. Pieter Emmer, *The Dutch in the Atlantic Economy, 1580–1880: Trade, Slavery, and Emancipation* (Aldershot, UK: Ashgate, 1998); Postma, *The Dutch in the Atlantic Slave Trade*, 68–69.

84. Christopher Bayly, *Indian Society and the Making of the British Empire* (Cambridge: Cambridge University Press, 1988), 71. On the ethnic issue, see also Christopher Bayly, *Imperial Meridian: The British Empire and the World, 1780–1830* (London: Longman, 1989), 147–55.

85. For a study of the significant later case of the Male revolt in Bahia, see João José Reis, *Slave Rebellion in Brazil: The Muslim Uprising of 1835 in Bahia*, trans. Arthur Brakel (Baltimore: John Hopkins University Press, 1993).

Chapter 12: Projects and Policies

1. The bulls and treaties are in various collections of printed sources. See especially António Joaquim Dias Dinis, ed., *Monumenta Henricina* (Coimbra, Portugal, 1971), 12:71–79 (bull *Romanus Pontifex* by Nicholas V, 8.1.1455), 286–88 (bull *Inter Cetera* by Callistus III, 13.3.1456); A. da Silva Rego, ed., *As Gavetas da Torre do Tombo* (Lisbon: Centro de Estudos Históricos Ultramarinos, 1968), 7:286–320 (treaty of Alcáçovas, 4.9.1479), 320–39 (bull *Eterni regis clementia* by Sixtus IV, 21.6.1481); João Martins da Silva Marques, ed., *Descobrimentos portugueses, Documentos para a sua história* vol. 3, *1461–1500* (Lisbon: Instituto de Alta Cultura, 1971), 384–90 (bull *Inter Caetera* by Alexander VI, 4.5.1493), 432–53 (treaty of Tordesillas, 7.6.1494). See also Júlio Valdeón Baruque, ed., *El testamento de Adán* (Lisbon: CNCDP, 1994).

2. Alonso de Espinosa, *The Origin and Miracles of the Holy Image of Our Lady of Candelaria, Which Appeared in the Island of Tenerife, with a Description of That Island*, trans. and ed. Clements Markham (1594; repr., London: Hakluyt Society, 1907), 97.

3. Jack D. Forbes (*Africans and Native Americans: The Language of Race and the Evolution of Red-Black Peoples* [Urbana: University of Illinois Press, 1993]) creates a convincing case for a wider enslavement of Native Americans than is commonly acknowledged.

4. Francisco de Solano, *Ciudades hispanoamericanas y pueblos de índios* (Madrid: CSIC, 1990); Clara Garcia and Manuel Ramos Medina, eds., *Ciudades mestizas: intercâmbios y continuidades en la expansión occidental* (Mexico City: Condumex, 2001).

5. Alain Musset, *Villes nomades du nouveau monde* (Paris: EHESS, 2002).

6. Berta Ares Queija, "Mestizos, mulatos y zambaigos (virreinato del Peru, siglo XVII)," in *Negros, mulatos, zambaigos: Derroteros africanos en los mundos ibéricos*, ed. Berta Ares Queija and Alessandro Stella (Seville: Escuela de Estúdios Hispano-Americanos, 2001), 75–89.

7. Magnus Mörner, *La mezcla de razas en la história de América Latina*, trans. Jorge Pratigowski (Buenos Aires: Paidos, 1969).

8. H. Hoetink, *The Two Variants in Caribbean Race Relations: A Contribution to the Sociology of Segmented Societies*, trans. Eva M. Hooykaas (London: Institute of Race Relations, 1967). This book is largely outdated, but the author spotted the contrast between legislation on manumission in the Spanish and English cases.

9. Carlos Malheiro Dias, ed., *História da colonização portuguesa do Brasil* (Porto: Litografia Nacional, 1924), 3:309–12 (letter of donation of the captaincy of Pernambuco to Duarte Coelho, September 5, 1534).

10. The debate on these Jesuit activities is not closed. See John Monteiro, *Os negros da terra: Índios e bandeirantes nas origins de de São Paulo* (São Paulo: Companhia das Letras, 1994); Karl-Heinz Arenz, "De l'Alzette à l'Amazone: Jean-Philippe Bettendorff et les jésuites en Amazonie portugaise (1661–1693)," 2 vols. (PhD diss., Université de Paris IV-Sorbonne, 2007).

11. Manuel Fernandes Thomaz, *Repertório geral ou índice alphabetico das leis extravagantes do Reino de Portugal*, 2nd ed., 2 vols. (Coimbra, Portugal: Imprensa da Universidade, 1843).

12. Francisco Bethencourt, "Low Cost Empire: Interaction between Portuguese and Local Societies in Asis," in *Rivalry and Conflict: European Traders and Asian Trading Networks in the 16th and 17th Centuries*, ed. Ernst van Veen and Leonard Blusse (Leiden: CNWS, 2005); Francisco Bethencourt, "The Political Correspondence of Alburquerque and Cortes," in *Correspondence and Cultural Exchange in Europe, 1400–1700*, ed. Francisco Bethencourt and Florike Egmond (Cambridge: Cambridge University Press, 2007).

13. Linda M. Heywood and John K. Thornton, *Central Africans, Atlantic Creoles, and the Foundation of the Americas, 1585–1660* (Cambridge: Cambridge University Press, 2007).

14. Charles R. Boxer, *Portuguese Society in the Tropics: The Municipal Councils of Goa, Macau, Bahia, and Luanda, 1510–1800* (Madison: University of Wisconsin Press, 1965).

15. Charles R. Boxer, *The Dutch Seaborne Empire, 1600–1800* (1965; repr., London: Penguin, 1990), 248.

16. S. Arasaratnam, *Ceylon and the Dutch, 1600–1800: External Influences and Internal Change in Early Modern Sri Lanka* (Aldershot, UK: Ashgate, 1996).

17. George M. Frederickson, *White Supremacy: A Comparative Study in American and South African History* (Oxford: Oxford University Press, 1981).

18. Christopher Bayly, *Imperial Meridian: The British Empire and the World, 1780–1830* (London: Longman, 1989), 149.

19. D. MacGalvray, "Dutch Burghers and Portuguese Mechanics: Eurasian Ethnicity in Sri Lanka," *Comparative Studies in Society and History* 24, no. 2 (1982): 264–79.

20. See John H. Elliott, *Empires of the Atlantic World: Britain and Spain in America, 1492–1830* (New Haven, CT: Yale University Press, 2006), 79–87.

21. Winthrop D. Jordan, *White over Black: American Attitudes toward the Negro, 1550–1812* (Chapel Hill, NC: University of North Carolina Press, 1968).

22. Louis Sala-Molins, *Le Code Noir ou le calvaire de Canaan* (Paris: PUF, 1987). This book includes a reproduction of the code of 1685 and variants of the 1724 code for Louisiana.

23. William B. Cohen, *The French Encounters with Africans: White Responses to Blacks, 1530–1880* (Bloomington: Indiana University Press, 1980); Gretchen Gerzina, *Black England: Life before Emancipation* (London: John Murray, 1995), 5.

CHAPTER 13: DISCRIMINATION AND SEGREGATION

1. Richard M. Morse, *The Urban Development of Latin América, 1750–1920*, 2 vols. (Stanford, CA: Center for Latin American Studies, 1971); Francisco de Solano, ed., *Historia y futuro de la ciudad iberoamericana* (Madrid: CSIC, 1986).

2. Clara Garcia and Manuel Ramos Medina, eds., *Ciudades mestizas: Intercâmbios y continuidades en la expansión occidental, siglos XVI–XIX* (Mexico City: Condumex, 2001), mainly the chapters by Decio de Alencar

Guzmán, Pilar Gonzalo Aizpuru, and Solange Alberro; Guillermo Lohman Villena, ed., *La ciudad ibero-americana* (Buenos Aires: Ministerio de Obras Publicas y Urbanismo, 1987), mainly the chapters by Jose Alcino Franch, Jose de Mesa, Teresa Gisbert, Ramon Gutierrez, Jorge E. Harding, and Alberto de Paula.

3. Javier Aguilera Rojas, ed., *La ciudad hispanoamericana: El sueño de un orden* (Buenos Aires: Ministério de Obras Publicas y Urbanismo, 1989).

4. Richard Kagan, *Urban Images of the Hispanic World, 1493–1793* (New Haven, CT: Yale University Press, 2000), mainly 19–44.

5. Tamar Herzog, *Defining Nations: Immigrants and Citizens in Early Modern Spain and Spanish America* (New Haven, CT: Yale University Press, 2003), particularly 17–63.

6. Francisco Dominguez Compañy, *La vida en las pequeñas ciudades hispanoamericanas de la conquista* (Madrid: Centro Iberoamericano de Cooperación, 1978).

7. Francisco de Solano, *Ciudades hispanoamericanas y pueblos de indios* (Madrid: CSIC, 1990).

8. Quoted in Solange Alberro, "La ciudad de México a finales del siglo XVII: Un crisol de sociedad mestiza," in *Ciudades mestizas: Intercâmbios y continuidades en la expansión occidental*, ed. Clara Garcia and Manuel Ramos Medina (Mexico City: Condumex, 2001), 173–86.

9. Decio de Alencar Guzmán, "Constructores de ciudades: Mamelucos, indios y europeos en las ciudades pombalinas de la Amazonia," in *Ciudades mestizas: Intercâmbios y continuidades en la expansión occidental*, ed. Clara Garcia and Manuel Ramos Medina (Mexico City: Condumex, 2001), 89–99; Rubenilson Brazão Teixeira, "De la ville de Dieu à la ville des hommes: La sécularisation de l'espace urbain dans le Rio Grande do Norte" (PhD, Ecole des Hautes Etudes en Sciences Sociales, 2002), especially part II.

10. Walter Rossa, *Indo-Portuguese Cities: A Contribution to the Study of Portuguese Urbanism in Western Hindustan* (Lisbon: CNCDP, 1997).

11. Antonio de Morga, *Sucesos de las Islas Filipinas*, ed. Patrício Hidalgo Nuchera (1609; repr., Madrid: Polifeno, 1997), 81.

12. Henry Kamen, *Spain's Road to Empire: The Making of a World Power* (London: Penguin, 2003), 207–8.

13. Robert R. Reed, *Colonial Manila: The Context of Hispanic Urbanism and Process of Morphogenesis* (Berkeley: University of California Press, 1978).

14. John H. Elliott, *Empires of the Atlantic World: Britain and Spain in America, 1492–1830* (New Haven, CT: Yale University Press, 2006), 181, 262; Dauril Alden, "Late Colonial Brazil," in *Colonial Brazil*, ed. Leslie Bethell (Cambridge: Cambridge University Press, 1987), 288.

15. Carl H. Nightingale, "Before Race Mattered: Geographies of the Color Line in Early Colonial Madras and New York," *American Historical Review* 113, no. 1 (2008): 48–71. The Iberian historical background is the weak point.

16. Elliott, *Empires of the Atlantic World*, 74.

17. Jack P. Greene, *Pursuits of Happiness: The Social Development of Early Modern British Colonies and the Formation of American Culture* (Chapel Hill, NC: University of North Carolina Press, 1988), 48–51.

18. Nightingale, "Before Race Mattered."

19. A.J.R. Russell-Wood, "Acts of Grace: Portuguese Monarchs and Their Subjects of African Descent in Eighteenth Century Brazil," *Journal of Latin American Studies* 32 (2000): 307–32.

20. Jonathan I. Israel, *Diasporas within a Diaspora: Jews, Crypto-Jews, and the World Maritime Empires (1540–1740)* (Leiden: Brill, 2002); Nathan Wachtel, *La foi du souvenir: Labyrinthes marranes* (Paris: Seuil, 2001); James C. Boyajian, *Portuguese Trade in Asia under the Habsburgs, 1580–1640* (Baltimore: Johns Hopkins University Press, 1993); José Pedro Paiva, "The New Christian Divide in the Portuguese-Speaking World (Sixteenth to Eighteenth Century)," in *Racism and Ethnic Relations in the Portuguese-Speaking World*, ed. Francisco Bethencourt and Adrian Pearce (London: British Academy, 2012), 269–80.

21. Charles R. Boxer, *The Church Militant and Iberian Expansion* (Baltimore: Johns Hopkins University Press, 1978).

22. For extensive information (not an interpretation) on this case, see Carlos Mercês de Melo, *The Recruitment and Formation of the Native Clergy in India (16th–19th Century)* (Lisbon: Agência Geral das Colónias, 1955).

23. Boxer, *The Church Militant and Iberian Expansion, 26.*

24. Francesco Ingoli, *Relazione delle Quattro Parti del Mondo*, ed. Fabio Tosi, intro. Josef Metzler (Vatican City: Urbaniana University Press, 1999).

25. D.G.E. Hall, *A History of South-East Asia*, 4th ed. (London: Macmillan, 1981), 750–54.

26. Paulino Castañeda Delgado, *El mestizaje en Indias: Problemas canónicos* (Madrid: Deimos, 2008).

Chapter 14: Abolitionism

1. Olaudah Equiano, *The Interesting Narrative and Other Writings*, ed. Vincent Carretta (1789; repr., London: Penguin, 2003), 65.

2. David Brion Davis, *The Problem of Slavery in Western Culture* (Oxford: Oxford University Press, 1966), chapters 10–11.

3. Equiano, *The Interesting Narrative and Other Writings*, 167–68.

4. Ibid., 337.

5. See Christopher Leslie Brown, *Moral Capital: Foundations of British Abolitionism* (Chapel Hill: University of North Carolina Press, 2006).

6. John Pinfold, ed., *The Slave Trade Debate: Contemporary Writings For and Against* (Oxford: Bodleian Library, 2007); Kenneth Morgan, ed., *The British Transatlantic Slave Trade*, vol. 3 (London: Pickering and Chatto, 2003); J. R. Oldfield, ed., *The Abolitionist Struggle: The Opponents of the Slave Trade* (London: Pickering and Chatto, 2003); J. R. Oldfield, *Popular Politics and British Anti-Slavery: The Mobilisation of Public Opinion against the Slave Trade, 1787–1807* (Manchester: Manchester University Press, 1995).

7. Seymour Drescher, *Abolition: A History of Slavery and Antislavery* (Cambridge: Cambridge University Press, 2009), 220, 250.

8. For images of materials in the Franklin Smith collection, see Pinfold, *The Slave Trade Debate*; see also reproductions from the Bodleian Library exhibition, http://www.bodley.ox.ac.uk/dept/scwmss/projects/abolition (accessed June 15, 2011).

9. William Blake, *The House of Death* (c. 1795), color print, finished in pen, chalk, and watercolor, 480 x 603 millimeters, Fitzwilliam Museum, Cambridge (number 1769). This image has been interpreted as a madhouse or mental slavery; David Bindman, *Mind-forg'd Manacles: William Blake and Slavery* (London: Hayward Gallery, 2007), 80–81. The song of innocence "The Little Black Boy" also stresses the blurring of skin colors: "When I from black and he from white cloud free." William Blake, *The Complete Poetry and Prose*, ed. David V. Erdman, rev. ed. (New York: Anchor Books, 1988), 9.

10. João Pedro Marques, *The Sounds of Silence: Nineteenth century Portugal and the Abolition of the Slave Trade,* trans. Richard Wall (Oxford: Berghahn, 2006); Nelly Schmidt, *L'abolition de l'esclavage: Cinq siècles de combats, XVIe–XXe siècle* (Paris: Fayard, 2005).

11. José Andrés-Gallego and Jesús María García Añoveros, *La Iglesia y la esclavitud de los negros* (Pamplona, Spain: EUNSA, 2002), 22–31. This book is also important for the following paragraphs.

12. Frank Bartholomew Costello, *The Political Philosophy of Luis de Molina, S. J. (1535–1600)* (Rome, 1974); Alan Watson, "Seventeenth Century Jurists, Roman Law, and the Law of Slavery," in *Slavery and the Law*, ed. Paul Finkelman (Madison: Madison House, 1997), 367–77.

13. Alonso de Sandoval, *Un tratado sobre la esclavitud*, ed. Enriqueta Vila Vilar (1627; repr., Madrid: Alianza, 1987), 142–49 (book 1, chapter 17). Sandoval offers reports of inquiries to his colleagues in Africa and conversations with slave traders in Cartagena to denounce the bad treatment to African slaves.

14. Francisco José de Jaca, *Resolución sobre la libertad de los negros y sus originarios, en estado de paganos y después ya cristianos*, ed. Miguel Anxo Pena González (Madrid: CSIC, 2002); Miguel Anxo Pena González, *Francisco José de Jaca: La primera propuesta abolicionista de la esclavitud en el pensamiento hispano* (Salamanca: Publicaciones Universidad Pontificia, 2003).

15. Richard Gray, "The Papacy and the Atlantic Slave Trade: Lourenço da Silva, the Capuchins, and the Decisions of the Holy Office," *Past and Present* 115 (1987): 52–68. For the consultation of the Roman Inquisition, revealing that the acceptance of Mendonça's request was limited, see Andrés-Gallego and García Añoveros, *La Iglesia y la esclavitud de los negros*, 88–89.

16. Andrés-Gallego and García Añoveros, *La Iglesia y la esclavitud de los negros*, 9–11.

17. Jean Bodin, *Les six livres de la république* (Paris: Jacques Du Puys, 1576), book 1, chapter 5.

18. Hugo Grotius, *De Jure Bell ac Pacis*, ed. James Brown Scott, trans. John Damen Maguire, 4 vols. (1625; repr., Washington, DC: Carnegie Institution, 1913–25), book 1, chapter 3 § 8; book 2, chapter 5 § 27–30; book 3, chapters 7 and 14.

19. Thomas Hobbes, *Human Nature and De Corpore Politico*, ed. J.C.A. Gaskin (1640; repr., Oxford: Oxford University Press, 1994), 78, 93, 126–29; Thomas Hobbes, *Leviathan*, ed. C. B. Macpherson (1651; repr., London: Penguin, 1985), part 1, chapter 13; part 2, chapter 20.

20. Samuel Pufendorf, *On the Duty of Man and Citizen*, ed. James Tully (1673; repr., Cambridge: Cambridge University Press, 1991), 129–31.

21. John Locke, *Two Treatises of Government*, ed. Peter Laslett (1689–90; repr., Cambridge: Cambridge University Press, 1988), 141, 169–70, 236–37, 283–85.

22. Montesquieu, *De l'esprit des lois*, ed. Laurent Versini (1748; repr., Paris: Gallimard, 1995), book 15. For an even clearer position against slavery, see Montesquieu, *Pensées: Le spicilège*, ed. Louis Desgraves (Paris: Robert Laffont, 1991), 174–76, 466, 643, 1782, 1838, 1847, 1916, 1925, 2194.

23. Denis Diderot and Jean d'Alembert, eds., *Encyclopédie, ou dictionnaire raisonné des sciences, des arts et des métiers* (Paris, 1755), 5:934–43. For articles by Chevalier de Jaucourt on slavery and the slave trade, see *Encyclopédie, ou dictionnaire raisonné des sciences, des arts et des métiers* (Neuchatel, 1765), 16:532–33. For analysis, including on the influence of George Wallace, see Davis, *The Problem of Slavery in Western Culture*, 416.

24. Jean-Jacques Rousseau, *Discours sur l'origine et les fondements de l'inégalité parmi les hommes*, ed. Jean Starobinski (1755; repr., Paris: Gallimard, 1969), 113–14; Jean-Jacques Rousseau, *Du contrat social*, ed. Bruno Bernardi (1762; repr., Paris: Flammarion, 1969), 46, 50–54.

25. Guillaume-Thomas Raynal, *Histoire philosophique et politique des établissements et du commerce des Européens dans les deux Indes*, 7 vols. (The Hague: Chez Gosse Fils, 1774), particularly 4:187–235, 7:139–146.

26. Marquis de Condorcet, *Réflexions sur l'esclavage des nègres*, ed. Jean-Paul Doguet (1781; repr., Paris: Flammarion, 2009).

27. Adam Ferguson, *An Essay on the History of Civil Society*, ed. Fania Oz-Salzberger (1767; repr., Cambridge: Cambridge University Press, 1995).

28. Davis, *The Problem of Slavery in Western Culture*, 106–11.

29. David Hume, "Of the Populousness of Ancient Nations" (1752), in *Selected Essays*, ed. Stephen Copley and Andrew Edgar (Oxford: Oxford University Press, 1998), 223–74.

30. Benjamin Franklin, *The Autobiography and Other Writings on Politics, Economics, and Virtue*, ed. Alan Houston (Cambridge: Cambridge University Press, 2004), 215–21, 369–71.

31. Victor Riqueti de Mirabeau, *L' ami des hommes, ou traité de la population*, 6 vols. (The Hague: Benjamin Gibert, 1758), mainly 3:233–59. For an extended analysis of the influence of the Physiocrats, see Davis, *The Problem of Slavery in Western Culture*, 427–34.

32. Adam Smith, *An Inquiry into the Nature and Causes of the Wealth of Nations*, ed. Kathryn Sutherland (1776; repr., Oxford: Oxford University Press, 1998), 80–81, 238–39.

33. Eric Williams, *Capitalism and Slavery* (Chapel Hill: University of North Carolina Press, 1944).

34. Seymour Drescher, *Capitalism and Antislavery: British Mobilization in Comparative Perspective* (Oxford: Oxford University Press, 1986); David Eltis, *Economic Growth and the Ending of the Transatlantic Slave Trade* (Oxford: Oxford University Press, 1987); Thomas Bender, ed., *The Antislavery Debate: Capitalism and Abolition as a Problem in Historical Interpretation* (Berkeley: University of California Press, 1992); Seymour Drescher, "Capitalism and Slavery after Fifty Years," *Slavery and Abolition* 18, no. 3 (1997): 212–27; S.H.H. Carrington, *The Sugar Industry and the Abolition of Slave Trade* (Gainesville: University Press of Florida, 2002); David Richardson, "The Ending of the British Slave Trade in 1807: The Economic Context," in *The British Slave Trade: Abolition, Parliament and People* ed. Stephen Farrell, Melanie Unwin, and James Walvin (Edinburgh: Edinburgh University Press, 2007), 127–40; David Rydan, *West Indian Slavery and British Abolition, 1783–1807* (Cambridge: Cambridge University Press, 2009).

35. Benjamin Lay, *All Slave-keepers That Keep the Innocent in Bondage, Apostates Pretending to Lay Claim to the Pure Holy Christian Religion* (Philadelphia, 1737). See Davis, *The Problem of Slavery in Western Culture*, 291–332.

36. Davis, *The Problem of Slavery in Western Culture*, 291–364.

37. Arthur F. Cowin, *Spain and the Abolition of Slavery in Cuba (1817–1886)* (Austin: University of Texas Press, 1967); Christopher Schmidt-Nowara, *Empire and Antislavery: Spain, Cuba, and Puerto Rico, 1833–1874* (Pittsburgh: University of Pittsburgh Press, 1999); Rebecca J. Scott, *Slave Emancipation in Cuba: The Transition to Free Labor* (Princeton, NJ: Princeton University Press, 1985).

38. Leslie Bethell, ed., *The Independence of Latin América* (Cambridge: Cambridge University Press, 1987); Drescher, *Abolition*, 181–204.

39. João José Reis and Flávio dos Santos Gomes, eds., *Liberdade por um fio: História dos Quilombos no Brasil* (São Paulo: Companhia das Letras, 1996).

40. Leslie Bethell, *The Abolition of the Brazilian Slave Trade* (Cambridge: Cambridge University Press, 1970).

41. Robert E. Conrad, *The Destruction of Brazilian Slavery, 1850–1888* (Berkeley: University of California Press, 1972).

42. José Capela, *Escravatura: A empresa do saque. O abolicionismo (1810–1875)* (Porto, Portugal: Afrontamento, 1974); Valentim Alexandre and Jill Dias, eds., *O império africano, 1825–1890* (Lisbon: Estampa, 1998), 52–60, 192–98, 287–93, 457–71, 589–96; Marques, *The Sounds of Silence*; Francisco Bethencourt, "Race Relations in the Portuguese Empire," in *Encompassing the Globe: Portugal and the World in the 16th and 17th Centuries; Essays*, ed. Jay A. Levenson (Washington, DC: Smithsonian Institution, 2007).

43. Pieter C. Emmer, *The Dutch Slave Trade, 1500–1850*, trans. Chris Emery (New York: Berghahn Books, 2006).

44. Jeremy D. Popkin, *You Are All Free: The Haitian Revolution and the Abolition of Slavery* (Cambridge: Cambridge University Press, 2010); David Barry Gaspar and David Patrick Geggus, eds., *The French Revolution and the Greater Caribbean* (Bloomington: Indiana University Press, 1997); Carolyn Fick, *The Making of Haiti: The Saint Domingue Revolution from Below* (Knoxville: University of Tenessee Press, 1990).

45. Laurent Dubois, *A Colony of Citizens: Revolution and Slave Emancipation in the Slave Caribbean, 1787–1804* (Chapel Hill: University of North Carolina Press, 2004); Frédéric Régent, *Esclavage, métissage, liberté: Le Révolution Française en Guadeloupe, 1789–1802* (Paris: Grasset, 2004); David Patrick Geggus, ed., *The Impact of the Haitian Revolution on the Atlantic World* (Columbia: University of South Carolina Press, 2001).

46. Nelly Schmidt, *Victor Schœlcher* (Paris: Fayard, 1994).

47. See Drescher, *Abolition*, 245–332.

48. Lynn Hunt, *Inventing Human Rights: A History* (New York: W. W. Norton, 2007).

49. Jean-Pierre Brissot, quoted in Schmidt, *L'abolition de l'esclavage*, 81: "Non seulement la Société des Amis des Noirs ne sollicite point en ce moment l'abolition de l'esclavage, mais elle serait affligée qu'elle fût proposée. Les esclaves ne sont pas mûres pour la liberté; il faut les y préparer: telle est la doctrine de cette Société."

50. See George Boulukos, *The Grateful Slave: The Emergence of Race in Eighteenth-Century British and American Culture* (Cambridge: Cambridge University Press, 2008). Boulukos rightly points out the extension of this idea to iconography—namely, the image of the kneeling slave with the caption "Am I not a Man and a Brother?"

51. Montesquieu, *De l'esprit des lois*, book 15, chapter 5.

52. Jean-Jacques Rousseau, *Discours sur l'origine et les fondements de l'inégalité parmi les hommes*, ed. Jean Starobinski (1755; repr., Paris: Gallimard, 1969).

53. Voltaire, *Romans et contes*, ed. René Pomeau (Paris: Flammarion, 1966), particularly *Candide ou l'optimisme* and *L'ingénu*.

54. Raynal, *Histoire philosophique et politique*, 4:168–74.

55. Condorcet, *Réflexions sur l'esclavage des nègres*, especially chapter 8.

56. Alexis de Tocqueville, *Sur l'esclavage*, ed. Seloua Luste Boulbina (Arles, France: Actes Sud, 2008).

57. Maria Lúcia Garcia Pallares-Burke, *Gilberto Freyre: Um vitoriano dos trópicos* (São Paulo: UNESP, 2005).

58. Abbé Grégoire, *De la noblesse de la peau*, ed. Jacques Prunar (1826; repr., Grenoble: Jerôme Million, 1996), 39.

59. Drescher, *Abolition*, 294–371.

Part IV: The Theories of Race

1. Lisbet Koerner, *Linnaeus: Nature and Nation* (Cambridge, MA: Harvard University Press, 1999), 65–71. This book also refers to the frontispiece of *Flora Lapponica* (1737), in which Linnaeus placed himself at the forefront of a fantastic Lapland landscape, playing a shamanist drum. I have been unable to find any reference to the painter, Martin Hoffman, in the main dictionaries of artists, or in published collections of art and portraits. This is not the place for a discussion of the accuracy of the costumes worn by Linnaeus, but for the nineteenth-century ethnographic photographs of Saami, see http://saamiblog.blogspot.com/2008/01/saami -pewter-embroiderie-belts-purses.htlm (accessed September 3, 2010).

2. Koerner, *Linnaeus: Nature and Nation*; Wilfrid Blunt, *Linnaeus: The Compleat Naturalist* (1971; repr., London: Frances Lincoln, 2001).

3. Michel Foucault, *Les mots et les choses: Une archéologie des sciences humaines* (Paris: Gallimard, 1966), particularly chapter 5. See also the English translation: Michel Foucault, *The Order of Things: An Archaeology of the Human Sciences* (London: Tavistock, 1970). Foucault's schematic approach using compartmentalized historical periods, inspired by Gaston Bachelard, has since been criticized by several authors, especially Claude Blanckaert in the collective book *L'histoire des sciences de l'homme: Trajectoires, enjeux et questions vives* (Paris: L'Harmattan, 1999).

4. Jorieke Rutgers, "Linnaeus in the Netherlands," *Tijdshrift noor Skandinavistiek* 29, nos. 1–2 (2008): 103–16; Patricia Fara, "Carl Linnaeus: Pictures and Propaganda," *Endeavour* 27, no. 1 (2003): 14–15.

5. Ferdinand Denis, *Une fête brésilienne célébrée à Rouen en 1550* (Paris, 1850).

6. Carl Linnaeus, *Lachesis Lapponica or a Tour in Lapland*, trans. Charles Troilius and James Edward Smith, 2 vols. (London: White and Cochrane, 1811); see also Carl Linnaeus, *Flora Lapponica* (Amsterdam, 1737).

7. Kroener rightly analyzes Linnaeus's scientific life according to these different dimensions.

8. Martin J. S. Rudwick, *Bursting the Limits of Time: The Reconstruction of Geohistory in the Age of Revolution* (Chicago: University of Chicago Press, 2005); Martin J. S. Rudwick, *Worlds before Adam: The Reconstruction of Geohistory in the Age of Reform* (Chicago: University of Chicago Press, 2008).

9. Jacques Roger, *Buffon: Un philosophe au jardin du roi* (Paris: Fayard, 1989).

10. Alessandro Scafi, *Mapping Paradise: A History of Heaven on Earth* (Chicago: University of Chicago Press, 2006).

11. Isaac de La Peyrère, *Man before Adam*, (London, 1656); Richard H. Popkin, *Isaac La Peyrère (1596–1676): His Life, Work, and Influence* (Leiden: Brill, 1987).

12. Giuliano Glozzi, *Adamo e il nuovo mondo: La nascita dell'antropologia come ideologia coloniale; Dalle genealogie bibliche alle teorie razziali (1500–1700)* (Florence: La Nuova Itália Editrice, 1977), 306–47.

13. David N. Livingstone, *Adam's Ancestors: Race, Religion, and the Politics of Human Origin* (Baltimore: Johns Hopkins University Press, 2008).

14. On the importance of theological reasoning for the reflection on races, see Colin Kidd, *The Forging of Races: Race and Scripture in the Protestant Atlantic World, 1600–2000* (Cambridge: Cambridge University Press, 2006).

15. Arthur O. Lovejoy, *The Great Chain of Being: A Study of the History of an Idea* (Cambridge, MA: Harvard University Press, 1933).

16. Aristotle, *Histoire des animaux*, trans. Pierre Louis, 2 vols. (Paris: Les Belles Lettres, 1969).

17. Stephen Jay Gould, *The Mismeasure of Man* (New York: W. W. Norton, 1996).

18. Hannah Franziska Augstein, ed., *Race: The Origins of an Idea, 1760–1850* (Bristol: Thoemmes Press, 1996), ix–x.

CHAPTER 15: CLASSIFICATIONS OF HUMANS

1. Carl Linnaeus, *Systema naturæ* (Lugduni Batavorum, Netherlands: Theodorum Haak, 1735). See the facsimile edition with an introduction by M.S.J. Engel-Ledeboer and H. Engel (Nieuwkoop, Netherlands: B. De Graaf, 1964).

2. Carl Linnaeus, *A General System of Nature*, trans. William Turton (London: L. Allen, 1806), 1:9. I have checked the original, Latin, 13th edition for the description of the varieties of humans: Carl Linnaeus, *Systema naturæ* (Vindobonæ: Ioannis Thomae, 1767–70), 1:28–33.

3. Here I draw on Buffon, *De l'Homme*, texts from 1749–77, organized and presented by Michèle Duchet with a postface by Claude Blanckaert (Paris: L'Harmattan, 2006).

4. François Bernier, "Nouvelle division de la Terre, par les différentes espèces ou races d'hommes qui l'habitent," *Journal des Sçavans*, April 24, 1684, 148–55; see also Siep Stuurman, "François Bernier and the Invention of Racial Classification," *History Workshop Journal* 50 (Fall 2000): 1–21. This vision, though, particularly of black people in different continents, had already been suggested; see Alonso de Sandoval, *Un tratado sobre la esclavitud*, ed. Enriqueta Vila Vilar (1627; repr., Madrid: Alianza, 1987), book 1.

5. Cornelius de Pauw, *Recherches philosophiques sur les Américains* (1768–69), preface Michèle Duchet, 2 vols. (1774; repr., Paris: Jean Michel Place, 1990); Guilaume Thomas François Raynal, *Histoire philosophique et*

politique des établissements des Européens dans le deux Indes, rev. ed., 12 vols. (1770; repr., Paris: Amable/Coste, 1820–21).

6. Thomas Jefferson reported this anecdote, adding that Raynal was "a mere shrimp." Franklin could not have made this joke against the tall and proud Buffon. See Antonello Gerbi, *The Dispute of the New World: The History of a Polemic, 1750–1900*, trans. Jeremy Moyle, rev. ed. (1955; repr., Pittsburgh: University of Pittsburgh Press, 1973), 242.

7. Jean Chardin, *Voyage de Paris à Ispahan*, ed. Stéphane Yerasimos, 2 vols. (1686; repr., Paris: La Découverte, 1983). The significant passages are in ibid., 1:143, 154, 181–82. Other travelers, particularly Bernier, shared this vision.

8. Voltaire, *Dictionnaire philosophique*, ed. Béatrice Didier (Paris: Imprimerie Nationale, 1994). In any case, these prejudices are far from the ferocity attributed to Voltaire by Léon Poliakov. The philosopher's target was, as usual, the Jewish origins of Christian superstition.

9. Immanuel Kant, "On the Different Races of Human Beings" (1775–77), in *Anthropology, History, and Education*, ed. Günther Zöller and Robert B. Louden (Cambridge: Cambridge University Press, 2007), 82–97.

10. Immanuel Kant, "Determination of the Concept of a Human Race" (1785), in *Anthropology, History, and Education*, ed. Günther Zöller and Robert B. Louden (Cambridge: Cambridge University Press, 2007), 143–59.

11. Johann Gottfried von Herder, *Philosophical Writings*, trans. and ed. Michael N. Foster (Cambridge: Cambridge University Press, 2002), 60. The argument is developed through the greater part of the texts in this collection, but I highlight ibid., 54–64, 69–77, 161–62 (texts published in 1767–68 and 1772).

12. Ibid., 220 (text published in 1778).

13. Ibid., 154–55, 160–61, 220–21, 255–56.

14. Ibid., 62, 282.

15. Ibid., 152–53, 248.

16. Ibid., 297, 318, 328–32, 350 (text published in 1774).

17. *The Works of the Late Professor Camper on the Connexion between the Science of Anatomy and the Arts of Drawing, Painting, Statuary, &c. &c. in Two Books*, trans. T. Cogon (London: C. Dilly, 1794).

18. Miriam Claude Meijer, *Race and Aesthetics in the Anthropology of Petrus Camper (1722–1789)* (Amsterdam: Lodopi, 1999).

19. Charles White, *An Account of the Regular Gradation in Man and in Different Animals and Vegetables* (London: C. Dilly, 1799).

20. Johann Friedrich Blumenbach, *The Anthropological Treatises*, trans. and ed. Thomas Bendishe (London: Anthropological Society, 1865).

21. Georges Cuvier, *Le règne animal*, 4 vols. (Paris: Deterville, 1817), particularly 1:94–99. For the description of the Hottentot female exhibited in Paris, and examined and autopsied by Cuvier, see Georges Cuvier and Geoffroy Saint Hilaire, *Histoire naturelle des mammifères* (Paris: A. Balin, 1824–29), 1:1–7.

22. Jean-Baptiste Lamarck, *Philosophie zoologique*, 2 vols. (Paris: Dentu, 1809), particularly 1:ii–iv, viii, 5 (which noted in italics the *progression* in the composition of the organization), 7–8, 89, 107, 113; 2:159, 252, 320, 341, 349. For the first airing of his main ideas, see Jean-Baptiste Lamarck, *Recherches sur l'organisation des corps vivants* (Paris: Maillard, 1802). Here, the notion of acquired forms, successively transmitted by generation, was formulated. Lamarck's interest in the natural environment—he hinted that the origins of life lay in the sea—led to the launch of studies on meteorology. On the similarity between Lamarck's and Erasmus Darwin's ideas, see Ludmilla Jordanova, *Lamarck* (Oxford: Oxford University Press, 1984).

23. Geoffroy Saint Hilaire, *Cours d'histoire naturelle des mammifères* (Paris: Pichon et Didier, 1829) ; Geoffroy Saint Hilaire, *Principes de philosophie zoologique* (Paris: Pichon et Didier, 1830); the reference to Lamarck is inscribed in the title. See Toby A. Appel, *The Cuvier-Geoffroy Debate: French Biology in the Decades before Darwin* (Oxford: Oxford University Press, 1987).

24. Pietro Corsi, *The Age of Lamarck: Evolutionary Theories in France, 1790–1830*, trans. Jonathan Mandelbaum, rev. ed. (Berkeley: University of California Press, 1988).

25. Etienne Serres, *Recherches d'anatomie transcendante et pathologique* (Paris, 1832); Etienne Serres, *Précis d'anatomie transcendante appliquée à la physiologie* (Paris, 1842).

26. Julien Joseph Virey, *Histoire naturelle du genre humain*, rev. ed., 3 vols. (1801; repr., Paris: Crochard, 1824).

27. Ibid., 3:436–37.

28. Ibid., 2:32.

29. Ibid., 2:2–20.

30. Ibid., 1:408–50.

31. Ibid., 1:28–39.

32. Claude Blanckaert, "J. L. Virey, observateur de l'homme," in *Julien-Joseph Virey: Naturaliste et anthropologue*, ed. Claude Benichon and Claude Blanckaert (Paris: Vrin, 1988), 97–182.

33. Virey, *Histoire naturelle*, 1:298–99.

34. Ibid., 2:64–65, 106–7.

35. Blanckaert, "J. L. Virey, observateur de l'homme."

36. James Cowles Prichard, *Researches into the Physical History of Mankind*, 3rd ed., 5 vols. (n.l.: Sherwood Gilbert and Piper, 1836–47); see also the introduction to the edited edition by George W. Stocking (Chicago: University of Chicago Press, 1973).

37. James Cowles Prichard, *Ethnographical Maps* (London: H. Baillière, 1843).

38. Adrien Balbi, *Introduction à l'atlas ethnographique du globe* (Paris: Rey et Gravier, 1826).

39. Henry Home, Lord Kames, *Sketches of the History of Man*, 4 vols. (Dublin, 1775).

40. Hannah Franziska Augstein, *James Cowles Prichard's Anthropology: Remaking the Science of Man in Early Nineteenth-Century Britain* (Amsterdam: Rodopi, 1999).

41. Alexander von Humboldt, *Cosmos: A Sketch of the Physical Description of the Universe*, trans. E. C. Otté, intro. N. A. Rupke (1848; repr., Baltimore: Johns Hopkins University Press, 1997), 1:351–59.

Chapter 16: Scientific Racialism

1. Mike Rapport, *1848 Year of Revolution* (London: Little, Brown and Company, 2008); Jonathan Sperber, *The European Revolutions, 1848–1851* (Cambridge: Cambridge University Press, 1994).

2. For a reproduction of the declarations of human rights along with a discussion of their limits and consequences, see Lynn Hunt, *Inventing Human Rights: A History* (New York: W. W. Norton, 2007).

3. US constitutional documents, http://memory/loc.gov (accessed June 20, 2011).

4. Paul Spickard, *Almost All Aliens: Race and Colonialism in American History and Identity* (New York: Routledge, 2007), chapter 3; David Brion Davis, *Inhuman Bondage: The Rise and Fall of Slavery in the New World* (Oxford: Oxford University Press, 2008), 141–56, 175–204, 250–322. Congressional laws and debates from 1774 to 1873, http://memory.loc.gov/ ammem/amlaw/lawhome/html (accessed June 20, 2011).

5. Christopher Bayly, *Recovering Liberties: Indian Thought in the Age of Liberalism and Empire* (Cambridge: Cambridge University Press, 2012).

6. Tony Ballantyne, *Orientalism and Race: Aryanism in the British Empire* (Houndmills, UK: Palgrave, 2002).

7. Robert Knox, *The Races of Men: A Fragment* (London: Henry Renshaw, 1850).

8. Ibid., 2, 6, 21, 26.

9. Ibid., 2.

10. Ibid., 69.

11. Ibid., 56–57.

12. Ibid., 55.

13. Ibid., 46–58.

14. Ibid., 18, 26–27, 123, 140.

15. Ibid., 48–49, 59.

16. Ibid., 65–67, 89, 97, 114.

17. Ibid., 158.

18. Ibid., 194–96.

19. Ibid., 157.

20. Ibid., 141.

21. Ibid., 283–84.

22. Ibid., 181–82.

23. Ibid., 222.

24. Ibid., 42.

25. Nancy Stepan, *The Idea of Race in Science: Great Britain, 1800–1960* (London: Macmillan, 1982).

26. Catherine Hall, *White, Male, and Middle Class* (Cambridge, UK: Polity, 1992); Catherine Hall, "The Nation Within and Without," in *Defining the Victorian Nation: Class, Race, Gender, and the Reform Act of 1867*, ed. Catherine Hall, Keith McClelland, and Jane Rendall (Cambridge: Cambridge University Press, 2000); Catherine Hall, *Civilising Subjects: Metropole and Colony in the English Imagination, 1830–1867* (Cambridge, UK: Polity, 2002); Robert Young, *Colonial Desire: Hybridity in Theory, Culture, and Race* (London: Routledge, 1995).

27. Peter Mandler, "The Problem with Cultural History," in *Cultural and Social History* 1, no. 1 (2004): 94–117; see also by Peter Mandler, "'Race' and 'Nation' in Mid-Victorian Thought," in *History, Religion, and Culture: British Intellectual History, 1750–1950*, ed. Stefan Collini, Richard Whatmore, and Brian Young (Cambridge: Cambridge University Press, 2000), 94–117.

28. Sadiah Qureshi, "Robert Gordon Latham, Displayed Peoples, and the Natural History of Race, 1854–1866," *Historical Journal*, 54, no. 1 (March 2011): 143–66.

29. Robert G. Latham, *The Ethnology of the British Islands* (London: John Van Voorst, 1852), 259–60.

30. Arthur de Gobineau, *Essai sur l'inégalité des races humaines* (1853–55), in Arthur de Gobineau, *Œuvres*, ed. Jean Gaulmier and Jean Boissel (Paris: Gallimard, 1983), 1:133–1174 (text), 1216–471 (critical notes). I translated the quotations.

31. Gobineau, *Œuvres*, 1:195.

32. Ibid., 1:179, 237, 632, 964, 1013, 1134.

33. Ibid., 1:313.

34. Ibid., 1:175.

35. Alexis de Tocqueville, *Lettres Choisies: Souvenirs, 1814–1859*, ed. Françoise Mélonio and Laurence Guellec (Paris: Gallimard, 2003), 1088–96. See especially the letter to Gobineau written on November 17, 1853.

36. Gobineau, *Œuvres*, 1:347.

37. Ibid., 1:198–211.

38. Ibid., 1:1164–65.

39. Ibid., 1:248–55, 622.

40. Ibid., 1:252–55, 275–80.

41. Ibid., 1:242–47.

42. Ibid., 1:312.

43. Ibid., 1:268.

44. Ibid., 1:286, 287.

45. Ibid., 1:288–97.

46. Ibid., 1:343–44.

47. Ibid., 1:306–7.

48. Ibid., 1:339–40.

49. Ibid., 1:341–42.

50. Ibid., 1:622, 725.

51. Ibid., 1:345, 488, 561, 613.

52. Ibid., 1:980–1016, 671–76.

53. Ibid., 1:699.

54. Ibid., 1:1041.

55. Ibid., 1:1058.

56. Ibid., 1:473.

57. Ibid., 1:711.

58. Ibid., 1:430.

59. Ibid., 1:602.

60. Samuel George Morton, *Crania Americana* [and] *Crania Aegyptiaca*, intro. Robert Bernaconi (1839/1844; repr., Bristol: Thoemmes, 2002), 67, 90.

61. On the demolition of Morton's methods, see Stephen Jay Gould, *The Mismeasure of Men* (New York: W. W. Norton, 1996), chapter 3.

62. Morton, *Crania Americana* [and] *Crania Aegyptiaca*, 1–3.

63. Ibid., 55 (in the second text).

64. For an analysis of this phenomenon, see George M. Frederickson, *The Black Image in the White Mind: The Debate on Afro-American Character and Destiny, 1817–1914*, rev. ed. (Hanover, NH: Wesleyan University Press, 1981), chapter 3.

65. John Campbell, *Negro-Mania: Being an Examination of the Falsely Assumed Equality of the Various Races of Men* (Philadelphia: Campbell and Power, 1851); Charles Hamilton Smith, *The Natural History of the Human Species, Its Typical Forms, Primeval Distribution, Filiations, and Migrations* (Edinburgh, 1848).

66. Josiah Clark Nott and George Robins Gliddon, eds., *Types of Mankind* (Philadelphia: Lippincott, Grambo and Co., 1854); see also the development of this line of inquiry in Josiah Clark Nott and George Robins Gliddon, eds., *Indigenous Races of the Earth, or New Chapters of Ethnological Enquiry* (Philadelphia: J. B. Lippincott and Co., 1857). Burke published ten issues of the *Ethnological Journal* in 1848–49 in London with the revealing subtitle *A Magazine of Ethnography, Phrenology, and Archaeology, Considered as the Elements of the Science of Races, with the Application of This Science to Education, Legislation, and Social Progress*.

67. Louis Agassiz, *An Essay on Classification*, ed. Edward Lurie (1857; repr., Cambridge, MA: Belknap, 1962); see also the version edited by John M. Lynch (Bristol: Thoemmes, 2003).

68. Professor and Mrs. Louis Agassiz, *A Journey in Brazil* (Boston: Ticknor and Fields, 1868), 129, 246, 260, 292, 296–98.

69. Joel Williamson, *The Crucible of Race: Black-White Relations in the American South since Emancipation* (Oxford: Oxford University Press, 1984).

70. See Urs App, *The Birth of Orientalism* (Philadelphia: University of Pennsylvania Press, 2010).

71. Giovanni-Paolo Marana, *L' espion turc dans les cours des princes chrétiens*, ed. Françoise Jackson (1684–88; repr., Paris: Coda, 2009), 452–54. This book was an extraordinary success, with successive editions and translations in English, Italian, and German; it inspired Montesquieu to write *Lettres Persanes*.

72. John Zephaniah Holwell, *Interesting Historical Events to the Province of Bengal and the Empire of Hindostan* (London: T. Becket and P. A. de Hondt, 1765); Anquetil-Duperron, *Zend-Avesta*, 3 vols. (Paris: N. Tilliard, 1771); Charles Wilkins, *Bhagvad-Geeta* (London, 1785); William Jones, *Institutes of Indian Law* (Calcutta, 1796).

73. Friedrich Max Müller, *Rig-Veda Sanhita, the Sacred Hymns of the Brahmans*, 6 vols. (London, 1849–74).

74. Voltaire, *Essai sur l'histoire générale et les mœurs et l'esprit des nations*, books 11–17, *Œuvres Complètes* (Geneva: Frères Cramer, 1756).

75. Thomas R. Trautmann, *Aryans and British India* (Berkeley: University of California Press, 1997).

76. Tony Ballantine, *Orientalism and Race: Aryanism and the British Empire* (Houndmills, UK: Palgrave, 2002).

77. Léon Poliakov, *The Aryan Myth: A History of Racist and Nationalist Ideas in Europe*, trans. Edward Howard (London: Chatto and Windus, 1974).

78. William Z. Ripley, *The Races of Europe: A Sociological Study* (London: Kegan Paul, 1899).

Chapter 17: Darwin and Social Evolution

1. Bouda Etemad, *La possession du monde: Poids et mesures de la colonisation* (Brussels: Complexe, 2000), 172.

2. Erasmus Darwin, *The Collected Writings*, ed. Martin Priestman, 9 vols. (Bristol: Thoemmes, 2004).

3. Janet Browne, *Charles Darwin*, 2 vols. (London: Jonathan Cape, 1995–2002); Charles Darwin, *Evolutionary Writings*, ed. and intro. James A. Secord (Oxford: Oxford University Press, 2008).

4. Charles Darwin, *Voyage of the Beagle*, ed. Janet Browne and Michael Neve, 1st abridged ed. (1839; repr., London: Penguin, 1989), 172. I will also quote from James Secord's edition of the selected writings, which used the important second edition of the *Voyage* published in 1845.

5. Darwin, *Evolutionary Writings*, 24.

6. Ibid., 25.

7. Ibid., 23.

8. Ibid., 28–36.

9. Thomas Robert Malthus, *An Essay on the Principle of Population* [1798], intro. Donald Winch, ed. Patricia James (1798; repr., Cambridge: Cambridge University Press, 1992), 56–57, 61–63, 66–67, 72–73, 226, 331 (the main link to Darwin's reflection), 343–45.

10. Darwin, *Evolutionary Writings*, 37–38.

11. Charles Darwin, *Journal of Researches into the Natural History and Geology of the Countries Visited during the Voyage of H. M. S. Beagle*, ed. R. D. Keynes (1839; repr., London: Folio Society, 2003), 403–4, 417–19, 432–33, 445–50.

12. J. C. Beaglehole, ed., *The Journals of Captain James Cook on His Voyages of Discovery*, 5 vol. (London: Hakluyt Society, 1955–74).

13. Darwin, *Evolutionary Writings*, 88–89.

14. James A. Secord, *Victorian Sensation: The Extraordinary Publication, Reception, and Secret Authorship of the Vestiges of the Natural History of Creation* (Chicago: University of Chicago Press, 2000).

15. Charles Lyell, *Principles of Geology*, ed. James A. Secord (1831; repr., London: Penguin, 1997).

16. Malthus, *An Essay on the Principle of Population*.

17. Charles Darwin, *On the Origin of Species by Means of Natural Selection, or the Preservation of Favoured Races in the Struggle for Life*, ed. J. Endersby (1859; repr., Cambridge: Cambridge University Press, 2009), 9–13.

18. Ibid., 372. See mainly 55–165, 318–76 (quote from the last chapter).

19. Thomas Henry Huxley, *Evidence as to Man's Place in Nature* (London: Williams and Norgate, 1863).

20. Darwin, *On the Origin of Species*, 354–76.

21. Charles Darwin, *The Descent of Man, and Selection in Relation to Sex*, ed. and intro. James Moore and Adrian Desmond (1871; repr., London: Penguin, 2004).

22. Ibid., 74, 86.

23. James Moore and Adrian Desmond, introduction to *The Descent of Man, and Selection in Relation to Sex*, by Charles Darwin (London: Penguin, 2004); Adrian Desmond and James Moore, *Darwin's Sacred Cause: Race, Slavery, and the Quest for Human Origins* (London: Allen Lane, 2009).

24. Darwin, *The Descent of Man*, 144; William Edward Hartpole Lecky, *History of European Morals*, 2 vols. (London: Longmans, 1869) (the significant passage is in ibid., 1:124).

25. Darwin, *The Descent of Man*, 159.

26. Ibid., 167–68.

27. Edward Burnett Tylor, *Researches into the Early History of Mankind and Development of Civilization* (London: John Murray, 1865).

28. Darwin, *The Descent of Man*, 171–72.

29. Ibid., 194–240.

30. Ibid., 213–21.

31. Ibid., 222. Broca, however, sustained distinctive features of the Jews.

32. Darwin, *Evolutionary Writings*, 222 (edited with useful sections on responses and reviews).

33. Auguste Comte, *Cours de philosophie positive*, 3rd ed., 6 vols. (1830–42; repr., Paris: J. B. Baillière, 1869); the significant quote is in ibid., 5:7.

34. Karl Marx and Friedrich Engels, *The Communist Manifesto*, trans. David Aaronovitch (1848; repr., London: Vintage, 2010); Karl Marx, *Early Writings*, trans. and ed. B. T. Bottomore (London: Watts, 1963); Karl Marx, *A Contribution to the Critique of Political Economy* (1859), trans. S. W. Ryazanskaya (1859; repr., London: Lawrence and Wishart, 1971); Karl Marx, *Capital: A Critique of Capitalist Production*, ed. Friedrich Engels (vols. 2–3), trans. Samuel Moore and Edward Aveling, 3 vols. (1867–94; repr., London: Lawrence and Wishart, 1955–59).

35. Paul Crook, *Darwin's Coat-Tails: Essays on Social Darwinism* (New York: Peter Lang, 2007).

36. Richard Hofstadter, *Social Darwinism in American Thought, 1860–1915* (Philadelphia: University of Pennsylvania Press, 1944).

37. Robert M. Young, "Darwinism Is Social," in *The Darwinian Heritage: Charles Darwin Centenary Conference*, ed. David Kohn (Princeton, NJ: Princeton University Press, 1985), 609–38.

38. Mike Hawkins, *Social Darwinism in European and American Thought, 1860–1945: Nature as Model and Nature as Threat* (Cambridge: Cambridge University Press, 1997).

39. Linda L. Clark, *Social Darwinism in France* (Tuscaloosa: University of Alabama Press, 1984); Jean-Marc Bernardini, *Le darwinisme social en France (1859–1918): Fascination et rejet d'une idéologie* (Paris: CNRS, 1997).

40. Herbert Spencer, *On Social Evolution*, ed. J.D.Y. Peel (Chicago: University of Chicago Press, 1972).

41. Herbert Spencer, *The Principles of Sociology*, 3 vols. (London: Williams and Norgate, 1876–96); the significant reference, concerning "primitive men," is in ibid., vol. 1, part I.

42. Tylor, *Researches into the Early History of Mankind*, 232, 234.

43. Herbert Spencer, ed., *Descriptive Sociology or Groups of Sociological Facts*, 3 vols., 8 parts (London: William and Norgate, 1873–81).

44. Spencer, *The Principles of Sociology*, vol. 1, part II.

45. Benjamin Kidd, *Social Evolution* (London: Macmillan, 1894).

46. Ibid., 56.

47. Ibid., 58.

48. This was the title of an essay: William Graham Sumner, *The Conquest of the United States by Spain and Other Essays*, ed. and intro. Murray Polner (Chicago: Henry Regnery, 1965).

49. William Graham Sumner, *Folkways: A Study of the Sociological Importance of Usages, Manners, Customs, Mores, and Morals* (Boston: Ginn, 1906).

50. William Graham Sumner, *Essays*, ed. Albert Galloway Keller and Maurice R. Davie, 2 vols. (New Haven, CT: Yale University Press, 1934).

51. This is where I diverge from the linear and schematic vision of Claude Lévi-Strauss, *L'anthropologie face aux problèmes du monde moderne*, (1986; repr., Paris: Seuil, 2011), 107–8.

52. G. Vacher de Lapouge, *L' aryen: Son role social* (Paris: Albert Fontenoing, 1899).

53. William Z. Ripley, *The Races of Europe: A Sociological Study* (London: Kegan Paul, 1899).

54. Madison Grant, *The Passing of the Great Race or the Racial Basis of European History* (London: G. Bell and Sons, 1917); Madison Grant, *The Conquest of a Continent or the Expansion of Races in America* (New York: C. Scribner's Sons, 1933).

55. Lothrop Stoddard, *The Rising Tide of Color against White World-Supremacy*, intro. Madison Grant (New York: C. Scribner's Sons, 1920).

56. Jonathan Peter Spiro, *Defending the Master Race: Conservation, Eugenics, and the Legacy of Madison Grant* (Burlington: University of Vermont Press, 2009), xi–xii.

57. Nicolas Bancel, Pascal Blanchard, Gilles Boëtsch, Éric Deroo, and Sandrine Lemaire, *Zoos humains: Au temps des exhibitions humaines* (Paris: La Découverte, 2002).

Part V: Nationalism and Beyond

1. Michael Mann, *The Dark Side of Democracy: Explaining Ethnic Cleansing* (Cambridge: Cambridge University Press, 2005).

Chapter 18: The Impact of Nationalism

1. Miroslav Hroch, *Comparative Studies in Modern European History: Nation, Nationalism, Social Change* (Aldershot, UK: Ashgate, 2007); Miroslav Hroch, *Social Preconditions of National Revival in Europe: A Comparative Analysis of the Social Composition of Patriotic Groups among the Smaller European Nations*, trans. Ben Fowkes (Cambridge: Cambridge University Press, 1985).

2. On the infamous case of the forced conversion and kidnap of the child Edgardo Mortara in 1858, with direct intervention by the Roman Inquisition and the Vatican, see David I. Kertzer, *The Kidnapping of Edgardo Mortara* (New York: Alfred A. Knopf, 1997).

3. Christopher Clark, *Iron Kingdom: The Rise and Downfall of Prussia, 1600–1947* (London: Allen Lane, 2006); Jonathan Steinberg, *Bismarck: A Life* (Oxford: Oxford University Press, 2011).

4. John W. Mason, *The Dissolution of the Austro-Hungarian Empire, 1867–1918*, 2nd ed. (London: Longman, 1997)

5. Achilles Kallos, *The Balkan Wars of Independence, 1821–1922: A Military and Political History* (London: Athena, 2006); Misha Glenny, *The Balkans, 1804–1999: Nationalism, War, and the Great Powers* (London: Granta, 1999).

6. Donald Quataert, "Population," in *An Economic and Social History of the Ottoman Empire*, ed. Halil Inalcik and Donald Quataert (Cambridge: Cambridge University Press, 1994), 2:777–97.

7. Ernest Gellner, *Nations and Nationalism* (Oxford: Blackwell, 1983); Eric J. Hobsbawm, *Nations and Nationalism since 1780* (Cambridge: Cambridge University, 1990). For a tempered look at this approach, which should be treated with caution as to time and place, see Anthony D. Smith, *The Ethnic Origins of Nations* (Oxford: Blackwell, 1986). None of these authors introduces a racial construction into the discussion, with the exception of a hint by Hobsbawm. Hroch (*Social Preconditions*) analyzes the social and national background of specific cases.

8. Reşat Kasaba, ed., *The Cambridge History of Turkey*, vol. 4, *Turkey in the Modern World* (Cambridge: Cambridge University Press, 2006).

9. Ronald Grigor Suni, ed., *The Cambridge History of Russia*, vol. 3, *The Twentieth Century* (Cambridge: Cambridge University Press, 2006).

10. Sebastian Conrad, *Globalization and the Nation in Imperial Germany*, trans. Sorcha O'Hagan (Cambridge: Cambridge University Press, 2010).

11. Jonathan M. Hess, *Germans, Jews, and the Claims of Modernity* (New Haven, CT: Yale University Press, 2002); Ronald Schechter, *Obstinate Jews: Representations of Jews in France, 1715–1815* (Berkeley: University of California Press, 2003).

12. Hans Rogger, "Conclusions and Overview," in *Pogroms: Anti-Jewish Violence in Modern Russian History*, ed. John D. Klier and Shlomo Lambroza (Cambridge: Cambridge University Press, 1992), 314–72; Léon Poliakov, *The History of Anti-Semitism*, trans. Miriam Kocham, vols. 3–4 (Philadelphia: University of Philadelphia Press, 2003).

13. John D. Klier and Shlomo Lambroza, eds., *Pogroms: Anti-Jewish Violence in Modern Russian History* (Cambridge: Cambridge University Press, 1992).

14. Peter Kenez, "Pogrom and White Ideology in the Russian Civil War," in *Pogroms: Anti-Jewish Violence in Modern Russian History*, ed. John D. Klier and Shlomo Lambroza (Cambridge: Cambridge University Press, 1992), 293–313.

15. Quataert, "Population."

16. Raymond Kévorkian, *The Armenian Genocide: A Complete History* (London: I. B. Taurus, 2011).

17. Donald Bloxham, *Genocide, the World Wars, and the Unweaving of Europe* (Edgware, UK: Valentine Mitchell, 2008).

18. David McDowall, *A Modern History of the Kurds* (London: I. B. Taurus, 1996).

19. Arnold Toynbee, *Turkey* (London: Ernest Benn, 1926).

20. *Ambassador Morgenthau's Story*, intro. Ara Sarafian (1918; repr., Princeton, NJ: Gomidas Institute, 2000), 94.

21. Vahakn N. Dadrian, *German Responsibility in the Armenian Genocide: A Revision of Historical Evidence of German Complicity* (Cambridge, MA: Blue Crane, 1996).

22. Ruth Harris, *The Man on Devil's Island: Alfred Dreyfus and the Affair That Divided France* (London: Penguin Books, 2010).

23. Wilhelm Marr, *Der Sieg des Judenthums über das Germanenthum* (Bern: Rudolph Costenoble, 1879).

24. Richard J. Evans, *The Coming of the Third Reich* (London: Allen Lane, 2003).

25. Ludwig Woltmann, *Der Historische Materialismus: Dartstellung und Kritik der Materialistischen Weltanschaung* (Dusseldorf: Hermann Michel, 1900); Ludwig Woltmann, *Politische Anthropologie* (Jena: Eugen Diederichs, 1903).

26. Houston Stewart Chamberlain, *The Foundations of the Nineteenth Century*, trans. John Lees, 2 vols. (London: John Lane, 1911).

27. Ibid., 1:xciii, 578.

28. Ibid., 1:lxv–lxvi.

29. Ibid., 1:389–90.

30. Ibid., 1:405, 483, 490–91.

31. Ibid., 1:492.

32. Ibid., 1:332.

33. Ibid., 1:xciv.

34. Ibid., 1:336.

35. Ibid., 1:421–22, 425, 434.

36. Ibid., 1:351–52.

37. http://www.ewtn.com/library/PAPALDOC/P9SILL/HTM (accessed September 20, 2011).

38. Karl Vogt, *Lectures on Man: His Place in Creation and in the History of Earth*, ed. J. Hunt (London: Longman, Green and Roberts for the Anthropological Society, 1864).

39. Chamberlain, *The Foundations of the Nineteenth Century*, 2:218, 377.

40. Adolf Hitler, *Mein Kampf* (1925), trans. James Murphy (London: Hutchinson, 1939).

41. Ibid., 270.

42. Ibid., 113.

43. Ibid., 114.

44. Ibid., 60, 205–6, 273.

45. Adolf Hitler, *My New Order* (1941), ed. Raoul de Roussy de Sales (New York: Octogon, 1973), 17.

46. Hitler, *Mein Kampf*, 77–78, 89.

47. Ibid., 66, 80.

48. Ibid., 84.

49. Ibid., 98.

50. Ibid., 118.

51. Ibid., 128.

52. Ibid., 145.

53. Léon Poliakov, *The Aryan Myth: A History of Racist and Nationalist Ideas in Europe*, trans. Edward Howard (London: Heinemann, 1974), 267.

54. Hitler, *Mein Kampf*, 288.

55. Ibid., 580.

56. Ibid., 162.

57. Ibid., 249.

58. Michael Burleigh and Wolfgang Lieppermann, *The Racial State: Germany, 1933–1945* (Cambridge: Cambridge University Press, 1991); Peter Longerich, *Holocaust: The Nazi Persecution and Murder of the Jews* (Oxford: Oxford University Press, 2010).

59. Leni Yahil, *The Holocaust: The Fate of European Jewry, 1932–1945*, trans. Ina Friedman and Haya Galai (Oxford: Oxford University Press, 1990).

60. For a reproduction of the main legislation, see Helmut Walser Smith, ed., *The Holocaust and Other Genocides: History, Representation, Ethics* (Nashville, TN: Vanderbilt University Press, 2002), 20–23.

61. Ritchie Robertson, "Varieties of Anti-Semitism from Herder to Fassbinder," in *The German-Jewish Dilemma from the Enlightenment to the Shoah*, ed. Edward Timms and Andrea Hammel (Lewiston, ME: Edwin Mellen, 1999), 107–21; Claudio Pogliano, *L'ossessione della razza: Antropologia e genetica nel XX secolo* (Pisa: Edizioni della Normale, 2005), 85–144.

62. See Yahil, *The Holocaust*; Longerich, *Holocaust*.

63. Jonathan Steinberg, *All or Nothing: The Axis and the Holocaust, 1941–1943*, 2nd ed. (London: Routledge, 2002).

64. Smith, *The Holocaust*, 41.

65. David Bankier and Israel Gutman, eds., *Nazi Europe and the Final Solution* (Jerusalem: International Institute for Holocaust Research, 2003).

66. Yahil, *The Holocaust*.

67. Guenter Lewy, *The Nazi Persecution of the Gypsies* (Oxford: Oxford University Press, 2000).

68. For the extraordinary impact of eugenics, see Alison Bashford and Philippa Levine, eds., *The Oxford Handbook of the History of Eugenics* (Oxford: Oxford University Press, 2010).

69. Yahil, *The Holocaust*.

70. Norman Cameron and Ribb Steven, trans., *Hitler's Table Talk, 1941–1945*, intro. Hugh Trevor-Roper (London: Weidenfeld and Nicholas, 1953), 33–35.

71. Ibid., 75, 87.

72. R. H. Stevens, trans., *The Testament of Adolf Hitler: The Hitler-Bormann Documents* (London: Cassell, 1960), 44.

73. Ibid., 45

74. Ibid., 56.

75. Ibid., 52.

76. Ibid., 53–54.

77. See Joshua Goode, *Defining Race in Spain, 1870–1930* (Baton Rouge: Lousiana State University Press, 2009); Gonzalo Alvarez Chillida, *El anti-semitismo en España: La imagen del judío* (Madrid: Marcial Pons, 2002); Joseph Perez, *Los judíos en España* (Madrid: Marcial Pons, 2005).

78. Jaime de Andrade [Francisco Franco], *Raza: Anecdotario para el guion de una pelicula* (Madrid: Delegación Nacional de Propaganda, 1942).

79. Irene Flunser Pimentel, *Judeus em Portugal durante a Segunda Guerra Mundial: Em fuga de Hitler e do Holocausto* (Lisbon: Esfera dos Livros, 2006).

80. Stevens, *The Testament of Adolf Hitler*, 47.

81. José Ortega y Gasset, *España invertebrada: Bosquejo de algunos pensamientos históricos* (Madrid: Calpe, 1921).

82. Patrícia Ferraz de Matos, *As cores do Império: Representações Raciais no Império Colonial Português* (Lisbon: ICS, 2006).

Chapter 19: Global Comparisons

1. Donald Bloxham, *Genocide, the World Wars, and the Unweaving of Europe* (Edgware, UK: Valentine Mitchell, 2008).

2. Speros Vryonis, *The Mechanism of Catastrophe: The Turkish Pogrom of September 6–7, 1955, and the Destruction of the Greek Community of Istanbul* (New York: Greekworks, 2005).

3. Vasily Grossman, *Life and Fate*, trans. Robert Chandler (London: Vintage, 2007).

4. Pavel Polian, *Against Their Will: The History and Geography of Forced Migrations in the USSR* (New York: Central European Press, 2004).

5. Adam Tooze, *Wages of Destruction: The Making and Breaking of the Nazi Economy* (New York: Viking Press, 2007).

6. Seymour Drescher, *Abolition: A History of Slavery and Antislavery* (Cambridge: Cambridge University Press, 2009), 415–56.

7. Ian Kershaw, *The End: Hitler's Germany, 1944–45* (London: Allen Lane, 2011).

8. José Bengoa, *Historia del pueblo Mapuche*, 6th ed. (Santiago: LOM, 2000); Isabel Hernández, *Autonomia o ciudadania incompleta: El pueblo Mapuche en Chile y Argentina* (Santiago: Pehuén, 2003).

9. http://www.funai.gov.br (accessed September 10, 2011).

10. William C. Sturtevant, ed., *Handbook of North American Indians*, vol. 4 (Washington, DC: Smithsonian Institution, 1988); Wilcomb E. Washburn, ed., *History of Indian-White Relations* (Washington, DC: Smithsonian Institution, 1988).

11. http://www.census.gov (accessed September 20, 2011).

12. http://www.bia.gov (accessed September 10, 2011).

13. Washburn, *History of Indian-White Relations*, especially the chapters on legal status, government agencies, rights movement, and education; Frederick E. Hoxie, "The Reservation Period, 1880–1960," in *The Cambridge History of the Native Peoples of the Americas*, vol. 1, part 2, *North America*, ed. Bruce G. Trigger and Wilcomb E. Washburn (Cambridge: Cambridge University Press, 1996), 183–258.

14. http://www.Censo2010.ibge.gov.br (accessed September 10, 2011).

15. Murdo J. MacLeod, "Mesoamerica since the Spanish Invasion: An Overview," in *The Cambridge History of the Native Peoples of the Americas*, vol. 2, part 2, *Meso-America*, ed. Richard E. W. Adams and Murdo

J. MacLeod (Cambridge: Cambridge University Press, 2000), 1–43; David-Maybury Lewis, "Lowland Peoples of the Twentieth Century," in *The Cambridge History of the Native Peoples of the Americas*, vol. 3, part 2, *South America*, ed. Franck Solomon and Stuart Schwartz (Cambridge: Cambridge University Press, 1999), 872–948.

16. http://www.law.cornell.edu/wex/civil_rights (accessed September 10, 2011).

17. This is just a schematic summary of a much more complex reality. See Joel Williamson, *The Crucible of Race: Black-White Relations in the American South since Emancipation* (Oxford: Oxford University Press, 1984); Barbara Young Welke, *Law and the Borders of Belonging in the Long Nineteenth Century United States* (Cambridge: Cambridge University Press, 2010).

18. Leon F. Litwack, "Hellhounds," in *Without Sanctuary: Lynching Photography in America*, ed. James Allen (Santa Fe, NM: Twin Palms, 2008), 8–37.

19. Amy Louise Wood, "Lynching Photography and the Visual Reproduction of White Supremacy," in *Lynching Reconsidered: New Perspectives in the Study of Mob Violence*, ed. William D. Carrigan (London: Routledge, 2008), 147–73.

20. Litwack, "Hellhounds"; see also Christopher Waldrep, ed., *Lynching in America: A History in Documents* (New York: New York University Press, 2006).

21. http://www.law.cornell.edu/wex/civil_rights (accessed September 10, 2011).

22. On the importance of feelings and beliefs in race, see Sarah Daynes and Orville Lee, *Desire for Race* (Cambridge: Cambridge University Press, 2008).

23. José Vasconcelos, *La raza cosmica: Misión de la raza iberoamericana; Notes de viajes a la América del Sur* (Barcelona, 1929). For the bilingual English edition, see José Vasconcelos, *The Cosmic Race*, trans. Didier T. Jaén (Los Angeles: California State University, 1979).

24. Gilberto Freyre, *Casa Grande e Senzala: Formação da família brasileira sob o regime de economia patriarcal* (Rio de Janeiro: Maya and Schmidt, 1933). For the English edition, see Gilberto Freyre, *The Masters and the Slaves: A Study in the Development of the Brazilian Civilization*, trans. Samuel Putnam (New York: Alfred A. Knopf, 1946).

25. Maria Lúcia Garcia Pallares-Burke, *Gilberto Freyre: Um vitoriano nos Trópicos* (São Paulo: UNESP, 2005).

26. Marvin Harris, *Town and Country in Brazil* (New York: Columbia University Press, 1956); Fernando Henrique Cardoso and Octávio Ianni, *Côr e mobilidade social em Florianópolis: Aspectos das relações entre negros e brancos numa comunidade do Brasil Meridional* (São Paulo: Editora Nacional, 1960); Fernando Henrique Cardoso, *Capitalismo e escravidão no Brasil meridional: O negro na sociedade escravocrata do Rio Grande do Sul* (São Paulo: Difusão Européia do Livro, 1962); Octávio Ianni, *As metamorfoses do escravo: Apogeu e crise da escravatura no Brasil meridional* (São Paulo: Difusão Européia do Livro, 1962).

27. António Sérgio Guimarães, *Racismo e anti-racismo no Brasil* (São Paulo: FAUSP, 1999); António Sérgio Guimarães, *Classes, Raças e Democracia* (São Paulo: FAUSP, 2002).

28. Bruce S. Hall, *A History of Race in Muslim West Africa, 1600–1960* (Cambridge: Cambridge University Press, 2011).

29. Michel Leiris, *L'Afrique fantôme* (1934), in *Miroir d'Afrique*, ed. Jean Jamin (Paris: Gallimard, 1996), 61–869 (with contemporary correspondence of the author).

30. Jan Bart Gewald, "Herero Genocide in the Twentieth Century: Politics and Memory," in *Rethinking Resistance: Revolt and Violence in Africa*, ed. Jon Abbink, Minja de Bruijn, and Klaas van Walraven (Leiden: Brill, 2003), 279–304; Henrik Lundtofte, "'I Believe That the Nation as Such Must Be Annihilated' . . . Radicalisation of the German Suppression of the Herero Rising in 1904," in *Genocide: Cases, Comparisons, and Contemporary Debates*, ed. Steven L. B. Jensen (Copenhagen: Danish Centre for Holocaust and Genocide Studies, 2003), 15–53; Sebastian Conrad, *German Colonialism: A Short History*, trans. Sorcha O'Hagan (Cambridge: Cambridge University Press, 2010).

31. Convention on the Prevention and Punishment of the Crime of Genocide, Resolution 260(III)A, UN General Assembly, December 9, 1948, http://www.hrweb.org/legal/genocide.hmt (accessed September 20, 2011).

32. Carolyn Hamilton, Bernard K. Mbenga, and Robert Ross, eds., *The Cambridge History of South Africa*, vol. 1, *From Early Times to 1885* (Cambridge: Cambridge University Press, 2010–11); Robert Ross, Anne Kelk Mager, and Bill Nason, eds., *The Cambridge History of South Africa*, vol. 2, *1885–1994* (Cambridge: Cambridge University Press, 2010–11).

33. George M. Fredrickson, *White Supremacy: A Comparative Study in American and South African History* (Oxford: Oxford University Press, 1981).

34. Paul Maylam, *South Africa's Racial Past: The History and Historiography of Racism, Segregation, and Apartheid* (Aldershot, UK: Ashgate, 2001); Sampie Terreblanche, *A History of Inequality in South Africa, 1652–2002* (Pietermaritzburg, South Africa: University of Natal Press, 2002).

35. Helmut Walser Smith, ed., *The Holocaust and Other Genocides: History, Representation, Ethics* (Nashville, TN: Vanderbilt University Press, 2002), 201–22; Alison Des Forges, *Leave None to Tell the Story: Genocide in Rwanda* (New York: Human Rights Watch, 1999). The vision of colonial legacy expressed by Mahmood Mamdani in *When Victims Become Killers: Colonialism, Nativism, and the Genocide in Rwanda* (Princeton, NJ: Princeton University Press, 2002) has been challenged in Hall, *A History of Race in Muslim West Africa*, 1–3.

36. See Frank Dikötter, *The Discourse of Race in Modern China* (London: Hurst and Co., 1992). For the following paragraphs, see also Frank Dikötter, ed., *The Construction of Racial Identities in China and Japan* (London: Hurst and Co., 1997).

37. For several examples of this early poetry, see Victor H. Mair, ed., *The Columbia Anthology of Traditional Chinese Literature* (New York: Columbia University Press, 1994), 450, 483, 630.

38. Blaine Kaltman, *Under the Heel of the Dragon: Islam, Racism, Crime, and the Uighur in China* (Athens: Ohio University Press, 2007); Gardner Bovingdon, *The Uyghurs: Strangers in Their Own Land* (New York: Columbia University Press, 2010).

39. Chi-yu Shih, *Negotiating Ethnicity in China: Citizenship as a Response to the State* (London: Routledge, 2002).

40. Françoise Grenot-Wang, *Chine du Sud: Le mosaïques des minorités* (Paris: Les Indes Savantes, 2005).

41. Nicole Constable, ed., *Guest People: Hakka Identity in China and Abroad* (Seattle: University of Washington Press, 1996).

42. Michael Weiner, "The Invention of Identity: Race and Nation in Pre-War Japan," in *The Construction of Racial Identities in China and Japan*, ed. Frank Dikötter, 96–117, especially 108.

43. Michael Weiner, ed., *Japan's Minorities: The Illusion of Homogeneity* (London: Routledge, 1997).

44. Richard Siddle, *Race, Resistance, and the Ainu of Japan* (London: Routledge 1996).

45. Naoko Shimazu, *Japan, Race, and Equality: The Racial Equality Proposal of 1919* (London: Routledge, 1998).

46. http://www.stat.gv.jp/english/data/kokusei/2010 (accessed September 25, 2011).

47. Siddle, *Race, Resistance, and the Ainu of Japan*.

48. Michael Weiner, *Race and Migration in Imperial Japan* (London: Routledge, 1994).

49. George Hicks, *Japan's Hidden Apartheid: The Korean Minority and the Japanese* (Aldershot, UK: Ashgate 1997); Sonia Ryang, ed., *Koreans in Japan: Critical Voices from the Margins* (London: Routledge, 2000).

50. David Blake Willis and Stephen Murphy-Shigematsu, eds., *Transcultural Japan: At the Borderland of Race, Gender, and Identity* (London: Routledge, 2008), particularly the chapters on Filipinos, Brazilian Japanese, Chinese, Okinawan, and Ainu.

51. George De Vos and Hiroshi Wagatsuma, eds., *Japan's Invisible Race: Caste in Culture and Personality* (Berkeley: University of California Press, 1966), xx.

52. Ibid., 9.

53. http://www.censusindia.gov.in (accessed September 25, 2011).

54. Louis Dumont, *Homo Hierarchicus: The Caste System and Its Implications*, trans. Marc Sainsbury, Louis Dumont, and Basia Gulati, rev. ed. (Chicago: University of Chicago Press, 1980).

55. R. S. Khare, ed., *Caste, Hierarchy and Individualism: Indian Critics of Louis Dumont's Contributions* (Oxford: Oxford University Press, 2006).

56. Gnana Prakasam, *Social Separatism: Scheduled Castes and the Caste System* (Jaipur, India: Rawat, 1998).

57. Rosa Maria Perez, *Kings and Untouchables: A Study of the Caste System in Western India* (New Delhi: Chronicle Books, 2004).

INDEX